ORDO

Band 30

ORDO

Jahrbuch für die Ordnung von Wirtschaft und Gesellschaft

Band 30

Begründet von

Walter Eucken

Franz Böhm

Herausgegeben von

Fritz W. Meyer

Hans Otto Lenel

Walter Hamm

Ernst Heuß

Erich Hoppmann

Ernst-Joachim Mestmäcker

Christian Watrin

Hans Willgerodt

unter Mitwirkung von

Friedrich A. v. Hayek

Gustav Fischer Verlag · Stuttgart · New York · 1979

Zur Verfassung der Freiheit

Festgabe

für

Friedrich A. von Hayek

zur Vollendung seines achtzigsten Lebensjahres

Das Foto von F. A. von Hayek wurde freundlicherweise vom Presse- und Informationsamt der Bundesregierung Bonn zur Verfügung gestellt.

ISBN 3-437-50239-5

Satz: Bauer & Bökeler Filmsatz KG, Denkendorf
Druck: Sulzberg-Druck GmbH, Sulzberg im Allgäu
Einband: Großbuchbinderei Koch, Tübingen
Printed in Germany

Vorwort

Am 8. Mai 1979 vollendet *Friedrich August von Hayek* das achtzigste Lebensjahr. Der in der ganzen Welt hochangesehene Gelehrte ist unserem Jahrbuch in besonderer Weise verbunden. Er hat es durch zahlreiche Beiträge von hohem Rang ausgezeichnet und wirkt daran seit Erscheinen des ersten Bandes im Jahre 1948 mit. Das Ordo-Jahrbuch hat deswegen begründeten Anlaß, seinen hervorragenden Autor und Mitarbeiter durch diese Festgabe zu ehren, die ihm zu seinem Geburtstage in Dankbarkeit und treuer Verbundenheit gewidmet ist. Autoren aus vielen Ländern haben sich darin vereinigt, um an den ordnungspolitischen Problemen weiterzuarbeiten, die *von Hayek* seit Jahrzehnten beschäftigt haben. Wir haben diesem Band den Titel «Zur Verfassung der Freiheit» gegeben und knüpfen damit an *von Hayeks* herausragendes Buch «Die Verfassung der Freiheit» an, in dem er die Grundprobleme einer freiheitlichen und menschenwürdigen Gesellschaft in umfassender Weise darstellt.

Damit werden zugleich die Gedanken aufgenommen, die *von Hayek* auch in unserem Jahrbuch vorgetragen hat. Eine Fülle von Themen hat er in seinen Ordo-Aufsätzen behandelt, doch ist ihnen ein Leitmotiv gemeinsam, das überhaupt sein ordnungspolitisches Denken beherrscht: Es geht um die Achtung vor der Einzelperson und vor ihren Freiheitsrechten, die nur gesichert sind, wenn Regeln und Gesetze herrschen, nicht die Willkür von Diktatoren und Majoritäten. Gegenüber ungeordneter Anarchie ist damit unübersehbar ein Trennungsstrich gezogen, also gegenüber dem falschen Individualismus, der keine Ordnung als ein System von Verhaltensregeln anerkennen will und dadurch den Umschlag des Chaos in die zentrale Organisation von Wirtschaft und Gesellschaft hervorruft. Die Einzelperson wird keineswegs isoliert gesehen, sondern ihr Interesse mit demjenigen der Gesellschaft verbunden. Allerdings bestreitet *von Hayek,* daß irgendjemand in der Lage und berechtigt sei, ein Gemeinwohl materiell genau festzustellen und dann durch Anordnung durchzusetzen. Durch die Regeln, nach denen Entscheidungen zustande kommen, soll es der Einzelperson zugestanden werden, sich im Rahmen geschriebener und ungeschriebener Gesetze an einem Suchprozeß nach günstigen Lösungen zu beteiligen, die sich allmählich ausbreiten und damit zum Vorteil aller ausschlagen. Wer behauptet, in einer Welt verschiedenartiger Wertvorstellungen und allgemeiner Ungewißheit über die Informationen zu verfügen, die notwendig wären, um das Wohl anderer umfassend und genau zu definieren, müsse sich den Vorwurf einer «Anmaßung von Wissen» gefallen lassen. Diesen Titel hat *von Hayek* für eine Ansprache gewählt, die er gehalten hat, als ihm im Jahre 1974 der Nobelpreis für Wirtschaftswissenschaften verliehen worden ist. Wir haben diese Ansprache im Ordo-Jahrbuch 1975 veröffentlicht.

Die Autoren dieser Festgabe haben immer wieder die philosophische Grundfrage in das Blickfeld gerückt, was der menschlichen Erkenntnis zugänglich ist und wohin uns bestimmte Arten von Rationalismus geführt haben und noch führen können. Der «konstruktivistische Rationalismus» hat zentral gelenkte politische und ökonomische Gestaltungen so stark gefördert, daß dadurch alle freiheitlichen Systeme mehr oder weniger in Gefahr geraten sind. So lag es nahe, dieser Entwicklung nachzuspüren und über verfassungsrechtliche Schranken nachzudenken, die einer solchen Entartung gesetzt werden können. Die Liberalen müssen sich immer wieder mit dem Staat, seiner Aufgabe, die Freiheit zu sichern, seinen Wucherungs-, Zerfalls- und Gleichschaltungstendenzen befassen. Kritik am Staat ist jedoch nicht ohne Meinungsfreiheit und eine freiheitliche Wirtschaftsordnung denkbar. Der Wettbewerb der Meinungen und der Wettbewerb der wirtschaftlichen Handlungen gehören zusammen. Für beides müssen faire Regeln entwickelt werden. Wie sie im einzelnen aussehen sollen, ist jedoch keineswegs endgültig geklärt. Unsere Autoren haben sich zum Teil kontrovers mit der Frage auseinandergesetzt, welchen Regeln der freiheitliche Suchprozeß nach besseren wirtschaftlichen Lösungen zu unterwerfen ist. In diesem Zusammenhang ist auch die Frage zu klären, welche verfassungsrechtlichen Grenzen für den Staatsapparat gesetzt werden sollen, sich Einnahmen zu verschaffen und die Steuerpolitik als Lenkungsinstrument zu benutzen. Wie soll im übrigen ein wettbewerblicher Suchprozeß fair bleiben, wenn der Staat durch selektive Struktur- und Forschungspolitik nicht nur die Wege beschränkt, auf denen gesucht werden darf, sondern auch den Suchenden in verzerrender Form differenzierte Hilfen gewährt? In jüngster Zeit hat *von Hayek* das Wettbewerbskonzept sogar auf das Währungssystem übertragen und durch diese auch für Liberale teilweise provozierenden Vorstellungen eine Fülle von fruchtbaren Diskussionen ausgelöst, die wirksam bleiben werden. Wer für eine freiheitliche Ordnung eintritt, kann ferner heute nicht mehr daran vorübergehen, daß sich ihr Schicksal zu einem wesentlichen Teil in den internationalen Wirtschaftsbeziehungen entscheidet. Auch dieser Aspekt wird in unserer Festgabe erörtert.

Friedrich August von Hayek hat in seinem persönlichen Lebensweg[1] und seinen wissenschaftlichen Veröffentlichungen die Verbindung von Rechts- und Wirtschaftswissenschaften gesucht. In beiden Fächern hat er den Doktorgrad erworben und die Beziehung der Wirtschaftsordnung zum Recht auch dann immer wieder eingehend untersucht, als er einer der international bedeutendsten Nationalökonomen geworden war. Gleichzeitig hat er, was bei einem Geld- und Konjunkturtheoretiker seines Ranges nicht verwundern kann, die dem Juristen nicht selten ungewohnte Denkweise in historischen und ökonomischen Abläufen oder Entwicklungen betont. Gleichwohl bleibt für ihn das Recht nicht ein Gegenstand täglicher Disposition oder beliebiger Mehrheitsentscheidungen, aber auch nicht ein Ergebnis historischer Zwangsläufigkeit, wie sie die Marxisten behaupten und der gegenüber es kein Entrinnen gibt. Die Macht der Ideen ist es, die nach *von Hayek* letztlich die Welt bewegt, und so hat er es stets als seine Pflicht angesehen, für die Ideen der Freiheit und der Vernunft einzutreten. Hierfür danken ihm Autoren und Freunde des Ordo-Jahrbuches.

Die Schriftleitung

---

[1] Eine Würdigung der Werke *von Hayeks,* eine Biographie und ein Schriftenverzeichnis finden sich in: *Fritz Machlup,* Würdigung der Werke von Friedrich A. von Hayek, Walter Eucken Institut, Vorträge und Aufsätze, 62, Tübingen 1977.

Inhalt

I. Philosophische Grundfragen

Karl Popper

Epistemology and Industrialization

Remarks on the Influence of Philosophical Ideas on the History of Europe*

> . . . Francis Bacon looked forward to an alteration in the form of production and to the effective control of nature by man, as a result of a change in the ways of thinking.
> *Karl Marx*[1]
> The belief that . . . it is ideas and therefore the men who give currency to ideas that govern . . . [has] long formed a fundamental part of the liberal creed.
> *F. A. von Hayek*[2]

I.

In a famous and highly dramatic passage of his chief work, *Plato* demands that philosophers should be kings and, vice versa, that kings – or autocratic rulers – should be fully trained philosophers.[3] *Plato's* proposal that philosophers should be kings has pleased many philosophers, and some of them have taken it very seriously. Personally I do not

* A lecture delivered in German on June 13th, 1959, at the School of Economics, the University of St. Gallen, Switzerland, as part of a series of lectures entitled ‹Europe: Inheritance and Future Tasks›, on the topic ‹The Influence of Philosophy upon some Fundamental Turning Points in the History of Europe›. The lecture (not previously published) has been revised for the present publication; I would like to thank *Jeremy Shearmur* for assisting me by providing the references in the footnotes, and *Larry Briskman, Knud Haakonssen,* and *Bryan Magee* for their criticisms and comments.

[1] The first motto is taken from *Karl Marx*, Capital, volume one, chapter 13, section 2 (the footnote on pp. 413f. of the Everyman's Library edition, J. M. Dent & Sons Ltd., London, E. P. Dutton & Co., Inc., New York, 1930 and subsequent impressions; cp. Lawrence & Wishart, London/Progress Publishers, Moscow edition, 1963 and subsequent impressions, footnote 2 on p. 368).

[2] *F. A. von Hayek*, The Constitution of Liberty, London 1960, p. 112.

[3] *Plato*, Republic 473 c-e. In my Open Society, 1945; 12th impr London 1977 chapter 8, pp. 151f. I translated the passage as follows: ‹Unless, in their cities, philosophers are vested with the might of kings, or those now called kings and oligarchs become genuine and fully qualified philosophers; and unless these two, political might and philosophy, are fused (while the many who nowadays follow their natural inclination for one of these two are suppressed by force), unless this happens, my dear Glaucon, there can be no rest; and the evil will not cease to be rampant in the cities – nor, I believe, in the race of men.›

find it an attractive proposal. Quite apart from the fact that I am against any form of autocracy or dictatorship, including the dictatorship of the wisest and best, philosophers do not seem to me particularly well suited for the job. Take for example the case of *Thomas Masaryk*, the creator, first president and, one might say, the philosopher-king of the Czechoslovak Republic. *Masaryk* was not only a fully trained philosopher but also a born statesman and a great and admirable man; and his creation, the Czechoslovak Republic, was an unparalleled political achievement. Yet the dissolution of the old Austrian Empire was also partly *Masaryk's* work; and this proved a disaster for Europe and the world. For the instability which followed this dissolution was largely responsible for the rise of Nazism and finally even for the downfall of *Masaryk's* own Czechoslovak Republic. And it is significant that *Masaryk's* doctrine that ‹Austria-Hungary, this antinational . . . state, must be dismembered›[4] (to use his own words) was derived from a mistaken philosophical doctrine: from the philosophical principle of the National State.[5] But this principle, the principle of political nationalism, is not only an unfortunate and even a mischievous conception, but actually one which it is impossible to realize, because nations – in the sense of those who advocate this principle – do not exist: they are theoretical constructs, and the theories in which they are constructed are wholly inadequate, and completely inapplicable to Europe. For the political theory of nationalism rests on the assumption that there are ethnic groups which at the same time are also linguistic groups, and which happen also to inhabit geographically unified and coherent regions with natural boundaries that are defensible from a military point of view: groups which are united by a common language, a common territory, a common history, a common culture, and a common fate. The boundaries of the regions inhabited by these groups should, according to the theory of the Nation State, form boundaries of the new national states.

It was this theory which underlay the *Masaryk-Wilson* principle of the ‹Self-determination of Nations›; and in its name the multi-lingual state of Austria was destroyed.

But no such regions exist; at least not in Europe nor, indeed, anywhere in the Old World.[6] There are few geographical regions in which only one native language is spoken; almost every region has its linguistic or ‹racial› minority. Even *Masaryk's* own newly created national state contained in spite of its small size several linguistic minorities,[7] and the principle of the National State played a decisive role in its destruction: it was this principle which allowed *Hitler* to appear in the role of a liberator, and which confused the West.

It is important to my present theme that the idea or theory of nationalism is a philosophical idea. It sprang from the theory of sovereignty – the theory that power in the state must be undivided – and from the idea of a superhuman ruler who rules by the grace of

[4] See T. *Masaryk*, The New Europe (The Slav Standpoint). London 1918, for private circulation, p. 68.

[5] It might, perhaps, be mentioned that *Masaryk's* nationalism was moderate and humane: ‹I have never been a national Chauvinist; I have not even been a nationalist . . .› (Ibid., p. 45). Nevertheless, he also said: ‹. . . we advocate the principle of nationality . . .› (ibid. p. 52) and demanded the dismemberment of Austria-Hungary into national states. (See also n. 53 to chapter 12 of my Open Society.) For a most interesting though different appraisal of *Masaryk's* views, see A. *van den Beld*, Humanity: The Political and Social Philosophy of Thomas G. Masaryk, The Hague and Paris 1975.

[6] Iceland may be a possible exception: cp. my Conjectures and Refutations, 7th impr., London 1978, p. 368.

[7] A. J. P. *Taylor* claims that ‹Czechoslovakia contained seven [nationalities]› that is, ‹Czechs, Slovaks, Germans, Magyars, Little Russians, Poles, Jews›. See The Hapsburg Monarchy, 1948; Peregrine Books Edition, 1964, p. 274.

God. *Rousseau's* replacement of the king by the people only inverted the view: he made of the people a nation – a superhuman nation by the grace of God. Thus the theory of political nationalism originated in a philosophical inversion of the theory of absolute monarchy. The history of this development seems to me characteristic of the rise of many philosophical ideas, and it suggests to my mind the lesson that philosophical ideas should be treated with a certain reserve. It also may teach us that there are fundamental ideas, such as the idea of political liberty, of the protection of linguistic and religious minorities, and of democracy, which remain fundamental and true even when defended by untenable philosophical theories.

The fact that an admirable man and a great statesman like *Masaryk* was led by certain philosophical ideas to commit so grave a mistake; that he accepted a philosophical theory which was not only untenable but, under existing conditions, almost bound to destroy his work as a statesman; all this, I believe, amounts to a strong argument against *Plato's* demand that philosophers should rule. But one could also adduce another and entirely different argument against *Plato:* one could also say that *Plato's* demand is superfluous, because the philosophers are ruling anyway – not officially, it is true, but all the more so in actual fact. For I want to advance the thesis that the world is ruled by ideas: ideas both good and bad. It is, therefore, ruled by those who produce these ideas – that is, by philosophers, though rarely by professional philosophers.

The thesis that it is the philosophers who actually are the rulers is, of course, not new. *Heinrich Heine* expressed it as follows in 1838:[8]

Mark this, ye proud men of action: Ye are nothing but unconscious instruments of the men of thought who, often in humblest seclusion, have appointed you to your inevitable task.*Maximilian Robespierre* was merely the hand of *Jean Jacques Rousseau* . . .

And *Hayek*, in his great work of liberal political philosophy, The Constitution of Liberty, has emphasised the relevance of this idea for us today, and its importance in the liberal tradition.[9]

Countless examples illustrate the political power of philosophical ideas. Marxism is a philosophy: *Marx* himself proudly quoted a review which described his theory, as expounded in Capital, quite correctly, as the last of the great post-Kantian philosophical systems.[10] His seizure of power, thirty four years after his death, in the person on *Lenin*, is almost an exact repetition of the seizure of power by *Rousseau*, sixteen years after his death, in the person of *Robespierre*.

Orthodox Marxism, of course, denies the thesis of the political power of ideas: it sees in ideas mainly the inevitable consequences of technical and industrial developments. What changes first, *Marx* teaches, is the technique of production; depending on this, the class structure of society; next, the prevalent ideas; and finally, when the whole substruc-

---

[8] *Heinrich Heine,* Zur Geschichte der Religion und Philosophie in Deutschland, 1833–4, book three (see p. 150 of *Wolfgang Harich's* edition, Frankfurt, 1966). The passage was quoted in my Open Society, volume two, chapter 15, p. 109.

[9] *Hayek* has long stressed this point which, as he says in the passage that I have used as a motto to this essay, has ‹long formed a fundamental part of the liberal creed›. See his The Constitution of Liberty, Chicago 1960; and London 1960, pp. 112f., the quotation in his text from *J. S. Mill*, and, in his footnote 14 on p. 445, from Lord *Keynes*.

[10] *Marx* does so in the ‹Author's Preface to the Second German Edition› of Capital, dated London, January 24th, 1873; see p. 871 of the Everyman edition of Capital, volume one; p. 27 of the Lawrence & Wishart edition, volume one.

ture has changed, the system of political power will also change.[11] But this theory – which contradicts our thesis of the power of philosophical ideas – is refuted by history; for example by the history of Russia since 1917. What came there first was the seizure of power; that is, what according to the theory should have come last. Next came *Lenin's* great idea: the idea that socialism is the dictatorship of the proletariat plus electrification.[12] And last came electrification, industrialization, the enforced change of the so-called economic ‹substructure›; and this change was imposed from above, by a new instrument of power, the new class dictatorship.

Later I shall endeavour to show that the first industrial revolution, the English Industrial Revolution – was also inspired by philosophical ideas.

A totally different example of the seizure of political power by a philosophy – a seizure of power by purely democratic means – has been brought to my attention by *Hayek*. The English philosopher and economist, *John Stuart Mill*, wrote in his Autobiography, published shortly after his death in 1873, that in the years around 1830 his circle (the so-called Philosophical Radicals) had adopted the following programme: they wanted to achieve an improvement in human society by ‹securing full employment at high wages to the whole labouring population›.[13] Seventy two years after his death *John Stuart Mill* seized political power in England; and no political party would dare today (1959) to challenge his programme.

II.

The political power of philosophical ideas – and often enough of harmful or immature or downright silly philosophical ideas – is a fact that might well depress and even terrify us. And indeed, it would be quite true to say that almost all our wars are ideological wars: religious wars or ideological-religious persecutions.

But we must not be too pessimistic. Fortunately there are also good, humane, and wise philosophical ideas, and they, too, are powerful. There is, first of all, the idea of religious tolerance and of respecting opinions which differ from our own. And there are the philosophical ideas of justice and of liberty. Countless men have sacrificed their lives for them. And if we mention ideological wars we must not forget such crusades of peace as the Nansen Aid of the International Red Cross in Geneva which saved more than a million citizens of the Soviet Union from death by famine in the years 1921 and 1922. And we must

---

[11] Thies brief account is based on the analysis of *Marx's* theory that I give in my Open Society, chapters 13–21. See especially chapter 15, pp. 108f.; footnote 13 on p. 326; and the references given there to *Marx's* ‹Preface› to his A Contribution to the Critique of Political Economy and his The Poverty of Philosophy. (But see also my Poverty of Historicism, London 1957; 9th impr. 1976.)

[12] Cp. my Open Society, volume two, pp. 83 and 108.

[13] See *John Stuart Mill*, Autobiography, chapter IV, first edition, 1873, p. 105, Houghton Mifflin/Oxford University Press edition, ed. *J. Stillinger*, 1969, 1971, p. 64. It seems that *Mill* believed at the time that the only means of realizing his programme was by the voluntary adoption of birth control by the ‹labouring classes›. (The quotation in the text continues: ‹through a voluntary restriction of the increase of their numbers›.) There is no reason to think that he gave up his support for birth control; but in his Autobiography, chapter VII (first edition, p. 231; *Stillinger* edition, p. 138) he indicates (possibly under the influence of his wife: note the sudden ‹we› instead of ‹I› on the page referred to) that a necessary additional means was a changed attitude towards private property, and the adoption of a form of socialism.

not forget that the idea of Peace on Earth is a philosophical as well as a religious idea, and that it was a philosopher, *Immanuel Kant*, who first formulated the idea of a World Federation or a League of Nations.

The idea of peace is a good example of our thesis of the political power of ideas. Obsessed as we are by the memory of two world wars and by the threat of a third, we all are inclined to overlook something important – the fact that since 1918 all Europe has acknowledged the idea of peace as fundamental. Even *Mussolini* and *Hitler*, whose ideology was openly aggressive, were forced, by the prevailing public opinion, to pose as friends of peace, and to blame others for the wars which they began. The fact that they had to make this concession to public opinion shows how strong was the will to peace. One must not underrate the moral victory won in 1918 by the idea of peace. It has not, it is true, brought us peace; yet it has created that opinion, that will to peace, which is a moral prerequisite for it.

This victory of the idea of peace can be regarded as a belated victory of *Erasmus* of Rotterdam, almost four hundred years after his death. To see clearly how badly Christian Europe stood in need of the teachings of the Christian humanist *Erasmus*, we should remember the attack made upon *Erasmus* by that great musician, poet, and fighter against the devil, *Martin Luther*.

Luther fought *Erasmus* because he saw that the idea of peace was linked with the idea of tolerance: ‹If I did not see these upheavals [*Luther* speaks of war and bloodshed] I should say that the word of God was not in the world. But now, when I do see them, my heart rejoices . . .›. ‹The wish to quieten these upheavals is nothing less than the wish to abandon the word of God and to suppress it.›, *Luther* wrote. And to *Erasmus's* appeal for peace and understanding he replied: ‹Stop lamenting, stop trying to cure [the ills of the world]! This war is the war of our Lord God. He started it, He sustains it, and it will never cease until all the enemies of His word have become dung under our feet.›.[14] We should remember here that *Erasmus* and his friends were not lacking in personal courage. Sir *Thomas More* and *John Fisher*, both friends of *Erasmus* and like himself champions of tolerance, died, not primarily as martyrs of Roman Catholicism, but rather, I believe, as martyrs of the idea of humanism, as opponents of barbarism, of arbitrary rule, and of violence. If today we look upon Christianity as a force for peace and tolerance, we testify to the spiritual victory of *Erasmus*.

III.

All I have said so far was meant to suggest an attitude towards philosophy which might perhaps be formulated like this. Just as there are good and evil religions – religions that encourage the good or the evil in man – so there are good and evil philosophical ideas, and true and false philosophical theories. We must therefore neither revere nor revile re-

---

[14] The quotations are from *Martin Luther's* De servo arbitrio, (The Bondage of the Will), 1525, a book that he wrote in reply to *Erasmus's* De libero arbitrio (A Diatribe or Discourse Concerning Free Choice), 1524. The translations are my own; see De servo arbitrio in D. *Martin Luthers* Werke, Kritische Gesamtausgabe (Weimarer Ausgabe), 18. Band, Weimar, 1908, p. 626; cp. *Luther's* Works, volume 33, Career of the Reformer III, Philadelphia 1972, pp. 52–3; or *Martin Luther*, Ausgewählte Werke, ed. *H. H. Borcherdt* and *G. Merz*, Ergänzungsreihe, erster Band, 1954, p. 35.

ligion as such, or philosophy as such; rather we must evaluate religious and philosophical ideas with critical and selective minds. The terrifying power of ideas burdens all of us with grave responsibilities. We must not accept or reject them unthinkingly. We must judge them critically.

The attitude I have just formulated may appear to many as obvious. But it is not by any means generally accepted, or even generally understood. It is in origin, rather, a specifically European or Western attitude; the attitude of critical rationalism. It is the attitude of the critical and rational tradition of European philosophy.

Of course, critical thinkers have existed outside Europe. But nowhere else, to my knowledge, has there existed a critical and rationalist tradition. And from the critical and rationalist tradition in Europe there grew, eventually, European science.

But even before it gave rise to modern science, critical rationalism created European philosophy. Or more precisely, European philosophy is just as old as European critical rationalism. For both were founded by *Thales* and *Anaximander* of Miletus.

Naturally, within European philosophy itself, uncritical and even anti-critical countercurrents kept forming, both of rationalist and of anti-rationalist persuasions. And nowadays[15] the anti-rationalist philosophy of ‹existentialism› is enjoying a great vogue.

Existentialism maintains, quite correctly, that in matters of real importance nothing can be proved, and that therefore one is always faced with the necessity of making decisions – fundamental decisions. But hardly anybody, not even the most uncritical and naive rationalist, would contest the assertion that nothing of importance can be proved, and that all that can be proved consists, at most, of mathematical and logical truisms.

It is, therefore, perfectly correct to state that we have to make free decisions all the time; a fact that, for instance, *Immanuel Kant*, the critical rationalist and the last great philosopher of the Enlightenment, saw very clearly. But of course this statement tells us nothing about what our fundamental decision will turn out to be: whether we decide for or against rationalism; whether we decide with *Erasmus* and *Socrates* in favour of listening to rational arguments, making our further decisions depend on critical and careful consideration of such arguments, and on self-critical reflection – or whether we leap headlong into the magic circle of an irrationalist existentialism, or rather, into the magic whirlpool of anti-rationalistic ‹commitments›.[16]

However that may be, European philosophy made a fundamental decision, fundamental for itself and for Europe, when twenty four centuries ago it decided in favour of critical rationalism and self-criticism. And indeed, without this self-critical tradition the current fashions of philosophical anti-rationalism could not possibly have arisen: it is just one of the traditions of critical rationalism that it never ceases to criticize itself.

IV.

What I have said so far bears heavily upon my main subject; yet it is only an introduction. For the task of outlining the influence of European philosophy on the history of Europe in one short hour confronted me with some difficult and fairly fundamental deci-

---

[15] Note that this passage was written in 1959.

[16] Decisions (‹making up our minds›) are unavoidable, even in science. What scientists do all the time is to decide, in the light of argument. But we should distinguish between critical and tentative decisions and dogmatic decisions or commitments: it is the latter type of decision which has given rise to ‹decisionism›.

sions. I decided to limit myself to three closely connected problems. I want to discuss the little-known role which a highly immature philosophical theory has played in the rise of the three most distinctive and characteristic forces in European history. The three forces I have in mind are the following:

(1) Our industrial civilization.
(2) Our science, and its influence.
(3) Our idea of individual freedom.

Thus industrialism, science, and the idea of freedom are my three chief subjects. It is fairly obvious that they are characteristically European subjects, provided we permit ourselves to treat American civilization as an offshoot of European civilization. How they link up with philosophy is perhaps less obvious.

It is my basic proposition that they are connected in an interesting way with a highly characteristic European theory of knowledge or epistemology: with that theory which *Plato* described in his famous simile of the cave in which he depicted the world of phenomena as a world of shadows – shadows cast by a real world hidden behind the world of phenomena. Admittedly *Plato's* belief in a world we can never learn to know could perhaps be called ‹epistemological pessimism›; and it has spread far beyond Europe. But *Plato* supplemented it, quite in the spirit of the old Ionian critical and rationalist tradition, with an unequalled epistemological optimism; and this epistemological optimism has remained part of our Western civilization. It is the optimistic theory that science, that is, real knowledge about the hidden real world, though certainly very difficult, is nevertheless attainable, at least for some of us. Man, according to *Plato*, can discover the reality hidden behind the world of phenomena, and he can discover it by the power of his own critical reason, without the aid of divine revelation.

This is the almost unbelievable optimism of Greek rationalism:[17] of the rationalism of the Renaissance: of European rationalism. *Homer*, though perhaps with a slight touch of irony, still appealed to the authority of the Muses; they are his sources, the divine fountainheads of his knowledge. Similarly the Jews and, in the Middle Ages, the Arabs and the Christians of Europe, appealed to the authority of divine revelation as the source of their knowledge. But the Ionian philosophers, beginning perhaps with *Thales*, argued. They appealed to critical argument and thus to reason: they thought of reason as capable of unveiling the secrets of a hidden reality. This is what I call ‹epistemological optimism›. I believe that this optimistic attitude existed almost exclusively in Europe: in the two or three centuries of Greek rationalism and in the three or four centuries of its European and American renaissance.

Corresponding to my three main subjects, industrialism, science, and freedom, I can now formulate my three chief theses. Summed up in one sentence they read:

Europe's industrialism, its science, and its political idea of freedom, that is to say, every one of those characteristic and fundamental aspects of European civilization which I have listed, is a product of what I have called epistemological optimism.[18]

I shall now try to substantiate this thesis for each of my three chief subjects.

---

[17] It will be clear from the context that I am using the term ‹rationalism› in its wide sense, and not in the narrow sense in which it is used in opposition to empiricism. (Cp. my Conjectures and Refutations, p. 6.)

[18] For a discussion of ‹epistemological optimism›, see ‹On the Sources of Knowledge and of Ignorance› in my Conjectures and Refutations, pp. 5 ff.

V.

When we seek to understand the distinctive character of European or Western civilization, one feature leaps to the mind. European civilization is an industrial civilization; it is based upon industrialization on the grand scale. It uses engines, sources of energy which are non-muscular. In this, European and American civilizations differ fundamentally from all the other great civilizations which are or were mainly agrarian and whose industry depended on manual labour.

I think there is no other feature that distinguishes our civilization so clearly from all the others – except perhaps European science. Literature, art, religion, philosophy, and even the rudiments of natural science, play their part in all other civilizations, for instance in those of India and China. But heavy industry on a grand scale seems to be unique as a form of production and indeed as a way of life. We find it only in Europe and in those parts of the world which have taken it over from Europe.

Like industrialism, the growth of science is a characteristic feature of Europe. And since they have developed almost simultaneously, the question arises whether industry is a product of the development of science or whether (as Marxism would have it) science is a product of industrialization.

I believe that neither of these interpretations is true, and that both science and industry are products of that philosophy which I have called epistemological optimism.

It is a fact that ever since the Renaissance the development of industry and the development of science have been closely linked and have closely interacted. Each is indebted to the other. But if we ask how this interaction came about, my answer is this. It was bound to take place right from the outset, for it stemmed from a new philosophical or religious idea – a peculiar new variant of the Platonic idea that the philosophers, that is, those who know, should also be those who wield the power. The peculiar new variant of that theory is expressed in the dictum that knowledge is power – power over nature. It is my thesis that both the industrial and the scientific development which took place after the Renaissance are realizations of this philosophical idea – the idea of the mastery of man over nature.

The idea of mastery over nature is, I suggest, the Renaissance version of epistemological optimism. We find it in the Neo-Platonist *Leonardo*, and in a somewhat claptrap form we find it in *Bacon*. *Bacon* was not, I believe, a great philosopher; but he was a visionary, and he is most important as the prophet of a new industrial and scientific society. He founded a new secularized religion and so became the creator of the industrial and scientific revolution.[19]

---

[19] Only quite recently, and many years after I first arrived at my not too favourable opinion of *Bacon's* philosophy as well as at the view that he was the prophet of the industrial revolution, I came across the admirable and highly original book by *Benjamin Farrington*, Francis Bacon, Philosopher of Industrial Science (American edition 1949, 1961; English edition, 1951). Though *Farrington's* philosophical standpoint is very different to mine, our results concerning *Bacon's* influence on the industrial revolution are strikingly similar. Indeed, *Farrington* quotes (on p. 136 of the 1961 American edition) the passage from *Marx's* Capital which I have now adopted as a motto to this essay. In that passage *Marx* says: ‹ . . . *Francis Bacon* looked forward to an alteration in the form of production and to the effective control of nature by man, as a result of a change in the ways of thinking›. I certainly agree with what *Marx* says here, though my interpretation hardly fits *Marx's* own view of the relation between ‹the mode of production of material life› and ‹the general character of the social, political and intellectual processes of life›. For *Marx*

VI.

Before going into details I would like to explain briefly my own opinion about this particular version of epistemological optimism.[20]

I am myself a rationalist, and an epistemological optimist, yet I am no friend of that mighty rationalist religion of which *Bacon* is the founder. My objection against this religion is purely philosophical; and I should like to emphasize that it has nothing whatever to do with the present hangover – the intellectual anti-climax of the nuclear bomb[21] (or with other undesirable unintended consequences of the growth of scientific knowledge and technology). My objection to the religion of mastery over nature, to the idea that knowledge is power, is, quite simply, that knowledge is something far better than power. *Bacon's* formula ‹knowledge is power› (‹nam et ipsa scientia potestas est›) was an attempt to advertise knowledge. It takes it for granted that power is always something good, and it promises that you will be repaid in terms of power if you make the unpleasant effort needed to attain knowledge. Yet I believe that Lord Acton was right when he said: ‹Power tends to corrupt; and absolute power corrupts absolutely.›[22] Of course, I do not deny that power can be tamed, that it may sometimes be used for very good things – for instance, in the hands of a good physician. But I am afraid that even physicians not infrequently succumb to the temptation to make their patients feel their power.

Kant once commented strikingly on the saying that truthfulness, and honesty, is the best policy. This, he said, was open to doubt; but he added that he did not doubt that truthfulness was better than any policy.[23] My remark that knowledge is better than all power is merely a variant of this remark of *Kant's*. To the scientist only truth matters, not power; it is the politician who cares about power.

The idea of mastery over nature is in itself perhaps neutral. When it is a case of helping our fellow men, when it is a case of medical progress or of the fight against starvation and misery, then of course I welcome the power we owe to our knowledge about nature. But the idea of mastery over nature often contains, I fear, another element – the will to power

---

says in his ‹Preface› to A Contribution to the Critique of Political Economy (cp. Lawrence & Wishart edition, 1971, pp. 20–21; *T. B. Bottomore* and *M. Rubel* (eds) *Karl Marx*, Selected Writings in Sociology and Social Philosophy, Penguin edition, 1963, p. 67) ‹The mode of production of material life determines the general character of the social, political and intellectual processes of life. It is not the consciousness of men that determines their existence but, on the contrary, their social existence determines their consciousness.›

[20] Cp. my paper referred to in footnote 18 above and my paper ‹Science: Problems, Aims, Responsibilities›, Federation Proceedings (Baltimore) 22, 1963, pp. 961–72.

[21] In the original lecture I mentioned at this point that my critical attitude towards *Bacon* predated the creation of nuclear weapons (I criticized *Bacon* in 1934), and that I remained a great admirer of *Albert Einstein* and *Niels Bohr* even though their theories fathered the atom bomb.

[22] Lord *Acton*, Letter to Mandell Creighton, April 5th, 1887. Cp. Lord *Acton*, Essays on Freedom and Power, ed. *Gertrude Himmelfarb*, Meridian Books, Thames and Hudson, London, 1956, p. 335.

[23] I referred to this in my Open Society, volume one, chapter 8, p. 139; see *Immanuel Kant*, On Eternal Peace, Appendix; (Kant's Gesammelte Schriften, ed. königlich preussische Akademie der Wissenschaften, VIII, Gruyter, Berlin and Leipzig, 1923, p. 370). Cp. *H. Reiss* (ed.), Kant's Political Writings, Cambridge University Press, 1971, p. 116: ‹It is true, alas, that the saying «Honesty is the best policy» embodies a theory which is frequently contradicted by practice. Yet the equally theoretical proposition «Honesty is better than any policy» infinitely transcends all objections, and is indeed an indispensable condition of any policy whatever.›

as such, the will to dominate. And to the idea of domination I cannot take kindly. It is blasphemy, sacrilege, hubris. Men are not gods and they ought to know it. We shall never dominate nature. The mountaineer is to be pitied who sees in mountains nothing but adversaries he has to conquer; who does not know the feeling of gratitude, and the feeling of his own insignificance in the face of nature. Power always is temptation, even power or mastery over nature. What the Sherpa *Tenzing* felt on the peak of Chomo Lungma – that is, Mount Everest – was better: ‹I am grateful, Chomo Lungma›, he said.[24]

But let us return to *Bacon*. From a rational or critical point of view *Bacon* was not a great philosopher of science. His writings are sketchy and pretentious, contradictory, shallow, and immature; and his famous and influential theory of induction, so far as he developed it (for most of it remained a mere project, and has remained so ever since), bears no relation to the real procedure of science. (It was the great chemist *Justus Liebig* who pointed this out most forcefully.[25]) *Bacon* never understood the theoretical approach of *Copernicus* or of *Gilbert* or of his contemporaries *Galileo* and *Kepler*;[26] nor did he understand the significance of mathematical ideas for science.[27] Yet hardly any philosopher of modern times can compete with *Bacon's* influence. Even today many scientists still regard him as their spiritual father.

VII.

This leads us to a question which one may call the historical problem of *Bacon*: how can we explain the immense influence of this logically and rationally quite unimportant philosopher?

I have already briefly hinted at my solution of this problem. In spite of everything I have said, *Bacon* is the spiritual father of modern science. Not because of his philosophy of science and his theory of induction; but rather because he became the founder and prophet of a rationalist church – a kind of anti-church. This church was founded not on a rock but on the vision and the promise of a scientific and industrial society, a society based on man's mastery over nature. *Bacon* promises the self-liberation of mankind through knowledge.[28]

In his Utopia, The New Atlantis, *Bacon* depicted such a society. The governing body of that society was a technocratic institute of research which he called ‹Salomon's House›.

It is interesting to note that *Bacon's* New Atlantis not only anticipated certain not too pleasant aspects of modern ‹Big Science›, but goes beyond them in its uninhibited

[24] *Tenzing Norgay*, Man of Everest (as told to James Ramsey Ullman), London, 1955; see p. 271.

[25] See *Justus von Liebig*, Ueber Francis Bacon von Verulam und die Methode der Naturforschung, Munich, 1863; English translation, ‹Lord Bacon as Natural Philosopher› I and II, Macmillan's Magazine, 8, 1863, pp. 237–49, 257–67.

[26] *Kepler* is not mentioned at all by *Bacon*. See *Ellis's* Preface to the Descriptio Globi Intellectualis, in The Works of *Francis Bacon*, edited by *James Spedding, Robert Leslie Ellis* and *Douglas Denon Heath*, Longmans & Co., London, 1862–75, Volume III, pp. 723–6.

[27] On *Copernicus*, see *Spedding, Ellis* and *Heath* (eds), The Works of *Francis Bacon,* III, p. 229 and V, p. 517 (also IV, p. 373); on *Galileo*, see II, p. 596 (*Bacon* on *Galileo's* theory of the tides) and, for example, V, pp. 541–2; on *Gilbert*, see III, pp. 292–3 and V, p. 202 (also V, pp. 454, 493, 515 and 537).

[28] Compare my ‹Emancipation Through Knowledge›, in The Humanist Outlook, edited by A. J. Ayer, Pemberton Publishing Company, London, 1968, pp. 281–96.

dreams of the power, the glory, and the wealth which the great scientist may attain. This becomes very obvious from *Bacon's* description of the more than papal pomp of one of the ‹Fathers of Salomon's House›; that is to say, one of the Directors of Research.[29]

A less questionable passage that may be found in *Bacon's* Novum Organum may be here of interest.[30]

Also our hopes are raised by the fact that some of the experiments made hitherto are of such a kind that nobody before had an idea of such things; rather, they would have been contemptuously set aside as impossibilities.

If prior to the discovery of firearms somebody would have described their effects, and would have said that an invention had been made by the means of which even the biggest walls and fortifications could be shaken and knocked down from a great distance, people might have, quite reasonably, deliberated about the various ways of utilizing the power of the existing machines and contraptions, and how one might strengthen them with more weights and more wheels, or increase the number of knocks and blows; but nobody would have dreamt of a fiery blast which suddenly and violently expands and blows up; one would, on the contrary, have discarded such a thing entirely, because nobody had ever seen an example of it . . .

Bacon then goes on to discuss in a similar vein the discovery of silk and of the mariner's compass; and he continues:

Thus there is much hope that Nature still holds many an excellent and useful thing in her lap that has no resemblance or parallel to what has been discovered hitherto, but, on the contrary, lies far away from all the paths of imagination, and from all that has been found so far. No doubt it will come to light in the circuitous course of the centuries, just as has happened with earlier inventions; but with the aid of the method which is here treated of, these things will be found far more surely and more quickly; and indeed, they might be accounted for and anticipated at once.

This passage from the Novum Organum is characteristic of *Bacon's* promise: Follow my new way, my new method, and you shall quickly attain knowledge and power. Indeed, *Bacon* believed that an Encyclopaedia containing a description of all important

---

[29] *Francis Bacon,* New Atlantis, in *Spedding, Ellis* and *Heath* (eds.), The Works of *Francis Bacon,* Volume III, pp. 114f: ‹The day being come, he made his entry. He was a man of middle stature and age, comely of person, and had an aspect as if he pitied men. He was clothed in a robe of fine black cloth, with wide sleeves and a cape . . . He had gloves that were . . . set with stone; and shoes of peach-coloured velvet . . . He was carried in a rich chariot without wheels, litter-wise; with two horses at either end, richly trapped in blue velvet embroidered; and two footmen on each side in the like attire. The chariot was all of cedar, gilt, and adorned with crystal; save that the fore-end had pannels of sapphires, set in borders of gold, and the hinder-end the like of emeralds of the Peru colour. There was also a sun of gold, radiant, upon the top, in the midst; and on the top before, a small cherub of gold, with wings displayed. The chariot was covered with cloth of gold tissued upon blue. He had before him fifty attendants, young men all, in white sattin loose coats to the mid-leg; and stockings of white silk; and shoes of blue velvet; and hats of blue velvet; with fine plumes of divers colours, set round like hat-bands. Next before the chariot went two men, bare-headed, in linen garments down to the foot, girt, and shoes of blue velvet; who carried the one a crosier, the other a pastoral staff like a sheep-hook; neither of them of metal, but the crosier of balm-wood, the pastoral staff of cedar. Horsemen he had none, neither before nor behind his chariot: as it seemeth, to avoid all tumult and trouble. Behind his chariot went all the officers and principals of the Companies of the City. He sat alone, upon cushions of a kind of excellent plush, blue: and under his foot curious carpets of silk of divers colours, like the Persian, but far finer. He held up his bare hand as he went, as blessing the people, but in silence.› This is *Bacon's* dream of the link of knowledge with power.

[30] The quotations are from Novum Organum, 109th Aphorism, cp. *Spedding, Ellis* and *Heath* (eds.), The Works of *Francis Bacon,* volume I, pp. 207f. The translation is my own; cp. *James Spedding's* translation in The Works of *Francis Bacon,* Volume IV, pp. 99f.

phenomena of the Universe could be completed soon: he believed that, given two or three years, he could read through the whole book of Nature and bring the task of the new science to its completion.

There is no need to say that *Bacon* was mistaken; not only about the magnitude of the task, but about his new method. The method he was proposing had nothing whatever to do with that of the new science of *Gilbert*, of *Galileo*, or of *Kepler*; or with the later developments of *Boyle* and of *Newton*.

Yet *Bacon's* promise of a scientific future, splendid and close at hand, had an immense influence on both English science and the English industrial revolution; the industrial revolution which spread first to Europe and later to America and, indeed, all over the world, and which has truly changed the world into a Baconian Utopia.

As is well known, the Royal Society and later the British Association for the Advancement of Science (and still later the American Association) were deliberate attempts to give effect to the Baconian idea of co-operative and organized research.

It may be of interest to quote at this stage a passage from the second charter of the Royal Society, of 1663, which is still in force. It says that the researches of the Members are to promote ‹by the authority of experiments the sciences of natural things and of useful arts [that is, industrial technology], to the glory of God the Creator, and the advantage of the human race›.[31] The conclusion of this passage is taken almost literally from *Bacon's* The Advancement of Learning.[32]

Thus this pragmatic-technological attitude was combined from the outset with humanitarian aims: the increase of general welfare and the fight against want and poverty. The English and European industrial revolution was a philosophical and religious revolution, with *Bacon* as its prophet. It was inspired by the idea of accelerating, through knowledge and research, the hitherto far too slow advance of technology. It was the idea of a material self-liberation through knowledge.

VIII.

But here one could raise an important objection. Was not the idea of applied knowledge, the idea that knowledge is power, already an influence in the Middle Ages? Was there not astrology that served the desire for power, and alchemy, the search for the Philosopher's Stone?

The objection is important and can help us to bring out more clearly the influence of epistemological optimism. For that peculiar optimism was lacking in the medieval alchemists and astrologers. They searched for a secret which, they believed, had once been known in antiquity but had later been forgotten. They looked for the key to wisdom in old parchments.

---

[31] Cp., for example, Sir *Henry Lyons*, The Royal Society 1660–1940, Cambridge University Press, 1944, Appendix I: ‹Second Charter: 22 April 1663›. The quotation in my text is from p. 329 of this Appendix.

[32] See *Spedding, Ellis* and *Heath* (eds), The Works of *Francis Bacon*, Volume III, p. 294: ‹ . . . for the glory of the Creator and the relief of man's estate›. Cp. also *Rawley's* Introduction ‹To the Reader› to New Atlantis (published in 1627): ‹ . . .a college instituted for the interpreting of nature and the producing of great and marvellous works for the benefit of men . . .› (ibid, volume III, p. 127).

And yet, they may have been right in hunting for lost treasures of wisdom. What they were seeking so eagerly may well have been, unknown to themselves, the greatness of ancient Rome and the Augustan Peace, or perhaps the greatness and the boldness of the critical and rationalist philosophy of the Presocratic philosophers.

However this may be, *Bacon* (and the Renaissance) felt differently on this point. Admittedly *Bacon* was an alchemist and a ‹magus› who believed in ‹natural magic›; but he also believed – and this is decisive – that he himself had found a key to new wisdom. It is this new selfconfidence that distinguishes *Bacon's* optimism; the confidence, completely unwarranted in his case, that he himself had the power to unveil the mysteries of nature without having to be initiated into the secret wisdom of the ancients. This power is independent of divine revelation, and independent of disclosure of mysteries in the secret writings of ancient sages. Thus *Bacon's* promise may be said to encourage enterprise and selfconfidence. It encourages men to rely on themselves in the search for knowledge, and so to become independent of divine revelation and of ancient traditions.

IX.

Bacon himself (and with him many other Renaissance sages) belonged to two worlds: he belonged to the old world of mysticism and word magic combined with the authoritarian faith in some lost secret, the (Neo-Platonic[33]) Wisdom of the Ancients.[34] At the same time he belonged to the new world of an anti-authoritarian confidence in our own power of adding to our wisdom and thereby of further increasing our power. This made *Bacon's* prophetic message apt to grow into a new religion, and ultimately into the new message of the Enlightenment. This new message of the European Enlightenment might perhaps be summed up in the somewhat equivocal formula: God helps those who help themselves; a formula which has sometimes been taken quite seriously as a statement of the responsibility imposed by God on us, and sometimes as a manifesto of the self-emancipation and the self-reliance of a secular, fatherless society.[35]

[33] I should perhaps have said, rather, Hermetic. See, notably, *P. Rossi*, Francis Bacon: From Magic to Science, Routledge & Kegan Paul, London, 1968 (first published in Italian in 1957); *Francis Yates*, Giordano Bruno and the Hermetic Tradition, London, 1964; and *Francis Yates*, ‹The Hermetic Tradition in Renaissance Science›, in *C. S. Singleton* (ed.) Art, Science and History in the Renaissance, Baltimore 1967. For a recent discussion see *D. K. Probst*, Francis Bacon and the Transformation of the Hermetic Tradition into the Rationalist Church, D. Sc. thesis, Université Libre de Bruxelles, Faculté des Sciences, Service de Chimie Physique II, 1972. I might also add that in the interesting discussion of *Bacon* in *Joseph Agassi's* Ph. D. thesis, ‹The Function of Interpretations in Physics›, submitted to the University of London in 1956, some suggestive remarks are made about certain resemblances between *Bacon's* demands that the mind should be prepared before learning takes place and the preparation needed before participation in the religious mysteries of the Cabbala.

[34] Cp. *Bacon's* De Sapientia Veterum, in *Spedding, Ellis* and *Heath*, volume VI, pp. 619–86 (translation ibid., pp. 689–764); and De Principiis Atque Originibus Secundum Fabulas Cupidinis et Coele, ibid., volume III, pp. 79–118 (translation ibid., volume V, pp. 461–500), which interpreted a number of classical myths as cosmological allegories.

[35] This term is a reference to the idea that our Western societies do not, by their structure, satisfy a need for a father-figure. I discussed these problems, briefly, in my (unpublished) William James Lectures delivered in Harvard in 1950. (Cp. my Conjectures and Refutations, p. 375.)

Christianity, perhaps more than any other religion, had always taught its believers to look forward to a life to come; to sacrifice the present for the sake of the future. Thus it laid the foundation of an attitude towards life that might be called ‹the European futurity neurosis›. It is a way of living at all times more in the future than in the present; of being obsessed with plans for the future, schemes for the future, investments in a better life to come. My conjecture is that epistemological optimism with its peculiar idea of self-reliance – that God helps those who help themselves – secularized Christianity, and turned its futurity neurosis into the idea of self-liberation through the acquisition of new knowledge and through participation in the new knowledge to come – the new growth of knowledge – and at the same time into the related but subtly different idea of self-liberation through the acquisition of new power, and of new wealth.

Thus we may say that the Baconian Utopia, like most Utopias, was an attempt to bring heaven down to earth. And so far as it promised an increase of power and of wealth through self-help and self-liberation through new knowledge, it is perhaps the one Utopia that has (so far) kept its promise. Indeed it has kept it to an almost unbelievable extent.[36]

X.

I may perhaps now remind you of my programme, which was to outline the decisive part played by philosophical ideas, and more precisely by epistemological optimism, in the development of three characteristic forces of European history:

(1) our industrial civilization;
(2) our science, and its influence;
(3) our idea of individual freedom.

I will now leave the first of those three points; not because I have exhausted it – it is a subject I could not exhaust in one lecture – but simply because I have to pass on to my second point, the evolution of modern science.

As I have pointed out before, the evolution of science and of industry and technology have interacted, and have enriched each other. I now only want to stress that this interaction shows a significant asymmetry. While modern industrial development has become unthinkable without modern science, the opposite is not the case: science is largely autonomous. No doubt the needs of industry have been a stimulus to its development, and any stimulus is welcome and useful. But what the scientist wants more than anything else is to know; and though he is grateful to anybody who gives him interesting problems to tackle, and the means of tackling them, what he wants is to know, and to be able to add to our knowledge.

---

[36] I offer this view as an alternative historical conjecture to the theories of *Max Weber* and *R. H. Tawney* about the relation between ‹Religion› and ‹the Rise of Capitalism› *(Max Weber*, The Protestant Ethic and the Spirit of Capitalism, 1904–5; *R. H. Tawney,* Religion and the Rise of Capitalism, Holland Memorial Lectures, 1922, first published 1926). The time at my disposal did not allow me to elaborate my conjecture – and even less to compare it critically with its competitors.

XI.

The science of the Renaissance may be regarded as the direct continuation of the Greek Cosmology of the Ionians and the Pythagoreans; the Platonists and the Aristotelians; the Atomists and the Geometers. The method of *Galileo* and of *Kepler* is a development of the rational, the hypothetical, the critical method of these forerunners of theirs.[37] Hypotheses are invented and criticized. Under the influence of criticism they are modified. When the modifications become unsatisfactory, they are discarded, and new hypotheses are advanced. One typical example is the Ptolemaic geocentric cosmology with its modifications and auxiliary hypotheses, the epicycles. When they became too cumbrous, *Copernicus* rediscovered the heliocentric cosmology of *Aristarchus*. The heliocentric hypothesis, too, led to grave difficulties; but they were triumphantly resolved by *Kepler* and *Newton*. Thus the method of science consists of boldly advancing tentative hypotheses and of submitting them to critical tests. Since *Einstein* we know that it can never lead to certainty; for whether *Newton* or *Einstein* is right, we have learned from *Einstein* at least one thing: that *Newton's* theory, too, is only a hypothesis, a conjecture, and perhaps a false one, in spite of its incredible success in predicting with the greatest precision almost all astronomical phenomena within our solar system, and even beyond.

Thus we have learned from *Einstein* that science offers us only hypotheses or conjectures rather than certain knowledge. But the modest programme of searching for hypotheses would probably not have inspired scientists: it might have never started the enterprise of science. What people hoped for, and sought, was knowledge – certain indubitable knowledge. Yet while searching for certain knowledge, scientists stumbled, as it were, upon the hypothetical, the conjectural, the critical method. For knowledge, whether certain or not, had to stand up to criticism. If it failed to do so, it had to be discarded. And so it came about that scientists got used to trying out new conjectures, and to using their imagination to the utmost while submitting themselves to the discipline of rational criticism.

Although nowadays we have given up the idea of absolutely certain knowledge, we have not by any means given up the idea of the search for truth. On the contrary, when we say that our knowledge is not certain, we only mean that we can never be sure whether our conjectures are true. When we find that a hypothesis is not true, or at least that it does not appear to be a better approximation to the truth than its competitors, then we may discard it. Hypotheses are never verifiable, but they can be falsified; they can be criticized, and tested.

It is the search for true theories that inspires this critical method. Without the regulative idea of truth, criticism would be pointless.

The experimental methods of *Gilbert, Galileo, Torricelli,* and *Boyle* are methods for testing theories: if a theory fails to satisfy an experiment, it is falsified, and has to be modified or supplanted by another one; by a theory, that is, which lends itself better, or at least equally well, to testing.

So much for the method of science. It is critical, argumentative, and almost sceptical.

---

[37] Lest I be misunderstood, my comments pertain not so much to scientists as individuals as to the scientific tradition – the friendly-hostile cooperation of scientists – which itself emerged from the very developments we are discussing. (See also my Objective Knowledge: An Evolutionary Approach, Oxford, 1972; 5th enlarged edn., 1979; chapter 4, section 9.)

XII.

But the great masters of this method were not aware of the fact that this was their method. They believed in the possibility of reaching absolute certainty in knowledge. A radical version of epistemological optimism inspired them (as it inspired *Bacon*). It led them from succes to success. Nevertheless it was uncritical, and logically untenable.

We can describe this radical and uncritical epistemological optimism of the Renaissance as the belief that truth is manifest: Truth may be hard to find; but once the truth stands revealed before us, it is impossible for us not to recognize it as truth: we cannot possibly mistake it. Thus nature is an open book. Or, as *Descartes* put it, God does not deceive us.

This theory is closely related to *Plato's* theory of anamnesis; to the theory that before our birth we knew the hidden reality, and that we recognize it again once we happen to catch sight of it, or perhaps even its faint shadow.

The idea that truth is manifest is a philosophical idea (or perhaps even a religious idea) of the greatest historical importance. It is an optimistic idea, a beautiful and hopeful dream, a truly sublime idea. I am even willing to admit that there may be a grain of truth in it; yet certainly not more than a grain. For the idea is mistaken. Again and again, even with quite simple things, we hold the truth in our hands and do not recognize it. And still more often we are convinced of having recognized the manifest truth while in fact we are entangled in errors.

The radical epistemological optimists, *Plato, Bacon, Descartes,* and others, were of course aware of the fact that we sometimes mistake error for truth; and in order to save the doctrine of manifest truth they were forced to explain the occurrence of error. *Plato's* theory of error was that our birth is a kind of epistemological fall from grace: when we are born we forget the best part of our knowledge, which is our direct acquaintance with truth. Similarly, *Bacon* (and *Descartes*) declared that error is to be explained by our personal shortcomings. We err because we stubbornly cling to our prejudices instead of opening our physical or mental eyes to the manifest truth. We are epistemological sinners: hardhearted sinners who refuse to perceive the truth even when it is manifest before our eyes. *Bacon's* method, therefore, consists in cleansing our minds of prejudices. It is the unbiased mind, the pure mind, the mind cleansed of prejudice, that cannot fail to recognize the truth.

With this theory I have reached a final formulation of radical epistemological optimism. The theory is of great importance. It became the cornerstone of modern science. It made the scientist a priest of truth, and the worship of truth a sort of divine service.

I believe that this respect for truth is indeed one of the most important and most precious traits of European civilization, and that it is rooted nowhere more firmly and deeply than in science. It is a priceless treasure we find in the treasure-house of science, a treasure which, I believe, far surpasses its technological utility.

Yet *Bacon's* theory of error is, in spite of its desirable consequences, untenable. Small wonder, therefore, that it has also led to undesirable consequences. I shall discuss some of these consequences in connection with my third and last point to which I am now coming, my analysis of the importance of epistemological optimism for the development of freedom, of European liberalism.

XIII.

In discussing my second point I have tried to show the way in which epistemological optimism is responsible for the development of modern science. At the same time I have tried to discuss epistemological optimism and to evaluate and criticize this peculiar philosophy.

All this we have to keep in mind when we now turn to glance at the development of modern liberalism. And since I am going to say something critical about it, I want first of all to state quite clearly and unmistakably that my sympathies are all for it. Indeed, while I am well aware of its many imperfections, I do think – with *E. M. Forster* (Two Cheers for Democracy) and *Pablo Casals* – that democracy is the best and noblest form of social life that has so far arisen in the history of mankind. I am not a prophet, and I cannot deny the possibility that one day it will be destroyed. But whether or not it will in fact survive we should work for its survival.

Now I think that the mainspring that keeps democratic societies going is the peculiar philosophy which I have just sketched: the belief in the sanctity of truth, together with the over-optimistic belief that truth is manifest, even though it can be temporarily obscured by prejudices.

This peculiar philosophy is, of course, much older than *Bacon*. It played a large part in almost all religious wars: each side regarding the other as benighted; as refusing to see the obvious truth; and perhaps even as possessed by the devil.

XIV.

Epistemological over-optimism has two very different philosophies opposed to it: a pessimism which despairs of the possibility of knowledge; and a critical optimism which realizes that it is human to err, and that fanaticism is usually the attempt to shout down the voices of one's own doubts. Up to the twentieth century critical optimists were rare. *Socrates, Erasmus, John Locke, Immanuel Kant* and *John Stuart Mill* were among the greatest of them.

The development of liberalism from the Reformation down to our own time took place almost entirely under the sway of an uncritical, epistemological over-optimism: the theory of manifest truth. This theory led liberalism along two roads. The first led straight from the Reformation to the demand for freedom of religious worship. The second led through some disappointments in the theory of manifest truth to the theory that there exists a conspiracy against truth. For, it was argued, if so many do not see the manifest truth – that truth which is so clearly visible – it must be on account of false prejudices, cunningly and systematically implanted into young impressionable minds so as to blind them to truth. The conspirators against truth were, of course, the priests of the competing churches: in the minds of the Protestants the Catholic Church, and vice versa.

Though based upon the mistaken doctrine of manifest truth, this second road led, nevertheless, to the valid and invaluable demand for freedom of thought, and to the demand for a universal and secular primary education; on the ground that those who are freed from the darkness of illiteracy and religious tutelage cannot fail to see the manifest truth.

And it led finally to the demand for universal suffrage; for if truth is manifest, the people cannot err; since they can recognize the truth, they can also recognize what is good and just.

I believe that this development was good and just, despite the epistemological over-optimism which is the main weakness of its theoretical basis. For it was the weakness of its theoretical basis that led to the terrible religious wars of the sixteenth and seventeenth centuries, and to the horrors of violent revolutions and civil wars. Here in the West, all this has finally led most of us to the Socratic insight that to err is human. We are not fanatics any longer. Most of us are only too willing to recognize our own shortcomings and mistakes. This insight, belatedly as it came to us, is a blessing. Like all blessings, though, it is a mixed blessing: it tends to undermine our confidence in our way of life, especially the confidence of those of us who have learned this lesson well.

I have come to the end of my historical sketch. In conclusion I wish to add only one further remark: The Socratic-Erasmic insight that we may be in error should certainly prevent us from waging a war of aggression. But our consciousness of our shortcomings and mistakes must not deter us from fighting in defence of freedom.

Summary

Epistemology and Industrialization

The author commences by discussing critically the Platonic thesis that philosophers should be kings and kings philosophers. He then turns to the thesis, familiar from the liberal tradition from *Heine* to *Hayek*, that philosophers, or some of them, are the rulers anyway, because of the impact of their ideas on the men of action. After some comments on the power of ideas for good and ill, and on the importance of the Western tradition of critical rationalism, the author turns to his main theme: the influence of European philosophy on the history of Europe.

Here, he concerns himself with three characteristic features of Western civilization: industrialization; science and its influence; and individual freedom. He suggests, as a historical conjecture, that all three are related to a distinctive theory of knowledge, which he calls «epistemological optimism»; a doctrine of which he is in some respects critical. The author's brief exploration of his conjecture includes a critical discussion of *Francis Bacon*, and of the doctrine «knowledge is power».

Chiaki Nishiyama

Anti-Rationalism or Critical Rationalism

I. Scientific Deliberation versus Actual Practice

It is not quite easy to tell whether The Constitution of Liberty is the magnum opus of Professor *Hayek*; for he wrote also two other major works; The Pure Theory of Capital, (Chicago: The University of Chicago Press, 1941), and Law, Legislation and Liberty, (Chicago: The University of Chicago Press, 1973–79). It is true that so far The Pure Theory of Capital has not been given as much attention by the contemporary economists as it should have. After all, under the influence of the Keynesian economists, the field of economics made its major efforts to develop flow analyses in the 1940's, 50's and 60's. Even as late as in the 1970's, this trend was not quite reversed, although the influence of the Keynesian economists has noticeably declined in the last ten years. This may be partly because even their major opponents called «Monetarists», including myself, have not really been different from them in so far as the primary attention of the latter has also still been centered about flow analyses.** Under such an intellectual climate in the last four decades, The Pure Theory of Capital has often had to be left outside of active discussions among economists. But sooner or later economists may well once again have to be confronted with the problem of capital and go back to that work. There are already several indications of the revival of economists' interests in the economic writings of Professor *Hayek*. A revolutionary effort which was initiated by *Axel Leijonhufvud* in 1968 in order to provide the economics of *Keynes* with its micro foundation, was triggered by his rediscovery of the Hayekian economics,[1] which insisted since as early as 1936 on the utmost

---

** An explanatory note on this passage may well be necessary. If we limit the theoretical system of Professor Hayek only to his monetary theory and cmpare it with that of Monetarists, we must say that it is really the analysis of Professor Hayek that has been money-flow (or credit-flow) oriented, whereas the emphasis of Monetarists has been on the stock of money. While, however, monetarists have been busy in exploring relationships among the different flows of such aggregates as general price level, national product and money supply, the capital theory of Professor Hayek has been stock-analysis oriented in the sense that it tried to analyze the problem of capital not as «an amorphous mass» nor as «a datum» but as «a result of the equilibrating process», by emphasizing the importance of changes in real factors and relative prices as well as of «the essentially nonhomogeneous nature of the different capital items.» Of course, it may well not be wise to differentiate the two in terms of stock-analysis v.s. flow-analysis. It may be far more appropriate to identify the system of Professor Hayek as a micro analysis and that of Monetarists as a macro type. In any case, it is undeniable that there has been a very significant difference between the two approaches. Nad I still maintain that the capital theory of Professor Hayek must and will be given much more attention than it already has. [In addition to *The Pure Theory of Capital,* see als his *Prices and Production,* 2nd ed., (London: Routledge & Kegan Paul Ltd., 1935) and *Profits, Interest, and Investment,* (London: George Routledge & Sons, Ltd., 1939).]

[1] *Axel Leijonhufvud,* On Keynesian Economics and the Economics of Keynes, (New York 1968), p. 70.

importance of an economic factor called »information» in the field economics or, more specifically, of the problem of how all the relevant information could be communicated to the different people who were involved in economic activities.[2] And the further development of a new field called «human capital theory»[3] may well also lead us to the re-examination of capital theory at large. At any rate, we are today observing the emergence of an epochal change of interests in the field of economics. I am rather certain that the economic writings of Professor *Hayek* will greatly assist such a change and contribute to the further development of economics. As to Law, Legislation and Liberty, I personally feel that the work tells us the Hayekian system more eloquently than The Constitution of Liberty and that this work alone can entitle Professor *Hayek* to one more Nobel Prize. But it is still so new; and its publication is to be completed only in 1979. We must wait for the appearance of the third volume.

In any case, there is no doubt that The Constitution of Liberty will become a classic, if it is not one already. Not only those who will be interested in freedom but also those who will dispute it in future may well have to refer themselves to this great work from time to time. While Professor *Hayek* was writing it, I had a lucky opportunity of being taught by him (almost all the time tutorially) and of being with him even thereafter for almost one decade in total. I am really the record holder of having been with Professor *Hayek* longer than any other student of his, though this may well prove only that I was the dullest. Under the guidance of Professor *Hayek*, I wrote my Ph.D.'s dissertation, which was on the methodology of the social sciences and especially of economics, and which greatly dealt with the works of *Bernard Mandeville*. The major issue between Professor *Hayek* and me during that period was whether we should use the term «anti-rationalism» in order to describe the position not only of *Mandeville* but also of *David Hume, Adam Ferguson, Adam Smith,* etc., who were the forerunners of those who came later to embrace «liberalism» in our sense of the term. Both of us thought that these people shared a very similar philosophical position. But while, at that time, it was Professor *Hayek* who was convinced that the term «anti-rationalism» was most appropriate for our purpose, it was I who was quite ambivalent about it even to the degree of obstinate reluctance, although I did come to identify their positions as «anti-rationalism» in my Ph.D.'s dissertation.

As can be seen from The Constitution of Liberty, Professor *Hayek* called his own position in that work «anti-rationalism».[4] But later he changed his mind and came to agree with Professor *Karl R. Popper* that we had better use the term «critical rationalism» instead of «anti-rationalism» in order to present our position. In the lecture he gave in our university, he asserted that:

«. . . The general social philosophy which I hold sometimes has been described as anti-rationalistic, and at least with regard to my main intellectual forebears in this respect, *B. Mandeville, David Hume* and *Carl Menger,* I have, like others, occasionally myself used that term. Yet this has given rise to so many misunderstandings that it seemed to me now a dangerous and misleading expression which ought to be avoided.

We have to deal here once again with a situation in which one group of thinkers have effectively claimed for themselves the only proper use of the good word and had in consequence come to be called rationalists. It was almost inevitable that those who did not agree with their views on the proper use of reason should have been called ‹anti-

---

[2] *F. A. Hayek,* «The Use of Knowledge in Society», Individualism and Economic Order, Chap. IV, (Chicago 1948). Hereafter, the title of this book will be abbreviated to I. & E.

[3] *Gary S. Becker,* Human Capital, (New York 1964).

[4] *F. A. Hayek,* The Constitution of Liberty, (Chicago 1960), p. 57 & p. 69. Hereafter, the title of this book will be abbreviated to C.o.L.

rationalists». This gave the impression as if the latter rated reason less highly, while in fact they were anxious to make reason more effective and pleaded that an effective use of reason required a proper insight into the limits of the effective use of individual reason in regulating relations between many reasonable beings.»[5]

And in the same lecture he announced that the word «critical rationalism» of Professor *Karl R. Popper*[6] «seems to me the best term for describing the general position which I regard as the most reasonable one.»[7] Well, certainly none of us would want to be viewed as if we negate reason as such. By the use of the term ‹anti-rationalism›, I myself have had to experience many serious misunderstandings and unnecessary objections. At a glance, therefore, it may well seem wiser to change the term to «critical rationalism». As a matter of fact, I myself argued in my Ph.D.'s dissertation that there was no great difference between what I called «anti-rationalism» and what Professor *Popper* called «critical rationalism», and that the difference between the two might be one of emphasis: it depended on which aspect of our arguments we wanted to emphasize most.[8] But now I very much doubt if this is really the case.

At the very outset of Chapter Two of The Constitution of Liberty, Professor *Hayek* wrote that: «The Socratic maxim that the recognition of our ignorance is the beginning of wisdom has profound significance for our understanding of society.» Indeed, in preparing a philosophical foundation for the work, he repeatedly emphasized the utmost importance for us to be aware of the «constitutional limitations of the individual mind».[9] This was because he firmly believed that only then we would be able to understand how our society really worked and what we could truly do for its genuine improvement and progress. It was *Bernard Mandeville* who succeeded for the first time in the history of mankind in presenting a genuinely evolutionary and systematic account of society, by asserting, for example, that: «we often ascribe to the Excellency of Man's Genius, and the Depth of his Penetration, what was in Reality owing to length of Time, and the experience of many Generations, all of them very little differing from one another in the natural Parts and Sagacity.»[10] And later *David Hume, Adam Ferguson, Adam Smith* and others came to follow suit in promoting still further the evolutionary theory of society. Only with their realization that our civilization was «indeed the result of human action but not of human design»,[11] they came to be able to recognize how indispensable liberty was for its advancement. Liberty alone allows people to engage in trials and errors on their own initiatives and from time to time accomplish some great things which nobody beforehand ever dreamed of. Echoing the assertions of those forebears, Professor *Hayek* maintained that: «Liberty is essential in order to leave room for the unforeseeable and unpredictable»,[12] or that «the case for individual freedom rests chiefly on the recognition of the

[5] F. A. Hayek, «Kinds of Rationalism», Studies in Philosophy, Politics and Economics, Chap. 5, (Chicago 1967), p. 84. Hereafter, the title of this book will be abbreviated to Studies.

[6] Cf., Karl R. Popper, The Open Society and Its Enemies, (Princeton 1950), pp. 410–17, esp. p. 417. Also see Karl R. Popper, The Poverty of Historicism, (Boston 1957). Hereafter, the former will be abbreviated to O.S.E., and the latter of P.o.H.

[7] Studies, p. 94.

[8] Chiaki Nishiyama, The Theory of Self-love, Ph.D.'s Dissertation, The University of Chicago, 1960, p. 60.

[9] C.o.L., Chap. II, and I. & E., p. 14.

[10] Bernard Mandeville, The Fable of the Bees: or, Private Vices, Public Benefits, (Oxford 1924), Vol. II, p. 343. Hereafter, the title of this book will be abbreviated to F.o.B.

[11] Adam Ferguson, Principles of Moral and Political Science, (Edinburgh 1792), p. 187.

[12] C.o.L., p. 29.

inevitable ignorance of all of us concerning a great many of the factors on which the achievement of our ends and welfare depends».[13]

In spite of his strong insistence on the importance of our awareness of the inescapable limitation of any individual mind, Professor *Hayek* never advocated to abdicate reason as such. Even when he described his position in The Constitution of Liberty as «anti-rationalism», he was really asserting an «intelligent use of reason».[14] His aim was to «continue the efforts which *David Hume* commenced when he ‹turned against the enlightenment its own weapons› and undertook ‹to whittle down the claims of reason by the use of rational analysis›[15].»[16] What he objected against was fundamentally to regard human reason as omnipotent and treat it as «an absolute».[17] Putting it differently, what he insisted was the impossibility for any human reason to grasp our society as a whole so that it could hope to improve it in its totality. In The Constitution of Liberty, Professor *Hayek* wrote, for example, that we should always «aim at piecemeal, rather than total construction, and use at each stage the historical material at hand and improve details step by step rather than, attempt to redesign the whole [of our civilization]».[18] The assertion that the progress of our society should always be a step-by-step, part-by-part process was also repeatedly made by Professor *Popper*[19] as well as by another great liberalist, the late Professor *Ludwig von Mises*.[20] The «piecemeal method» and the negation of «wholism» were the kernels of the «social engineering» that Professor *Popper* proposed.[21] When examined in this manner, whether we should describe the philosophical foundation of The Constitution of Liberty as anti-rationalism as Professor *Hayek* himself did in this work or as critical rationalism as he did later in the lecture mentioned before may well appear as if it were a matter of semantics as I suggested in my Ph.D.'s dissertation. But as soon as I finished that dissertation, I in fact came to believe that the problem involved was actually far more serious than that.

First of all, Professor *Hayek* emphasized not only the inescapable limitation of human reason but also the importance of what he called «non-rational factors», by saying that:

«The growth of knowledge and the growth of civilization are the same only if we interpret knowledge to include all the human adaptations to environment in which past experience has been incorporated. Not all knowledge in this sense is part of our intellect, nor is our intellect the whole of our knowledge. Our habits and skills, our emotional attitudes, our tools, and our institutions – all are in this sense adaptations to past experience which have grown up by selective elimination of less suitable conduct. They are as much an indispensable foundation of successful action as is our conscious knowledge. Not all these *non-rational* factors underlying our action are always conductive to success. Some may be retained long after they have become more an obstacle to success. Nevertheless, we could not do without them: even the successful employment of our intellect itself rests on their constant use.»[22]

---

[13] ibid., p. 29.
[14] ibid., p. 69.
[15] S. S. Wolin, «Hume and Conservatism», American Political Science Review, Vol. XLIII, 1954, p. 1001.
[16] C.o.L., p. 69.
[17] ibid., p. 69.
[18] ibid., p. 70.
[19] O.S.E., pp. 407, 571, 579. P.o.H., pp. 58, 91.
[20] *Ludwig von Mises*, Human Action, (New Haven 1949), pp. 7, 45–6.
[21] O.S.E.
[22] C.o.L., p. 26.

The anti-rationalism of Professor *Hayek* was clearer in his earlier artic'
dividualism: True and False». There he maintained that the anti-rationε
«regards man not as a highly rational and intelligent but as a very *irratiι*
being».[23] Or, in the same article, commenting on the individualism of.
others, he wrote that:

«It would scarcely be too much to claim that the main merit of the individualism whπ.
he [*Adam Smith*] and his contemporaries advocated is that it is a system under which bad
men can do least harm. It is a social system which does not depend for its functioning on
our finding good men for running it, or on all men becoming better than they now are,
but which makes use of men in all given variety and complexity, sometimes good and
sometimes bad, sometimes intelligent and more often *stupid*.»[24]

This remark of Professor *Hayek* on the early liberalists (in our sense of the term) re-
minds us the very similar comment of *Leslie Stephen* on *Bernard Mandeville*. *Stephen* stated that the fundamental position of *Mandeville* was «You are all Yahoos . . ., and I am a
Yahoo; and so — let us eat, drink, and be merry».[25] Our question is then whether we can
lightly call the philosophical foundation of the approach, which regards the individuals
from time to time as irrational, foolish, emotional or full of nonrational factors, as critical rationalism. I am rather certain that while Professor *Popper* may well also readily
admit such aspects of human nature, he will not make them the central issues in establishing the methodological foundation of the social sciences. But Professor *Hayek* as well as
Bernard Mandeville and others did. Why? It is because unless we come to understand
fully the significance of those features of all the individual, we will never be able to hope
to lay a secure foundation for the system of the social sciences, if not also of positive
science in general, as well as for liberalism in the eighteenth century sense of the term. As
a matter of fact, unless we do so, we can perhaps never understand why *positive science is
inseparable from liberalism* and why *the latter from the former*.

According to *Alfred N. Whitehead*, the medieval age was «preeminently an epoch of
orderly thought, rationalist through and through».[26] The birth of science was nothing
else than the revolt against this, or the revolt of reason against reason itself. *Whitehead*
described this process quite vividly that:

«*Galileo* keeps harping on how things happen, whereas his adversaries had a complete
theory as to why things happen. Unfortunately the two theories did not bring out the
same results. *Galileo* insists upon ‹irreducible and stubborn facts›, and *Simplicius*, his
opponent, brings forward reasons, completely satisfactory, at least to himself. It is a great
mistake to conceive this historical revolt as an appeal to reason. On the contrary, it was
through and through an antirationalist movement.»[27]

In grasping the fundamental nature of that historical revolution in this manner,
Whitehead, of course, was not quite happy; for he felt that because of this particular nature of its birth, science had been «degenerated into a medley of ad hoc hypotheses»,[28]
and that the historical revolt had «been exaggerated into the exclusion of philosophy
from its proper role of harmonising the various abstractions of methodological
thought».[29] I fully share the same feeling with him, although I have a great difficulty of

---

[23] I. & E., p. 16.
[24] ibid., p. 12.
[25] *Leslie Stephen*, Essays on Freethinking and Plainspeaking, (London 1873), p. 280.
[26] *Alfred N. Whitehead*, Science and the Modern World, (New York 1956), p. 17.
[27] ibid., p. 9.
[28] ibid., p. 18.
[29] ibid., p. 19.

accepting in its entirety the philosophy of science, which he later came to establish. In fact, while I greatly admire the basic feature of Professor *Popper's* methodology of science, I often can not agree with him either as soon as he comes to discuss specifically the methodology of the social sciences in detail. In order for us, however, to be able to understand the most basic nature of positive science and its inseparable relationship with liberalism in our sense of the term, we must once fully realize that both science and liberalism were through and through anti-rationalistic in their nature at the time of their birth.

Mandeville repeatedly insisted that reason played its own role entirely at the bidding and under the sway of some passion:

«All Human Creature are sway'd and wholly govern'd by their Passions, whatever fine Notions we may flatter our Selves with: even those who act suitably to their Knowledge, and strictly follow the Dictates of their Reason, are not less compell'd so to do by Some Passion or other, that sets them to Work, than others, who bid Defiance and act contrary to Both, and whom we call Slaves to their Passions.»[30]

Here, it may be necessary to note that according to *Mandeville*, «What we call the Will is properly the last Result of Deliberation, whether long or short, which immediately precedes the Execution of, or at least the endeavour to execute the Thing will'd».[31] But, then, *Mandeville* proceeded to write that:

«Hor. You make Stocks and Stones of us; It is not in our choice, to act, or not to act?

Cleo. [*Mandeville's* spokesman] Yes, it is in my choice now, either to run my Head against the Wall, or to let it alone; but, I hope, it does not puzzle you much to guess, which of the two I shall chuse.

Hor. But, don't we move our Bodies as we list? and is not every Action determin'd by the Will?

Cleo. What satisfies that, where there is a Passion that manifestly sways, and with a strict Hand governs that Will.»[32]

Passions bid the mind strongly or weakly to make a certain decision. The mind in return may make a decision in this way or that way according to the proportional strength of passions. What is evident from the process *Mandeville* so described is that whatever be the decision, it is thus by necessity the expression of some passion or other. It is thus *Mandeville's* contention that human reason is the tool of passions. True, it is also *Mandeville* who stated elsewhere that «Man is a rational Creature»[33], or that «Superiority of Understanding . . . gives us a Foresight, and inspires us with Hopes, of which other Creatures have little, and that only of things immediately before him».[34] Moreover, he did admit that man had not only «acquired» moral senses but also even «natural» inclinations such as would induce him to act morally. Indeed, it is he who asserted, for example, that should we see an «over-grown Sow» attacking an innocent child, we would certainly try to rescue it.[35] Professor *Hayek* was quite right, when he interpreted for us the theory of self-love not only of *Mandeville* but also of *David Hume* and *Adam Smith* that the «‹self›, for which alone people were supposed to care, did as a matter of course include their family and friends; and it would have made no difference to the argument if it had included anything for which people in fact did care».[36] As is well known, *Hume* and

---

[30] F.o.B., Vol. II, p. 281.
[31] *Bernard Mandeville*, Free Thoughts on Religion, the Church and National Happiness, (London 1729), p. 88.
[32] F.o.B., Vol. II, p. 299.
[33] ibid., p. 190.
[34] ibid., p. 300.
[35] F.o.B., Vol. I, pp. 255–56, 259.
[36] I. & E., p. 13.

Smith, differently from *Mandeville,* even came to propound the principle of sympathy. And Professor *Gary S. Becker,* whom I admire greatly, and who is a sincere liberalist in the present age, is now trying to establish a new field of economics in accordance to the principle of «altruism».[37]

But in the central point of *Mandeville's* argument was that even our altruistic acts should be regarded as »selfish« regardless of either whatever meritorious motives they had behind them or whatever good consequences they might bring about, in so far as human decisions were made in accordance to limited knowledge and moreover influenced by emotions. Such acts might become flawless by accident. But they can never truly be made perfect by conscious efforts and perhaps even less by unconscious endeavors and hence always must fundamentally be arbitrary impositions on others. Without doubt, it is a very ethical and altruistic act of a mother if she was drowned in her attempt to rescue her child who was drowned. Suppose, however, one or two infants were left behind and had to be sent to an orphanage. Whether her act was truly altruistic from the broader point of view is a very difficult question. As Professor *Hayek* stated, the point of utmost importance is the fact that «man *cannot* know more than a tiny part of the whole of society»; that «therefore all that can go into his motives are immediate effects which his actions will have in the sphere he knows»; and that «all man's mind can effectively comprehend are the facts of the narrow circle of which he is the center».[38]

If there were some omniscient men in our society, there may be little need for the freedom of the people. And even when nobody is omniscient, their liberty may not be quite essential in so far as some group of men can even approximately get hold of the total body of the knowledge that exists in our society. But the fundamental characteristic of such knowledge is that it is dispersed among the people and only in the hands of the individual. And the knowledge of each individual is basically in the process of constant adaptation to the changes of the circumstances that surround him. The introduction of large electronic computers and the increase of their memory capacity in whatever scale do not fundamentally change the situation. Electronic computer can work, only when data are fed into it. But data can never exhaust all the knowledge that exists in society. This is because the knowledge, which any society is potentially capable of producing, is always greater than the mere sum of all the knowledge of the individual members of that society, in so far as those members are allowed to interact freely with each other and compete with each other without restrictions, by using their knowledge and skills, both of which are inescapably very limited. Indeed, the toughest problems for any society, regardless of its political system, are always how to mobilize such knowledge and skills of all the individuals to the fullest degree and how to maximize the fruits of their mutual interactions. The freedom of each individual is *the* answer to this most difficult problem. Each individual must be made free so that he or she can fully use whatever limited knowledge, skills, inclinations, etc., which he or she has; unless, of course, the resultant acts are not detrimental to other individuals. Only out of the free interactions of those knowledge and skills, can we hope that our society may produce some great things which not even geniuses can ever foresee.

The most fundamental question involved here is not only whether we must allow each member of our society to be guided freely in his or her actions by those limited information and judgements which he or she can know or care: the question that is concerned

---

[37] *Gary S. Becker,* «The Effect of the State on the Family», the Paper presented at the 1978 Mont Pelerin Society General Meeting. Also see his «A Theory of Social Interactions», Journal of Political Economy, Vol. 82, No. 6, 1974.

[38] I. & E., p. 14.

with the problem of the freedom of each individual. But it also has a bearing of utmost importance on the methodology of positive science and especially of the social sciences. Indeed, a unique difficulty we often experience, whenever we read the works of *Mandeville, Hume* and *Adam Smith* or of Professors *von Mises, Hayek* and *Popper* lies in the fact that their works frequently discuss (1) the methodology of science or of the social sciences, (2) the theory of society or of economics and (3) the system of liberalism all at one time. In order for us to appreciate fully their great works, it seems thus that we had better first of all clearly differentiate these three and then proceed to analyze why there exist inseparable relationships among the three. Let us start from the problem of methodology. It may well seem platitudious to say that every science proceeds more or less explicitly by devising some hypotheses of greater or less generality, from which particular consequences are deduced. But this statement, which may well appear superfluous today, is the result of our poignant realization of the inescapable and universal limitation of our reason. Only thanks to the anti-rationalism of *Bernard Mandeville, David Hume* and others, we came to recognize that we had to rely upon hypotheses in our search for truth. Always we must first of all establish some hierarchical system of hypotheses and then test them by observation and experiment. In other words, the predominant method, which is employed by both the natural sciences and the social sciences, is hypothetico-deductive-observational method. As *William Stanley Jevons* once aptly put it,[39] scientific inquiry consists essentially in a «happy marriage» between hypothesis and experiment, deductive method being the link between these two. In so far as this aspect is concerned, there is no essential difference between the natural sciences and the social sciences. But there does exist the unity of method. In all cases, scientific inquiry makes use of the method of the fundamentally same nature. The function of science is to establish laws, concerning the behavior of empirical events in order to enable us to connect together our knowledge of the separately known events and make reliable predictions of events as yet unknown.

The usual process of formulating any system of hypotheses consists, in the first place, of observation of the subject matter under investigation. Guided, then, by something in the subject matter as well as by the previous knowledge of other subject matters, we invent some system of hypotheses. Of course, the concept, with which the primary hypothesis is concerned, ceases from time to time to be the properties of the things that are directly observable, and can be related to observable facts only by extremely complicated deduction. And only the hypotheses, which are deduced from the primary one, can be tested by empirical data. But the results of such tests will often either strengthen or weaken also the primary hypothesis. In construing the fundamental nature of scientific method as hypothetico-deductive-observational method, a strong emphasis is placed upon the role played by hypotheses or conjectures[40] in the conduct of scientific research. Indeed, no systematic inquiry in both the natural sciences and the social sciences has made progress apart from some hypotheses adapted to their specific topics. And it is *Bernard Mandeville* who strongly insisted on this point so many times. He wrote, for example, that «as all our Knowledge comes a posteriori; it is imprudent to reason otherwise than from facts»[41]; or that «more useful Knowledge may be acquired from unwearied Observation, judicious Experience, and arguing from Facts a posteriori, than the haughty attempts of entering into the first Causes, and reasoning a priori».[42] Then he proceeded to assert that:

---

[39] *William Stanley Jevons,* The Principles of Science, (New York 1958), pp. viii, 258–59, 737–38.
[40] P.o.H., p. 131. C. G. *Hempel,* «Studies in the Logic of Confirmation», Mind, Vol. LIV (1945).
[41] F.o.B., II, p. 261.
[42] ibid., p. 164.

«Cleo. [*Mandeville's* spokesman] . . . When Things are very obscure, I sometimes make Use of *Conjecture* to find my Way.

Hor. Do you argue, or pretend to prove any thing from those Conjectures?

Cleo. No; I never reason but from the plain Observations which every body may make on Man, the *Phenomena* that appear in the lesser World.»[43]

These assertions of *Mandeville* are striking indeed, since many of his predecessors were caged by rationalistic prepossessions and not only unable to realize the evolutionary aspect of law, language, market and other social institutions and phenomena but also often inclined to explain them dogmatically by deductions from some final certainties. Even *Felix Kaufman,* who questioned «why the observational test is to be considered an essential element in scientific procedure»[44], had to admit that: «The most obvious criterion of the success of methods (habits) of thought is indeed the confirmation by observational tests of the results to which they have led.»[45]

Precisely because of his awareness of the inevitable limitation of any reason, or, putting it in short, because of his anti-rationalism, *Mandeville* was successful for the first time in the history of mankind in presenting a truly evolutionary account of society as well as of various phenomena in society. He stated, for example, that:

«Knowing, a priori, belongs to God only, and Divine Wisdom acts with an original Certainty, of which, what we call Demonstration, is but an imperfect, borrow'd Copy . . . Wretched Man, on the contrary, is sure of nothing, his Existence not excepted but reasoning a posteriori.

The consequence of this is, that the Words of Art and human Invention are all very lame and defective, and most of them pitifully mean at first: Our Knowledge is advanced by slow Degrees, and some Arts and Sciences require the experience of many Ages, before they can be brought to any tolerable Perfection.»[46]

And *Mandeville* maintained even that «diligent Enquirers have often stumbled by Chance on useful Discoveries of Things they did not look for, and which human Sagacity labouring with Design a priori never have detected».[47] He then went on to explain how law, government, language, money, market, the division of labor, etc. had evolved. The great significance of this evolutionary theory of *Mandeville* lies in its emphasis on the point that social phenomena are not the simple results of isolated human actions but the products of the social process in which a plurality of individuals adjust their actions to those of others: i.e., in the words of *Mandeville,* «associating in Men turns to better Account».[48] His demand for the freedom of the individual comes from nowhere else than this evolutionary account of society. For example, he asserted that:

«. . . In the Compound of all Nations, the different Degrees of Men ought to bear a certain Proportion to each other, as to Numbers, in order to render the whole a well-proportion'd Mixture. And as this due Proportion is the Result and natural Consequence of the difference there is in the Qualifications of men, so *it is never better attained to, or preserv'd, than when no body meddles with it. Hence we may learn, how the short-sighted Wisdom, of perhaps well-meaning People, may rob us of a Felicity, that would flow spontaneously from the Nature of every large Society, if none were to divert or interrupt the Stream.*»[49]

43 ibid., p. 128.
44 *Felix Kaufman,* Methodology of the Social Science, (New York 1958), pp. 41–2.
45 ibid., pp. 43–44.
46 F.o.B., Vol. II, pp. 186–87.
47 ibid., p. 179.
48 ibid., p. 180.
49 ibid., p. 353. The underline is mine.

In short, the emphasis on the inevitable and universal limitation of human reason led *Mandeville, Hume, Ferguson, Smith* and others to form the hypothetico-deductive-observational method, which was thoroughly antirationalistic in its nature, when compared with the rationalism of the medieval thinkers, with, of course, exceptions of such as *Duns Scotus, William of Ockham, Pierre Abélard*, etc. It was thanks to this anti-rationalistic method that they were able to give the scientific accounts of various phenomena in society, according to which they also came to advocate liberalism in our sense of the term.

Although *Mandeville* wrote almost all the works in English in England, he was born in the Netherlands, attended the Erasmian School in Rotterdam, where *Pierre Bayle* was teaching at that time, and graduated from the University of Leyden. *Bayle's* influence on *Mandeville* is clear. Moreover, it is more than probable that in promoting the hypothetico-deductive-observational method, he was at least indirectly influenced by a great scientist Holland produced, *Christian Huygens*. *Isaac Newton* asserted that «the main Business of natural Philosophy is to argue from Phaenomena without feigning Hypotheses, and to deduce Causes from Effects, till we come to the very first Cause, which certainly is not mechanical».[50] In contrast to this, *Huygens* readily admitted at the beginning of his Treatise on Light that some of the suggestions he made were only hypothetical in their nature. He wrote there that:

«Whereas the Geometers prove their Propositions by fixed and incontestable Principle, here the Principles are verified by the conclusions to be drawn from them; the nature of these things not allowing of this being done otherwise. It is always possible to attain thereby to a degree of probability which very often is scarcely less than complete proof.»[51]

But the fundamentally hypothetical nature of scientific method especially in the social sciences has often been forgotten. A part of the reason for this may have been that differently from the natural sciences, the social sciences deal with beliefs, opinions, expectations, etc., which are held by particular people, and which «we cannot directly observe in the minds of the people but which we can recognize from what they do and say merely because we have ourselves a mind similar to theirs».[52] This «subjective» character of the approach of the social sciences led the social scientists from time to time to adopt the so-called introspective method and, in any case, choose as premises for their theoretical systems only those propositions, the individual reliabilities of which have already been well accredited for relatively simple situations. Here, the primary question was no longer the validities of those premises themselves but whether only appropriate premises were selected and combined so that they would allow the deduction of a process which might have brought about the social phenomena under investigation. In other words, the question was whether the intricate explanatory scheme, which was thus built, would be appropriate in its totality to account for the complex phenomena under observation. It cannot be denied that this particular situation in the field of the social sciences has helped to obscure the fundamentally hypothetical nature of whatever theory in this field[53].

More fundamentally, however, this basically always hypothetical nature of all the scientific theory was destined to be forgotten, in so far as it was suggested that hypotheses were provisional or tentative in their nature only in the sense that they were ultimately to be replaced by the theories that were verified by observed facts. Indeed, in so far as the people believed that at least some scientific hypotheses could decisively be verified by facts, they could easily overlook their intrinsically hypothetical nature. Here we owe

---

[50] *Isaac Newton*, Optics, (New York 1952).

[51] *Christian Huygens*, Treatise on Light, (Chicago 1945).

[52] *F. A. Hayek*, The Counter-Revolution of Science, (Glencoe, Ill. 1952), p. 28.

[53] *F. Kaufman*, op.cit., p. 236.

greatly to Professor *Popper* who reminded us that we in fact could never decisively verify any theory, or rather that it would often be so easy for us to verify scientific theories by facts that such verifications could not amount to anything. According to him, the real task of scientific test must be a genuine attempt to «falsify» hypotheses by facts.[54] And even when we failed to falsify any hypothesis, we should not regard it as finally confirmatory but proceed to test its reliability in both ways, i.e., by more new deductions and by further attempts to falsify them by more new empirical findings. Both in the natural sciences and the social sciences, scientific endeavors are in this sense endless efforts to form hypotheses and falsify them by facts. And the fundamentally contingent character of all the scientific truth is undeniable. But this does not mean at all that the philosophical foundation of science is agnosticism. As Professor *Popper* lucidly put it, «science aims at *true* theories, even though we can never be certain, about any particular theory, that it is true» but «science may progress (and know that it does so), inventing theories which, compared with earlier ones, may be described as better approximations to what is true».[55] Because of the fact that in the field of the social sciences we often use as the primary premises the propositions, the validities of which have been tested many times, we must not be led to disregard the basically hypothetical nature of all the theories in this field. All the truth we can hope to obtain in both the natural sciences and the social sciences is only a contingent truth in its fundamental nature. With this realization alone, can there be a hope of the progress of science and the need for freedom in scientific trials and errors.

True, it will be much easier to invent new hypotheses, if it is feasible to treat a few connected events as if they are closed systems, for which all the determining factors can be placed under an experimental control. But, in complex phenomena such as we find in society, (where the phenomena arise out of an infinite number and variety of human decisions channeled by the interplay of infinitely various actions of individuals and groups), there is no direct way of ascertaining even the presence and specific arrangement of that multiplicity of factors which must form the starting-point of deductive reasoning in the proposed system. Here, controlled experiment is almost always totally impossible. Finding himself in such a complex situation, any social scientist usually will not attempt to invent an utterly novel hypothesis. Instead he may well ask at first how far what he and others already know about some aspects of the complex phenomena can account for the regularities observed in those phenomena, and try to utilize such knowledge in order to establish an appropriate theory. This way of approach will almost definitely be more expedient than the former. But the point of importance is that this does not imply any methodological supremacy over the former. Fundamentally, *complete freedom* for inventing and proposing whatever hypotheses in whatever manner, *complete freedom* for scrutinizing the logical consistencies of those hypotheses, *complete freedom* to let them compete with each other and *complete freedom* to try to falsify them by facts are the indispensable essentials for the real advancement of not only the natural sciences but also the social sciences. It is neither rationalism nor even critical rationalism but only anti-rationalism that can make all these freedoms possible. After all, an anti-rationalist, *David Hume*, maintained that:

---

[54] *Karl R. Popper*, Logik der Forschung, (Wien 1935), secs. 80 ff.
[55] *Karl R. Popper*, «A Note on Berkeley as Precursor of Mach», The British Journal for the Philosophy of Science, vol. IV, May 1953–Feb. 1954, pp. 34–5.

«In a word, then, every effect is a distinct event from its cause. It could not, therefore, be discovered in the cause; and the first invention or conception of it, a priori, must be entirely arbitrary.»[56]

This statement, of course, does not imply at all that in our attempt to set up a system of hypotheses we must not search for existing knowledge, the reliability of which has already been well established, and utilize it, by squeezing its hidden implications out at the same time. Fundamentally, however, it does not make any difference at all whether we do this or instead rely upon some ideas which we may, for example, suddenly develop by intuition while we are half asleep. The former way may well have a better chance of successfully passing the tests of both logical scrutinization and observational falsification. This possibility, however, cannot conceal its basically hypothetical nature. In our theoretical appeal for a free enterprise system or a free society, we may well get frustrated by the slowness of the process, in which our theory becomes accredited. But in so far as our theory is a good approximation of what is true, its reliability will sooner or later be established on the basis of facts. We should never be led by our frustration to limit the freedoms mentioned above.

Any system of hypotheses, which is invariably private in its original nature, can increasingly acquire a public and objective character, as it goes through the process of free competition with other systems of hypotheses as well as the process of unfettered and rigorous falsifications that are to be done not only by the scientist who proposed that system but also by others. The point of great significance here is that only then, or, putting it differently, only when the four freedoms mentioned before prevail, scientific endeavors can become devoid of value-judgement. But, then, this lack of value-judgement is limited to the scientific sphere, where the anti-rationalism is prevalent. As soon as any system of hypotheses is put into practice, the anti-rationalism is lost. Because of the anti-rationalistic reasons that have thus far been explained, either in the natural sciences or the social sciences we can never attain the ultimate truth but only contingent ones. We might achieve some approximations of what is true. We might well fail many times to falsify a certain set of hypotheses. But we can never completely erase off the intrinsically hypothetical nature of whatever scientific knowledge we possess. In so far as our discussions of theories are limited within the domain of science, this nature is neither important nor harmful. But the ultimate purpose of our scientific inquiries lies in the utilization of their conclusions.

Especially in the field of the social sciences, there exists a unique difficulty in this regard. Here both the observer and the observed are human beings. Moreover, any social scientist, of necessity, thinks on the one hand and acts on the other; he not only meditates by himself but works with others from time to time; and he engages in scientific study and at the same time asserts his theory to others. As soon as thus in one way or another any theory in the field of the social sciences begins to be advocated to the public and especially put into practice, the fundamentally contingent nature of whatever reliability or validity it has becomes the problem that cannot lightly be overlooked. It is here that the value-judgement, which was intrinsically involved in any theory, activates itself. The anti-rationalism dictates that as soon as any social theory is moved to the outside of the field of pure science, it must be made clear that it is inescapably intertwined with some kind of value-judgement. This is precisely because we do not know any ultimate truth, nor have any perfect knowledge. As soon as, therefore, we assert and put into practice any theory

---

[56] *David Hume,* Enquiries concerning the Human Understanding and concerning the Principles of Morals, (Oxford 1955), Chap. 1.

in the social sciences, we unavoidably make value-judgement in one way or another; for even at best this fundamentally amounts to the application of an arbitrary selection of some aspects of what is true.

We are keenly aware of the inevitable limitations and imperfections not only of our knowledge and skills, but also of our emotions, inclinations, instincts, intuitions and drives, which influence our actions and behaviors. Should we be prohibited to say nothing else than the perfect truth and do nothing else but the actions based upon that truth, we in fact could not live for long. Knowing that our theory is neither flawless nor perfect, we must yet from time to time advocate it to the public and persuade them to practice it. It is precisely here that great cautions are called for, or, putting it differently, that Professor *Popper's* «critical rationalism» instead of anti-rationalism must become effective. The critical rationalism is now acutely in need in order to hold value-judgements in check. Moreover, when put into practice, the theory of society, which the anti-rationalistic approach establishes, is really an appeal for the wise use of reason, i.e., the use of reason with humbleness, precautions and the keen realization of its limitations; which means the assertion of critical rationalism. Or perhaps had we better say that it is the appeal for the use of reason not of the chosen few but of the common individuals at large. As soon as that theory of society is adopted for its practical application, it shifts its philosophical foundation from the anti-rationalism to Professor *Popper's* critical rationalism. It must be remembered, however, that without the anti-rationalism, we cannot come to realize the inevitable limitations of our knowledge, the inescapable presence of value-judgements in our theories and the need of the critical rationalism itself for those theories in their actual applications. In fact, as may become clearer later, without the anti-rationalism, we will never be able to establish a genuine theory of society itself.

The anti-rationalistic assertion that we are universally inescapably limited in our knowledge and skills, which are moreover influenced by our instincts, drives, emotions, inclinations and such other non-rational factors, has a grave bearing upon the question of individual responsibility. As the idea that responsibility belongs to society or to the social conditions, which surround each individual, has become popular and predominant, the feeling of personal responsibility has increasingly been destroyed. Basically, however, it seems that this destruction was brought about by the modern rationalism, which held an unwarranted belief that at least some of us were capable of grasping all what should be known about our society. In so far as some of us could become omniscient in this manner, whatever misconduct each individual would make should really be regarded as the result of the failure of utilizing that knowledge but could be remedied by such knowledge as soon as the case comes to be noticed. The indisputable fact is, however, that nobody can possess such knowledge. In so far as we are without exception inescapably very limited and imperfect, we must take our individual responsibilities for, in fact, all our own individual conducts. The anti-rationalism demands individual freedom. But, then, that individual freedom is inseparable from individual responsibility.

Be that as it may, because of the frequent difficulty to falsify theories by observable facts in the field of the social sciences, it may be asserted that the freedoms, which the anti-rationalism demands as the conditions of the genuine progress of science, are not really desirable. Or because of the unique characteristics of the social sciences, it may be suggested that only some specific types of approaches must be allowed. But, the matter, which is concerned with the methodological foundation of the social sciences, must not be confused with the technical question of how to devise appropriate premises. In the field of the social sciences, many of the important phenomena are not quantifiable. It is thus quite true that while a very naive and simple system of hypotheses, which are, however, full of quantified variables, is readily verified, a much better and very subtle but non-quantified system is often put outside of the attempts to falsify it. Nevertheless, only by allowing the four freedoms mentioned before, can we hope to test eventually even such a complicated system and falsify the simple ones that were once accepted before. In order to make the real progress of the social sciences possible, the anti-rationalism, which was maintained by *Mandeville, Hume, Smith* and others, seems essential. To some people, the term, anti-rationalism, may seem rather distasteful. But for those who are aware of the dark sides of the rationalism not only in the medieval age but also in the modern era, the term implies the coming of new lives for the common people at large and of the individual freedoms. As soon as, however, we move from the sphere of the social sciences as such to the field of actions and practices, we must make, as it were, a «Copernican inversion», by moving from the anti-rationalism to the critical rationalism. While the major emphasis of the former is on the inevitable limitations of reason, that of the latter is on the active use of reason, though with the keen awareness of such limitations.

II. The Emergent Properties of Social Phenomena versus Rational Expectation Theory

The methodological essence of the evolutionary approach to social phenomena, (the approach that was initiated and pursued by *Mandeville, Hume, Ferguson, Smith* and others), can be found in the statement *Carl Menger* once made:

«Eine jede Theorie, welcher Art dieselbe auch sein mag und welchen Grad der Strenge der Erkenntnis sie auch immer anstrebt, hat in erster Reihe die Aufgabe, uns die konkreten Erscheinungen der realen Welt als Exemplifikationen einer gewissen Regelmäßigkeit in der Aufeinanderfolge der Erscheinungen d.i. *genetisch verstehen zu lehren*. Eine jede Theorie strebt demnach vor allem danach, uns die komplicierten Erscheinungen des ihr eigenthümlichen Forschungsgebietes als Ergebnis des Zusammenwirkens der Faktoren ihrer Entstehung verständlich zu machen. *Dies genetische Element ist untrennbar von der Idee theoretischer Wissenschaften.*»[57]

This assertion of *Menger* ist remarkable indeed; for it succeeded in pointing out so clearly and concisely the most important aspect of the methodology of the social sciences. Yet strangely it has often been neglected by those who engaged in the study of social phenomena. Moreover, as well known, the methodology of *Menger* was bitterly attacked and criticized as physicalistic, mechanical, unrealistic in the sense of being too abstract, void of historical sense, etc. by the historical school. It was really ironical that he had to be accused, of all things, in such a manner. For what led him to the study of social phenomena was clearly nothing else than his deep reverence toward the wisdom that could be produced only by the interplays of the people's actions through the long process of human history, or, in the words of his own, toward «die ‹unverstandene Weisheit› in den auf organischem Wege entstandenen socialen Institutionen».[58]

The fact that it was really the methodology of *Menger* that was truly historical, organic and realistic becomes evident, as soon as we compare it with that of the historical school or more specifically with what *A. von Schelting* called the method of ideal construction of causal imputation in *Max Weber*.[59] What *Weber* called a «historical individual»[60] may

---

[57] *Carl Menger*, Untersuchungen über die Methode der Socialwissenschaften, und der Politischen Ökonomie insbesondere, (Leipzig 1883), S. 88.

[58] ibid., S. 283.

[59] *Alexander von Schelting*, Max Webers Wissenschaftslehre, (Tübingen 1934), SS. 334, 329–45.

[60] *Max Weber*, Gesammelte Aufsätze zur Wissenschaftslehre, (Tübingen 1951), SS. 177–78.

be described as a system in the sense that it is a selective ordering of some aspects of external reality. It is always a simplified picture of concrete phenomena. Therefore, it cannot by itself concretely exist except in a few very special cases. Though thus it always involves some one-sided exaggerations, such a conceptual scheme may still be able to retain its historical individuality. In the causal imputation of such a system, it is often broken down at first into a larger number of parts or smaller subsystems. According to *A. von Schelting*, for example, the first step in the procedure of causal explanation is to break down a historical individual into its constituent parts, of such a character that each of such parts can be subsumed under a general law which has been ascertained beforehand. (1. Gedankliche Analyse der komplexen Wirklichkeit des in Frage stehenden Hergangs; seine derart vorgenommene «Zerlegung» in «Bestandteile», daß diese sich je einer generellen Regel des Geschehens einfügen lassen. 2. Vorangegangene Gewinnung solcher Regeln des Geschehens.[61]) When such a breakdown, or what may be called «unit analysis», is followed far enough, it eventually arrives at the «smallest» units of the system of social phenomena under investigation. Now, the central issue between the historical school and *Carl Menger* was concerned with the methodologically permissible extent of such breakdown operations. The former insisted that even the smallest units should still retain the character of historical individuals or should remain to be realistic constructs to that extent. In contrast to this, *Menger* asserted that we should reduce the system of social phenomena to the «simplest elements possible», which would constitute that system, without considering if such elements were realistic or not. («Die theoretische Forschung... strebt nach der Feststellung dieser [einfachsten] Elemente ... ohne Rücksicht darauf, ob dieselben in der Wirklichkeit als selbständige Erscheinungen vorhanden, ja selbst ohne Rücksicht darauf, ob sie in ihrer vollen Reinheit überhaupt selbständig darstellbar sind.»[62])

At a glance, it looks as if the historical school is indeed realistically minded, whereas *Menger's* way will let us be bogged into the abstract world of formal analyses. But appearances are often deceptive. We cannot, of course, deny some usefulness of the analytical method of the historical school, which is discussed here. We must, first of all, admit the possibility that the smallest units, which this method will let us arrive at, not only make sense as the parts of the system of social phenomena under investigation but also refer in one way or another to some concrete realities. That is, it is not impossible for us to conceive such units as existing by themselves, or, in other words, as the «pure types» of some concrete phenomena, without involving anything else, from which they are distinguished. That is precisely why *Max Weber* came to call them «ideal types».[63] Let us then call the method discussed here «type-parts analysis».[64] As maintained by *Weber*, those type-parts are not restricted in their use to their definitions and empirical identifications as parts of a system of social phenomena, nor to their classifications. But, on occasion, such type-parts may be identified as common to a plurality of different systems of social phenomena. This possibility may enable us from time to time to investigate the behaviors of those type-parts under certain kinds of definable circumstances. In other words, we can perhaps occasionally make some judgements on causal relationships by formulating typical lines of developments for those type-parts. But we must notice here that the basis for such judgements can never be more than empirical generalization about the possible or probable behaviors of such type-parts, or of various combinations of

[61] *A. von Schelting*, op.cit., S. 262.
[62] *Carl Menger*, op.cit., S. 41.
[63] *Max Weber*, op.cit., S. 190.
[64] Cf. *Talcott Parsons*, The Structure of Social Action, (Glencoe, Ill. 1949), pp. 31–3, 605.

them, under given typical circumstances. It may, of course, enable us to «understand» (verstehen) probable causal relationship that is involved in a particular system of social phenomena. With the type-parts analysis, however, we can never hope to go beyond that and grasp even the approximations of the laws that may commonly or universally exist behind causal relationships.

This is because the type-parts analysis never goes beyond the descriptive plane. Its characteristic enthusiasm about first-hand contact with concrete facts is commendable. But it was precisely this enthusiasm that led the people of the historical school to overlook the truly historical and organic nature of social phenomena. In the field of physical science, type-parts may well refer to mechanistic parts, which can be observed without essential change of properties, even when they are separated from each other and taken out of the system which they consitute. If we like to know how a watch works, for example, we can simply disassemble it to various parts and study how those parts work under different circumstances. When we complete such a study and add up the knowledge thus acquired, we may well be able to tell how the total system of that watch itself works. But relationships between any system of social phenomena and its parts as well as interrelationships among those parts themselves are not analogous to the case of a watch at all. Within any system of social phenomena, interrelations among its parts determine the properties of those parts and hence of that system as well.

Indeed, the very characteristic of social phenomena lies in the fact that they have the properties that are *emergent* only on a certain level of complexity in interrelationships among their constituent parts. These *emergent properties* begin to evaporate and become no longer observable as the type-parts analysis is carried out. It becomes impossible for us to identify those *emergent properties*, when type-parts are isolated and considered apart from their mutual interrelationships with other type-parts of the same system of social phenomena. We cannot derive such *emergent properties* by a process of direct generalization of the elementary properties of type-parts. Suppose that there is a system of social phenomena called a system. Suppose further that we observe the properties of its type-parts under various conditions but not in the unique interrelationships among them, (the interrelationships which they had when they constituted a system), and that we then directly generalize the results of the observations and systematically combine all the conclusions of such generalizations. Even if we wish to apply the end result of such a procedure to a system in order to make judgement on a causal relationship that may be involved in that system, it can only be indeterminate. At best it may enable us to «understand» (verstehen) the causal relationship. Fundamentally, however, such an understanding can never be determinate. That is, we can never be sure if the assumed causal relationship will really prevail. That is why *Menger* emphasized the importance of what he called «genetic elements» and insisted that we must try to explain social phenomena «genetically», as we have seen before. If there are truly historical factors among social phenomena, they are those emergent properties; for they arise only out of historical process. And if there are genuinely organic factors among social phenomena, they are also those emergent properties; for they appear out of the complex interplays of individuals and groups in society.

According to *Menger,* what we observe in a nation's economy is «die Resultante all der unzähligen einzelwirtschaftlichen Bestrebungen im Volke».[65] Moreover, he maintained that: «Das Recht, die Sprache, der Staat, das Geld, die Märkte, alle diese Socialgebilde in ihren verschiedenen Erscheinungsformen und *in ihrem steten Wandel* sind zum nicht geringen Theile *das unreflectierte Ergebnis socialer Entwicklung:* die Güterpreise, die Zins-

---

[65] *Carl Menger,* op.cit., S. 87.

raten, die Bodenrenten, die Arbeitslöhne und tausend andere Erscheinungen des socialen Lebens überhaupt und der Volkswirtschaft insbesondere weisen genau die nämliche Eigenthümlichkeit auf.»[66] And the method, which *Menger* proposed to analyse those unintended resultants of the interactions of innumerable efforts of individual people in socio-historical process, was: «Daß wir die Menschheitsphänomene auf ihre ursprünglichsten und einfachsten constitutiven Faktoren zurückführen, an diese letzteren das ihrer Natur entsprechende Maß legen und endlich die Gesetze zu erforschen suchen, nach welchen sich aus jenen einfachsten Elementen, in ihrer Isolirung gedacht, compliciertere Menschheitsphänomene gestalten.»[67] We must once reduce any given system of social phenomena into the simplest elements, or the most elementary factors, which constitute that system, without considering whether they still retain the character of historical individuals, if we really like to know the causal relationships that may be involved in that system. This is precisely because only then we can hope to be able to observe what values those factors will take as they are combined together in the manner as we find in that system and begin to interact to each other over time. It is only by this method that we may well succeed in grasping the emergent properties that are unique to the system so that we may truly be able to analyze the causal relationships involved. The points that are especially emphasized here are two. The one is that the constituent parts of any system of social phenomena are influenced by other parts through their interactions, or, in other words, take various values, depending upon the impact effects of such interplays, so that they come to produce those emergent properties that characterize the system and make it indeed social, historical and organic in its nature. The other point is, in the words of *Menger*, that «one can never fully understand the causal interconnections of the various occurrences in a process, or the process itself, unless we view it in time and apply the measure of time to it».[68] We can meet this requirement only by allowing the elementary factors, or the constituent parts, of any system of social phenomena, to change their values through the process of development. While the emergent properties can thus perhaps be explained in a «genetic manner» as the resultants of the unique relations among the various values that the constituent factors took, we can now hope to arrive ultimately at the discovery of certain uniform modes of such relations, which may hold independently of any one particular system of social phenomena, in so far as other systems fundamentally share the similar manner of combinations of those factors.

Now, the essence of the analytical method, which we have seen in the above and may call «compositive method», was really «invented» by *Bernard Mandeville* and, if the word «invention» is too excessive, was successfully applied to social phenomena in a systematic manner, surely for the first time in the history of mankind. The works of *Hume, Ferguson, Smith* and others were fundamentally the continuations of his efforts and the improvements of his works. It is not well-known that the system of *Mandeville* had in fact two major principles: the principle of self-liking and that of self-love.[69] As we have seen before, the principle of self-liking reduced all the human actions, whether altruistic or egoistic, to self-liking. By so doing, he succeeded on the one hand in laying the foundations of the hypothetico-deductive-observational method in the field of the social sciences, and on the other in letting us realize that our civilization was principally the resultant of the trial and error type of adaptation efforts of innumerable individuals, *whose rea-*

---

[66] ibid., SS. 164, 163.
[67] ibid., S. 43.
[68] *Carl Menger,* Principles of Economics, Tr. & ed. by *J. Dingwall* & *B. F. Hoselitz.* (Glencoe, Ill. 1950). Chap. 1.
[69] *Chiaki Nishiyama,* op.cit., esp. pp. 194–95.

sons were invariably limited, to changing circumstances. What was then the purpose of the principle of self-love? The methodological significance of this principle lies in the fact that it amounted to compositive method, though in a rudimental form. Differently from self-liking, self-love was to take various forms such as anger, avarice, compassion, courage, cowardice, diligence, envy, fear, greediness, hunger, idleness, industriousness, integrity, imperfectness, laboriousness, laziness, lewdness, lust, modesty, pride, prowess, shame, thirst, unreasonableness, vanity, etc. In other words, in the system of *Mandeville* the concept of self-love was to represent a bundle of variables that were to take, as it were, various values. By combining together those variables as he thought fit to the varieties of the problems he chose, he went on to observe how those particular combinations of variables would behave through the process of history. It was thanks to such a method that he succeeded in giving the remarkably evolutionary or strikingly genetic accounts of language, common law, the division of labor, government, society in general, etc. Yet, he was humble enough to say that: «What I said . . . was a conjecture, which I recommend no farther to you than you shall think it probable.»[70] *Menger's* attempts to explain not only economic phenomena but also such social phenomena as language, law, religion and even state, or Professor *Hayek's* laborious efforts to explicate the emergence of what he calls «spontaneous order», the efforts that have already produced great results, are basically the continuations of the works that *Mandeville* and then *Hume, Josiah Tucker, Smith, Ferguson* undertook.

Since the adjective «evolutionary» has often been used in the above, it may be a good idea to mention here that the evolutionary theories of *Mandeville* and others were not asserting the survival of the fittest individuals but precisely its opposite, i.e., the eventual survival of the social institutions, customs and other conventions, which were fittest to the welfare of as many individuals as possible.[71] At any rate, what is rather noticeable in the works of *Mandeville* is his repeated emphasis on the great significance of the effects of the accumulation of past experiences in society; by saying, for example, that «joint Experience of many Ages, tho' none but Men of ordinary Capacity should ever be employ'd in them».[72] It is Professor *Hayek* who has been insisting on the importance of the factor identified as «adaptation» in the field of the social sciences for so long time. He stated, for example, in 1945 that «the economic problem of society is mainly one of rapid adaptation to changes in the particular circumstances of time and place»,[73] and in The Constitution of Liberty that «all institutions of freedom are adaptations to [the] fundamental fact of ignorance, adapted to deal with chances and probabilities».[74] Yet, when the type of the method, which *Menger* advocated, (and which he himself called «exact method»), was actually put into practice, all these important points have often been forgotten. It can perhaps be said that equilibrium theory, or even the price theory itself, is a system which was theoretically constructed essentially by that method. Such a system has a logical consistency and contains a particular set of variables, as the compositive method requires. Moreover, from time to time we do observe an actual tendency toward equilibrium such as described in the theory in economic phenomena. That is the very reason why equilibrium theory or the price theory was established. But, precisely from that coincidence between the theory and the reality, however vague it might be, many economists were led to assume once again the perfect rationality of men, their perfect knowledge, a

---

[70] F.o.B., Vol. II, p. 167.
[71] Cf. Studies, p. 111.
[72] F.o.B., Vol. II, p. 343.
[73] I. & E., p. 83.
[74] C.o.L., p. 30.

perfect market, or that all informations were free goods and instantaneously communicated to all the people. These points were criticized by Professor *Hayek* already in 1936. And, as stated before, Professor *Leijonhufvud* tells us that his remarkable contribution was greatly assisted by the rediscovery of Professor *Hayek's* statement in that year. However, many economists assert even today, for example, that labor market must be perfect in the sense that there exists a perfect mobility of labor, and that «life-time employment practices» in Japan must mean a great economic inefficiency. It becomes evident that such a belief is only ridiculous, as soon as we compare it with the actual performance of the Japanese economy. What those economists say really amounts to putting the cart before the horse. As I recently explained elsewhere,[75] those life-time employment practices were brought about, precisely because there existed an economic rationality in them.

An economy as a whole, or a society as a whole, can produce the results that appear impossible unless each individual is full of rationality, although in fact every individual is inescapably limited in his rationality. Why such a state of affairs is possible is the very question we must answer, or the very task we must take. In this regard, a new field of economics, which is known as «rational expectation theory» and has been developed in the last twenty years or so, is rather interesting. Its name sounds as if it assumed once again the «perfect rationality» of men. And the precursor in this field, Professor *John F. Muth,* asserted as a matter of fact that «dynamic economic models do not assume enough rationality».[76] But the actual emphasis of the theory is really on the following two. The one is that each individual improves the rationality of his expectations, by learning from his own experiences in the past, and adjusts his actions to his improved expectations or adapts his actions to his improved perceptions of his circumstances. (This includes his better utilizations of the informations that concern governmental policies. And what has been said here applies also to the case of each individual firm.) The other point emphasized is that even though what was said about each individual and each firm in the above may well still not make their expectations and actions rational enough to let them correspond to their changing circumstances to the satisfactory degree, the resultant of their mutual interactions and their combined effects have the possibilities of becoming so rational that they can correctly anticipate governmental actions and off-set whatever effects government intends to create by its policy measures. The corollary of such assertions is that the public can hardly be «fooled»[77] by governmental policies or that governmental interventions will increasingly become ineffective, as they are repeatedly practiced. When viewed in this manner, the name of the theory, which we have seen before, is not really appropriate. It had better be called «the *public's* rational expectation theory».[78] The public's rationality is assumed here because of the stochastic character of economy. What this means is that the more widely freedom and free competition prevail among different individuals, groups and firms, the more rational the public's expectations and actions will become.

---

[75] *Chiaki Nishiyama,* «How Should We Evaluate Teamworks», the Paper presented at the 1978 Mont Pelerin Society General Meeting.

[76] *John F. Muth,* «Rational Expectations and the Theory of Price Movement», Econometrica, Vol. 29, No. 3, Juli 1961, pp. 315–35.

[77] *R. E. Lucas,* «Some International Evidence on Output-Inflation Tradeoffs», The American Economic Review, Vol. LXIII, No. 3, June 1973, pp. 326–34.

[78] *Thomas J. Sargent* and *Neil Wallace,* « ‹Rational› Expectations, the Optimal Monetary Instrument, and the Optimal Money Supply Rule», Journal of Political Economy, vol. 83, No. 2, April 1975, pp. 241–54.

III. Conclusion

I now hope that what has been discussed thus far in this short article may shed light on why and how mutually inseparable from each other the anti-rationalism, the hypothetico-deductive-observational method, the compositive method, the evolutionary theory of society, (or as its recent illustration, the public's rational expectation theory), and the assertion of individual freedom are. It has from time to time been suggested as if our kind of liberalism has had hardly anything to do with historical science. But the real fact is exactly the opposite. The genuinely historical science was born together with liberalism in the eighteenth century or at the end of the seventeenth century. If either one of them was not born, so could not the other. It is really our kind of liberalists who have the true reverence toward our historical heritage. And precisely because of the profound reverence toward the resultants of the efforts of the innumerable individuals, we demand the freedom of individual people. But we are not against the improvements of various social institutions either. The true liberalism is nothing else than the deep-felt trust in the ordinary individuals. We must strive for yet better social arrangements to allow more the varieties of their developments and mobilize their fruits to the yet higher degree. After all, as we have seen, the social sciences were born also together with our liberalism. They are inseparable from each other and cannot exist without the other. There may well, of course, be still more turns and twists in the development of the social sciences. And some erroneous theories may yet succeed in deceiving the people from time to time. But such deceits can never last for long. Facts are with us and waiting for us to uncover them. Though every one of them is limited and imperfect, it is the common individuals who can make great achievements even to the unimaginable degree, if they are left free to make spontaneous efforts and interact with each other through socio-historical process. What the social sciences may yet discover and may yet attain will assist us in our endeavors to promote our social engineering activities. But, then, in such practices we must always bear in our mind the humbleness and cautions, which are the essential characteristics of Professor *Popper's* critical rationalism.

Summary

Anti-Rationalism or Critical Rationalism

This paper tries to explain why and how mutually inseparable the social sciences and our kind of liberalism are from the beginning of their simultaneous birth. Among the various social sciences, history and economics, (or what perhaps had better be identified as socio-historical sciences), are especially discussed. In order to understand the inseparable relationship mentioned above, we must once go back and examine how they came into being. It is asserted in this paper that when we do this, we will realize that their philosophical foundation was through and through «anti-rationalistic». Though the term «anti-rationalism» may sound not really tasteful to some people and will cause the unnecessary misunderstandings of our position, the paper attempts to make explicit that without this anti-rationalism, and not «critical rationalism», we will never be able to understand fully why and how the liberalism in the eighteenth century sense of the term can not exist without the genuinely socio-historical sciences, nor can the latter without the former. The anti-rationalism is an emphasis on the invariably inevitable limitations of reason as well as on the importance of emotions, inclinations and other non-rational factors in social phenomena. It views civilization fundamentally as the resultant of interplays of the only imperfectly rational actions of innumerous people. In its attempt to explain these points, the paper first pays its major attention to the works of *Bernard Mandeville*. At the same time, however, the paper asserts that as soon as we move from the field of pure science to that of practice, we must make, as it were, a «Copernican inversion», by changing our philosophical foundation from anti-rationalism to critical rationalism.

The second part of the paper tries to explain why the «compositive method» of *Carl Menger* is more suitable than the «type-parts analysis» of the *Max Weber*ian school to the «genetic» or «evolutionary» clarification of the «emergent» properties that are the very characteristics of social phenomena, and hence to the analytical detections of the causal relationships that may regularly be involved in those phenomena. More specifically, the paper asserts that the compositive method can explain why and how the individuals, who are without exception limited in their knowledge and skills, can yet come as a whole to form quite rational expectations and make great achievements. And the more they have their individual freedoms and free competitions among them, the greater those achievements yet will become. In order to explain these points, the paper will use as an illustration the so-called «rational expectation theory», or what perhaps had better be called «the public's rational expectation theory».

II. Politik und Verfassung

Giovanni Malagodi

The Market and Planning

With his book «The Road to Serfdom» *Hayek* established and later developed extensively two points of fundamental importance which have remained firm, becoming the basis for a renaissance of liberal thought in Europe and the USA over the years.

The first point was the superiority of the market as an instrument for economic activity and development. In pure theory, a collectivistic economy could reach the same results. In fact *Hayek* has shown this to be impossible. The IInd World War, if not entirely conclusive, supported his arguments. The natural resources at the disposal of Nazi Germany and Fascist Italy were inferior to those at the disposal of the Allies. So were those of Japan notwithstanding its conquests. Russia lost a large part of its resources as a consequence of the Nazi's military onslaught and was in any way, and particularly in the rest of its territory, far behind the Allies in point of development. The evident economic superiority of the Allies could therefore be explained by their control of larger supplies as also by the fact that they adopted, during the war years, a largely dirigistic management of their economies. However, on balance, I believe it to be indisputable that their superiority was largely due to the fact that their societies were fundamentally free and their economies fundamentally market economies. This had created over the years a reserve of attitudes, of skill, of know-how, of technological and psychological resources vastly superior both to those of Germany and Japan (even if the latter was far from the dirigism of the Nazis and of the Fascists) and to those of Soviet Russia. These reserves proved in the end to be decisive also at the psychological and political level. The resistance of Great Britain in face of tremendous political and military odds, the warlike resolve of the United States proved stronger than the ideological and military aggressiveness of Germany, Italy and Japan. Even the tenacity of Russia must be largely seen as the survival of a patriotic-religious ethos of national independence and personal dignity and heroism from less servile times.

What happened after the war was even more decisive in proving the superiority of freedom also on the economic plane. The return of the USA from a war-dirigistic to a free peace economy took place without substantial difficulties. Immense new resources were generated which allowed the USA to make an indispensable contribution to the re-building of Western and Central Europe and of Japan. If the contribution did not include the countries of Eastern Europe it was only because the Kremlin refused it for ideological prejudicies. The re-building took place in a free democratic framework and followed the guiding lines of a free market economy. Since 1950, the Marshall plan, Bretton Woods, the IMF, the Worldbank, the GATT and later the European Community have reversed the trend towards world disintegration of which *W. Roepke* had written in the middle thirties. The German «miracle» and later the Italian one were but the high-lights of a general growth of the western or western-type economies and of the societies in which they operated. They appeared the more remarkable in view of the recent nazi and fascist past of Germany and Italy. But the development in the central area of freedom, the United

States, was still more tremendous. The present rate of unemployment in the USA must not hide from us the almost incredible creation of new jobs in the same country in the past years. The technology which sent men to the moon and satellites to Mars and to Venus also transformed industry, agriculture, communications and trade. The world today sees Soviet Russia and Red China, both rich in natural resources and disposing of immense labour forces working under strict discipline, obliged to beg and borrow from the West the means to develop those resources, to meet to some extent the growing demands of their subjects and even to hold their own or improve their position in that arms-race for which they are largely responsible.

The economic difficulties which have troubled and are troubling the free industrialized countries during the last few years do not seem to contradict what we have just been saying. They neither stem from the freedom of the market, nor from the free democracy that goes with it and with which it goes, but from «market resistant forces» of which I will have to say something later on.

The second point which *Hayek* has established beyond dispute is the necessity of a market economy if man wants to be free also in the cultural, political and social respect. Without economic pluralism no other pluralism seems possible. Nobody has yet been able to negate this basic truth, neither in reasoning in theory nor through facts in practice. Unless man has freedom of choice in the economic field: freedom to choose his job, his employer, the relative size and form of his consumption and of his savings, the small or large enterprise he wants to engage in – he is not free in other fields. With the freedom of economic choice goes the freedom of thought, of religion, of expression, of political organisation and activity.

Freedom and justice are often proposed as a joint ideal nowadays. *Hayek* has shown the imprecise, vague character of the notion of social justice. Let us take it as meaning simply a state of affairs where the difference in riches and in security, in welfare between the citizens is «not excessive», leaving the measurement to the circumstances of place and time. It is not difficult to show that without freedom injustice prevails and that with freedom justice is established of necessity. The instances of some rough forms of justice without freedom are inconclusive. How «just» is such justice? How deep does it go, how long can it last, by the sacrifice of what other human values is it paid for?

The necessary connection between cultural and political freedom on the one hand, and the free market on the other hand was seen by *Hayek,* almost four decades ago, against the background of a growing wave of planned economy. Basically, against a growing wave of socialism.

Soviet Russia stood out, then as now, as the supreme example of a totally planned economy to which corresponded, as they correspond to-day, a totalitarian society and a totalitarian state.

To the lack of freedom, nay the denial of freedom in words and deeds, corresponded in Fascist Italy and in Nazi Germany economic systems which under various names, «corporativism», «planned economy», largely even if not totally rejected the free market and laboured to replace it by the establishment of one form or another of centralized direction of the economy under a State becoming as a consequence increasingly authoritarian.

In a free society and for a free market the law – as *Hayek* points out – is really equal for all. It is a general rule of conduct whose applications must not and can not be foreseen, thus being meant to favour nobody and to discriminate against nobody. In a fully centralized society and economy, and to a growing extent in a growingly centralized one, in a totalitarian and to a growing extent in an authoritarian State (and in the latter even if it dresses itself in a democratic garb), the law changes its character. It becomes, in fact if not always in words, an administrative and discriminatory measure. Its main purpose is to take from *Paul* to give to *Peter*. It enjoins on both *Paul* and *Peter* what their work should be, how managed and how paid; the measure and nature of their comsumption, the size and use of their savings. Beyond a certain limit, social security in the larger sense of the word, becomes the «welfare State» and the welfare State cannot be a free State.

Exceptions to the freedom of the market must be made – so *Hayek* tells us following the classics – for some public infrastructures and services and also regarding war, both to prepare for it and to wage it. But if a nation goes beyond this, its freedom is forfeit.

Hayek remarked in later years that in practice the connection between a growing measure of centralized planning and a diminishing measure of cultural and political freedom had shown itself to be slower and less far-reaching in practice than could be logically anticipated. The socialdemocratic regimes of Western and Northern Europe are still free to-day. The growing elements of planning in other regimes, however much they may be orientated towards the market, have equally failed to destroy the liberties of the citizen. It can be said with truth that they have interfered less with social life than with the economy, with its resiliency and inventiveness, its capacity to regain balance after a crisis, to develop without inflation and all this in the face of increasing objective difficulties. These qualities appear to-day to be appurtenant as much as ever to the economies where the market subsists and where they also are seen, politically, to have a greater chance to remain stronger.

This brings us to reflect again on the immense spiritual and human force of liberty. Where it is deeply rooted in the history and in the minds of the citizen, it can withstand larger doses of centralized or semi-centralized planning without withering away. In fact, it constitutes by itself a barrier against the spreading of total dirigism.

There is one other theorem of «moderate» or «gradualistic» socialism which no one has ever been able either to demonstrate in theory nor to substantiate in fact. It is the assumption that a market economy, a «capitalist» system can finance without hitch its own demize. That a social-democratic or socialist government can count to an almost unlimited amount on the resources produced by a market economy in order to introduce without pain new «elements of socialism» into the economy itself until the point is reached where it is entirely purged of capitalism and turned into a fully socialist, centrally managed economy. It goes almost without saying that the attempt to do so only contrives to weaken the market to the point where it hardly functions any more, and not to create the conditions for an «easy» transition to socialism. It goes also almost without saying that the contradiction explodes sooner and more violently in a transformation economy, i.e. in one in which natural resources are scarce and the demands of a large population are great and which therefore depends to a decisive extent on foreign trade to keep itself going and growing. This is, inter alia, the case of the UK and of the country where I am writing, Italy.

More than twenty years ago, two very eminent Italien liberal thinkers, *Benedetto Croce* and *Luigi Einaudi,* discussed among themselves (the discussion has been printed in a very interesting volume à deux voix) the relationship between liberalism and what *Croce* called «liberism», between spiritual and political freedom and economic freedom. *Einaudi* was on *Hayek's* side. *Croce,* seeing in liberalism the «religion of liberty» and in liberty a universal principle governing all human things, expressed the belief that liberty could subsist even in the absence of the free market. In the end, faced with *Einaudi's* arguments, *Croce* reluctanly agreed that at least in the world of to-day, the two stand and fall together.[1]

---

[1] *Benedetto Croce – Luigi Einaudi,* Liberismo e Liberalismo, a cura di Paolo Solari, Milano–Napoli, (Ricciardi) 1957.

There is, however, an element of permanent and fundamental value in *Croce's* original position. Unless we assume that there is in freedom an unlimited capacity to enlighten men and women and to master the difficulties with which they are more and more faced in their daily lives, it becomes impossible to understand how freedom has managed and manages to survive up to now the growing encroachments of dirigism and of outright planning and by what means we can hope to confront those that I call «market-resistant» factors so as to ensure in the near and not-so-near future the strengthening of free institutions on all planes and not only a precarious life, marked by their diminishing effectiveness.

In what do the «market-resistant» factors consist? In a general way I would call by such name the socio-political and economic distortions that are not and can not be automatically corrected by the operation of the market.

The market can and does very effectively correct the mistakes of those who produce at to high a cost and favours those who have succeeded in combining the factors of production in a better way. It corrects an excess of productive capacity in one field and a lack of it in another field. It encourages and facilitates the replacement of outworn technologies by new and more efficient ones. It anticipates to some extent the needs of to-morrow and opens the way to satisfy them. All in all, it stimulates productivity and economic growth and thereby the creation of the larger resources needed to finance its own survival and development and to take care of the requested improvements in the conditions and remuneration of work by men and women.

There are however facts that are not amenable, or at least not entirely and rapidly amenable to the working of the market mechanism.

That some aspects in the life of the commonwealth: the building of infrastructures, public services, defense, are beyond the market and the initiative and control of individuals, we have already recalled. But these aspects are changing and there are others. And they grow apace. And to understand how to master them without losing liberty, indeed enlarging it and strengthening it is the task of our times.

Here again *Hayek's* growing concern with constitutional problems and with those that are called to-day problems of «social engineering» is a major stimulant of our thoughts and of our action as liberals.

It may be useful to define briefly, at this point, what I mean, later on, by «necessary» or «unavoidable» planning. By such words I will indicate a measure of conscious direction of the economy and therefore, in a liberal view, of the market, by a public body or by a looser or tighter system of public bodies. A measure, as I understand it, going beyond and sometimes considerably beyond the conscious direction, the planning which is eo ipso required by those aspects of our economic life which are of themselves beyond the market and which I have just enumerated. Aspects, however, as I also indicated, that are changing and growing with respect to their traditional forms and dimensions.

I realize how «personal» concepts such as «a measure», «growing» or «traditional» are. But I believe they are sufficiently indicative for this brief inquiry.

I would divide the «market-resistant» factors into two main groups, «subjective» and «objective».

First among the subjective factors appear to be the pseudo-intellectual and passionate factors.

Under the pressure of more or less real factors and of the fact that these either correspond to the specific interests of large sectors of the population, or go back to real difficulties, there has come to be born over the last decades and among the intellectual élites, a growing fashion and passion for a growing measure of «public control». The cry «down with the anarchy of the market», against the «exploitation of man by man» and the ensuring «alienation». In favour of planning, of nationalization of industry and of nationalization of the media, in short of conformity in all things.

This fashion constitutes a very powerful incentive to fight the market without knowing its mechanisms, its pros and cons, to fight it in the name of democracy and liberty, indeed of a liberty often degenerating in anarchical permissiveness.

To such a fashion we can but answer culturally and with our deeds. Culturally by patient reasoning – and here lies the great value of the neo-liberals which have been gaining ground over the last few years and of whom *Hayek* has been an anticipator and is a leader. In deeds, by showing in fact the greater capacity of freedom to satisfy both the spiritual and the physical needs of man.

Among the subjective factors I would also include feelings and attitudes that are rooted in the specific – or can we use the old word: egoistic? – interests of important sectors of the population.

In the name of justice, the poorer classes have been asking and ask for a larger share of the national product. In the name of equality, they ask for a more uniform distribution of the said product. To those ends, they more and more exert pressure on the political system in order that it should intervene to «correct» the natural results of the market, either by supporting their claims to pay increases and working conditions not sufficiently related to productivity or by requesting large and swift increases in the social services. In a growing measure they make such pressure more effective through sudden and carefully planned economic disorder, from «wild cat strikes» to the scientific exploitation of the «strategic positions» of small groups in the industrial system.

The pressures, in turn, being normally divorced from a careful consideration of the resources to be shared and of the inner logic of their production, tend to generate both demand and cost-push inflation and therefore to limit new investment and technological development and to cause unemployment and balance of payments difficulties.

Here again the answer is in the first place cultural, a patient work of enlightenment. At the same time, it involves one of the most important if not perhaps the most important internal problem of contemporary democracies: the problem of the trade unions.

Under different political circumstances, e.g. in an oligarchical society without the universal franchise and the organisation of labour, some would imagine that the answer could be left entirely or almost entirely to market forces: bankruptcies, mass dismissals of workers, large scale unemployment, reduction of wages etc.

Such things are impossible to-day. Not only do they not correspond to the political structure of our societies, but we are averse from them because we believe, on the one hand in the defense of the poor against hazards of which they are largely innocent, and on the other hand in the need for society to grow above present conditions through the exercise of responsibility if society must remain free, solve its problems in the framework of liberty and not fall into the toils of dictatorship, be it black or red. A dictatorship which would mean, among other things, the destruction of the market, immediate or medium-term, or its withering away.

Besides being cultural, our answer must be factual and constitutional.

Enlightenment is not only a matter of explaining and teaching. It is also a matter of taking reasonable positions and then holding them. Here lies a great responsibility for entrepreneurs and for statesmen and politicians alike.

A responsibility which can, and to my mind must take two directions.

The first must be an attempt to bring the trade unions into the system of checks and balances which is the system of free democracies. The unions have performed and perform a great and useful function in improving the bargaining position of their members. They overstep their usefulness when they become instruments of an excessive pressure and deny, in fact or in words, the functions of the market. By doing so, they incur a trilemma. Either they take over government, cease to be advocates and become judges, leaving the democratic system lopsided. Or they create anarchy, cause the fall of democratic government and the rise of a dictatorship and cease to function as real unions. Or they accept their proper place as one of the impelling forces, checks and balances of liberty.

Attempts have been made towards this goal. In France and Italy, the unions sit together with the entrepreneurs and with governement-chosen experts in a consultative «Council for economy and labour». In fact, such Councils are rarely listened to. The distance is too great between their structure with its purposes of internal equilibrium and the actual situation. The European Community has set up a social council to the same purpose. It appears to be slightly more effective. In the UK, a few years ago, the «*Heath* show-down» on «who governs the country» left things very much where they were.

In fact, the unions are reluctant to surrender their apparently unlimited powers. For the same reason they resist the proposals to set up a system of co-directorship in at least some large industries. They refuse a system of profit-sharing or tend, even in Germany and in Sweden, to divert it towards the «unionization» of industry through the control of company capital stocks by the unions themselves.

They also resist, more or less according to circumstances, any kind of incomes policy. They prefer irresponsibility at the price of massive inflation, unemployment and stagnation.

An incomes policy is obviously a dirigistic instrument. Can a liberal accept it? Can he favour it? This is a crucial point. An incomes policy, once introduced, tends to become compulsory and to embrace, if not all incomes, then most of them. These are illiberal aspects. But if the labour situation is not largely amenable to the checks and balances of the market, we must look for something else. Otherwise, we would be making the same mistake as the unions. We would be working, in the name of unlimited freedom, towards the destruction of the conditions for the existence and functioning of the market.

The problem is, in the last resort, a problem of political limits. Within proper limits, with unions made constitutionally a part of the democratic system, the great instrument of responsibility learnt through responsibility would come into full play. The alternative risks being chaos. Those democracies function better, to-day, where in some way the problem has been put on the rails towards a solution. Such is the case, e.g., of Germany, of Sweden, of the USA and in a peculiar way of Japan.

I come now to those I have called objective factors of resistance to the market.

«Objective» in the sense that they exist and make themselves felt independently from ideologies or special interests.

The first of these, I believe, is the sheer increase in the numbers of population, in the coming into being and the growth of the «masses».

There must be the same percentage and therefore a larger number of first class men and women in a larger mass. But if the mass augments very rapidly, and especially where the traditions of a liberal democracy and of a market economy are weaker, then the mass tends to dilute the relatively small groups on which lies the responsibility to guide their communities in the right direction. The average becomes lower, and the lowering tends to become cumulative. In recent years this has been accentuated by the slowing down, indeed the cessation, actual or potential, of the increase in population in the more developed countries, while it continues at a fast rate in the others.

The management of the commonwealth and the running of a market economy require qualities of responsibility, of self-denial, of compromise, of putting invisible and distant advantages before immediate and gross ones. Such qualities tend to lose their weight in a mass society. Their place is taken – as a great historian wrote more than a century ago –

by the «terrible simplifiers» who believe in authoritarian management from the center. A tendency which goes easily together with egalitarian and socialist inclinations. It is not by chance that many of the new «Less Developed Countries», born to independence after World War II, call themselves «socialist» and are so to a considerable extent, even if some of the elements of a market economy and some of the trappings of a free democracy are allowed to exist.

Clearly this state of internal and international affairs reflects itself heavily on the remaining free countries and free markets. The human and political necessity of ensuring internal development and avoiding excessive tensions and clashes, as also of trading with the LDC.s (Less Developed Countries) and with the N.I.C.s (New Industrialized Countries) and of helping them to grow and to diversify, forces the States and the producers of the D.F.C.s (Developed Free Countries) to internal and external arrangements which do not always correspond, or only in part, to the logic of a market economy. There are compensations in larger trade and greater occasions for investment. But strains are also set up in addition to the others of which I have spoken and will speak.

Here allow me to say that the answer to the problem is again cultural and political. We must spread responsibility and understanding by our example and not only by our teaching. We must protect our political freedom and ensure the functioning of our market economies. This requires a measure of adaptation to conditions which in themselves are not necessarily favourable. It requires a conscious effort to understand and «plan» our answer.

The problem of the masses is made more acute by their concentration in urban areas and away from the land.

The problem of our enormous, often monstruous cities can not be left to solve itself. Everywhere (and always, I dare say, even under easier circumstances) the development of large cities has required a great deal of planning. The very structure of the city and of its quarters, city-walls and ring-roads, the situating of public buildings and markets, the network of services, they all require intervention, the favouring of some as against others according to the discretionary views of those in power. The temptation to submit housing to their control in all its phases lies very near. It must be resisted. Market incentives are not incompatible with urban planning. They should be developed.

Similar problems arise with infrastructures. The complexity of modern life, the growth of cities and of trade, the localization of industries at one or other of the possible intersections between raw materials, energy, labour, distribution and markets impose a series of difficult and to a large extent discretionary choices in a field which was in other times much simpler and clearly motivated by elementary and evident preferences. Transportation is a good example. The Prince has always taken care of roads, bridges and harbours. To-day, the competition for the resources available, both in respect of other uses and of other infrastructures is often frantic. Is it better, e.g. for the *Mezzogiorno* of Italy to develop local roads and railways or connections with the markets in the Po valley? Or new tunnels and bridges in the Alps, aiming at the markets and the supplies of central and northern Europe? Railways or roads? Harbours for coastal traffic, or try to capture a growing part of the trade between Europe, the Near and the Far East?

The proper answer requires a careful assessment of present market conditions, but a least as much of potential conditions. An evaluation of the probable, but always uncertain social repercussions e.g. on labour conditions, on urban housing, on local agriculture, on the need for this or that sort of schooling. The resulting actions have a deep and often decisive influence on the chances of the labour forces and of the entrepreneurs now working in the market and on those who wish to join them. Even in a country wedded to a free economy, such actions can be, if at all, only to a limited extent the result of the working of the market. They are, again, very largely the result of conscious decisions, good or bad, by those in power: parliaments, governments, social forces.

A similar reasoning applies to regional policies. Such policies aim deliberately at correcting the imbalances in infrastructures, in productive capacities, in public services, in wealth and welfare as between the different parts of a country or of a community of countries. They are aimed in part towards a larger global production of wealth and welfare in the community or country concerned. But no less to «better» viz. less unequal conditions as between their regions. The decisions directed towards such purposes are, again, or should be based on a careful study of actual and potential conditions, but the end result is very much discretionary.

I have but to mention ecology without needing to develop the theme. The choice between lower costs to-day and a better environment to-morrow weighs heavily on some and not on others. It influences the localization of investments, their amount and their yield, the employment they give, the pattern of internal and international trade (e.g. coal versus oil).

Looking at public and social services, let us first dispose, at least in our thinking, of the unwholesome tendency to increase them for their own sake and to concentrate them in public hands, whereas in many instances they would be run better and more cheaply, to the general advantage, by private capital and managers. Even so, the number, the variety and the volume of these services has grown and is still growing under the pressure of the increase both in population and in its expectancies. I abstain from repeating what I have just said about the choice between them, their organization and efficiency, their rate of development, and the consequences. I will rather say a word here about their global cost. The demand, even a reasonable demand for them very often exceeds the means available. In some cases (e.g. medical services at very low prices) it may turn out to be practically almost unlimited. They are a relatively new and very large addendum in the sum of the resources requested by the Commonwealth from itself.

One particular public service which has come to weigh very heavily in that sum, much more than formerly, both in absolute and relative terms, is defence. Nuclear defence devours huge sums for research and for development. So-called «conventional» armaments become more and more sophisticated and multiply in number. Highly qualified manpower is both required and absorbed. Especially the first sort of armaments (nuclear) require an increasing peace-time expenditure also for their own defense against the risk of accidents and of falling into irresponsible hands.

It would take us very far if we tried to cover the field of the «Club of Rome». What is the balance between available natural resources and their consumption? Must we aim at «zero growth», perhaps at «reverse growth» before we are caught in the nut-cracker of growing demand and dwindling possibilities? The picture of exponential growth and ensuing disaster which was first painted was too black. But it seems to me that one valid conclusion remains. Under present and foreseeable world circumstances (population, expectancies, economic growth, defense) the «terms of trade» as between mankind and our earth tend to move against mankind. Very probably we must anticipate the need for more research, more capital and more labour being necessary to obtain the same results we now obtain from less. Technology can probably help us in the future as it has in the past (e.g. it could give us energy from fusion). But on balance, and at least up to now, the signs of pressure seem to be evident. The case of oil is typical. The sudden and dramatic increase of its price in 1973 was the immediate result of a political decision by OPEC. The decision, however, was proposed and made possible not only by the monopoly of oil lying in OPEC's hands, but also by the sudden realization that oil resources, including potential ones, if very large, are not inexhaustible within a not too distant future.

This raises a great problem. Oil, we said, is in the hands of a monopoly. The setting of prices and of conditions for its sale do not, therefore, correspond in themselves to the requirements of a free market. But is there not, beyond this, a more general need to husband world resources? To apportion them on a «just» basis? To make sure that the capital and labour needed to develop increasingly expensive reserves of raw materials are made available in time and in the proper measure, even if this entails taking them away, by an «act of the Prince», from other, less essential forms of investment and/or consumption? The heavy taxes most States already impose on oil products seem to point in such direction.

If one takes the sum total of these various needs: the growing numbers and the expectations of the masses, the cities, infrastructures, ecology, defense, social services, the growing cost of natural resources – then we are faced with the largest of «market-resistant» factors and at the same time with a central responsibility of any government. Particularly, I would add, of a free democratic government which by definition allows the pressures to become manifest, to organize, to exert themselves in competion among themselves as also in mutual support.

How large a part of the national product can be allotted to what has come to be known as the «public sector»? How should and can the resources be raised? How to spend them?

An important word of caution before going further. Nowadays, everywhere, the «public sector» includes a large number of enterprises and services which either are overblown as an effect of bureaucracy's tendency to grow beyond what is needed, or should altogether not be there but in the private sector. I am not now discussing this point, although it is one of the great, indeed almost mortal dangers to our free societies and perhaps to all organized societies as such. The quarrel with this state of affairs has been growing larger over the last ten or fifteen years. It has gone into irrefutable examples and details. The low and decreasing productivity of the public sector is by now grudgingly admitted even by the so called «progressive left». In some cases public intervention is an almost undiluted consequence of statist superstition («bailed out» entreprises kept artificially alive – cold-blooded nationalizations). In other cases, the excess in fixed assets and in man-power er is so to say grafted on to services that are public by needs.

What I am occupied with here is however not with unnecessary and excessive public expenditure, but with the limits and control of useful expenditure. I contend, in fact, that you cannot lead the fight against excesses effectively if you lump together in an indiscriminate manner needed and unneeded public expenditure.

Nor is it of avail to admit en passant that some public expenditure is needed, having more or less in mind a state of affairs where such expenditure was limited by itself.

To combat excesses one must be just towards needs. And needs are to-day much larger than in the past, even the recent past. Otherwise, one uncovers one's flank to the counter-thrust of the statist that from showing that one is wrong in denying or passing-over certain real needs, proceeds to depict one as being unaware of the real state of human affairs. And as one is at the same time in favour of the market economy, his adversary equally proceeds to equate such an economy with insensitiveness and incapacity to provide for essential requirements, and from there to argue the necessity to replace the market more and more with public intervention even if he is forced to admit that it does not work well.

An analogous case must be made with regard to planning. It is easier for the dirigiste to promote and indeed to offer planning as the only rational tool available, if he is faced with the refusal of planning where it is obvious that it cannot be done without even in a market economy. It is, to my mind, only by recognising the existence and the force of subjective and objective market-resistant factors, that such factors can be limited to their proper functions, stopped from destroying the market, indeed made to serve it in its character as the most useful tool man has devised to further his own welfare and also to ensure his freedom.

I now revert to the question of how much the public sector can take of the national product and how it can be used. I speak of the public sector (of what we have come to call in Italy the «enlarged public sector») because everywhere, in different forms, to the drawings and expenditures of the central and of local governments have been added those of various other public bodies, such as autonomous public services (e.g. railways and electricity), productive units (e.g. in coal, oil and natural gas, industry, even agriculture), social security and medical care organisations.

It is in view of the ensemble of these that one must ask oneself a few fundamental questions. Is their total sum such as to leave sufficient resources for consumption, investment and production? If not, is this not a primary reason for the «unholy alliance» of inflation and stagnation? Where do we draw the limit? And how do we evaluate, inside the limit, the claims of the different components of the enlarged public sector?

This is, in fact, the «budget exercise» in its modern form. I believe it can be shown that the budget was always a primary factor in determining the conditions and the running of the economy as a whole (and this apart from its often decisive influence on the state of the public mind and on the political balance). How much more that is so to-day. The requirement for compatibility between public and private and for a proper mix of public expenditures is in fact the old budget in its modern form. It is not a fad if finance ministers now submit to their parliaments an economic review together with the figures for State taxation and expenditure stricto sensu.

Taxation raises again tremendous questions. Together with its traditional forms, direct and indirect, go vastly increased local taxation, social security dues, the rates at which public services are offered to the citizen and in some cases also the prices for the products of public enterprises. Last not least, tariffs still exist and influence the picture notwithstanding the E.E.C. and the GATT-rounds.

How much the Prince taxes in which various forms, how the total is apportioned between them are essential components in a system of economic compatibilities in order to allow (or not to allow) the market to function properly. And so is public borrowing, internal and external, and the concession of incentives to certain groups of semi-private or private borrowers.

There is no country left, to-day, where the management of the enlarged public sector is not decisive.

It is decisive for the money market and the banks, starting with the central bank. It is decisive for the balance of payments. Other factors are obviously at work too. There are the other «market-resistant» ones. There is the market itself, how it runs, how it reacts. But the point I want to make here is that the extent and character of public finance, – on the taxing, on the borrowing and on the spending side – is so large, quite apart from excesses, that it entails a measure of conscious management (call it planning, or programming if you like) vastly superior to the past. Add to it the other examples I have given and you begin to have the picture. In which – I will repeat in order to avoid misunderstandings – the market is not lost, only put in a new setting.

A system of compatibilities must therefore be drawn up year per year (and now and then be adapted during the year) if one does not want to make the working of the market impossible or very difficult through an insufficiency of resources, taxation, wasteful expenditure, inflation. Also very difficult through the lack of a proper basis on which to calculate the other phases of public action.

In a system of compatibilities the cost and conditions of labour are another decisive element. This brings us back to the difficult problem of an incomes policy. In the measure in which public finances are handled properly, the need for an «authoritative» incomes policy diminishes, labour becomes more amenable to the impulses, to the checks and balances of the market.

The same applies, albeit to a smaller degree, to the other forms of public intervention. The more they are restricted to what is really needed and reasonable; the more they avoid excesses of any kind (of expenditure as of regulations) – the better the economy will function as a whole and the better the market will do its irreplaceable job of ensuring the continuous adaptation of the factors of production to the ever-changing realities. This includes labour, to my mind, even under contemporary conditions. The attitudes and the behaviour of labour in Germany or in the USA contrasted with Italy and the UK are a telling example. It can be remarked that the difference in attitudes is more a condition of the political mind. True. But is such a condition independent of a proper management also of the economic side of market-resistant factors by the governments concerned?

Among the duties involved in such management are also those relating to the monetary system in its external aspects. A healthy economy has obviously less to fear also with respect to the international monetary system. But one's own health is not sufficient if the others are seriously ill. The case of the starkly overvalued Swiss frank, of staid Swiss financiers asking for «a little inflation» is typical. The attempt to leave the currency markets to their own devices since 1971–73 has not worked well. Some «dirty floating», some reciprocal aid, some recourse to traditional instruments such as the bank rate completed with banking reserve requirements et sim. have not fundamentally changed a picture where the parities of purchasing power and the differentials in inflation rates have often been overshadowed by abrupt and very strong changes in the market rates that not even the strongest Central banks and Treasuries have been able to stem. To some extent the underlying trends have pushed the various countries, with the assistance of the I.M.F., towards correcting their basic policies. But in no case up to now to a sufficient degree.

There are, I believe, three large market-resistant factors in the international monetary picture. One is the unprecedented fact of a group of countries, the OPEC, which after having suddenly multiplied by 4 or by 5 the price of one of the main, perhaps the crucial commodity in world trade, have proved themselves, as a group, incapable of spending more than a part of their receipts, or of lending a significant part of their unspent receipts to LDC.s in order to stimulate their imports from the D.C.s. This, together with the prevailing international inflation, has accentuated both such inflation and the stagnation of several economies and has created a huge pool of totally uncontrolled «xeno-dollars» or «xeno-currencies» which seem capable of little more than accentuating speculative operations on this or that currency. A second factor is the apparent capability of the American economic system to withstand an enormous external deficit and a marked devaluation of the dollar without up to now developing a corresponding internal policy really capable of correcting the imbalance. Lastly the peculiar social structure of Japan, now a main actor in world trade, has again made the Japanese economy much less subject to external market pressures than would be in itself theoretically justified.

The attempt made in 1972–73 to rebuild a world monetary system after the breakdown of Bretton Woods did not succeed. However much, or little, disputed in theory, the problem of bringing some stability into world exchange rates is felt to be strongly there. Slowly there seem to emerge the outlines of a regional solution. A dollar zone, a yen zone, a European zone. For the purpose of these remarks on the free market and planning, I will confine myself to the latter. The «snake» of European currencies, born in 1972, rapidly shedded the pound, the lira, the French franc. An attempt is now underway to revamp it. The preconditions indicated in 1972–73 by the British and the Italian treasury would be met. A partial pooling of reserves; enlarged reciprocal credits; massive transfers of resources from the richer to the poorer regions and nations of the E.C.; reciprocal surveillance on economic and financial policies of an IMF type; support from the IMF itself; measures intended to ensure a symmetry of obligations between debtor and creditor countries: these seem to be the main ingredients intended to produce sufficient stability as between E.C. currencies and in respect of a «basket» of the same (a sort of «parallel currency») and make a «common float» with respect to the dollar possible.

I will not even try to go further into this most arduous subject. I will limit myself to point out that the measures taken or intended, all require a high degree of conscious planning and intervention by the Governments, and have greatly different consequences for the various economic groups operating in the markets. Protectionism, however, which is raising again its ugly head, would be much worse. It seems to be again a case where some degree of conscious direction, with all its dangers, is needed to avoid the total breakdown of the market economies.

It is not necessary to spend many words to point out that the problems of the so-called «North-South Dialogue», connected as they are also with the problems of the international monetary and financial system, seem to be of a similar character.

The DC.s have resisted up to now the request by the L.D.C.s to create a huge dirigistic, inter-State organisation to take care of all trade in all raw materials and stabilize their prices. Something however seems necessary, on a commodity basis and country by country, taking account of the political, social and economic conditions in each, if one wants to avoid a breakdown in the economies of many L.D.C.s with the consequent serious repercussions on world trade and on what there exists of political stability. The increase in the price of oil and the wild fluctuations on the currency markets increase these dangers.

I will just mention the problem of trade and financial relations with the communist countries selling, buying and lending by a large number of free market operators in competition among themselves to individual States, viz. to counterparts which are «entirely» and not only commodity-wise monopolistic, poses a number of political problems. Which commodities («strategic» or «semi-strategic»)? on what terms? in what currencies? for a total credit risk of how much? with what repercussions on the political and military picture? The case for deliberation by the State or even more by a group of allied or «communitary» States (as in fact happens in part) is very strong.

Again, the market is indispensable as an instrument of development and efficiency, but it cannot work, in this case, if not under conditions which are largely the fruit of deliberations taken outside the market and for reasons partially extraneous to the market itself.

The trade in question is not yet very large. But considering the size, the needs, the potential riches of the communist countries on one side, and the need to produce and trade of the industrial free countries, especially in Europe, it is called to grow.

Looking back at this brief paper, I feel brought once more to the conclusion that we live to-day in a paradoxical situation. Perhaps we have always lived in it, although noticing it less because it was less acute.

In order to safeguard the working of the free market we must limit planning. To limit planning to what is really needed, we must plan.

To deny all need for planning runs counter to «subjective» market-resistant factors: statism and egalitarianism, which we have good grounds to consider as being, all included, erroneous. These subjective factors are however very strong, deeply rooted in history and partially justified by a past of excessive inequalities, of excessive uncertainties in the life of the masses, of an unwarranted opposition by the ruling élites to the State taking action also where it appeared appropriate and has produced positive results (e.g. legislation on the hours, the conditions, the security of labour). Such attitudes and resistances have been largely overcome in our countries (in fact, it can be said with reason that often we have gone too far in the opposite direction). But they are still alive in some groups, and especially they are suspected to be lurking round the corner. And certainly they are alive in some of the N.I.C.s and of the L.D.C.s which are now turning themselves rapidly into industrial producers and exporters. We cannot therefore just dispose of them out of hand. While opposing any exaggeration, we must make it clear that we do not intend the working of the market to produce by itself insecurity and inequality. That in fact the market, properly organized, makes for more security, more equality in the points of departure, better conditions of life than a centralized economy, unavoidably accompanied by a totalitarian regime as it is, and that we are constantly at work improving the organisation of the market without destroying its positive capabilities.

But then we are faced also by the «objective» market-resistant factors. There again, planning and public intervention have come to be regarded by many and by the masses as magic remedies to the difficulties and ills in which such objective factors are embodied. Together with the kind of human failings to which mass-democracy is prone, this has generated excesses of planning and intervention which we can and must combat unremittingly. But we can and must not deny the reality of the difficulties and of the ills and the need for some measure of conscious public action to overcome them. We must analyze them one by one and define the action needed under varying circumstances. In doing so, we must devise the ways and means which limit the freedom of the market less and in any case do not jeopardize it. On such conditions we will be strengthening the market, not making it weaker.

What we are looking for is in each case an approach which allows for a combination, a synthesis between macro-economics and micro-economics. Between guidelines for the economy as a whole, including the market, and the feelings and interests which motivate the actual decisions of the men and women at work in the market, as well as in the public sector itself.

It is often said that we are looking for «flexible» planning (what we call «programming» in Italy). What does that mean? I believe the answer is that we are looking for a state of things in which:
– the public sector knows and respects its limits, qualitatively and quantitatively, and:
– while continuously revising its plans in the light of their results and of the indications of the market, it:
– gives the market a certain number of assumptions on which it can work for at least a definite period of time.

Among such certainties I would like to underscore the internal and external value of the currency in the measure in which it depends on the functioning of one's own economy.

In shouldering the inexcusable responsibility for planning in the sense I have indicated, the State, viz. public institutions in the largest sense, including the bureaucracy, the parties, the unions and public opinion at large must be aware that we live in circumstances where political and technological reasons compel one to make decisions, private and public, well ahead of execution and where at the same time the unexpected explodes continuously, suddenly and grandly – both much more than ever before.

This state of affairs is connected not only with the rapid changes in our increasingly complex societies, but also with the size of the markets in which we work and trade. The volume of production and of internal and international trade has grown over the last fifty, twenty, ten years in an incredible way. Up to now, depressions, inflation, vaguaries in currency rates, unexpected crises such as the one in oil have not arrested or reversed the general trend. However partially distorted or fettered, the market economy still embraces the largest part of mankind and by far the largest part of production and exchanges. It has shown and shows its inner strength by resisting attacks and adverse tendencies and by continuing to underpin the remaining free democracies. Aided by the breathless development of technology (rooted, let me note in passing, in the same soil of individual freedom in the sciences as in the counting-shops and factories), the market economy has resisted the challenges of protectionism, of cartelisation, of autarky, of statism. Outside the frontiers of the communist States it has reached more than ever for the world as a whole. In doing so it has created for itself the challenge of size. Size, with the diversity of the structures that come to be embraced in the area of market economy (e.g. the UK, Germany, the USA, Japan, South Korea) causes problems which are to a certain extent market-resistant, if for no other reason because of the different time-lags involved in the action of market factors in this new dimension. This has produced the multinationals and the European Community. The managers of a multinational are confronted with the difficult task of producing the same goods or the same services under widely different conditions, to each set of which they must conform in a continuous process of private connected with public planning. The E.C. is meant to cut through the tangle by merging a dozen developed markets into one market.

The merger was found to be not too difficult until it was a matter of eliminating tariffs, in the framework of a relatively stable world monetary system and with the assistance of the GATT rounds, i.e. the progressive reduction of tariffs on a world basis. It has run into very serious delays since it has become a matter of coordinating public policies and finances and of transfering resources under the so-called regional policy. As I have already pointed out, the process implies a high degree of planning, made more complex by the need to enmesh the plans of the Community as a whole with those of the member States and of their regions. Such planning is the price to be paid in order to create an area of free market economy large enough to hold its own in world competition and to avoid a relapse of the European states into an autarchy disastrous for them and for others, leading as it would to a renewed disintegration of the international system, including its political aspects.

Citizen and governments must also be aware that public planning is clumsier and slower than private planning, including the activities, e.g. infrastructures, for which the public hand is naturally responsible. Not seldom when a public project is completed, it appears to be insufficient or out-of-date.

We also know and must make clear the inborn tendency of public intervention to grow as a thing good in itself, which it is not, and far beyond necessity. Public means political and political means the search of power – a search which is unlimited, even to its own detriment.

This does not mean that we can do without public planning. We must understand and measure its reasons in order to keep it within its proper bounds. By simply denying it any raison d'être, or overlooking it, we would not strengthen the case for the market but weaken it, theoretically and politically.

The task of turning planning from a danger into an instrument useful to the market is cultural, constitutional and political. I will allow myself here only a few words on these three aspects.

First and foremost we must educate public opinion and its leaders. You cannot force man to be free. You can awaken and strengthen his natural inclination towards freedom. You can fight against attempts to make him walk the road to serfdom by false pretences.

There are two main tools. The first includes the school and the press. Hence also the decisive importance which, as liberals, we attribute to both. But we recognize that society in its entirety is a school to itself. Therefore the second tool is for us the education to liberty in all fields through liberty and responsibility, in the awareness that all fields are one.

Constitutionally, I believe that the main open problems, with regard to planning, are two. To one I have already referred. It is the bringing of the unions into the system of checks and balances on which a free democracy rests. The other is «quasi-constitutional». It is the obligation for government and parliament to collect, digest, discuss and take their decisions, especially in the economic and social field (but there is an economic and financial side also to e.g. defence, or schooling) on the basis of a thoroughgoing picture of «enlarged» public finance in the framework of the economic situation and trends in the country, in the Community to which the country belongs and in the world economy. Incoherent, disjointed debates and decisions by the Prince are the mortal enemies of a free market economy. Compatibility is all, if we can adapt the words of a great poet. I believe less in the deficit or the volume of money being restricted by law to a percentage e.g. of the national product. What a law can establish, another law can change. Circumstances can require a change quite outside any «perverse» scheme or prejudice.

We have entered the political field at this point. It should be the first concern of all those engaged in governing, from the benches of the majority or from those of the opposition, to ask themselves, on any question: how do we solve it and further the interests of freedom? Freedom understood in its all-embracing capacity to foster at the same time the spiritual, the social and the economic interests of man.

The critical position taken up in some of my remarks is not a battle against, but in favour of the market. Human nature being what it is, man tends to want freedom for himself while denying it to others when it impedes his own. Out of the request for freedom the market economy is born. Out of its denial protectionism, monopoly and statism are born. To enjoy the advantages of the free market, we must protect it against such dangers. Legislation on contract and private property is the first bulwark, planning properly applied and limited, the second.

Summary

The Market and Planning

The economic development after World War II has verified two important theses of F. A. v. Hayek: first, market economies are superior to collectivist economies; second, a market economy is a necessity, if one wants to be free also in cultural, political and social respect. Countries with a liberal tradition prove to be more resistant to measures of centralization than those without. Yet, the danger cannot be denied that many market economies are gradually undermined with more and more market-economy elements being replaced by socialist ones. This danger is immanent to most Western economies in form of so-called subjective and objective «market-resistant-factors». The first category includes the passion of some intellectuals for more public control, the claim of some interest groups to correct the natural results of the market, and those actions of the trade-unions, which are not related to bargaining for higher wages. Objective factors are the increasing population, the urbanization, the necessity of infrastructures, regional policy, ecology, the demand for-public and social services, defence and the growing costs of natural resources.

Subjective factors may be contained by convincing their proponents of their being wrong. Objective factors do need public planning. But on the other hand it is necessary to limit the destruction of the market. This leads to a paradoxical situation. Planning must be limited, but for the very purpose of limiting planning to the necessary minimum, there has to be some planning.

What is the way out of this dilemma? The author suggests a «flexible» way of planning, limiting the public sector quantitatively and qualitatively, continuous comparisons of the results of public planning in the light of the market results and improvements of the market mechanism.

George J. Stigler

Why Have the Socialists Been Winning?

The massive growth of governments in the twentieth century has been the most conspicuous single change in the organization of social life, – a growth so large and so pervasive that it would be as difficult to deny as the existence of the Pacific Ocean. The task I have set myself here is to explore the reasons for the growth of government, on the ground that we are not likely to predict, let alone control, a movement we cannot explain.

This growth requires no explanation for a socialist: justice simply formed an irresistible merger with democracy. Of course there are numerous phenomena which require explanation even if one accepts this relaxing view: for example, nations differ widely in the degree to which they have transferred the conduct of economic life over to the state, and do the loose notions of democracy and justice help us to explain these differences?

In any event a different explanation for the growth of the state is required for those of us who believe that the result of this growth has been a large reduction in aggregate output, quite possibly with a deterioration in the moral quality of society. The task of explanation is not only more difficult but also more important for those who oppose the growth of government. I suppose that it is conceivable that one can control a social development that one does not understand, perhaps by stopping that development through the decisive use of power. But that kind of policy is repugnant to our principles, and we do not even have a strong temptation to become unprincipled because the power is on the other side. If we are to predict and perhaps to control the role of government in the future, we need to know why it has been growing. I propose to examine the leading explanations for the present age of collectivism.

I. The Theory of Mistakes

Overwhelmingly the most popular explanation for the growth of government, among those opposed to the trend, has been that it was a mistake: a mistake in the literal sense that a misinformed populace has acted against its own interests. The mistake has presumably been induced and certainly fostered by the socialists and interventionists. The socialists have denounced the system of private enterprise and individualism with enormous vigor and persistence, presenting an indictment filled with charges that are always exaggerated and often false. The socialists have simultaneously promised vast and unrealizable benefits from the socialization of life.

It is easy enough to illustrate gross libels of private enterprise. Of the literature in this tradition, which in volume is strictly infinite relative to the reading life of a person, I choose only one example, Professor *Richard Tawney*, the well-known historian and one-time colleague of Professor *Hayek*, and only one passage from his famous book, The Acquisitive Society.[1]

[1] The Acquisitive Society, New York 1920, pp. 34-35.

«Because rewards are divorced from services, so that what is prized most is not riches obtained in return for labor but riches the economic origin of which, being regarded as sordid, is concealed, two results follow. The first is the creation of a class of pensioners upon industry, who levy toll upon its product, but contribute nothing to its increase, and who are not merely tolerated, but applauded and admired and protected with assiduous care, as though the secret of prosperity resided in them. . . .The rentier and his ways, how familiar they were in *England* before the war! A public school and then club life in *Oxford* and *Cambridge*, and then another club in town; *London* in *June*, when *London* is pleasant, the moors in *August*, and pheasants in *October*, *Cannes* in *December* and hunting in *February* and *March*; and a whole world of rising bourgeoisie eager to imitate them, sedulous to make their expensive watches keep time with this preposterous calendar!

The second consequence is the degradation of those who labor, but who do not by their labor command large rewards; that is of the great majority of mankind. And this degradation follows inevitably from the refusal of men to give the purpose of industry the first place in their thought about it. When they do that, when their minds are set upon the fact that the meaning of industry is the service of man, all who labor appear to them honorable, because all who labor serve, and the distinction which separates those who serve from those who merely spend is so crucial and fundamental as to obliterate all minor distinctions based on differences of income. But when the criterion of function is forgotten, the only criterion which remains is that of wealth, and an Acquisitive Society reverences the possession of wealth, as a Functional Society would honor, even in the person of the humblest and most laborious craftsman, the arts of creation.»

These are the two fundamental themes of socialist criticism: gross inequalities of income arise under capitalism, and production is directed by profit rather than by use. The themes have been repeated by so many people so often that they have constituted a socialized form of the classical Chinese torture.

The promises of the socialists have almost always been conveniently vague; indeed one could make a good case that socialism has seldom had any clear goal beyond the removal of capitalistic evils. One famous exception is *Edward Bellamy*, and I must resist the temptation to quote extensively from Looking Backward.[2] Still, he deserves quotation on at least two points. The first concerns the organization of labor in the good society (attained in the year 2000):

« . . .we hold the period of youth sacred to education, and the period of maturity, when the physical forces begin to flag, equally sacred to ease and agreeable relaxation. The period of industrial service is twenty-four years, beginning at the close of the course of education at twenty-one and terminating at forty-five. After forty-five, while discharged from labor, the citizen still remains liable to special calls, in case of emergencies causing a sudden great increase in the demand for labor, till he reaches the age of fifty-five, but such calls are rarely, in fact almost never, made.» (pp. 63-64)

Bellamy's vision of the socialist society was more accurate than most: he promised both high productivity and suppression of individual preferences, so his prophecy was at least half right. Even such limited foresight failed him in the area of politics:

«[Mr. *West*] ‹But with no state legislatures, and Congress meeting only once in five years, how do you get your legislation done?›

‹We have no legislation›, replied Dr. *Leete*, ‹that is, next to none. It is rarely that Congress, even when it meets, considers any new laws of consequence, and then it only has power to commend them to the following Congress, lest anything be done hastily. If you will consider a moment, Mr. *West*, you will see that we have nothing to make laws about. The fundamental principles on which our society is founded settle for all time the strifes and misunderstandings which in your day called for legislation.» (p. 208)

This blindness to the persistence of real problems under any conceivable social system ist the hallmark of the Utopian. I cannot refrain from noting finally a curious anticipation

[2] Looking Backward, Houghton Mifflin 1890.

of Professor *Hayek's* proposal that the selection of political leaders be made by citizens over the age of 40 (ibid., p. 189).

Many people, to repeat, attribute the growth of statism to the changes of opinion brought about by this kind of literature. I consider it a major complaint to make against such an explanation of a vast, persistent social movement that it rests on mistaken behavior of the public: if left in this form, the explanation is vacuous. Any behavior, even correct behavior, is consistent with a mistake having been made. Unless a theory is presented of the kinds of mistakes that will be made, there is no possible test of the mistake hypothesis. And no one, so far as I know, had offered even a mistaken theory of mistakes. If random blizzards of opinion blow societies one way and then another, there is nothing for us to do but to hope that the wind will shift, and to fear that it may increase in intensity.

The fundamental objection to the «mistake» theory, however, is that it flies in the face of both our general knowledge of society and the facts of socialization in our times. If deception by intellectuals were the motive force of social change, we would expect to observe numerous occasions on which a group of conservatives with large powers of persuasion had captured the public's fancy, and succeeded in initiating a regime of declining governmental activity. After all, which socialist philosopher has been as profound as *Hayek*, which socialist propagandist has been as lucidly logical as *Friedman*? In fact intellectuals largely – although not wholly – respond to the demands of their times: like *Detroit,* they produce to demand, rather than contrive that demand. Indeed, per educated person employed, *Detroit* may well turn out a larger variety of products. Persistent and widespread social phenomena do not have adventitious causes.

Nor does the domestic or international pattern of support for socialization of economic life suggest that it is the uneducated or socially backward classes that provide the chief support for socialization. If the professors of *America* had chosen our *President*, it would have been *McGovern* from 1968 to 1976. If highly educated and even civilized peoples were less susceptible to misleading socialist arguments, we would not expect to find nations such as *Britain* and *Sweden* among the leaders in the race to expand the role of government.

II. The Bias of Political Processes

No other explanation by conservatives for the rise of socialism is remotely so popular as the deception theory I have just discussed. An alternative theory that is growing in popularity, however, is that the political process is strongly biased toward collectivism, and thus systematically misrepresents the public's true preferences. The bias theory can be viewed as a theory of rational behavior because individuals behave rationally, given the political institutions under which they live; but it can also be viewed as nonrational because the political institutions they have devised are inefficient.

The bias in the process is this: we are presented with two kinds of policies: those which greatly benefit the few and slightly injure the many, and those (including repeal of the first kind of policy) that benefit the many slightly and injure the few greatly. Hence for almost every individual policy proposal of a socialist variety, there will be a cohesive, well-financed, articulate special group to support it, and a large, poorly-informed majority that, if it is informed correctly, will be weakly opposed, but often this majority will be simply unaware of the proposal.

For example, the dairy farmers about a city will seek a milk marketing order which will raise the price of milk (say) 5 c a quart. Each of these farmers will gain perhaps $15,000 a year from the policy. Each consumer in the city will lose $10 or $20 a year. The dairy farmers will use effective lobbyists and political contributions to promote the policy. The rational consumer could not afford to spend more than an hour or two a year to become acquainted with the effects of the milk marketing order and to oppose it. No wonder that each of us vigorously supports the 15 policies that benefit us appreciably and pretty much ignore the 800 policies that individually harm us slightly.

I believe that there is much truth in this explanation. One may address certain perplexing questions to its supporters, however. Why did this kind of political machinery produce no large growth of state action before 1900 in the *United States*? Why has the center of governmental activity been moving from local governments to federal governments, when the bias of the machinery is surely more severe at the federal level? Thus why did we abandon the choice of U. S. Senators by state legislatures in 1914, when this was a powerful support of state sovereignty? Did the public support these shifts of power by mistake?

There may be good answers to such questions – in one or two cases I believe that there are – but in any event there is a substantial amount of truth in the argument that the present policy machinery is biased toward governmental growth. It is less clear that there is any satisfactory way of dealing with the problem.

The growth of public expenditures has been so rapid in the last two decades that a slowing down and possibly a backlash would seem to be highly probable. One manifestation of that reaction is the wave of proposals to place limits on spending. This is by no means the first such wave: severe limits were put on many state governments' debts already by the 1850's, and debts and tax rates of local governments have long been regulated. I find it strange that the proponents of spending limits have not looked at this extensive experience, which – it is my impression – had little effect on the long term trend of public expenditures.

Even if we get such limits and they resist the enormous forces for expansion of public spending, these limits will certainly not dispose of the problem of growth of government. There are literally thousands of public regulatory policies, usually involving little public spending, that have substantial effects on the vigor of economic enterprise and the distribution of income. If suitable numbers could be assigned to the income redistributions effected by these policies, I would not be surprised if in the aggregate they are of the same magnitude as direct governmental redistributions: simply consider what an extensive panoply we have of tariffs, quotas, entry and occupational controls, price regulations, conferrals of tax exemption, and the like. This avenue of income redistribution will surely grow even more rapidly if direct public expenditures are curtailed.

III. The Rational Theories

The rational theories of the growth of government explain that growth as the result of the purposeful use of public power to increase the incomes of particular groups in the society. The poor tax the rich, the farmers tax the urban consumers, the airlines levy noncompetitive prices on their passengers – and in each such case the power of the state is invoked by the particular group. On this view, the modern state is engaged in the wholesale redistribution of income, not only through direct taxes and welfare programs of expenditures but also through a large network of regulatory policies.

I pointed out that the mistake theory is not a theory at all until someone produces a theory of which mistakes will be made. The rational theories face a similar problem. Every public policy or tax or expenditure program will have beneficiaries, and it is reasonable to believe that the beneficiaries will support and the losers oppose the policy. Therefore the rational theories will have to tell us which groups will be successful in the rivalry for political power before they become useful in explaining the growth of the state. And it must be said at once that only a small amount of progress has been made in devising a theory of which groups will control the state. Nevertheless I believe that political life is rational and that the successful explanations for the growth of government lie in this direction.

I cannot hope to support this claim adequately at this time. I am tempted to say that there is not sufficient time to present the case for the rational theories, and hope that you will infer that the argument would require an hour or more. In fact a full argument may require a decade or more. Still, here are two small appetizers.

Applying the theory to the regulation of individual industries – electric power generation, airlines, trucking, television, etc., we have consistently found strong benefits for the producer groups in terms of protection from competition. Our theory predicts that strongly situated consumers will also benefit from these regulatory policies and this has been found especially in U.S. energy policies, where northeastern consumers have been vast beneficiaries of natural gas price controls. On the other hand, we have had very modest success in explaining which industries receive tariff protection.

The direct income redistribution policies have of course been of special interest, and since the appearance of Director's law the field has attracted numerous scholars. Since three of those scholars are *Gary Becker, Harold Demsetz* and *Sam Peltzman*, we have every reason to be optimistic about the appearance of a useful explanation for the rise of heavily progressive income taxation and huge welfare programs.

The scientific problem is not to explain why the poor tax the rich: to paraphrase the *Duke of Wellington*, anyone who cannot understand that cannot understand anything. It is to explain why this development waited until about 1925 to begin accelerating, why it has gone much farther in *Sweden* than the *United States*, why it is proceeding more slowly in *Japan* than in *Western Europe*, and so on. The most obvious explanation for these differences is that universal suffrage is fairly modern, but the extent of the suffrage has only the loosest association with the observed facts. (For example, if breadth of suffrage were decisive, the *United States* should have socialized earlier than the *United Kingdom*.)

It appears to me that much more is to be explained by three developments: First, modern economic systems have made very aggressive levels of taxation feasible. The predominance of the corporate form, the decline of single proprietors, the proliferation of written records, make it possible to tax at rates *John Stuart Mill* considered wholly impossible.

Second, there has been a large increase in the concentration – to use a word from industrial organization – of the population in fewer nations. We often use a measure of concentration – the *Herfindahl* index – which allows us to ask: what number of nations of equal size is equivalent in (let us say) power to an observed distribution of nations by size? In 1815 the nations of *Europe* had only modest concentration: *Russia* was largest with 23% of *Europe's* population, and the distribution among nations was equivalent to eight nations of equal size. Now *Russia* and *Poland* have 46% of *Europe's* population and the index of concentration of population has risen to the equivalent of four nations of equal size. The total number of independent nations fell from 54 to 23 between 1815 and 1970. The ability of individuals to discipline overlygreedy states by migrating has sharply declined.

Third, *Becker* and *Peltzman* have provided largely complementary theories of the state as an income redistributing agency. *Peltzman* has emphasized the demand for income redistribution. In *Peltzman's* theory, and probably everyone else's, the greater the income disparity between rich and poor the larger the income redistribution program of the state. His second main implication is a good deal less obvious: the more equal the incomes of the poor, and of the rich, separately, the larger will be the role of the government. *Becker's* theory also takes the existing redistributive policies of the state as yielding the income distribution which is desired by the members of the society. He emphasizes the influence of the costs of redistribution – costs that include deadweight losses as well as administrative costs – on the extent to which income is redistributed. Indeed the first two forces making for more government that I discussed above (ease in collecting taxes and fewer possibilities of migration) are particular reasons that the redistribution of income has become easier. (*Demsetz* has sought the main explanation for the rise of government in the increased specialization of modern societies.)

Truth in talking can easily be carried too far, as *Frank Knight* was fond of saying, but I will concede that no rational theory of the state has yet received a strong vote of confidence from empirical tests.

IV. Concluding Remarks

Suppose the rational theory of the growth of government is correct, – suppose that it is soon developed to a stage where it is commended to even its critics as a useful explanation of the changing role of government. That would seem to imply that with our existing political institutions – our freely chosen political institutions – the large and growing role of government has been what the public as a whole has wanted: democratic majority rule likes what we have been doing. Do we not then face the hard choice between becoming collectivists and becoming non-democratic in our desired political institutions?

Let me be more explicit on what becoming a collectivist would mean. It would not mean joining the appropriate majority socialist party of one's nation, and heartily endorsing the choices of the most recently elected legislators. We could still argue for a much larger role of the price system. Thus we could say that if the citizens of the *United States* wanted purer air or cleaner lakes or safer factories than were provided in the absence of state control, that the price system is usually vastly more economical than direct regulation in achieving these goals. In such a case there is no dispute over goals, only over the costs of different methods of achieving them. I would consider this an extremely valuable function of the conservative economist even in a socialized society. *Friedman's* demonstration of the role of money in income fluctuations is a striking example of this kind of work.

Again, becoming a collectivist would not mean that we concurred in every program designed to help a particular group. Consider the benefits to the members of the American labor unions which are conferred by the minimum wage law. This law overprices young, untrained, inexperienced and handicapped workers, pushing them into uncovered occupations, unemployment or withdrawal from the labor force, and thus increases the demand for the more productive workers who constitute the membership of the unions. If we could devise a method of supplementing the union members' wages by the amount of these gains, and still preserve the employment opportunities for the unskilled workers, we would be able to increase our aggregate income.

To become collectivists, in short, would be to become market socialists – to ask us to take out a license from *James Meade* to practice economic reform in the *United States*. Whether there is a large role in the modern world for market-oriented socialists is a question I will not attempt to discuss.

The alternative is to abandon total acceptance of present day democratic institutions. I must hasten to say that this is not to argue for totalitarianism in any form. Indeed, some alternative political systems that would insure a substantial reduction in the governmental role could be even more democratic in the sense that public policies could be closer to the desires of the individual citizens. We have been so prone to dispute the popular goals of income redistribution, however, that we have devoted little attention to more efficient methods of fulfilling existing goals.

One possible route to a reduced role of the state is to create competitive pressures on government such that any group – the well-to-do, the highly productive – can escape one government by moving to another. If the main tax, subsidy and regulatory programs of the *United States* were conducted by the 50 states instead of the single Congress, there would appear states whose policies suited any group large enough to form a substantial part of that state's population. Strongly progressive taxation, highly restrictive regulations of businesses, and extensive restrictions on personal choice – would all become escapable for those who found them heavy burdens. Of course this competition would restrict the powers and resources of other states and that is why such a decentralization of political life could not be achieved by an appeal to the citizens under today's political institutions.

The second possible route toward a reduced role of government would be through the restriction of the franchise to property owners, educated classes, employed persons, or some such group. *Dicey* implicitly blamed the development of the modern welfare state on an unlimited electorate. Such restrictions on voting, if they were attainable, would surely change the policies of government. I am not at all clear that the narrow electorate would engage in less income redistribution through the state.

A related route would be to reduce the power of simple majorities. Requirements of larger than simple majorities to pass economic legislation might reduce the exactions of smaller minorities, and of course the bicameral system had as a main purpose the blunting of majority rule. Is it not striking that the long established trends in political structure and practice are exactly the reverse of those favorable to our policies?

It is not congenial to us to contemplate departures from simple majoritarian political systems. It is so much more pleasant to look elsewhere for the reversal of our defeats, – especially to the turning of the tide of public opinion. How wonderful it will be if the public has decided on a liberal society, how wonderful if on June 6 of 1978 when the famed Proposition 13 carried in *California*, the reaction became a viable political force in the *United States*. Yet surely changes of political tastes are more convenient than probable, and I doubt that they will allow us believers in decentralized economic and political life to escape the hard question: are we a permanent minority?

If the liberal values we cherish have become minority views, I do not propose that we abandon them. Indeed my own attachment to them grows with the realization of how widely they are rejected. If in fact we seek what many do not wish, will we not be more successful if we take this into account and seek political institutions and policies that allow us to pursue our own goals?

Summary

Why Have the Socialists been Winning?

The explanations for the great expansion of government in the last hundred years throughout the western world fall into two groups. The more popular group explains this development by the wide-spread misunderstanding by the voters of the immense achievements and basic virtues of private enterprise, on the one hand, and the failures of socialism, on the other. On this reading of the trend toward socialism, the primary task of the liberals (in the correct, traditional sense) is to educate the public.

The less popular explanation is that the growth of the government is due to the explicit and well-informed desires of politically powerful groups in the society – farmers, welfare recipients, businessmen, professional men, etc. It is this explanation that is commanding growing acceptance among the economists who study public regulation and the political process, and it is the explanation I accept.

The latter explanation presents a serious difficulty to the liberal: is he simply to acquiesce to a policy that is increasingly inefficient and is not ethically attractive? Only partial answers to this uncomfortable question are given in the paper.

Ludwig M. Lachmann

The Flow of Legislation and the Permanence of the Legal Order

I.

Few economists will deny that the market operates within a framework of legal and other institutions, that its *modus operandi* may be helped or hindered by the varying modes of this framework, and that the outcome of market processes will not be unaffected by changes in it. That the obvious implications of these facts for the operation of the modern market economy are so rarely understood is of course to some extent due to the circumstance that in the products of the textbook industry they are commonly ignored. This neglect is largely the result of the fact that in the general equilibrium model of neoclassical economics institutions do not qualify as «data» of the system, and hence are abstracted from. This merely goes to show that, contrary to a view widely held today, abstraction is not a procedure in which arbitrary choices may be made to suit our «analytical convenience», and that, in a significant sense, the quality of abstraction reflects the quality of the abstracting mind.

To the classical economists, as *Lord Robbins* has often reminded us, the economic importance of institutions was well-known. In opposing the mercantilist view that the production of wealth was not a matter to be left to chance, but required the constant attention of, and carefully designed action by, the state bureaucracy (at their time a fairly recent creation), the classical economists held that, if only the institutions of property and contract were firmly entrenched and safeguarded, the market would give rise to a continuous process in the course of which far more wealth would be produced than the wisest of bureaucracies could ever have designed. As they, however, were, in the terminology we have recently learnt from Sir *John Hicks*,[1] *plutologists*, interested primarily in the production and distribution of wealth, and not in exchange or market processes as such in any respect other than as agencies of the growth of wealth, they had little reason to go beyond emphasizing property and contract as the basis of the institutional order of their time.

Today we face an altogether different situation. In the first place, as heirs of the *catallactic revolution* of the 1870s, in which the interest of economists became concentrated on market events such as prices and relative quantities of various goods, and emphasis shifted from the production and distribution of (abstract) wealth to the exchange of concrete goods and services, we have to review the classical teaching on the institutional basis of economic activity. Modern economists regard production as a form of exchange. It is evident that the catallactic perspective with its emphasis on contractual relations in a

---

[1] *J. R. Hicks:* ‹Revolutions› in economics, in *Sp. Latsis* (Ed.): Method and Appraisal in Economics, Cambridge 1976, ESP. pp. 212–16.

multitude of markets, while production and distribution would take place even in a subsistence or a manorial economy, calls for another look at the institutional basis of the market economy. The current revival of Austrian economics, moreover, with its emphasis on the market as a multitude of related, though not necessarily consistent, processes rather than a state of equilibrium, makes it incumbent on us to pay particular attention to the legal norms and institutions on which the complex network of market transactions rests.

Secondly, it goes without saying that our world is far more complex than was that of the classical economists and that, quite apart from the consequences of the movement of economic thought just mentioned, there is evidently a good case for having another look at the relationship between the market economy of our days and its institutional basis.

Finally we can hardly ignore the fact that a good deal of the legislation currently emanating from the *Sozialstaat* of our time, designed to gratify the various appetites of the modern mass electorate, has served to provide obstacles to market processes and to undermine the legal order on which the market must rest.

What follows is offered as a modest and preliminary contribution towards the exploration of some of the problems indicated.

Our field is cognate to the one *Hayek* chose for Law, Legislation and Liberty, (1973, 1976), but it also differs from it in some important respects. We are both dealing with relations between law and legislation and concerned about the threat posed to the legal order of the modern market economy by attempts to enact a normative order inspired by the spurious ideal of *social justice*. On the other hand, *Hayek* paints his landscape on a much broader canvas than we would dare to touch. In his work we have a whole political philosophy for our time within which relations between law and legislation play a part, even a prominent part (in chapters 4 to 6 and 8), but only one part among many all the same. «I soon discovered that to carry out what I had undertaken would require little less than doing for the twentieth century what *Montesquieu* had done for the eighteenth.»[2] We have nothing comparable to offer, needless to say, and shall confine ourselves to exploring a fairly narrow strip of land in the border area between economics and the sociology of law.

We both reject the thesis of legal positivism that law is nothing but the sediment of past legislation, but we reach this position by somewhat different paths. *Hayek* reaches this conclusion by an argument derived from the nature of law and justice and from the historical fact that law is old and legislation a fairly recent phenomenon. We, on the other hand, at first accept the positivistic thesis at its face value, but then demonstrate that, if taken in its strictest form, it leads us to absurd conclusions, viz. the legal world in a state of chaos. In this way we hope to discover what tacit assumptions legal positivism has to make to avoid these conclusions. It will then become apparent that these tacit assumptions may be valid in some circumstances of history, but not in others, so that the thesis of positivism, so far from being a universal thesis about the identity of law and legislation, proves to be plausible only in circumstances in which legislation operates under some constraint.

We hope that, by emphasizing the part such constraints play in the legal order, our argument will serve to cast light on some of our contemporary dilemmas. At the same time we shall come to learn that our problem is linked to some sociological problems of even wider significance, viz. the complementarity of new and old institutions within the social order in a changing world, and, in particular, the modes of complementarity of what *Menger* called *organic* and *pragmatic institutions*, those that emerge as part of a sponta-

---

[2] F. A. *Hayek:* Law, Legislation and Liberty, Vol. I, London 1973, p. 4.

neous order of society and those that owe their existence to some act of the «common will».

II.

A permanent legal order and a continuous flow of legislation are evidently incompatible notions. Even where the new laws, the particles of this flow, do not replace other laws that formerly existed, but are, so to speak, «new additions» to the edifice of the legal order, they must have some effect on some part of the latter. Those who deny this incompatibility must have a conception of the legal order not unlike the way a merchant is looking at his stock, i. e. as consisting entirely of exchangeable parts, so that the stock may be maintained even when every single component has been replaced. Economists would speak of a homogeneous aggregate, but know that such homogeneity precludes all complementarity.

The coherence of the legal order, however, requires consonance, hence heterogeneity, of the norms composing it. New legal norms cannot be simply added to, or replace, old norms, they have to fit into the existing order. We could hardly speak of a legal system if we meant by it a mere aggregate of norms. The practical relevance of all this lies in the circumstances *Max Weber* described as follows: «To those who had interests in the commodity market, the rationalization and systematization of the law in general and, with certain reservations to be stated later, the increasing calculability of the functioning of the legal process in particular, constituted one of the most important conditions for the existence of economic enterprise intended to function with stability and, especially, of capitalistic enterprise, which cannot do without legal security.»[3] In other words, if A lends B 10 000 DM (to choose the most stable of currencies) for twenty years, how, in a world of continuous legislation, can either creditor or debtor be sure that at the end of this period the present legal norms governing repayment of debt will still be in force in such a form that the repayment is «calculable»? If so, what might inspire such confidence in the permanence of the present legal order? If not, what do we have to assume about the nature of the expectations governing long term loans?

It is readily seen that any attempt to answer these or similar questions will have to rest on the assumption that, whatever the stream of legislation in the next twenty years may turn out to be, certain tacit conventions will be observed which impose some constraint upon the range of legislative change. It may be that legislative change is expected to be confined to what might be described as «the outer range of the legal order». New legislation would not affect the «inner core», the «lawyer's law», in other words the civil law. We find a good example in *Hayek*: «Of British legislation it could be said in 1901: 'ninetenths of each annual volume of statutes are concerned with what may be called adminis-

---

[3] *Max Weber* on Law in Economy and Society, ed. by *Max Rheinstein,* Cambridge (Mass.) 1954, p. 305. Consider also the following passage: «It is a curious fact of history that although the older books are full of discussions of the principle that law implies general rules, there is almost no explicit recognition that the enactment of general rules becomes meaningless if government considers itself free to disregard them whenever it suits its convernience . . . Perhaps there is also operative here a confusion arising from the fact that we realize that normally a lawgiver can change any one of his laws simply by repealing it and providing a quite different law for the governance of events thereafter happening.» *Lon L. Fuller,* Law and Human Interaction. Sociological Inquiry, Vol. 47, Nos. 3–4, 1977, p. 76.

trative law, and an analysis of the content of the General Acts during the last four centuries would probably show a similar proportion.»[4]

Alternatively, in our example, lender and borrower may believe in the permanence of the legal order in the sense that legislative change, even though affecting the civil law, would not affect its principles, but be confined to the revision of norms flowing from them. Such a belief would of course involve the distinction between «inner core» and «outer range» merely on another level. Obviously no such constraints upon the flow of legislation can ever be taken for granted. Belief in them will be more warranted in some periods of history than in others. Experience of historical change is unlikely to leave it unscathed.

Behind our conundrum there loom much wider issues. Unable as we are to do justice to them in the present context, they simply cannot be ignored. Professor *Talcott Parsons* has recently complained about the place of «Law as an intellectual stepchild».[5] So, as social scientists, we had better take heed.

Legal institutions are part of the institutional order of society. The question we have raised is merely an instance of the more general question how an institutional order can persist even though institutions change in the course of history. Behind it there lies the even more complex question of the complementarity of old and new institutions in a changing world. How can we be sure that they will actually fit into the same order? One is tempted to think of the institutional order as of an array of hinges: the institutions within each hinge can move a good deal, if within limits, but the hinges themselves cannot. The matter is of particular relevance to «*the market order of catallaxy*», the subject of *Hayek*'s chapter 10. There must be a good deal of flexibility in it of course, but some elements must persist, otherwise how could we talk of an order? We suggest that, while within the catallaxy prices and quantities of goods and services, produced and exchanged, must indeed be flexible and will actually change each market day, the *order of catallaxy* must derive its quality as an order from the permanence of its institutional framework, and in particular the legal norms forming part of it. Such permanence alone permits economic agents to «take their orientation» from them in making their plans of action. Otherwise all intertemporal transactions must become precarious.[6]

III.

We must now turn aside to consider a noteworthy recent example of legislation disrupting the existing legal order, the German *Mitbestimmungsgesetz* of 1976 which provides that half the members of the supervisory board of German industrial joint-stock

---

[4] *F. A. Hayek:* Law, Legislation and Liberty, loc. cit., p. 127.

[5] *Talcott Parsons:* Law as an Intellectual Stepchild. Sociological Inquiry, Vol. 47, 1977, p. 11.

[6] It is tempting, in this context, to make use of *Menger's* distinction between institutions of *Organic* and of *Pragmatic* origin. The latter are those which owe their origin to an act, legislative or otherwise, by a political association, or those holding power in it, while the former «present themselves to us as the unintended result of individual efforts of members of society, i. e. of efforts in pursuit of individual interests» and are largely «the unreflected result of social development» (*«Das unreflectirte Ergebniss socialer Entwickelung»*). But while it may be tempting to say that flexible organic institutions evolve within the «interstices» of the more durable pragmatic order, there is no warrant for such interpretation in *Menger's* work. In fact he took the opposite view. *Carl Menger,* Untersuchungen über die Methode der Socialwissenschaften, 1883, pp. 161–66.

companies must be elected by the workers (where there are more than 2000 of them) while the other half is elected by shareholders. The supervisory board (*Aufsichtsrat*) is an institution peculiar to German company law and unknown in Anglo-Saxon countries. Its main function is to appoint management (*Vorstand*) and take major policy decisions.[7]

The main motive of this legislation was of course narrowly political, – it is a typical piece of «social legislation». We shall ignore such arguments as that it is «a major step on the way to industrial democracy». We are interested in it solely from the point of view elucidated in this paper: How does such legislation fit into the legal order required by a market economy? If new legislation requires some constraint imposed upon it by the need to observe certain «tacit conventions» lest it disrupt the legal order, has any such convention been observed in this particular case? What are the principles of company law requisite in a modern industrial economy that aspires to the rank of a catallaxy, a market order?

We shall of course be told that modern joint-stock enterprise has in any case been created by a century's legislation, that the legislator in this field always had to weigh the interests of different groups, and that the new legislation is following the trend of permitting workers to participate in entrepreneurial decision-making. In order to deal with arguments such as this it is necessary to go back to the principles underlying a market order.

Company Law, as it has emerged in the Western world in the course of time, is a delicate web within which many interests, some conflicting, some complementary, have been woven into a pattern of harmony. (No doubt its very success in this task encouraged the advocates of codetermination to hope that, having achieved so much, the pattern of harmony might be expected to accommodate a few more interests without undue strain.) In this it is a true mirror image of the catallaxy as a whole.

On the other hand, there is no company law of which it could be said that it preceded legislation. As soon as the resources for organizing joint ventures with limited liability and the opportunities for their use were present, there also arose the need to give them an adequate legal form, e. g. in the form of a royal charter, or in some other way. Participants in the venture needed this minimum of «calculability». Modern joint-stock enterprise is of course a creation of the market (in *Menger's* terminology an «organic institution»), but it could not have come into existence without a legal form expected to be permanent. It comprehends elements of *order* as well as of *organization*. The relationship between directors and shareholders, e. g., partakes of both. In the study of joint-stock enterprise, if anywhere, we learn to apply the distinction between ideal types and reality.

Company law, in short, the joint creation of market growth and the legislative embodiment of ideas pertaining to the market, is the final product of a long process of interaction of business men and lawyers who invested their experience, their ingenuity and their skills in it. In discussions of it we do well to remember *Max Weber's* point that law, whatever social forces it may respond to, is always, in the first place, the product of lawyers (in

---

[7] See the following writings: *Franz Böhm*, Das wirtschaftliche Mitbestimmungsrecht der Arbeiter im Betrieb. Ordo, Band 4, 1952. *Charles Hanson*, The Bullock Report and the West German system of Codetermination. Three Banks Review, December 1977. *Ernst Heuss*, Einige kritische Überlegungen zum Sachverständigengutachten über die Mitbestimmung in der Unternehmung. Ordo, Band 21, 1970, pp. 194–216. *Hans Willgerodt*, Der Liberale Standpunkt und die Mitbestimmungsfrage. Ordo, Band 21, 1970, pp. 218–42. *Hans Willgerodt*, Vermögensstreuung und Mitbestimmung der Eigentümer. Wirtschaftspolitische Chronik, Heft 2, 1972. For the United Kingdom the Report of the Bullock Committee, Cmnd. 6706, January 1977 is of importance. For a succinct version of *Böhm's* argument against codetermination see also his famous article in the Frankfurter Zeitung of 22 October 1966: «Es geht um die Menschenwürde».

our world academically trained). As so often in history, we have here an institution which bears the imprint of the minds of its creators long after they have vanished from the scene.

Unfortunately a deeper understanding of the nature of modern joint-stock enterprise and its environment has not been helped in recent years by the spreading notion of the «separation of ownership and management», now widely believed to be one of its outstanding characteristics. The modern shareholder, we are told, has lost all interest in his company, rarely attends the annual meeting and is, in any case, owing to lack of information, incapable of exercising any influence on, let alone control over, management. Thus the modern «giant enterprise» has become a law unto itself. This notion has of course been used as a weapon for the expansion of government control. It also has helped to foster an atmosphere favourable to the claims of the advocates of codetermination, at least by creating confusion about these issues in the minds of social scientists and lawyers.

This notion rests, briefly, on a failure to understand the role of the Stock Exchange in the modern market economy. Here the Stock Exchange «monitors» the performance of managers. Brokers, investment analysts et al. devote time and effort to this purpose. The daily fluctuations of market prices reflect continuously the results of this activity by specialists. The shareholder watches these prices and draws his conclusions. When he disapproves of some action by his managers he «votes with his feet» – he sells. Far from being a passive spectator of the deeds and vicissitudes of his company, he is active in the most obvious way the modern division of functions between specialist observers and «the public» demands. Owners and managers, so far from being «separated» from each other, are linked together *indirectly through the market*. Managers, in public statements, often deny that stock exchange prices are of any interest to them. They know very well, however, that their creditors watch their performance and are by no means insensitive to the daily verdicts of specialist observers, and they cannot prevent shareholders from learning these verdicts.

Those who espouse the notion of the separation of ownership and management have failed to understand the function of the stock market as an intermediary of information.

We now come to the main issue. Economists distinguish between flows and stocks, between streams of goods and services and the sources of these streams. While workers sell their services, capital owners entrust the *sources* of capital services to the enterprise of their choice. In adverse circumstances they suffer not merely, as workers also might, a loss of income, but a capital loss. It seems evident that he who entrusts his capital, the source of his income stream, to others must be able to demand that these are responsible to him for their conduct, in particular where he lacks the ordinary rights of a creditor and cannot withdraw his capital. If, however, managers are responsible for their management of the (durable and often specific) capital instruments of the company, they bear such responsibility towards the owners, and not towards somebody else. Otherwise responsibility has no meaning. The worker members of the supervisory boards share in the control of management, but do not share in this responsibility.

Moreover, what exactly are the codeterminators to help determine? It is not a question of labour relations. In modern industry labour interests can hardly be said to be underrepresented. The position of the firm vis-à-vis its customers and suppliers is given in the market. Here, as in other market relations, little can be «determined» by a single firm, unless it held a complete monopoly, which hardly ever happens.

There is, however, one matter in respect of which each firm does enjoy some discretion. It concerns its capital. A merchant turns over his stock. A firm turns over its capital by means of depreciation. The decision, how much to set aside for depreciation out of gross revenue each year is indeed a crucial decision which, like all such, must depend on expectations. Where a wrong decision is made a capital loss will be suffered subsequently. It becomes clear, from the very nature of this case, why workers' representatives, even were they qualified for participating in such decisions, would be unable to discharge such responsibility towards those they do not represent.

It lies in the nature of productive processes that decisions concerning stocks, their rate of turnover and their composition at different points of time, are always and necessarily more crucial decisions than decisions concerning flows. The more durable and specific capital goods become, the heavier the responsibility of the decision-makers, the more crucial the nature of their decisions. It is perhaps clear (not only to economists, one hopes) why any attempt to hand decision-making power concerning capital to those who bear no responsibility to capital owners is bound to undermine not merely the legal order but the market economy. At the same time we can now see that company law, as it had developed until «codetermination», was indeed an «organic growth». Political arguments cannot affect the nature of the responsibility for capital decisions.

This is most clearly seen in the case of unsuccessful firms. It is in the interest of society that capital should flow from levels of low to levels of high profitability. In a market economy competition and the motivation of capital owners will bring this about. Are we to believe that workers' representatives will quietly see capital flow out of their unsuccessful enterprise to be invested elsewhere? Yet this is precisely what should happen. Company law, as it had evolved before codetermination, was shaped in such a way as to make it happen. If the power of those who have an interest in preventing it from happening is increased to the point of making them «codeterminators», can the catallaxy remain unscathed? Changes in organization can and do affect the market order.

IV.

What do we learn from our exercise?

That politicians will readily sacrifice any principles they may hold for the sake of gaining votes, seek to erode all limits to their power, such as constitutional safeguards, and thus help to undermine the very order which confers legitimacy on their power is, alas, not a novel insight. That friends of the market economy have good reason to pay close attention to its legal and institutional framework, the more so since the style of late classical formalism that has dominated economic thought for three decades can hardly be said to provide an atmosphere congenial to such work, is also not exactly new. In fact the ORDO school has for many years taken a special interest in this framework.

That we must not expect ideal types to find full reflection in the real world is an old truth that perhaps bears repetition. Order and organization are such ideal types. It is hard to imagine any order in which, in reality, problems of organization may not arise. We saw a good example in the joint-stock company, a typical product of the modern market order, in which such organizational problems as the relationship between managers and shareholders naturally arise. Legal institutions may well come into existence in response to social needs, but nonetheless have to be given their concrete shape by lawyers whose mentality they reflect. Needless to say, it is in their concrete and permanent form alone that they can serve as points of orientation to agents. For this reason, if for no other, the legal order requires permanence.

Behind all this there remain the wider issues to which we alluded. There is the problem of the complementarity of old and new legal norms, feasible perhaps, we saw, if both are subject to, and thus, in legal logic, inferable from, the same principles, but not where these principles are in fact, if not in words, actually eroded. There is the, even wider, problem of the flexibility of the institutional order which must contain both, flexible and immutable elements and which we likened to an array of hinges: the hinges, immutable and known as such, permit other elements to «turn» within limits. We have elsewhere suggested the distinction «between the *external* institutions which constitute, as it were, the outer framework of society, the legal order, and the *internal* institutions which gradually evolve as a result of market processes and other forms of spontaneous individual action». It still seems to us «that it is within a scheme such as this that the praxeological theory of institutions ... most readily finds its place».[8]

One of the tests to be applied to a legal order is whether intertemporal transactions are possible within it without turning transactors into gamblers. It is a sobering thought that the permanent inflation of our age has by now had precisely the same effect, and has made the same contribution to the subversion of the social order of a free society as would a stream of legislation incompatible with the principles of the market order. This, again, is not new. Some economists have pointed out in recent years that continuous inflation must erode the basis of contract as an institution.

It is certainly important to realize that the nature of the relationship between the market and its legal and institutional framework is complex, that we must beware of undue simplification, and that, if the market may be jeopardised by clumsy legislation pandering to ignorance, it is also true that the legal order may be subverted by economic processes such as inflation, and that influences can run in both directions.

It is therefore to be hoped that, hard as is the task of conceptual clarification in such a field, all those concerned about the order of a free society will give unceasing attention, critical and constructive, to the grave problems some features of which we have attempted to adumbrate here.

Summary

The Flow of Legislation and the Permanence of the Legal Order

As the classical economists knew, the market economy is embedded in a framework of legal and other institutions. The quality of the market depends, among other factors, on the quality of this framework. This remains as true today as it was two centuries ago, as does the corollary notion that the market economy rests on the twin pillars of the institutions of property and contract.

Today this is not widely appreciated. Neoclassical formalism, whose style of thought has come to dominate academic economics since the Second World War, ignores it. Such facts are abstracted from. A broad belt of secondary reality in the form of statistical time series shields our formalists from any contact with the real world. Characteristically, today we find an awareness of the significance of our framework only in those schools of thought, (like the ORDO school, or among those whose work is inspired by *Mises* or *Weber*) in which a vivid sense that the social sciences are concerned with meaningful human action is alive.

---

[8] *L. M. Lachmann,* The Legacy of Max Weber. Heinemann, London 1970, p. 81. (German translation: Drei Essays über Max Webers geistiges Vermächtnis. Tübingen 1973).

Hayek's «Law, Legislation and Liberty», for all its dissent from *Weber*, falls into the same tradition. The «market order of catallaxy» comprises laws as well as market phenomena.

In the sociology of law, thus broadly conceived as an area adjacent to Economics as one of the humanities, there arises the question «Is the annual flow of legislation in the modern state compatible with the permanence of the legal order»? Without the latter intertemporal market transactions are impossible, yet the former is a fact of experience. We suggest that in modern society the gap has been bridged by means of tacit conventions which it is our task to make explicit.

Behind our question there loom much wider issues, formidable enough to make us tread warily. (It is not for nothing that *Talcott Parsons* recently spoke of «Law as an intellectual stepchild».) These are the problems of institutional change in a changing world. Some institutions must be flexible enough to adjust to change, while others, by contrast, must be sufficiently resistent to change to make the outcome of intertemporal transactions predictable. With institutional change the complementarity of old and new institutions becomes a problem.

The German Codetermination Act of 1976 (Mitbestimmungsgesetz) raises a number of problems of this nature. Company Law, in its long process of evolution, has thus far provided the market with the institutional framework it required. Now these institutions are forced into the Procrustean bed of political expediency. Property rights are infringed.

It should be evident to all who are concerned with the market (not merely to economists) that, in the nature of the case, the law must grant stronger protection to those who entrust the stocks they own to others to be managed by them, than to those who sell time segments of a flow of services, as in the latter case the problem of confidence does not arise. Stocks and flows are different things and require different forms of protection. Also, in unsuccessful companies, codetermination may impede the flow of capital out of them that the market requires.

The true function of ideal types is to serve us as criteria of classification for real events. We must not confuse them with reality.

Egon Tuchtfeldt

Ideensysteme als Bezugsrahmen der Politik

«Was sind wir eigentlich? Liberale? Konservative? Sozialisten? Und wenn
wir das eine oder das andere sind, warum sind wir es, und wohin führt es
uns?»
Wilhelm Röpke

I. Politische Positionen

Um die unterschiedlichen Standorte des politischen Denkens und der ihnen verpflich-
teten Gruppierungen zu kennzeichnen, ist die heute so viel benutzte Dichotomie «rechts –
links» oder, meist gleichbedeutend verwendet, «reaktionär – progressiv» kaum geeignet.
Wird damit doch nur ein Feindbild konstruiert, das die eigene Position als allein richtig
profiliert. Um die Topographie der politischen Landschaft zu charakterisieren, erscheint
jene ältere Dreiteilung besser geeignet, die Konservative (Rechte), Liberale (Mitte) und
Sozialisten (Linke) unterscheidet. Graphisch dargestellt lassen sich die drei Positionen
auf einer Linie abtragen. Diese eindimensionale Darstellung erscheint auf den ersten
Blick plausibel. Bei näherer Betrachtung bleiben jedoch wichtige politische Fragen offen,
so
1. Warum wollen (fast) alle Parteien heute «Parteien der Mitte» oder «Volksparteien»
   sein (obwohl doch der Begriff «Partei» schon vom Wortsinn her auf einen Teil des
   Ganzen hindeutet)?
2. Warum ist die politische Mitte, im Sinne des Liberalismus verstanden, in fast allen
   Staaten so schwach?
3. Warum finden Mitte-Links-Koalitionen in der veröffentlichten Meinung im allgemeinen eine bessere Beurteilung als Mitte-Rechts-Koalitionen?

Sicherlich ließen sich noch weitere offene Fragen zur Dreiteilung der politischen Land-
schaft formulieren. Zu denken wäre hier etwa an den offenkundigen Hang zur Fraktionsbildung und weiter an die Spaltungstendenzen bei allen drei Gruppierungen. Auch
die verschiedentlich feststellbaren Übergänge und Verbindungen zwischen extremer
Rechter und extremer Linker könnten erwähnt werden. Alle diese Fragen deuten auf die
Verbesserungsbedürftigkeit der eindimensionalen Darstellung hin.
In seinem 1960 erschienenen Werk «The Constitution of Liberty» schrieb *F. A. von
Hayek*, dem die nachfolgenden Ausführungen aus Anlaß seines 80. Geburtstages gewid-
met sind, zu diesem Problemkreis: «Das Bild, das von den relativen Positionen der drei
Parteien allgemein gegeben wird, trägt mehr zur Unklarheit als zur Klärung ihrer wahren
Beziehungen bei. Sie werden gewöhnlich als verschiedene Positionen auf einer Linie dar-
gestellt, die Sozialisten links, die Konservativen rechts und die Liberalen ungefähr in der
Mitte. Nichts könnte irreführender sein. Wenn wir ein Diagramm haben wollen, wäre es

entsprechender, sie in einem Dreieck anzuordnen, in dem die Konservativen eine Ecke einnehmen und die Sozialisten nach der zweiten und die Liberalen nach der dritten Ecke ziehen.»[1] Im folgenden soll diese Anregung aufgegriffen und versucht werden, die Dreiecksdarstellung der Ideensysteme näher auszuführen.[2]

II. Ideensysteme oder Ideologien?

Liberalismus, Konservatismus und Sozialismus sind gesamtgesellschaftliche Ideensysteme oder, anders formuliert, innerlich zusammenhängende Vorstellungen über das, was unter bestimmten Grundannahmen für Mensch und Gesellschaft als wünschenswert angesehen wird. Als Ideensysteme müssen sie von den historisch-konkreten Ausprägungen parteilicher Art unterschieden werden.[3] *Hayek* hat an anderer Stelle darauf hingewiesen, daß zudem im Laufe der geschichtlichen Entwicklung die gleichen Bezeichnungen von den diversen Gruppen für sehr verschiedene Dinge benutzt worden sind.[4]

Damit wird der meist gebräuchliche Begriff «Ideologie» für die drei Ideensysteme bewußt vermieden – wie dies übrigens auch bei *F. A. von Hayek* durchgehend der Fall ist.[5] Schon 1941 hatte er dargelegt, wie *Napoleon I.* zu Beginn des 19. Jahrhunderts den damals üblichen Begriff der Ideologie im Sinne der menschlichen Ideengeschichte mit einer zweiten, abqualifizierenden Bedeutung versah, weil die Forschergruppe der «Ideologen»

---

[1] *F. A. von Hayek*, The Constitution of Liberty, London 1960, S. 398 (deutsch: Die Verfassung der Freiheit, Tübingen 1961, S. 482 f.); weitere Angaben aus diesem Werk beziehen sich auf die deutsche Ausgabe.

[2] *Hayeks* Vorschlag eines politischen «Wertedreiecks» ist später verschiedentlich aufgegriffen worden, doch gebührt ihm diesbezüglich die Priorität. Vgl. hierzu beispielsweise *H. G. Frank*, Der Standort des fortschrittlichen Bildungstechnikers in den ideologischen Kämpfen unserer Zeit. In: *B. Wellmann* (Hrsg.), Die Umwelt-Revolte, Köln 1972, S. 139 ff. *Frank* unterscheidet liberale, konservative und kollektivistische Ideologien (ohne Bezug auf *F. A. von Hayek*). – Eine weitere, jedoch anders konzipierte Dreiecksdarstellung, das «Social Triangle», findet sich bei *K. E. Boulding*, The Economy of Love and Fear. A Preface to Grants Economics, Belmont 1973, S. 103 ff. *Boulding* gliedert die sozialen Interaktionen in die drei Möglichkeiten «Exchange», «Threat» and «Love». Im Rahmen seiner diesbezüglichen Dreiecksdarstellung spricht er von «the pattern of human history in the proportions of *the three social organizers*» (a.a.O., S. 107, im Original nicht kursiv). Ein Bezug zu *Hayek* liegt nicht vor.

[3] Irgendwelche Ähnlichkeiten mit bestehenden Parteien sind daher auch rein zufälliger Natur.

[4] «Die Schwierigkeit, der wir gegenüberstehen, liegt nicht bloß darin, daß die geläufigen politischen Bezeichnungen notorisch mehrdeutig sind, oder darin, daß dieselbe Bezeichnung für verschiedene Gruppen sogar fast das gerade Gegenteil bedeutet. Die viel schlimmere Erscheinung ist, daß Menschen, die in Wirklichkeit widersprechende und unvereinbare Ideale haben, häufig unter ein und demselben Namen vereinigt werden. Namen wie ‹Liberalismus›, ‹Demokratie›, ‹Kapitalismus› und ‹Sozialismus› bezeichnen heute nicht mehr zusammenhängende Ideensysteme; sie bezeichnen ein Konglomerat von ganz heterogenen Grundsätzen und Tatsachen, die der geschichtliche Zufall mit diesen Worten in Zusammenhang gebracht hat, die aber fast nichts gemein haben, als daß sie zu verschiedenen Zeiten von denselben Leuten oder auch nur unter demselben Namen vertreten worden sind» (*F. A. von Hayek*, Individualismus und wirtschaftliche Ordnung, Erlenbach-Zürich 1952, S. 11).

[5] Anders als etwa *L. von Mises*, der «World Views» und «Ideologies» unterscheidet. Vgl. *L. von Mises*, Human Action, 3. Aufl., Chicago 1966, S. 178 f.

am Collège de France die individuelle Freiheit gegen den Diktator verteidigte.[6] Diese zweite Bedeutung gewann dann durch *Karl Marx* vollends die Oberhand, für den «Ideologie» gleichbedeutend mit «falschem Bewußtsein» war.

Seither ist es weitgehend üblich geworden, die Auffassung des Gegners als «ideologisch» abzuqualifizieren. Über Ideologiekritik und Wissenssoziologie hat dieser negative Ideologiebegriff Eingang in die Wirtschafts- und Sozialwissenschaften gefunden. So spricht, um hier nur ein Beispiel zu erwähnen, *H. Giersch* davon, daß den Ideologien «ein verzerrtes Bild der sozialökonomischen Wirklichkeit zugrunde liegt. Das Wirklichkeitsbild mag veraltet sein, auf naiven Vorurteilen beruhen oder bestimmte weltanschauliche oder interessenbedingte Wunschvorstellungen zur Grundlage haben.»[7]

In neuerer Zeit scheint sich, vor allem ausgehend von den USA, eine Entwicklung anzubahnen, die den alten vornapoleonischen Ideologiebegriff wiederbeleben möchte. So sieht beispielsweise *T. Parsons* in einer Ideologie ein System gesellschaftlicher Überzeugungen.[8] *C. J. Friedrich* definiert Ideologien als Systeme von Ideen und Impulsen für politisches Handeln.[9]

Gleichwohl dürfte es zweckmäßig sein, den immer noch umstrittenen Ideologiebegriff zu meiden und statt dessen den Ausdruck Ideensysteme zu verwenden. Hierfür spricht auch die als Folge der marxistischen Vereinnahmung des Ideologiebegriffes vielfach anzutreffende Zuordnung dieser Ideensysteme zu sozialen Schichten oder historischen Situationen.

III. Partielle Interpretation der Ideensysteme

Die *schichtspezifische* Deutung stützt sich auf die Annahme von Bindungen zwischen den Ideensystemen und bestimmten sozialen Schichten oder Interessenlagen. Hierunter fällt die frühere marxistische Ansicht, man könne den Liberalismus dem Bürgertum (der «Bourgeoisie») zurechnen, den Konservatismus der Aristokratie und dem Klerus und den Sozialismus der «Arbeiterklasse». Ähnliche Zuordnungen finden sich bis heute, wenn auch wesentlich differenzierter (so unter Fortlassung der Aristokratie und des Klerus), bei Autoren aus dem sozialistischen Lager. Als eines der jüngsten Beispiele sei *H. Reithofer* erwähnt, der zwar vorsichtigerweise nur von «Hauptträgern» spricht, aber unter dieser Bezeichnung doch folgende Zuordnung vornimmt:

[6] Vgl. *F. A. von Hayek*, The Counter-Revolution of Science. In: Economica, New Series, Vol. 8 (1941); wiederabgedruckt in *ders.*, The Counter-Revolution of Science. Studies in the Abuse of Reason, Glencoe 1952 (deutsch: Mißbrauch und Verfall der Vernunft, Frankfurt a. M. 1959). «Das Wort Ideologie in dem Sinne, in dem es von jener Gruppe gebraucht wurde, bedeutet einfach das Studium der menschlichen Ideen . . .» (a.a.O., S. 157). *Hayek* gebraucht statt dessen Ausdrücke wie «position», «attitude» oder «political philosophy».

[7] *H. Giersch*, Allgemeine Wirtschaftspolitik, Bd. I: Grundlagen, Wiesbaden 1960, S. 135. – *Giersch* stellt der Ideologie die Konzeption gegenüber, die er als widerspruchsfreien Zusammenhang von Grundsätzen, Zielen und Instrumenten definiert (a.a.O.).

[8] Vgl. *T. Parsons*, The Social System, London 1952, S. 359.

[9] Vgl. *C. J. Friedrich*, Totalitäre Diktatur, Stuttgart 1957, S. 26. – Zur neueren Ideologie-Diskussion vgl. ferner *Th. Geiger*, Ideologie und Wahrheit, Stuttgart-Wien 1953, *L. Rosenmayr*, Über den Ideologiebegriff. In: *L. Rosenmayr* und *S. Höllinger* (Hrsg.), Soziologie Forschung Österreich, Wien-Köln-Graz 1969, S. 149 ff. (mit einer deutlichen Unterscheidung der beiden Ideologiebegriffe), sowie *E. Lemberg*, Ideologie und Gesellschaft. Eine Theorie der ideologischen Systeme, Stuttgart-Berlin-Köln-Mainz 1971.

Konservatismus	Mittelstand (Kleinbürger, Landwirte, zum Teil Beamte)
Liberalismus	Großbürgertum, gehobene Angestellte
Sozialismus	Arbeiterschaft.[10]

Sicherlich sind damit Beziehungen angesprochen, die es im Laufe der Geschichte bei bestimmten Ideensystemen gegeben hat. Generelle Beziehungen dieser Art anzunehmen, widerspricht aber gerade den historischen Erfahrungen. Die Landwirte beispielsweise, die durchgängig dem Konservatismus zugeordnet werden, waren in der Zeit der Laisser-faire-Politik (nach der Bauernbefreiung!) bis in die achtziger Jahre des 19. Jahrhunderts eher liberal. Erst der Konkurrenzdruck des überseeischen Getreides, der mit der Einführung des Dampfschiffs begann, ließ sie in das konservative Lager abwandern. Wäre die seit den Zeiten von *Marx* und *Engels* übliche Zuordnung des Sozialismus zur «Arbeiterklasse» gerechtfertigt, gäbe es angesichts des Rückgangs der Selbständigen und der Zunahme der unselbständig Beschäftigten eigentlich keinen Grund, warum nicht die sozialistischen Parteien – allgemeine, freie und geheime Wahlen vorausgesetzt – mühelos die absolute Mehrheit in den Parlamenten erreichen. Die neuere Wählerforschung hat ergeben, daß Arbeitnehmer in erheblichem Umfang auch liberal oder konservativ wählen. Nach der sozialistischen Selbstinterpretation müßte hier also massenweise ein «falsches Bewußtsein» vorliegen! Ebenso ist es eine bekannte Tatsache, daß die Führungskader linker Parteien mancherorts in signifikantem Umfang dem Großbürgertum und der Aristokratie entstammen. Offenkundig reicht die schichtspezifische Erklärung der Ideensysteme nicht aus.

Aber auch die *situationsbezogene* Interpretation der Ideensysteme kann nicht mehr als mögliche Beziehungen andeuten. Danach sind liberale Ideen eine bloße Reaktion auf Zwangsordnungen. So wird beispielsweise der Siegeszug des Wirtschaftsliberalismus als Konsequenz des Merkantilismus und seiner vielfältigen Reglementierung angesehen oder der Erfolg des deutschen Neoliberalismus nach 1948 als Reaktion auf die Entbehrungen infolge der Konsumgüterrationierung. Das Vorrücken konservativer Ideen wird auf raschen ökonomischen und sozialen Wandel zurückgeführt, der ganze Branchen oder Schichten bedroht. So wird etwa ein Zusammenhang zwischen der *Metternich*schen Restaurationspolitik und dem raschen Industrialisierungsprozeß gesehen. Auf der gleichen Linie liegt die Deutung einer wie immer auch verstandenen konservativen «Tendenzwende» als Folge des beschleunigten Sozialwandels in der Gegenwart. Ebenso kann der Sozialismus seine Triebkräfte aus Situationen beziehen, die als «ungerecht» oder als «Unterdrückung» empfunden werden. Man denke beispielsweise an die Sklavenaufstände in der Antike oder an die Gesellenaufstände im Mittelalter, an die Bauernkriege usw.

Bezüge zwischen Ideen und historischen Situationen sind vermutlich in vielen Fällen vorhanden gewesen. Als ausschließliche Interpretationsbasis für politische Ideen dürften sie zu schmal sein, wie schon die Kritik an der Unterbau-Überbau-Hyothese des Historischen Materialismus gezeigt hat.

---

[10] *H. Reithofer*, Die ausgleichende Gesellschaft. Strategien der Zukunftsbewältigung, Wien-München-Zürich 1978, S. 25.

IV. Ideensysteme als sozialphilosophische Grundhaltungen

Wichtiger als schichtspezifische oder situationsbezogene Zuordnungen der drei Ideensysteme Konservatismus, Liberalismus und Sozialismus ist ihre primäre *sozialphilosophische* Erklärung, also der Regreß auf grundsätzliche Werthaltungen des Menschen. Ob die Identifikation mit einer solchen Werthaltung bewußt als menschliche Wahlhandlung erfolgt oder durch vorhandene psychische Dispositionen beeinflußt wird, kann hier unberücksichtigt bleiben.

Entscheidend ist für diese dritte Interpretation, daß sich die ideellen Grundeinstellungen des Menschen zur Gesellschaft bis in die Antike zurückverfolgen lassen, also der vielfach angenommene bewußtseinsmäßige Bruch zwischen vorindustriellen und industriellen Zeiten nicht zutrifft. Selbstverständlich hat es wichtige Zusammenhänge zwischen der Französischen Revolution (besser: den Ideen der Aufklärung) und dem damaligen Liberalismus gegeben – ebenso wie das Auftauchen der damaligen Ausdrucksformen des Konservatismus und des Sozialismus mit den Folgen eben dieses Liberalismus zusammenhängt. Nur ist damit lediglich etwas über das Aktuellwerden von vorhandenen Werthaltungen unter bestimmten historischen Bedingungen ausgesagt; die Grundintentionen als solche sind zeitlos. So kann es eigentlich nur verwundern, daß selbst *K. Mannheim* den Konservatismus mittels eines etwas merkwürdig anmutenden Kunstgriffs erst mit *Chateaubriands* Zeitschrift «Le Conservateur» 1818 beginnen läßt. Er unterscheidet nämlich eine generelle menschliche Haltung, die er aber als Traditionalismus bezeichnet, vom Konservatismus «als einem spezifisch historischen und modernen Phänomen» und begründet diese Unterscheidung auch noch sprachgeschichtlich.[11]

Werfen wir darum einen kurzen Blick auf die Erscheinungsformen des liberalen, konservativen und sozialistischen Denkens in vorindustriellen Zeiten. In seinem dreibändigen Werk «Die Ortsbestimmung der Gegenwart» schildert *A. Rüstow* im zweiten Band den «Weg der Freiheit», also der Grundidee des liberalen Denkens, von der griechischen Polis bis zum Beginn des 19. Jahrhunderts.[12] *F. A. von Hayek* weist in seiner «Verfassung der Freiheit» auf die zentrale Bedeutung *Ciceros* für den modernen Liberalismus hin.[13]

[11] *K. Mannheim*, Das konservative Denken. In: Archiv für Sozialwissenschaft und Sozialpolitik, Bd. 57 (1927); wiederabgedruckt in *ders.*, Wissenssoziologie, Berlin und Neuwied 1964, S. 412. An späterer Stelle heißt es dazu: «Daß diese beiden Erscheinungen, Traditionalismus und Konservatismus, zwei besondere Phänomene sind, von denen das Letztere in einer besonderen historisch-soziologischen Situation zuerst entsteht, darauf deutet ja bereits der zuverlässigste Führer in der Geschichte, die Sprache, hin. Es muß nämlich auffallen, daß das Wort Konservatismus erst in der neuesten Entwicklung aufkam. *Chateaubriand* war es, der zum ersten Male dem Worte seine spezifische Prägung verlieh, als er seiner Zeitschrift, die den Ideen der politisch-kirchlichen Restauration dienen sollte, den Titel ‹Le Conservateur› gab. In Deutschland wurde das Wort erst in den 30er Jahren heimisch. In England wurde es erst 1835 rezipiert» (S. 417 f.). Angesichts dieser Perspektive ist es nur konsequent, wenn *Mannheim* davon spricht, daß der Traditionalismus zum Konservatismus erstarrt (S. 419) und nicht umgekehrt, wie es eher der Fall sein kann.

[12] Vgl. *A. Rüstow*, Ortsbestimmung der Gegenwart, Bd. 2: Weg der Freiheit, 2. Aufl., Erlenbach-Zürich und Stuttgart 1963.

[13] «Cicero wurde die wichtigste Autorität für den modernen Liberalismus, und wir verdanken ihm viele der wirksamsten Formulierungen des Begriffs der Freiheit unter dem Gesetz. Von ihm stammt der Begriff von allgemeinen Regeln oder ‹leges legum›, die die Gesetzgebung leiten, die Vorstellung, daß wir den Gesetzen gehorchen, um frei zu sein, und die Idee, daß der Richter nur der Mund sein soll, durch den das Gesetz spricht. Kein anderer Autor zeigt so deutlich, daß in der klassischen Periode des Römischen Rechts vollkommen verstanden wurde, daß zwischen Gesetz und Freiheit kein Gegensatz besteht, und daß die Freiheit von bestimmten Eigenschaften des

Ansonsten bildet das elfte Kapitel seiner «Verfassung der Freiheit» eine Fundgrube für die Rolle des Freiheitsideals im 17. und 18. Jahrhundert, also vor Beginn des industriellen Zeitalters.[14]

Aber auch das Gleichheitsideal, die Grundidee des Sozialismus, läßt sich bis auf antike Wurzeln zurückverfolgen. Die Isonomie, wie die Demokratie im Sinne des gleichen Rechtes für alle Vollbürger bis zum vierten vorchristlichen Jahrhundert in Griechenland genannt wurde, drängte mit einer gewissen Notwendigkeit zur Ausdehnung auf den sozialen Bereich. Hierzu berichtet *R. von Pöhlmann*: «Mit der Idee einer so engen Gemeinschaft, wie sie eben die Polis verwirklichen sollte, war es ja auf die Dauer unvereinbar, wenn durch die Ungleichheit von Besitz und Einkommen Gegensätze in der Gesellschaft entstanden, welche die Einheitlichkeit des Bürgertums völlig zerstören mußten. So stellte sich ganz folgerichtig der Gedanke ein, daß die überkommene Ordnung des Güterlebens durch eine zwangsweise gesellschaftliche Regelung der Güterverteilung im Sinne jener Prinzipien umzugestalten sei. Der Demokratismus im hellenistischen Stadtstaat erzeugt als sein logisch notwendiges Komplement den Sozialismus.»[15] Daß auch im Römischen Reich sozialistische Auffassungen vertreten wurden, insbesondere in den letzten Jahrhunderten seines Bestehens, hat *R. von Pöhlmann* in seinem erwähnten Werk ausführlich dargelegt. In diesem Zusammenhang ist auch an sozialkritische Tendenzen bei den frühen Christen zu erinnern. Sozialistisch-kommunistische Strömungen und Aufstände lassen sich vom Beginn des Mittelalters bis in das 19. Jahrhundert hinein immer wieder feststellen (Mazdakiten in Persien im fünften und sechsten Jahrhundert, Patarener in Italien im 13. und 14. Jahrhundert, Lollardenaufstand in England 1381, Taboriten in Böhmen im 15. Jahrhundert, Bauernkriege des 16. Jahrhunderts, Wiedertäuferherrschaft in Münster 1534/35, die Leveller im England des 17. Jahrhunderts, dann in Frankreich Ende des 18., Anfang des 19. Jahrhunderts die verschiedenen Richtungen des Babeufismus, Blanquismus, Cabetismus, Saint-Simonismus und Fourierismus, sowie *Wilhelm Weitlings* Handwerksburschenkommunismus und *Robert Owens* Genossenschaftssozialismus).[16] Alle diese Ansätze sind durch den Anspruch des Marxismus, «wissenschaftlicher Sozialismus» zu sein, als mehr oder minder utopische Frühformen in den Hintergrund gedrängt und dadurch abgewertet worden, obwohl sie in ihrer jeweiligen Zeit *die* Ausdrucksformen der sozialistischen Grundideen waren.[17]

Ebenso fällt es nicht schwer, konservative Ideen schon in der Antike nachzuweisen. *Platon* und *Aristoteles* sind diesbezüglich zu nennen; *Pindar* und *Thukydides* werden von *A. Rüstow* noch besonders hervorgehoben.[18] Die konservative Prägung des Mittelalters

---

Rechts abhängt, nämlich ihrer Allgemeinheit und Gewißheit, und den Beschränkungen, die sie dem Ermessen der Behörde auferlegt» (*F. A. von Hayek*, Die Verfassung der Freiheit, a.a.O., S. 206 f., mit weiteren Hinweisen auf die Bedeutung *Ciceros* für *Hume* und *Montesquieu*).

[14] Vgl. *F. A. von Hayek*, Die Verfassung der Freiheit, a.a.O., S. 195 ff.

[15] *R. von Pöhlmann*, Geschichte der sozialen Frage und des Sozialismus in der antiken Welt, Bd. 1, 3. Aufl., München 1925, S. 126.

[16] Zusammenfassung nach *G. Bartsch*, Kommunismus, Sozialismus, Anarchismus. Wurzeln, Unterschiede und Gemeinsamkeiten, Freiburg-Basel-Wien 1976. Vgl. hierzu ferner *K. Kautsky*, Vorläufer des neueren Sozialismus, 2 Bde., Berlin(Ost) 1947.

[17] Wissenssoziologisch mag hier eine wichtige Rolle gespielt haben, daß der vormarxistische Sozialismus vor allem eine bäuerliche, daneben eine handwerkliche Bewegung darstellte, die genossenschaftliche Produktionsformen bevorzugte. Dieser Unterschied macht sich bis heute in der sowjetisch-chinesischen Rivalität bemerkbar und in der stärkeren Attraktivität des chinesischen Modells für manche Entwicklungsländer.

mit seinen hierarchischen Strukturen im weltlichen und geistlichen Bereich und der Ableitung politischer Entscheidungen auf allen Ebenen (Subsidiaritätsprinzip!) aus transzendentalen Bezügen ist unbestritten. *Augustinus, Thomas von Aquino, Dante, Petrarca* und das christliche Naturrecht kennzeichnen die zeitlosen und zugleich positionalen Ideen des damaligen Konservatismus.[19]

V. Das einfache Wertedreieck

Die von *F. A. von Hayek* angeregte Dreiecksdarstellung der politischen Ideensysteme läßt sich nach den bisherigen Ausführungen wie folgt formulieren:

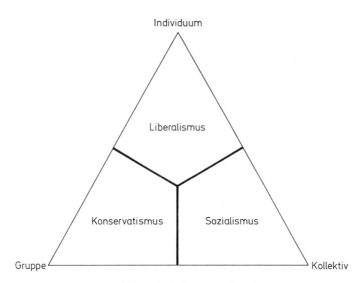

Abb. 1: Einfaches Wertedreieck

[18] Vgl. *A. Rüstow*, Ortsbestimmung der Gegenwart, Bd. 3: Herrschaft oder Freiheit, Erlenbach-Zürich und Stuttgart 1957, S. 199 f. Allerdings interpretiert *Rüstow* im Sinne seiner Überlagerungstheorie das konservative Denken als Ideologie der Oberschicht, die sich von der vorher einmal überlagerten Unterschicht bedroht sieht. Vgl. kritisch dazu *W. E. Mühlmann*, Rassen, Ethnien, Kulturen. Moderne Ethnologie, Neuwied-Berlin 1964, S. 248 ff.

[19] *G.-K. Kaltenbrunner* (Hrsg.), Rekonstruktion des Konservatismus, 3. Aufl., Bern und Stuttgart 1978, wendet sich in seinem einführenden Beitrag («Der schwierige Konservatismus») zu diesem Sammelband gegen die «zeitlose» Interpretation und tritt für eine «positionale» Deutung des konservativen Ideensystems ein (a.a.O., S. 41). Unseres Erachtens schließt eine sozialphilosophische (also «zeitlose») Perspektive die partiellen schichtspezifischen oder situationsbezogenen Zuordnungen nicht aus, sondern enthält sie als jeweilige historische Aktualisierungen – so problematisch sie im Einzelfall auch sein mögen, was übrigens ebenso für den Liberalismus und den Sozialismus gilt. – Zu den konservativen Grundideen vgl. auch *G. Weippert*, Das Prinzip der Hierarchie, Hamburg 1932.

Die Zuordnung des Individuums, der Gruppe und des Kollektivs zu den drei Ideensystemen entspricht den Sozialfiguren, die jeweils von konstitutiver Bedeutung für den Liberalismus, den Konservatismus und den Sozialismus sind.[20]
Unter der Annahme eines reinen Verhältniswahlrechts und des Bestehens dreier Parteien, die den Ideensystemen entsprechen, könnte man sich eine Art «politische Normalverteilung» vorstellen: Jede Partei erhält ungefähr ein Drittel der Wählerstimmen. Eine Regierungsbildung wäre dann nur durch Koalition von mindestens zwei Parteien möglich. Einschränkungen des reinen Verhältniswahlrechts bis hin zum Majorzsystem würden eine «Verzerrung» dieser «Normalverteilung» zur Folge haben.

Als Erklärungshypothese für die politische Praxis ist das einfache Wertedreieck jedoch ungeeignet, weil es die unverkennbaren Tendenzen zur Fraktionsbildung innerhalb der drei Ideensysteme vernachlässigt. Gerade *F. A. von Hayek* hat immer wieder großes Gewicht darauf gelegt, zwei Arten des Liberalismus zu unterscheiden. Eine ähnliche Zweiteilung ist auch beim Sozialismus und beim Konservatismus geboten.

VI. Zwei Arten des Liberalismus

In der Tat zeigt die Geschichte der politischen Ideen und ihrer Realisierungsversuche deutlich die Notwendigkeit, die Ideensysteme in sich zu differenzieren. Die «Scheidelinien der Sozialphilosophie und der Wirtschaftspolitik» (*W. Röpke*) verlaufen nicht zwischen, sondern mitten durch die Ideensysteme.[21] So weist der Liberalismus einen Flügel auf, der zum Konservatismus tendiert, und einen zweiten, der eine große Affinität zum Sozialismus besitzt. Vereinfachend kann man sie Rechts- und Linksliberalismus nennen. *F. A. von Hayek* hat über Jahrzehnte immer erneut auf den fundamentalen Unterschied zwischen diesen beiden aufmerksam gemacht, die er als wahren und als falschen Liberalismus, Individualismus oder Rationalismus bezeichnet.[22]
Die wichtigsten Merkmale können schematisch folgendermaßen gegenübergestellt werden:

[20] Analog wäre eine Zuordnung zu den Postulaten der Französischen Revolution (liberté = Liberalismus, égalité = Sozialismus, fraternité = Konservatismus) denkbar. Vgl. hierzu die interessante Untersuchung von *M. U. Rapold*, Demokratie und Wirtschaftsordnung, Zürich o. J. (1958). Warum der «Grundwerte-Kanon» heute an Stelle der Gleichheit (vor dem Gesetz) die (distributive) Gerechtigkeit und an Stelle der Brüderlichkeit die Solidarität enthält, kann hier aus Platzgründen nicht näher erörtert werden. Bemerkt sei nur, daß auch die Reihenfolge «Freiheit – Gerechtigkeit – Solidarität» in unserem Wertedreieck durch eine Linksdrehung, die Reihenfolge «Freiheit – Solidarität – Gerechtigkeit» dagegen durch eine Rechtsdrehung dargestellt werden könnte. Zur heutigen «Grundwerte-Diskussion» vgl. auch *G. Gorschenek* (Hrsg.), Grundwerte in Staat und Gesellschaft, München 1977.

[21] Vgl. *W. Röpke*, Jenseits von Angebot und Nachfrage, 4. Aufl., Erlenbach-Zürich und Stuttgart 1966, S. 338.

[22] Vgl. hierzu vor allem *F. A. von Hayek*, The Road to Serfdom, London und Chicago 1944 (deutsch: Der Weg zur Knechtschaft, Erlenbach-Zürich 1945), *ders.*, Individualism: True and False, Dublin und Oxford 1946 (deutsch in *ders.*, Individualismus und wirtschaftliche Ordnung, a.a.O., S. 9 ff.), *ders.*, The Constitution of Liberty, a.a.O., *passim*, *ders.*, Freiburger Studien, Tübingen 1969 (insbesondere den Beitrag «Arten der Ordnung», S. 75 ff.), und *ders.*, Die Irrtümer des Konstruktivismus, Tübingen 1975.

Rechtsliberalismus	Linksliberalismus
Empirisch-evolutionäres Denken	Konstruktivistischer Rationalismus
Angloschottische Moralphilosophie (*Locke, Hume, Ferguson, Smith*) und *Montesquieu*	Französische Aufklärung (*Descartes, Rousseau*) und Utilitarismus (*Bentham*)
Ambivalentes Menschenbild	Optimistisches Menschenbild
Spontane Ordnung durch allgemeine Verhaltensregeln (Privatrecht, Strafrecht, Gewohnheitsrecht, Ethik)	Organisation durch Anordnungen (Verwaltungsrecht, Staatsrecht, Maßnahmegesetze)
Rechtsstaat (Gewaltenteilung, Föderalismus, Selbstverwaltung)	Sozialstaat (Zentrismus)
Politik nach Grundsätzen	Politik nach quantifizierten Zielen
Offene Zukunft	«Machbare» Zukunft

Die mangelnde Berücksichtigung (oder Kenntnis) dieser grundlegenden Unterschiede, die sich im Detail noch weiter differenzieren lassen (z. B. im Hinblick auf das empirische und das jakobinische Demokratieverständnis[23]), hat entscheidend zur Schwäche liberaler Parteien beigetragen, wie sie seit langem in Europa zu verzeichnen ist.

VII. Differenzierung des Sozialismus und Konservatismus

Ebensowenig wie der Liberalismus sind auch die beiden anderen Ideensysteme homogene Gebilde. Sie weisen ebenfalls in sich einen Rubicon auf, der zwei ganz verschieden orientierte Richtungen entstehen läßt.

So spaltete sich der *Sozialismus* im Zuge heftiger parteiinterner Auseinandersetzungen (Revisionismus-Debatte) gleichfalls in einen rechten und einen linken Zweig. Während der rechte Zweig, die Sozialdemokratie, ihr Grundziel – die Herstellung von mehr Gleichheit im Sinne distributiver Gerechtigkeit – durch Reformen anstrebt, also insofern das rechtsstaatlich-parlamentarische Prinzip anerkennt, will der linke Zweig, der Kommunismus, durch die «Revolution des Proletariats» den Einparteienstaat, in welchem die Kommunistische Partei als «Avantgarde der Arbeiterklasse» elitäre Funktionen ausübt. Der Rubicon zwischen beiden Richtungen des Sozialismus wird also durch den Unterschied zwischen parlamentarischem Sozialstaat und totalitärem Machtstaat charakterisiert. An die Stelle des Rationalismus tritt der Voluntarismus, an die Stelle der Vergesellschaftung des Staates die Verstaatlichung der Gesellschaft.[24]

---

[23] Vgl. hierzu W. *Röpke*, Jenseits von Angebot und Nachfrage, a.a.O., S. 103 ff. und S. 386 f., sowie E. *Fraenkel*, Deutschland und die westlichen Demokratien, Stuttgart 1964, S. 70.

[24] Aus der größeren Durchschlagskraft des Voluntarismus resultiert zugleich die Schwäche von Volksfrontexperimenten, die entweder zerbrechen, wenn der demokratische Sozialismus stark genug bleibt, oder in ein kommunistisches Regime übergehen, wenn die kommunistischen Kader sich durchsetzen.

Daß sich neben den beiden Hauptvarianten des Sozialismus (Sozialdemokratie und Kommunismus) noch weitere Fraktionen herausbilden können, so beispielsweise eine sich nur sozialistisch nennende Partei, die links von der Sozialdemokratie steht, hängt mit den außerordentlich starken Zentrifugalkräften der erwähnten Scheidelinie zusammen. Hingegen unterscheidet sich die chinesische Variante des Kommunismus von der russischen weniger in der Zielsetzung als in den Auffassungen über die anzuwendenden Mittel und die stärkere agrarische Komponente des chinesischen Kommunismus.[25]

Am meisten Schwierigkeiten bereitet (scheinbar) die systematische Erfassung des *Konservatismus* und seiner verschiedenen Spielarten. Im Nachwort zur «Verfassung der Freiheit» widmet sich *F. A. von Hayek* denn auch ausdrücklich dem Verhältnis von Liberalismus und Konservatismus und legt dar, warum er sich nicht als Konservativer betrachtet.[26] Indem er einerseits die nationale Komponente des Konservatismus und die damit oft verbundenen Staatseinflüsse auf die Wirtschaft ablehnt, andererseits aber konstitutionalistische Denker wie *Burke, Acton* oder *Tocqueville* durchaus akzeptiert, deutet er zugleich an, wo der Rubicon innerhalb des konservativen Ideensystems verläuft. Die Scheidelinie liegt hier zwischen der konstitutionellen und der nationalen Variante.

Ähnlich wie der Rechtsliberalismus beruht der Konservatismus auf einem eher skeptischen Menschenbild. Der Mensch ist ambivalent strukturiert; er besitzt die Fähigkeit sowohl zum Guten wie zum Bösen. Er ist weder Tier noch Engel, um ein oft zitiertes Wort von *Pascal* zu erwähnen. Stärker als der Rechtsliberale weiß der Konservative aber um die vielfältigen Möglichkeiten des Scheiterns in dieser Welt, um die Tragik menschlichen Handelns. Er sucht daher Halt in den Institutionen, in den Traditionen, in den religiösen Bindungen und in kleinen überschaubaren Bezügen (Familie, Nachbarschaft, Gemeinde, Region).[27]

Die konstitutionelle Variante des Konservatismus hat mit dem Rechtsliberalismus manche Gemeinsamkeiten, allen voran die strenge rechtsstaatliche Orientierung auf empirisch-evolutionärer Grundlage. Jenseits dieses Rubicon ist der nationale Konservatismus demgegenüber voluntaristisch und machtstaatlich orientiert (bis hin zum Einparteienstaat). Er steht damit dem Kommunismus näher als dem Konstitutionalismus.[28] Viele Mißverständnisse lassen sich vermeiden, wenn man diese sozialphilosophischen Scheidelinien innerhalb der Ideensysteme berücksichtigt. Aus dem einfachen wird dann das differenzierte Wertedreieck, das mindestens sechs Richtungen unterscheidet.

---

[25] Vgl. hierzu auch die Bemerkungen in Fußnote 17.

[26] Vgl. *F. A. von Hayek*, Die Verfassung der Freiheit, a.a.O., S. 492.

[27] Bemerkenswert ist *Hayeks* Äußerung zur transzendentalen Orientierung des Konservatismus: «Im Gegensatz zum Rationalismus der Französischen Revolution liegt der wahre Liberalismus nicht im Streit mit der Religion, und ich kann die militante und wesentlich unliberale Einstellung, die den kontinentalen Liberalismus des 19. Jahrhunderts anfachte, nur bedauern. Daß sie nicht zum Wesen des Liberalismus gehört, zeigt sich bei seinen englischen Vorfahren, den Old Whigs, die eher zu eng mit einem bestimmten religiösen Glauben verbunden waren. Was den Liberalen hier vom Konservativen unterscheidet, ist jedoch, daß er, so tief auch seine eigenen spirituellen Überzeugungen sein mögen, sich nie für berechtigt halten wird, sie anderen aufzudrängen und daß für ihn das Ewige und das Zeitliche verschiedene Bereiche sind, die auseinander gehalten werden sollten» (*F. A. von Hayek*, Die Verfassung der Freiheit, a.a.O., S. 491).

[28] Zu erwähnen wäre hier beispielsweise der «revolutionäre Konservatismus» in der Weimarer Republik. Vgl. *A. Mohler*, Die konservative Revolution in Deutschland 1918–1932, 2. Aufl., Darmstadt 1972. – Die konservative Komponente im Kommunismus zeigt sich in der Sowjetunion in den Erstarrungstendenzen der hierarchisch aufgebauten Parteielite, ferner überall dort, wo kommunistische Parteien sich in parlamentarischen Demokratien als staatserhaltende Ord-

VIII. Einbeziehung utopischer Komponenten

Solange nur die Ideensysteme diskutiert werden, besteht die Gefahr, eine wesentliche Quelle der politischen Programmatik zu übersehen, nämlich das utopische Element. Neben den politischen Ideen, die sich mehr auf die Gestaltung der Gegenwart richten, stehen die Utopien als Zukunftsbilder einer idealen Gesellschaft. In ihren sozialphilosophischen Wurzeln sind sie nicht immer genau zu trennen.[29]

Wie *H. Giersch* dargelegt hat, weisen die Zukunftsbilder einer idealen Gesellschaft gewisse Gemeinsamkeiten auf:

1. Sie verabsolutieren eine einzelne Grundidee (daher lassen sich auch liberale, konservative und sozialistische Utopien unterscheiden).
2. Sie unterstellen einen Menschen, der sich utopiekonform verhält (daher wird den Erziehungsmaßnahmen in den Sozialutopien großes Gewicht beigemessen).
3. Die ideale Zukunftsgesellschaft ist konfliktfrei.
4. Gegenüber der Außenwelt herrscht das Autarkieprinzip.[30]

Wie die Ideensysteme reichen auch die Utopien bis in die Antike zurück. *Platons* «Staat» stellt die erste konservative Utopie dar, in der das Prinzip der Hierarchie verabsolutiert wird.[31] Auf einen gemeinsamen Nenner gebracht, lassen sich die konservativen Sozialutopien durch den Begriff des *Ständestaates* charakterisieren.

Als Beispiel für eine sozialistische Utopie ist vor allem die «Utopia» von *Thomas Morus* zu nennen, der die ganze Literaturgattung der Sozialutopien zugleich ihre Bezeichnung verdankt. Die «Utopia» wurde von *K. Kautsky* eine «machtvolle Verherrlichung des Kommunismus» genannt.[32] Die Faszinationskraft sozialistischer Utopien, die auf der Verabsolutierung der Gleichheitsidee beruhen, hat im Laufe der Jahrhunderte immer wieder zu diesbezüglichen Experimenten geführt, die seit *Marx* und *Engels* durch die Rubrizierung in die Kategorie des «utopischen» im Gegensatz zum «wissenschaftlichen» Sozialismus allerdings eine Abwertung erfahren haben. Aus der Verabsolutierung der

---

nungskräfte gerieren (Eurokommunismus in Südeuropa!). – Im weiteren ist auch an die Ähnlichkeiten zwischen Rechts- und Linkstotalitarismus zu denken, die durch die derzeitige Verengung des Totalitarismusbegriffes auf den Rechtstotalitarismus (= Faschismus) wegdiskutiert werden. Vgl. hierzu *G. Schmidt*, Politik als Heilslehre. Zur Idee des Totalitarismus, Mainz 1970.

[29] Vgl. hierzu *K. Mannheim*, Ideologie und Utopie, 3. Aufl., Frankfurt a. M. 1952, und die dortige Bibliographie, S. 269 ff. – Zu einigen kritischen Aspekten vgl. ferner *E. Tuchtfeldt*, Zur heutigen Problemstellung der Wissenssoziologie. In: Zeitschrift für die gesamte Staatswissenschaft, Bd. 107 (1951), S. 723 ff.

[30] Vgl. *H. Giersch*, Allgemeine Wirtschaftspolitik, a.a.O., S. 62 f. – Zu Utopien generell vgl. ferner *L. Mumford*, The Story of Utopias, New York 1922, *J. O. Hertzler*, History of Utopia Thought, London 1923, sowie vor allem *E. Bloch*, Freiheit und Ordnung. Abriß der Sozial-Utopien, Berlin 1947, und *F. E. Manuel* (Hrsg.), Wunschtraum und Experiment. Vom Nutzen und Nachteil utopischen Denkens, Freiburg i. Brsg. 1970. Einige besondere Aspekte behandelt *J. Starbatty*, Die Entzauberung der «Utopia» – Zur Frage des Christlichen in der utopischen Ethik. In: *Chr. Watrin* und *H. Willgerodt* (Hrsg.), Widersprüche der Kapitalismuskritik (Festschrift für Alfred Müller-Armack), Bern und Stuttgart 1976, S. 215 ff.

[31] Die nicht selten anzutreffende Ansicht, es handele sich hier um eine sozialistische Utopie, ist unzutreffend. *Platon* wendet sich mehrfach gegen die Idee der Gleichheit, worauf auch *K. R. Popper* in seiner Kritik an *Platons* Sozialutopie aufmerksam macht. Vgl. *K. R. Popper*, Die offene Gesellschaft und ihre Feinde, Bd. 1: Der Zauber Platons, Bern 1957, S. 136 ff. und S. 344 ff.

[32] *K. Kautsky*, Vorläufer des neueren Sozialismus, Bd. 3: Die beiden ersten großen Utopisten, 2. Aufl., Stuttgart-Berlin 1922, S. 49. – Zu *Thomas Morus* vgl. ferner die Literaturangaben im Aufsatz von *J. Starbatty* (s. Fußnote 30).

Gleichheitsidee resultiert der Rätestaat, dessen Bedeutung für die heutige Neue Linke zugleich deren utopisches Element erkennen läßt.

Als utopische Ausdrucksform der liberalen Grundidee ist der libertäre Anarchismus im Sinne totaler Freiheit zu nennen. Ihr erster Vertreter war *W. Godwin* («Untersuchung über soziale Gerechtigkeit», 1793), der selbst die Institution der Familie und die Schulpflicht als Freiheitsbeschränkungen ablehnte.[33] Da eine völlig herrschaftslose Ordnung, in der es auch keine Herrschaft des Gesetzes gibt, vernünftigerweise nicht vorstellbar ist, wäre es aus heutiger Sicht wohl eher angebracht, die in den USA entwickelte Idee des *Minimalstaates* als utopische Verabsolutierung der Freiheitsidee aufzufassen. Damit werden auch zeitgenössische «Libertarians» wie vor allem die Amerikanerin *Ayn Rand* («The Virtue of Selfishness: A New Concept of Egoism», 1966, und «Capitalism: The Unknown Ideal», 1967) dem utopischen Bereich zugerechnet. Zumindest stehen sie – aus europäischer Perspektive – am Rande dieses Bereiches.

IX. Das differenzierte Wertedreieck

Nach Einführung des «sozialphilosophischen Rubicons» bei jedem der drei Ideensysteme und der utopischen Bereiche an den drei Ecken kann nun das in Abb. 1 gebrachte einfache Wertedreieck wesentlich differenziert werden:

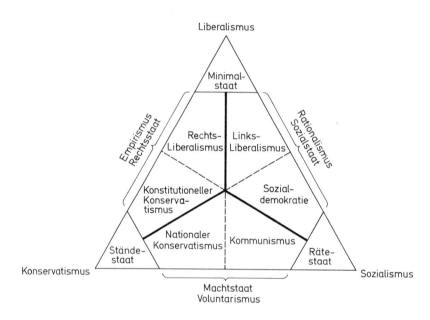

Abb. 2: Differenziertes Wertedreieck

---

[33] Zur Vermeidung von Mißverständnissen sei erwähnt, daß neben dem Individual-Anarchismus (*W. Godwin, M. Stirner*) die verschiedenen Strömungen des Sozial-Anarchismus (*P. Proudhon, M. Bakunin, P. Krapotkin*) eine größere Bedeutung erlangt haben.

Die «Scheidelinien der Sozialphilosophie» (*W. Röpke*), die in Abb. 1 die drei Ideensysteme voneinander abgrenzten, verlaufen jetzt in der in den Abschnitten VI und VII dargelegten Weise quer durch den Liberalismus, den Konservatismus und den Sozialismus. Dadurch werden die Affinitäten und Abneigungen deutlich, die in der politischen Praxis zwischen den verschiedenen Richtungen bestehen und in ihren ideenmäßigen Hintergründen oft nicht verstanden werden.

Eine weitere Ausfächerung wäre ohne weiteres möglich, indem man beispielsweise dem Umstand Rechnung trägt, daß sich auch innerparteilich oft mehr als zwei Fraktionen bilden. Der Erklärungswert der Abb. 2 würde dadurch jedoch nicht wesentlich gewinnen.

X. Ideensysteme und wirtschaftspolitischer Interventionsgrad

Die Darstellung der politischen Positionen in Dreiecksform, wie sie *F. A. von Hayek* angeregt hat, läßt noch einen weiteren Zusammenhang deutlich werden, der vor allem zwischen Liberalen und Konservativen seit jeher zu Komplikationen geführt hat. Die übliche Gegenüberstellung von Marktwirtschaft und Zentralverwaltungswirtschaft oder von Individualismus und Kollektivismus hat eigentlich nie eine befriedigende Erklärung für das wachsende Ausmaß der Staatstätigkeit geliefert.[34]

Das Wertedreieck in der dargestellten Form bietet für diese Problematik eine relativ einfache Erklärung. Der Rechtsliberalismus ist aufgrund seiner Prinzipien darauf angelegt, die Staatstätigkeit zu beschränken. Linksliberalismus und Sozialismus tendieren infolge ihrer konstruktivistischen Ideen zu einer Ausdehnung der Staatstätigkeit. Der Konservatismus neigt, wenn auch unter Betonung des Subsidiaritätsprinzips, ebenfalls zu mehr Staat. «Ordnung erscheint dem Konservativen als das Ergebnis ständiger Pflege durch die Behörde, die zu diesem Zweck die Befugnis haben muß, zu tun, was unter den besonderen Umständen erforderlich ist, und nicht durch strenge Regeln gebunden sein darf.»[35]

Ordnet man dazu noch, wie bereits in Abb. 1 geschehen, dem Konservatismus die Sozialfigur der Gruppe zu, konkret die Verbände, die meist mit Interventionswünschen zu ihren Gunsten an den Staat herantreten, so läßt sich mittels des Wertedreiecks zeigen, daß von zwei Ecken her ein Zug nach mehr Staat ausgeübt wird, dagegen nur aus einer Ecke ein Zug nach mehr Markt:

---

[34] Es sei denn, man beschränkt sich hier auf die schon von *L. von Mises* herausgearbeitete «Interventionsspirale» bei marktinkonformen Eingriffen, die dann von *F. A. von Hayek* und *W. Röpke* weiterentwickelt worden ist.

[35] *F. A. von Hayek*, Die Verfassung der Freiheit, a.a.O., S. 485. Einige Zeilen später kommt *Hayek* auf das zurück, was er als Hauptpunkt seiner Ablehnung des Konservatismus bezeichnet: «Das ist die charakteristische Unbesorgtheit des Konservativen gegenüber den Maßnahmen der eingesetzten Behörde und seiner vornehmlichen Sorge, daß diese Behörde nicht geschwächt wird, anstatt dafür zu sorgen, daß ihre Macht in Schranken gehalten wird. Das ist mit der Erhaltung der Freiheit schwer zu vereinbaren. Im allgemeinen kann man wohl sagen, daß der Konservative nichts gegen Zwang oder Willkür einzuwenden hat, solange diese für Zwecke ausgeübt werden, die ihm die richtigen scheinen» (a.a.O.).

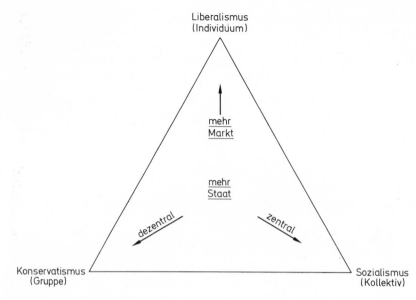

Abb. 3: Wertedreieck und Interventionsgrad

Daß der Sozialismus dabei mehr zentrale, der Konservatismus mehr dezentrale Interventionen (Selbsthilfeorganisationen!) zur Folge hat, ändert am Gesamteffekt kaum etwas. Im «Zeitalter der Experimente» (W. Eucken) bewirkt das Parallelogramm der politischen Kräfte, wenn erst einmal die Ideen des konstruktivistischen Rationalismus sich hinreichend ausgebreitet haben, eine Tendenz zu «mehr Staat».

XI. Hypothesen für politisches Verhalten

Außer dem Zusammenhang zwischen den Ideensystemen und dem wirtschaftspolitischen Interventionsgrad lassen sich aus dem differenzierten Wertedreieck noch weitere generelle Erklärungsansätze für politisches Verhalten ableiten. So zeigt es, um hier nur einige wichtige Punkte herauszugreifen:

1. Die «sozialphilosophischen Scheidelinien» (W. Röpke) mitten durch die Ideensysteme, also der Empirismus, Rationalismus und Voluntarismus, haben in der Praxis ein stärkeres Gewicht als die Grundideen des Liberalismus, Sozialismus und Konservatismus. Jedes der drei Ideensysteme weist daher (mindestens) zwei Fraktionen auf, die jeweils eine größere Affinität zu einem der beiden anderen Ideensysteme besitzen als zur benachbarten Fraktion, weshalb Spaltungstendenzen nicht zu vermeiden sind.

2. Verbindungen zwischen Parteien mit ähnlicher empiristischer, rationalistischer oder voluntaristischer Position kommen leichter zustande als zwischen zwei «politischen Großfamilien».[36] Beispiele hierfür liefern die liberal-konservativen Koalitionen zwi-

---

[36] Der Ausdruck «politische Großfamilie» stammt von E. Gruner, Die Parteien in der Schweiz, 2. Aufl., Bern 1977.

schen Rechtsliberalismus und konstitutionellem Konservatismus, die beide dem Rechtsstaat verpflichtet sind (das Streben nach dezentraler staatlicher Autorität macht die Konservativen sozusagen zum «geborenen» Partner für die Rechtsliberalen), oder die sozial-liberalen Koalitionen zwischen Sozialdemokratie und Linksliberalismus, die beide den Sozialstaat verwirklichen wollen. Daß dann auch zwischen der nationalen (voluntaristischen) Variante des Konservatismus und dem Sozialismus Affinitäten bestehen, mag manchen vielleicht auf den ersten Blick schockieren, obwohl schon *F. A. von Hayek* darauf aufmerksam gemacht hat, daß der «Nationalismus oft die Brücke vom Konservatismus zum Kollektivismus bildet: von Gedanken an ‹unsere Industrie› oder ‹unsere Naturschätze› ist es nur ein kleiner Schritt zu der Folgerung, daß diese nationalen Vermögenswerte im nationalen Interesse gelenkt werden sollen.»[37] Dem nationalen Konservatismus und dem Kommunismus sind gemeinsam die voluntaristische Einstellung und der expansionistische Machtstaat – ein Tatbestand, der durch die Verengung der Totalitarismus-Diskussion weitgehend verdrängt worden ist.[38]

3. Große Koalitionen, bei denen in der politischen Praxis mindestens ein «ideeller Rubicon» laufend durch Kompromisse bewältigt werden muß, sind in der Regel nur unter besonderen innen- und/oder außenpolitischen Umständen möglich, weil normalerweise die zentrifugalen Kräfte zu stark sind.[39]

4. «Volksparteien», welche die relative oder absolute Mehrheit der Wählerstimmen gewinnen wollen, müssen sich in ihren Programmen mehr am Schwerpunkt als an den Ecken des Wertedreiecks orientieren, also möglichst vielen wertedifferenzierten Gruppen entgegenkommen. Sie verlieren damit notwendigerweise an programmatischer Schärfe.[40]

5. Die Standorte der verschiedenen Parteien lassen sich an Hand des Wertedreiecks lokalisieren. Im Laufe der Entwicklung kann sich auch der Standort einer Partei verändern – mehr zum Schwerpunkt, mehr zu einer Ecke oder mehr zu den Seiten hin. Solche Standortverschiebungen können beispielsweise eintreten, wenn eine jüngere, durch andere Erfahrungen geprägte (oder bestimmte Erfahrungen nicht mehr besitzende)

---

[37] *F. A. von Hayek*, die Verfassung der Freiheit, a.a.O., S. 490.

[38] Vgl. hierzu die Bemerkungen in Fußnote 28. – Daß diese Verbindung dann ein nationaler Sozialismus ist, wird durch die historischen Erfahrungen bestätigt. Nach dem heutigen Stand der Forschung läßt sich die Verbindung von Nationalismus und Sozialismus bis zur taboritischen Bewegung des 15. Jahrhunderts in Böhmen zurückverfolgen. Vgl. hierzu ausführlich *R. Kalivoda*, Revolution und Ideologie. Der Hussitismus, Köln-Wien 1976. – Schon vor der Spaltung der russischen Sozialisten (1903) war es 1896 zur Spaltung der tschechischen Sozialisten gekommen, wobei sich ein national orientierter Flügel verselbständigte und sich auch bereits als nationalsozialistisch bezeichnete. Dieser Spaltung lag die damals in Böhmen sich ausbreitende, stark taboritisch beeinflußte Ansicht zugrunde, der Sozialismus könne nur auf nationaler Ebene erfolgreich sein. *Mussolini*, anfangs noch Sozialist, hat während seines Aufenthalts im damals noch österreichisch-ungarischen Trient mit tschechischen Nationalsozialisten Kontakt gehabt und ist von deren Gedankengängen fasziniert gewesen. Sein späteres faschistisches Konzept hat er dann bewußt als Verbindung von Nationalismus und Sozialismus entwickelt.

[39] Eine Ausnahme von der hier formulierten Regel bildet die Schweiz, insofern dieses Land seit Jahrzehnten von einer «Großen Koalition» zwischen konservativen, liberalen und sozialen Demokraten regiert wird. Dieser «Sonderfall Schweiz» resultiert aus der größeren Spannweite des politischen Grundkonsenses im Vergleich zu anderen Industriestaaten. Instruktive Darlegungen hierzu bringt *K. W. Deutsch*, Die Schweiz als ein paradigmatischer Fall politischer Integration, Bern 1976.

[40] In der Nähe der «sozialphilosophischen Scheidelinien» nimmt allerdings die Instabilität zu. Sie kann sich beispielsweise in Form des Parteiwechsels von Abgeordneten äußern.

Generation in die Führungspositionen einrückt. Eine Annäherung an die Ecken, also an die utopischen Bereiche, dürfte eine Abschwächung des sozioökonomischen Wandels voraussetzen.[41]

Diese (und weitere mögliche) Folgerungen verdeutlichen, daß sich aus dem differenzierten Wertedreieck, auch in seiner immer noch rigoros vereinfachenden Form, Hypothesen für politisches Verhalten ableiten lassen, die für manche Vorgänge und Tendenzen in der Praxis als Erklärungsmuster dienen können.

Summary

Political Ideas as Patterns of Political Behaviour

Usually, the political spectrum is represented by a straight line with the socialists on the left-hand side, the conservatives on the right-hand side and the liberals in the middle. This presentation, however, leaves many questions unanswered. Hence, F. A. *von Hayek* suggested as early as in 1960 arranging the basic political positions in form of a triangle, each of them occupying one angle. In this article, F. A. *von Hayek's* suggestion is discussed in some more detail.

First, the more common explanations of political systems of thoughts are examined. Those interpretations drawing on social strata and historical situations are of partial explanatory value only. Compared with them, the socio-philosophical interpretation of the liberal, the socialist and the conservative principles (liberty, equality, hierarchy) are valid at all times.

The simple presentation in form of a triangle is particularly insufficient to account for the formation of parliamentary parties and the splitting tendencies within each of the three positions. Taking into consideration that each of them is intersected by a «socio-philosophical demarcation line» (W. *Röpke*), characterized by empiricism, rationalism and voluntarism, six different positions can be distinguished. When furthermore including the utopian fields in the far end of each angle which stand for the idealization of a principle (liberty = minimum state; equality = soviet system; hierarchy = corporate state), the result is a differentiated «triangle of values», which is giving the possibility to formulate a number of explanatory hypotheses for political behaviour.

---

[41] Diese Feststellung ist für den Ständestaat unmittelbar einleuchtend; sie gilt aber auch für den Rätestaat. Hier ist beispielsweise an die blutige Unterdrückung des Kronstädter Aufstandes 1921 zu denken, der das im Zuge der bolschewistischen Oktoberrevolution eingeführte Rätesystem verteidigen wollte. *Lenin* mag vorübergehend selbst an die dauerhafte Realisierbarkeit eines Rätesystems geglaubt haben (zumindest propagandistisch hat sich diese Idee sehr erfolgreich ausgewirkt, weil sie viele Russen damals glauben ließ, an Stelle des vorausgegangenen Feudalsystems würde nun das Volk regieren). Infolge der Ineffizienz des «Kriegskommunismus» (die Produktion war 1921 auf rd. 20% des Vorkriegsstandes gesunken) mußte *Lenin* zur Idee der kommunistischen Kaderpartei zurückkehren, die als Machtelite diktatorisch herrscht. An das ursprüngliche Rätesystem erinnern nur noch die Bezeichnungen.

Hans Heinrich Rupp

Zweikammersystem und Bundesverfassungsgericht

Bemerkungen zu einem verfassungspolitischen Reformvorschlag F. A. von Hayeks

I.

Das heute weithin geäußerte Unbehagen an der Praxis der parteienstaatlichen Demokratie der Bundesrepublik hat viele Ursachen.

Ein Teil dieses Unbehagens ist sicherlich künstlich gezüchtet und nicht zuletzt Ergebnis der Strategie, die politische Wirklichkeit auf einen utopischen Hintergrund zu projizieren, die dabei in Erscheinung tretenden Diskrepanzen zwischen Utopie und politischer Wirklichkeit dem «System» anzulasten und solchermaßen einer «Systemüberwindung» psychologisch den Weg zu bereiten.

Daß diese Methode in der Bundesrepublik auf so erstaunlich fruchtbaren Boden fiel – der Studentenaufstand Ende der 60er Jahre legt dafür eindrucksvoll Zeugnis ab – und noch immer fällt, ist ein Problem für sich, das hier nicht zu erörtern ist. Hier geht es um jenes Unbehagen, das tatsächlich institutionelle Mängel und Schwächen des politischen Systems der Bundesrepublik im Auge hat, also um jene «Staatsverdrossenheit», die nicht eingeredet, sondern echt ist.

Als einer dieser Mängel werden immer wieder und von verschiedener Seite die ständig schneller rotierende parlamentarische Gesetzgebungsmaschinerie, die zunehmende Perfektionierungssucht des Gesetzgebers, das Überhandnehmen von Maßnahmegesetzen, die oft schon geändert werden müssen, bevor sie in Kraft treten, die Reglementierungsdichte und die Regelungsintensität des gesetzgeberischen Zugriffs (beispielsweise im Schulrecht) beklagt und es wird darauf hingewiesen, daß der steigenden parlamentarischen Hektik sinkende Rechtsetzungsqualität, abnehmender Sachverstand bei zunehmendem politischem Einfluß von Regierung und Ministerialbürokratie korrespondiere und das Parlament zeitlich und sachlich nicht mehr in der Lage sei, seinen eigentlichen verfassungsmäßigen Aufgaben, nämlich Festsetzung der für alle geltenden Gesetze und Kontrolle der Regierung, zu genügen.

Bei solchen und ähnlichen Einwänden muß man freilich differenzieren: Sofern sie sich gegen die parlamentarische Rechtssetzungsprärogative als solche, also gegen einen allgemeinen «Gesetzesvorbehalt» richten, sind sie unbegründet. Denn nicht zuletzt unter dem Druck des Bundesverfassungsgerichts und der Verwaltungsgerichte ist das Parlament verfassungsrechtlich gehalten, Exekutive und Judikative vollzugsfähige Rechtsmaßstäbe an die Hand zu geben und regelungsbedürftige Probleme nicht vor sich heroder von sich wegzuschieben. Relikte einer für das deutsche Staatsdenken des vorigen

Jahrhunderts charakteristischen Rechtssetzungshoheit der Krone bestehen nicht mehr. Häufig richtet sich allerdings der Einwand gesetzgeberischer Reglementierungssucht gerade gegen dieses Grundprinzip und nicht gegen legislatorische Mängel und Auswüchse. Diese müssen dann nur dafür herhalten, um die parlamentarische Rechtssetzung als solche zu diskreditieren und an ihre Stelle wieder jene vorkonstitutionelle Rechtssetzungsgewalt der Exekutive treten zu lassen, die nach aller Erfahrung zu noch viel perfektionistischerer Reglementierung neigt. Die beispielsweise von den Schulverwaltungen angestimmte Klage über die gesetzliche «Verrechtlichung» des Schulwesens ist, aus solcher Sicht gesehen, von handfestem Eigeninteresse geprägt und ein Versuch zur Wiedererlangung ministerialeigener Reglementierungsgewalt. Ähnliches gilt für die Stimmen, die in die Kritik an der überschäumenden legislatorischen Springflut einstimmen, aber unerwähnt lassen, daß ein Teil dieser quantitativen Springflut qualitativ auf das Konto einer Rechtspolitik geht, die, von hektischem Reformeifer erfaßt, ohne Rücksicht auf Gediegenheit ständig Neues produziert – oft mehr zum Schaden als zum Vorteil des Rechtswesens und der Rechtssicherheit.

Was bleibt, ist dennoch ein beklagenswerter Befund: Ein überlasteter Bundestag, der unter Anweisung von Regierung und Ministerialbürokratie zum Gesetzgebungsautomaten zu werden droht, Abgeordnete, die nicht mehr die Zeit, Kraft und Muße finden, über das Heute hinauszublicken und sich der friedensstiftenden Funktion des für alle geltenden Gesetzes bewußt zu werden, Bürger auf der anderen Seite, denen das Gesetzesrecht fremd und ungewiß wird, die sich an die Unbeständigkeit und Unverläßlichkeit des Rechts gewöhnen wie an den Wandel der jeweils herrschenden politischen Richtung – all dies sind Symptome eines sehr ernst zu nehmenden Befundes, der dringend nach einer Therapie verlangt.

II.

An einer solchen Therapie fehlt es bislang gänzlich. Zwar hat schon *Ernst Forsthoff* frühzeitig auf die rechtsstaatliche Problematik der «Maßnahmegesetze» aufmerksam gemacht[1], doch hat die deutsche Staatsrechtslehre diese Frage alsbald wieder fallen lassen. Erst *Günter Dürig* hat 1973 auf der Mannheimer Tagung der Vereinigung der Deutschen Staatsrechtslehrer den Faden wieder aufgenommen und bemängelt, daß der Kampf gegen das Maßnahmegesetz zu schnell abgebrochen worden sei[2] und daß Protest dagegen erhoben werden müsse, das «Ad-hoc-Gesetz, das Punktgesetz, das Maßnahmegesetz» geradezu als den Gesetzestyp des Sozialstaates schlechthin zu kennzeichnen. Aus der Sicht der betroffenen Staatsbürger sähen die Dinge ganz anders aus, und das Verlangen nach Dauer und Verläßlichkeit der Gesetze sei ungebrochen. Dem Gesetz müsse wieder Würde und Qualität, Dauer und Beständigkeit gegeben werden. Wie allerdings diese Forderung angesichts einer verwalteten Welt und zunehmender Komplexität der Lebensverhältnisse rechtstechnisch erfüllt werden könnte, bleibt offen. Erwähnenswert in diesem Zusammenhang ist schließlich, daß auch die Beratungen der vom Deutschen Bundestag 1970 eingesetzten Enquête-Kommission Verfassungsreform in der in Betracht stehenden Frage nicht weitergeführt haben[3]. Zwar hat die Kommission nach eigenem

---

[1] Über Maßnahme-Gesetze, Gedächtnisschrift für *Walter Jellinek*, München 1955, S. 221; der Beitrag ist auch abgedruckt in: *Ernst Forsthoff*, Rechtsstaat im Wandel, Stuttgart 1964, S. 78.

[2] Veröffentlichungen der Vereinigung der Deutschen Staatsrechtslehrer Bd. 32 (1974) S. 247 ff.

[3] Schlußbericht der Enquête-Kommission Verfassungsreform vom 9.12.1976, BT-Drucks. 7/5924.

Zeugnis Möglichkeiten untersucht, wie das Parlament von einem Teil seiner Routinearbeit entlastet werden könne, um mehr Zeit für die Diskussion der politischen Grundsatzentscheidung zu erhalten, und wie es zu verhindern sei, daß es «seinen nach der Verfassung ihm gebührenden Platz im Steuerungssystem unseres Staatswesens allmählich an die Regierung verliere»[4], doch ist der Lösungsvorschlag der Kommission widersprüchlich und dürftig. Er konzentriert sich auf das konventionelle Regelungsschema, das Parlament im Wege einer Änderung des Art. 80 GG von seinen Rechtssetzungskompetenzen dadurch zu entlasten, daß dafür der Regierung ein verstärktes Verordnungsrecht übertragen wird. Wie auf diese Weise allerdings das Parlament gegenüber der Regierung gestärkt und «wieder zu einem echten Gegenpart der Regierung» gemacht werden soll, ist nicht recht ersichtlich. Aber davon abgesehen kann es kaum als Reform bewertet werden, wenn man des Rätsels Lösung ausschließlich aus der Sicht einer Kompetenzkürzung des Parlaments sieht und zu der traditionellen Stärkung der ohnedies übermächtigen Exekutive auf Kosten des Parlaments Zuflucht nimmt. Eine solchermaßen angestrebte Entlastung des Parlaments ist zu teuer erkauft, im übrigen auch wohl nur von geringem Nutzen. Denn die Wiedereinführung eines selbständigen, d. h. gesetzesvertretenden und damit wirklich parlamentsentlastenden Verordnungsrechts der Regierung ließe sich nicht nur kaum vom Gesetzgebungsrecht des Parlaments abgrenzen, sondern verstieße gegen Fundamentalnormen des grundgesetzlichen Konzepts und könnte daher selbst durch förmliche Verfassungsänderung nicht bewirkt werden (Art. 79 Abs. 3 in Verbindung mit Art. 20 Abs. 2 GG). Die Enquête-Kommission hat daher nicht von ungefähr eine solche konkurrierende Gesetzgebung der Regierung im Ergebnis verworfen. Die Vorschläge der Enquête-Kommission bleiben daher im Bereich bloßer Randkorrekturen, treffen aber nicht das eigentliche Problem.

III.

Ganz andere Qualität besitzt ein Vorschlag, den *F. A. von Hayek* schon 1963 gemacht und immer wieder aufgegriffen hat[5]. Dieser Vorschlag geht das Problem frontal an, meidet die ausgetretenen Pfade konventioneller Lösungsmuster und hat überdies den Vorteil, in der Linie der grundgesetzlichen Basiskonzeption zu liegen. Er hat allerdings den Nachteil, den durch ängstlichen Blick auf das politisch «Machbare» eingeengten Bereich verfassungspolitischen und verfassungsrechtlichen Denkens mutig zu verlassen, nach Neuem zu suchen und deshalb kaum auf Verständnis der in jenem engen Denken befangenen Zeitgenossen zu stoßen. Soweit ersichtlich, hat sich denn auch die deutsche Staatsrechtslehre mit dem Vorschlag *F. A. von Hayeks* noch nicht auseinandergesetzt. *Von Hayeks* Lösungskonzept ist von bestechender Einfachheit: Es teilt die bisherige Legislative sachlich und organisatorisch sozusagen in zwei Hälften, also in ein Zweikammersystem auf, und zwar dergestalt, daß der einen Kammer die auf Dauer und Beständigkeit angelegten allgemeinen Rechtsregeln, der zweiten Kammer dagegen die laufenden legislatorischen und sonstigen parlamentarischen Tagesgeschäfte anvertraut werden sollen. *Von Hayek* ist der Auffassung, daß rechtsstaatliches government under the law nur erreicht werden könne, wenn die zweite Kammer, die die laufenden Geschäfte führt und die

---

[4] Kommissionsbericht S. 89.
[5] Recht, Gesetz und Wirtschaftsfreiheit, abgedruckt in *F. A. von Hayek*, Freiburger Studien, Tübingen 1969, S. 47.

Regierung kontrolliert, unter Regeln steht, über die sie nicht selbst verfügt, sondern die von einer anderen demokratischen Körperschaft bestimmt werden, «die gewissermaßen die langfristigen Prinzipien festlegt». Zum Funktionieren dieses Systems wäre es also notwendig, daß die von der ersten Kammer erlassene Rechtssetzung Bindungswirkung gegenüber der Gesetzgebung der zweiten Kammer erhielte, was freilich keineswegs mit der gängigen Derogationsautomatik der Nichtigkeit verbunden zu sein brauchte. Andererseits müßte Vorsorge getroffen werden, daß sich die erste Kammer nicht auf Kosten der zweiten Kammer ausbreitet. *Von Hayek* sieht dieses Problem und erkennt, daß die Einhaltung der Zuständigkeitsabgrenzung «ein starkes Verfassungsgericht» voraussetze, «das jede der beiden Körperschaften innerhalb der von der Verfassung gezogenen Grenzen hielte».

Was die Organisation und Zusammensetzung der beiden Kammern betrifft, so geht *von Hayek* davon aus, daß die parlamentarische Kompetenzfülle als solche erhalten bleiben solle, aber nichts im Wege stehe, diese Aufgaben unter zwei Vertretungskörperschaften aufzuteilen, die – entsprechend der Unterschiedlichkeit ihrer Aufgaben – auch nach verschiedenen Prinzipien demokratisch gewählt und entsprechend zusammengesetzt sein sollten. Die erste Kammer – so schlägt *von Hayek* vor – müßte eine stabile, auf lange Sicht arbeitende Körperschaft sein, deren Mitglieder nur schrittweise zu ersetzen und nach einer langen Amtsperiode nicht wiederwählbar wären. So lasse sich beispielsweise daran denken, daß jedes Jahr die jeweils Vierzigjährigen aus ihrer Mitte Vertreter auf fünfzehn Jahre entsendeten und jedes Jahr ein Fünfzehntel der ersten Körperschaft ersetzt werde.

Die zweite Kammer – «Regierungsversammlung» – dagegen, die mit wesentlich kurzfristigeren Aufgaben betraut sei, könne die Form der heutigen Parlamente behalten, wobei – wie dies praktisch bereits heute weitgehend der Fall sei – die Regierung auch formell als Ausschuß dieser Versammlung bzw. ihrer Majorität fungiere. Auf solche Weise entstünde zugleich eine neue und wirksame Form der Gewaltenteilung.

Ohne auf Einzelheiten der *Hayekschen* Reformskizze einzugehen, läßt sich aus verfassungsrechtlicher Sicht dazu folgendes sagen:
1. Die Zuteilung von Gesetzgebungsbefugnissen an zwei Kammern ist bekanntlich nicht ungewöhnlich. Ungewöhnlich ist nur die Idee einer vertikalen kompetenzrechtlichen Aufteilung dieser Aufgaben nach dem Kriterium der Richtlinien- und Geschäftsführungsfunktion. Durchforscht man indessen das geltende Recht, so stellt sich heraus, daß diese Merkmale als kompetenzabgrenzende Prinzipien absolut kein Novum sind. Das Kommunalrecht – Abgrenzung der Befugnisse des Bürgermeisters von denen des Rats – bietet dafür hinreichende Beispiele. Aber auch auf der Ebene der förmlichen Gesetzgebung ist dem geltenden Recht eine Kompetenzabgrenzung zwischen verschiedenen gesetzgebenden Körperschaften nach dem vergleichbaren Kriterium etwa der «Rahmengesetzgebung» oder der «Grundsatzgesetzgebung» nicht unbekannt (vgl. Art. 75 GG); solche Kriterien gelten allerdings nur für das Verhältnis der Gesetzgebungskompetenzen des Bundestags zu denjenigen der Landesparlamente. Immerhin belegt dieser Vergleich, daß solche Kriterien als legislative Kompetenzabgrenzungen durchaus bekannt und gebräuchlich sind. Auf dieser Linie liegt es auch, wenn die Enquête-Kommission Verfassungsreform eine zusätzliche Gesetzgebungskategorie dieser Art vorschlägt, nämlich die sog. «Richtliniengesetzgebung», die ebenfalls im Verhältnis von Bundes- und Landesgesetzgebung eine neue Rechtssetzungsverteilung schaffen soll[6]. Bemerkenswert hieran ist noch ein weiterer Aspekt: Auch die Kommission sieht, daß offen gefaßte gesetzgeberische

---

[6] Vgl. Schlußbericht, a. a. O., S. 127.

Kompetenzabgrenzungen, sollen sie nicht von einer Seite überspielt werden, einer starken verfassungsgerichtlichen Kontrolle bedürfen. Deshalb schlägt die Kommission gerade in dieser Hinsicht eine Verschärfung der verfassungsgerichtlichen Überprüfung vor[7] – auch in dieser Hinsicht eine beachtenswerte Parallele zu der Gedankenführung *von Hayeks*.

2. Sucht man nach Parallelen, so finden sich auch für den von *von Hayek* angenommenen Vorrang der Richtliniengesetzgebung (der ersten Kammer) vor der Alltagsgesetzgebung (der zweiten Kammer) vergleichbare Vorbilder. Es zeigt sich nämlich immer wieder, daß die Verfassungspraxis mit dem undifferenzierten Rangunterschied von Verfassungsgesetz einerseits und «einfachem» Gesetz andererseits nicht auskommt, sich vielmehr selbst dort, wo «einfache» Gesetze durch ein und dasselbe Gesetzgebungsorgan erlassen werden, aus qualitativen Unterschieden normative Rangunterschiede ergeben. Paradigmatisch für dieses noch wenig erörterte Phänomen[8] ist das sog. Haushaltsgrundsätzegesetz vom 19.8.1969[9], in dessen § 1 der Bundestag nicht nur die Länderparlamente, sondern seine eigene Gesetzgebung an die von ihm festgelegten Grundsätze des Haushaltsrechts bindet. Auch hier zeigt sich: Ein Rangunterschied innerhalb der sog. einfachen Gesetzgebung ist keineswegs so ungewöhnlich, wie dies auf den ersten Blick scheinen könnte. Wollen auf Dauer angelegte Programm-, Plan- oder Richtliniengesetze ihre Funktion erfüllen, so lassen sie sich eben nicht durch jedes Vollzugsgesetz, nur weil es auch Gesetzesqualität besitzt, nach der Derogationsregel der lex posterior wieder aus den Angeln heben. Ähnlich ist das Verhältnis von Rechtsnormen, welche das Rechtssetzungs*verfahren* regeln, zu solchen Rechtsnormen, die in diesem Rechtssetzungsverfahren ergehen. Auch hier haben zwar beide Normenkategorien Rechtssetzungsqualität und sind in der Regel sogar durch ein und dasselbe Organ erlassen worden; aber auch hier verlöre das Verfahrensgesetz seinen Sinn, wenn der ergehende Rechtssetzungsakt das Verfahren zur Entstehung seiner selbst beliebig gestalten könnte. Auch Parallelen für Rangunterschiede innerhalb des «einfachen Gesetzesrechts» liegen daher genügend vor.

3. Das *Hayeksche* Reformmodell würde schließlich auch der Reaktivierung der rechtsstaatlichen Gewaltenteilung zugute kommen.

Daß das *Montesquieusche* Gewaltenteilungsschema unter den realen Bedingungen der parteienstaatlichen Demokratie der Gegenwart weithin seine machtbegrenzende Funktion eingebüßt hat und daß von einer wirksamen Kontrolle der Regierung durch das Parlament nicht mehr die Rede sein kann, wenn die Regierungsmitglieder zugleich derselben politischen Partei oder denselben politischen Parteien, welche auch die maßgebliche Mehrheit im Parlament bilden, nicht nur angehören, sondern auch dort Führungsämter besitzen, wird kaum mehr bestritten. Aber alle bisherigen Vorschläge, etwa mit dem bundesstaatlichen System der föderalen Machtbalance eine neue Art funktionsfähiger Gewaltenteilung auszubauen oder mit einer Institutionalisierung und rechtlichen Absicherung des Status der parlamentarischen Opposition die Möglichkeiten politischer Kontrolle zu reaktivieren und zu beleben, können als gescheitert gelten: Das bundesstaatliche System der Bundesrepublik tendiert je länger, desto eindeutiger zum zentralstaatlichen Unitarismus, und die parteipolitische und ideologische Polarisierung macht auch vor den Landesgrenzen nicht halt. Die rechtliche Absicherung der Regierungskontrolle

---

7 Schlußbericht S. 130.
8 Vgl. dazu *Breuer*, Selbstbindung des Gesetzgebers durch Programm- und Plangesetze? Deutsches Verwaltungsblatt 1970, S. 101; *Püttner*, Unterschiedlicher Rang der Gesetze? Die öffentliche Verwaltung 1970, S. 322; *Rupp*, Die Grundrechte und das Europäische Gemeinschaftsrecht, Neue Juristische Wochenschrift 1970, S. 353 (358 N. 34).
9 BGBl III 63–14.

durch die Opposition aber würde der jeweiligen Regierungsmehrheit gerade jene Prämie auf den legalen Machtbesitz abverlangen, von der sie zehrt, also einem Selbstverzicht gleichkommen. Der *Hayeksche* Vorschlag hat den Vorteil, daß er auch hier ausgetretene Pfade meidet, die nun einmal in der politischen Praxis bestehende Einheit von parlamentarischer Mehrheit und Regierung seinem Lösungsmuster zugrunde legt und an ganz anderer Stelle die Etablierung politischer Balance und Kontrolle versucht, und zwar in einer originellen Weise, die selbst der zunehmenden parteipolitischen Totalpolarisierung Widerstand böte: Im Gegensatz zu der kürzeren Amtszeit der Mitglieder der «Regierungsversammlung» schlägt *von Hayek* für die Mitglieder der Richtlinienkörperschaft eine langfristige Amtszeit von beispielsweise 15 Jahren vor, also eine Amtszeit, welche die kurzlebigen parteipolitischen Konstellationen überdauerte und in Perioden mit ganz anderen politischen Mehrheitsverhältnissen hineinragte. Die Tendenz eines dadurch erreichbaren Balanceeffekts würde sich verstärken, wenn – wie dies *von Hayek* vorschlägt – jedes Jahr immer nur ein bestimmter Bruchteil der Abgeordneten gewählt würde und dies nicht von allen Bürgern, sondern nur jeweils von und aus dem Kreis derjenigen Bürger, die ein bestimmtes Lebensalter erreicht haben, das eine gewisse politische Erfahrung, Reife und Verläßlichkeit erwarten läßt. Damit würde nicht nur die Grundsatz- und Richtliniengesetzgebung von modischen Sprüngen, kurzlebigen Wahlgeschenken und hektischem Wechselfieber verschont, sondern zwischen den beiden Kammern in dreifacher Weise ein Verhältnis politischer Distanz, Unabhängigkeit und Eigenständigkeit erzeugt, das der Gewaltenteilung nur zugute käme.

Doch wie immer man über diesen Lösungsvorschlag denken mag: Die Möglichkeiten seiner realen Umsetzung in politische Wirklichkeit sind unter den gegenwärtigen politischen Verhältnissen der Bundesrepublik minimal. Aber gerade dieser Umstand sollte die Wissenschaft vom Staat veranlassen, über den *Hayekschen* Vorschlag ernsthaft nachzudenken, ihn in die öffentliche Diskussion zu bringen und mit ihm auf die politische Praxis Einfluß zu nehmen. Bestechende wissenschaftliche Ideen haben sich noch immer dadurch ausgezeichnet, daß sie für das zeitgenössische Denken ungewohnt und fremd waren.

IV.

Daß der Vorschlag *von Hayeks* auf der richtigen Linie liegt und Mängel des derzeitigen politischen Systems der Bundesrepublik trifft, die nach einer Korrektur verlangen, wird indirekt durch Reaktionen und Kompensationen bestätigt, die sich – bislang als solche noch wenig gewürdigt – im System der politischen Herrschaftsorganisation der Bundesrepublik abspielen. Nach allem Anschein wächst dem *Bundesverfassungsgericht* im Sinne jener inneren Folgerichtigkeit des *Hayekschen* Entwurfs in immer stärkerem Maße die Rolle einer zweiten Kammer zu, also eine Ersatzfunktion, die nach einer Verortung verlangt, sie aber bisher noch nicht gefunden hat. Beleg für diesen stillschweigenden Wandel im Gefüge der grundgesetzlichen Ordnung könnte die sich gerade in letzter Zeit häufende Kritik an der Rechtsprechung des Bundesverfassungsgerichts sein, die in dem Vorwurf gipfelt, das Bundesverfassungsgericht schwinge sich zum Gesetzgeber des Gesetzgebers auf, verstehe sich als «Dritte Kammer» und überschreite die der Rechtsprechung gegenüber der Politik gesetzten Grenzen[10]. Diese Kritik gehört heute fast schon

---

[10] Vgl. dazu beispielsweise *Hoffmann-Riem*, in: *Friedrich Kübler* (Hrsg.), Medienwirkung und Medienverantwortung, Baden-Baden 1975, S. 20 ff (41 ff); *Menger*, Verwaltungsarchiv 1976, S.

zum guten Ton; an ihr beteiligen sich nicht nur die Gewerkschaften, sondern auch die politische Publizistik, maßgebende Politiker und einige Richter des Bundesverfassungsgerichts selbst[11]. Jüngst hat sich auch der Bundeskanzler an dieser öffentlichen Kritik beteiligt[12]. Alle diese Indikatoren eines Verfassungswandels sind freilich mit Vorsicht zu genießen: Die Kritik entspringt zum großen Teil der Verärgerung darüber, daß es das Verfassungsgericht – entsprechend seinem grundgesetzlichen Auftrag – wagt, sich über Gesetzgebungsbeschlüsse der jeweiligen parlamentarischen Mehrheit hinwegzusetzen und sie durch das eigene Dictum zu ersetzen. Wiederholt wurde deshalb die demokratische Legitimation solcher Verfassungsrechtsprechung massiv in Zweifel gezogen und die sorgenvolle Frage: «Quo vadis Bundesverfassungsgericht» (*Delbrück*) gestellt. Solche Reaktionen sind indessen an sich nichts Ungewöhnliches und haben die Rechtsprechung des Bundesverfassungsgerichts von Anfang an begleitet. Gesetze werden immer von der Mehrheit gemacht, und deshalb pflegt die Aufhebung eines Gesetzes immer von den Regierungsparteien kritisiert zu werden. Auch der Widerstand des supreme court gegen den New Deal des amerikanischen Präsidenten *Roosevelt* hatte bekanntlich massive Kritik ausgelöst und zu dem berühmt-berüchtigten «court packing»-Plan geführt, also zum Versuch einer personalpolitischen Lösung der Konflikte. Schließlich ist auch der häufig erhobenen Klage, neuerdings würden politische Probleme nicht mehr politisch, sondern vom Bundesverfassungsgericht entschieden, weil jedermann, sage ihm eine politische Entscheidung nicht zu, sein Glück beim Bundesverfassungsgericht versuche, mit Skepsis zu begegnen. Schon 1835 hatte *Alexis de Tocqueville* in seiner Analyse der Demokratie in Amerika beobachtet, daß es in den Vereinigten Staaten kaum eine politische Frage gebe, die nicht früher oder später zu einer gerichtlichen Frage werde, und kein politisches Ereignis vorkomme, in dem man nicht die Autorität des Richters anrufe[13]. Diese Tendenz wird sich in der Bundesrepublik in dem Maße verstärken, in welchem die politische Polarisierung zunimmt und damit die Möglichkeit politischer Konsense oder wenigstens Kompromisse schwindet und eine Blockierung des politischen Entscheidungsprozesses eintritt. All dies ist daher eher eine normale Begleiterscheinung und Zeugnis einer wirksamen Verfassungsgerichtsbarkeit denn ein Beleg für eine bedenkliche Entartung dieser Institution und einen tiefgreifenden Strukturwandel im Gefüge der grundgesetzlichen Ordnung[14].

Gleichwohl läßt sich nicht bestreiten, daß das Bundesverfassungsgericht seine Kompetenzen extensiv handhabt und sich nicht nur als Rechtsschutzorgan, sondern als «Hüter der Verfassung» in einer Weise versteht, die den Bereich rein kassatorischer Gesetzeskontrolle und fallbezogener Selbstbeschränkung weit verläßt. Häufig hat man den Eindruck, daß das Bundesverfassungsgericht einen ihm vorgelegten Anlaßfall nur benutzt, um sich grundsätzlich zu allgemeinen Verfassungsproblemen zu äußern und den Gesetzgeber zu einem ganz bestimmten legislatorischen Programm innerhalb einer bestimmten Zeitspanne zu verpflichten. Damit Hand in Hand geht ein extensives Selbstverständnis des Gerichts von der Bindungswirkung der eigenen Entscheidungen, obiter dicta und Ausle-

---

315; *Delbrück*, in: FS Menzel, Berlin 1976, S. 83 ff; *Grimm*, Juristenzeitung 1976, S. 703; *v. Mutius*, Verwaltungsarchiv 1976, S. 403; *J. Ipsen*, Zeitschrift für Rechtspolitik 1978, S. 153 ff; *Zuck*, Zeitschrift für Rechtspolitik 1978, S. 189; *Vogel*, Die öffentliche Verwaltung 1978, S. 665 mit weiteren Nachweisen.

[11] Vgl. die Nachweise bei *Vogel*, a. a. O., Fußnoten 9 bis 12.

[12] Vgl. den Bericht in der FAZ vom 3.10.1978, S. 1.

[13] *Alexis de Tocqueville*, Über die Demokratie in Amerika, Bd. I, deutsche Ausgabe Stuttgart 1962, S. 111, 311.

[14] Vgl. dazu *Rupp*, Die öffentliche Verwaltung 1976, S. 691.

gungsergebnisse, das den gesetzgeberischen Gestaltungsspielraum zwangsläufig immer stärker einengt und erhebliche Probleme birgt, weil sich das Bundesverfassungsgericht nur selbst für befugt hält, von seiner eigenen Rechtsprechung und den von ihr für tragend erklärten Rechtsgrundsätzen abzuweichen. All diese Symptome können hier nicht im einzelnen belegt werden, sie sind jedem Kenner der Rechtsprechung des Bundesverfassungsgerichts geläufig. Was im vorliegenden Zusammenhang interessiert, ist die Erklärung dieser Symptome als eigenartige Kompensation, mit welcher die Verfassungswirklichkeit offenbar mit einer gewissen Zwangsläufigkeit auf institutionelle Schwächen des politischen Systems antwortet und die das Verfassungsgericht in die Ersatzrolle eines Grundsatzgesetzgebers hat geraten lassen. Diese Deutung würde die diagnostische und therapeutische Richtigkeit des *Hayekschen* Lösungsentwurfs eindrucksvoll belegen und auch eine Erklärung dafür geben, warum gerade dem Bundesverfassungsgericht dieses Rolle zuwuchs und warum seine Rechtsprechung bestimmte Eigentümlichkeiten aufweist. Auch dabei würden nämlich interessante Parallelen zum *Hayekschen* Lösungsentwurf sichtbar: Die Amtszeit der Richter des Bundesverfassungsgerichts dauert 12 Jahre, ist also auf Beständigkeit und Unabhängigkeit vom Rhythmus parlamentarischer Mehrheitsverhältnisse angelegt. Die Richter müssen das 40. Lebensjahr überschritten haben; sie dürfen weder dem Bundestag, dem Bundesrat, der Bundesregierung noch den entsprechenden Organen eines Landes angehören. Der Modus ihrer Wahl ist kompliziert und auf Vermeidung der unmittelbaren Widerspiegelung des parteipolitischen Kräftefeldes angelegt. Ihr richterlicher Status und der Status des Gerichts als selbständiges Verfassungsorgan verbürgt rechtliche Unabhängigkeit, und die Vorschrift, daß ein Teil der Richter des Bundesverfassungsgerichts aus der Richterschaft der obersten Gerichtshöfe des Bundes gewählt werden muß, kann nur im Sinne einer Verstärkung dieser Tendenz gedeutet werden. In diesem Zusammenhang ist auch zu erwähnen, daß die Richter je zur Hälfte vom Bundestag und vom Bundesrat gewählt werden, also von Verfassungsorganen, in welchen – wie die Verfassungswirklichkeit beweist – durchaus verschiedene parteipolitische Mehrheitsverhältnisse herrschen können.

Bemerkenswert im Sinne einer Parallele zum Vorschlag *von Hayeks* ist ferner, daß die Amtszeit der Bundesverfassungsrichter nicht zu einem einheitlichen Zeitpunkt, sondern individuell verschieden abläuft, so daß innerhalb einer politischen Wahlperiode immer nur einige wenige Richter nachzuwählen sind, so daß die Kontinuität des Spruchkörpers und der Spruchpraxis erhalten und das Bundesverfassungsgericht vom Wechsel der parlamentarischen Mehrheitsverhältnisse weitgehend verschont bleibt.

Schließlich hat das Bundesverfassungsgericht im Sinne der ihm zugefallenen gesetzgeberischen Ersatzfunktion – wie schon erwähnt – Sorge dafür getragen, daß seine Entscheidungen, obiter dicta und Interpretationsergebnisse nicht nur den Rang formeller Gesetze besitzen, sondern praktisch den Parlamentsgesetzen vorgehen. Das Bundesverfassungsgericht hat dies erreicht mit Hilfe einer extensiven Auslegung jener Vorschrift, nach der die Entscheidungen des Bundesverfassungsgerichts alle Verfassungsorgane, Gerichte und Behörden des Bundes und der Länder binden. Auf diese Weise ist das eingetreten, was *von Hayek* der ersten Kammer vorbehalten wissen wollte, nämlich die Festlegung allgemeiner Rechtsregeln, unter denen auch die Regierungsversammlung stehe. Das Bundesverfassungsgericht hat im Verlaufe seiner Rechtsprechung eine Fülle solcher Rechtsregeln und Rechtsgrundsätze geschaffen und – so ließe sich überspitzt sagen – das Legislativorgan der *Hayekschen* ersten Kammer in gewisser Weise ersetzt. Vielleicht ist es auch dieser Umstand, der die eigenartige Schwäche der bundesverfassungsgerichtlichen Rechtsprechung gegenüber jenem grundgesetzlichen Fundamentalsatz erklärlich macht, der das Postulat der Allgemeingeltung grundrechtsbeschränkender Gesetze enthält und das Einzelfallgesetz verbietet. *Von Hayek* sieht mit Recht in dieser Verfassungsnorm des Art. 19 Abs. 1 Satz 1 GG einen Grundpfeiler des Rechtsstaates, und er rügt mit ebensolchem Recht das Leerlaufen dieser Verfassungsnorm bis zur Bedeutungslosigkeit. Das ist in der Tat der Fall und das Bundesverfassungsgericht war an dieser Entwicklung nicht unbeteiligt[15] und hat das Gebot der Allgemeingeltung der Gesetze auf ein nichtssagendes und bereits im Gleichheitssatz des Art. 3 GG enthaltenes Willkürverbot reduziert, mit der Folge, daß der eigentliche Gehalt jener Fundamentalnorm auf Null geschrumpft ist, das Parlament sich immer tiefer in der Maßnahme- und Ad-hoc-Gesetzgebung verliert und auf das Bundesverfassungsgericht umso intensiver jene legislatorische Ersatzkompetenz der Grundsatzbestimmung zukommt. Vielleicht war es die unbewußte Vorstellung des Bundesverfassungsgerichts, sich selbst als Hort und Hüter der elementaren Rechtsgrundsätze zu fühlen, die mitursächlich dafür war, daß es der Maßnahmegesetzgebung des Parlaments freien Lauf lassen zu können glaubte.

Doch wie immer man darüber denken mag: Offenbar waren auch bei dieser Entwicklung Zwangsläufigkeiten am Werk, die aus inneren, im politischen System selbst angelegten Schwächen resultieren. Insoweit ist das allgemeine Unbehagen an der Rechtsprechung des Bundesverfassungsgerichts letztlich an die falsche Adresse gerichtet: Das Bundesverfassungsgericht folgt nolens volens anscheinend nur einer im politischen System der Bundesrepublik angelegten Zwangsläufigkeit und ersetzt gewissermaßen eine legislatorische Funktion, die unter den heutigen Bedingungen heimatlos geworden ist, aber auf die die rechtsstaatliche Demokratie nicht verzichten kann. In Wahrheit richtet sich daher der Vorwurf, das Bundesverfassungsgericht schwinge sich zum Gesetzgeber des Gesetzgebers auf, gegen diejenigen, die diesen Vorwurf erheben, und gegen die Unfähigkeit der politischen Kräfte und der Verfassungslehre, jener heimatlos gewordenen Funktion der Grundsatzgesetzgebung denjenigen Stellenwert und Ort im Verfassungs- und Organisationsgefüge der Bundesrepublik zu verschaffen, der ihr gebührt. Die stillschweigende, unbewußte und aus vordergründiger Perspektive gescholtene Übernahme dieser Funktion durch das Rechtsprechungsorgan Bundesverfassungsgericht ist aus vielerlei Gründen mehr als problematisch. Der *Hayeksche* Vorschlag geht in die richtige Richtung. Er ist es wert, ernsthaft erörtert zu werden[16].

Summary

A Two-Chamber-System and the Federal Constitutional Court – Notes on a Proposition of F. A. von Hayek for a Constitutional Reform

The rapidly increasing mass of laws ultimately causes such discomfort, because in the contemporary distributive and welfare state the amount of universal rules with long-term validity is losing ground to the detriment of legal security and legal validity. This development is accompanied by a loss of authority on the part of the parliamentary legislature and a weakening of the balance of powers intended by the constitution. The ordinary at-

---

[15] Vgl. dazu *Rupp*, Art. 3 als Maßstab verfassungsgerichtlicher Gesetzeskontrolle, in: *Christian Starck* (Hrsg.), Bundesverfassungsgericht und Grundgesetz, Tübingen 1976, Bd. II, S. 364 (368 ff).

[16] Verfasser verdankt die Anregung zur Befassung mit diesem Thema *Erich Hoppmann* und vielen mit ihm geführten Diskussionen. Ihm sei daher auch an dieser Stelle für seinen Rat und Beistand herzlich gedankt.

tempts and propositions to cure these structural deficiencies of the based on political parties democracy have proved insufficient or inadequate. It is for this reason that *von Hayeks* proposition to modify organization and functions of the legislature deserves special interest. *Von Hayek* suggests that, according to the criterion of universal rules with long-term validity on the one hand and parliamentary routine work on the other, the legislative power should be divided into two chambers – each especially deviced for its particular task. This proposition is supported by the fact that, for the lack of such a two-chamber-system, the role of legislator for universal rules seems inevitably to be falling to the Federal Constitutional Court. In view of this, the growing criticism of the jurisdiction of the Federal Constitutional Court appears superficial and addressed to the wrong party. It fails to realize the true problem, i.e. that it is a compensation for fundamental institutional structural deficiencies.

III. Freiheit, Gleichheit und Staat

Charles K. Rowley

Collective Choice and Individual Liberty*

It is suggested in this paper that welfare economists, with few exceptions, have offered intellectual sustenance to the advance of government power in Western economies via an excessive emphasis upon a restricted and value-based analytical approach. It is further suggested that welfare economists, by identifying incorrectly the Paretian values which underpin their analysis with liberal ethics have failed to devise constitutional safeguards against the erosion even of minimal individual liberty in societies wherein individuals gain satisfaction from meddlesome behaviour. Finally, an alternative approach, based on a more general notion of liberty derived from classical liberalism is outlined which certainly would go far to restoring the lost balance between the individual and the state in all Western societies and which might even resolve the dilemma of the impossible Paretian liberal which has recently plagued the economic journals.

I. The Suspect Analytical Approach

The suspect analytical approach is that initiated by *Kenneth Arrow*[1] and subsequently refined and extended by a host of enthusiasts working in the field of collective choice. *Arrow's* seminal contribution was to establish the impossibility of devising a «desirable» constitution for the effecting of collective choices on the basis of diverse individual preferences. Undoubtedly, *Arrow's* initial intention was simply to determine whether certain axioms, well-established in the economic analysis of individual choice, might be applicable equally in situations where individual choices were translated into collective choices. As such, his contribution must be respected as a logical progression in scientific analysis. Unfortunately, as we shall outline later, both *Arrow* himself,[2] in subsequent work, and others who moved into the field that he had established, have given rise to false paradigms concerning the true nature of a collective choice and, as such, however unwittingly, have offered sustenance to bureaucratic socialism.

In Arrowian collective choice, each individual in society is assumed to possess a well-defined preference ordering over all social states. This ordering is an insufficient basis for collective choice in view of the diversity of individual preferences. Thus, individual preferences are «aggregated» in collective choice into what is termed a «welfare judgment» via a «constitution», which simply is a mechanism for selecting a socially preferred action from any profile of feasible alternatives. It was to the characteristics of such a «constitution» that *Arrow* directed attention. Following the well-established axioms governing

* References at the end of the article.

individual choice, *Arrow* suggested as desirable the socalled condition of collective rationality (which requires that collective choices should represent a complete ordering over an unbounded domain). Simply (and approximately) this condition is satisfied when (1) each collective choice is at least as socially preferred as itself (reflexivity), (2) for any three alternative choices, if a is preferred to b and b is preferred to c, then a is preferred to c (transitivity), (3) society is able to choose, on a basis either of preference or of indifference, between any two conceivable social states (connectedness) and (4) all conceivable social states are countenanced (unbounded domain).

Secondly, *Arrow* advanced as desirable for any constitution the Pareto condition, sometimes referred to as the condition of positive association of social and individual values. Simply (and approximately) this condition requires that if all individuals in society are indifferent between two social states then so is society and that if all individuals in society consider one social state to be at least as good as another whilst one individual strictly prefers the former to the latter state, then society prefers the former to the latter state.

Thirdly, *Arrow* suggested as desirable for any constitution the independence of irrelevant alternatives condition. Simply (and approximately) this condition requires that if the ordering of individual preferences over all social states does not change, then the consideration only of some smaller grouping of such states should not disturb the latters' ordering as reflected by the constitution for all social states. In essence, this rules out the taking account of individual intensities of preference which might lead to a changed collective ordering over the remaining social states if one or more social state were to disappear.

Fourthly, *Arrow* suggested as desirable for any constitution the condition of non-dictatorship and non-imposition. This condition clearly implies that no individual within or without society should be capable always of imposing his/her will in collective choice without reference to the preferences of other individual in society.

Arrow's General Possibility Theorem, which was proved in his initial contribution to collective choice theory, states that if the domain of collective choice contains at least three social states, given diversity in individual preferences over these social states, there does not exist any constitution capable of satisfying simultaneously each of the four desirable conditions outlined above. This result is perfectly general. The consequences for collective choice, therefore, would appear to be serious indeed for those who hold the conditions in question to be essential or even indeed only highly appealing.

Inevitably, *Arrow's* contribution awakened intellectual interest in collective choice theory and generated a great deal of academic activity initially in evaluating the proof and subsequently in exploring the degree to which any one or more condition must be relaxed or eliminated in order for the theorem to fail. Such is the nature of much economic theory and it is not the intention of this paper to criticise the methodology employed. Rather is criticism directed towards the false paradigms which now permeate the collective choice literature.

The first such paradigm is that of the dictatorial social decision-maker. Following criticisms by *Little* to the effect that *Arrow's* collective choice analysis contained totalitarian notions, *Arrow* endorsed the notion of the dictatorial social decision-maker in 1967 by a supportive reference to a concept put forward by *Bergson* (actually as a criticism rather than as a proposition):

«But some may be inclined nevertheless to a different conception, which allows still another interpretation of *Arrow's* theorem. According to this view, the problem is to counsel not citizens generally but public officials. Furthermore, the values to be taken as data are not those which would guide the official if he were a private citizen. The official is envisaged instead as more or less neutral ethically. His one aim in life is to implement the values of other citizens as given by some rule of collective decision-making.»[2]

Thus, collective choice is viewed as a two-stage procedure. The first stage – the choice of a constitution – requires the public official to inject his own ethical beliefs about the proper form of the constitution (presumably with some deference to *Arrow's* «desirable properties». The second stage requires the public official to choose between alternative attainable collective actions according to a social welfare (or choice) function that is derived from the constitution and from individual preference orderings. Thus, the social choice function reflects the value system of the public official, who has selected the constitution, and renders such an official a dictator, however benevolent may be his intentions.

The second false paradigm which permeates modern collective choice theory is that of the existence of omniscient and impartial government – the assumption that full information is available to society (the public official) concerning all individual preferences and that social welfare will be maximised by reference to a constitution strictly adhered to. Such a conception, central to Arrowian collective choice, is derived from a philosophic approach which *Hayek*[9] has designated as «constructivist rationalism», which was first fully developed by *Descartes* and which was consolidated by *Hobbes*[11] and *Rousseau*[14] into the concept of the «social contract». The essential approach of the constructivist rationalists is grounded on the false assumption that all relevant information is available to some one mind and that the mind in question is capable of constructing from such information from a position of ethical neutrality the particulars of a desirable social order. This fallacy has been designated by *Hayek* as «synoptic delusion».

For, in reality, the assumptions of constructivist rationalism are totally invalid. Societies typically are highly complex, individuals' preferences over attainable social states are not widely disseminated nor are they always stable. In such circumstances no public official, however capable, could be fully informed as to the precise configurations of all individual preferences at any point in time, let alone as to the manner in which such preferences might adjust through time. Planning frameworks for society, promulgated on the basis of this false paradigm, are dangerously misdirected and constitute an ongoing persistent threat to individual liberty.

II. The Impossible Paretian Liberal

The large majority of welfare economists in the Western world subscribe to a value-system which is designated as Paretian, after *Vilfredo Pareto*. Simply (and approximately) Paretian welfare economics requires that each individual is the best judge of his own welfare and that any change in society which improves the welfare of at least one individual without reducing the welfare of any other individual is a Pareto-preferred change. Since welfare comparisons between individuals are assumed to be impossible, any situation in which no change is possible without harming at least one individual (if necessary after attempted compensation) is deemed to be a Pareto optimum. Since any Pareto optimum is derived from an initial distribution of rights (more colloquially of income) there exists an infinity of Pareto optima, each reflecting a change in the initial income distribution in society.

For welfare economists reared in the apparently liberal tradition of classical and neo-classical economies, the Paretian approach, with its emphasis upon the primacy of individual preferences and the potential veto of changes harmful even to the few, has long proved highly attractive. Prior to 1970, the only real challenge to this hegemony of methodology was from those of the old and new left who rejected explicitly the so-called liberal tradition. Well over 90 per cent of the welfare economics literature was Paretian or neo-Paretian in nature.

It is less than surprising therefore that *Amartya Sen's* 1970 theorem[17] to the effect that it was not possible simultaneously to pursue Paretian and liberal ideologies should provoke a strong and continuing debate in the leading economic journals, in some quarters with the blood running in the gutters. Employing essentially the methodology of *Arrow* (for which he is later criticised), *Sen* centred attention upon a particular category of social states which arguably might be taken to be the concern only of the individual involved, e. g. should Jack sleep on his back or on his belly, should Sheila read or not read a particular saucy book. The existence of such «protected spheres» for all individuals in society was demanded in a weak condition which *Sen* now calls «weak libertarianism». In the 1970 article, *Sen* proved that the Pareto principle was incompatible even with minimal liberalism. His more general proof here is only illustrated by reference to a simple example.

Let us define the Pareto principle (Condition P) as implying that whenever all individuals prefer alternative a to alternative b, then collective choice also should order a as preferred to b. Let us define minimal liberalism (Condition L) as allowing each individual to be decisive in collective choice over at least one pair of social outcomes (i.e. if Individual 1 or Individual 2 prefers to sleep on his back or on his belly then collective choice should confirm this preference). Finally, let us hold with *Arrow* in requiring the constitution to be capable of ordering social states for all possible configurations of individual preferences. This is called the unrestricted domain condition (Condition U). The «impossibility of the Paretian liberal» theorem establishes a conflict between these conditions for collective choice (U, P and L). Let us illustrate by an example which is due to *Sen*.

Consider a society comprising two individuals, Man A, who is a prude and Man B, who is lascivious, facing social alternatives involving a book, «Lady Chatterley's Lover», which can be read either by Man A, or by Man B, or by neither. Suppose that Mr. A (the prude) ranks most highly the outcome that the book should not be read; but if it must be read he would read it himself rather than allow Mr. B his pleasure. Suppose that Mr. B (the lascivious) ranks most highly the outcome that Mr. A should read the book as a means of self-education, but would read it himself rather than that it should go to waste. Now, according to Condition P, the collective choice rule should register the outcome that Mr. A reads the book is socially preferred to Mr. B's reading the book. But, according to Condition L, Mr. A prefers not to read the book, whilst Mr. B prefers to read the book. The results are inconsistent and the collective choice rule fails.

In societies wherein individuals do not respect necessarily each other's personal choices, even within the «protected sphere» as defined by *Sen*, the dilemma posed must be disturbing for would-be Paretian liberals. For it turns out that a principle reflecting liberal values even in a very mild form cannot be combined with the Pareto principle, given an unrestricted domain for collective choice, even when such «desirable» Arrowian characteristics as «transitivity of social preferences» and «independence of irrelevant alternatives» (both required by *Arrow*) are ignored. It is interesting to note that *Sen* appears to endorse in his analysis the false paradigms of the dictatorial social decision-maker and of omniscient and impartial government.

III. Attempts to Escape from the Sen Dilemma

The many attempts to escape from *Sen's* theorem may be classified by reference to which condition (L, P or U) is redefined or over-ridden.

A number of economists have challenged *Sen's* concept of liberalism (Condition L) and by redefinition have resolved their dilemma. *Hillinger* and *Lapham,*[10] for example, define liberalism as «the desire not to coerce individuals to accept choices that they would not have made voluntarily». They claim that with this definition, liberalism is a special case of condition P when the actions of one individual do not impinge on the welfare of others, but that condition L is silent when such actions do impinge on others, leaving condition P decisive. In the view both of *Sen* and ourselves this definition of liberalism is an empty box. Other economists, like *Blau,*[4] advocate «modified liberalism» under which liberal privileges alternatively are withheld (a) for all if every individual's preferences are meddlesome, (b) for all if some individual's preferences are meddlesome and (c) for those whose preferences are meddlesome. In essence, this restricts the domain of collective choice to protect condition P. Such a solution is not «modified liberalism» but «illiberal».

Despite overwhelming support among economists for condition P, a few have examined the implications of constraining its applicability. *Farrell,*[7] for example, explores the possibility of «amending» an individual's preferences so that «he is deemed indifferent between any pair of states for which some other individual is to be decisive». But having explored the possibility, he rejects it on the ground that the Pareto relation on the «amended» preferences may be the exact opposite of the Pareto relation on the «true» preferences.

Sen,[18] however, almost alone, looks favourably upon the *Farrell* «amendment», noting that it eliminates the «pernicious consequences» of the mechanical use of condition P. He justifies the «amendment» however on what we consider to be unjustifiable grounds, namely that the «amendment» might be viewed as self-denial by those with meddlesome preferences, rather than as a process of an outside observer denying the Pareto preference. Surely, this is little more than a sleight of hand. For if the meddlesome preferences really were outweighed by libertarian notions the «amendment» would be unnecessary.

A small number of economists, most notably *Bernholz*[3] and *Nozick,*[13] have argued that the domain of collective choice might be bounded as a means of escaping from *Sen's* dilemma. *Nozick,* for example, proposes that liberal rights should be accorded priority and that such rights should set the constraints within which collective choices should be made. In such a framework, condition P would determine a partial ordering with which the social ordering must be consistent, whilst liberal rights would restrict the configurations of individual preferences for which the collective choice rule is well-defined. *Bernholz* argues that «an assumption of unrestricted domain is certainly not justified, since nobody would dream of applying one decision-rule like the rule of liberalism under all circumstances».

IV. Sugden's New Framework of Collective Choice

In an important paper, *Sugden*[19] takes issue with *Arrowian* collective choice theory, claiming that it permits value judgments only about the relative merits of different social outcomes. Since *Sugden* takes the view that a belief in the value of individual liberty is a belief about what are the proper means of social decision-making, he contends that liberal values simply cannot be expressed within the framework of *Arrow's* theory. For this reason, if *Sen's* analysis is to be rendered relevant to the debate on individual liberty, *Sugden* contends that the dictatorial social decision-maker must be dispensed with and that the constitution must be reinterpreted as a description of a procedure by which decisions are taken by individuals in society. Such procedures, *Sugden* designates as voting rules, and the constitution as a voting system.

In such circumstances, *Sugden* contends that *Sen's* impossibility theorem does not pose a dilemma. For there is no reason to require either that the voting system that a liberal recommends should be consistent with any constitution that a public official might devise or even that a liberal necessarily would wish to endorse the actual outcome of the voting rule that he himself selects. To illustrate the essential difference between *Sugden* and *Sen* let us refer to a simple example due to *Nozick* (1973) and to *Sen* (1976).

Consider a situation in which it is feasible for *Nozick* to live either in Massachusetts (x) or in New York (y). *Nozick* prefers x to y. To *Sen* (1970) minimal libertarianism would assign the pair [x, y] to *Nozick,* implying that the constitution should be such that if *Nozick* prefers x to y, so should society. *Sugden* rejects this outcome as illiberal, on the ground that it amounts to *Nozick's* being compelled (by the public official) to live in Massachussetts. To *Sen* (1976) a liberal might wish to include an additional choice, namely that *Nozick* should be allocated the right to choose between x and y, with the choice itself remaining within the domain of the collective choice.

Both views are rejected by *Sugden* who points out that since *Nozick* is not the social decision-maker, his choice between x and y cannot lie within the domain of collective choice. Rather, it is *Nozick's* being free to choose among a set of alternatives that lies within the domain of collective choice. A liberal would express a commitment to *Nozick's* freedom of choice as to where to live, even though he might not like the outcome of that choice.

The *Nozick* example is deceptively appealing in that there is no apparent conflict of freedoms for the liberal to resolve. Such was not the case with *Sen's* original example concerning «Lady Chatterley's Lover», the reading of which was available only to one of the two individuals, Mr. A and Mr. B. In such latter circumstances, both individuals cannot be accorded the «freedom to read or not to read». *Sugden* would have this dilemma resolved by reference to the property rights in the book, arguing that an individual's claim to «freedom to read» extends only to those books of which he is the rightful owner. The owner of the book would have the right to choose, therefore, that he should read the book, that the other individual might read the book if he wished so to do, or indeed that the book should remain unread (which indeed would be the outcome if Mr. A owned the book. But the choice itself is outside the domain of collective choice.

V. A Return to Reality

Sugden's claim that *Sen*-type dilemmas arise not from any defects in the concept of liberty but rather from the inability of collective choice theory to accommodate concepts central to liberal philosophy undoubtedly is correct. However, by concentrating attention exclusively upon *Sen*-type examples, *Sugden* failed to encompass important issues in collective choice which fall outside «the protected sphere». Typically, liberals are concerned less with such latter issues than with wider issues of collective choice which impinge on many or indeed on all individuals in society and in which individuals' freedoms genuinely are in conflict. It is to the handling of these wider issues, to the constitution required and to the attitudes which must be fostered if a liberal order is to be safeguarded that the remainder of this paper is devoted.

Liberalism in the classical (whiggist) sense here employed[12,8,9,15,16] is concerned with the maintenance and extension of individual freedoms (political, intellectual and economic), where freedom is defined as the absence of coercion of some individuals by others (negative freedom in the sense of Isaiah Berlin). Thus, *Sen's* definition of minimal libertarianism indeed does provide a minimal basis for classical liberalism, but is too limited to make an operational contribution to wider issues of collective choice. In an attempt to fill this gap and to render the debate on liberty and collective choice more relevant to real world conditions, it is essential to outline, albeit briefly, five notions which in our view are central to liberal thinking.

Firstly, there is the notion that the act of choice by individuals is itself ethically desirable. From *Mill*[12] onwards, liberals have emphasized the importance in individual development of nurturing a capacity to choose among alternatives and to assume responsibility for the choices made. Thus is it that the means (i.e. voting rules) are important to liberals and ends only to *Arrow* in collective choice.

Secondly, there is the notion that information on individual preferences is not and cannot be widely disseminated in society. *Hayek*[9] in particular has exposed the «synoptic delusion» inherent in the «constructivist rationalist» Arguably, constructivist rationalism has reached its economic zenith with Arrowian collective choice theory. For liberals, societies are highly complex, and no single mind can possibly be fully informed as to the configuration of individual preferences. Without a suitable voting system, therefore, the preferences of a few will be imposed upon society.

Thirdly, there is the notion that any order in society which encourages the establishment of realisable expectations is likely, other things being equal, to be more harmonious than one that does not. The rules of conduct and social organisations which develop, in an environment characterised by uncertainty, manifest themselves in a regularity of action and in a matching of expectations with outturns. This order, which for the most part is self-generating, is designated by *Hayek* as a «spontaneous order». Such an order, by its nature, encompasses circumstances beyond the comprehension of a single mind. Correspondingly, individuals are able to exercise less control over its details than would be the case with a continued order. Spontaneous orders may be illiberal. But liberal orders must to an extent be spontaneous.

Fourthly, there is the notion that any discretionary power accorded to representative government will be abused in illiberal fashion. In rejecting the notion of the social decision-maker in favour of representative government, liberals are acutely aware of the vote-pressures to which politicians react, and of the distortive influences of pressure groups and bureaucracies. Recent contributions to public choice theory are not favourable to the platonic notion of impartial government.

Fifthly, there is the notion that discretionary power within the market-place also will be abused. Liberals traditionally have been hostile to the development or maintenance of private power, whether in the product or in the factor markets. For such power constitutes a threat to individual freedom by offering the opportunity for certain individuals to impose their will arbitrarily upon others. Such power, in the liberal view, will be abused, if it exists.

VI. Towards a Liberal Constitution

It has been suggested already that liberals can live quite happily with impossibility theorems such as those by *Arrow* and by *Sen*. For liberals are concerned more with means than outcomes, with freedom to choose than with choices. The first step towards a liberal constitution therefore is the selection of an appropriate voting system. Equality before the law, which is an important safeguard of individual freedom, requires that individuals in society (unless excluded by reason of age or of lunacy) shall have the same share in making the law. Extended more generally to collective choice, majority rule in some form (in our view proportional representation) offers the closest approximation to this ideal. Certainly, liberals have fought hard both to establish majority rule and to extend the franchise whence it is applicable.

Liberals endorse the unrestricted domain assumption utilised by *Arrow* and by *Sen*, recognizing that the potential exclusion of individuals from participation in collective choice is illiberal. However, liberals would support the notion that where individuals' preferences over social states are sharply dichotomous, the domain might be partitioned, perhaps via devolution and federalism, to avoid coercive solutions. They also endorse the Paretian condition in the sense that if all individuals in society voted in favour of meddlesome policies then it would be illiberal of a liberal observer to force such a society to be free.

However, it may often be the case that individuals who are naturally meddlesome, nevertheless, may enjoy meddling in the affairs of others less than they dislike the meddling by others in their own affairs. In such circumstances, liberals would commend to the electorate the case for introducing restrictions on the constitution, especially to protect the rule of law from disruption by governments which respond to tactical voter manoeuvrings, and to promote the supremacy of freedom of choice in occupation and consumption over freedoms of contract and coalition. The detailing of such restrictions is beyond the scope of this paper. Even in a meddlesome society, there may be substantial support for such overall protection.

In the last analysis, of course, the maintenance of a liberal society depends upon the values of individuals in society. *Sen*[18] is correct in stating that «the ultimate guarantee for individual liberty may rest not on rules for social choice but on developing individual values that respect each other's personal choices». But the reasons why he is correct lie not in the writings of those who remain enmeshed in Arrowian collective choice theory, but rather in the contributions of those like *Mill*[12] and *Hayek*[8, 9] which provide a basis for liberal philosophy and which offer realistic guidelines for a «constitution of liberty».

References

[1] *Arrow, K. J.*: «Social Choice and Individual Values» (2nd Ed. 1963) Wiley.

[2] *Arrow, K. J.*: «Values and collective decision-making» in Laslett and Runciman (eds) Philosophy, Politics and Society, Blackwell, Oxford 1967, Vol. 3, pp. 215–232.

[3] *Bernholz, P.*: «Is a Paretian Liberal Really Impossible?» Public Choice 19, 1974, pp. 99–107.

[4] *Blau, J. H.*: «Liberal Values and Independence» Review of Economic Studies 42, 1975, pp. 395–402.

[5] *Breton, A.*: «The Economic Theory of Representative Government», Macmillan 1974.

[6] *Descartes, R.*: Principles of Philosophy, Everyman's Library Edn. No. 570.

[7] *Farrell, M. J.*: «Liberalism in the theory of social choice», Review of Economic Studies, 43, 1976, pp. 3–10.

[8] *Hayek, F. A.:* «The Constitution of Liberty», Routledge and Kegan Paul 1960.
[9] *Hayek, F. A.:* Law, Legislation and Liberty, Vol. 1, Rules and Order, Routledge and Kegan Paul 1973.
[10] *Hillinger, C.* and *Lapham, V.:* «The Impossibility of a Paretian Liberal», Journal of Political Economy 1971, pp. 1403–5.
[11] *Hobbes, T.:* «Leviathan» Everyman's Library, Edn. No. 691.
[12] *Mill, J. S.:* «Liberty» in Everyman's Library, Edn. No. 482.
[13] *Nozick, R.:* «Distributive Justice», Philosophy and Public Affairs, 1973, pp. 45–126.
[14] *Rousseau, J. J.:* The Social Contract, Everyman's Library, Edn. No. 660.
[15] *Rowley, C. K.* and *Peacock, A. T.:* «Welfare Economics: A Liberal Restatement», Martin Robertson, 1975.
[16] *Rowley, C. K.:* «Liberalism and Collective Choice: A Return to Reality», Manchester School, September 1978.
[17] *Sen, A.:* «The Impossibility of a Paretian Liberal», Journal of Political Economy, 1970, pp. 152–157.
[18] *Sen, A.:* «Liberty, Unanimity and Rights» Economica 1976, pp. 217–246.
[19] *Sugden, R.:* «Social Choice and Individual Liberty» (forthcoming 1978).

Summary

Collective Choice and Individual Liberty

Welfare economists, following the approach of *Arrow,* are guilty of advancing beaureaucratic socialism in Western countries, because they have promulgated false paradigms about the true nature of collective choice. *Arrow's* conclusions are based on the false assumptions that firstly, a public official is capable of aggregating individual preferences into a welfare judgment, without changing into a dictatorial social decision-maker and that secondly, there is an omniscient and impartial government. Many Liberals, opposing *Arrow's* theory, refer to Paretian welfare economics emphasizing the primacy of individual preferences and the potential veto of changes harmful even to the few. *Sen,* however, drawing attention to a special category of social states, so-called «protected spheres», irrefutably proved that a principle, reflecting liberal values, cannot be combined with the Pareto principle. All theoretical attempts to overcome the *Sen* Dilemma have failed. *Sugden,* therefore, redefines the Arrowian constitution as a procedure through which decisions are made by individuals and distinguishes liberal decision-making from decision-making by way of a voting system. Only a new approach, based on the general notion of liberty, derived from general classic liberal assumptions (preference of choice by the individual to collectivist choice, impossibility to widely disseminate information on individual preferences, existence of a «spontaneous order», necessity to abolish discretionary power within representative government and markets) would restore the lost balance between the individual and the state.

Michael Zöller

Handeln in Ungewißheit

F. A. v. Hayeks Grundlegung einer freiheitlichen Sozialphilosophie

Seit der Stiftung eines Nobelpreises für Wirtschaftswissenschaften im Jahre 1968 ist auch freiheitliches politisches Denken preiswürdig geworden. So hebt das Nobelpreiskomitee im Falle *F. A. v. Hayek*s die fachübergreifende Arbeitsweise und die über den Bereich der Wirtschaftswissenschaften hinausreichende Bedeutung des Laureaten hervor. Dieses Urteil findet auch insofern eine – freilich negative – Bestätigung, als einflußreiche sozialwissenschaftliche Theorien sich gerade dort in Aporien verfangen, wo die Wiederaufnahme jener sozialphilosophischen Tradition für sie fruchtbar werden könnte, die *F. A. v. Hayek* in zahlreichen Studien aktualisiert hat.[1]

I.

Die moderne politische Theorie, die in ihren unterschiedlichen Varianten vor der Aufgabe steht, Orientierungspunkte jenseits der Repräsentation organisierter Interessen (und damit auch Kriterien zur Relativierung solcher Interessen) auszuweisen, erweckt insgesamt den Eindruck, als bleibe nur die Wahl, entweder die Objektivität eines interessentranszendierenden Systems oder die Subjektivität interessengeleiteten Handelns zu betonen. Systemvernunft und Handlungsrationalität miteinander zu verbinden, also Systemvernunft ohne Vernichtung der Subjektivität denken zu wollen (und umgekehrt), gilt dagegen als eine vergebliche Absicht, mit der allenfalls noch einige katholische Naturrechts-Theoretiker sich abmühen mögen.[2]

Tatsächlich bestimmt die Hervorhebung entweder des Systemaspekts oder aber umgekehrt des Aspekts der sozialen Handlung die prominenten politischen Theorien.

Diese Dichotomie zeigt sich bereits in der jeweiligen Beschreibung der Ausgangslage. Wer, wie die Vertreter der kritischen Theorien, jede Stabilisierung von Formen des sozialen Austausches als Affirmation betrachtet, der betont dann etwa am sogenannten Spätkapitalismus die totale und unausweichlich manipulative Strukturhaftigkeit. Wer ande-

---

[1] Dies gilt v. a. für die in dem Sammelband «Freiburger Studien» (Tübingen 1969) zusammengefaßten Aufsätze.

[2] So bezeichnet *Friedrich Jonas* den Versuch, Systemvernunft und Handlungsrationalität miteinander zu verbinden, als das Kennzeichen des «katholischen» Theorie-Typus, womit er wohl v. a. auf die mangelnde Verallgemeinerungsfähigkeit eines solchen Denkansatzes verweisen will. (*Friedrich Jonas*, Die Institutionenlehre Arnold Gehlens, Tübingen 1966, S. 90).

rerseits, wie *Parsons*, die Stabilität von Systemen zum Gegenstand des Interesses macht, der hebt chaotische Strukturlosigkeit und Komplexität als den «Naturzustand» hervor, von dem alle Überlegungen auszugehen haben, um anschließend das «Hobbesian problem of order»[3] in den Mittelpunkt seiner Theorie zu stellen.[4]

Insgesamt gerät dadurch die politische Theorie in jene Situation, die *Schopenhauer* in seiner Parabel von den Stachelschweinen umschrieben hat: Sie möchten wegen der Kälte zusammenrücken, müssen jedoch wegen der Stacheln Abstand halten. *Karl Heinz Messelken* benutzt dieses Bild, um das Verhältnis zwischen Systemtheorie und Konflikttheorie zu kennzeichnen. Während die Systemtheorie «die Interessenreziprozität zu ihrer Grundannahme» mache und von dieser Voraussetzung aus «immer nur Integration und nicht Konflikt, immer nur Stabilität und nicht Wandel» erklären könne, gerate die Konflikttheorie in die Schwierigkeit, «von ihrer Grundannahme her immer nur Konflikt und nicht Integration, immer nur Wandel und nicht Stabilität begreifen zu können».[5] *Messelkens* Arbeit erschien 1968. Seither sind andere Theorien und andere Autoren in den Mittelpunkt des Interesses getreten, doch hat dies an der Grundstruktur des von *Messelken* geschilderten Problems nichts geändert. Das Stachelschwein-Dilemma läßt sich an der neueren Kontroverse zwischen *Luhmann* und *Habermas* mindestens ebenso gut illustrieren, wie an der Gegenüberstellung von *Parsons* und *Dahrendorf*.

Hinweise darauf, daß bei *Habermas*, wie in der gesamten sogenannten kritischen Theorie, institutionelle Probleme stets in anthropologische uminterpretiert werden, und daß dabei in der Tradition eines postulativen bürgerlichen Subjekts idealistischer Prägung und nicht auf der Ebene politischer Institutionen räsonniert wird[6], finden sich in der Literatur mittlerweile in großer Zahl. Vor allem *Bernard Willms* hat hervorgehoben, daß *Habermas*, der in seiner Argumentation stets «von der Handlungsebene ausgeht» mit «einem bestimmten Theorietypus» nämlich mit solchen Theorien, die «von der Systemebene» ausgehen, «offenbar nichts anfangen» kann. So gibt es auch einen *Hegel*, den *Habermas* nicht rezipiert, und zwar den *Hegel* der Rechtsphilosophie. Dies führt zu dem paradoxen Ergebnis, daß dem von *Habermas* beklagten Verfall «der einst emanzipativen liberalen Öffentlichkeit mit nichts anderem gesteuert werden soll, als eben wieder mit Öffentlichkeit».[7] Dies bedeutet auch, daß Vernunft unter solchen Voraussetzungen nicht als Systemvernunft denkbar ist, und daß soziales Handeln nicht verstetigt und berechenbar gemacht, also auch nicht im *Hegel*schen Doppelsinn des Wortes aufgehoben werden kann. Politik wird daher auf Kommunikation reduziert.

Luhmann wendet denn auch zu Recht gegen *Habermas* ein, man dürfe den Abbau von Institutionen nicht mit Aufklärung verwechseln.[8] Doch während *Habermas* außerstande ist, Vernunft auch in institutionelle Zusammenhänge zu stellen, verflüchtigt sich in systemtheoretischen Argumentationen nur allzuleicht das Subjekt vernünftiger Reflexion und vernünftigen Handelns. Bei *Parsons* und *Luhmann* werden nicht soziale Systeme als

---

[3] *Talcott Parsons*, Gesellschaften. Evolutionäre und komparative Perspektiven, Frankfurt 1975, S. 36, 71 und 118.

[4] Dazu auch: *Manfred Hennen*, Krise der Rationalität – Dilemma der Soziologie. Zur kritischen Rezeption Max Webers, Stuttgart 1976, S. 27.

[5] *Karl-Heinz Messelken*, Politikbegriffe der modernen Soziologie. Eine Kritik der Systemtheorie und Konflikttheorie, Köln und Opladen 1968, S. 100.

[6] *Friedrich H. Tenbruck*, Zur Kritik der planenden Vernunft, Freiburg und München 1972, S. 109.

[7] *Bernard Willms*, Kritik und Politik. Jürgen Habermas oder das politische Defizit der kritischen Theorie, Frankfurt 1973, S. 19 und 119. Siehe auch *Michael Zöller*, Die Unfähigkeit zur Politik. Politikbegriff und Wissenschaftsverständnis von Humboldt bis Habermas, Opladen 1975.

[8] *Jürgen Habermas / Niklas Luhmann*, Theorie der Gesellschaft oder Sozialtechnologie, Frankfurt 1971, S. 376f.

Handlungszusammenhänge interpretiert, sondern umgekehrt. Es geht eben nicht um eine Handlungstheorie, sondern um «Gleichförmigkeiten, die hinreichend stabil sind, um sie für pragmatische Zwecke innerhalb gewisser Grenzen als konstant» unterstellen zu können.[9] Handlungen interessieren unter dem Aspekt ihrer Funktionalität oder Dysfunktionalität für die «stabilitätsverbürgenden Gleichförmigkeiten», also für den Bestand von Systemen.

Daher glaubt *Luhmann* auch, es sei gelungen, «alteuropäische» Problemstellungen, wie sie besonders in den Begriffen Vernunft und Herrschaft zum Ausdruck kommen, nicht nur durch «abstrahierende und entmoralisierende Umdeutung» in eine systemtheoretische Terminologie zu übersetzen, sondern sie auch der Sache nach als obsolet zu erweisen. Die Systemtheorie habe «sich von Vernunft und von Herrschaft emanzipiert . . . Vernunft und Herrschaft sind für sie weder im Sinne der alteuropäischen Lehrtraditionen kongruent gesetzte, noch im Sinne der dagegen reagierenden Aufklärungstradition kontradiktorische Begriffe; sie sind überhaupt keine brauchbaren Begriffe mehr».[10] Die solcherart in die begriffsgeschichtliche Rumpelkammer verwiesenen «alteuropäischen» Bestände nahmen jedoch subtile Rache, indem sie, von *Luhmann* jeweils nur mühsam terminologisch verkleidet, an entscheidenden Stellen wieder aufstanden und die Grenzen systemtheoretischen Argumentierens markieren. Daß es nicht gelingt, Recht, Politik und letztlich auch die Person in Systemfunktionen umzuinterpretieren, zeigt sich vor allem an systemtheoretischen Dauerthemen wie dem Problem der Grenzziehung zwischen Subsystemen oder der Diskussion um die Rolle des politischen Systems, das den einzelnen Normen und Verhaltensweisen ihren jeweils funktional richtigen Ort zuweisen soll. Es geht dabei also darum, ein Subsystem zu konstruieren, dessen im systemtheoretischen Zusammenhang unlösbare Aufgabe *Luhmann* zutreffend umschreibt, wenn er von einem Subsystem spricht, das von «höherer Komplexität» sein müsse als «das System, dem es angehört».[11] Die Festlegung von Grenzen zwischen Systemen oder Systemteilen und die Durchsetzung von Normen innerhalb bestimmter Systeme werden daher, wie *Luhmann* schließlich erklärt, zu einer «Machtfrage».[12]

Die Ansprüche der «alteuropäischen» Herrschaftsvorstellungen und vieler damit verbundener Begriffe sind durch die terminologische Umformung keineswegs abgewehrt oder in funktionale Imperative verwandelt worden. Sie sind nur auf eine andere Ebene verlagert worden und machen sich nun wieder geltend. In der «Machtfrage» tritt also die Banalität zum Vorschein, daß Systeme sich nicht durch den Imperativ der Systemerhaltung selbstgenügsam zu rechtfertigen vermögen, sondern daß auch ihre Rechtfertigung auf subjektive Interessen rekurriert, die nicht als funktionalisierte systeminterne Normen, sondern nur mit Hilfe «alteuropäischer» Begriffe zu beschreiben sind.

II.

Bleibt es also wegen des Stachelschweindilemmas der Sozialphilosophie bei der Unbegründbarkeit einer interessentranszendierenden Norm, so daß die «Machtfrage» *Luhmann*s nichts anderes zum Ausdruck brächte, als den Tatbestand des Pluralismus?

---

9 *Talcott Parsons*, Soziologische Theorie, Neuwied und Berlin 1964, S. 37.
10 *Habermas / Luhmann* (siehe Anmerkung Nr. 8) S. 401.
11 *Niklas Luhmann*, Soziologie des politischen Systems, in: Luhmann, Soziologische Aufklärung Band 1, 4. Aufl., Opladen 1974, S. 169.
12 *Niklas Luhmann*, Theorie der Verwaltungswissenschaft, Köln und Berlin 1966, S. 81.

«Vermag niemand festzustellen, was gerecht ist, so muß jemand festsetzen, was Rechtens sein soll», schreibt *Gustav Radbruch*.[13] Diese Kurzfassung des rechtspositivistischen Dogmas ist jedoch zumindest unvollständig. Sie müßte eigentlich lauten: Wenn niemand festzustellen vermag, was gerecht ist, andererseits aber festgesetzt werden muß, was Rechtens sein soll, so muß diese Festsetzung so vorgenommen werden, daß sie der zugrundeliegenden Ungewißheit Rechnung trägt. Diese vermeintlich wertrelativistische Aussage besitzt jedoch ausschließenden und damit wertenden Charakter. Sie legitimiert nicht beliebige Wertsetzungen, sondern nur solche, die sich in ein bewußtes Verhältnis zur Tatsache ihrer eigenen Unbeweisbarkeit setzen, diese also selbst als einen Wert begreifen. Die Unbeweisbarkeit von Werten führt also noch nicht zu der oft angenommenen Unvermeidlichkeit des Wertrelativismus, denn einem konsequenten Relativisten ergeht es wie dem Kreter *Epimenides* mit seinem Satz «Alle Kreter lügen».[14] Die Feststellung, daß Werte unbeweisbar sind, bleibt nicht folgenlos, denn als Ausschließung der für beweisbar gehaltenen Werte und der aus solcher Beweisbarkeit folgenden Geltungszumutungen impliziert sie positiv formuliert die Unverfügbarkeit der Personen, an die solche Zumutungen zu richten wären.

Die Notwendigkeit, der Ungewißheit von Werten wertend Rechnung zu tragen, führt damit zu dem gleichen Ergebnis, zu dem ein über die Möglichkeiten seiner eigenen ideologiekritischen Infragestellung aufgeklärtes Naturrechtsdenken gelangen muß. Immer wieder ist ja die Kritik an verschiedenen Ausprägungen dieses Naturrechtsdenkens als der Versuch verstanden worden, «die Lösung des Naturrechtsproblems wenigstens per modum exclusionis voranzutreiben».[15] Dieser Absicht, Essentialismen, zirkuläre Argumentationen und Hypostasierungen zeitgebundener Meinungen zu eliminieren, um das zentrale Anliegen, nämlich die Suche nach einem das positive Recht transzendierenden Geltungsgrund, zu retten, ist freilich durch eine Historisierung des Problems nicht gedient. Hinter *Rudolf Stammler*s Forderung nach einem Naturrecht mit «wechselndem Inhalt»[16] oder der von *Alfred Verdross* eingeführten Unterscheidung zwischen «primären, dem allgemeinen Wesen des Menschen angemessenen Grundsätzen des Naturrechts» und sekundären, veränderlichen naturrechtlichen Normen, «die den konkreten Verhältnissen einer bestimmten Periode entsprechen»[17], steht die von *Verdross* auch ausgesprochene Hoffnung, Normen infolge eines allmählichen Erkenntnisfortschritts doch noch aus wissenschaftlicher Evidenz gewinnen zu können.[18] Im Gegensatz zu der von *Verdross* vertretenen Meinung besteht das Problem des Naturrechtsdenkens, und jeder Suche nach Normgewißheit, aber darin, daß auch «mit fortschreitender Erkenntnis der menschlichen Natur die verkürzten Menschenbilder» mit Sicherheit nicht «überwunden werden können» und daß es eine intersubjektiv ansinnbare normenstiftende und legitimationskräftige Gewißheit über positive Kenntnisse nicht geben kann.

Die Suche nach einer Grundnorm wird daher zu der Aufgabe, ein zentrales Prinzip von notwendiger Allgemeinheit zu finden, das sich ohne Inanspruchnahme von Wesensbehauptungen oder Annahmen über den notwendigen Verlauf der Geschichte und derglei-

---

[13] *Gustav Radbruch*, Rechtsphilosophie, 6. Aufl., Stuttgart 1963, S. 179.

[14] Siehe dazu: *Karl Engisch*, Auf der Suche nach der Gerechtigkeit. Hauptthemen der Rechtsphilosophie, München 1971, S. 256.

[15] *Ulrich Matz*, Rechtsgefühl und objektive Werte. Ein Beitrag zur Kritik des wertethischen Naturrechts, München 1966, S. V.

[16] *Rudolf Stammler*, Die Lehre vom richtigen Rechte, Leipzig 1926.

[17] *Alfred Verdross*, Statisches und dynamisches Naturrecht, Freiburg 1971, S. 93.

[18] «Man kann aber hoffen, daß mit fortschreitender Erkenntnis der menschlichen Natur die verkürzten Menschenbilder überwunden werden können ...» (*Verdross*, a.a.O., S. 14).

chen formulieren läßt, das also eine in Verhaltensregeln konkretisierbare Gewißheit ausdrückt, ohne auf positives Wissen zurückgreifen zu müssen.

Die Festsetzung einer solchen Grundnorm wäre daher als der Versuch zu beschreiben, sich zu der unaufhebbaren Ungewißheit und der Notwendigkeit des Handelns in Ungewißheit in ein bewußtes Verhältnis zu setzen. Diese Forderung ist identisch mit jener, die Unverfügbarkeit des anderen zu respektieren, weshalb das Ergebnis einer erkenntnisrelativistischen Betrachtung sich zuletzt mit dem harten Kern einer auch gegen ideologiekritische Einwände vertretbaren naturrechtlichen Position deckt. Wenn etwa *Hans Welzel* die «Frage nach der Rechtsgeltung» schließlich so beantwortet, daß ein allgemein verpflichtendes Sollen jedenfalls daraus folge, «daß jeder Mensch seinen Mitmenschen als ebenso verantwortliche Person wie sich selbst respektieren muß»[19], so ist mit diesem personalistischen Prinzip eine zwar positiv formulierte, aber nur in negativen Verhaltensregeln konkretisierbare Grundnorm genannt. Diese Grundnorm ist nicht das ausformulierte Ergebnis einer fortschreitenden «Erkenntnis der menschlichen Natur», sondern die Konsequenz der Unmöglichkeit solcher Erkenntnis, also dessen, was *Edmund Burke* als konstitutive Unkenntnis[20] bezeichnet hat. Der Mitmensch soll, so könnte die zutreffendere, weil negativ formulierte Fassung der *Welzel*schen Schlußfolgerung lauten, deshalb als verantwortlich gelten, weil es nicht zu verantworten ist, ihm seine Verantwortung abzunehmen. Seine Irrtümer sollen wenigstens seine eigenen sein.

III.

So zu argumentieren, also die konstitutive Ungewißheit und die Unverfügbarkeit der Person gleichzusetzen, und beides als zwei verschiedene Aspekte der gleichen Grundnorm zu betrachten, bedeutet entgegen einem naheliegenden Mißverständnis nicht, das pluralistische Dilemma in eine abstrakte Verbindlichkeit umzubiegen, die gewissermaßen besser wäre als gar keine, sondern bedeutet, eine nur vermeintliche Not als die Tugend zu erkennen, die sie immer schon war. Wie die Unbeweisbarkeit von Werten mehr und anderes bedeutet, als die faktische Pluralität von Wertvorstellungen, so ist auch das Handeln in Ungewißheit nicht nur die immer schon gültige Umschreibung der politischen Handlungssituation, sondern, soweit es als solches erkannt und anerkannt wird, die einzige Garantie für ein ohnehin relatives Maß individueller Freiheit. Nur die Nicht-Identität zweier verschiedener Arten von Geltungsansprüchen vermag der Attraktion globaler Menschlichkeitsziele entgegenzuwirken und vom entschlossenen Sprung in eine bessere Menschheitszukunft abzuhalten.

Besteht also die einzige legitimationskräftige Tatsache, d.h. die einzige normenbegründende Feststellung, die auf notwendige Zustimmung rechnen darf, in der konstitutiven Ungewißheit und der Unverfügbarkeit der Person, als deren positiv formulierter Konsequenz, so wird es zur Aufgabe der Politik und der politischen Theorie, sich zu diesem Umstand in ein bewußtes Verhältnis zu setzen. Einem politischen Denken, das dem Rationalitätsmodell des Machens und Herstellens verhaftet ist oder sich in den Dichotomien von Natur und Kultur, gemacht und vorgefunden, änderbar und nicht veränderbar,

---

[19] *Hans Welzel*, An den Grenzen des Rechts. Die Frage nach der Rechtsgeltung, Opladen 1966, S. 30.

[20] *Edmund Burke* (The Works of the Right Honourable Edmund Burke, London 1803–1827) spricht (Vol. 6, S. 6) von der «unavoidable uncertainty».

bewegt und sich daher in den wechselnden Verabsolutierungen des Handlungsaspekts oder des Systemaspekts, also dem oben geschilderten Stachelschweindilemma der politischen Theorie, verfängt, ist dies freilich nicht möglich. Politische Theorie als Theorie des Handelns in Ungewißheit steht daher zunächst vor der Aufgabe, sich in der Beschreibung von Handlungszusammenhängen von einem Rationalitätsmodell zu lösen, das menschliche Handlungssituationen als den Ausdruck eines bewußten, auf eben diese Handlungsfolgen gerichteten Willens interpretiert. Wenn «Rationalität im strengen Sinne verlangt … daß der Handelnde ein klares Wissen über die Zwecke, die Mittel und die Sekundäreffekte hat»[21], dann kann nicht umfassender als durch diese Formel umschrieben werden, daß es unmöglich ist, soziale Handlungssituation im Rahmen eines Modells (zweck-)rationaler Orientierung angemessen zu verstehen. Dies gilt für die Einschätzung sowohl der Ausgangsbedingungen wie auch der Zwecke und Folgen des Handelns. So ist auch die spezifische Rationalität der Wissenschaft nur unter der Voraussetzung und um den Preis einer institutionalisierten arbeitsteiligen Entlastung von der Verantwortung für Zwecke und Folgen denkbar.

Die menschliche Handlungssituation ist also durch einen unaufhebbaren Umstand gekennzeichnet, der in einem Gesetz von der Konstanz der Problemmenge ausgedrückt werden könnte.[22] In der Terminologie *Kants* geht es dabei um die «verschuldeten» Bestandteile der menschlichen Unmündigkeit, aus denen es darum auch keinen «Ausweg» geben kann. Entsprechend dem Gesetz von der Erhaltung der Problemmenge bedeutet auch ein theoretisch möglicher Fortschritt der Erkenntnis, oder eine Mehrung des gesicherten Wissens, nur eine Verschiebung und Umdefinition von Problemen. Solches gesichertes Wissen geht, wie der *Gehlen*sche Begriff der Hintergrundserfüllung besagt, als routinisierte Praxis in Alltagssicherheit ein, weshalb die Schwierigkeiten sich an der solcherart immer wieder verschobenen Grenze zwischen routinisierten und noch nicht routinisierten Handlungsformen ergeben. «Weil wir unser Wissen ständig bis zur Sicherheitsgrenze ausnützen, läßt sich die Überforderung des Wissens durch dessen Mehrung nie aufheben.»[23]

Vor allem *Friedrich H. Tenbruck* hat in seiner «Kritik der planenden Vernunft»[24] darauf hingewiesen, daß den Theorien des rationalen Handelns insofern ein Irrtum zugrundeliegt, als sie es für möglich halten, Zwecke in einem geordneten System von Präferenzen zu fixieren. Da aber nur das zum erkennbaren Zweck wird, was nicht schon durch die Umstände befriedigt ist, sind «unsere Bedürfnisse durch unsere Zwecke nie zu erschöpfen».[25] Die Zusammensetzung der Präferenzen wechselt also nicht einfach, d. h. es werden nicht einfach neue Zwecke eingesetzt, sondern die «Präferenzstrukturen» bilden sich in Folge vorheriger Zweckrealisierungen um, ein Vorgang, der sich nicht als (zweck-)rationaler Handlungsablauf beschreiben läßt. So verwendet der Mensch beträchtliche Aufmerksamkeit und Energie darauf, die Struktur seiner Präferenzen immer wieder umzubauen und die «Gratifikationsbilanz» zu «frisieren». Er entwickelt, wie *Tenbruck* schreibt, eine Vielzahl von «Innentechniken der Bedeutungsinvestition», d. h. er sublimiert die Fähigkeit, sich immer wieder in neuen Gegebenheiten einzurichten[26] und einer

---

[21] *Hans Peter Dreitzel,* Rationales Handeln und politische Orientierung, in: *Koch / Senghaas* (Hrsg.), Texte zur Technokratiediskussion, Frankfurt 1970, S. 17.

[22] Siehe z. B. *Niklas Luhmann,* Theorie der Verwaltungswissenschaft, Köln und Berlin 1966, S. 93.

[23] *Friedrich H. Tenbruck,* Wissenschaft, Politik und Öffentlichkeit, in: *Mayer / Ritter / Matz* (Hrsg.), Politik und Wissenschaft, München 1971, S. 329.

[24] *Tenbruck,* siehe Anmerkung Nr. 6.

[25] *Tenbruck,* a. a. O., S. 24.

[26] *Tenbruck,* a. a. O., S. 77 und S. 117f.

unerwarteten Lage «positive Seiten abzugewinnen», wie es in einer rationale Ansprüche dementierenden Weise umgangssprachlich heißt.

So ist es in der Literatur längst zu einem Gemeinplatz geworden, darauf hinzuweisen, daß Situationen, Alternativen und Vorlieben kaum je so klar umrissen oder so stabil sind, wie Spieltheorien oder Entscheidungstheorien voraussetzen.[27] Dennoch fällt es der politischen Theorie schwer, aus dieser Unangemessenheit des Modells rationalen Verhaltens die Konsequenz zu ziehen. Verantwortlich für diese Lernverweigerung dürfte die tief eingewurzelte Denkgewohnheit sein, die Ergebnisse menschlichen Handelns auch als die Ergebnisse eines auf genau diese Folgen gerichteten menschlichen Willens zu interpretieren. Es ist das Verdienst F. A. v. Hayeks, gegen diesen von ihm als konstruktivistisch bezeichneten Denkstil vor allem durch die Erinnerung an die sogenannte schottische Aufklärung immer wieder angekämpft zu haben.

IV.

Ordnung ist, wie *Hayek* schreibt, «für einfach denkende Menschen das Ergebnis der ordnenden Tätigkeit eines ordnenden Wesens».[28] Eine derartige antievolutionistische Denkweise beinhaltet nicht nur ein Vorurteil zu Gunsten des ordnenden Anordners, sondern auch zu Gunsten einer Ordnungsvorstellung, die nur in der hierarchisch strukturierten, zweckorientierten und durch Befehl und Anordnung gesteuerten Organisation ihre Entsprechung findet. Ordnungen werden daher als entweder aus der Natur oder aus Übereinkunft folgend verstanden. Demgegenüber betont *Hayek*, daß «ein Großteil dessen, was wir Kultur nennen . . . weder völlig unabhängig von menschlichem Handeln entstand, noch planmäßig geschaffen wurde».[29] Infolge der alten Gewohnheit, die Erscheinungen in «natürliche» und «künstliche» zu unterteilen, sei jedoch nie deutlich geworden, daß eigentlich eine Dreiteilung erforderlich sei. Neben solchen Erscheinungen, die im Sinne völliger Unabhängigkeit von menschlichem Handeln «natürlich» zu nennen wären, und jenen, die im Sinne eines «Produkts menschlichen Entwurfs» als «künstlich» oder «vereinbart» gelten dürfen, wäre eine gesonderte mittlere Kategorie «zu berücksichtigen», die alle jene ungeplanten Ordnungen und Regelmäßigkeiten umfaßt, deren Existenz wir im menschlichen Zusammenleben feststellen und deren Erklärung die Aufgabe der Sozialtheorie ist».[30] Beispiele für ein solches Handeln nach Regeln, die nicht entworfen wurden, sondern sich durchsetzten, weil sie eine erfolgreichere Praxis ermöglichten als andere Regeln, findet *Hayek* besonders in Fertigkeiten wie der Beherrschung der Sprache oder handwerklichem und sportlichem Geschick. Die «Dinge, die wir können, ohne zu wissen, wie wir sie zustande bringen», seien Beispiele für Regeln, «die sich durchsetzten, weil die erfolgreichen imitiert wurden». Auf diese Weise entstehen Regelordnungen, «die uns nicht positiv sagen, was wir tun sollen, sondern nur was wir nicht tun dürfen». Auch Ordnungen setzen sich daher in einem Selektionsprozeß durch, «in dem die Gruppen, die eine wirksamere Ordnung bildeten, andere verdrängten oder von den anderen imitiert wurden».[31] Zum Gegenstand der Sozialwissenschaften werden daher in er-

---

[27] Siehe z. B. *Anatol Rapoport*, Verschiedene Bedeutungen von «Theorie», in: *Robert H. Schmidt* (Hrsg.), Methoden der Politologie, Darmstadt 1967, S. 327.
[28] *Hayek*, a. a. O., (siehe Anmerkung Nr. 1), S. 32 f.
[29] *Hayek*, a. a. O., S. 36.
[30] *Hayek*, a. a. O., S. 98.
[31] *F. A. v. Hayek*, Die Irrtümer des Konstruktivismus, Tübingen 1975, S. 8 f.

ster Linie die «ungeplanten Ordnungen und Regelmäßigkeiten», also die ungeplanten Handlungsfolgen, ein Hinweis, der von *Popper* aufgegriffen wurde.[32]

Dies kann eine sozialwissenschaftliche Theorie jedoch nur dann leisten, wenn sie weder den Systemcharakter, noch den Konfliktcharakter von Handlungszusammenhängen verabsolutiert. Daher ist auch von verschiedenen Autoren vorgeschlagen worden, soziale Prozesse nicht funktionalistisch, sondern im Rahmen einer Theorie des sozialen Austausches zu interpretieren. Die Diskussion um diese Alternative hat sich besonders an *Robert K. Merton*s Unterscheidung zwischen offiziellen und inoffiziellen Strukturen entzündet. In seinem Aufsatz über «manifeste und latente Funktionen» hatte Merton die amerikanischen «Parteimaschinen» und ihre Praxis der Vergabe von öffentlichen Aufträgen an Firmen und der Gewährung sozialer Hilfen für einzelne als Beispiel für eine Selbstregulierung als Ausdruck funktionaler Notwendigkeiten interpretiert. Die funktionalen Unzulänglichkeiten der offiziellen Struktur erzeugen also nach *Merton* eine inoffizielle Struktur, die zu einer wirksameren Befriedigung vorhandener Bedürfnisse führt.[33] Dagegen wurde, etwa von *Alfred Bohnen*, eingewandt, die Hypothese von der funktionalen Selbstregulierung beinhalte die unrealistische Annahme, überall dort, wo «den Armen» nicht wirksam geholfen werde, würden eben deshalb sofort entsprechende Kräfte mobilisiert. Es müsse wohl die Möglichkeit des sozialen Austausches hinzukommen, d. h. «die Armen» müßten, wie es das Beispiel der Parteimaschinen ja nahelegt, in der Lage sein, Wählerstimmen gegen Hilfe zu tauschen.[34] Gesetzeshypothesen über «individuelles Verhalten in sozialen Situationen» wären also geeignet, «an die Stelle der überaus problematischen Selbstregulierungshypothese» zu treten und damit auch einen Erklärungsansatz überflüssig zu machen, «der bestimmte soziologische Probleme unter dem Aspekt des Systemcharakters von Gesellschaften zu lösen versucht».[35]

Freilich darf dieser fruchtbarere Erklärungsversuch nicht zu der Illusion verführen, daß Tauschprozesse geeignet seien, gesellschaftliche Harmonie herzustellen. Entgegen den ebenso häufigen wie unbegründeten Fehldeutungen[36] steht ein solches Harmonieverlangen auch im Falle *Adam Smith*s nicht hinter dem Versuch, soziale Entwicklungen mit Hilfe der «unsichtbaren Hand» zu verstehen.[37] Vielmehr geht es um die Logik der «invisible hand», die man, wie *Watrin* abgrenzend gegen harmonistische Mißverständnisse und gegen die von *Albert* hervorgehobenen «Souveränitätsfiktionen»[38] formuliert, lieber als die «Erklärung mittels der Idee der unbeabsichtigten Konsequenzen individuell rationalen Handelns» bezeichnen sollte.[39] Es sind daher auch nicht irgendwelche erwünsch-

---

[32] *Hayek*, Freiburger Studien (siehe Anmerkung Nr. 1), S. 101.

[33] *Robert K. Merton*, Social Theory and Social Structure, New-York 1957, S. 66f.

[34] *Alfred Bohnen*, Interessenharmonie und Konflikt in sozialen Austauschbeziehungen. Zur ökonomischen Perspektive im soziologischen Denken. in: *Hans Albert u. a.* (Hrsg.), Sozialtheorie und soziale Praxis (Eduard Baumgarten zum 70. Geburtstag), Meisenheim am Glan 1971, S. 154ff. Zur Theorie sozialer Austauschprozesse siehe außerdem: *Peter M. Blau*, Exchange and Power in Social Life, New York – London – Sydney 1964.

[35] *Bohnen*, a. a. O., S. 157.

[36] Siehe dazu v. a. *Viktor Vanberg*, Wissenschaftsverständnis, Sozialtheorie und politische Programmatik. Zur Analyse des Gegensatzes zwischen liberalem und totalitärem Politikverständnis, Tübingen 1973, S. 22f.

[37] Dazu v. a. *Robert Nozick*, Anarchie – Staat – Utopia, München 1976, S. 32.

[38] Z. B. *Hans Albert*, Rationalität und Wirtschaftsordnung, in: *Albert*, Aufklärung und Steuerung, Hamburg 1976, S. 67f.

[39] *Christian Watrin*, Ordnungspolitische Aspekte des Sozialstaates, in: Soziale Probleme der modernen Industriegesellschaft (Schriften des Vereins für Socialpolitik, N. F., Bd. 92) Berlin 1977, S. 975.

ten Ergebnisse, wie die optimale Güterversorgung, die das Einräumen von Freiheit rechtfertigen, sondern es ist die Unmöglichkeit verbindlich ansinnbarer Zwecke und die Unmöglichkeit umfassender, planvoll und rational organisierter Handlungszusammenhänge, die Freiheit erfordert.[40] *Hayek* stellt diesen Zusammenhang her, indem er die
«unavoidable uncertainty» mit der Theorie einer freiheitlichen Ordnung verbindet. Da
menschliche Handlungssituationen zwar ihrerseits «Ergebnisse menschlichen Handelns», nicht aber «menschlichen Entwurfs» sind[41], ist die «unvermeidliche Unkenntnis
der meisten Umstände, die das Handeln anderer bestimmen, von dem wir nichtsdesto-
weniger Nutzen ziehen . . . der letzte Grund, der die persönliche Freiheit so wichtig
macht».[42] Dieser Rechtfertigungszusammenhang zwischen der persönlichen Freiheit
und der Notwendigkeit zum Handeln in Ungewißheit war es auch, der *Hume, Mandeville* und *Ferguson* dazu veranlaßte, gegenüber dem «Funktionalisten» *Hobbes* darauf zu
bestehen, daß die Analyse sozialer Gegebenheiten, also jener Verhältnisse, in die Nationen nach *Ferguson* «hineinstolpern», nicht vom Systemgedanken, sondern von den
Handlungen der einzelnen auszugehen habe. Ein derartiges Argumentieren setzt sich freilich immer wieder dem Mißverständnis aus, im Sinne einer utilitaristischen Souveräni-
tätsfiktion den Menschen «wie er geht und steht» rechtfertigen zu wollen. Gemeint ist jedoch gerade nicht, daß jedes beliebige Interesse als ein gerechtfertigtes auftreten kann,
sondern daß, weil niemand richtige oder wahre Bedürfnisse bestimmen kann, nicht jeder,
sondern niemand eine solche Definitionskompetenz besitzt, und daß deshalb die stets
notwendige antizipierende Beschreibung von Bedürfnissen und Handlungszielen als politisches Handeln nach Regeln vonstatten gehen muß, die es als ein prinzipiell revidierbares
Handeln in Ungewißheit ausweisen.

V.

Einzugestehen, daß «die Präferenzen der individuellen Personen . . . das einzige Kriterium für das Allgemeinwohl» sind, «das nicht zum Totalitarismus führt»[43], bedeutet also
noch keineswegs anzunehmen, daß in diesen Präferenzen der individuellen Personen ein
Fundament der Gewißheit entdeckt sei. Was aus dieser Präferenzsouveränität an Gewißheit folgt, reduziert sich letztlich wieder auf eine negative Regel: Niemand kann beanspruchen, die Präferenzen anderer ohne deren Zustimmung zu definieren. Damit ist noch
nicht einmal gesagt, daß die «individuellen Personen» auch nur über ihre eigenen Präfe-

---

[40] Weshalb die Verwechslung der einen Rechtfertigung mit der anderen die ständige Selbstgefähr-
dung des Liberalismus ausmacht. So schon bei *Wilhelm v. Humboldt*, der neben die formale Definition («Mannigfaltigkeit der Situationen») die Definition mittels eines positiv beschriebenen
Ziels («höchste und proportionierlichste Entfaltung der Persönlichkeit») stellt. Dazu im einzelnen *Michael Zöller*, a. a. O., (siehe Anmerkung Nr. 7).

[41] So übersetzt *Hayek* die zentrale Formulierung bei Ferguson: «Every step and every movement of
the multitude, even in what are termed enlightened ages, are made with equal blindness to the future; and nations stumble upon establishments, which are indeed the result of human action, but
not . . . of any human design.» (Zit. nach *Hayek*, a. a. O., S. 141, Anm. Nr. 56).

[42] *Hayek*, a. a. O., S. 14.

[43] *Gerard Radnitzky*, Die Sein-Sollen-Unterscheidung als Voraussetzung der liberalen Demokratie,
in: *K. Salamun* (Hrsg.), Sozialphilosophie als Aufklärung (Festschrift für Ernst Topitsch). Erscheint noch 1978, hier zit. nach dem vervielfältigten Manuskript.

renzen Zuverlässiges wissen könnten, sondern es ist wiederum nur festgehalten, daß ihre Irrtümer ihre eigenen sein sollen.

Ein politisches Denken, das Handlungssituationen nicht als Glieder innerhalb einer Kette rationaler Handlungsabläufe versteht, das also davon ausgeht, daß der Mensch «nicht das Produkt seines Willens zur Produktion dieses Produkts» ist[44], wird sich dementsprechend auch nicht als eine Anweisung zur zweckrationalen Durchordnung von Präferenzen und zur optimalen Einsetzung geeigneter Mittel begreifen, sondern als den Versuch, Regeln des Umgangs mit der Ungewißheit zu entwickeln. Die dem politischen Handeln mögliche Rationalität bestimmt ein derartiges politisches Denken daher auch nicht von der möglichst weitgehenden Realisierung positiv beschreibbarer politischer Nah- oder Fernziele her. Vielmehr könnte Politik unter der Voraussetzung der unavoidable uncertainty in dem Maße rational heißen, als es ihr gelingt, das stets notwendige Überschreiten des gegebenen Maßes an Wissen und Übereinstimmung dem Umfang nach gering und der Art nach revidierbar zu halten.

Gerade die Prämisse eines allerdings negativ, nämlich als Unverfügbarkeit der Person, formulierten Personalismus steht daher auch der Versuch entgegen, den Handlungsaspekt im Sinne einer Ausschließlichkeit gegen den Systemaspekt auszuspielen. Die Aufgabe, die konstitutive Ungewißheit als die Unverfügbarkeit der Person einerseits und den Zwang zum Handeln andererseits miteinander in Beziehung zu setzen, könnte im Gegenteil als die allgemeinste Beschreibung der Absicht jeder Theorie der Institution gelten. Ist es die tatsächliche Wirkung von Institutionen, Spannungen nicht zu lösen, sondern, wie *Arnold Gehlen*s zutreffende funktionale Definition besagt, zu stabilisieren, so kann es nur darum gehen, solche Spannungen im *Hegel*schen Doppelsinn «aufzuheben», sie also erträglich zu machen, ohne sich über ihr Fortbestehen und ihre Unauflöslichkeit zu täuschen. Darüber hinaus bedarf es jedoch, entgegen der von *Gehlen* zwar nicht ausdrücklich geäußerten, aber praktisch befolgten Auffassung, keiner weiteren Ausfüllung mehr. Die Funktion ist mit dem Rechtfertigungsgrund identisch, d. h. daß es überhaupt unauflösliche Spannungen gibt, kann bereits als der allen institutionalisierbaren Widersprüchen zugrundeliegende Hauptwiderspruch zwischen Handlung und Gewißheit eingesetzt werden.

«Hinter jeder Institutionenlehre», so schreibt *Friedrich Jonas*, «steht die mehr oder weniger deutliche Voraussetzung, daß der Mensch einen Defekt hat, und eben gegen diese Voraussetzung polemisiert die Naturlehre der Aufklärung.»[45] Der erste Teil dieses Satzes sollte nun in dem Sinne wörtlich genommen werden, daß es sich um einen, und zwar nur einen Defekt von unauflöslicher Art handelt, nämlich um den der konstitutiven Ungewißheit. «Mängel» verschiedener Art, die als Folge wechselnder anthropologischer Theorien in ihrer institutionenbegründenden Funktion als je ein Defekt gegeneinander ausgetauscht werden könnten, führen im Unterschied zu dem Grunddefekt der Erbungewißheit zu der am Beispiel *Gehlen*s zu beobachtenden keineswegs zwingenden Verknüpfung von Anthropologie, Kulturkritik und funktionaler Umschreibung der Leistungen von Institutionen.[46] So wird auf dem Umweg über die «Mängel», die ja nur eine negativ formulierte Fassung der jeweils zugrundeliegenden Vorstellung vom Normalzustand oder vom Wesen des Menschen darstellen, die Theorie der Institution zu einer mehr oder weniger philosophisch oder naturwissenschaftlich orientierten Anthropologie. Tritt da-

---

[44] *Hermann Lübbe*, Geschichtsphilosophie und politische Praxis, in: *Lübbe*, Theorie und Entscheidung, Freiburg 1971, S. 118.

[45] *Friedrich Jonas*, a. a. O., (siehe Anmerkung Nr. 2) S. 15.

[46] Dazu im einzelnen: *Helmut Schelsky*, Zur soziologischen Theorie der Institution, in: *Schelsky* (Hrsg.), Zur Theorie der Institution, Düsseldorf 1970, S. 22.

gegen der niemals mit ausreichender Kenntnis aller relevanten Umstände, aller denkbaren Ziele, aller denkbaren Mittel und aller möglichen Nebenwirkungen ausgestattete und dennoch unter Handlungszwang stehende Mensch an die Stelle des Mängelwesens und ersetzt seine Erbungewißheit als der institutionenbegründende Defekt die Vielzahl denkbarer Mängel, so erweist sich auch die Entgegensetzung von Institution und Subjektivität oder von Institution und Aufklärung als eine Scheinalternative.

Institution kann nur solange als gegenaufklärerisches Prinzip gelten, wie Aufklärung von der universellen Kompetenz des Herstellens ausgehend alles Kontingente für verfügbar hält und in einer Verwechslung von Aufklärung und Emanzipation nicht der Ausgang aus selbstverschuldeter Unmündigkeit, sondern der Auszug aus der Geschichte gemeint ist. Andernfalls ist Institution nicht Gegenprinzip, sondern Voraussetzung der Aufklärung, nicht die zu beseitigende Ursache, sondern die notwendige Folge der Entfremdung.

Institutionen stabilisieren also die Spannung zwischen Handlung und Gewißheit, indem sie entweder das Bewußtsein erweitern oder gegenüber dem Handeln in Ungewißheit Rationalitätsregeln des Verhaltens zur Geltung bringen. Zur Erweiterung des Bewußtseins tragen sie durch Erinnerung und Antizipation auf zweierlei Weise und sozusagen auch in zwei Richtungen bei. Sie vergegenwärtigen in verdichteter Form frühere Argumente, erinnern also an Geschichte im Sinne der jeweils bewußt zu treffenden Entscheidung, «wie man aufgrund des Bisherigen jetzt neu sein will».[47] Da der Mensch «auf ein Arsenal von Mitteln» angewiesen ist, das er weder aus dem biologischen Instinktvorrat der menschlichen Gattungsnatur noch durch informatorisches Wissen oder aus dem rationalen Kalkül gewinnen kann, bezeichnet *Leszek Kolakowski* die Tradition als «das einzige Arsenal dieser Mittel».[48] Freilich gibt die Tradition ebenso wie «die Natur» keine Kriterien zu ihrer eigenen Beurteilung ab, sie ist also ihrerseits keine Quelle von Verbindlichkeit. Sie hält lediglich gegenüber einem Handeln, das auch als die Entscheidung, wie man aufgrund des Bisherigen jetzt neu sein will, ein Handeln in Ungewißheit bleibt, den Horizont anderer Möglichkeiten offen und erlaubt es, mehr Wissen zu berücksichtigen, als der Handelnde je aktuell besitzen kann.

Diese Funktion, das Bewußtsein zu erweitern und die Handlungsfreiheit durch Vervielfachung der Wahlmöglichkeiten zu erhöhen, können aber sogenannte sinnvermittelnde Institutionen nur soweit und nur solange erfüllen, als sie sich ihre Besonderheit der Handlungs- und Entscheidungsentlastung erhalten. Wenn soziale Strukturen ihre Bindekraft verlieren, dann gewinnen damit umgekehrt jene Orientierungsmöglichkeiten an Bedeutung, die außerhalb oder jenseits der Repräsentation von Interessen oder überhaupt jenseits der Widerspiegelung von Wirklichkeit liegen. Institutionen der Weltauslegung und der Sinnvermittlung müßten sich deshalb eigentlich darin bestärkt finden, ihre Aufgabe im Präsenthalten früherer Entscheidungen, also in Erinnerung oder im Entwerfen denkbarer anderer Zustände, also in Antizipation, zu sehen. Ihre Leistung und ihre Stärke bestünde in Distanz, Differenz oder Skepsis, jedenfalls in Nicht-Identität. Stattdessen lassen sich aber gerade solche Institutionen allzuleicht einreden, sie hätten «Realitätsdefizite» und «Modernitätsrückstände» zur Anpassung an die Wirklichkeit «aufzuarbeiten» und arbeiten schließlich sich selbst bis zur Angepaßtheit und Ununterscheidbarkeit auf, indem sie Identität anstreben.

Neben der Erweiterung des Bewußtseins und der Vermehrung der Wahlmöglichkeiten, also insgesamt der Vergrößerung des Handlungsspielraums bringen Institutionen beson-

---

47 *Max Müller*, Philosophische Anthropologie, Freiburg und München 1974, S. 157.
48 *Leszek Kolakowski*, Der Anspruch auf die selbstverschuldete Unmündigkeit, in: *Leonhard Reinisch* (Hrsg.), Vom Sinn der Tradition, München 1973, S. 3.

ders dort, wo sie für abgegrenzte Sachbereiche das Verhalten in regelmäßig wiederkehrenden oder vergleichbaren Situationen regeln, auch Erfahrungen zum Ausdruck, indem sie die Zahl der denkbaren Handlungsalternativen begrenzen. Sie erscheinen dann als eine Rationalitätsregel des Wandels, da sie gegenüber dem Handeln in Ungewißheit die Beweislast zugunsten früherer Entscheidungen verteilen. Dieser Aspekt widerleglicher, aber nur unter erhöhtem Aufwand an Überzeugungskraft widerlegbarer Vermutungen zugunsten der Ergebnisse vorausgegangenen menschlichen Handelns führt daher auch eine an sozialen Handlungszusammenhängen orientierte Theorie der Institution in die Nähe der juristischen oder rechtsphilosophischen Betrachtungsweise: «Der Jurist lernt, daß die höchstrichterliche Rechtsprechung für ihn als Richter nicht verbindlich ist, daß er von ihr abweichen kann, aber nur, wenn er sich mit ihren Gründen auseinandersetzt ... Der Jurist geht aus von einer Vermutung zugunsten der höchstrichterlichen Rechtsprechung, allerdings von einer widerleglichen Vermutung. Demjenigen, der korrigieren und weiterführen will, obliegen die Begründungspflicht und die Argumentationslast. Dieser methodische Ansatz gewährleistet, daß sich das Abweichen von der höchstrichterlichen Rechtsprechung auf der Höhe des Problembewußtseins bewegt...»[49]

VI.

Institutionalisierten Verhaltensregeln sowohl die Aufgabe einer Erweiterung des Handlungsspielraumes durch Vermehrung der Wahlmöglichkeiten als auch jene der Handlungshemmung zuweisen zu wollen, mag auf den ersten Blick als widersprüchlich erscheinen. Es handelt sich bei diesem Widerspruch jedoch wiederum nur um die institutionell zu stabilisierende Spannung zwischen Handlung und Gewißheit, weshalb sowohl Erinnerung und Antizipation als die Repräsentation anderer Handlungsmöglichkeiten wie auch die vor dem Veränderungswillen aufgebaute Schwelle der Beweislast nur die konstitutive Ungewißheit des Handelns im Bewußtsein der Handelnden präsent halten. Der Versuch, die Berücksichtigung der Handlungsbedingungen durch institutionalisierte Verhaltensregelungen auf Dauer zu stellen, könnte daher auch als Äquivalent für die «Lehre vom irrenden Gewissen» beschrieben werden, die nach *Robert Spaemann* das «missing link zwischen der klassischen Naturrechtslehre und der modernen Subjektivitätsphilosophie» darstellt.[50]

Setzt man an die Stelle des irrenden Gewissens in terminologischer Modernisierung die Berücksichtigung des entscheidenden Unterschiedes zwischen kognitiven und politischen Geltungsansprüchen, so könnte man ebenso gut sagen, das «missing link» sei von *F. A. v. Hayek* wiedergefunden worden. Er hat eine zweite, allzu oft vergessene Aufklärungstradition erneuert und damit den heruntergekommenen Begriff des Liberalismus wieder brauchbar gemacht.

---

[49] *Martin Kriele,* Einführung in die Staatslehre. Die geschichtlichen Legitimitätsgrundlagen des demokratischen Verfassungsstaates, Reinbek bei Hamburg 1975, S. 41.
[50] *Robert Spaemann,* Die Utopie der Herrschaftsfreiheit, in: Merkur Nr. 26, Jg. 1972, S. 743.

Summary

Acting under Uncertainty. F. A. von Hayek's Foundation of a Liberal Social Philosophy

By one-sidedly emphasizing the subjective aspect of social action or the objective systems aspect, modern political theories are faced with the dilemma that their way of thinking is either too subjective for their concepts to be institutionalized or that they describe the objectiveness of systems contexts in a way that is incompatible with the «modern subjectiveness of reflection» *(Gehlen)*.

It is *F. A. von Hayek*, who has shown the way out of this dilemma: The fact that values are beyond proof represents a value in itself, one that has to be acknowledged in a liberal society. Recognizing that values are beyond proof implies that there is no one to decide about their validity. If the constitutive uncertainty of reality is the only legitimating factor, i. e. the only factor to establish norms, which may count on the necessary consent, then it is the task of practical politics and political theories to become aware of this phenomenon. Actions do, in spite of this, not necessarily become unsystematical and irrational. The circumstances of men, being an orderly system, can be «the result of human action but not the execution of any human design». With this fundamental statement, a too frequently forgotten enlightenment tradition is resumed, i. e. the «Scottish» one which, contrary to the totalitarian consequences of the «French» one, is in harmony with liberal constitutional requests and is not under the coercion to comprehend subjectiveness and systems rationality as irreconcilable opposites.

Arthur Seldon

Individual Liberty, Public Goods and Representative Democracy

Lessons from the West and Escape for the East

«If it is assumed that whatever the majority decides is just, even if what it lays down is not a general rule, but aims at affecting particular people, it would be expecting too much to believe that a sense of justice will restrain the caprice of the majority: in any group it is soon believed that what is desired by the group is just.»

« . . . since the theoreticians of democracy have for over a hundred years taught the majorities that whatever they desire is just, we must not be surprised if the majorities no longer even ask whether what they decide is just. Legal positivism has powerfully contributed to this development by its contention that law is not dependent on justice but determines what is just.»

F. A. Hayek
Economic Freedom and Representative Government, Institute of Economic Affairs, London, 1973.

«If . . . dividing supreme power into two independent democratic assemblies, or some better device, is not applied in the next 10 years or so, the public loss of faith in the ideal of democracy itself will continue to evaporate, especially if government acquires even more power over economic life and even more power to dispense arbitrary, discriminate benefits to group interests that will, in turn, therefore, be increasingly disposed to organise pressure on it.»

F. A. Hayek
The Coming Confrontation, Institute of Economic Affairs, London, 1978.

As incomes rise in Western societies, individuals can pay more for more goods and services in the market, yet government has paradoxically taken more of them in taxes and supplied more goods and services in return. As incomes become more equal by the operation of competition, contract and mobility, the «free» supply by government of goods and services financed by redistributive, «progressive» taxation becomes less necessary, desirable or justifiable; yet taxes become increasingly generalised payment for government supply. This twin quixotic development requires more attention from market economists concerned with the translation of economic liberalism into public policy.

I. Growth of Government: West and East

Relatively to the rising trend in real income, the individual in Europe, North America and Australasia (although probably not in the market oases of Taiwan, South Korea or Hong Kong and elsewhere in Asia) has been losing control over the disposition of his income. An expansion in public goods, not least defence to protect societies against Communist expansion, might explain and justify a larger proportion of even rising real income being taken in taxes. But most of the increasing taxes have been taken to provide wholly or largely private goods and personal benefits that could have been supplied by developing markets.

Even in the market oases of Asia, not least Taiwan and Hong Kong, the same false justification for higher «public» (government) expenditure is heard from government officials and other advisers urging politicians to take the fiscally easy and (wrongly thought) politically popular course of raising more revenue from rising incomes to provide more private goods, not least education and medical care, on the ground that, as economic growth makes these societies richer, they can «afford» to spend more on public benefits. Politicians in emerging societies would be better advised to observe where this schoolboy howler of a *non sequitur* and circular reasoning has led the liberal West.

It may already have occurred to the more astute of public men in the East as well as the West that rising real incomes may make it *possible* for government to raise more tax revenue to spend on «free» (or nominally-priced) government services but also make it *unnecessary*, since by definition rising personal real incomes enable more people to pay more in the market. In the market oases less government expenditure on public health and associated environmental services has been made possible by the conquest of infectious and contagious disease. The argument for more expenditure on measures to contend with the pollution externalities of noise, smell and congestion is over-exaggerated because it does not always allow for the extent to which the externalities can be internalised by pricing. And the new public health service of information to inculcate living habits that preserve health, now gaining credence in the West, is likely to require far less revenue than the 19th century public health measures against infection and contagion.

The East, moreover, could learn from the West, especially Britain, about the political difficulty of phasing out private/personal benefits as incomes rise, even where the reasons for installing them had been valid in the first place.

II. False Arguments for Government Supply of Private Goods

In Britain, and in much of Western Europe, the justifications for the government supply of the largely non-public goods, especially education and medical care, the two largest state benefits in kind that with other social benefits comprise a half of British government (central and local) expenditure, go back a century, from poverty in the 1860's to Keynesian demand management since the 1940's.

The medley of arguments, justifications and pretexts number mainly nine, and they have not been adequately contested. The 19th century argument of («primary») poverty was that many people lacked the earnings or wealth to pay for the desirable quantum of education, medical care and other «social services». The later argument of irresponsibility, dignified by *Seebohm Rowntree* and other British observers of social conditions as «secondary poverty», was that, even where earnings or wealth became adequate, they would not necessarily be used to pay for the desired services. After R. H. *Tawney* came the argument of equality developed by the *Fabians* and R. M. *Titmuss*: only state supply, they insisted, could ensure equality of access. A fourth argument, derived from the sociologists, was the parity of esteem that again required government supply rather than payment in the market. The fifth argument was Fabian-economic: centralised government supply of transport and power reaped the economies of large scale technique, financing, and management. The sixth argument, of similar vintage, was that transport and power for lighting and heating was a «natural monopoly» requiring the power of *eminent domain* to facilitate lowest-cost production and distribution. The seventh, and more recent, was, and is, the argument of externality – that some services would be under-produced in the market because they rendered «social benefits» the value of which individuals would not comprehend and for which they would not voluntarily pay; they would therefore have to be taxed and so be forced to pay indirectly for collective production on the required larger scale. The opposite proposition, that some products/services, which imposed «social costs» on third parties who could not be compensated, would therefore be over-produced in the market, formed the eighth argument for government supply. (Since all goods/services have external effects, benefits or costs, if the legal framework is not designed to internalise all externalities, there was nothing left for the market at all.) The ninth argument was the most generalised: government had to control enough of total expenditure (whether, it seemed, there was any justification for individual items or not) to be able to offset fluctuations in private demand in the market, and so keep the economy on an even keel and avoid the opposite excesses of under-employment and over-exuberant price rises.

All of these nine justifications of government expenditure have been rejected, some in recent years. Keynesian countervailing «public» expenditure does not survive the combined critique of Friedman-ite monetarist diagnosis of inflation and unemployment and Buchanan-ite dissection of the *political* inability of government to offset budget surpluses symmetrically with deficits.[1] The appeal to social cost has been undermined by the explanation that divergences between private and social costs and benefits can often be removed by shifting the boundaries of property rights so that effects that were external can be made internal. «Natural monopoly» and economies of large scale that produce monopoly are better left in private hands even if subject to anti-trust law, because they do not survive innovation which introduces new techniques that reap more economies from medium or small scales; in contrast, state control confirms and perpetuates the monopoly, which then requires economic, political and social upheaval to dislodge. Equality and parity of esteem are even more remote in the state economy, where access is determined by differences in political, cultural, racial, religious, class, economic or other forms of power, in which the lowly (the «disadvantaged», «under-privileged» and «deprived» of the new sociology) cannot hope to achieve equality, than in the market, where the inequality of income and wealth can more readily be corrected. Irresponsibility is itself the result of the divorce between payment and service that is the hallmark of state supply of «free» services. And poverty does not require state supply but state redistribution of tax revenue to «top up» low incomes by purchasing power, untied in cash or earmarked by voucher.

---

[1] *J. M. Buchanan* and *R. E. Wagner*, Democracy in Deficit: The Political Legacy of Lord Keynes, New York and London, 1977. The argument is refined and applied to the British economy in *J. M. Buchanan, John Burton* and *R. E. Wagner*, The Consequences of Mr. *Keynes*, Institute of Economic Affairs, London, 1978.

The case for state supply of services, except public goods, has for a century been the creation of intellectuals, a gigantic hoax on the common people that politicians from *Bismarck*, through *Roosevelt* to *Bevan* and *Butler* have gladly embraced because it validated their urge for power, which they variously rationalised as compassion, public service or patriotism. The growth of the state since the 19th century has been the tragedy of the West that will destroy civilisation if it is not resisted and itself destroyed. It has destroyed the individual spirit in Eastern Europe, in large parts of China, and is spreading to Africa where it will probably require armed revolution to overthrow. The market oases of Asia can resist it before it grows further. In the Western World it will now require tenacious strategies to resist and repulse.

III. Weakness in the Case for Government Supply

It is surprising that, despite the intellectual weakness of the arguments for enlarging the province of the state, and their rebuttal by a long line of liberal economists, political scientists, philosophers and historians from *David Hume* and *Adam Smith* 200 years ago to *Karl Popper* and *Friedrich Hayek* in our day, the expansion of the state has proceeded remorselessly. Two kinds of emergencies – war and slump – gave power-hungry politicians the plausible excuse that in crises there was no time for the niceties of intellectual argument about the relative merits of market and state in economic affairs. The growth of the state began a century ago in Britain, but was first accelerated to formidable proportions by the 1914–18 war and then by the 1930–33 depression. It was further enlarged during and after the 1939–45 war. It is difficult to believe that the British Welfare State would have been created in 1946–48 if it had not rested on false analogy with the community action of the war years, and if economists and others, many absorbed in supervising and then running down war-time controls, had been able to put the case against state welfare. Without the 1939–45 war it is doubtful if Keynesian deficit financing or the *Beveridge-Bevan-Butler* welfare state would have been established.

Even so, liberals could have deployed more effectively two arguments against the expansion of the state that might have weighed with what *Hayek* has called the «second-hand dealers in ideas» who shape opinion and influence policymakers, and even with power-hungry politicians.

First: however plausible any of the nine arguments for expanding the state, they remained hypotheses difficult to rebut conclusively since the unknown is always possible. The most their protagonists – Conservatives like *Bismarck* in Germany, «liberals» in the USA like *Roosevelt*, liberal economists in Britain like *Beveridge*, Socialist ideologues like *Bevan*, Conservative politicians like *Butler* – could claim was small-scale pilot experiments to discover whether the hypotheses were supported by testing in the real world of fallible men, imperfect institutions, self-interested bureaucracies. If they were not rebutted by successive experimentation they might then be extended on a larger scale.

Second: even if experimentation had suggested that state supply had advantages that justified wider application, which I doubt, there was never under any circumstances, even those of war or slump, a conclusive case for establishing it on a national scale with power to exclude other methods, techniques or systems. For to do so would be to exclude the possibility of discovering even better methods, techniques or systems that might emerge with the evolution of individual aspirations, social institutions, industrial or commercial innovation. But if no other method, technique or system could emerge because it was suppressed, the only way of demonstrating that state supply was the best system available to man would have been destroyed. However plausible the hypothesis in favour of state supply, and however persuasive the evidence of success in early experiments, the exclusion of alternatives was too high a price to pay for *exclusive* state supply.

There is therefore never, under any circumstances, and even, as Professor W. A. Niskanen[2] has demonstrated, in public goods such as armament research and manufacture, a conclusive case for abolishing the market. That is the truth that liberals in Europe, North America and Australasia have failed to press home with sufficient intellectual tenacity on opinion-formers and policy-makers against the infinitely inferior case for exclusive state supply. Fortunately it is not too late to do so in the Western world or in Asia.

There are reasons for supposing this truth will be heeded more in the future than in the past. For there is now evidence from the thirty years of British post-war experience that state supply has failed. How far the lessons will be learned and applied will depend on the resistance from the older ideas favouring state supply, from the institutions created by state supply, and from the interests that would lose income or property if state supply were run down – government employees organised in trade unions and professional associations with bureaucratic power to influence the course and pace of events.

Two examples from Britain may suffice to illustrate these possibilities, tendencies to reform, and resistances to change. They also indicate the lessons that other Western countries and the emerging market societies of the East could learn if they are not too blind to see.

The case for the British *National* Health Service or for British *universal* comprehensive state education is intellectually so weak that no social political scientist should have given it a moment's credence. Yet, under the influence of political ideologues and bureaucratic trade unions, medical care and education in Britain are being made monopolies that are gradually excluding any alternative method, technique or system of organising medical care or education. The wholly state-owned hospitals in the National Health Service, for example, are gradually ejecting the one per cent of «pay» beds for which patients could pay for a choice of doctor, privacy, maintenance of contact with family or work, or personal comforts. Politicians are allowing non-medical employees such as porters organised in trade unions to have more authority in decisions on medical treatment. And all state schools are gradually being standardised into «comprehensives» in which children of all rates of intellectual advance are taught together, and private schools in which children of similar intellectual capacity are taught together are discouraged. All this – and much more – is being done in the name of equality and the «right» of employees to have decisive influence on the conduct of the «public» services in which they work.

These developments are proceeding without evidence that the hypothesis – that «employee participation» will improve the National Health Service, or that quicker children will galvanise the slower to work and learn more quickly – are substantiated in practice. The sanctity of equality is used to reinforce these trends to exclusive monopoly state supply.

I must add that there are economists and other academics who support the trend not only to state supply but to state monopoly in both. Here is a development that liberals in the West and the East must recognise quickly before it is too late. As state supply extends, it is natural for the state to encourage and finance research into ways of improving the efficiency of its services in order, if nothing more, to win popular support for them and to reduce its requirement of tax revenue. It is also natural for the state to ignore or discour-

---

[2] Bureaucracy and Representative Government, Chicago 1971; Bureaucracy: Servant or Master, Institute of Economic Affairs, London 1973.

age research into ways of improving on state supply, which in practice means discovering ways of making the market work better.

Such developments would have appalled liberals in the 19th century. They should be used by liberals in our day to condemn the politicians, academics and others who tolerate them without thought for their consequences for the future of civilisation.

IV. The Political Creation of Social Conflict

The fundamental flaw in, and the fearsome consequences of, the growth of the state in Western society are clear. The error is that the state has used the same political machinery for private goods that it has to use for deciding the nature and scale of public goods.

The state decides the nature and scale of public goods by majority decisions and committee procedures. Majorities of citizens elect political parties into power, and they in turn decide by majorities in Parliaments or other legislatures or in Cabinet Rooms how much to raise in tax revenue and how to distribute it between defence and other public goods.

1. The misuse of political machinery for private goods

This is the only method government can use. It is crude, arbitrary, clumsy and wasteful, since it does not reflect individual preferences. Refinements are possible: two-thirds or other proportions instead of simple majorities; proportional representation in varying forms to replace first-past-the-post majority voting and prevent government based on minorities; referenda or plebiscites on single issues, or small groups of issues, instead of crude take-it-or-leave-it votes for or against all 27, 49 or 163 planks in the platforms of political parties; varying devices from entrenched clauses to Supreme Courts to prevent governments elected by temporary majorities from riding roughshod over minorities; and others. But there is nothing better that government can do to respect and reflect individual preferences, or the preferences of small groups or uncommon minorities. Since public goods are defined as those that cannot be refused to people who refuse to pay for them, they must be financed by voluntary agreement to pay «compulsorily» by taxes. And tax revenues must be spent by the decisions of majorities and committees.

As government in Britain, and elsewhere in the West, has extended to embrace personal/private services, it has used essentially the same majority/committee procedures to decide the distribution of tax revenues between state education, health care, housing subsidies, pension subsidies (through so-called «social insurance») and many more. The most it can do to respect and reflect the preferences of small groups (but not individuals) is to decentralise such personal/private services to regional or local authorities. But even here decentralisation is limited by the collectivist/egalitarian anxiety to avoid differences between richer and poorer areas, which in Britain are reduced by «block grants» from central government, thus restoring the reality of central state control over education, medical care, housing, and many other nominally «local» services.

This is the flaw in the conduct of state-provided private/personal services. The consequence is a vast growth in *unnecessary* social conflict. There is increasing personal dissatisfaction with government services, especially the most intimate of education and medical care that affect the concern of husbands and wives for each other and of parents for infant and adolescent children: increasingly they feel their family lives are ruled by outsiders. And there is intensifying tension between minorities and majorities because of the electoral power of majorities to decide how minorities shall live. No wonder, as *Hayek* says, groups organise themselves to influence legislatures.

In Britain, as in the USA, there is increasing anxiety to escape from standardised «public services». If individuals were given the choice between paying taxes for government services and paying in the market for private/personal services more nearly «tailored» to their individual or family circumstances, requirements and preferences, many more than now would prefer to pay in the market. In Britain there is no such choice: an individual who would rather pay in the market for a private service has also to pay government for the «public» service he does not use. Short of such a choice in practice, a second-best method of discovering private preferences is the field survey of a national sample asked to state its preferences between the two alternatives, *with their relative costs indicated as nearly as possible.*

The two very different results are highly revealing. In the absence of a clear choice, roughly 5 per cent of British families contract out of state education, despite paying taxes for it, and pay in the market for private education; and roughly $2^{1}/_{2}$ per cent contract out of the National Health Service (or most of it) despite paying taxes for the whole of it, and also pay in the market, through insurance, for private medical care. In contrast, with price-labels attached to both to make the preference significant since demand is meaningless without reference to price, the Institute of Economic Affairs has revealed that the true order of magnitude of the preference for private over government services has risen from 30% for education in 1965 to 52% in 1978, and from 30% for medical care to 58%.[3] The early results of these pioneering researches into these hypothetical demand curves, which indicates the reality behind the crude public choices made in the ballot box and the widespread inability to relate «public» service benefits to their costs in taxes, attracted the attention of Professor *J. M. Buchanan* who discussed them in his celebrated pioneering *Public Finance in Democratic Process* in 1965, sub-titled «Fiscal Institutions and Individual Choice».

These findings indicate the massive suppression of individual preferences by a state system that does not allow contracting out. Little wonder that more and more British citizens feel they are locked into a state system from which they cannot escape except by the large penalty of «paying twice» – once in their taxes for the state service they want to reject and once in prices (fees, charges, insurance premiums, etc) for the private service they prefer.

2. Rising tide of resentment and social conflict

This sense of resentment is producing more explicit tension and conflict as individuals come to understand that their denial of personal choice, their dissatisfactions, «imprisonment», and the political and bureaucratic lack of respect for their private personal or family sensitivities, are *unnecessary*. It is the consequence of using the majority/committee procedure of the political process in the ballot box for services in which, I would argue, the British increasingly sense that it is technically feasible for them to increase

---

[3] The measure was calculated as the response to education and health vouchers worth 2/3 of the cost of paying for a private service. If the voucher had represented the full cost, the responses would presumably have been higher, and the increase faster: *Ralph Harris & Arthur Seldon,* (Overruled on Welfare), IEA, London, 1979.

personal choice by rejecting the unsatisfying (state) supplier. Moreover they know that their rising incomes would enable them to pay (in the market) if they did not have to «pay twice». This growing social conflict arising from the resentment against the coercion of majorities takes numerous forms in Britain. (There are parallels in the USA, Europe, Australia, Asia and Africa.)

a. Regional (national)

A regional, or national, form is that of the people of Scotland and Wales who (rightly) resent the political majority power of the more numerous English to decide the education, medical care and many other personal services the people of Scotland and Wales must use, and pay for in taxes (unless they pay twice). A religious or sectarian form of social conflict arises from resentment of the Catholics of Northern Ireland that so-called «social» but essentially personal services (not least housing) are decided by majorities of Protestants. Within England (and Scotland and Wales and Northern Ireland) racial/religious tension is created among minorities of Catholics, Baptists, Jews and, more lately, Pakistanis who must send their children to schools decided by white, Anglo-Saxon, Protestant majorities. In all three cases there would be less coercion and less social tension, and therefore less cause for «nationalism» in Scotland, civil war (since 1969) in Northern Ireland, and disaffection in England, if the state withdrew from personal «social» services and confined itself to public goods. The Scots, the Catholics, the Jews and Pakistanis would still be outvoted on defence, etc, where opinion does not run on national or religious lines, but not on the conditions of their intimate personal and family lives.

b. Occupational

A second group of social tensions is occupational. The minority of risk-takers, innovators, exceptionally talented (in art, culture, sport, etc as well as industry and commerce) and the exceptionally skilled are pillaged and coerced by the progressive taxation voted by the majority of people who seek security, are not innovators, are only modestly talented, or are unskilled or medium-skilled. The minority of self-employed who are entrepreneurially-minded and independent-spirited are coerced by legislation on employment security, etc, passed by government to appease the large majorities of employees. Established majorities of doctors, actuaries, lawyers, architects, printers, dockers and others are enabled by politically-created legal privileges to exclude minorities of would-be new entrants by prescribing unnecessarily costly training or apprenticeship, superfluous staffing (transport, printing, etc), and other protective devices.

c. Bureaucratic/syndicalist

A third form of friction is created by the use by minorities of articulate activists and manipulators of the political majority/representative/committee system, particularly in education and medical care, to dominate or coerce majorities of passive citizens, who moreover tend to be in the lower-income groups. The «representative» committee which has to operate in the absence of a pricing mechanism has lately been claimed in Britain by the supporters of state economy, notably Mr. Anthony Wedgwood Benn, the energetic Minister for Energy, to be more democratic than the market because it is «accountable» to the citizen who elects it and whom it «represents». This new apologia has been made necessary by the growing disillusionment with conventional «public ownership» (nationalisation) of fuel, transport, education and medical care, because of bureaucratic remoteness and insensitivity to individual circumstances, and the growing syndicalist tendency of the employees, reinforced by laws that endow their trade unions with privileges, to regard the «public services» primarily as means of maintaining jobs and only secondarily as services for the consumer.

d. Cultural, sexual, urban/rural

Yet a fourth form of friction derives from the realisation that cultural elites derive privileges for themselves from government subsidies for minority arts (opera, museums, etc) at the expense of the majority of (usually lower-paid) taxpayers who hardly use them.

A source of friction exploited by Women's Liberationists to demand «equal rights» even in unique circumstances (such as equal pensions despite differences in life expectancy) is the use of the legislature by majorities of politically active men to pass laws that coerce majorities of domestically-minded women.

A recent form of friction is a small but telling example of the tyrannical use by majority power in representative democracy. Politicians with strong support in large towns have moved to outlaw rural pursuits such as fox-hunting by relatively small minorities of countrymen.

Inequality in income and power

Critics of the market complain that people with relatively low income or wealth have less purchasing/voting power in the market than others with relatively high income or wealth. They therefore advocate one-man-one-vote in the polling booth (to by-pass inequality of income/wealth) as the more equitable democratic system of deciding the use of resources. This was the impetus behind the British Welfare State, the American Great Society, Swedish Social Democracy and other manifestations of state supply. And, until the last ten years or so, liberal economists and politicians in Britain paid too little attention to means of evening up incomes without disproportionately adverse effects on incentives.

Yet, even without such measures as negative (or reverse) income taxes or vouchers, liberal economists could have pointed to what was evident from history down the centuries, and not least in Soviet Russia. They could have replied that, if there is no market in which each man's pound or dollar, or Deutschmark, or franc is the same as everyone else's, access will be based on much more arbitrary differences in power, cultural or political, that are more difficult to correct or remove. None of the tensions and incipient conflicts reviewed above can be removed by re-arranging voting systems, making «representative» institutions more «accountable», or devising constitutional safeguards for minorities. Given the political machinery of majority decisions by representatives, the only way the Catholics of Northern Ireland can remove their vulnerability to dominance by Protestant majority is by shooting Protestants and breeding Catholics, so that the Protestant majority is replaced by a Catholic majority. But that would replace Protestant dominance by Catholic dominance, and Catholic grievance by Protestant grievance. And much the same is true of the other forms of friction. There is no solution by political/constitutional reforms so long as government provides private goods.

The only certain method of removing the friction is to remove its cause: the power of majorities to coerce minorities, or of minorities with power to coerce majorities without power. That means depriving men of power over the personal/private lives of other men, and confining political majority decisions to public goods. If the Catholics in Northern Ireland were not taxed to finance schools (or housing) controlled by Protestants but initially had vouchers, and ultimately kept their taxes, so that they could pay fees (or rents) for schools (housing) of their choice, there would be much less cause for avoidable friction. They might still dislike the choices of the Protestants in public goods, but they could no more complain that the Protestants did not make Catholic choices than claim they would make Protestant choices.

The market minimises *group* conflict; state economy maximises group conflict. Liberal economists have not exploited the strength of their case to the full.

V. Social Welfare Function and Individual Frustration

The state economy also maximises *individual* frustration; and the market minimises it.

The «social welfare function» was a figment of the state planners' imagination, or a product of the wishful thinking that individual preferences could be assimilated in broad categories sufficiently to make allocation by central authority of resources among competing employments feasible, and more equitable and efficient than in a market order. Although *Arrow* recognised the impossibility of such a theorem, the suspicion or hope that it might one day be found practicable lingers on. *J. M. Buchanan* has said[4] that, although *Arrow* conceded the impossibility, he «would have been happier if he could have been able to demonstrate that a social welfare function could be constructed», and he «was, and to my knowledge remains, an advocate of social planning». Collective choice theorists continue to examine the restrictions on individual preferences required to generate consistent social orderings.

Opponents of the market claim that government can or would reflect public references more faithfully. What evidence is there for or against this view? In theory it would be feasible to erect a structure of prices and purchasing power, and see how citizens expressed their preferences. I have described above how wide a gap there is in Britain between freely expressed preferences and government allocation of resources. In public goods, supplied collectively and consumed jointly by the populace, no private preferences can be elicited by such «second-best» methods. But more can be done by adapting techniques than has been done by government to validate its claims to serve the national interest by reflecting public preferences. The only evidence it can now point to is that the electorate elects one political party rather than another; and it claims that electoral approval provides evidence of agreement with the elected party's policies.

This is a very unconvincing assertion. First, even the claim to represent a majority cannot be supported; since the 1939–45 war every British government, Conservative or Labour, has been elected by a minority of votes cast (and by as little as a third or a quarter of the total electorate). Second, there has often been little or no choice between the two main parties.[5] Third, there has never so far been an opportunity to indicate preferences on single issues, as there are in Swiss referenda or American «propositions». The only issue put to the vote has been on constitutional matters: adherence to the Common Market (in June 1976) and Scottish/Welsh devolution (March 1979). Otherwise both parties have

---

[4] The Economics of Politics, Readings 18, Institute of Economic Affairs, London 1978.

[5] As Professor *Gordon Tullock* has led us to expect, their policies tended to converge: they were described jocularly or cynically as *Butskellism* (after the Conservative *R. A. Butler* and the Socialist *Hugh Gaitskell*) in the 1950s and *MacWilsonism* (after the Conservative *Harold MacMillan* and the Socialist *Harold Wilson*) in the 1960s.

opposed referenda. Neither therefore can claim to have «represented» the electorate because it has never given them the opportunity to record a clear vote in support of any single one of its policies – from the National Health Service in 1946 to the trade union closed shop in 1974.

But if the political parties refuse to discover latent public preferences, independent organisations can try to discover what can be discovered. (At least, they have not yet been suppressed.) And even if they have to use second-best methods that yield imperfect results, they can make available information on which a tentative judgement can be made about the claim of government to reflect public preferences.

Just as in 1963, 1965, 1970 and in 1978 the Institute of Economic Affairs used sample survey methods to discover how far the British people would prefer to pay for «public» services in the market rather than through government if they had a clear choice by not having to pay twice, so in 1978 it went further to discover how the British would like their taxes spent if they could not have them returned. The findings would provide a rough check on the existence of a social welfare function and begin to indicate how far government was reflecting public preferences, whether in public or private goods.

The findings were published in early 1979[6]. More than 70% thought government expenditure on one or more of a group of seven public goods and private benefits, together representing about $^3/_4$ of total government expenditure (defence, education, health care, roads, housing, unemployment benefit, retirement pensions) should be different from the proportion currently spent by government. This is a first attempt at an elusive social statistic, but it suggests severe doubt about the claim that British government faithfully reflects the preferences of the people whom it loudly and often claims to «represent».

VI. Cash Limits and Pricing Disciplines on Government

If government is not reflecting public preferences, and the solution is not, or not only, to control it by constitutional reform but also to reduce its province to public goods, how is the contraction to be achieved?

The revolt against the state has begun in the USA, in the California vote on Proposition 13 to limit local taxes. A modern *Lenin* might have argued, turning *Marx* on his head, that the people would first resist and roll back the state in the country where it had encroached most on personal/private lives. That country, apart from those like the Communist societies of Europe or Asia where rebellion is suppressed by force, is Great Britain. The British Welfare State, above all in education, medical care, housing and pensions, has invaded personal and family lives to a point at which resistance and rebellion might have been expected at any time since 1948. It is the Welfare State rather than nationalisation of fuel and transport that is now provoking rebellion, because technical/market conditions prevented the state from establishing complete monopoly. Nationalised coal has faced competition from private oil, and nationalised railways from private road and air transport. The consumer of fuel and transport has never felt so much at the mercy of a state monopoly as the consumer of state education or state medicine.

It was natural for the rebellion of the citizen against the state provision of personal /private goods to take the oblique form of resistance to high taxation. In Britain resentment against high taxation, or against particular forms of taxation, has historically

---

[6] (Over-ruled on Welfare) Institute of Economic Affairs, 1979.

provoked armed rebellion or constitutional revolution. Wat Tyler led a Peasants' Revolt against taxation from the English county of Kent in 1381; the Glorious (because bloodless) English Revolution of 1688 was a revolt against the powers of the monarchy, *inter alia* to tax. The American Revolution of 1776 was a declaration of independence from Britain because its Government did not sense how its colonial subjects would react to taxation. The bloody French Revolution of 1789 was stoked by unacceptable taxation. The epidemic of European Revolutions in France, Germany, Italy and elsewhere in 1848 were aggravated by the over-taxation of petty princes or provinces. The American tax revolt of 1978 was ignited by a rejection of local taxes in California.

Rebellions against taxes are not directly rejections of big government and its invasion of personal/private lives. Professor *Milton Friedman* has rightly assessed the California vote for tax limitation as encouraging but not adequate on these grounds. But, to the extent that government spending is limited to tax revenue, a vote against taxation is a vote against government spending, and therefore a vote for cutting government down and rolling back the state. Government may have income from trading; it can borrow; and it can inflate its revenue by printing money. And to the extent that the people limit its revenue by refusing to pay taxes, government may resort to all these three – and possibly new and unknown – methods of maintaining its spending power. But a vote to limit taxation is a natural first step in voting to limit the size of government. An electorate that has voted to limit taxation has warned government that it is not likely to approve expansion in government spending. A vote for lower taxes is not a vote for higher tax revenue.

In Britain changing public attitudes to taxation have been recognised by both main political parties, but they have thought mainly of spending limitation: «expenditure ceilings» or «cash limits». Here Professor *Friedman* has proposed defined cuts in expenditure of X per cent, with the tactical advantage that individual Ministers of Departments would be out-manoeuvred into disputing among themselves on how the total reduction should be divided among them instead of using their familiar tactics of justifying additional expenditure for themselves without reference to any of the others, which is invariably persuasive because additional expenditure brings a positive even if relatively small return. There is little doubt that this internal bargaining would be a formidable step in the effort to reduce the size and power of government as a whole.

Nevertheless the control over government that economists of the Austrian school would wish to urge, in addition to the «cash limit» approach, would be more market-oriented. To use terminology that not all liberal economists find congenial, the «cash limit» approach is macro-economic. The micro-economic approach would be to reduce the size of government by introducing prices for government-supplied personal/private services.

The micro-economic method would have three fundamental advantages over the macro-economic. Cash limits leave the decisions on slimming or «taming» government with politicians and bureaucrats. Pricing would transfer the decisions on cutting down, or cutting out, government to taxpayers/consumers. Even if, say, a 10% cut in the total budget were translated by political bargaining/trading between politicians and between bureaucracies into 15% in defence, 8% in law and order, 6% in health, 4% in education and 2% in roads, cash limits would entail the probability that government would use them to «cut» the highly-desired flowers as well as the dispensable weeds in personal/private services. Individual preferences may be, say, to maintain or even increase government expenditure on police and roads, which many people in Britain may wish, and reduce it on education and health care, leaving individuals to pay more for them privately. Cash limits are not likely to reflect individual preferences with such refinement.

Secondly, charging would make cutting government expenditure more likely than would cash limits since it would transfer the political unpopularity of reducing education, health, housing or other ostensibly desirable welfare services from politicians to the public. Professor *Buchanan* has pointed to the political unrealism of Keynesian «demand management»: that it supposed politicians would be equally ready to create budget surpluses by raising taxes as budget deficits by cutting taxes. He argued that politicians en-

Table 1: The Scope for Charging to avoid Over-Government
(Britain in a recent year)

	Percentages	
	of total govern ment expen- diture	of gross national product
1. Public goods with inseparable benefits (charging impracticable or uneconomic)		
Military defence	10	6
Civil defence	*	*
External relations (embassies, missions, EEC. etc.)	2	1
Parliament & law courts	1	*
Prisons	*	*
Public Health	*	*
Land drainage & coast protection	*	*
Finance & tax collection	1	1
Other government services	*	*
	15	8
II. Public goods with some separable benefits (charging partly practicable)		
Government (central & local) and public corporation current & capital expenditure	6	3
Roads and public lighting	3	2
Research	1	*
Parks, pleasure grounds, etc.	1	*
Local government services (‹misc›)	2	1
Police	2	1
Fire services	*	*
Records, registration, surveys	*	*
	14	8

joy spending and dislike taxing. *Pro tanto*, politicians do not enjoy announcing reduction in welfare (or other) services but, as Governor *Jerry Brown* of Californa has shown, learn to enjoy cutting taxes as soon as public opinion shows it wants taxes cut. Charging thus has political as well as economic advantages over cash limits.

Such a method of reducing government expenditure would be especially applicable in

	Percentages	
	of total govern ment expen diture	of gross national product
III. Substantially or wholly separable benefits (charging substantially practicable)		
Education	12	7
National Health Service	9	5
Personal social services	2	1
School meals, milk & welfare goods	1	*
Employment service	1	*
Libraries, museums & art galleries	1	*
Housing	9	5
Water, sewage, refuse disposal	2	1
Transport & communications	5	3
	40	22
IV. Subsidies, grants, pensions and other (mostly) cash disbursements		
Agriculture, forestry, fishing, food	3	1
Cash benefits for social insurance etc.	16	9
Miscellaneous subsidies, grants, lending, etc. to private/personal sector	3	2
	22	13
V. Interest on National Debt	9	6
Total government expenditure	100	56

* Less than one per cent

Source: Charge, pages 46–7.

Britain, and its experience would be a guide to other Western countries whose governments have gone down the same road as the British but do not yet provide personal/private services on as large a scale, and to countries in the East which could be tempted to venture down the same road. A year ago I tried to estimate the scope for pricing («charging») for British Government services and emerged with the approximation that no more than one-third of all government services were public goods in which joint consumption made charging impracticable (or uneconomic because the revenue might fall short of the costs of collection) and no less than some two-thirds comprised essentially separable personal/private services for which charging was practicable, probably economic, and highly desirable.[7] What would be the comparable German, French, American or other figures? – probably much higher than in the market oases that have had unexampled rates of economic growth because their «public» sector is smaller, their bureaucracies fewer, and their taxation lower.

A third advantage of charging is that it is more likely than «cash limits» to prune personal/private goods out of the «public sector» and leave government with public goods. Taxpayer/consumers cannot, by definition, reduce their individual expenditure on public goods except by emigration. Charging would in time reduce the demand for government supply of personal/private goods, since charging for, say, formerly «free» state education, or charging a market rate for, say, formerly subsidised local government homes, etc, is tantamount to reducing the price of private education and housing. Parents and tenants would therefore raise their demand for private education and housing. In time, most personal/private goods would be transferred out of government into the market. And government would be left providing public goods.

VII. The West's Road the East Could Avoid

Western countries which have over-expanded government now confront, or before long will confront, taxpayer-citizens increasingly frustrated by government supply of personal/private goods. They have a choice of methods by which to extricate themselves from their error. Taiwan, Hong Kong, Japan and other market societies which have not yet over-expanded their government services can avoid the error by leaving personal/private services to develop in the market where they can be paid for directly by consumers with rising incomes. And for consumers with low incomes the solution is not to operate on the side of supply and provide these services by government without charge («free») or at a below-market price, but to operate on the side of demand and ‹top up› low incomes by a reverse income tax or vouchers until incomes rise sufficiently to dispense with such temporary expedients.

The market societies in the East will be tempted by a plausible argument that was once dominant in the West, and still bemuses some politicians and bureaucrats, but has become discredited by events. It was that, as incomes rise, government can «afford» to spend more on social/welfare services. As argued above, the more valid principle is that, as national income rises, government should spend less, because an increase in national income implies that private incomes have also risen.

The danger in acting on the former Western fallacy of raising government revenue *pari passu* with national income is that government expenditure tends to rise faster than na-

---

[7] Charge, London, 1977.

tional income because it is politically easy to extract larger tax revenues out of people whose incomes are rising. This has been the experience of almost all Western countries, which have found their governments spending a gradually *rising* proportion of national income. Although personal expenditure has risen absolutely, it has fallen as a percentage of national income. And the process continues for decades, until taxpayers wake up to the truth that if their incomes are rising they do not have to pay higher taxes to enable government to provide them with services they can pay for themselves, with all the added advantages of choice between competing suppliers in the market.

The political difficulty of reducing government once it has grown large is again illustrated by the state of Tennessee, which, three months before California's Proposition 13, approved (by a two-to-one majority) an amendment to its Constitution to limit the increase in state government spending to the ‹estimated rate of growth of the state's economy›, that is, its national income. This principle of raising government spending proportionately with national/personal income has been heralded as an historic victory of the people over government. Given the vested interests of politicians who love power, bureaucrats who love influence, and state employees (from teachers to firemen) who love their jobs, the claim is understandable. But it goes only half-way to the right relationship between government expenditure and national income. There is no reason at all why the first should rise faster or at the same rate as the second. The right relationship is *inverse*: expenditure should *fall* as national/personal income rises.

But it is more difficult to reduce than to enlarge government. And in the decades when government expenditure rises faster, or even at the same rate, as national income, rising taxation burdens industry, weakens incentives to work, acquire skills, train for management, take risk, start new businesses. All these qualities have helped build the economy and prosperity of Taiwan, Hong Kong and Japan, and their impairment could alter the general direction of effort, enterprise, growth, therefore income and standards of life, and so their safety and national security.

Of even more intimate concern for Chinese and Japanese culture could be the repercussions of the over-expanded state on family life. After 30 years of the Welfare State, both British political parties have «rediscovered» the family, and have belatedly recognised the alarming signs of its disintegration in the increasing births outside marriage, a high rate of divorce, juvenile delinquency, truancy and even arson in (state) schools.

Yet all these and more symptoms of breakdown of the family are not surprising when the state has interposed itself between parents and children. When the state supplies schools, parents feel they do not have much influence in their children's education, and children sense their impotence. When the state provides medical care, parents feel they cannot do much to help their children in sickness or accident, and their children do not look to them for help. When the state (or local government) supplies housing (as it does for one British family in three), parents are seen by their children as having almost no control over the conditions in which they live. And when the state provides pensions in retirement and generally takes care of old people, the bonds between parents and children are stretched, weakened and broken.

How the Chinese family, with Catholic and Jewish families among the most closely knit in the world, and the Japanese family (70 per cent of which have their aged parents living with or near them), would stand up to these strains is for Chinese and Japanese leaders to judge; and the people will judge them. It may be that they would stand up well. But there is no reason to subject them to the strains in the first place. On the contrary, there is strong reason for avoiding the strains by refining the market as the Taiwan, Hong Kong and Japanese economies develop, so that individual and family preferences can be expressed without the direct intervention of government, which can then concentrate its resources on the provision of public goods that their people want but cannot provide by private trading in the market.

Not least, the market oases of Asia could also escape the increasing corruption and rejection of the law evidenced in India and other countries in Asia that have tried to replace the market by government but have succeeded only in driving the open market «underground» into black or grey markets. The contempt for the tax laws in Southern Europe has lately spread to historically law-abiding Britain, where a new form of tax «avoision» has appeared: a mixture of tax avoidance (legal) and tax evasion (illegal) that expresses in the taxpayer's mind a blurring of the moral distinction between the two that used to be acceptable because it was thought that what was legal was moral and what was illegal was immoral.

This distinction has lost its influence on British public attitudes and behaviour. In the first place, there is something artificial and hypocritical in the distinction between tax avoidance and evasion if what is moral avoidance one year can be made immoral evasion in the following year by a change of mind among politicians or bureaucrats concerned with self-interest as much as with public well-being. Secondly, governments are not necessarily capable of moral behaviour solely because they represent majorities: sheer numbers do not transform immorality into morality. «Majorities», as Hayek says, «no longer even ask whether what they decide is just». Third, as recounted above, post-war British governments have not even represented majorities. Fourth, while government has a moral authority to tax all citizens to provide public goods, no such morality extends to taxes levied to supply private goods that taxpayers can arrange with less coercion themselves. Fifth, government which levies taxes that the populace indicates it resents by increasing «avoision» may be regarded as more immoral than the citizenry that avoids or evades them.

Such attitudes would spread in any society where growing government made necessary high and rising taxation. The East could not escape the economic consequences of high taxation experienced by the West.

VIII. Salute

Such are the lessons from the enlargement of the state that liberal economists using the market analysis refined by *Hayek* can teach the East to escape. In saluting his 80th birthday, the leaders and peoples of the market oases of Asia could be as much indebted to him as are the people of the West who are at last heeding his warnings against abandoning the market.

Summary

Individual Liberty, Public Goods and Representative Democracy – Lessons from the West and Escape for the East

As incomes rise and become more equal in competitive societies, individuals can pay for more goods and services in the market: yet British government has since the last world war, and further back for a century, increased its supply. Some of the expansion has been in defence and other public goods, but most of it has been in private/personal/family benefits: education, health care, housing, pensions, transport, fuel, and other services. These tendencies have recently become evident in the market oases of Asia as well as in industrial countries of the West.

The nine arguments for expanding the government supply of goods and services – poverty, irresponsibility, equality of access, parity of esteem, economies of centralisation, natural monopoly, external benefits, external detriments, demand management – have been increasingly seen to be vulnerable and unfounded. But liberal economists could have used two general arguments against state supply: first, that the hypothetical case for government provision was at most an argument for experimentation, not for comprehensive national supply; second, that even if experimentation had indicated that state supply has advantages, they did not justify monopoly. To allow private production and distribution in the market was the only way to demonstrate the superiority of state supply. Exclusion of possibly superior private alternatives was too high a price to pay for the supposed advantages of exclusive state supply.

In practice, even in Western countries with «liberal» traditions, state supply has been increasingly exclusive and has led to deterioration in the quality of state services. The evidence is most clearly apparent in British medical care and education.

The extension in the Western democracies of state services from public to private goods has created unnecessary social conflict. The majority/committee procedures necessarily used by government have suppressed individual preferences. The resulting tensions and conflicts are increasingly seen in Britain. The existence of suppressed preferences is evidenced by field studies that demonstrate a wide gap between the small private sectors in medicine and education that are «allowed» to exist by the side of state medicine and education and the much larger market supply that would result from the creation of unbiased choice through reverse income taxes and/or voucher systems. These developments in Britain and in other industrial countries in Europe, North America and Australasia show undesirable economic and political consequences that the market oases of Asia could avoid.

State economy maximises group conflict and individual frustration; markets minimise them. Further field surveys in Britain suggest that the social welfare function was a figment of the state planners' imagination or wishful thinking.

The defenders of state supply have resorted to the false claim that democratic «representative machinery» can make it accountable to the citizen. This machinery is less egalitarian than the market: the inequalities that arise in the market from inequality in income and wealth are less difficult to modify than is the inequality of cultural, «social», economic or political power which decide access to services in state economy. State «representative machinery» is usually manipulated by articulate activist individuals or groups, usually more literate and moneyed than the average, and is therefore inegalitarian as well as arbitrary and «unjust».

The further claim that public preferences are respected by the machinery of party politics in representative government is no more convincing. In Britain the party in government has not represented majorities of electors since the 1939–45 war; there has often been little or no choice between their policies; and there has been no opportunity for the citizen to record preferences on single services.

The task of confining government supply to public goods will require not only macro-economic «expenditure ceilings» or «cash limits». It will require also micro-economic market pricing or charging, which would be more refined in reflecting individual citizen preferences and be more certain to contract government since it would transfer unpopular political decisions from government to individuals in the market.

Taiwan, Hong Kong, South Korea and Japan have made the fastest post-war economic advance because they have based their economies on open markets and have, so far, avoided the errors of the West in expanding the functions of government from public to private/personal/family services. The recent advice reaching their governments from officials, academics and politicians that, as their national incomes rise they can «afford» to spend more on «social welfare», etc, is an error based on a misconception. There is still time for them to avoid it. The proper relationship between government expenditure and national income is not direct but inverse: as national income and therefore personal incomes rise, government expenditure should fall.

If the market oases of Asia follow the errors of the West they will confront new problems of resistance to government, a weakening respect for law in general, increasing tax «avoision», undermining of the family unit, retarded economic growth, decelerating living standards, weakening national security.

Otmar Issing

Markt, Freiheit und wirtschaftliche Sicherheit*

«Freiheit, die nur gewährt wird, wenn im voraus bekannt ist, daß ihre Folgen günstig sein werden, ist nicht Freiheit. Wenn wir wüßten, wie Freiheit gebraucht werden wird, würde sie in weitem Maße ihre Rechtfertigung verlieren. Wir werden die Vorteile der Freiheit nie genießen, nie jene unvorsehbaren neuen Entwicklungen erreichen, für die sie die Gelegenheit bietet, wenn sie nicht auch dort gewährt ist, wo der Gebrauch, den manche von ihr machen, nicht wünschenswert erscheint. Es ist daher kein Argument gegen individuelle Freiheit, daß sie oft mißbraucht wird. Freiheit bedeutet notwendig, daß vieles getan werden wird, das uns nicht gefällt. Unser Vertrauen auf die Freiheit beruht nicht auf den voraussehbaren Ergebnissen in bestimmten Umständen, sondern auf dem Glauben, daß sie im Ganzen mehr Kräfte zum Guten als zum Schlechten auslösen wird».
F. A. von Hayek, Die Verfassung der Freiheit, S. 40.

Das Studium der Marktbeziehungen steht seit jeher im Mittelpunkt nationalökonomischer Forschung; während jedoch die Klassiker den Staat in ihre positiven und normativen Überlegungen einbezogen, wurde seine Existenz später (außerhalb der traditionellen Finanzwissenschaft) im wesentlichen nur in Form des Trägers wirtschaftspolitischer Entscheidungen berücksichtigt. Der modernen Finanztheorie und der Neuen Politischen Ökonomie verdanken wir eine Rückbesinnung auf die Position der Klassiker und damit eine wesentliche Erweiterung des Gegenstandes wirtschaftstheoretischer Betrachtungen. Eine wichtige Rolle spielt dabei die Erkenntnis, daß der Marktmechanismus, also die Steuerung der Wirtschaft über die Preise, nur eines der Systeme darstellt, in denen Entscheidungen in einer Gesellschaft getroffen werden; *Dahl/Lindblohm* nennen daneben Bürokratie, Demokratie und Verhandlungen[1]. In einer vollständigen Systematik wäre ferner auch der Einfluß von Tradition und Zufall zu nennen[2].

Die Vorzüge des Marktes als Allokationssystem liegen im Prinzip des Tausches zum gegenseitigen Vorteil der Partner; in der Freiwilligkeit der Marktbeziehungen manifestiert sich ein Stück menschlicher Freiheit, während etwa die hierarchische Struktur des Zuteilungssystems «Bürokratie» nicht ohne Zwang auskommt. Das Marktsystem stößt jedoch dort auf seine Grenzen, wo im Prozeß des Tauschverkehrs die Kosten nicht ausschließlich von den unmittelbaren Kontrahenten getragen, sondern zu einem mehr oder minder großen Teil auf die Allgemeinheit abgewälzt werden. Auf der politischen Ebene, sei es durch diktatorische Anordnung oder demokratische Abstimmung, ist dann zu entscheiden, inwieweit die externen Kosten individueller Handlungen durch die Allgemeinheit getragen, durch Internalisierung den Verursachern angelastet werden oder ihre Entstehung verhindert wird.

* Für kritische Anregungen danke ich meinen Kollegen *E. Heuß, J. Klaus, H. C. Recktenwald* und *C. Watrin* sowie meinen Mitarbeitern *H. Brehm* und *R. Fuchs.*

[1] *Dahl R. A., Lindblohm Ch. E.,* Politics, Economics and Welfare, New York 1953, S. 171 ff.

[2] Eine Übersicht findet sich bei: *Frey B. S.,* Gesellschaftliche Entscheidungssysteme, WiSt, April 1976, S. 153 ff.

Die Diskussion um die gesellschaftliche Tolerierung des Konsums gesundheitsgefähr-dender Produkte (Alkohol, Tabak, Rauschgift) zeigt die Möglichkeiten abgestufter Re-aktionen in Form von preispolitischen Maßnahmen, öffentlicher Mißbilligung und so-zialem Druck bis hin zum Verbot, durch das individuelle Freiheitsrechte schlechthin be-seitigt werden.

Für einen Staat, der sich als (wohlwollender) Vormund des Individuums sieht, leiten sich derartige Eingriffe unmittelbar aus diesem Selbstverständnis ab. Die liberale Staats-auffassung hat mit dieser patriarchalisch-diktatorischen Auffassung gebrochen; sie be-tont die Freiheitsrechte des einzelnen gegenüber dem Staat und setzt eine Grenze für die individuelle Freiheit im wesentlichen nur dort, wo die Freiheit des anderen tangiert wird.

Gerade in den modernen Industriegesellschaften, die sich gerne auf ihren liberalen Sta-tus berufen, kann man nun eine seltsame Ambivalenz gegenüber dem angesprochenen Phänomen registrieren. Vom Erfordernis des Jugendschutzes einmal abgesehen scheint es ausgesprochen schwerzufallen, zwischen verschiedenen, teilweise nur graduell unter-schiedlich schädlichen Arten des Konsums zu diskriminieren. Auf der anderen Seite resul-tiert offenbar das kollektive Urteil über den gesellschaftlich nicht tolerablen Mißbrauch der individuellen Konsumfreiheit in zunehmendem Maße aus der Weigerung, die Folge-kosten in Form von sozialen Einrichtungen zu tragen. Die Freiheit gerät damit unverse-hens aus dem Rang des unbestritten höchsten Gutes in den politischen Streit um die Prio-ritäten zwischen einer Mehrzahl verschiedener Werte, unter denen eben auch materielle Größen ihren Platz beanspruchen.

Sofern ein trade-off besteht zwischen Beschränkungen der Freiheit und den gesell-schaftlichen Kosten, die aus der Inanspruchnahme individueller Freiheiten herrühren, hat dieser seine Wurzel in dem Empfinden einer sozialen Verpflichtung, den Einzelnen gegebenenfalls auch in einer selbstverschuldeten Notlage durch kollektive Anstrengun-gen wirtschaftlich sicherzustellen; dies wäre als ein spätes Erbe einer Entwicklung anzu-sehen, die sich von ersten, das Marktgeschehen lediglich in krassen Fällen korrigierenden sozialpolitischen Maßnahmen bis hin zum Sozial- oder Wohlfahrtsstaat vollzogen hat. Unmittelbare Beschränkungen des privaten Konsums aus «sozialen Kostenerwägungen» heraus stellen allerdings bis heute relativ seltene Ausnahmen dar; nicht auszuschließen ist freilich, daß in der Zukunft solche Überlegungen eine größere Rolle spielen und zu Ver-boten oder Einschränkungen besonders gefährlicher Verkehrsmittel, risikoreicher Sportarten etc. führen.

I. Wirtschaftliche Sicherheit und Freiheit

Weitaus umfangreicher sind dagegen die Konflikte, die sich zwischen individueller Freiheit sowie dem Ausmaß und vor allem der Art staatlicher Maßnahmen zur wirt-schaftlichen Sicherheit ergeben. Ohne auf die umfangreiche und wohl niemals endgültig abgeschlossene Debatte um den Begriff näher einzugehen, sei hier im Sinne *von Hayeks* Freiheit als Abwesenheit von Beschränkung und Zwang verstanden[3]. Terminologische

---

[3] *F. A. von Hayek,* Die Verfassung der Freiheit, Tübingen 1971, S. 22. Von zahlreichen Autoren wird dagegen unter Freiheit das Ausmaß der Möglichkeiten verstanden, die Freiheitsrechte dank der Verfügung über entsprechende Ressourcen auch tatsächlich ausnutzen zu können. Freiheit ist dann eine Frage des Lebensstandards. In den Worten von *Rawls* kommen die beide im Grunde völlig verschiedenen Ebenen deutlich zum Ausdruck: «Wir unterscheiden also folgendermaßen zwischen der Freiheit und ihrem Wert: Die Freiheit besteht in dem gesamten System der gleichen

Schwierigkeiten, wenn auch ganz anderer Natur, bereitet ebenfalls die Definition der wirtschaftlichen bzw. sozialen Sicherheit. Die Auffassung, daß man darunter die staatliche Sicherung eines bestimmten Existenzminimums zu verstehen habe, dominiert zwar weitgehend in der theoretischen Literatur[4]; in der politischen Diskussion hat sich dagegen die Vorstellung der Garantie des einmal erarbeiteten Lebensstandards weitgehend durchgesetzt[5]. Weiterhin kann man beobachten, daß der in dieser Weise geschützte bzw. als schutzbedürftig betrachtete Personenkreis ständig ausgedehnt wurde. Wie soziale Sicherheit aber auch immer definiert werden mag, es bleibt die Tatsache, daß in der Bundesrepublik Deutschland das «Sicherungsnetz» für weite Kreise der Bevölkerung engmaschig gezogen ist. Inwiefern soll es nun möglich sein, daß Art und Umfang der Sozialleistungen, die für sich betrachtet als gewaltiger Fortschritt erscheinen, mit der persönlichen Freiheitssphäre in Konflikt geraten?

Beispielhaft soll dieser Zusammenhang zunächst anhand der gesetzlichen Krankenversicherung demonstriert werden, die bisher als leistungsfähig und – etwa im Vergleich zum englischen System – gleichzeitig ein hohes Maß an Freiheit gewährend eingestuft wird. Ihren freiheitlichen Charakter verdankt sie dem Umstand, daß die Nachfrager in der Vergangenheit kaum reglementiert wurden und die Anbieter durch erhebliche finanzielle Anreize motiviert waren. An einer marktlichen Regelung fehlte im wesentlichen «nur» ein Element, nämlich der Preismechanismus. Der Versicherte hat für die Kosten nicht direkt, sondern indirekt in Form von einkommensabhängigen Beiträgen aufzukommen; die individuell in Anspruch genommenen Leistungen erwirbt er praktisch zum Nulltarif.

Ein derartiges Allokationssystem, das eine im Grunde eigenartige Mischung von Elementen der Hierarchie (Beitragserhebung) und des Marktes verkörpert, stellt jedoch keine Dauerlösung dar, sondern ist von der Konstruktion her zum Scheitern verurteilt. Die Gründe dafür bedürfen mittlerweile kaum mehr der näheren Erläuterung: Die einzelnen Nachfrager verhalten sich individuell rational und behandeln die Leistungen des Gesundheitssektors als freies Gut; Appelle an die soziale Verantwortung bleiben demgegenüber wirkungslos. Die zum Preis von Null nachgefragte «Sättigungsmenge» droht schließlich einen Umfang zu erreichen, der nicht mehr finanzierbar ist. In diesem Zeitpunkt, in dem eine Reform des bisherigen Systems unausweichlich wird, werden die Weichen gestellt. Als Alternativen bieten sich an eine verstärkte Steuerung über den Markt, d. h. unter Einschluß des Preismechanismus, soweit dieser anwendbar ist, oder eine Abwendung vom Markt hin zur Reglementierung. Dieser zweite Weg begegnet aus naheliegenden Gründen wesentlich geringeren politischen Widerständen und läßt sich damit leichter durchsetzen; an seinem Ende droht aber zwangsläufig die Zuteilung durch den Apparat der Gesundheitsbürokratie und damit der Zwang sowie die Beseitigung des Anreizsystems für die Produzenten. Warteschlangen, Vorzugsbehandlungen für Funktionsträger etc. sind die bekannten Begleiterscheinungen des reglementierten Systems.

---

bürgerrechtlichen Freiheiten; der Wert der Freiheit für einzelne oder Gruppen hängt von deren Fähigkeit ab, innerhalb dieses Rahmens ihre Ziele zu erreichen. Die Freiheit ist als gleiche Freiheit für alle gleich; es entsteht kein Problem des Ausgleichs für geringere Freiheit. Doch der Wert der Freiheit ist nicht für jedermann der gleiche». *Rawls J.*, Eine Theorie der Gerechtigkeit, Frankfurt 1975, S. 233.

[4] Allerdings finden sich auch hier Ausnahmen. So definiert etwa *G. Weisser* soziale Sicherheit als Schutz der Lebenslage vor bestimmten Gefahren der Verschlechterung. *Weisser G.*, Soziale Sicherheit, Handwörterbuch der Sozialwissenschaften, 9. Band, Stuttgart 1956, S. 396.

[5] Diese Feststellung trifft für die Bundesrepublik: *v. Bethusy-Huc, V.*, Das Sozialleistungssystem der Bundesrepublik Deutschland, Tübingen 1976[2], S. 222.

An diesem Beispiel läßt sich im übrigen zeigen, daß die Auffassung eines vermeintlichen trade-offs zwischen sozialer Sicherheit und individueller Freiheit durchaus auf einem Trugschluß beruhen kann. So steht in der Hinwendung zur Reglementierung zwar am Anfang eine Entscheidung für die soziale Sicherheit auf Kosten freiheitlicher Formen der individuellen Vorsorge, doch endet dieses System in letzter Konsequenz in einem Zustand, in dem eine geringere Qualität der Versorgung und damit der Sicherheit einhergeht mit einer Beseitigung der persönlichen Freiheit für alle Beteiligten.

II. Allokation der meritorischen Güter

Keine Alternative für eine freiheitliche Gesellschaft gibt es zum Markt als Steuerungssystem bei den Gütern, die man gemeinhin dem privaten Sektor zurechnen kann; Schwierigkeiten bereiten dagegen die Allokation öffentlicher Güter und insbesondere die Verteilung der sog. meritorischen Güter. Aber auch hier läßt sich die These, daß das Zurückdrängen von Marktelementen tendenziell freiheitsbeschränkend wirkt, vielfach belegen. Dazu sei hier ein Ausschnitt aus dem Bildungssektor gewählt, dessen «Produktion» nach allgemeinem Verständnis in der Liste der meritorischen Güter ganz obenan zu stehen pflegt.

Freiheit in der Wahl akademischer Berufe setzt zweierlei voraus, nämlich Freiheit in der Wahl des Studiums und bei erfolgreichem Abschluß die Chance, den erwählten Beruf ausüben zu können. In einer reinen Marktlösung hätte jeder einzelne die Kosten seiner Ausbildung und das voraussichtliche spätere Einkommen ins Kalkül einzubeziehen. Mit dem Hinweis auf den «materialistischen» Charakter und ähnlichen Vorwürfen erfährt die Anwendung ökonomischer Kriterien auf die Organisation des Bildungssektors überwiegend schroffe Ablehnung. Auch wenn die Gegenposition zur Marktlösung nur selten in dieser Klarheit beschrieben wird, kann sie in der nüchternen Sprache der Ökonomie wie folgt umrissen werden: freie Wahl des Universitätsstudiums ohne jede Kostenbelastung und Übernahme der Absolventen zum garantierten Lohn.

Ein System dieser Art könnte jedoch nur so lange funktionieren, als – aus welchen Gründen auch immer – die Zahl der Eintrittsberechtigten so niedrig bleibt, daß die Ausbildungskapazitäten ausreichen und das Angebot an Absolventen die Nachfrage nicht übersteigt. Nimmt die Zahl der Studierwilligen zu, ergeben sich zwangsläufig Diskrepanzen auf dem Akademikermarkt insgesamt und speziell innerhalb der einzelnen Teilmärkte. Freiheitsbeschränkende Zwangseingriffe werden unvermeidbar, Fehlallokationen können nicht ausbleiben; diese nehmen vor allem dann teilweise groteske Formen an, wenn zwischen der Reglementierung des Zugangs zu den einzelnen Studiengängen und der Situation des jeweiligen Teilarbeitsmarktes kein Zusammenhang besteht, also etwa die Zulassung dort stark beschränkt wird, wo die Absolventen gute Berufschancen besitzen (und umgekehrt).

Zukunftsbezogene Handlungen stehen unter dem Vorzeichen der Unsicherheit, der Marktprozeß trägt diesem Umstand durch unablässige Anpassungen der individuellen Angebots- und Nachfragepläne Rechnung, für die der Marktpreis die entsprechenden Signale gibt. Planung als der Versuch einer gedanklichen Vorwegnahme der Zukunft kann die Ungewißheit als solche nicht beseitigen, sie kann aber die Ebene bestimmen, auf der sie sich äußert. Zunächst einmal muß sie jedoch die Freiheit der individuellen Entscheidung beseitigen – die Freiheit der Berufswahl hat in einem reglementierten Bildungssystem keinen Platz; eine «effiziente» Planung des Ausbildungssystems setzt ferner in letzter Konsequenz eine Planung der gesamten Wirtschaft voraus, da die Nachfrageseite anders nicht als fester Bestandteil in das Gesamtsystem integrierbar ist. Soweit die Mengenplanung gelingt bzw. durch den Zwangscharakter des Systems garantiert wird, verlagert sich die Folge der Ungewißheit auf die Preise, d. h. am Arbeitsmarkt auf die Entlohnung: Der Reallohn der einzelnen Berufsgruppen bleibt die Variable, sofern eine Gleichgewichtslösung überhaupt angestrebt wird.

Allokationsmechanismen, in denen Elemente staatlicher Reglementierung und freiheitlicher individueller Entscheidungen gleichzeitig zum Tragen kommen, zeigen ganz spezifische Defekte. So etwa dann, wenn der Zugang zu einem bestimmten Studium beliebig offen steht, keine kostenmäßigen Restriktionen (Nulltarif) vorliegen und der Staat als (im wesentlichen) einziger Nachfrager nach den Absolventen gleichzeitig die Menge und den (Lohn-)Preis bestimmt oder durch Gesetz den Nachfragepreis festlegt. Prognosen oder selbst absolut zuverlässige Daten über den «Bedarf», d. h. die konkret nachgefragte Menge, sind in Zeiten der «Akademikerschwemme» vor Studienbeginn für den einzelnen keine wesentliche Entscheidungshilfe, da er einmal die Reaktionen der anderen nicht kennt und außerdem nicht voraussehen kann, ob er am Ende innerhalb des festen Kontingents derer sein wird, die – zum garantierten Lohn – Anstellung erfahren oder nicht.

Die Beseitigung des Preismechanismus als eines entscheidenden Bestandteils eines Allokationssystems, das auf freien individuellen Entscheidungen beruht, erhöht die individuelle Unsicherheit bis zum Extrem, wenn lediglich ein Teil der Absolventen in den Genuß der fixierten Entlohnung kommt, die restlichen aber keine Chance besitzen, eine Anstellung in dem gewünschten Beruf zu erhalten. Ein funktionsfähiger Markt würde dagegen auf eine Situation des Angebotsüberschusses mit sinkender Entlohnung reagieren und damit zu einer Erhöhung der Nachfrage beitragen; die Unsicherheit wird in diesem Prozeß nicht beseitigt, sie verlagert sich jedoch auf die Entlohnung – im Gegensatz zum Plansystem allerdings unter Wahrung der Freiheit der individuellen Entscheidung. Im übrigen würden von den (relativen) Lohnbewegungen auf den einzelnen Teilmärkten Signale ausgehen, die von den Studienanfängern jeweils im Rahmen ihrer Entscheidung berücksichtigt werden könnten und daher geeignet wären, das Ausmaß der Preisschwankungen zu verringern[6].

III. Der Arbeitsmarkt

Der Arbeitsmarkt stellt einen Sektor dar, auf dem die Marktelemente im Laufe der Zeit immer weiter über das aus «sozialen» Gründen erforderliche Maß hinaus verdrängt wurden. Gleichzeitig kann man hier besonders deutlich die Folgen einer Entwicklung studieren, die sich daraus ergeben, daß mit der Fixierung bestimmter Parameter die Anpassung auf andere Variable verlagert wird.

Beinahe schon unter die trivialen Sätze ist die Aussage zu rechnen, daß die Tarifpartner zwar den Nominallohn festlegen können, nicht aber den Reallohn, bei dem die Vollbeschäftigung erreicht wird. Die sozialen Kosten eines darüber hinaus erhöhten Reallohnes

---

[6] Es wäre interessant, die Informationskosten der verschiedenen Systeme miteinander zu vergleichen und auf ihre Allokationsfunktion hin zu überprüfen. Gesamtwirtschaftlich (und gesellschaftlich) wäre ferner die Wirkung einer individuellen Kostenbeteiligung als Alternative zum Nulltarif in die Überlegung einzubeziehen.

der Beschäftigten lassen sich an der entsprechenden Rate der Arbeitslosigkeit ablesen. Bei der nun schon Jahre anhaltenden Unterbeschäftigung und pessimistischen Prognosen über die absehbare Entwicklung des Arbeitsmarktes richten sich gesetzliche Maßnahmen und Vereinbarungen der Tarifpartner zunehmend nicht mehr nur auf den Preis (Lohn), sondern unmittelbar auch auf die Menge (Beschäftigung), die durch Schutzbestimmungen vor Kündigungen, Rationalisierungsvorhaben und ähnlichem gesichert werden soll.

Durch administrative Regelungen dieser Art werden wiederum die Risiken, die aus der Unsicherheit über die Zukunft resultieren, als solche nicht beseitigt; werden daher einzelne Gruppen vor diesen Risiken geschützt, kann das nur heißen, daß sie von anderen getragen werden müssen. Zu diesen rechnen zunächst einmal die Arbeitslosen, die nicht eingestellt werden, weil etwa die Unternehmen das Risiko einer durch die Schutzbestimmungen erzwungenen künftigen Überbeschäftigung nicht tragen wollen oder können. Da sich die Unternehmen also im Falle eines Absatzrückganges nicht marktgerecht verhalten können, sinkt auch die Investitionsneigung; eine mögliche Schaffung von Arbeitsplätzen unterbleibt.

Auch bei der Regelung der Arbeitsverhältnisse könnte jedoch ein Rückgriff auf Marktelemente dem Bedürfnis der Beschäftigten nach mehr wirtschaftlicher Sicherheit Rechnung tragen, ohne die Wirtschaft deswegen in einem Dickicht von Reglementierungen erstarren zu lassen. Wirtschaftliche Sicherheit als knappes Gut hat ihren Preis; marktmäßig wäre daher eine Lösung zu nennen, in der dieser Preis individuell entsprechend dem Ausmaß der in Anspruch genommenen Sicherung zugerechnet würde. So könnte man sich beispielsweise durchaus differenzierte Vereinbarungen vorstellen, die jeweils unterschiedliche «Mischungen» aus Lohnhöhe und Arbeitsplatzgarantie darstellen. Die kollektive Verordnung von wirtschaftlicher Absicherung trägt dagegen den unterschiedlichen individuellen Präferenzen nicht Rechnung und verlagert darüber hinaus einen Teil der Kosten auf Gruppen, die sich gegen diese Belastung nicht wehren können, selbst aber nicht in den Genuß der Vorteile kommen[7].

Der Konflikt zwischen den Begünstigten und Benachteiligten ist daher in solchen marktwidrigen Reglementierungen schon vorprogrammiert. Sein Ausbruch kann hinausgeschoben werden durch finanzielle Leistungen an die Gruppe derer, die von den Segnungen der genannten «Sicherheitsmaßnahmen» ausgeschlossen sind. In einem System dieser Art werden sich etwa die Zahlungen der Arbeitslosenversicherung immer mehr von ihrer ursprünglichen Absicht, nämlich der Existenzsicherung in einer vorübergehenden (konjunkturellen), unverschuldeten Notlage, entfernen und den Charakter eines dauerhaften Transfers annehmen; er wird von den Beschäftigten erbracht, die in den Genuß der vielfältigen Maßnahmen der sozialen Sicherung des Arbeitslebens (im eigentlichen Sinne) kommen, und an die gezahlt, die nicht zuletzt wegen dieser Reglementierungen arbeitslos bleiben. Mit der Ausdehnung der wirtschaftlichen Sicherheit der Beschäftigten steigt freilich auch der Preis für das politische «Stillhalten» der Nichtbeschäftigten. Wegen der zunehmenden Belastung der «Aktiven» mit Abgaben und der wachsenden Honorierung der «Inaktiven» verringert sich jedoch zwangsläufig der Abstand zwischen dem finanziellen Ertrag der beiden Situationen. Die kaum vermeidbare Bruchstelle des Systems ist dann erreicht, wenn entweder die Gruppe der Beschäftigten revoltiert und/oder eine zunehmende Präferenz für den Status des Unbeschäftigten den Rahmen des Finanzierbaren sprengt.

---

[7] In der Diskussion des Verhältnisses von Freiheit und Ungewißheit betont *Heuß,* daß die Ungewißheit geradezu die Bedingung für die Existenz der Freiheit ist. (*Heuß, E.,* Freiheit und Ungewißheit, Ordo 1965, S. 53). Es bedeutet daher eine Pervertierung dieses Komplementaritätsverhältnisses, wenn die Tatsache der Ungewißheit als Anlaß für die Beseitigung der Freiheit dient.

IV. Individuelle Freiheit und sozialer Rahmen

Diesem Aufsatz wurde ein Zitat *von Hayeks* vorangestellt, aus dem ein Satz wiederholt werden soll: «Unser Vertrauen auf die Freiheit beruht nicht auf den voraussehbaren Ergebnissen in bestimmten Umständen, sondern auf dem Glauben, daß sie im Ganzen mehr Kräfte zum Guten als zum Schlechten auslösen wird». Damit die Ausübung individueller Freiheit dieser Hoffnung gerecht werden kann, bedarf es jedoch eines Gesamtrahmens, innerhalb dessen die individuellen Handlungen zu einem sozial akzeptablen Ergebnis führen können – nicht von ungefähr trägt das *Hayeksche* Werk den Titel «Verfassung der Freiheit». Es ist das Verdienst der klassischen Nationalökonomen, insbesondere von *A. Smith*, den Markt als ein System entdeckt zu haben, das die auf eigenen Vorteil gerichteten Handlungen zu einem für die Gemeinschaft vorteilhaften Zusammenwirken koordiniert. Zu den Voraussetzungen, die erfüllt sein müssen, damit der Markt diesem Anspruch genügt, zählt vor allem, daß der einzelne für die Folgen seiner Aktivitäten verantwortlich bleibt, die Vorteile genießen kann und die Nachteile tragen muß. Regelungen, die aus sozialen oder anderen politischen Motiven heraus diesen Zusammenhang grundsätzlich beseitigen, zerstören das Fundament, auf dem das liberale Plädoyer für die Freiheit beruht – der Mechanismus zur sinnvollen Koordination der individuellen Handlungen wird unterbrochen, individuell rationales Verhalten erhält schließlich den Charakter der Sozialschädlichkeit. Von dieser Feststellung bis zur Beseitigung der individuellen Freiheit ist dann nur noch ein kleiner Schritt.

Summary

Market, Liberty, and Economic Security

The market process represents only one of various systems within which decisions are reached in a society. Another one is bureaucracy. While the latter goes hand in hand with coercion, the exchange in markets is based on voluntary actions. There are, however, also limits to the market mechanism, i.e. when individual actions produce negative external effects.

Modern industrial states tend to restrict the individual liberty to consume unhealthy products (alcohol, tobacco, drugs) on the grounds of the social costs caused by the damage, which results from consuming these goods. Thus, liberty is involved in a kind of trade-off with financial values. Still more important is the fact that the alleged trade-off between liberty and economic security may prove a fallacy. To obtain more security, a social security system may initially only slightly restrict individual liberty, but it may well end with both liberty and security being highly diminished.

Bureaucratic regulations also predominate in the education sector; more confidence in the market would increase both, individual liberty and social security. Still a further example is the labour market, which is nowadays almost paralysed by all kinds of general restrictions. The scope of liberty would be wider if everyone could, at his cost, choose the degree of his social security.

Christian Watrin

Grenzen der Gleichheit in einer freiheitlichen Ordnung

> «Die Nationen unserer Tage können nicht bewirken, daß bei ihnen die gesell-
> schaftlichen Bedingungen nicht gleich seien; von ihnen jedoch hängt es ab, ob
> die Gleichheit sie in die Knechtschaft oder in die Freiheit, zur Gesittung oder
> in die Barbarei, zum Wohlstand oder ins Elend führt.»
> *Alexis de Tocqueville*

I. Freiheit und Gleichheit als Themen der ordnungspolitischen Diskussion

Es wird allgemein anerkannt, daß in einer freiheitlich-demokratischen Ordnung, die nicht zur Anarchie verkommen oder in die Despotie umschlagen soll, für jeden gleiche Grenzen seiner allgemeinen Handlungsfreiheit gelten müssen. So wird nicht nur die Freiheit, über Einkommen autonom zu disponieren, durch staatliche Zwangsabgaben zur Finanzierung öffentlicher Güter eingeschränkt, sondern Freiheitsbeschränkungen gibt es auch dort, wo individuelles oder kollektives Handeln die Handlungsfreiheit anderer in einer Weise, die als unzulässig angesehen wird, beeinträchtigen oder gefährden kann. So ist es ein großer Fortschritt in der Rechtsentwicklung, daß die Beschränkung der Wettbewerbsfreiheit anderer durch Kartellabsprachen oder Lieferboykotts nicht mehr als Ausübung eines legitimen Freiheitsrechtes mißverstanden, sondern als Verstoß gegen die Grundlagen einer freiheitlichen Wirtschaftsordnung aufgefaßt wird.

Wenn es aber als sinnvoll und notwendig erachtet wird, Grenzen der Freiheit festzule-gen, dann ist auch zu fragen, ob in der freiheitlichen Ordnung analog auch Grenzen der Gleichheit bestimmt werden müssen. Gibt es akzeptable Gründe – etwa unter Berufung auf Freiheitsrechte –, Ungleichheiten zwischen Menschen zu dulden, m. a. W. läßt sich überhaupt die Ansicht vertreten, daß eine Ordnung, die Ungleichheiten zuläßt, als frei-heitlich bezeichnet werden kann?

Es gibt hierzu viele Antworten, und das Verhältnis von Freiheit und Gleichheit hat in der Geschichte des westlichen Denkens nicht erst seit der «Revolution der Gleichheit» im achtzehnten Jahrhundert zahlreiche Interpretationen erfahren. Niemand dürfte heute bereit sein, mit öffentlichem Anspruch die Gleichheit von Menschen im Sinne ihres *glei-chen Ranges* in Zweifel zu ziehen, wie das die Rassentheorie unseres Jahrhunderts mit entsetzlichen Folgen für die Diskriminierten tat. Auch die von *Aristoteles*[1] vertretene Auffassung, nach der von Natur aus die einen Menschen zum Sklavendienst und die an-deren zu entsprechender Herrschaft bestimmt sind und nach der «der Sklave (so gut wie) ein Teil seines Herren, gleichsam ein lebendiger aber abgetrennter Teil seines Körpers»

---

[1] *Aristoteles*, Aufzeichnungen zur Staatstheorie (Politik), übersetzt von *Walter Siegfried*, Köln 1967, S. 26 f.

ist, über den diesem die uneingeschränkte Herrschaft zusteht, wird heute ebenso allgemein abgelehnt wie jeder Versuch, zu den Ordnungsprinzipien der Alten Gesellschaft zurückzukehren und etwa erbliche Ämter neu zu schaffen[2].

Das entscheidende Datum für die neuere Geschichte des Problems ist ohne Zweifel die Französische Revolution, die die Freiheit, die Gleichheit und die Brüderlichkeit auf ihre Fahnen schrieb. *Dahrendorfs*[3] Urteil unterscheidet sich nur in Nuancen von *Tocquevilles* Analyse, wenn er bemerkt, daß durch diese Revolution die Idee der Gleichheit zur treibenden Kraft in der europäischen Geschichte geworden sei. Allerdings sollte in Erinnerung gerufen werden, daß die Ordnung der Alten Gesellschaft zwar keine allgemeine Gleichheit und auch keine individuelle Freiheit im heutigen Sinne kannte, wohl aber ein gestuftes System von Gleichheit und Freiheiten innerhalb mehr oder minder selbständiger Korporationen, der Städte, der Grundherrschaften, des Adels und der Kirche. Durch die geistigen Väter und dann durch die politischen Träger der Französischen Revolution aber wurde diese gestufte Sozialordnung zunächst in Zweifel gezogen und dann verdrängt. Das seit zwei Jahrhunderten bestimmende Ordnungsmodell stellt Individuen und Staat ohne Vermittlung durch Stände oder partikuläre Gewalten einander gegenüber und faßt die Bürger als *freie und gleiche Menschen* auf. Das historische Verdienst der Französischen Revolution wird allgemein in der Durchsetzung der allgemeinen Gleichheit im Sinne der Abschaffung von Standesprivilegien gesehen. Die politischen Bestrebungen, Gleichheit im Sinne der staatsbürgerlichen Gleichheit zu verwirklichen und das allgemeine Wahlrecht an die Stelle des Dreiklassenwahlrechts treten zu lassen, hatten erst später Erfolg.

Die Diskussionen über Gleichheitsfragen in der Gegenwart unterscheiden sich von den älteren Debatten dadurch, daß der Grundsatz der politischen Gleichheit (das Staatsbürgermodell) auf den *gesellschaftlichen* Bereich übertragen werden soll, also auf jenen Sektor, in dem nach den klassisch-liberalen Anschauungen der einzelne im Rahmen der Grenzen der Rechtsordnung sich frei entfalten und betätigen kann. In der deutschen Diskussion mag dieser Gesichtspunkt gelegentlich zu kurz kommen im Zuge der Verengung der Aufmerksamkeit auf Bildungsfragen und der Betrachtung von Schulen als Stätten, in denen die Gleichheit junger Menschen durch den Abbau sogenannter Milieuschranken gefördert werden soll. Eine weiter gesteckte Behandlung des Gleichheitsproblems muß jedoch von folgendem Argumentationsmuster ausgehen: Der Hauptvorwurf gegen eine freiheitliche Ordnung heutigen Zuschnitts läßt sich auf die Formel bringen, daß der Bereich des Politischen, besonders aber die Wahlen, durch die Gleichberechtigung und damit die Gleichheit aller Bürger ausgezeichnet sei. Jeder verfügt nur über eine Stimme. Im Bereich des Marktes hingegen sei Ungleichheit vorherrschend, da der Wettbewerb — selbst dort, wo die Konkurrenten möglicherweise einmal von der gleichen Linie aus starteten, — Differenzierung und wirtschaftliche Ungleichheit erzeuge, die wieder in politische Macht umschlage.

---

[2] Siehe hierzu die klassische Argumentation von *Alexis de Tocqueville,* Über die Demokratie in Amerika. Übersetzung aus dem Französischen, Ausgabe der dtv-bibliothek, München 1976, S. 819.

[3] *Ralph Dahrendorf,* Einleitungsreferat zum Thema «Revolution der Gleichheit – Ende oder Beginn der Freiheit?» Bergedorfer Gesprächskreis zu Fragen der freien industriellen Gesellschaft. Protokoll Nr. 47 vom 4. März 1974. Herausgegeben vom Bergedorfer Gesprächskreis, Hamburg-Bergedorf. o.O., o. J., S. 6.

II. Konzeptionen der Gleichheit

Auf eine Nachzeichnung der neueren Problemgeschichte des Verhältnisses von Freiheit und Gleichheit soll hier zugunsten einer Erörterung von zwei Grundpositionen verzichtet werden. Sie seien plakativ bezeichnet als die demokratisch-egalitäre und die freiheitlich-nichtegalitäre Konzeption.

1. Der demokratisch-egalitäre Entwurf

Seit Beginn des neunzehnten Jahrhunderts wird von sozialistischen und marxistischen Geistesströmungen die Auffassung vertreten, daß eine freiheitliche Ordnung besonders im Bereich der wirtschaftlichen Beziehungen der Menschen untereinander nichttolerable Ungleichheiten schaffe. Zwar habe die bürgerlich-demokratische Entwicklung im neunzehnten Jahrhundert die juristische und politische Gleichheit durchgesetzt, die «materielle» oder gesellschaftliche Gleichheit fehle hingegen noch weitgehend.

Aus diesem Befund werden zwei verschiedene Schlußfolgerungen gezogen. Die erste ist die radikal-marxistische Antwort, daß das weithin bestehende private Eigentum an Produktionsmitteln zur Klassenspaltung zwischen Kapitalisten und Proletariern führe, die – solange jenes bestehe – nicht «aufgehoben» werden könne. Die moderne Marktwirtschaft, sprich: der «Kapitalismus», sei deswegen keine Gesellschaft von Gleichen. Die Ungleichheit zwischen Kapitalisten und Proletariern könne jedoch nicht im Rahmen der bestehenden Ordnung, sondern nur im Zuge einer radikalen Systemänderung überwunden werden, an deren Ende die Beseitigung der Ungleichheit des Eigentums bei den Produktionsmitteln durch Vergesellschaftung stehe, da nur das Gemeineigentum aller an den Gütern höherer Ordnung die Gleichheit der Bürger und damit auch die Aufhebung der Klassenspaltung gewährleiste.

Das Gemeineigentum an den Produktionsmitteln wird somit zum Vehikel der Gleichheitsverbürgung. Wenn aber das private Produktionsmitteleigentum in Gemeineigentum überführt sei, dann – so wird weiter argumentiert – könnten alle Bürger gleichberechtigt und aktiv nicht nur an der Bildung des politischen Willens teilnehmen, sondern auch an der Leitung der Wirtschaft und der anderen gesellschaftlichen Einrichtungen mitwirken. Die Bürger eines Landes aber wären erst dann wirklich gleich und damit auch frei, wenn sie in allen wichtigen Bereichen des gesellschaftlichen Lebens gleichberechtigt mitbestimmten[4].

In der marxistischen Version fällt allerdings der Zeitpunkt des Eintritts in die Gesellschaft der Gleichen erst mit dem Erreichen der «Überfluß»gesellschaft zusammen, von der es heißt, daß sie irgendwann in der Zukunft realisiert werden würde. Die ordnungspolitische Frage nach der Verfassung dieser Gesellschaft wird damit umgangen und für die Gegenwart der realen sozialistischen Gesellschaften die Suspendierung der Gleichheitsregel zugelassen. Am Beispiel der Güterverteilung läßt sich das leicht demonstrieren. Im *Marxschen* Epigramm heißt es für die Zukunftsgesellschaft: «Jeder nach seinen Fähigkeiten, jedem nach seinen Bedürfnissen». Diese Formel, die gerne als die Verteilung nach dem Bedarfsprinzip gedeutet wird, erweckt bei den weniger Begabten und Leistungsschwächeren den Eindruck, daß sie den gleichen Anteil an den irdischen Gütern wie die Fähigeren und Begabteren erhalten werden.

---

[4] Siehe hierzu die knappe Darstellung im Artikel: Gleichheit, soziale. In: Marxistisch-Leninistisches Wörterbuch der Philosophie. Hrsg. von *Georg Klaus* und *Manfred Bücher*, ro-ro-ro-Handbuch, 1972, Bd. 2., S. 456.

Dieses ideale Ergebnis soll aber erst in der zweiten Phase der kommunistischen Gesellschaft, wenn «der enge bürgerliche Rechtshorizont ganz überschritten» ist, dadurch erreicht werden, daß die Talentierten dann uneigennützig für die Mehrung des allgemeinen Wohlstands sorgen. Sie verzichten ihrerseits auf das sprichwörtlich größere Stück am gemeinsamen Kuchen, dessen sie noch aus Gründen der Leistungsanreize in der ersten Phase der kommunistischen Entwicklung bedürfen, in der sie «in jeder Beziehung, ökonomisch, sittlich geistig noch behaftet (sind) mit den Muttermalen der alten Gesellschaft».[5] Mit diesem Versprechen läßt sich für die irdische Welt des realen Sozialismus das Leistungsprinzip und damit die wirtschaftliche Ungleichheit in Anspruch nehmen, denn auf dieser Gesellschaftsstufe «erhält der einzelne Produzent – nach den Abzügen (für die Finanzierung öffentlicher Güter, C. W.) – exakt zurück, was er ihr (der Gesellschaft, C. W.) gibt».[6] Nach den zahlreichen Erfahrungen mit den Versuchen, die erste Stufe des Kommunismus in die Tat umzusetzen, heißt das, daß dort, wo nicht die Geldstimmen der Verbraucher und der Wettbewerb der Unternehmer, sondern politische Gremien den Wert einer Leistung bestimmen, die jeweils Herrschenden ihren eigenen Beitrag hoch bewerten und daß dort gleichzeitig neue Systeme der gesellschaftlichen und wirtschaftlichen Ungleichheit zwischen Privilegierten und Nichtprivilegierten geschaffen werden.

Die zweite Schlußfolgerung aus dem Befund der «materiellen» bzw. gesellschaftlichen Ungleichheit hingegen schlägt zur Lösung des Problems der Gleichheit die Mitwirkung und Mitbestimmung aller in den wesentlichen gesellschaftlichen Lebensbereichen vor, allerdings ohne die Einschränkung, daß erst Kollektiveigentum und klassenlose Gesellschaft geschaffen sein müßten, um die spannungslose Koexistenz von Freiheit und Gleichheit zu ermöglichen. Die gleiche Teilhabe an den gesellschaftlich wichtigen Entscheidungen auf der Basis demokratischer Regeln soll auch hier sowohl Freiheit als auch Gleichheit verbürgen. Diesseits des Reichs der unerreichbaren Überflußgesellschaft wird die Lösung des Problems von Freiheit und Gleichheit darin gesehen, daß durch die Partizipation alle gleichberechtigt werden und dadurch auch frei sind. In der voll demokratisierten Gesellschaft ist jeder Konflikt zwischen der Idee der Freiheit und der Gleichheit im *Hegelschen* Sinne «aufgehoben». Freiheit setzt Gleichheit voraus und die demokratische Gleichheit in allen Angelegenheiten soll ihrerseits Freiheit bedingen.

Da das Problem nicht in die fiktive Welt des vollendeten Kommunismus verschoben wird, ist nach den institutionellen Bedingungen zu fragen, wie denn die möglichst gleiche Teilhabe aller an den wesentlichen Entscheidungen in die Tat umzusetzen ist. Der mittlerweile hinreichend bekannte und in manchen Bereichen ansatzweise in die Praxis umgesetzte Lösungsvorschlag ist das Partizipationsmodell. Sein Grundgedanke ist einfach: Die demokratische Teilhabe des Bürgers erstreckt sich nicht nur auf den politischen, sondern auch auf den gesellschaftlichen Raum.

Demokratisierung ist dabei als ein Prozeß vorzustellen, der sich allmählich vollzieht und in dem die Rechte auf gleiche Teilhabe nicht über Nacht, sondern nur schrittweise verwirklicht werden können. Ob und inwieweit die Partizipationsgesetzgebung in den Unternehmen, den Universitäten, den öffentlichen Betrieben und den Schulen oder die gegenwärtig erörterte Demokratisierung der Wirtschaft auf überbetrieblicher Ebene, die die Lenkung oder zumindest Vorstrukturierung der Investitionen durch Wirtschafts- und Sozialräte zum Gegenstand hat, ein erster Schritt auf diesem Wege ist, sei offengelassen. Entscheidend ist die Grundfrage, ob demokratische Teilhabe entsprechend den Grund-

---

[5] *Karl Marx*, Politische Schriften, 2. Bd. Hrsg. von *Hans-Joachim Lieber*, Darmstadt 1971, S. 1022 (Kritik des Gothaer Programms).
[6] Ebenda.

annahmen der demokratisch-egalitären Konzeption unter realistischen Annahmen tatsächlich auch Aussicht auf gleiche Teilhabe eröffnet.

Die Grundprämisse des Modells, daß Demokratie – oder genauer: demokratische Teilhabe – die Gleichheit aller Beteiligten dadurch verbürgt, daß jeder Teilnehmer nur eine Stimme in die Waagschale werfen kann, hält nur vordergründig einer Überprüfung stand. Die Zuweisung der Macht- und Entscheidungsbefugnisse durch Wahlakte verändert die für den Ausgangszeitpunkt zunächst angenommene Gleichheit zwischen den Staatsbürgern grundlegend. Die Gewählten erlangen anders als ihre Wähler ein Mandat auf Zeit, das sie berechtigt, Maßnahmen zu ergreifen, die auf den Widerspruch, ja die Mißbilligung der von ihnen Repräsentierten treffen können und dies häufig auch tun. Die Kontrolle der Macht des demokratisch gewählten Souveräns ist deswegen ein zentrales Problem jeder freiheitlichen Ordnung. Das gilt um so mehr, wenn die Politik professionalisiert wird und Abgeordnete, die im Sinne der klassisch-liberalen Demokratielehre die Inhaber eines freien Mandats sind, mannigfachen politischen Zwängen unterliegen.

Dieser Einwand gewinnt an Gewicht angesichts der in der Realität nicht bestehenden Gleichheit der Startchancen von Teilnehmern an demokratischen Abstimmungen. Gleiche Teilhabe würde voraussetzen, daß jeder auch eine gleiche Chance hat, gewählt zu werden. Selbst in der kleinen Gruppe, in der der Einsatz von knappen Ressourcen zu Wahlkampfzwecken nur eine untergeordnete Rolle spielt, ist das, wie die Theorie der informellen Gruppenbeziehung zeigt, wenig wahrscheinlich. Für die große Gruppe (im *Olsonschen* Sinne)[7] aber besteht schon in der Phase der Wahl keine Gleichheit der individuellen Wahlchancen, da der Zugang zu und die Kontrolle von Wahlkampfmitteln nach aller Erfahrung ungleich verteilt und je nach Interessenlage (etwa bei Bewerbung um die Wiederwahl) auch verschieden nutzbar sind. Es wird zwar der Eindruck zu erwecken versucht, daß im «Reiche der Selbstverwaltung aller durch alle»[8] diesen Problemen nur wenig Gewicht beizumessen wäre; tatsächlich ist jedoch die Ungleichheit zwischen den Teilnehmern an demokratischen Wettbewerbs- und Entscheidungsprozessen eine sozialstrukturelle Tatsache, die der ideologischen Überhöhung demokratischer Verfahren entgegenzusetzen ist.

Deswegen ist, wie *Max Weber* hervorgehoben hat, auch zu beachten, daß der Name «Demokratisierung» irreführend wirken kann, denn «der Demos im Sinn einer ungegliederten Masse ‹verwaltet› in größeren Verbänden nie selbst, sondern wird verwaltet und wechselt nur die Art der Auslese der herrschenden Verwaltungsleiter und das Maß von Beeinflussung, welches er oder richtiger: andere Personenkreise aus seiner Mitte durch die Einwirkung einer sogenannten ‹öffentlichen Meinung› auf den Inhalt und die Richtung der Verwaltungstätigkeit auszuüben imstande sind.» Deswegen muß Demokratisierung auch «nicht etwa notwendig Zunahme des aktiven Anteils der Beherrschten an der Herrschaft innerhalb des betreffenden Sozialgebildes bedeuten».[9]

Ungleichheit besteht aber nicht nur zwischen Wählern und Gewählten, sondern auch zwischen den Gewinnern und den Verlierern einer Abstimmung. Es gilt zwar als demokratische Tugend, sich einer Mehrheitsentscheidung zu beugen. Aber es ist zweifelhaft, ob die Unterordnung unter den Willen der anderen in – wie gefordert wird – «allen rele-

---

[7] *Mancur Olson Jr.*, Die Logik des kollektiven Handelns. Kollektivgüter und die Theorie der Gruppen, Tübingen 1968, S. 3 f.

[8] *Heinz-Dietrich Ortlieb*, Die mißverstandene Freiheit oder woran eine egalitäre Gesellschaft zugrunde geht. In: Hamburger Jahrbuch für Wirtschafts- und Gesellschaftspolitik, 23. Jahr (1978) S. 15.

[9] *Max Weber*, Wirtschaft und Gesellschaft. Studienausgabe herausgegeben von *Johannes Winckelmann*, Zweiter Halbband, Köln und Berlin 1964, S. 724 f.

vanten gesellschaftlichen Bereichen», also gerade dort, wo die freiheitlich-nichtegalitäre Ordnung die Chance zur unabhängigen und eigenen Gestaltung der Lebensverhältnisse bietet, ein erstrebenswertes Ziel und überdies menschlich auf Dauer ertragbar ist. Die Verfechter der egalitären Vorstellung haben hier keine befriedigende Antwort zur Hand. Sie überspielen das Problem der unterliegenden Minorität entweder dadurch, daß sie unterstellen, alle Beteiligten seien stets einer Meinung, was im Grunde die demokratische Abstimmung überflüssig macht, oder sie halten die uneingeschränkte Macht der Mehrheit über die Minderheit für rechtens. Letzteres aber widerspricht, wie *von Hayek* nicht müde wird zu betonen, den Prinzipien einer freiheitlichen Ordnung[10].

Schließlich aber ist bei dem Programm der Gleichheit durch demokratische Teilhabe zu beachten, daß im politischen Prozeß nicht abstrakte Individuen, sondern konkrete Menschen handeln, deren Interessen gerade hinsichtlich des politischen und gesellschaftlichen Geschehens in der Regel höchst unterschiedlich gelagert sind und deren Bereitschaft, Zeit und Mittel in die Teilnahme an den jeweiligen demokratischen Willensbildungsprozessen zu investieren, folglich sehr verschieden sein kann. Gerade das aber bedingt im politischen Leben Ungleichheit zwischen den Wählern, zwischen den gut und den schlecht Informierten, zwischen den nicht und den gut Organisierten. Demokratische Entscheidungsverfahren verbürgen somit keineswegs die angenommene allgemeine Gleichheit unter den Gesellschaftsmitgliedern. Demokratie – verstanden als Verfahren der Mehrheitsabstimmung in gemeinsamen Angelegenheiten – kann deswegen auch nicht die allein ausschlaggebende Verfassungsregel in einer freiheitlichen Ordnung sein, wie seit *Tocqueville* die Mahner vor den Gefahren der verschiedenen Wege in den demokratischen Totalitarismus immer wieder betont haben[11].

2. Der freiheitlich-nichtegalitäre Entwurf

Die zweite Konzeption, die hier als die freiheitlich-nichtegalitäre Alternative bezeichnet wird, unterscheidet sich von den bisher erörterten Varianten dadurch, daß sie nicht unterstellt, Freiheit und Gleichheit könnten ohne Spannungsverhältnis nebeneinander bestehen. Ebenso wie in einer freiheitlichen Ordnung die Freiheitsrechte nicht schrankenlos sein können, wenn das Ganze nicht schaden nehmen soll, bedarf auch die Forderung nach Gleichheit der Grenzen.

Der Konfliktpunkt kann so umschrieben werden: Inwieweit darf die menschliche Freiheit, die das Recht auf individuelle Entfaltung verbürgt, aus Gründen der Herstellung oder Sicherung der Gleichheit eingeschränkt werden? Anders ausgedrückt: Wo Freiheits-

---

[10] Siehe hierzu besonders *Friedrich A. von Hayek*, Die Verfassung der Freiheit, Tübingen 1971, passim.

[11] Siehe *Friedrich A. von Hayek*, Grundsätze einer liberalen Gesellschaftsordnung. In: Derselbe, Freiburger Studien, Tübingen 1969, S. 109. Die kritischen Hinweise liberaler Autoren auf die Gefahren und Risiken demokratischer Abstimmungsverfahren werden gelegentlich dahin mißverstanden, daß es sich um eine Ablehnung der Ideale handelt, die – in einer weiteren Fassung – oft mit dem Begriff Demokratie verbunden werden. Siehe hierzu jedoch die klärende Bemerkung *von Hayeks* (a.a.O.) und seinen Hinweis, daß es beim Liberalismus um das Ausmaß der Regierungsgewalt geht, während unter Demokratie die Allokation von Entscheidungsmacht bei bestimmten Wahlkörpern unter Beachtung bestimmter Verfahrensregeln zu verstehen ist. Die wieder im Vormarsch begriffene jakobinische Demokratiekonzeption, die allein am Mehrheitsprinzip orientiert ist, verwischt den entscheidenden Unterschied zwischen totalitärer und freiheitlicher Demokratie. Siehe auch *Jakob L. Talmon*, Die Ursprünge der totalitären Demokratie, Köln und Opladen 1961, S. 2 ff.

rechte gewährleistet werden, entstehen zwischen Menschen in bezug auf Wohlstand, Einkommen, Macht und Autorität, Ungleichheiten, weil die Fähigeren ihre Talente besser einzusetzen verstehen als die weniger Begabten und die von der Natur Vernachlässigten oder die schlechter Ausgestatteten. Inwieweit aber haben die Fähigeren ein Recht, ihre Talente einzusetzen oder ihre besseren Ausgangspositionen zu nützen?

Auf den ersten Blick entsteht der Eindruck eines unausweichlichen und letztlich nicht zu bewältigenden Konfliktes zwischen beiden Leitideen. Das ist jedoch eine zu dramatische Sicht des Spannungsverhältnisses, denn es gibt ohne Zweifel wichtige Gebiete, in denen Freiheit und Gleichheit im Rahmen einer freiheitlichen Ordnung miteinander vereinbar sind. Ein ständiges Leitmotiv des westlichen Denkens ist die Vorstellung, daß sich die Menschen in der liberalen Gesellschaft – vor allem etwa beim Gütertausch und bei Verträgen – einander als Freie und Gleiche gegenübertreten. Zu den selbstverständlichen Gleichheiten in einer freiheitlichen Ordnung aber zählen auch die Gleichheit vor dem Gesetz, der Grundsatz der gleichen Freiheitsrechte für alle, das allgemeine Wahlrecht, die Gleichheit im Zugang zu öffentlichen Ämtern oder das Verbot der staatlichen Ungleichbehandlung aus Gründen der Rasse, des religiösen Bekenntnisses und des Geschlechtes.

Diese verschiedenen Ausprägungen des Gleichheitsprinzips, dessen Auslegung im einzelnen Schwierigkeiten bereiten mag, ohne daß die Grundsätze kontrovers sind, können vielleicht am ehesten unter dem Sammelbegriff «Gleichberechtigung» zusammengefaßt werden. Die Erfüllung der oben genannten Gleichheitsbedingungen schließt jedoch nicht aus, daß die tatsächlichen Ungleichheiten zwischen Menschen nach wie vor gewaltig sind, nicht nur im Hinblick auf Lebensalter, Lebensaussichten, Gesundheit und Intelligenz oder die Einbettung in soziale Bezüge wie Familie, Freunde, Bekannte, Nachbarschaft und Kollegen oder die Staatsbürgerschaft in einem armen oder reichen Land, sondern auch im Hinblick auf das individuelle biologische und kulturelle Erbe und das jeweilige Lebensschicksal.

In den letzten beiden Jahrzehnten sind Unterschiede in der natürlichen Situation der Menschen Gegenstand zahlloser Erörterungen und Programme gewesen. Dabei ging es beispielsweise darum, ob Unterschiede des Geschlechts Ungleichheiten rechtfertigen, so den unterschiedlichen Zugang von Frauen zu Berufen, Unterschiede zwischen Frauen- und Männerlöhnen[12] und viele andere Aspekte der tatsächlichen oder vermeintlichen Diskriminierung nach Geschlechtern. Ferner wurde heftig erörtert, wie die genetischen Anlagen von Menschen zu veranschlagen seien. Ist es zutreffend, daß Begabungen vererblich sind oder kann davon ausgegangen werden, daß – wie auch die klassischen Ökonomen annahmen – Menschen in einem Zustand natürlicher Gleichheit geboren werden, so daß später auftretende Unterschiede im Berufserfolg oder in der Leistungsfähigkeit im wesentlichen auf Milieufaktoren rückführbar sind?

Die beiden zuletzt skizzierten Positionen führen zu unterschiedlichen politischen Empfehlungen. Wer von der Idee ausgeht, daß die Menschen bei der Geburt in ihren natürlichen Anlagen gleich sind, wird dazu neigen, die Herstellung oder Wiederherstellung der Gleichheit unter den Menschen zu verlangen. Im Bereich der Erziehung bedeutet das die Forderung nach Abbau der Milieufaktoren von der frühkindlichen Phase an, d. h. die Beseitigung sogenannter Bildungsbarrieren durch Akte staatlicher Erziehungsorgane. Nach der Auffassung des Deutschen Bildungsrates im Strukturplan für das Bildungswesen[13]:

---

[12] Hier ist die in der öffentlichen Diskussion fast ausschließliche Konzentration der Aufmerksamkeit auf die Lohnsätze und die Vernachlässigung aller Gesichtspunkte des Lebenseinkommens, einschließlich der wegen der höheren Lebenserwartung von Frauen vergleichsweise längeren Rentenzahlung, problematisch.

[13] Zitiert nach *Klauer*, Ein Diplom für jedermann? Frankfurter Allgemeine Zeitung Nr. 236/1973, S. 14.

«Die Gleichheit der Chancen wird in manchen Fällen nur durch die Gewährung besonderer Chancen zu erreichen sein.» Wird dieser Grundsatz nicht pragmatisch im Sinne des sozialen Ausgleichs für erlittene Benachteiligungen, sondern konsequent gehandhabt, so birgt er die Gefahr, zur negativen Diskriminierung zu führen, zur bewußten Politik der Einebnung der verschiedenen Talente und Fähigkeiten, kurz zur Redressierung der Unterschiede. Gleichheit kann dann bedeuten, daß für ethnische Minoritäten ein proportionaler Anteil an öffentlichen Positionen reserviert wird, ohne daß Rücksicht genommen wird auf das Prinzip des gleichen Zugangs für alle, oder daß die Fähigkeiten des begabten Kindes nicht entwickelt, sondern eher zurückgedrängt werden, um die möglichst weitgehende Egalisierung innerhalb der jeweiligen Altersstufe zu erreichen.

Diesen Vorschlägen liegt ein abstraktes Menschenbild zugrunde. Es wird nicht versucht, jeden einzelnen als unverwechselbare Persönlichkeit, als Geschöpf Gottes oder der Evolution zu verstehen, dessen Lebenslauf und Schicksal einmalig ist, sondern es wird ein die Individualität menschlicher Existenz in Abrede stellendes Idol postuliert, das der Bedeutung von existentiellen und weitgehend nicht aufhebbaren Unterschieden zwischen Menschen entweder nicht ausreichend Rechnung trägt oder sie sogar in Abrede stellt. Daraus folgen Programme, die im Wege der Anwendung des Zwangs durch staatliche oder gesellschaftliche Organe die Chancen der individuellen Entfaltung zurückdrängen und die – im äußersten Fall – bis hin zum Einsatz der Mittel einer Erziehungsdiktatur reichen. Es ist deswegen zu fragen, ob es bessere Lösungen gibt.

Im Anschluß an *John Rawls'* Buch «Eine Theorie der Gerechtigkeit»[14], das dem Gleichheitsproblem besondere Aufmerksamkeit widmet und oft wegen seiner egalitaristischen Grundtendenz gelobt wird, läßt sich argumentieren, daß in neuerer Zeit die Probleme des menschlichen Zusammenlebens in großen Gesellschaften aus zwei konkurrierenden Perspektiven gesehen werden: (1) der Betrachtung sozialer und ökonomischer Beziehungen unter dem Gesichtspunkt des Konflikts oder (2) ihrem Verständnis als eine Veranstaltung der friedlichen Kooperation.

Der erste Gesichtspunkt wurde in der Geschichte des politischen Denkens von *Thomas Hobbes* betont, von *Karl Marx* in seiner Theorie des Klassenkonfliktes auf die Spitze getrieben und durch die *Dahrendorfsche* Konfliktlehre in die Gegenwart transplantiert. Die Konfliktlehre durchzieht mittlerweile Legionen von Traktaten sozialwissenschaftlichen, politischen und literarischen Inhalts[15]. Pflichtet man ihr bei, dann ist Ungleichheit gesellschaftlich untragbar, da sie im Konfliktfall zum Sieg des Stärkeren über den Schwächeren, zur Übervorteilung der weniger Geschickten durch den Geschickteren und damit zur Befestigung der Ungleichheit unter Menschen führt. Die Ungleichheit wird im sozialen und wirtschaftlichen Prozeß stabilisiert, es gibt Herrschende und Beherrschte, Ausbeuter und Ausgebeutete, und Freiheit und Gleichheit sind Fiktionen, die allenfalls der Verschleierung von Herrschaftsverhältnissen dienen. Wenn man aber nicht an die Katharsis der *Marxschen* Revolution glaubt, dann müßte es nach dieser Auffassung allein aus Gründen der Sicherung der sozialen Koexistenz geboten sein, alles zu tun, um eine möglichst weitreichende Gleichheit zwischen den Menschen zu schaffen, denn nur so können die das gesamte gesellschaftliche Leben durchziehenden Konflikte auf ein noch erträgliches Maß heruntergeschraubt werden. Gleichheitspolitik sichert so, auch wenn sie die Freiheit erheblich einschränkt oder sogar aufhebt und selbst wenn sie den Grundsatz der Gleichbehandlung verletzt, das soziale Zusammenleben.

---

[14] *John Rawls*, Eine Theorie der Gerechtigkeit, Frankfurt am Main 1975.
[15] Siehe hierzu *Thomas Nipperdey*, Ist Konflikt die einzige Wahrheit der Gesellschaft? Mensch und Gesellschaft in den hessischen Rahmenrichtlinien. Frankfurter Allgemeine Zeitung vom 24. und 25. Oktober 1973.

Die Betrachtung der menschlichen Gesellschaft unter dem Konfliktaspekt hat jedoch den Mangel, daß sie das in Wirklichkeit vorhandene hohe Ausmaß der tatsächlich bestehenden Kooperation zwischen Menschen nicht erklären kann. Personen in höchst ungleichen sozialen und ökonomischen Rollen arbeiten in Unternehmen zusammen. Die Arbeitsteilung auf nationalen und internationalen Märkten, die nichts anderes darstellt als indirekte Produktion, schafft wirtschaftliche Kommunikationsbeziehungen zwischen Menschen in aller Herren Ländern. Das Prinzip aber, das diesen friedlichen Beziehungen zugrundeliegt, ist: die Ausnutzung von Ungleichheiten, und zwar der individuellen Fähigkeiten und Talente, der ökonomischen und der sozialen Ausstattung, kurz der komparativen Vorteile. Die menschliche Gesellschaft kann somit aufgefaßt werden als ein Unternehmen der Zusammenarbeit zum gegenseitigen Vorteil, als ein Positiv-Summenspiel, in dem es Interessenübereinstimmungen aber auch Konflikte gibt. Erstere bestehen, weil die gesellschaftliche Zusammenarbeit die Ausnutzung der Vorteile der Arbeitsteilung in einem Maße ermöglicht, das allen Bestrebungen, nur auf der Basis eigener Anstrengungen oder denen einer kleinen Gruppe zu leben, weit überlegen ist[16]. Ein Hauptsatz der ökonomischen Theorie lautet: Handel ist der Autarkie überlegen, weil er Vorteile für alle Beteiligten erzeugt[17]. In der menschlichen Kooperation aber treten Interessenkonflikte auf, weil es den Beteiligten nicht gleichgültig ist, wie die Ergebnisse der Zusammenarbeit verteilt werden, denn in der Regel zieht jeder einen größeren einem kleineren Anteil vor. In den einfachen Sätzen der Tauschtheorie ausgedrückt: Über die Aufteilung des potentiellen Handelsgewinns können Meinungsverschiedenheiten bestehen, die allerdings in dem Umfang abnehmen, wie an die Stelle von zwei Tauschpartnern eine große Zahl von Beteiligten tritt und jeder Marktteilnehmer den sich aus der Interaktion ergebenden Preis als gegeben ansieht[18]. Mit der Betonung der Vorteile der marktlichen Interaktion für die Beteiligten, dem Hinweis auf die individuellen Gewinne aus freiwilligen Tauschhandlungen, den sich auf ihnen aufbauenden komplexen Strukturen der Arbeitsteilung und damit der indirekten Produktion aber stehen die Ökonomen im Streit der sozialwissenschaftlichen Meinungen allein. Andere Sozialwissenschaften bevorzugen eher einseitige Konflikt- oder – früher auch – Harmoniemodelle. Die Frage, ob deren Erklärungskraft jedoch dem ökonomischen Ansatz überlegen ist, ist erst wenig erörtert.

Die *Rawlssche* Lösung, die an das ökonomische Paradigma anknüpft, besteht nun in dem Vorschlag, die freie Gesellschaft so zu verfassen, daß die Ungleichheiten in der natürlichen Ausstattung oder in den gesellschaftlichen Ausgangspositionen allen zugute kommen. Nicht durch Redressierung der Unterschiede (etwa durch das Zurückdrängen der Talente der besonders Begabten) soll Gleichheit erzwungen werden. Es wird vielmehr eine andere Lösung bevorzugt: Die ungleiche Ausstattung des einzelnen mit Fähigkeiten und Talenten, die die Folge eines im wesentlichen unbekannten Evolutions- und Selektionsprozesses ist, in dem nicht nur natürliche, sondern auch kulturelle Faktoren eine Rolle spielen, wird als eine vorgefundene Tatsache aufgefaßt, der in der freiheitlichen Ordnung dadurch Rechnung getragen wird, daß soziale und wirtschaftliche Ungleichheiten so zu gestalten sind, daß sie folgende Bedingungen erfüllen: Es muß vernünftigerweise erwartet werden können, daß sie für jedermann von Vorteil sind, bzw. unter Berücksich-

---

[16] Eine interessante allgemeine Begründung findet sich bei *James M. Buchanan,* The Limits of Liberty, Chicago/London 1964, S. 29 ff. – Derselbe, A Hobbesian Interpretation of the *Rawlsian* Difference Principle, Kyklos Bd. 29, 1976, S. 10.

[17] Eine aktuelle Interpretation dieses Satzes findet sich in dem Aufsatz von *Hans Willgerodt,* Bemerkungen zum Freihandelsproblem, Ordo Bd. 29 (1978) S. 343 ff.

[18] *James M. Buchanan,* Markets, States and the Extent of Morals. American Economic Review. Papers and Proceedings. Vol. 68 (1978) S. 364.

tigung der zweiten Formulierung des *Rawlsschen* Prinzips, soziale und wirtschaftliche Ungleichheiten müssen so beschaffen sein, daß sie den am wenigsten Begünstigten den größtmöglichen Vorteil bringen.

Auf die verschiedenen Formulierungen der Gerechtigkeitsgrundsätze bei *Rawls*[19], die intuitive und die systematische Version, kann hier nicht im einzelnen eingegangen werden. Die zweite Formulierung stellt im wesentlichen einen Versuch dar, mit den aus der Wohlfahrtsökonomik bekannten Schwierigkeiten der Amalgamierung von individuellen Präferenzrangfolgen zur sozialen Nutzenskala fertig zu werden und an die Stelle der problematischen Bestrebungen der Utilitaristen, die gesellschaftliche Nutzensumme zu ermitteln, ein einfaches und eindeutiges Wohlfahrtskriterium zu setzen. Vor allem will *Rawls* verhüten, daß unter der Annahme eines kardinalen Nutzenmaßes Ungleichverteilungen dadurch gerechtfertigt werden, daß der Schlechterstellung einiger ein höherer kollektiver Nutzen gegenübergestellt wird. An einer wichtigen Stelle[20] schreibt er in bezug auf die Verfassungsregeln, die in einer von ihm als «original position» beschriebenen Ausgangsposition gewählt werden: «Ich behaupte, daß die Menschen im Urzustand zwei ... Grundsätze wählen würden: einmal die Gleichheit der Grundrechte und -pflichten, zum anderen den Grundsatz, daß soziale und wirtschaftliche Ungleichheiten, etwa verschiedener Reichtum und verschiedene Macht, nur dann gerecht sind, wenn sich aus ihnen Vorteile für jedermann ergeben, insbesondere für die schwächsten Mitglieder der Gesellschaft. Nach diesen Grundsätzen kann man Institutionen nicht damit rechtfertigen, daß den Unbilden einiger ein größerer Gesamtnutzen gegenüberstehe, daß einige weniger haben, damit es anderen besser geht. Es ist aber nichts Ungerechtes an den größeren Vorteilen weniger, falls es dadurch auch den nicht so Begünstigten besser geht».

Wenn die Existenz sozialer und wirtschaftlicher Ungleichheiten nicht ohne weiteres, wie die Anhänger egalitaristischer Positionen annehmen, ein Grund ist, eine Verletzung von Gerechtigkeitsgrundsätzen anzunehmen, dann ist damit noch nicht die schwierige Frage entschieden, wie die Verfassung einer nichtegalitaristischen freiheitlichen Ordnung zu gestalten ist und wie in Einzelfragen verfahren werden soll.

Rawls' institutionelle Vorschläge zur Ausgestaltung einer gerechten Ordnung können hier nicht im einzelnen erörtert werden. Es sei lediglich auf seine Auffassung hingewiesen, daß eine Marktwirtschaft mit funktionsfähiger Wettbewerbspolitik bei offenen Märkten, mit Vollbeschäftigung der Ressourcen, hinreichend breiter Eigentums- und Vermögensstreuung, angemessenen Regeln der Besteuerung, Garantie eines Mindestlebensstandards, fairer Chancengleichheit und der Garantie gleicher Freiheiten für alle als eine Ordnung angesehen werden kann, in der die sich ergebende Einkommensstreuung seinen Gerechtigkeitsvorstellungen genügt[21]. Der im vorliegenden Zusammenhang entscheidende Punkt aber ist die Interpretation des Problems der Verteilungsgerechtigkeit als eine Frage der Verfassung der Grundinstitutionen der menschlichen Gesellschaft. *Rawls* gehört in diesem Punkt zu den Vertretern des Grundsatzes der *Verfahrensgerechtigkeit*.

---

[19] *Rawls*, a.a.O., S. 81 und S. 336.
[20] Ebenda S. 31 f.
[21] *John Rawls*, A Theory of Justice, Oxford University Press 1973, S. 87. Die zitierte Passage ist in der deutschen Übersetzung nicht enthalten (vgl. a.a.O. S. 108). Die entsprechende Passage findet sich jedoch auch in älteren Schriften von *Rawls*. So in Constitutional Liberty and the Concept of Justice, Nomos VI (Justice) New York 1963, S. 117, zitiert bei *F. A. Hayek*, Law, Legislation and Liberty, Bd. 2, London 1976, S. 179. Zu weiteren Einzelheiten der Ordnungspolitik siehe *Rawls'* Ausführungen auf S. 338 ff., S. 344 ff. Ferner *Chr. Watrin*, Eine liberale Interpretation der Idee der sozialen Gerechtigkeit. Bemerkungen zum Buch von *John Rawls* «Eine Theorie der Gerechtigkeit». Hamburger Jahrbuch für Wirtschafts- und Gesellschaftspolitik. 21 Jahr (1976) S. 55 ff.

Die Frage nach der Gerechtigkeit ist das vorrangige Kriterium, an dem sich die Zulässigkeit oder Unzulässigkeit von Ungleichheiten in einer freiheitlichen Ordnung entscheidet. Folglich werden auch Gerechtigkeit und Gleichheit nicht wie im egalitaristischen Denken einander gleichgesetzt. Ferner wird der Vorrang allgemeiner Regeln betont und die Herstellung von Gleichheit im Sinne einer allgemeinen Einkommensgleichheit – wie immer diese Vorstellung interpretiert werden mag – wird nicht zum Ziel erhoben. Ebensowenig aber wird die Forderung erhoben, daß in jeder beliebigen Situation jeder bestehende Wohlstandsunterschied durch den Nachweis eines Nutzens für die am wenigsten Begünstigten zu rechtfertigen ist, sondern es wird ein gerechtes System der Zusammenarbeit als System öffentlicher Regeln gefordert[22].

Damit ergibt sich zwischen den Positionen von *Rawls* und *Hayek* in einem zentralen Punkt eine weitgehende Übereinstimmung[23], obwohl beide Autoren von verschiedenen sozialphilosophischen Positionen aus argumentieren. Für *Hayek* ist das Argument ausschlaggebend, daß mit der spontanen Ordnung des Marktes eine egalitaristische Politik, die auf eine weitgehende Angleichung oder Gleichheit der Ergebnisse des Marktprozesses ausgerichtet wäre, nicht vereinbar ist und nur zu verwirklichen wäre, wenn zentrale Werte der freiheitlichen Ordnung geopfert würden[24]; denn in einer Gesellschaft, in der jeder sein Wissen nutzen darf, um seine Ziele zu verfolgen, sind die Ergebnisse etwa des Wettbewerbs- und Entdeckungsprozesses auf Märkten notwendig ungleich und sie können keinem vorher postulierten Verteilungsprofil entsprechen[25]. Folglich kann nach *Hayek* der Maßstab der Gerechtigkeit nur auf das Handeln des einzelnen bezogen werden. Nur der einzelne kann gerecht oder ungerecht sein. Das Gesamtergebnis der menschlichen Interaktion aber kann Konsequenzen haben, die weder von einem einzelnen Akteur beabsichtigt noch irgendwie vorhersehbar waren. Folglich ist es unzulässig, auf die Ergebnisse eines unpersönlichen komplexen Prozesses, in dem neben Leistung und Fleiß auch noch Zufälle und unbekannte Faktoren eine Rolle spielen, das Kriterium der Gerechtigkeit anzuwenden. Wohl aber kann die Gerechtigkeitsfrage sinnvoll im Hinblick auf das Verfahren, das «game of catallaxy» (*Hayek*)[26], gestellt werden[27]. Das System der allgemeinen «Spiel»-regeln aber ist in seiner Wirkungsweise nicht voll determiniert und schließt Zufälle nicht aus, so daß Marktergebnisse weder im meritokratischen Sinn, noch im Sinn einer Erfolgsethik nur als »Verdienst« der Betreffenden aufgefaßt werden können[28]. Ähnlich wie bei einem fairen Spiel eine Partei unverdient gewin-

---

[22] Siehe *Rawls*, a.a.O., S. 124 ff.

[23] Vgl. auch das Vorwort *von Hayeks* zu Law, Legislation and Liberty, Bd. 2, a.a.O., S. XIII und den Text auf S. 100. Bei der Würdigung der *Hayekschen* Position sollte in Betracht gezogen werden, daß er trotz seiner Kritik an der heutigen Verwendung des Begriffs soziale Gerechtigkeit keine Einwände prinzipieller Art gegen die *Rawlssche* Konzeption von sozialer Gerechtigkeit erhebt, die sich auf die Fairness von Systemen von allgemeinen Regeln gründet (vgl. a.a.O., S. 63). Im wesentlichen scheint mir *Hayeks* Kritik des Begriffs soziale Gerechtigkeit von der Sorge getragen zu sein, daß mit dessen Hilfe neue willkürliche Formen der Herrschaft gerechtfertigt werden. Er betont deswegen, daß Gerechtigkeit ein zentraler Aspekt jeder freiheitlichen Ordnung sei und daß es echte Gerechtigkeitsprobleme im Zusammenhang mit dem wohlüberlegten Entwurf politischer Institutionen gebe (a.a.O., S. 100).

[24] *Hayek*, Law, Legislation and Liberty, Bd. 2 a.a.O., S. 67.

[25] Vgl. ebenda, S. 69.

[26] Ebenda, a.a.O., S. 71.

[27] Das ist auch eine der Grundideen von *Rawls*.

[28] Zur Ablehnung der Meritokratie siehe *Rawls*, a.a.O., S. 124 f. *Hayeks* Hinweise, daß Marktergebnisse für den einzelnen zu bitteren Erwartungsenttäuschungen führen können, laufen auf dasselbe Ergebnis hinaus (Law, Legislation and Liberty, S. 72, 74, 94).

nen kann, sind auch in der spontanen Ordnung des Marktes «unverdiente» Einkommen möglich. Sie werden hingenommen, weil die übrigen Vorteile der Marktordnung im Hinblick auf die Entfaltungsmöglichkeiten der menschlichen Freiheit von keinem anderen System, auch nicht dem der demokratischen Selbstverwaltung, übertroffen werden. In einer Ordnung, in der die demokratische Abstimmung das wesentliche Instrument ist, um gemeinsame Entscheidungen zustandezubringen und in der folglich Märkte als Koordinationsverfahren keine Rolle spielen, ist die Freiheit des einzelnen auf die Teilnahme am demokratischen Prozeß beschränkt. In einer marktwirtschaftlichen Ordnung jedoch, die den Raum des Politischen begrenzt, hat der einzelne im Rahmen des rechtlich Zulässigen auch die Garantie der allgemeinen Handlungsfreiheit, d. h. das Recht auf freie Entfaltung seiner Persönlichkeit im Rahmen der Gesetze.

Hayek und *Rawls* sind der Auffassung, daß das Prinzip der Verfahrensgerechtigkeit als eine Grundregel für die Verfassung einer freien Gesellschaft sich aber noch aus anderen Gründen empfiehlt. Die Unzahl der Einzelumstände, in denen sich jeder Mensch in jedem Augenblick seiner Existenz befindet, und die Tatsache, daß jeder durch die besonderen Umstände seines Lebens verglichen mit seinen Mitmenschen in einer anderen Position ist, legt zunächst aus praktischen Gründen die Beschränkung auf die Verfahrensgerechtigkeit nahe, da nur so vermieden werden kann, daß den unendlich verschiedenen Einzelumständen und den sich verändernden Stellungen einzelner Menschen nachgegangen werden muß. Nur so kann der fruchtlose Versuch verhindert werden, Grundsätze aufzustellen, die mit den ungeheuer vielfältigen Einzelheiten des täglichen Lebens fertig werden müßten[2]. Die faktisch bestehende Ungleichheit der Lebenssituationen hat aber auch zur Folge, daß jeder Versuch, gleiche Ergebnisse herzustellen, wegen der Komplexität der Situationen die Möglichkeiten politisch-administrativen Handelns weit überschreitet, wenn die Voraussetzungen und Bedingungen einer freiheitlichen Ordnung eingehalten werden sollen.

Aber selbst wenn die Bereitschaft besteht, ein hohes Maß an staatlichem Zwang einzusetzen, so sind die Erfahrungen negativ. In den Frühphasen sozialistischer Gesellschaften hat es zahlreiche Versuche gegeben, entweder die Gleichheit der laufenden Einkommen[30] oder eine erhebliche Reduktion der Einkommensunterschiede durchzusetzen. Diese Großexperimente haben nicht nur gezeigt, daß die erzwungene Einkommensangleichung erhebliche Effizienzeinbußen erzeugt und alle schlechter stellt. Gleichzeitig lassen die feh-

---

[29] *Rawls,* a.a.O., S. 108.

[30] Vom ökonomischen Standpunkt aus gesehen ist es keineswegs unproblematisch, die Periodeneinkommen als Ausgangspunkt zu wählen. Ein konsequenter Egalitarist müßte Lebenseinkommen, die Lebenserwartung, die Ausbildungszeiten, das zeitweilige Ausscheiden aus dem Arbeitsprozeß und anderes in Rechnung stellen. Allerdings wäre sein Problem auch dann noch nicht gelöst, da neben den monetären Einkommen auch die nichtmonetären Einkommen, u. a. die Verwendung von Lebenszeit als Freizeit, doch ebenfalls gleich verteilt werden müßten, wenn nicht die Arbeitslasten in einer Gesellschaft ungleich sein sollen. Wäre es aber andererseits nicht gesamtwirtschaftlich nützlich, Personen mit geringerer Freizeitpräferenz ein höheres Einkommen zukommen zu lassen, da sie mehr für die Sicherung der Lebensbedürfnisse ihrer Mitmenschen tun als diejenigen, die die Muße vorziehen? Aber auch dann ist das Problem noch nicht gelöst, denn es ist zu fragen, ob nur Inländer oder auch Ausländer einzubeziehen sind und inwieweit zukünftige Generationen berücksichtigt werden sollen, denn deren Lebenschancen sind von den Spar- und Investitionsanstrengungen ihrer Vorfahren abhängig, die jedoch naturgemäß nicht für ihre Konsumverzichte von jenen entschädigt werden können. Die ungeklärten Fragen eines akzeptablen Gleichheitsmaßes werden bei *Amartya Sen* deutlich (Ökonomische Ungleichheit, Frankfurt, New York 1975, S. 36 ff.), der selbst eine starke Vorliebe für den egalitaristischen Standpunkt hat.

lenden Leistungsanreize sehr schnell auch die Situation eintreten, daß selbst die dringlichsten Güter nur unzureichend hergestellt werden und verfügbar sind. Es bleibt dann nur die Wahl, vermehrten politischen Druck auf die Betroffenen auszuüben. Am Ende aber steht regelmäßig der Abbruch des Experiments, seine Verwerfung als «Gleichmacherei» und der Übergang zum sogenannten System der «materiellen Anreize». Diesen Gefahren aber setzt sich jede Politik aus, die nicht vom Standpunkt einer – wie auch immer unvollkommenen – Verfahrensgerechtigkeit ausgeht, sondern statt dessen den Versuch unternimmt, etwa die Einkommens- und Vermögensstreuung allein an vorab aufgestellten Verteilungsprofilen zu messen und entsprechend zu verfahren.

Der Ansatz einer der freiheitlichen Ordnung gemäßen Vorgehensweise ist die Verfassung ihrer wichtigsten Institutionen, in einer Weise, daß für alle die gleichen Regeln gelten und daß wegen der eminenten politischen Gefahren, die jeder Versuch, «Gleichheit» in «materieller» Hinsicht zu erzwingen, heraufbeschwört, darauf verzichtet wird, durch den Einsatz staatlicher Zwangsmittel etwa die Gleichheit der Einkommen durchzusetzen.

Diese Auffassung schließt nicht ein System solidarischer Hilfen für die in Not geratenen aus, denn eine Gesellschaft kann auch als eine Gefahrengemeinschaft aufgefaßt werden, in denen der einzelne durchaus ein Recht auf Hilfe von seinen Mitmenschen hat, wenn ihn Schicksalsschläge treffen, gegen die Selbstvorsorge normalerweise nicht erwartet werden kann oder, wie im Falle von Katastrophen, nicht möglich ist. Wenn auch freiwillige Hilfen den Vorzug verdienen, so können doch historische Situationen auftreten, in denen ein hohes Maß an staatlichem Zwang zur Umverteilung unverzichtbar ist[31].

Die Mittel und Wege aber, mit denen dem Grundsatz, für alle gleiche und allgemeine Regeln anzuwenden, Rechnung getragen werden kann, können im Detail sehr verschieden aussehen, wie an zwei Beispielen kurz gezeigt werden soll.

(1) Die staatliche Finanzierung von Kunst- oder Bildungsgütern hat bekanntlich oberhalb der Grenze, wo sie jedem zur Verfügung stehen, einen diskriminierenden Effekt derart zur Folge, daß die Nichtbenutzer bzw. -konsumenten gleichwohl zur Finanzierung herangezogen werden, während die Nachfrager der entsprechenden Güter zwar ebenfalls zur Finanzierung beitragen, aber ihr Konsum subventioniert wird. Juristisch ließe sich hier argumentieren, daß der Gleichheitsgrundsatz nicht gebietet, alles gleich zu behandeln, also kein generelles Verbot von Differenzierungen bei ungleichen Tatbeständen ausspricht[32]. Trotzdem wäre auch aus dieser Sicht zu fragen, ob eine zulässige Ungleichbehandlung vorliegt. Die *Rawlssche* Regel hilft hier weiter. Danach wäre eine ungleiche Subventionierung von Konsumakten oder Investitionen in künftige Berufsfertigkeiten dann in einer freiheitlichen Ordnung zuzulassen, wenn gezeigt werden kann, daß sie jedermann, besonders den Unbegabten und Amusischen, von denen einmal angenommen sei, daß sie zu den am schlechtesten Gestellten gehören, einen Vorteil bringt. Der unmittelbare Nutzen der Benutzer von Bildungsstätten, die nicht von jedermann besucht wer-

---

[31] Zu denken ist etwa an die durch Kriege entstehenden Katastrophen und die Notwendigkeiten der Umverteilung durch staatlichen Akt zugunsten derjenigen, die in besonders hohem Maße Opfer der Auseinandersetzungen wurden. Dies hat beispielsweise in Deutschland nach dem Zweiten Weltkrieg eine große Rolle gespielt. Es hatte zunächst den Anschein, daß der gesellschaftliche Zusammenhalt ohne eine tiefgreifende Umverteilung der übriggebliebenen Vermögen in Frage gestellt sei. Im Zuge der schnellen Wohlstandsmehrung, die im Rahmen der marktwirtschaftlichen Ordnung erzielt wurde, verlor das Problem des Kriegslastenausgleichs jedoch schnell an politischer Bedeutung und öffentlicher Beachtung.

[32] Zur allgemeinen Interpretation des Gleichheitsgrundsatzes siehe *Eckehart Stein,* Staatsrecht, 5. Aufl., Tübingen 1976, S. 238.

den, etwa des tertiären Bildungssystems, in Form von höheren Einkommen und der Kunstbeflissenen in Form des Kunstgenusses liegt auf der Hand. Die Verbesserung der Position derjenigen, die keinen unmittelbaren Nutzen davontragen, aber kann nur behauptet werden, wenn positive externe Effekte ins Feld geführt werden. Es wäre also nachzuweisen, daß die höhere Bildung einiger und der feinere Kunstverstand anderer die soziale und kulturelle Umwelt positiv beeinflussen und so auf lange Sicht auch die Lage derjenigen verbessern, die nicht unmittelbar an diesen Gütern interessiert sind.

Auch wenn Argumente zu Gunsten dieses Wirkungszusammenhangs sprechen, so ist damit noch nicht die Frage des Maßes der Subventionierung entschieden, besonders dann nicht, wenn die Nichtkonsumenten zu den weniger oder am wenigsten günstig Gestellten in einer Gesellschaft gehören sollten. Deswegen kann eine der Gleichheitsidee angemessenere Lösung so beschaffen sein, daß die betreffenden Güter, oberhalb des Niveaus, auf dem sie jedem direkt zuteil werden, teilweise oder doch weitgehend aus der Steuerfinanzierung herausgenommen werden. Die Lage der Nichtinteressierten verbessert sich dann unmittelbar im Umfang der bei ihnen anfallenden Entlastung von Zwangsabgaben, ihr Freiheitsspielraum für den Konsum der von ihnen höher geschätzten Güter wird gleichzeitig erweitert. Diejenigen, die unmittelbar an Kunst und Bildung interessiert sind, erhalten allenfalls in dem Umfang eine Subvention, wie ihr Konsum nachhaltig positive Wirkungen für Dritte hat. Der unter diesen Umständen zu entrichtende Preis dürfte erheblich über dem heute im tertiären Bildungssystem üblichen Nulltarif liegen und auch der Kunstgenuß dürfte teurer werden. Wenn die höheren Bildungs- und Kunstgüter von den besser Verdienenden nachgefragt werden, dann läuft der Vorschlag rebus sic stantibus auf eine gleichmäßigere Einkommensverteilung hinaus. Diese aber wäre im vorliegenden Fall nicht nur mit den Grundideen einer Gesellschaft freier Menschen vereinbar, sondern sogar aus verschiedenen Überlegungen auch geboten. Die Freiheit der Einkommensverwendung wird bei einigen erhöht. Die Subventionierten aber können ihren Anspruch gegen die Allgemeinheit und damit auch gegen die Nichtinteressierten allenfalls auf das schwache Argument positiver Verkettungen[33] (Effekte) stützen, kaum aber auf die sachlich gewichtigeren Gründe der Abwendung von Not oder des sozialen Ausgleichs. Der Nachweis aber, daß die Handlungsweise des einen anderen nützt, kann kaum als allgemeine Regel für die Unterstützung jeder solchen Tätigkeit durch die Gemeinschaft herangezogen werden, es sei denn, man wäre bereit, absurde Konsequenzen in Kauf zu nehmen[34]. *Rawls*[35] verweist daher auch die Finanzierung von Kunst, Wissenschaft und Kultur, besonders von Theatern und Universitäten, auf den Weg, freiwillige Spenden einzuwerben und faire Entgelte zu erzielen, ein Standpunkt, dem *Hayek* kaum widersprechen dürfte[36].

Der Einwand, daß unter diesen Umständen zu wenig von den beiden «meritorischen» Gütern nachgefragt würde, ist kaum stichhaltig, wie die Erfahrung in jenen Ländern zeigt, die der privaten Initiative mehr Raum bieten. Die dort sich entfaltenden Eigeninitiativen führen sowohl zu neuen Wegen und Experimenten, Kunst- oder Bildungsgüter an die potentiell Interessierten heranzutragen, als auch zu einem viel höheren Maße an

---

[33] *Rawls*, a.a.O., S. 101.

[34] Man könnte sonst auf die Idee verfallen, die Körperhygiene öffentlich zu subventionieren (zum Nulltarif?), da ja die eigene Sauberkeit auch anderen nützt.

[35] *Rawls*, a.a.O., S. 367.

[36] *Hayeks* Vorstellungen zur Verfassung der Institutionen von Erziehung und Wissenschaft sind in seinem Buch: Die Verfassung der Freiheit, a.a.O., S. 462, niedergelegt.

individueller Bereitschaft, für den Erwerb nicht nur monetäre Opfer zu bringen, sondern sich die Güter wirklich anzueignen[37].

Ihr eigentliches Gewicht aber gewinnt die Subventionsproblematik erst im engeren Bereich der Wirtschaft. Es gibt zwar zahlreiche Untersuchungen darüber, wie Subventionsbegehren von Firmen oder Verbänden im politischen Prozeß durchgesetzt werden und wie teils aus vordergründigen wahltaktischen Erwägungen Subventionen an private Haushalte für verschiedene Zwecke und teilweise ohne Beachtung des Grundsatzes der Gleichbehandlung vergeben werden. Die ordnungspolitische Frage, nach welchen allgemeinen Regeln Produktions-, Arbeitsplatzerhaltungs- und Haushaltssubventionen aber zugänglich sein sollen und wie besonders in den ersten beiden Fällen das staatliche Ermessen einzuschränken und dem Gleichheitsgrundsatz zu unterwerfen ist, ist – zumindest auf der Seite der Ökonomen – noch offen, und zwar trotz der praktischen Bedeutung, die mittlerweile die staatliche Struktur- und Technologiepolitik erlangt hat. Wie immer man die Frage nach den allgemeinen Wohlstandswirkungen dieser Politiken beantwortet, eine Gleichbehandlung der Bürger im Hinblick auf diese staatlichen Leistungen ist in vielen Fällen offensichtlich nicht gegeben, selbst wenn der Begriff der Gleichheit der Tatbestände, die zur Erlangung der Hilfen erfüllt sein müssen, eng ausgelegt wird.

(2) Das zweite Beispiel betrifft die Vermögensstreuung: Wenn die Fähigeren ihre Talente in dem Umfange einsetzen und für sich nutzen, in dem dadurch gleichzeitig der allgemeine Wohlstand angehoben wird, dann ist es unvermeidbar, daß in Einzelfällen nicht nur hohe Einkommen, sondern auch Vermögensakkumulationen entstehen. Von der Ertragsseite her gesehen ist zwar der Anteil der Besitzeinkommen am Volkseinkommen wahrscheinlich auf weniger als ein Fünftel zu veranschlagen und säkular stark rückläufig.[38] Außerdem ist es nicht so leicht, wie häufig angenommen wird, Vermögen über längere Zeit zu erhalten und sie auf Kinder und Kindeskinder zu übertragen, denn eine funktionierende Wettbewerbswirtschaft bewirkt in erheblichem Umfang die gesellschaftliche

---

[37] Ein Vergleich der Kulturszene in den Vereinigten Staaten und in Deutschland ist in diesem Zusammenhang lehrreich. Die Leiter staatlich finanzierter Museen können beispielsweise nur mit Resignation feststellen, daß sich hierzulande nicht die Scharen von Helfern finden, die sich in amerikanischen Museen freiwillig und kostenlos als Führer zur Verfügung stellen. – Trotz aller Hindernisse im einzelnen bieten die marktfinanzierten Theaterprogramme der zahlreichen New Yorker Bühnen international mehr beachtete Aufführungen als die sorglos mit öffentlichen Mitteln umgehenden hochsubventionierten deutschen Bühnen. – Die durch den Abbau der akademischen Selbstverwaltung und die Politisierung der Entscheidungsorgane allmählich immer stärker unter die politisch-bürokratische Kontrolle geratenden deutschen Universitäten aber drohen ineffizient zu werden und haben wachsende Schwierigkeiten, auch nur noch im imitatorischen Wettbewerb international Schritt zu halten. – Zur Experimentierfreudigkeit und zum Rang künstlerischer Leistungen in den Vereinigten Staaten siehe z. B. den Bericht von *Dietmar Polaczek*, Meet me in Valhalla! *Wagners «Ring der Nibelungen»* in Seattle: Wie in Amerika Oper gemacht wird, Frankfurter Allgemeine Zeitung, Nr. 186 vom 28. 8. 1978, S. 15. – Zur kritischen Beurteilung deutscher Universitäten durch ausländische Beobachter siehe: International Council on the Future of the University. Bericht über deutsche Universitäten von der Kommission für deutsche Universitäten, Stuttgart 1978.

[38] Siehe hierzu *Josua Werner*, Verteilungspolitik, Stuttgart und New York 1979, S. 15, und seinen Nachweis, daß die Arbeitsquote (Lohnquote zuzüglich der errechneten Arbeitseinkommen der Selbständigen am Volkseinkommen) mittlerweile über 80 v. H. liegt. – Ähnlich *Jan Tinbergen*, Ein Beitrag zur Integration einiger Theorien der zukünftigen Einkommensverteilung. Hamburger Jahrbuch für Wirtschafts- und Gesellschaftspolitik, 23. Jahr (1978), S. 89, der berichtet, daß die Kapitaleinkommen auf 20 v. H. oder weniger gefallen seien.

Aneignung privater Leistungserfolge[39]. Trotzdem läßt es sich nicht leugnen, daß in den glücklicheren Fällen die Startchancen der so Begünstigten im wirtschaftlichen Wettbewerb, wenn auch keineswegs immer, günstiger sein können als diejenigen der vergleichsweise schlechter Gestellten.

Vom Standpunkt der Gleichheit her gesehen ist diese Verletzung der Chancengleichheit anstößig. Das Problem ist allerdings komplex. Soll es den besser gestellten Eltern erlaubt werden, verstärkt in die Ausbildung ihrer Kinder zu investieren, um ihnen so eine bessere Startbasis zu vermitteln, oder wird das Elternrecht und das Recht auf freie Persönlichkeitsentfaltung durch die oft aus der Gleichheitsidee abgeleitete Forderung dominiert, Chancengleichheit in dem Umfange herzustellen, daß jeder von der gleichen Linie – etwa beim Eintritt ins Berufsleben – aus startet? Kann letzterem nicht entgegengehalten werden, daß in einer Wirtschaft, die auf der Wahlfreiheit der Konsumenten aufbaut und diesen gestattet, kostspielige Automobile zu kaufen und aufwendige Hobbies zu betreiben, auch der Kauf besserer Schulausbildung für die eigenen Nachkommen ein Ziel ist, das durch die Freiheitsrechte verbürgt wird, so daß Gleichheitsforderungen zurücktreten müssen? Ist es zudem nicht für alle nützlicher, daß Menschen in Wissen und Bildung statt in Tand und Spielzeuge investieren?

Und wie ist der Erbvorgang zu regeln? Soll der Vermögensübergang mit einer so hohen Steuer belastet werden, wie es in einigen Wohlfahrtsstaaten der Fall ist, daß praktisch Vermögen aufgelöst werden, wenn sie mehr als zwei Erbgängen unterlegen haben? Oder sollte gar dem Vorschlag des Buches Leviticus (Lev 25, 20) gefolgt werden, das bereits in biblischer Zeit andeutungsweise empfahl, bestehende Vermögen in jedem Halljahr umzuverteilen, um Vermögensakkumulation auf der einen und Verarmung auf der anderen Seite zu vermeiden?

Beide Vorgehensweisen wären vom Standpunkt der allgemeinen Wohlstandsverbesserung her höchst abträglich. Die Möglichkeit der Vererbung ist ein wesentliches Motiv der Kapitalakkumulation. Sie würde wahrscheinlich erheblich geschwächt, wenn der Erbgang mit konfiskatorischen Steuern belastet würde. Eine periodische Vermögensumverteilung, wie immer sie zu Wege gebracht würde, würde ihre Schatten auf die Investitionsbereitschaft schon jahrelang vorauswerfen. Investitionen und Kapitalakkumulation aber sind wesentliche Voraussetzungen für die wirtschaftliche Entwicklung. Sie zu behindern heißt allen schaden. *Robbins*[40] plädiert daher für ein Erbrecht, das Anreize bietet für private Stiftungen oder für die Aufteilung von Vermögen auf viele Erben. In einem von zwei Kriegen und Inflationen betroffenen Land wird es ferner nicht ohne zusätzliche Vermögenspolitik gehen, deren Ausgestaltung mit einer freiheitlichen Ordnung vereinbar gemacht werden kann.[41]

Das Verhältnis zwischen Freiheit und Gleichheit ist weder das der Harmonie noch das des völligen Konfliktes. Gerade die durch den Wettbewerb und den gesetzlich-institutionellen Rahmen der Märkte geprägte marktwirtschaftliche Ordnung hat auch starke ma-

---

[39] Siehe hierzu *Hans Willgerodt*, Die gesellschaftliche Aneignung privater Leistungserfolge als Grundelement der wettbewerblichen Marktwirtschaft. In: *Heinz Sauermann* und *Ernst-Joachim Mestmäcker* (Hrsg.), Wirtschaftsordnung und Staatsverfassung. Festschrift für Franz Böhm, Tübingen 1975, S. 695 f.

[40] *Lionel Robbins,* Liberty and Equality. Hrsg.: The Institute of Economic Affairs, London 1977, S. 22.

[41] Vgl. *Hans Willgerodt, Karl Bartel, Ulrich Schillert,* Vermögen für alle. Probleme der Bildung, Verteilung und Werterhaltung des Vermögens in der Marktwirtschaft (Schriftenreihe der Ludwig-Erhard-Stiftung, Band 2), Düsseldorf – Wien o.J., S. 393 ff.

teriell egalisierende Kräfte hervorgebracht. Die Frage, inwieweit eine Marktwirtschaft allgemeine und freiheitlich-rechtsstaatliche Regeln zuläßt, die gleichwohl eine Tendenz zur Vermeidung starker Wohlstandsunterschiede begünstigen, gehört deswegen zu den wichtigen ordnungspolitischen Fragen.

Summary

On the Limits of Equality in a Free Society

Two models are discussed in this essay. The first one, the democratic egalitarian conception, proposes to secure equality by democratic procedures not only in politics but also in the fields which classical-liberal theory leaves open to individual autonomy. The core of the idea, the new interpretation of democratization or participation, is that everybody will become a free and equal citizen of a society, if he not only has the right to vote in the political process either himself or via an elected representative but in all those cases as well which are of interest to him. It is argued that the egalitarian belief that all men are equal in the democratic decision-making process is not correct.

The second model, the non-egalitarian and libertarian view, is based on the idea that a conflict can arise between liberty and equality. But there are many ways to handle it. The central idea which was developed by *Hayek* and *Rawls* is that the social and economic inequalities, which are the outcome of an evolutionary process, should be taken into account in a way that furthers human welfare. Therefore the institutions of a free society should be properly devised and should allow for economic inequalities as far as they promote human welfare.

Gottfried Dietze

From the Constitution of Liberty to its Deconstitution by Liberalistic Dissipation, Disintegration, Disassociaton, Disorder

I. Introductory Remark

Like *Montesquieu* and *Adam Smith, Friedrich August von Hayek* is a liberal of measure. While freedom ranks high in his scale of values, he does not tend to be corrupted by it and to incline toward anarchy, that great tempter of liberalism. The idea of order is recurrent in his publications.[1]

Hayek's social thought is mainly concerned with the constitution of liberty, with liberal order. It emphasizes the rule of law as a means of securing the freedom of the individual from undue infringements by the government. However, recent years have shown that individuals increasingly have been deprived of their safety by the unlawful acts of others, that the liberal order and its rule of law are jeopardized by crime.

In the following, the problem of crime in liberal societies will be discussed and remedies suggested.

---

[1] The word «order» is in the title of the book, The Sensory Order (London and Chicago 1952). International order is dealt with in «A Self-Generating Order for Society,» in *John Nef*, ed., Towards World Community (The Hague 1968), 39, and in the last chapter of The Road to Serfdom (London and Chicago 1944), entitled, «The Prospects of International Order», from which can be concluded that the preceding chapters dealt with the internal order of society. The idea of that order is evident in: Individualism and Economic Order (London and Chicago 1948). It is obvious in The Constitution of Liberty (Chicago 1960), whether that title implies a constituting of liberty, the organization of liberty, a system of laws or a law basic to society or government. In that work, praised by *Henry Hazlitt* as «the twentieth-century successor to *John Stuart Mill's* essay ‹On Liberty›» (Newsweek, Feb. 15, 1960), the concept of order in society is discussed at some length, as it is in later publications: «Arten der Ordnung», ORDO, XIV (1963), p. 3–20, and «The Principles of a Liberal Social Order», Il Politico, XXXI (1966), 601. The first volume of Law, Legislation and Liberty (Chicago 1973) has the title Rules and Order. Order is its «central concept», «indispensable . . . for the discussion of all complex phenomena.» The «Old Whig» makes plain that he discusses order in spite of «its frequent association with authoritarian views. We cannot do without it . . .» «It is clear that every society must . . . possess an order . . . As has been said by a distinguished social anthropologist, ‹that there is some order, consistency and constancy in social life, is obvious. If there were not, none of us would be able to go about our affairs or satisfy our most elementary needs›.» (Pp. 35 f.; quoting *E. E. Evans-Pritchard*, Social Anthropology (London 1951), 49).

II. Liberals and Crime

Our time, characterized by fights for, and guarantees of, rights, abounds in crime.

The age of *Paine* at the beginning of modern liberalism, hoping for an increasing emancipation and protection of men through popular government, today is felt by many people to have been a dreamworld. Men are realizing that they are living in an age of pain. For some, the pain began decades ago when property rights were discriminated against by democratic majorities. For others, it began recently when they were shocked by the riots of the 'sixties. For still others, it became evident with the enormous growth of crime. Riot can be compared to a clenched fist used for the fight for rights. It can be added that riots seem to have spawned crimes just as opening fists spawn fingers. The fight for rights has turned into a plight of rights. The recognition of democratic rights and majority rule did not only result in a disparagement of freedom of contract and property, in socialisms and welfare states brought about by the socialists of all parties, but also in serious threats to law and order through crime. At a time of an abundance of rights, property and even life have become insecure. More than ever before during the liberal era, the law-abiding citizen today lives in fear of being illegally attacked and injured by his fellow-men. «These are the times that try men's souls.» The words *Thomas Paine* in 1776 put at the beginning of his work on the American crisis can be applied to today's crisis of the liberal world. And just as then Americans fought for liberal ideas, today's liberals, if they want to maintain their way of life, must assert freedom under law.

The modern liberal era often is believed to have begun with the American Declaration of Independence and *Adam Smith's* Inquiry into the Nature and Causes of the Wealth of Nations. Today, after liberal nations have acquired the wealth predicted in that work as a result of free enterprise, they face death in a large measure on account of riots and crimes. *Smith's* arguments against absolutism and mercantilism aided the emancipation of the troisième état. Two hundred years later liberalism is threatened by the blatant emergence of the troisième dessous. The middle class, which according to *Euripides* maintains states, is challenged by the criminal class, which jeopardizes the maintenance of states. In the progression of democracy, cut-throat competition, a legal aspect of laissez-faire, had its throat cut by social legislation. Yet today, criminal cut-throats abound. Superman Poor has become complemented by superman Criminal. And whereas the poor have been aided by social legislation, criminals now have their way through law negation.

Hayek drew the distinction between Old and New Whigs; between traditional and rational liberals.[2] Without doubt, many liberals did not agree, and were disillusioned with others. It has been pointed out that socialism was aided under the banner of liberalism.[3] Certainly the present permissiveness under the banner of liberalism is about as bad. The growth of problems in liberal society seems to be the following. Originally, as a reaction against the police state under absolute monarchs, only a minimum of police was considered proper. Then, more police was put up with as «good» police. Later on, still more police came about as a result of the increase of governmental control and regulation. Recently, that bad police has been complemented by one which in a derelict manner winks at crime.

Perhaps *John Adams*, an Old Whig, envisaged the last stage. To him, «property is surely a right of mankind as really a liberty . . . The moment the idea is admitted into so-

---

[2] *Hayek,* The Constitution of Liberty, esp. 397. ff.
[3] See *Alpheus T. Mason,* Free Government in the Making (1949) ch. 16, entitled «Liberal Variations.»

ciety that property is not as sacred as the laws of God, and that there is not a force of law and public justice to protect it, anarchy and tyranny commence.»[4] Symbolic of classic liberalism, this statement contains everything relevant to the problem at hand. It mentions liberal values: property, the right of mankind, liberty, society, the laws of God, the force of law and public justice. It mentions the antipodes of a liberal society: anarchy and tyranny. An exegesis and some speculation on what might be inferred from it are in order.

Adams states that anarchy and tyranny commence the moment property rights are not respected. The very moment the principle of the sacrosanctity of property is deserted, a chain of events begins. However, something commencing seldom will reach pitch right away. In a word, the moment property is disregarded only the seed is sown for the growth of anarchy and tyranny. Another important feature of the statement is that it speaks of anarchy and tyranny, not of anarchy or tyranny. Disrespect for property rights plants the seeds for both, not just for one of the two. Anarchy and tyranny are twins springing from a disregard for property. Will one of them grow faster than the other? Will one of them show its face fully before the other?

Unlike natural twins, anarchy and tyranny are little alike. While they may be present at the same time, the one may be stronger than the other. Also, the one may lead to the other. *Adams* was well aware of the critical situation of his country. He feared the threat of anarchy and tyranny. *Shays's* Rebellion in his home state and legislation in other states were clear symptoms of the tyranny of debtors over creditors, of legal insecurity and anarchy. Yet he also knew that law was to secure the protection of the individual, including his property. And since the end is more important than the means, he, who later on as President filled judicial posts with men he hoped would protect private property, probably was worried mainly by the tyrannic designs of social movements, and considered the turnover of old laws, implying a trend toward anarchy, a mere by-product of those designs. Fear of despotism came first, that of anarchy, second. Therefore, *Adams* could be expected to have written «tyranny and anarchy commence.»

Yet he wrote «anarchy and tyranny commence.» There must have been some reason for doing so. *Adams* probably realized that the tyranny Americans were experiencing on account of discriminations against property rights was still in its infancy; that it affected mainly a few and therefore was not yet an all-out tyranny. Americans were still free to adopt new laws by ordinary procedures which would not have been possible had there been an unbearable despotism. Similarly, there did not yet exist an all-out anarchy. Generally, the laws were enforced. Legislation and constitution-making was done according to the law. The sequence, «anarchy and tyranny,» suggests that *Adams* thought of future development. Infringements upon property, implying the tyranny of the poor over the rich, would result not only, as they did at his time, in an anarchy that mainly hurt property owners, but in one under which the whole society suffered. The general insecurity would prompt the call for a dictatorship, for an all-out tyranny which could restore law and order and at least protect the individuals' lives.

Liberal democracies may well have reached this stage. The increase of crimes, combined with trends not to punish them, has created a situation that approaches anarchy. There is a call for law and order, often based upon the assumption that only some kind of dictatorship, preferably a strongman, can restore law and order. Just as *Adam Smith* two hundred years ago inquired what in absolutism prevented the wealth of nations and suggested ways and means to bring about that wealth, people today ask what in liberalism

---

[4] «Defence of the Constitutions of the United States of America», in *Charles Francis Adams*, ed. The Works of John Adams (Boston 1850–56), VI 8f. Cf. *Jefferson's* letter to *John Dickinson* of Dec. 19, 1801. Writings, X, 302; Marbury v. Madison, 1 Cranch 137 (1803).

makes wealthy nations sick and how their health can be restored. Liberal nations are wealthier than others. Unfortunately, they are rich not just in material goods, or in rights. They have become rich in riots and crimes, which in a large measure are due to an abundance of rights.

This suggests that liberal striving may have lost measure. Liberals today must re-examine liberal vagrancies and variations. There must be an inquiry into the nature and causes of the failing health of wealthy nations, of the not-so-lingering death threatening them. Needless to say, suggestions for saving liberalism must be measureful. One hybris should not be replaced by another. On the other hand, many illnesses have been cured by measures which, in spite of their radical nature, still had measure. What is to be done?

In 1902, *Lenin* asked that question to save communism. The Marxist movement was then threatened by dissolution on account of the «diffused, illdefined, but very persistent tendencies» advanced by revisionists and «Economists» who made undue concessions to the bourgeoisie, to liberalism and adulterated orthodox Marxism. *Lenin* asked for the liquidation of «confusion, disintegration, and vacillation», and proposed militant, centralized action. At that time, the bourgeoisie and liberalism were at their height. Generally well established, they were supported by governments, notably in the Western nations, but also in *Russia* – certainly against the Marxists. Communists were fighting an uphill battle. In the beginning of «What is to be done» *Lenin* stated they could survive only if they joined in their common effort:

> «We are marching in a compact group along a precipitous and difficult path, firmly holding each other by the hand. We are surrounded on all sides by enemies, and are under their almost constant fire. We have combined voluntarily, especially for the purpose of fighting the enemy and not to retreat into the adjacent marsh, the inhabitants of which, right from the very outset, have reproached us with having separated ourselves into an exclusive group, and with having chosen the path of struggle instead of the path of conciliation. And now several in our crowd begin to cry out: Let us go into this marsh! And when we begin to shame them, they retort: How conservative you are! Are you not ashamed to deny us the right to invite you to take a better road!»[5]

Today, it is all too evident that *Lenin's* suggestions have won his movement many a victory. Liberalism has been vanquished in quite a few nations that were taken over by the communists. It is threatened in other countries not only on account of the enormous increase of Soviet might, but also because of internal weaknesses. On a world scale, the party of liberty[6] is probably worse off today than was the Marxist movement at *Lenin's* time. Much as he criticized that movement, he was confident it was growing. Liberalism, on the contrary, has been weakening for generations.

One of liberalism's problems is that it is too much on the defensive. Liberals are not marching. They are gingerly treading, trying to hold their ground. Individualists, they are not in a compact group, holding each other by the hand. However, they certainly are surrounded on all sides by enemies, and are under almost constant fire. The path along which they are cautiously groping their way is precipitous and difficult. They have been threatened by despotism and anarchism, forces that probably are more destructive to liberalism than capitalism and revisionism were to *Lenin's* group. Many liberals throughout the past decades have retreated into the marsh of socialism, explaining their action from liberal motives. More recently, others have retreated into the marsh of anarchism, justifying their move in a similar manner. They all have reproached the remaining genuine liberals for separating themselves into an exclusive group, for having chosen the path of conciliation instead of the path of struggle. And now several in the diminished

---

[5] What Is To be Done, ch. 1, A (1902)
[6] This expression is used by *Hayek*, The Constitution of Liberty, 407.

hard core begin to cry out: Let us go into this marsh where the socialists are! And others begin to shout: Let us go into the marsh where the anarchists are! And when the unreconstructed Old Whigs begin to shame them, they retort: How conservative you are![7] Are you not ashamed to deny us the right to invite you to take the better road?

To deny the right to take a better road is exactly what true liberals always have been loathe to do. Unlike *Lenin*, they have not been thinking of revenge against those who swerved from what they considered the true path. A revitalization of liberalism will, of course, swerve from *Lenin's* suggestions for the revitalization of Marxism. *Lenin* called for a collective, all- Russian organization of communists. Liberals, being individualists, resent collectivism and abhor being organized. *Lenin* wanted an all-Russian newspaper as a collective organizer. Liberals reject collective organizers and want newspapers to freely represent different opinions. For the communists, there can be one truth as expressed by an official party newspaper with the symbolic title Pravda – Truth. Liberals realize that so far human beings have not been able to discover the whole truth which in fairness could be imposed upon others. Liberals believe that generally accepted truths may turn out to be false, that such truths can be freely challenged and refuted.[8]

Why, then, was *Lenin* mentioned? Can an archenemy of liberalism be cited for the preservation of liberalism? First, an enemy should never be ignored. If someone is out to silence me, I cannot afford to be silent about him if I want to exist. *Lenin* has been one of the great theorists and practitioners of communism and one of the major destroyers of liberalism. To pass him over would be as indefensible as to ignore the abundance of rights, riots and crimes which has jeopardized liberal democracies. Destroyers ought not to be slighted by those who do not sufficiently defend themselves against destruction. *Lenin's* spirit hovers over the world, be it communist or liberal, a world in which communism has been advancing, and liberalism, in retreat. In addition, to give an enemy the silent treatment would be intolerant and incompatible with liberalism. Furthermore, some statements are classic. The words quoted are of such a quality. People may not like Sparta and its way of life. Yet they have stood in admiration and awe before the Spartans' willingness to sacrifice themselves for their order, much as that order may have been an ordeal. The inscription of Thermopylae is a lasting and moving monument of heroism out of duty.[9] *Lenin's* passage is a timeless testimony of devotion to a cause. It tells of the brotherhood of fighters. It shows their loneliness in hostile surroundings, their constant fear of being deserted by friends who do not have the strength to endure. Uncompromising, it denounces the agility, opportunism and cowardice of those who balk and demonstrates the stubborn courage of those who stick to their ideal and their charted course of realizing it.

Lenin, then, could well teach liberals a lesson. They could consider some of his ideas for the improvement of their condition, just as communists have felt that the writings of *Ludwig von Mises* could improve their economy.[10] The plight of today's liberals is so great that they cannot afford to discard a remedy just because they dislike its author. I shall not dwell here on the fact that liberal democracies have constantly been losing ground to

[7] Especially in the United States, classic liberals often are considered conservatives and decried as reactionaries. Calling liberals «conservatives» is due to the fact that modern American «conservatives» try to preserve the liberalism of the formative period of the United States which was influenced by *Adam Smith*.

[8] See *John Stuart Mill*, On Liberty and Representative Government (*R. B. McCallum* ed.; Oxford 1946) 40 f., 46 f.

[9] *Heinrich Böll* later ridiculed that attitude in: Wanderer, kommst du nach Spa . . . (Opladen 1950).

[10] See *Oskar Lange*, «On the Economic Theory of Socialism», (1938) in *Oskar Lange* and *Fred Taylor*, On the Economic Theory of Socialism (Benjamin Lippincott, ed.; New York 1964), 58.

communist movements on the international scene. This is too obvious to need comment. The brotherhood of these democracies, as it was formalized by organizations such as NATO and SEATO, has been decimated through the agility, opportunism and cowardice of some of its members. Neither shall I deal with the fact that similar attitudes of liberals have contributed to the advance of socialism which in liberal democracies is likely to have a debilitating effect.[11] The discussion shall be confined to the plight of liberal democracies due to the increase of that dangerous product of the riot of rights and riots, namely, crime. Crime contributes to the present plight of liberal democracies vis à-vis other nations. It undermines law and authority, weakening national orders from the inside. Weak orders invite attacks. National security depends upon peace within as well as from without.

The threat to the peace of today's liberal societies on account of crime in a large measure is due to the fact that crime is not sufficiently fought. Law-abiders have turned into crime-connivers. Those who permit, or wink at, crime, threaten the peace about as much as those who commit it. Criminals are guilty by definition. Their guilt seems to be incomparably greater than that of law-abiding citizens. On the other hand, it may be asked whether from the point of view of social responsibility those who permit crimes are more guilty than those who commit them. Obeying the law, they supposedly have a social conscience, wheras criminals often do not and frequently consider their actions justified. From among the law-abiding citizens, a substantial share of blame for today's abundance of crime goes to extremist liberals.

Penal reforms from the enlightenment on, usually motivated by a legitimate quest for freedom, have reached a stage where they can be said to encourage crime. The police-state under monarchical despotism seems to have been replaced by the crime-state under democratic absolutism, the terror of the government complemented by that of criminals, be they alone or in gangs. Few liberals have hindered this development. This omission is due not merely to the fact that liberals traditionally have opposed state interference with the activities of individuals and therefore have a proclivity of giving criminals the benefit of that attitude. Neither does it just result from the general atmosphere created by *Brecht's* and Hollywood's heroization of little crooks and big gangsters making people crime-conditioned admirers of criminals. The liberals' reluctance to fight crime in a large measure is due to agility, opportunism and cowardice.

Once courageous fighters for freedom from established despotism, liberals have become established easy-going going-alongers, putting up with the tyranny of criminals. No longer does the determined bourgeois fight the roi. He has developed into the bourgeois gentilhomme whose gentility has become a challenge to the loi. It used to be that men, with the courage of liberals who fought the despotism of powerful governments, would rush to the defense of individuals attacked by criminals. They no longer do. They are afraid of getting hurt and do not want to get involved. Adult young men and women heard the cries of *Kitty Genovese* being stabbed to death in their front yard, rushed to their windows and watched the spectacle. They did not come to her aid although there was only one attacker, and did not even bother to lift up the telephone and call the police. Even the victims of crime no longer defend themselves, handing over their property rather than fighting for it. *Patrick Henry's* reputed statement, «Give me liberty, or give me death!», meant as a polemic against governmental oppression, could be today's battlecry for defying crime. However, few people think of it in an age in which it is assumed that

---

[11] *Carl Schmitt* warned that liberal permissiveness might lead to national socialism and communism in: Legalität und Legitimität (München und Leipzig, 1932). See also his remark, following the reprint of that work, in: Verfassungsrechtliche Aufsätze (Berlin 1958), 345 ff.

Henry would not have uttered his words had he really been faced by death, when the theory «rather dead than red» has been honored by a «rather red than dead» practice. Agility, opportunism and cowardice has prompted liberals to give in to crime, to live with it under governments that have proved to be only too willing to go along with a capitulation to crime.

Liberalism has no activists who could be compared to a *Lenin* or *Stalin*, a *Mussolini* or *Hitler*, its powerful destroyers who also were successful in suppressing what their laws labelled crime. The Soviet Union, built by *Lenin* and *Stalin,* did not get a crime problem under succeeding governments. Its collective leadership still is based upon a strong ever-present police. Italy did not have a problem of crime under *Mussolini*, who took issue with *Beccaria*. Today, she has enormous problems of law and order, which in a large measure account for the present *Mussolini* cult. Many Italians are longing for the times when the streets were safe. More and more inhabitants of West Germany are about to follow suit. Despotism certainly seems to offer an effective remedy against crime.

Nevertheless, despotism cannot be the solution for the problem of crime in liberal societies, if only because for liberals despotism is the crime by definition. Liberals generally have been wary of strongmen, even if the latter came from their ranks and were highly motivated. Since, then, despotism appears to be the most effective way of fighting crime and since liberals reject despotism, can there be any hope that liberal societies can cope with crime? Since liberals resent governmental activity, can they become active in the fight for law and order? Still, there is a chance. It lies in the re-activation of the rule of law. A re-assertion of this traditional means of preserving the freedom of the individual in society will secure liberty from the government and aid the citizens' protection from their fellow men. The latter could be achieved through emergency measures which perhaps could master the present waves of crime. But the liberals' task cannot end here. The protection of the individual from crime must also be provided for in a long-range program that consolidates liberal society and makes a re-emergence of crime improbable.

III. Emergency Measures Against Crime

If legal aspects of freedom – rights – can be curtailed when a nation is threatened, illegal abuses of freedom – crimes – must be fought a fortiori. The need for the restriction of freedom grows with the danger of liberty to society and the individuals composing it. If traditional rights of man, «the great rights,» [12] can be curtailed, there is no reason why an upstart right such as that of rioting should not also be restricted, the more so if it is deemed not so great a right at all, but a semi-right at best. And if rioting can be punished, even more so must be acts about the criminal character of which there is no doubt. From among crimes, those must be given special attention which add insult to injury by flagrantly ridiculing the government and even making it an accomplice to crime.

It has been generally admitted that the rights of man can be curtailed through emergency measures. In saying so, we need not think of *Hobbes*, whose philosophy was prompted by fears of disintegration following the execution of *Charles I.* To prevent anarchy the protagonist of absolute monarchy felt it necessary for individuals to surrender their rights to the king so that he might be able to at least secure their lives. Neither

[12] *Cf. Edmond Cahn*, ed.; The Great Rights (New York 1963). *Thomas Hobbes*, Leviathan (London 1651).

need we think of the man generally considered the most famous exponent of reason of state. An admirer of republican Rome and its dictatorship, *Machiavelli* felt that unusual conditions call for unusual measures [13], that ordinary procedures in times of emergency would prevent the necessary speedy action and that dictatorial restrictions of the rights of the individual were appropriate. The recent revival of interest in *Hobbes* and *Machiavelli* has in a large measure been due to the recognition that anarchical threats to liberal societies justify some kind of strong man rule. Especially *Machiavelli's* dictator, no tyrant but a republican commissar who may temporarily restrict freedom in order to save it in the long run, has appeal. On the other hand, *Machiavellianism* is too much tainted by low morality and reason of state, to be acceptable to liberals.

Rousseau made suggestions for emergencies that have been said to be both subtle and astonishingly realistic.[14] Impressed by the dictator of the Roman republic, he maintained that political institutions never must be so rigid that they could not be suspended when the existence of the state is at stake. Whenever the fatherland is in jeopardy, a condition that must be so obvious that it is recognized by everybody, responsibility for public safety must be transferred to the ablest person. Depending upon the intensity of the emergency, this commission of a dictator can take two forms. Either the executive power is concentrated in one or two persons who must make sure that the laws are strictly enforced, or if the danger is so great that adherence to existing laws proves to be a handicap, a chef suprême must be appointed who can suspend existing laws for the period of emergency and can do everything – except make laws. For he must use his extraordinary powers to restore the original state of legality. However, *Rousseau* probably will not be trusted by liberals either. Too conducive to democratic despotism are his emphasis on nationalism and his suggestion that individuals surrender their rights to the general will.

Yet liberals need not despair for want of acceptable defenders of emergency power for the preservation of liberal orders. They can take comfort in great minds whose liberalism few men will doubt. In The Spirit of the Laws, *Montesquieu* is not content with advocating liberty by virtue of, and according to, the law. He, who leaves no doubt about his hatred of despotism, recognizes the limitations of liberalism. In a book devoted to the discussion of liberty, following the famous book XI on the separation of powers and constitutional government, he discusses in what manner the use of liberty is, and can be, suspended in a republic. «In countries where liberty is most esteemed, there are laws by which a single person is deprived of it, in order to preserve it for the whole community.» After this statement at the beginning of the relevant chapter, he finishes saying «that there are cases in which a veil should be drawn for a while over liberty, as it was customary to cover the statues of gods.» The great defender of liberty defends limitations on liberty. Just as the government is supposed to be limited by freedom, freedom can temporarily be limited by the government. Free government implies restrictions of the individual as well as the government for the sake of freedom under law. Whereas *Montesquieu* describes freedom in all its aspects and details, he says quite generally that there are cases in which for a while it can be restricted and admits that in republics – which to him imply the maximal possible recognition of the freedom of the individual – any case may warrant temporary restrictions of freedom should this be essential for the preservation of liberty in the long run. For a man of measure like *Montesquieu*, this admission does not open the door for arbitrary restrictions of liberty in cases of emergency. Still, the philosopher on

---

[13] N. *Machiavelli* Discorsi sopra la prima deca di Tito Livio (Milano 1830) I, cap. 30, 33-35.
[14] J. J. *Rousseau*, Contrat Social, book IV, ch. 6.

the balance of powers obviously wants too much liberty given the appropriate measure, and balanced through the prudent checks of emergency powers.[15]

Montesquieu, one of the first and perhaps the greatest of the philosophers of modern liberalism, was followed by other liberals. Those who framed, commented upon, and ratified the American constitution believed that emergency powers were implicit in the new document. «It never seems to have been seriously considered in the Convention of 1787, the Federalist, or the debates in the state ratifying conventions that the men who were to govern in future years would ever have to go outside the words of the Constitution to find the means to meet any crisis. The provisions of the document and the government which they ordained were to be adequate for war as well as peace, for rebellion as well as internal calm.»[16] This is not surprising. After all, the American constitution resulted from the emergency of the American revolution, the threat of national disintegration, and serious challenges to traditional rights of men. It was likely to embody ways and means to ward off, and cope with, future crises. From the Whiskey Rebellion of 1794 to the Student Rebellions in the early 1970s, emergency powers were used in the United States, generally at the cost of human rights, to combat strikes, riots, civil war, economic and international crises, etc. *Lincoln*, the «Whig in the White House», used emergency powers and did not shy away from suspending habeas corpus and from doing other things which he was not supposed to do under the strict wording of the constitution.[17] From *Theodore Roosevelt's* «steward» theory to the «Stuart» concept of the presidency [18] under *Franklin D. Roosevelt* and his successors, emergency powers were used, for the sake of public order, now increasingly interfering with economic rights.

German constitutions prior to 1848 provided in so many words for emergency powers. They followed Art. 14 of the French constitutional charter of 1814 which made clear that while normally the king subjected himself to the laws, in times of crisis he could make all decrees and undertake all measures that were in the interest of public security. Art. 73 of the constitution of the Great Duchy of Hesse of 1820 is an example. Even under constitutions in which specific emergency provisions were missing, notably the old constitutions of Baden, Bavaria and Württemberg, the monarch and his government were not restricted by positive law from carrying out emergency measures. The Prussian constitution of 1848 stated that in case of war, sedition or riot, quite a few civil rights could be suspended. So did the constitution of 1850, which was complemented by a law of 1851, providing for emergency powers in a state of siege. The constitution of the empire basically took over Prussian law, introducing in Art. 68 a general clause under which existing Prussian practices were expanded, especially during World War I. The Weimar constitution, a democratic reaction of Prussianism, left far-reaching emergency powers in the executive. Its Art. 48 gave to the popularly elected President so many of these powers that it has been considered another dimension of Prussian-imperial practice. Its «constitutional dictatorship», evident in the last years of the republic, was a transition to the totalitarianism of the Third Reich. Due to *Hitler's* abuse of power, the men who made the Bonn

---

[15] Spirit of the Laws, book XII, ch. 19: « . . .the practice of the freest nation that ever existed induces me to think that there are cases in which a veil should be drawn for a while over liberty, as it was customary to cover the statues of Gods.»

[16] *Clinton Rossiter*, Constitutional Dictatorship, (Princeton 1948), 212.

[17] See *Gottfried Dietze*, «Lincoln's Constitutional Dilemma», Jahrbuch des Öffentlichen Rechts, N.F., XVI (1966), 5. The expression «Whig in the White House» was coined by *David Donald*, «Abraham Lincoln: «Whig in the White House,» in *Graebner*, ed.; The Enduring Lincoln, (Urbana, Ill. 1959), 47.

[18] See *Edward S. Corwin*, The Constitution and what it Means Today (8th ed., Princeton 1946), 80 f.

Basic Law refrained from inserting emergency provisions. However, as a result of disorders, emergency laws were passed in 1968.[19]

The French were reluctant to follow *Rousseau's* advice that one never must suspend the sacred power of the laws unless the welfare of the fatherland is at stake. The idea prevalent in Germany, that Staatsnotrecht, état de nécessité, justified executive government, generally was disliked by French jurists, who viewed it as a *Hegelian* idea of state preeminence. Still, they recognized the need for emergency measures under certain situations, and saw to it that such measures would be provided for by the laws. The use by *Charles X* in 1830 of Art. 14 of the constitutional charter of 1814 led to its replacement in that year by article 13 of the new constitution. Under that provision, the king no longer could suspend or disregard the laws. According to the principle of légalité, emergency measures were to be in conformity with the laws. The latter provided for a state of siege which was used by the wealthy bourgeoisie to strengthen its position against royalists and proletarians in the uprisings of 1832. Laws of August 9, 1849 and April 3, 1878 sepcified the powers of the government. A state of siege could be declared only by the legislature, and only in case of war or armed rebellion. The possibilities of infringements upon the rigths of the individuals were strictly defined. However, when World War I showed that the ordinary state of siege was insufficient, there came about, under the theory of circonstances exceptionelles, the practice of décrets-lois to speed up the legislative process. The Council of State created the concept of légalité élargie, which according to *Duguit* came dangerously close to the actes de gouvernement of the eighteenth century.[20] The enlarged legality was complemented in the Fourth Republic by the creation of an état d'urgence which could bring about further restrictions of civil rights and be declared whenever attacks against the public order were threatening. The Fifth Republic put an end to the primacy of legislative competency in times of emergency. Art. 36 of its constitution provides that the state of siege would now be declared by the government. An ordinance of April 15, 1960 transferred the power to declare the state or urgency to the government which for twelve days can take far-reaching measures without parliamentary approval. Art. 16 of the constitution confers wide emergency powers to the President of the Republic who becomes «the judge of the national interest.» It brought about an absolutely new dimension of state sovereignty, which is unique in French constitutional history after the French revolution, making the President of the Republic a «commissar-dictator» in the sense of *Carl Schmitt*, a man who suspends the constitution in order to save it.

Inter arma silent leges: When an emergency is to be fought, the constitution can be silent. Its force is dormant, like that of a patient under anesthesia. However, suspending a constitution involves greater risks than anesthetizing an individual. The latter will awaken and be his own self again. Those treating him do not want much else. Those suspending a constitution do away with checks and restrictions upon their ambitions and thus become more powerful. Since men in power generally will be in pursuit of power, they will be reluctant to relinquish it. The re-emergence of the original constitution amounts to a submergence of those who suspended it. In permitting it, rulers deprive themselves of power. They hardly can be expected to do so. In a word, a constitution, once suspended, seldom will be the same again.

Suspending merely a constitutional provision sounds less serious. Actually, it could be more dangerous. The suspension of the whole constitution creates a strong awareness that the situation is highly unusual and probably generates a pressing desire to get things

---

[19] 17. Gesetz zur Ergänzung des Grundgesetzes vom 24. Juni 1968. Bundesgesetzblatt I (1968) 709.
[20] See A. *Mathiot*, «Théorie des circonstances exceptionelles», in L'évolution du droit public. Études offertes à Achille Mestre (Paris 1956).

back to normal. The suspension of just a particular provision is unlikely to do so. People will be more willing tu put up with it. This will encourage suspensions of further provisions. In the end, the whole constitution may gradually fade away. The suspension of human rights is especially risky. It is likely to have in its wake the slighting of other rights. It hits the hard core of liberalism and jeopardizes constitutional government.

Yet wherever we look, the suspension of human rights is characteristic of emergency actions. During the Civil War, *Lincoln* suspended habeas corpus. In World War I, *Oliver Wendell Holmes* permitted infringements of freedom of speech in the case of a «clear and present danger» even though that freedom seemed to be absolutely protected by the First Amendment.[21] The right of a religous group not to salute the American flag, upheld by the Supreme Court in times of peace, was denied by the same court just a few months later during World War II.[22] Rights were restricted not only in times of war, but in those of peace. The reason for this policy was summed up in the statement that the constitution is not a suicide pact.[23] The situation has been similar in other nations. Whether one looks to Britain, France, Germany or elsewhere: in emergencies, civil rights are out.

This does not necessarily mean that the lights are going out. Emergency measures can keep constitutionalism alive. Trimming rights in an emergency is comparable to dimming lights on the road or in an air attack. It is necessary for survival. The willingness to suspend human rights also can be explained from the fact that these rights – nowadays often called «civil rights» – are, unlike the rights devided from civil law, not concerned with the free relationships of equals. Provisions concerning civil rights are public, not private, law. They define the positions of the government and the governed and thus determine the existence of governments as much as that of individuals. Just as the denial of civil rights will result in tyranny, their licentious extension is likely to bring about anarchy. In society, human rights are not unlimited. The adjective «civil» implies limitations by civil society which presumably is a civilized society. Society is the guarantor as much as the limitator of rights. In restricting human rights and making them civil, society guarantees that part of human rights which the citizen can claim. Restrictions of their rights are the price people pay for living in the security of a society under government. The price is commensurate to the full enjoyment of not-so-full, but measureful, rights – the proper price for the proper good. Since an emergency is a step toward anarchy, the danger that an undue extension of human rights could result in anarchy appears to be especially great in emergencies. If anarchy means lawlessness, it must mean the end of civil law, a law characterized by a great deal of freedom. The restriction of civil rights in emergencies, then, may be necessary for the survival of civil law and the civility of free government.

Nevertheless, caution is advisable when civil rights are suspended, no matter how great the emergency may be. For suspension of the great rights can all too easily result in the great beast Leviathan, which can be run by human beasts which are far more dangerous than *Nietzsche's* blond beast which did not fare well at all in the democratic, egalitarian French Revolution. Therefore, emergency powers ought to be strictly defined before an emergency comes about, by laws which bind those who exercise them. Such definitions ought to be specifically written down rather than generally concluded from customary law. While freedom appears to be safest under customary law, its restrictions seem to be the least dangerous if provided for by precise written norms. The latter ought to be made

---

[21] Schenck v. United States, 249 U. S. 47 (1919).
[22] Minersville School District v. Gobitis, 310 U. S. 586 (1939); West Virginia State Board of Education v. Barnette, 319 U. S. 624 (1942).
[23] See *Fraenkel*, ed., Der Staatsnotstand. See Justice *Jacksons's* dissent in Terminiello v. Chicago, 337 U. S. 1, 37 (1948).

according to liberal theory and practice by those who are the least likely to be negligent in the protection of the rights of man: the people acting as constituent power. In order to make doubly sure there will be no unnecessary infringements, the degree of possible curtailments of rights ought to be further defined by that constituted power which, according to liberal theory, is the closest to the people, the legislature. The Legislator in the sense of *Rousseau* must be aided by the ordinary legislature in protecting freedom from emergency measures.

Constitutions even permitted restrictions of rights according to executive rather than legislative discretion. In Germany, a fast effective mastering of emergency situations was given priority over far-reaching protections of human rights due to the recognition that the modern liberal state, threatened as it is by anarchy, cannot afford a time-consuming handling of emergencies by clumsy legislatures. The nation that brought forth the Declaration of the Rights of Man and Citizen for a long time rejected the German practice for being incompatible with the idea of légalité. Frenchmen boasted of not having a provision similar to that of Art. 48 of the Weimar constitution. However, with Art. 16. of the constitution of the Fifth Republic, they adopted a provision which gives to the chief executive emergeny discretions that go beyond those of Art. 48. The French President today can be more of a commissary dictator in the sense of *Carl Schmitt* than the Reich President could. It can be said, then, that our time has recognized that emergencies warrant restrictions of human rights not only by the legislature, but also by the executive.

From the general admission of the need to curtail civil rights in emergencies follows a fortiori that riots and crimes must be limited.

There is no reason not to restrict riots, even if a right to riot is admitted. Otherwise, this right would be preferred over that of speech, assembly, and association – important rights which can be curtailed in times of emergency. It would be strange indeed if a right to riot – at best a newcomer to the rights of man – would be considered more important than classic, long established rights. However, a right to riot is not generally admitted. Not being legally protected in normal times, it cannot well be safer in emergencies than rights which are so protected. If an emergency justifies infringements upon rights, then certainly something not qualifying as a right cannot enjoy protection. Furthermore, riots are more likely to produce emergencies for law and order than speeches, assemblies, or associations. It would be absurd, in fighting emergencies, to protect riots as much as the latter. Finally, riot under most legal systems is a crime. Warranting all the prosecution crimes deserve in normal times, it must, like other crimes, be prosecuted in emergencies.

The prosecution of crimes is especially necessary in liberal societies. Crime and punishment: if the liberal state is crime-ridden, it must punish. This remark ought not to be misleading. I do not have in mind the Marxist proposition that crimes are the result of the unequal possession of goods characteristic of liberal society and that, therefore, punishments basically are bourgeois means to oppress the poor. The falseness of that thesis is obvious. Certainly crimes such as treason, murder, rape and arson cannot generally be explained from an unequal distribution of property. Neither do I mean that a liberal state must be a police state. A liberal police state is a contradiction in terms. What I think of is that the liberal state, in creating Magna Cartas for criminals through its criminal laws, probably whetted the appetite for crime. This appetite is due not only to the improbability under liberal law of exemplary punishment. It is also due to a liberal inclination toward the mildness and absence of penalties. It is here maintained that liberal society must punish in order to kill the appetite for crime.

Liberal society is loosely structured and held together by a minimum of laws and regulations. Guaranteeing a maximum of freedom, it approaches anarchy. In view of this danger, liberal government must carefully enforce its few laws and regulations, irrespective of how strict they are. For it is not so much the leniency of the laws that is characteristic of the liberal state, but their clarity.[24] This general rule applies, of course, to criminal law. It implies that liberalism is compatible with capital punishment, perhaps the clearest, and certainly the most unequivocal, of all punishments. The need for a strict enforcement of criminal laws – including those providing for the death penalty – has been seen by great liberals.[25] Their attitude is quite natural. The elimination of a socially unbearable behavior was the reason for the formation of civil society. Criminal law, having for its objective that elimination, is thus rudimentary to the protection of society from anarchy, basic to public and private law. There are many things liberal society can endure. It cannot afford suffering crime. Therefore, liberal governments must strictly execute criminal law as well as other law. Since a normative effect is likely to be deterrent, non-execution of the law will take away that effect and even make law a laughing stock. The deterrent effect of criminal law usually will increase with the degree of punishment.[26] Non-execution of severe penalties probably will result in the non-execution of lesser ones, lead to the negation of all punishment and, ultimately, to that of the law.

These considerations apply to times of emergency a fortiori. For such times will bring liberal society even closer to anarchy and speed up its fall. The greater the threat of anarchy, the greater the need for law and its enforcement, and the punishment of crime.[27] Punishments must be especially rigorous with respect to crimes which openly defy law and order and add insult to injury. The brazen criminal has always generated greater wrath than the ordinary crook who usually works clandestinely. While in a liberal state this does not mean that the former should be punished more severely than the law provides, it is imperative that punishment be as severe as the law provides. And emergency legislation should stipulate severe punishments. This applies especially to criminals who boast that they want to destroy the liberal establishment.

In a way, every criminal is at war with the legal order, for every crime is an attack upon that order. Yet liberal society in general has refrained from applying the law of war to crime, feeling that criminal law will do. This is justified, for the ordinary criminal, from petty thief to murderer, may well be a good patriot who likes the liberal order he lives in, because he thrives in it. He does not want to overthrow it. A liberal society thus will apply the liberal principle nulla poena sine lege in the sense of the law of peace, although application of the principle, nullum crimen sine poena, might be considerably more effective in the fight against crime.[28]

---

[24] See *Dicey*, Introduction to the Study of the Law of the Constitution (10th ed. by E. C. S.*Wade*, London 1959), 189 f.; *H. W. R. Wade*, «The Concept of Legal Certainty», Modern Law Review, IV (1941), 183; *F. A. Hayek* The Constitution of Liberty, 208 f.

[25] See, for instance, *Eduard Lasker*, Rede über die Todesstrafe (Berlin 1870).

[26] Terrorists may be (as were the original assassins) so fanatic that they do not worry over the degree of punishment. Ordinary people do. It was the fear of death which *Hobbes* recognized justly as the greatest of all fears and made many Germans acquiesce in the *Hitler* régime. People generally believe that the death penalty is the greatest deterrent to crime, as is quite obvious in present attempts to restore it. To deny that the death penalty is the supreme deterrent is tantamount to asserting that a severe penalty for a crime is no greater deterrent than a light one, which must lead all differentiations of punishment ad absurdum.

[27] In Spain, threatened as it generally has been by anarchy, there usually would be a strict enforcement of the laws, including those providing for capital punishment. In a letter to *Pierre F. Goodrich* of August 18, 1952, *Wilhelm Röpke* wrote that *Lord Acton's* statement that power tends to corrupt and that absolute power corrupts absolutely does not imply that anarchy would not be worse than despotism.

[28] For a distinction between these principles, see *Carl Schmitt*, «Der Führer schützt das Recht», Deutsche Juristen-Zeitung, XLIX (1934), 945.

However, the question must be asked whether in emergencies the law of war might be applicable to criminals who, like guerillas, have put themselves into a state of war with the liberal order. When the American ambassador was kidnaped in Rio, the kidnapers wanted the release of a number of fellow guerillas from jail in return for the ambassador's freedom, threatening to kill him if their demands were not met. Some young Brazilian officers, obviously remindful of their flag's tribute to order and progress, suggested the kidnapers be told that unless the ambassador was released unharmed by a certain day, some of the imprisoned guerillas would be executed; that unless he was released the day following those executions, more would be shot, and so on. Had this kind of procedure been applied to the first conspicuous case of guerilla kidnaping and blackmail, it might well have stifled such crimes in the bud. It would also have been defensible under the law of war's internationally accepted provisions of reprisals.[29] After all, guerillas created, and consider themselves in, a state of war. They are committed to do away with their enemies, probably in a more objectionable manner than regular combatants would. This prompts the question whether reprisals against guerillas are not more justified than reprisals in regular wars.

Although, in the case at hand, the execution of the imprisoned guerillas would have been caused by the kidnapers blackmailing the government, liberals are likely to shy away from retaliation of the kind described. In that case the Brazilian government also could have applied the principle casum sentit dominus, and let the person concerned suffer the damage. Backed by the United States, it could have made clear that the demands of the kidnapers would not be met, even at the risk of sacrificing the ambassador. Citizenship implies the willingness to bring sacrifices for the order one's country stands for, not to compromise that order by permitting oneself to be intimidated by, and even make deals with, criminals. This obligation increases in the case of public servants. They should serve their country, from which they receive salary, at least as uncompromisingly as the soldier in the line of battle. And the higher their rank, the greater the obligation. An ambassadorship, representing a head of state to another head of state, implies more than cocktail parties and a pleasant life. The honor to serve in an eminent post must be matched by the gladness to die for the honor of that post.

The sissified way the case was dealt with reflected liberal tremor rather than determination. Its «solution» was no solution at all, spawning, as it did, further problems requiring solutions. A tragic example was set. Under pressure from the United States, the government of Brazil submitted to the demands of the kidnapers and blackmailers. The result was a chain of kidnapings and blackmailings throughout the world, with liberal governments giving in and becoming the laughing stock of criminals and non-liberals. Wherever kidnaping and blackmail were punishable governments became participants in the very crimes they were supposed to prosecute. An individual committing a crime threatens the freedom of others and the law and order of society. The threat increases if many individuals commit criminal acts. Still, even in the case of a riot of serious crimes, the legal order can be preserved if the government enforces the laws. That order is jeopardized as soon as crimes no longer are prosecuted. Non-prosecution of crimes amounts to government sanction of crime. It is the death blow to law and order and the freedom they protect, the ultimate negation of what according to liberal doctrine is considered the primary purpose of government.

---

[29] See *L. Oppenheim*, International Law (2d ed., London 1912), II, 36 ff.; *Friedrich Berber*, Lehrbuch des Völkerrechts (München 1964), III 88ff.

Experience has shown that standing up to blackmail and abiding by the law pays off.[30] It could be asked whether a clear and present danger to the law entitles the government to protect the legal order the way an individual can if he defends himself against illegal attacks by actions not ordinarily permitted. Quod ius bovi licet Jovi. It will be argued that the government's use of such actions is more dubious. Being on a larger scale, it involves a greater challenge to the law. However, this argument could be countered by saying that national emergencies constitute more of a challenge to the law than does an attack upon an individual and therefore justify a broader application of normally unadmissible means. *Goethe*, one of the great humanists who admitted that he could have committed any crime and yet defended the death penalty, perhaps even would have gone so far as to say that in an emergency the government can act illegally and unjustly to prevent disorder.[31]

In order to survive, liberals must recognize the truth of their existential situation and concede extraordinary measures against extraordinary threats. They may not agree with *Goethe*. They may be reluctant to admit that in an emergency caused by crimes and riots, ordinarily illegal government actions are warranted for the defense of the public order. Too much has the belief that only formulated law justifies governmental action become part of the liberal credo. Too much does legality loom in the liberal mind. Yet, regardless of the proclivity for a legality which could be a «legality that kills»,[32] liberals cannot get around the plain fact that the existential minimum of a liberal society requires the enforcement of that ethical minimum, the law.[33] If it wants to survive, liberal government must not suffer crime, even less bow to crime and become an accomplice to it.

The suggestion that emergencies be handled with swift efficiency takes us to a long-range program which may prevent the kind of emergencies liberal democracies are now experiencing. The fact that these emergencies in a large measure are due to an abundance and perversion of rights, suggests the remedy.

IV. Long Range Remedies Against Crime

The survival of a society of free and responsible individuals presupposes the restoration of proper rights.

The present riot of rights has been matched by an abundance of riots and crime. Since right will produce wrong as rarely as wrong will bring about right, the increase of crime is unlikely to be the result of a proper growth of proper rights, but rather will be due to an

---

[30] When hijackers wanted to take over an Ethiopian plane a few years ago, they were overwhelmed, strapped into first-class seats and had their throats slit. Ethiopian Airlines has not had a problem of hijacking ever since. On the other hand, the fact that the West German government did not comply with the wishes of those who occupied the German embassy in Stockholm, did not prevent the kidnaping of *Schleyer*. The firm attitude of the *Schmidt* government on the latter occasion, however, is generally believed to have put an end to kidnaping in West Germany.

[31] In «Belagerung von Mainz 1793», *Goethe* writes that he would prefer an injustice to disorder. His attitude toward the death penalty was the topic of *Eberhard Schmidt's* inaugural lecture at the University of Heidelberg in 1947, at a time when, on account of *Hitler's* cruel abuse of that penalty, the large majority of Germans were opposed to it, prohibiting it in the Basic Law of 1949.

[32] See *Fernand Auburtin*, Une Législation qui tue (Paris 1922).

[33] Cf. *Georg Jellinek*, Die sozialethische Bedeutung von Recht, Unrecht und Strafe (2d ed., Berlin 1908), 45.

improper increase of improper rights. A long-range program for the reduction of crime must, therefore, in a large measure be concerned with the impropriety of the present scale of rights and suggest the restoration of proper rights. But the task cannot end here. Since the protection of those rights is the purpose of the rule of law, suggestions must be made for the proper appreciation of that rule by rulers and ruled alike.

The propriety of rights must be restored by a re-appreciation of property rights.

Re-appreciation of property rights for the restoration of the propriety of rights? This indicates that property rights are not considered proper in spite of the fact that these rights usually were deemed proper by definition: the word property often has been used in lieu of propriety. To the Latins, proprietas meant «propriety» as well as «property.» In old French, propriété connoted something good, but, also, something owned. The Italian proprietà and the Spanish propiedad mean both «property» and «propriety.» The Oxford dictionary defines «propriety» as «property» and as «in conformity with good manners or polite usage.» «Goods», a kind of property, denote something proper, or good. The German Gut means property, the adjective «gut» means «good». Les biens in French mean property, as in biens meubles and biens immeubles. Bien is the adverb of bon, «good.» Property rights are unique among the rights of man. Language, that reliable judge, considers no other right as synonymous to propriety. In view of this legitimation, it must be surprising that the propriety of property should stand in need of emphasis. Yet great indeed is that need. For the rights of property in the past decades have been seriously discriminated against in what can be considered a major challenge to a value central to civilization and inextricably connected with the rule of law. This development has been due to a variety of factors, most of which are connected with the march of democracy. The democratic revolutions in England, America and France were accompanied by desires to bring about more equal distributions of property, i.e., to infringe upon property rights. However, in all these revolutions the egalitarian forces were outnumbered by the liberal ones who felt that property rights should be protected as much as life and liberty.

In the communist revolution in Russia, on the other hand, the egalitarian forces had their way. Egalitarianism came to the fore also in liberal nations. Property rights became disparaged. This development went parallel to what *Tocqueville* envisaged as the inevitable march of democracy. Its speed may have differed in the various nations. About its general trend, there can be no doubt. One of its aspects is the broadening of the suffrage. Since the latter implied the abolition of property qualifications, it meant that poorer and poorer segments of the population were given the vote. Naturally, these men and women were not much interested in protecting what they did not have. Rather, they would favor a more equal distribution of ownership and infringements upon existing property rights. *Marx* launched his attack against the property-owning bourgeoisie at about the same time *Proudhon* wrote that property is theft. The result was a challenge of property rights by the foes of liberalism. However, the attack was not confined to them. Property rights were hurt by liberals themselves. Their attacks, generally made under the banner of «social justice», was made on a wide front, by theologians, economists, jurists. They contributed to the riot of crime liberal nations have been experiencing these past years, characterized by restrictions of property rights, and by violence. In a large measure, this was due to the fact that people often did not realize that the permission of some infringements upon these rights would lead to more and the admission of some violence, to greater and greater violence, a destruction of the order of civil rights, to that of the liberal order itself. This possibility appears to be especially great if property rights are violated. For of all rights, those of property are the most essential to the law, the lynchpin around which the law turns. To say that democratic rights are more important than property and non-violence or peace means sanctioning violence. And the admission of violence and the destruction of property is an admission of crime. No matter how important democratic rights are for the democratic process, – and their preferred position has been defended on that ground – it must never be forgotten that democracy, important as it is for freedom, is according to liberal doctrine, not an end in itself, but a means for the protection of the rights of the individual, among which those of property figure prominently.

Disturbances through riots and crimes thus can be attributed in a large measure to the disparagement of property. Their abundance is not surprising, for publicly sanctioned violations of property have grown by leaps and bounds. If social legislation is the order of the day, the order of the day is likely to be disorder. *Marx*, seeing in laws protecting property a means for the oppression of the proletariat, proposed the disorder of revolution as a means of attacking property rights. Liberal societies have increasingly sanctioned infringements of property rights through social legislation in order to ward off Marxism. In doing so, they actually have encouraged crime and disorder. Certainly, if the government makes laws infringing upon private property, there is no reason why criminals should respect private property and refrain from disregarding the property rights of others, even with violence. Since most crimes are crimes against property, legal discriminations against property could well encourage the better part of all crimes.

An important long-range remedy against crime, then, is the restoration of property rights to their traditional rank. But there is another major remedy, one that traditionally protected property rights, and without which propriety can hardly be restored to the body politic, namely, the rule of law.

It will be remembered that *John Adams* wrote: «Property is surely a right of mankind as really as liberty ... The moment the idea is admitted into society that property is not as sacred as the laws of God, and that there is not a force of law and public justice to protect it, anarchy and tyranny commence.» This statement is as much one in defense of the rule of law as it is one in favor of property. *Adams* distinguishes the «force of law and public justice» from «anarchy and tyranny», the former corresponding to the rule of law, the latter constituting major challenges to it.

From among these challenges, most authors emphasized that of despotism. As a matter of fact, the idea of the rule of law traditionally has implied the restriction of governmental power and the protection of the individual's life, liberty and property. The barons at Runnymede thought so when they asked *John* to sign the Magna Carta. Even under theistic kingship in France, *Bodin*, in spite of his advocacy of royal sovereignty, emphasized that the king was under the laws of the realm. The rule of law, made popular through *Dicey's* exposition at the height of the liberal era, thus is a concept that precedes its popularization, as does its German counterpart Rechtsstaat, in which the syllable «right» or «law» symbolically precedes that of «state.» As *Triepel* remarked: «Many legal ideas which were emphasized and developed by liberalism ... are much older than liberalism, have survived liberalism and will survive us.»

He added: «If the timeless Rechtsstaat is given the attribute ‹liberal›, something that is usually done in order to denounce the Rechtsstaat; if with the same purpose in mind one speaks of the ‹bourgeois› Rechtsstaat to signify the Rechtsstaat of the bourgeoisie which fears for its ‹security›; if, in distinction to that kind of Rechtsstaat, one construes a ‹social› Rechtsstaat, it can only be said that all these are distortions against which we, men of the law, all of whom it is hoped favor the Rechtsstaat, ought to protest. For here an eternal value is pulled down into the dust of finite-littleness.[34] These words were spoken shortly

---

[34] *Heinrich Triepel* in: Veröffentlichungen der Vereinigung der Deutschen Staatsrechtslehrer VII (1932), 197.

before *Hitler* came to power, when the liberal and social Rechtsstaat of the Weimar Republic suffered from crime and approached political anarchy which the government tried to cope with by means of constitutional dictatorship. They show how the rule of law has been provided with adjectives such as «liberal», «bourgeois,» and «social.» *Triepel*, the teacher of *Gerhard Leibholz*, obviously felt that the Rechtsstaat was liberal by definition, that it did not stand in need of the adjective «liberal.» He regretted the use of adjectives which indicated that the rule of law was an empty form that could be filled with any kind of content, be it «social», «socialist», even «national-socialist». As a matter of fact, jurists, on account of the formalization of the rule of law, in good conscience claimed that the *Hitler* regime was a Rechtsstaat.[35] *Triepel* resented this formalization achieved at the cost of liberty, which brought about the decline of the Rechtsstaat,[36] a decline that went about parallel to that of property rights. Yet the advocate of the rule of law with its liberal values, also was the author of a work on hegemony.[37] To him, a «liberal Rechtsstaat» was redundant. It was likely to be all too liberal and tending toward anarchy. In liberal societies freedom exists under law. It cannot well exist without the law of the state.

In view of the increase of riots and crime in these societies, this must be kept in mind. While liberals favor the rule of law because it protects them from governmental restrictions, limits the rulers' power and provides for weak government according to the principle, «that government is best that governs least,» they must beware of sentimentalizing law out of existence. They must not forget that the rule of law implies more than limitations upon the government. It is a rule of law and implies sanction. It must be enforced by the government vis-à-vis individual citizens who are expected to obey it. Much as the rule of law is to curb governmental power and its abuse, it also is to implement the authority of rulers over the ruled. In a word, much as the Rechtsstaat has been threatened by Staatsrecht, the latter is necessary for the former's existence. Staatsrecht gives the Rechtsstaat pep. One concept of the rule of law gives the other vigor.[38]

A vigorous rule of law that protects proper rights, then, is necessary in order to restore propriety to liberal society. This restoration must exist from the top to the bottom, as must obedience to the laws. The rulers themselves must set the example. It was urged that they refrain from being accomplices to criminals, from bowing to crime, from suffering it. But this alone won't do. The fact that this had to be urged shows how the propriety of governments has declined. A few years ago, it would have been taken for granted that rulers fight crime. Today, this is no longer so. Liberal democracies have come a long way from the time of *Edmund Burke*, the great Whig supporter of the Americans' quest for rights, and his fellow-liberal *James Madison*, father of the American constitution. To both, representatives were natural aristocrats in the *Jeffersonian* sense, far above crime.[39] Today, after a long march of democracy, the members of governmental bodies no longer enjoy that prestige. There is corruption among them. They are not too careful about avoiding conflicts with the laws. Some of them, even in the highest positions, commit criminal acts. In 1944, *Hayek* could bewail that «the worst get on top».[40] Those he had in mind have been complemented by criminals. Liberalism made great progress when des-

---

[35] See *Gottfried Dietze*, Two Concepts of the Rule of Law (Indianapolis 1973), 36 f.

[36] See *F. A. Hayek*, «Entstehung und Verfall des Rechtsstaatsideales», in *Albert Hunold*, ed., Wirtschaft ohne Wunder (Zürich 1953), 33; The Constitution of Liberty, ch. 16.

[37] *Heinrich Triepel*, Die Hegemonie (Stuttgart 1938).

[38] See *Dietze*, Two Concepts of the Rule of Law.

[39] For *Jefferson's* concept of the natural aristocracy, see his letter to *John Adams* of Oct. 28, 1813. Writings, XIII, 394 ff.

[40] *F. A. Hayek*, The Road to Serfdom, 134 ff.

potism, symbolized by *Louis XIV's* statement «L'Etat c'est moi», was challenged by enlightened absolute monarchy in which, according to *Frederick the Great*, the king was the first servant of the state. Today liberalism, barely surviving under absolute democracy with its socialist trimmings, can be invigorated not only by making government more limited, but also by making democratic representatives more obedient to the laws. They should consider themselves the first servants of the people.

With honesty restored in the government, propriety has a better chance of pervading the rest of society. Young *Lincoln's* appeal to his countrymen is good advice today to those living under governments of the people, for the people, by the people:

> Let every American, every lover of liberty, every well wisher to his posterity, swear by the blood of the Revolution, never to violate in the least particular, the laws of the country; and never to tolerate their violation by others. As the patriots of seventy-six did to the support of the Declaration of Independence, so to the support of the Constitution and Laws, let every American pledge his life, his property, and his sacred honor; – let every man remember that to violate the law, is to trample on the blood of his father, and to tear the character [charter?] of his own, and his children's liberty. Let reverence for the laws, be breathed by every American mother, to the lisping babe, that prattles on her lap – let it be taught in schools, in seminaries, and in colleges; – let it be written in Primmers, spelling books, and in Almanacs; – let it be preached from the pulpit, proclaimed in legislative halls, and enforced in courts of justice. And, in short, let it become the *political religion* of the nation; and let the old and the young, the rich and the poor, the grave and the gay, of all sexes and tongues, and colors and conditions, sacrifice unceasingly upon its altars.

In that speech, *Lincoln* admitted that there are bad laws, suggesting that such laws be abolished in legal ways. Yet he also made it clear that as long as these laws were on the books, they ought to be strictly observed.[41] For the sake of legal security, he was willing to put up with a few bad laws. After all, they were the exception to the mass of good laws characteristic of a liberal body politic. Whether liberals in today's consumer society, prosperous as they generally are, will be able and willing to sacrifice unceasingly upon the altars of reverence for the laws, is perhaps the existential question of liberalism.

In the restoration of reverence for the laws and proper rights, – in the reassertion of the rule of law – an important role falls upon the United States. She claims leadership in the liberal world, upon which she has exercized a great influence. She was first in formulating modern bills securing proper rights, as well as in instituting judicial review for the protection of the rule of law from the arbitrariness of one, a few, or the many, and thus brought the development of the rule of law to a climax. It was also in the United States that the rights of man reached greater dimensions than anywhere else in the world, as did, in the past decades, riots and crime.

VI. Concluding Remark

Hayek considered constitutionalism «The American Contribution» to the constitution of liberty. He quoted *Lord Acton's* praise of America as a country from which «the plain ideas that men ought to mind their own business, and that the nation is responsible to Heaven for the acts of State . . . burst forth like a conquerer upon the world they were des-

---

[41] «Address Before the Young Men's Lyceum», 112. in *Roy P. Basler*, ed., The Collected Works of Abraham Lincoln (New Brunswick, N. J., 1953), I, 112.

tined to transform, under the title of the Rights of Man.»[42] An existential question for the preservation of liberal order today is whether these rights have corrupted those who have minded their own business too much, be it in fights for rights that seem to be exaggerated and perverted, or in the commission of, or acqiescence in, crime. Recent experience shows that like power, rights tend to corrupt.

Hayek's addressing The Road to Serfdom «To THE SOCIALISTS OF ALL PARTIES» was a warning to the concrete massed power of socialists, the enormity of which was symbolized by capital block letters, not to continue on the road to serfdom. It was followed by an admonition «to the unknown civilization that is growing in America», to which he addressed The Constitution of Liberty. That admonition was not put in capital block letters, perhaps because it was uncertain: The unknown civilization could grow into serfdom under socialist auspices, into anarchy on account of crime. In either case, the growth would be malignant to the known American civilization which contributed constitutionalism to the constitution of liberty and was not jeopardized by tyranny and anarchy. *Hayek* thus shows the relevance of the American development for all liberal societies. Many translations testify to the fact that The Constitution of Liberty was intended to convey its liberal message to the whole world.

Hayek's The Political Ideal of the Rule of Law, published in Cairo in 1955, when the problem of crime was a minor one in liberal societies, contains a section on «Law and Order». A subtitles «What Can Not be Done Under the Rule of Law», is followed by one, «The Socialist Revolt Against the Rule of Law». Today, it must be added that the socialist revolt has been complemented by that of the criminals. It must be asked what can be done under the rule of law to remedy the situation. For just as a nation is responsible to Heaven for acts of State, it is responsible for omissions of State, especially those which facilitate criminal acts.

Perhaps from liberal convictions or gentlemanly inhibitions, the aristocrat *Friedrich August von Hayek* has refrained from accusing socialists of bad intentions. Can liberals afford that attitude in their present existential struggle? To survive after the replacement of aristocracy by democracy, they must examine whether the principle noblesse oblige ought to be replaced by that of duresse oblige. Hardship makes obligatory an examination whether its promoters have evil motives. Free expression is not infringed upon by free expressions of opinions that it is prompted by the desire to do mischief. As was evident in the American Founders' distrust of human nature, human actions can derive from vicious human designs.[43] While the badness of human actions often will be difficult to prove, especially if such actions are in conformity with the laws, and an accusation often will have the effect of being considered proof of the goodness of the accused, liberals, if they want to survive, must be on the lookout for what is inimical to them and not shy away from denouncing the bad intentions of their non-liberal enemies and foes.

In the case of criminals, liberals are freed from the inhibitions they might have in denouncing legal, though illiberal, actions. Lawbreakers are hors de la loi. Their evil designs are obvious. In fighting them, liberals may go, as Chancellor *Helmut Schmidt* pointed out during the *Schleyer* affair, to the limits of the Rechtsstaat about which I gave a few indications.

The political ideal of the rule of law probably has as little of a chance of being realized as *Hegels* ideal state. It can only be approached. Its defense requires a realistic concept of

---

[42] The Constitution of Liberty, 176.
[43] Cf. *Ludwig von Mises*, Human Action (3rd rev. ed., Chicago 1966); *Hayek*, Law, Legislation and Liberty, vol. I, ch. 2.

the political that calls for fight against the enemies and foes of liberal orders and helps to restore the militancy liberals displayed in 1640, 1776, 1789 and 1848.[44]

Summary

From the Constitution of Liberty to Its Deconstitution by Liberalistic Dissipation, Disintegration, Disassociation, Disorder.

This article is addressed to the liberals of all parties with a view of reminding them of the need for liberal order.

From *Montesquieu* and *Adam Smith* to *Hayek*, great liberals have emphasized the rule of law. To them, that rule limited governmental power and regulation for the sake of the freedom of the individual. However, it also implied restrictions upon individuals for the sake of society and their fellow-individuals.

It is praiseworthy that liberals always have pointed out the risks of big government. On the other hand, some of those who call themselves liberals seem to be inclined toward rejecting aspects of government that are essential to the maintenance of the liberal order. Their extremism dangerously drifts away from that moderation which has been considered a landmark of genuine liberalism, a prerequisite for the existence of a free society and which *Wilhelm Röpke* expressed with the words, Maß und Mitte, measure and mean.

It is here maintained that measure is the treasure of liberalism, that liberal Maß must be pitted against the mass and mess of anarchistic trends as much as against the mass and mess of governmental regulations. Few people doubt that liberalism has been threatened by various types of despotic government. But quite a few people seem to be unaware that liberalism increasingly has become jeopardized by the liberalistic quaternion of perverted liberalism: dissipation, disintegration, disassociation, disorder. These discords of liberalism contribute about as much to the deconstitution of liberty as do the socialists of all parties. They are internal·threats to liberalism that are perhaps more dangerous than more external ones. Each of them may appear by itself. It also may form part of a liberalistic sham of events. An intoxication with freedom all too easily leads to liberalistic dissipation which in its individualistic hybris is likely to bring about disintegrating pluralistic excesses which tend to tempt individuals to disassociate themselves from society by committing crimes, or, in a liberalistic fashion, taking the law into their own hands. In the end, liberal order falls to its perversion, liberalistic disorder.

The essay perhaps even makes some suggestions on what is to be done by liberals to save liberalism.

---

[44] See *Gottfried Dietze*, «Rights, Riots, Crimes: On an Aspect of Carl Schmitt's Relevance for Today's Liberal Democracies», Revue Européenne des Sciences Sociales et Cahiers Vilfredo Pareto, XVI (1978), No. 44: Miroir de *Carl Schmitt*, 77. The article draws a few comparisons between *Hayek* and *Schmitt*. Cf. *Hayek*, Law, Legislation and Liberty vol. I, 71.

Hans Willgerodt

Wirtschaftsordnung und Staatsverwaltung

Man spricht kein Geheimnis aus, wenn man feststellt, daß viele Liberale ein gebroche-
nes Verhältnis zum Staat und zur staatlichen Verwaltung haben. Sie betonen die tyranni-
schen Möglichkeiten, die in jeder staatlichen Organisation angelegt sind. Der Staat sei
nämlich darauf angewiesen, die Kompetenz als oberste Entscheidungsinstanz in Anspruch zu nehmen und sich hierfür mit den erforderlichen Machtmitteln zu versehen. Un-
zählig sind die liberalen Warnungen vor dem Machtmißbrauch, der mit einer Ausdehnung der Staatstätigkeit verbunden sein müsse.

Meist ging es den Liberalen darum, die Privatautonomie und die private Wirtschaft vor
freiheitsbeschränkenden und die Marktkräfte lähmenden Einflüssen zu bewahren, die
vom Staat und seiner Verwaltung ausgehen können. Daß die Staatsverwaltung die Wirtschaft und die Wirtschaftsordnung deformieren können, ist ein im liberalen Schrifttum
geläufiges und immer wieder neu erörtertes Thema. Um Nachteile für die Privatautonomie und Wirtschaft der Privaten abzuwehren, wird eine bestimmte Staatsverfassung gefordert. «Wirtschaftsordnung und Staatsverfassung» ist denn auch ein Standardtitel liberaler Veröffentlichungen[1].

In jüngster Zeit wird – anknüpfend an eine im Kern schon bei *Adam Smith* und *John
Stuart Mill* angelegte Konzeption – zusätzlich geprüft, ob die Staatsverwaltung die von
den Bürgern gewünschten öffentlichen Leistungen zweckmäßig und kostengünstig er-
bringt; das heißt, die Liberalen haben das finanzpolitische und finanzwissenschaftliche
Grundproblem wieder entdeckt, das sie in einer bestimmten Phase vereinfachten Mo-
delldenkens aus den Augen verloren hatten. Die Sichtweise bleibt aber gleichwohl extrem
kritisch, indem alle – ohne Zweifel vorhandenen – Schwächen der staatlichen Bürokratie
pointierend hervorgehoben werden und der Versuch unternommen wird, diese Schwächen auf die Verhaltensweisen der staatlichen Bürokraten zurückzuführen[2]. Der homo
bürocraticus soll in einer Art von Modellanalyse ähnliche didaktische Funktionen erfüllen wie einst der homo oeconomicus für die Marktanalyse. Es wird davon ausgegangen,

---

[1] Vgl. *Franz Böhm*, Wirtschaftsordnung und Staatsverfassung, Tübingen 1950; *Heinz Sauermann*
und *Ernst-Joachim Mestmäcker* (Herausgeber), Wirtschaftsordnung und Staatsverfassung, Festschrift für *Franz Böhm* zum 80. Geburtstag, Tübingen 1975. Das Problem selber begleitet die
klassische Nationalökonomie seit ihren Anfängen, so daß die Nationalökonomen immer zugleich auch Staats- und Verfassungstheoretiker gewesen sind. Wo man diesen Aspekt vernachlässigt hat, weist die Nationalökonomie deutliche empirische und analytische Defekte auf; in jüngster Zeit sind diese Defekte so stark in das Blickfeld gerückt worden, daß die entgegengesetzte Gefahr einer Überbetonung und einer Vernachlässigung der bewährten volkswirtschaftlichen Allo-
kations- und Kreislauftheorie zugunsten wolkiger politökonomischer Denkgebilde besteht.

[2] *C. Northcote Parkinson*, Parkinson's Law and other Studies in Administration, Cambridge
(Mass.) 1957; *William A. Niskanen*, Bureaucracy and Representative Government, Chicago und
New York 1971; ders., Bureaucracy: Servant or Master? Lessons from America, (London) 1973;
The Institute of Economic Affairs (Herausgeber), The Economics of Politics, Readings 18, (Lon-
don) 1978, mit zahlreichen weiteren Literaturhinweisen, insbesondere auf Veröffentlichungen
von *James M. Buchanan, Gordon Tullock, Charles K. Rowley.*

daß der staatliche Verwaltungsfunktionär im eigenen Interesse handelt und sich darin vom privaten Wirtschaftsbürger nicht unterscheidet. Während aber Wettbewerb und Markt dafür sorgen, daß unter bestimmten Nebenbedingungen die Verfolgung des Privatinteresses durch Einzelbürger nicht gegen das Interesse anderer verstößt, sondern damit harmoniert, gebe es entsprechende Regelsysteme in der Staatsverwaltung nicht oder nur in unvollkommener Form. Der staatliche Bürokrat sei persönlich an der Expansion der Staatstätigkeit über das Maß hinaus interessiert, das die Bürger für nützlich halten, weil Gehalt und Einfluß des Bürokraten davon abhängen. Unwirtschaftlichkeit zeichne den öffentlichen Bereich aus, weil er nicht konkursfähig sei. Die politischen Wettbewerbe um Wählerstimmen seien aus Gründen, die im einzelnen untersucht werden, kaum geeignet, dieses Problem zu lösen. Daher sei es in erster Linie notwendig, die Staatstätigkeit einzuschränken; in zweiter Linie müsse darüber nachgedacht werden, wie die staatliche Verwaltung durch Verfassungsreformen, vielleicht auch durch Einbau marktähnlicher Elemente, funktionstüchtiger gemacht werden könnte. Ohne Zweifel hat diese Diskussion zu beachtlichen Einsichten geführt und die wissenschaftlichen Verfechter der These, dem Staat müsse wegen des «Marktversagens» ein ständig wachsender Handlungsspielraum eingeräumt werden, in arge Verlegenheit gebracht. Die kommunistische, aber nun auch von Nichtkommunisten vertretene Ansicht, der «Kapitalismus» überlebe zur Zeit nur deswegen, weil der Staat im Dienste der «Monopole» die Wirtschaft stabilisiere, ist schon wegen der dahinter stehenden Fehleinschätzung staatlicher Möglichkeiten reichlich naiv. Die Vertreter der «Stamokap»-Thesen verfügen selten über ausreichende Verwaltungserfahrung, und noch seltener dürfte ihnen die moderne liberale Bürokratietheorie bekannt sein.

Gleichwohl argumentiert die neuere liberale Bürokratiekritik teilweise etwas zu einfach, weil sie – ähnlich wie einst *Karl Marx* den «Kapitalisten» – nunmehr den staatlichen Bürokraten als den unvermeidlich auftretenden Theaterschurken ansieht, der als Person zwar nicht schlechter sei als wir alle, der aber innerhalb des modernen staatlichen Systems unvermeidlich gemeinschädliche Eigenschaften entwickeln müsse. Bereits *Adam Smith* hat darauf hingewiesen, daß die Menschen nicht nur Ziele zu ihren eigenen machen, die nur auf Kosten anderer erreicht werden können, sondern daß man auch auf Anerkennung durch andere Wert legt.[3] Für den Staatsfunktionär gilt dies nicht minder, und

---

[3] Vgl. *Martin Ricketts, Adam Smith* on Politics and Bureaucracy, in: The Economics of Politics (siehe Fußnote 2), S. 173–182. Die zahlreichen Mißverständnisse über die Rolle, die *Adam Smith* dem Egoismus angeblich zuschreibt, beruhen nicht zuletzt darauf, daß seine Erörterung dieser Frage in seinem Buch Theory of Moral Sentiments nicht herangezogen wird. Er beginnt dort seine Untersuchung mit der Feststellung, daß die Menschen Sympathie und Mitleid mit anderen empfinden und deren Situation also zum Teil als eigene empfinden mit der Folge, daß eigene Handlungen entsprechend orientiert werden (*Adam Smith,* Theorie der ethischen Gefühle, herausgegeben von *Walther Eckstein,* Leipzig 1926 – nach der 6. Auflage von 1790; 1. Teil, I. Abschnitt, 1. Kapitel, S. 1 ff.). *Smith* legt außerdem dar, daß die Menschen nach Anerkennung und auch nach einer Anerkennung streben, die sie objektiv wirklich verdienen (ebendort, 3. Teil, 2. Kapitel, S. 171 ff.). Zur Frage des vermeintlichen Widerspruchs zu der im «Wealth of Nations» vertretenen Konzeption vgl. die Einleitung von *Walther Eckstein,* ebendort, S. LIII ff. Die sozialethische Diskussion des «Widerspruchs» leidet darunter, daß sich die Autoren nicht in den empirischen Realismus des *Adam Smith* hineindenken können: Einerseits erkennt *Smith* richtig, daß der Mensch durchaus fähig und darauf angewiesen ist, in der Gemeinschaft mit anderen zu leben und diesen anderen nützlich zu sein, wobei das «Entgelt» in bloßer Anerkennung oder sogar in einfacher Selbstbestätigung bestehen kann, andererseits verkennt er nicht, daß der Altruismus nicht die normale Verhaltensweise für alle bei allen Handlungen sein kann und daß Handlungen zum Schaden anderer eine große Bedeutung haben, so daß eine Ordnung geschaffen werden muß, die vor allem gemeinschädliches Verhalten zurückdrängt.

es wäre wirklichkeitsblind, den Personen, die im Staatsdienst stehen, allgemein einen hemmungslosen Egoismus zu unterstellen. Die vielen Beamten, die auch heute noch Gesundheit und Leben im öffentlichen Interesse einsetzen, sprechen deutlich gegen allzu zynische Vereinfachungen. Außerdem wird nicht genügend beachtet, daß auch private Großunternehmen und Verbandsorganisationen über Bürokratien verfügen, die keineswegs so vollkommen über Wettbewerb und Märkte gezügelt werden, daß eine strenge Scheidelinie zur staatlichen Bürokratie gezogen werden kann, wenn die Verhaltensweise beurteilt werden soll.

Richtig ist jedoch die jetzt stark betonte Einsicht, daß das Verhalten der staatlichen Verwaltung von ihrem Aufbau, der staatlichen Gesamtordnung und den Aufgaben abhängt, die man der staatlichen Bürokratie zuweist. Uns soll im Folgenden die besondere Frage beschäftigen, wie die Staatsverwaltung selber ihren Charakter, ihre Leistungsfähigkeit und ihre innere Organisation verändert, wenn man sich für verschiedene Wirtschaftsordnungen entschieden hat. Das Thema lautet also nicht mehr: «Wirtschaftsordnung und Staatsverfassung», sondern «Wirtschaftsordnung und Staatsverwaltung». Gefragt wird nicht, was mit den Privaten und der Wirtschaft geschieht, wenn der Staat eine bestimmte Wirtschaftsordnung zuläßt oder anstrebt; vielmehr geht es um die Folgen für den Staat selber und seine Verwaltung, wenn eine bestimmte Wirtschaftspolitik getrieben wird. Diese Sicht ist ungewohnt, obgleich sich vor allem die liberalen Klassiker immer wieder auch mit dieser Frage eingehend befaßt haben.[4]

In scheinbarem Widerspruch zu ihrer angeblichen Staatsfeindlichkeit haben die Vertreter des politischen Liberalismus und Anhänger marktwirtschaftlicher Ordnungen den modernen Staat und seine Verwaltung in ungewöhnlichem Maße geprägt. Es stellt keinen übermäßig großen Fehler dar, wenn man diesen Staat geradezu als eine liberale Erfindung bezeichnet. Freilich ist dies nicht unbestritten. Die Entstehung einer modernen Staatsbürokratie wird vielfach als eine Leistung des absoluten Fürstenstaates und der von ihm bevorzugten merkantilistischen Wirtschaftspolitik betrachtet. Was den bloßen Behördenaufbau und äußere Organisationsmerkmale angeht, ist diese traditionelle Lehre nicht einmal ganz unrichtig. Aber erst in der marktwirtschaftlichen Ordnung des 19. Jahrhunderts hat die Staatsverwaltung jene Merkmale entwickelt, durch die in Anlehnung an *Max Weber*[5] eine moderne Staatsbürokratie gekennzeichnet ist: Diese Verwaltung gehorcht Gesetzen und Regeln; sie ist daher für den Bürger kalkulierbar. Ferner hat sie abgegrenzte Zuständigkeiten, wobei die zuständigen Beamten über die notwendige Fachkompetenz verfügen. Die Verwaltung unterliegt festgelegten Kontrollen; sie kann sich vor allem die zu verwaltenden Mittel nicht selbst beschaffen, sondern erhält sie zugeteilt und muß über die Verwendung abrechnen. Vorgänge und Handlungen werden in Akten festgehalten, schon um Kontrollen zu ermöglichen, Mißverständnisse auszuschließen und Rechtssicherheit zu wahren. Die Beamten, deren Kompetenz durch Ausleseverfahren ermittelt wird, werden so gestellt, daß von ihnen Unbestechlichkeit gefordert werden kann.

Auf den ersten Blick scheint es, als seien diese Merkmale in keine systematische Bezie-

---

[4] Hinzuweisen ist vor allem auf *Adam Smith,* An Inquiry into the Nature and Causes of the Wealth of Nations (1776), der sich eingehend mit der zweckmäßigen Organisation von Landesverteidigung, Rechtsprechung, öffentlichen Arbeiten und Erziehungswesen befaßt (Buch V), ferner auf *John Stuart Mill,* On Representative Government (1861), deutsch: Betrachtungen über Repräsentativ-Regierung, Leipzig 1873 (*John Stuart Mill's* Gesammelte Werke, Autorisirte Uebersetzung unter Redaction von *Theodor Gomperz,* 8. Bd.).

[5] *Max Weber,* Wirtschaft und Gesellschaft, in: Grundriß der Sozialökonomik, III. Abteilung, 3. Aufl. Tübingen 1947, 1. Halbband, S. 124 ff.

hung zu verschiedenen Wirtschaftsordnungen zu bringen. Jeder Staat, gleichgültig, welche Staats- und Wirtschaftsverfassung er besitze, sei doch auf eine solche Bürokratie angewiesen, so daß sie insoweit ein ordnungsindifferentes Werkzeug sei. Nähere Prüfung zeigt indessen, daß dies nicht zutrifft.

Betrachtet man die Zusammenhänge zunächst historisch, so steht fest, daß die Verwaltung des merkantilistischen Staates vielfach keinen festen Regeln unterworfen war, sondern bestenfalls internen Verwaltungsvorschriften. Nach außen wurde häufig in weiten Ermessensspielräumen und nach Gutdünken interveniert; Fachkompetenz und Kontrollen ließen zu wünschen übrig und die Zuständigkeiten waren nicht selten unklar oder überhaupt nicht geregelt.[6] Selbst soweit es hieran nicht mangelte, fühlte sich aber der merkantilistische Landesherr für alles zuständig, konnte also grundsätzlich nicht festlegen, daß seiner Bürokratie irgendein Lebensbereich prinzipiell entzogen sei. Man fühlt sich an moderne Phraseologien von «Daseinsfürsorge» durch den Staat erinnert, wenn man in der Hofkammerordnung des Markgrafen *Karl Friedrich von Baden* aus dem Jahre 1766 folgendes liest: «Unsere fürstliche Hofkammer ist die natürliche Vormünderin unserer Unterthanen. Ihr liegt ob, dieselben vom Irrtume ab und auf die rechte Bahn zu weisen, sie sofort und auch gegen ihren Willen zu belehren, wie sie ihre eigenen Haushaltungen einrichten sollen» und «sie, ob sie nun wollen oder nicht, frei, opulent und gesittet zu machen.»[7] Trotz dieses Totalitätsanspruches existierte aber keine durchgehend straffe Zentralverwaltungswirtschaft, sondern Elemente von Eigenwirtschaft, Marktverkehr und Staatseingriff waren in unsystematischer und jedenfalls buntscheckig-variabler Weise miteinander gemischt. Die von *Max Weber* angeführte Kalkulierbarkeit der Bürokratie war kaum gegeben.

Demgegenüber hat sich der liberale Staat des 19. Jahrhunderts Schranken auferlegt und die eigene Zuständigkeit abgegrenzt. Somit war es auch möglich, in die Kompetenzen der Bürokratie eine genauere Ordnung zu bringen. Auch in der Wahl politischer und wirtschaftspolitischer Mittel wurde die vorher übliche pragmatische Beliebigkeit aufgegeben. Man kann dies allein schon daran ablesen, daß die Währungspolitik nicht mehr handelspolitischen Zwecken dienstbar gemacht wurde, umgekehrt aber auch Handelsschranken nicht mehr in den Dienst der Währungspolitik gestellt wurden. Die Behauptung ist also unzutreffend, die merkantilistische Bürokratie habe durch ihr Beharrungsvermögen an ihren früheren Prinzipien auch in der liberalen Ära mehr oder weniger festhalten können[8], so daß es eine marktwirtschaftlich-liberal denkende und handelnde Staatsverwaltung eigentlich gar nicht gegeben habe. Daß solche Legenden sich verbreiten konnten, liegt nicht zuletzt daran, daß die Liberalen die Reformen der Staatsverwaltung, die sie unternommen haben, wenig oder überhaupt nicht plakatieren wollten. Sie waren so sehr mit der Aufgabe beschäftigt, die Grenzen der Staatstätigkeit abzustecken und den rechtlichen Ordnungsrahmen der Marktwirtschaft zu schaffen, daß ihnen ihr eigener Beitrag zur Begründung des modernen Staates und seiner Verwaltung nicht betonenswert erschien. Trotzdem bot erst der Übergang zum liberalen Rechtsstaat und der von ihm abhängigen marktwirtschaftlichen Ordnung die Möglichkeit, die Unvollkommenheiten des

---

[6] Vgl. *Eli F. Heckscher,* Der Merkantilismus, 1. Band, Jena 1932, S. 150 ff. und passim.

[7] Zitiert nach *Alexander Rüstow,* Ortsbestimmung der Gegenwart, 2. Bd., Weg der Freiheit, Erlenbach-Zürich 1952, S. 311.

[8] Es kommt in diesem Zusammenhang weniger auf die Quantität als auf die Qualität der Staatstätigkeit an, die eben im 19. Jahrhundert gegenüber der Zeit des Merkantilismus fundamental geändert worden ist. Es kann keine Rede davon sein, daß der liberale Rechtsstaat des 19. Jahrhunderts «vorwiegend Postulat» geblieben sei. (So *Thomas Ellwein;* vgl. *Renate Mayntz,* Soziologie der öffentlichen Verwaltung, Heidelberg, Karlsruhe 1978, S. 48).

merkantilistischen Verwaltungsapparates zu überwinden und die Verwaltung selber zu einem brauchbaren staatlichen Instrument zu machen.

Weil die Liberalen dieses von ihnen immer etwas mürrisch betrachtete staatspolitische Verdienst psychologisch verdrängt haben, ist eine fundamentale Erkenntnis praktischer Verwaltungskunst in Vergessenheit geraten: Die öffentliche Verwaltung ist um so funktionsfähiger, je klarer ihre Aufgaben definiert sind. Eine klare Definition der staatlichen Verwaltungsaufgaben ist im merkantilistischen Interventionsstaat erschwert, wenn nicht unmöglich; also kann dort auch die Staatsverwaltung nicht voll effizient sein.

Mag in der liberalen Ära der Umfang der Staatstätigkeit rein quantitativ unverändert geblieben sein oder gar mit wachsender Wirtschaft absolut und als Prozentsatz vom Volkseinkommen zugenommen haben. Zunächst war dies für das Funktionieren der Staatsverwaltung weniger wichtig. Den die Verwaltung vielleicht erschwerenden Ausweitungen der öffentlichen Haushalte standen Rationalisierungsvorteile gegenüber, und zwar in erster Linie die Tatsache, daß nunmehr die Sphäre der Privatautonomie in langfristig beständiger und klarer Form von den Möglichkeiten des öffentlichen Eingriffs abgegrenzt wurde. Dies gab nicht nur dem Bürger, sondern vor allem auch dem Beamten Sicherheit über seine Befugnisse und Aufgaben.

Die liberale Propaganda hat, um dies durchzusetzen, an die Bürger appellieren müssen, um sie notfalls als revolutionäres Potential gegen den merkantilistischen Allmachtstaat einsetzen zu können. Es hätte allzuviel an intellektueller Raffinesse bedurft, um massenwirksam darzustellen, daß die liberalen Trennungsgrundsätze nicht nur dem Bürger mehr Freiheit gewährten, sondern zugleich der Staatsverwaltung zu einer größeren Wirksamkeit verhelfen mußten. Außerdem wäre die Betonung dieses Sachverhaltes für die liberalen politischen Zwecke gefährlich gewesen; denn die Macht, die der merkantilistische Obrigkeits-, Regulierungs- und Ausbeutungsstaat angewandt hatte, war an sich verdächtig geworden und verdiente in den Augen der Öffentlichkeit keine Stärkung. So konnte es denn bis zum heutigen Tage gelingen, einer Fehlinterpretation zum Range kaum bestrittener wissenschaftlicher Dignität zu verhelfen, nämlich der Ansicht, der Liberalismus habe die Staatsverwaltung geschwächt und vernachlässigt. *Lassalles* Formel vom «Nachtwächterstaat», den die Liberalen begünstigt hätten, ist noch immer beliebt. Diese Formel erscheint heute ziemlich makaber, will sie doch andeuten, daß der liberale Staat ein schwächlicher Filzpantoffelstaat gewesen sei. Den allgemeinen Landfrieden hat er jedenfalls wirksamer sichern können als der neomerkantilistische Staat der Gegenwart. Es kam seltener vor, daß sich der Staat durch organisierten Terrorismus einschüchtern ließ und etwa einem Teil nicht nur der Bürgerschaft, sondern sogar seiner eigenen Beamten den gesetzlichen Schutz gegen illegale Gewaltanwendung vorenthielt, wie es heute, etwa bei Lehrern und Hochschullehrern, an der Tagesordnung ist.

Die Liberalen wußten sehr wohl, daß jede entwickelte Marktwirtschaft nicht nur Nachtwächter, aber allerdings auch diese, braucht, außerdem aber davon abhängig ist, daß die Staatsverwaltung ihre Aufgaben ordnungsgemäß erfüllt. *Adam Smith* selber, übrigens ein durchaus kundiger Staatsbeamter, hat einen bei näherer Betrachtung recht umfänglichen Katalog von Staatsaufgaben erstellt, die in der Marktwirtschaft erfüllt werden müßten. Allerdings hat er seine Zusammenstellung mit einer unbarmherzigen und sehr ins Detail gehenden Kritik der Staatsverwaltung seiner Zeit verbunden.[9] Neben den leider nicht mehr ganz selbstverständlichen Aufgaben des Staates, für äußere und innere Sicherheit einschließlich Rechtspflege zu sorgen, erwähnt er einen dritten Bereich, den wir heute etwas vage mit «Infrastrukturpolitik» bezeichnen würden. *Adam Smith* definierte

---

[9] Vgl. Anm. 4; *Eberhard Wille* und *Martin Gläser*, Staatsaufgaben bei *Adam Smith* – eine Würdigung unter Allokationsaspekten, Ordo Band 28 (1977), S. 34–76.

diesen Bereich freilich eindeutiger, als das heute üblich ist: Es sollte sich um Produktionen handeln, die gesellschaftlich und wirtschaftlich notwendig, aber privatwirtschaftlich nicht rentabel sind[10]. Heute werden dagegen zahllose privatwirtschaftlich rentable Produktionen von der öffentlichen Verwaltung übernommen und erst dadurch nachträglich unrentabel gemacht, womit alle Grenzen zwischen notwendiger und überflüssiger Staatstätigkeit merkantilistisch verschwimmen. *Adam Smith* und viele nach ihm haben die Notwendigkeit und Abgrenzung der Staatstätigkeit betont, im Interesse des Wohlstands der Nation, aber doch vornehmlich auch der Privatautonomie und der privaten Wirtschaft. *Max Weber* hat ebenfalls den Bedarf des sogenannten Kapitalismus an stetiger, strafferer, intensiver und vor allem kalkulierbarer Verwaltung hervorgehoben[11].

Die entgegengesetzte Frage, ob denn nicht ein funktionierendes Staatswesen etwa auch eine Marktwirtschaft braucht und speziell die Staatsverwaltung dann leistungsfähiger wird, ist zwar nicht völlig unterdrückt, aber seltener und meist nicht ausführlich behandelt worden. Es wäre gleichwohl merkwürdig, wenn dieser Zusammenhang völlig übersehen worden wäre. Allerdings haben ihn vor allem Verwaltungsfachleute bemerkt, die nicht immer Zeit und Neigung hatten, ihn auch in gelehrten Werken zu schildern. Ihnen blieb nicht verborgen, daß die Staatsverwaltung bei weitreichenden, aber diffusen Kompetenzen, die täglich wechseln, an Wirksamkeit einbüßen muß und daß bei einer marktwirtschaftlichen Ordnung mit ihrer Abgrenzung der Sphären dieses Problem lösbar ist. So hat der französische Reformminister *Turgot*, ein erfahrener Verwaltungsbeamter, unter *Ludwig XVI.* versucht, das französische Staatsschiff durch liberale Reformen vor der Revolution zu bewahren. Der Staat trieb durch die Ineffizienz und Korruptheit seiner Verwaltung dem Abgrund zu und es bedurfte einer selbstmörderischen Einsichtslosigkeit des Königs und der ihn lenkenden feudalen Interessenten, dies nicht zu sehen und den einzigen Staatsmann zu entlassen, der das Unheil hätte abwenden können.[12] Wie *Heckscher* hierzu treffend bemerkt, wurden erst Revolution und Liberalismus zu Testamentsvollstreckern der Rationalisierungsversuche, die der Merkantilismus nicht vollenden konnte.[13]

Auch in Preußen bedurfte es erst einer Katastrophe, um die erstarrte Staatsverwaltung zu reformieren. Die Vorstellungen, die man sich noch immer weithin von der angeblichen Rationalität der merkantilistischen preußischen Staatsverwaltung macht, sind ziemlich abwegig. Hören wir dazu einen sachverständigen Zeugen aus der Zeit des preußischen Zusammenbruchs, den Hofrath und Ober-Licent-Inspector *August Wilhelm Rehberg* mit seiner Schrift «Über die Staatsverwaltung deutscher Länder und die Dienerschaft des Regenten», Hannover 1807. Als Hannover vor der Schlacht von Jena und Auerstedt für einige Zeit an Preußen gefallen war, konnte er mit dem preußischen Verwaltungssystem eingehende Bekanntschaft machen. Ihm fällt vor allem die unablässige Intervention und Betriebsamkeit der preußischen Verwaltung auf, die mangelnde persönliche Bindung der Beamten an bestimmte Aufgabenbereiche, ein übertriebener Formalismus sowie mangelnde Selbständigkeit und damit starke Verantwortungsscheu der Beamten, ferner eine allgemeine Planungs- und Zahlengläubigkeit und die Unwirtschaftlichkeit einer egalisierenden, zentralisierenden und alle regionalen Besonderheiten mißachtenden Reglementierung. Hierzu einige Leseproben:

«... Das ganze statistische Treiben, woran unser wissenslustiges Zeitalter so vielen Gefallen findet, worin die Gelehrten und Geschäftsmänner einander die Hände bieten,

---

[10] *Adam Smith*, An Inquiry ... the Wealth of Nations, Book V, Part III, erster Satz.
[11] Wirtschaft und Gesellschaft, a.a.O., S. 129.
[12] Vgl. *Alexander Rüstow*, a.a.O., S. 404 ff.
[13] A.a.O., S. 433 ff.

und welches den letztern, vorzüglich in den preußischen Staaten, so viele Arbeit verursacht, ist in speculativer Hinsicht von sehr zweifelhaftem Werthe; in praktischer ist es geradezu verderblich: und es ist der erste große Fehler der neuern Staatsverwaltung, daß sie so vieles wissen will, was sie nicht zu wissen braucht, und gar nicht wissen kann. Die Regierung bedarf bey vielen ihrer wichtigsten Geschäfte sorgfältig gesammelter Nachrichten. Aber die häufige Beschäftigung damit, verleitet auch die besten Köpfe zu einem Misbrauche.»[14]

«. . . Der ruhige Geist einer solchen (republikanischen H.W.) Staatsverfassung ist nicht so nachforschend; er fragt wenig, so lange es von selbst gut geht: dahingegen eine Regierung, welche strebt den ganzen Staat ganz eigentlich zu ihrem Werkzeuge zu machen, allenthalben unaufhörlich nachspürt, ob es nicht noch etwas zu regieren gebe, und immer alles besser machen will.»[15]

«. . . So vereinigen sich die gränzenlose Begierde nach Vergrößerung, und die übermüthigen Ansprüche auf Alleinweisheit in der Verwaltung, um eine Staatskunst zu bilden, die mit gleicher Verblendung im äussern und im innern ihrer Zerstörung zueilte. Die Folgen der allgemeinen Beschränktheit aller Staatsdiener, Unterwürfigkeit eines jeden unter Vorgesetzte, und Abhängigkeit aller Sachen und Menschen von unwesentlichen Formen, zeigen sich am deutlichsten, wenn ausserordentliche Begebenheiten das System, wodurch alles zusammengehalten ward, gewaltsam sprengen. Wenn der Feind einbricht, und jeder sich selbst rathen muß, weil Anfragen nach Instruction nicht mehr statt finden, . . . so sucht man vergeblich Männer, die fähig sind nach eigner Einsicht zu handeln, unter denen, die solches nie wagen durften . . .»[16]

Nach der Niederlage fanden sich indessen mit der Sprengung des alten Systems sehr wohl auch in Preußen die Männer, die zur Entscheidung bereit waren: *Stein* und *Hardenberg*. Beide waren in jahrzehntelangem Staatsdienst ergraut und übrigens ebensowenig Preußen von Geburt wie die militärischen Reformer *Scharnhorst* und *Gneisenau*. Preußen wurde durch liberale Reformen wiederbegründet. Man ging zur Gewerbefreiheit und zu marktwirtschaftlichen Prinzipien über. Der neue Geist wird erkennbar an einer Geschäftsinstruktion für die preußische Verwaltung vom 26. Dezember 1808, in der es heißt: «Es ist dem Staat und seinen einzelnen Gliedern am zuträglichsten, die Gewerbe jedesmal ihrem natürlichen Gange zu überlassen, d. h. keines derselben durch besondere Unterstützungen zu begünstigen und zu heben, aber auch keine in ihrem Entstehen, ihrem Betriebe und Ausbreiten zu beschränken, insofern das Rechtsprinzip dabei nicht verletzt wird oder sie nicht gegen Religion, gute Sitten und Staatsverfassung verstoßen.»

Auf dieser Grundlage vollzog sich der wirtschaftliche und politische Aufstieg Preußens zur innerdeutschen Hegemonialmacht während des 19. Jahrhunderts, wobei eine liberale Außenwirtschaftspolitik Startvorteile gegenüber dem protektionistischen Österreich bot.

---

[14] *August Wilhelm Rehberg,* Ueber die Staatsverwaltung deutscher Länder und die Dienerschaft des Regenten, Hannover 1807, S. 25 f. Zu dem preußischen Versuch, eine detaillierte Totalstatistik über sämtliche Daten des erworbenen hannoverschen Gebietes zu erstellen, bemerkt er: «Diese statistischen Administratoren hätten lieber jedem Hausvater im Lande aufgeben sollen, Wochenberichte über das Gewerbe der Familie und dessen Ertrag einzusenden: unter Vorbehalt, demnächst allenfalls auch die losen Knechte zu ähnlicher Berichts-Erstattung anzuhalten. Dem zufolge wäre die eine Hälfte der Einwohner beständig beschäftigt zu protocolliren, was die andre beschickt. Würde aber auch am Ende im Ideale eines statistisch bearbeiteten Landes nichts mehr producirt, so würde doch controlirt, daß nichts unbemerkt producirt werden könnte.»

[15] Dsgl., S. 13.

[16] Dsgl., S. 71.

Auch im 20. Jahrhundert findet man immer wieder überzeugte Liberale und Anhänger der Marktwirtschaft in Schlüsselstellungen der Staatsverwaltung. Oft kommt ihre Stunde, wenn merkantilistische und interventionistische Experimente Wirtschaft und Staat ruiniert haben. Namen wie *Luigi Einaudi* in Italien, *Jacques Rueff* in Frankreich, *Ludwig Erhard* und *Alfred Müller-Armack* in Deutschland, *Reinhard Kamitz* in Österreich stehen für einen Typ des liberalen Staatsfunktionärs, der stark von wissenschaftlichen Überzeugungen geprägt ist. In England wurden viele liberale Nationalökonomen in der Planung der britischen Kriegswirtschaft verwendet, mit eindeutigem Erfolg, während man in Deutschland weder nationalökonomische noch gar liberale Ratgeber heranziehen wollte[17]. Es kann die These gewagt werden: Selbst eine zentral geleitete Wirtschaft funktioniert besser, wenn sie von Personen gelenkt wird, die ihren wirtschaftlichen Sachverstand an Problemen einer Marktwirtschaft geschult haben. Genug der Beispiele!

Fragen wir uns nun, von welchen Grundsätzen sich die Liberalen leiten lassen, wenn sie zur Sanierung der Staatsverwaltung gerufen werden, und rücken wir dabei vor allem die wirtschaftspolitischen Maßnahmen in das Blickfeld, um die Beziehungen zwischen Wirtschaftsordnung und Funktionsfähigkeit der Staatsverwaltung im einzelnen genauer zu erkennen. Die Hauptleistung liberaler Reformer besteht darin, die Staatsverwaltung zu beschränken und die Kraft der Bürokratie auf strategisch wichtige Aufgaben zu konzentrieren. Dem Staatsapparat wird die hierfür erforderliche Disziplin auferlegt. Möglichst viele Aufgaben werden dem Markt und der Planung des Einzelbürgers überlassen, Bewirtschaftungsbürokratien werden abgebaut. Vor allem aber wird die so gut wie immer verloren gegangene währungs- und finanzpolitische Stabilität wiederhergestellt. Man ist es gewohnt, diese monetäre und fiskalische Restriktion vorzugsweise als disziplinierendes Werkzeug gegenüber der privaten Wirtschaft anzusehen, die nicht mehr länger mit der enthemmenden Droge der Inflation versorgt wird. Mindestens ebenso wichtig ist jedoch der Umstand, daß solche Restriktionen der Staatsbürokratie eindeutige Planungsgrenzen setzen. Dadurch wird die Verwaltung gezwungen, wesentliche von unwesentlichen Staatstätigkeiten und Staatsausgaben zu unterscheiden und von krebsartigen Behördenwucherungen abzusehen. Qualität und Wirksamkeit der Staatsverwaltung nehmen durch solche Entfettungskuren ebenso zu wie gleichzeitig das Wachstum der Wirtschaft, von dem die staatlichen Entfaltungsmöglichkeiten abhängen. Im übrigen besteht die liberale Verwaltungskunst aus einer Fülle von Warnungen, damit nicht der Staat unversehens von einem Komplementärfaktor zu einem Surrogat der Bürgerfreiheit und Schmarotzer an der Privatwirtschaft degeneriert. Es ist also das Staatsversagen, das als Störfaktor gefürchtet wird und durch eine unendliche Kette von empirischen Fällen belegt werden kann.

Es leuchtet ein, daß solche staatliche Askese trotz ihrer wohltätigen Wirkungen für den Staat selber wenig beliebt ist. Politiker, die mit dem wirksamen, aber begrenzten Instrumentarium einer liberalen Staatsverwaltung erfolgreich sein wollen, müssen über ein Mindestmaß an Verständnis für das Funktionieren einer rechtsstaatlichen Ordnung und einer auf Privatautonomie beruhenden Marktwirtschaft verfügen. Der Seufzer des schwedischen Reichskanzlers *Oxenstierna*, mit wie wenig Weisheit doch die Welt regiert werde, hat jedoch nichts von seiner Aktualität verloren: Fleißige, aber mittelmäßige Politiker wollen im demokratischen Staat auf leichteren Wegen politische Erfolge erringen, indem sie die Staatstätigkeit ausdehnen, Wählergruppen begünstigen und mit gesetzgeberischer und administrativer Aktivität den Anschein erwecken, als erreichten sie in har-

---

[17] Über die chaotische Art der deutschen Wirtschaftslenkung im zweiten Weltkrieg informiert: *Erich Welter,* Falsch und richtig planen, Heidelberg 1954.

ter Arbeit für das Vaterland auch dort etwas, wo sie gar nichts bewirken können. Nachdem die Liberalen für eine Regeneration von Wirtschaft und Staat gesorgt haben, sind oft genügend Reserven aller Art vorhanden, um eine publikumswirksame Politik staatlicher Expansion – verkleidet als Wohlfahrtsförderung – einzuleiten.

Natürlich fehlt es hierzu nicht an wissenschaftlichen Begründungen. In zahlreichen Varianten wird vorgetragen, das marktwirtschaftliche System sei in sich unstabil und müsse nicht nur im Wege des nachträglichen Krisenmanagements, sondern durch antizipierende Regelung und Steuerung der sozio-ökonomischen Prozesse stabilisiert werden. Mit den Instabilitäten der Marktwirtschaft und dem sogenannten Marktversagen sowie den möglichen Gegenmitteln beschäftigen sich die Nationalökonomen seit vielen Jahrzehnten. Auch die Möglichkeiten staatlicher Gegensteuerung sind in aller Ausführlichkeit theoretisch und empirisch geprüft worden. Der Beweis, daß der Staat aus Stabilisierungsgründen das öffentliche Budget ständig ausweiten und im Wege der Feinsteuerung immer stärker in die Privatautonomie eingreifen müsse, konnte nicht geführt werden. Das Problem hinreichend zuverlässiger Prognosen konnte nicht gelöst werden; selbst soweit Richtungsprognosen möglich sind, folgt aus ihnen häufig ebenso oft, daß die Staatstätigkeit stabilitätsgerecht eingeschränkt werden sollte. Ein ständiges, dem Wirtschaftsverlauf entgegengerichtetes staatliches Gegensteuern versetzt allerdings die Staatsverwaltung in ein ununterbrochenes Wechselfieber. Das Angebot an komplementären Staatsleistungen wird auf diese Weise unstetig, insbesondere bei den Staatsinvestitionen. Versucht man statt dessen, durch Einnahmevariationen und gegenhaltende Steueränderungen zum Ziel zu kommen, so werden bei den heutigen Steuersätzen die Daten für die Planungen der Wirtschaft ständig unsicherer. Die immer mehr vordringenden Erhaltungs- und Sozialschutzinterventionen wirken im Verein mit staatlicher Strukturverzerrungspolitik eher destabilisierend auf Wirtschaft und Verwaltung.

Demgegenüber gehen wirklich stabilisierende Ordnungs- und Wettbewerbsgesetze eindeutig auf liberalen Rat zurück. Die großen Kodifikationen des modernen Zivilrechtes und der angrenzenden Gebiete des öffentlichen Rechtes, ja alle wirklich beständigen Ordnungsgesetze überhaupt sind ein Geschöpf der liberalen Ära und ihrer Fortwirkungen. Nach solchen Stabilisierungen strebt aber unsere Zeit nur noch wenig. Vielmehr wird ohne viel Überblick über das Ganze der Rechtsordnung und über die Funktionsgrundsätze der modernen Marktwirtschaft mit punktuellen Interventionen operiert. Man sieht einen Mißstand, erläßt eilig ein unüberlegtes Gesetz, das ihn beheben soll, ruft damit an anderer Stelle neue und größere Übel hervor, zu deren Korrektur abermals neue Gesetze dienen und so fort. Erreicht wird damit nichts, außer einer Verunsicherung der Wirtschaft und einer Kräftevergeudung in der staatlichen Verwaltung. Daß die Wirtschaft auf diesem merkantilistischen Wege nicht genesen kann, ist oft gesagt worden.[18] Kaum ausreichend gesehen wird aber, daß schließlich auch die Staatsverwaltung selber ein Opfer dieser Politik werden muß. Einstweilen verhallen die Proteste geplagter Steuer-

---

[18] Eine praxisnahe Darstellung findet sich in: Industrie- und Handelskammer zu Koblenz, Gängelwirtschaft statt Marktwirtschaft? Paragraphendirigismus lähmt unternehmerische Dynamik, Teile I und II November 1977, Teil III Juli 1978. Weniger bekannt ist, daß es auch eine dirigistische Selbstlähmung der staatlichen Verwaltung gibt, die sich derselben Lenkungstechniken bedient, wie sie gegenüber der privaten Wirtschaft angewandt werden. Die unmittelbar mit dem Bürger verkehrenden Ausführungsbehörden werden unaufhörlich mit ständig wechselnden Organisationsregeln, Verwaltungsvorschriften, Erlassen und Anordnungen überschwemmt. Die Vertraulichkeit des dienstlichen Schriftverkehrs verhindert Dokumentationen, wie sie von der privaten Wirtschaft zusammengestellt werden können. Bei relativ selbständigen Behörden wie Universitäten läßt sich allerdings der von den Lenkungsinstanzen hervorgerufene Leerlauf und Organisationswirrwarr kaum noch verheimlichen.

beamter noch ebenso ungehört wie die Ruminationen eines Bundeskanzlers, der seine eigene Gasrechnung nicht lesen kann und als Leiter des Staatsapparates an das Publikum appelliert, der Bürokratie bei Baubewilligungen zu einer schnelleren Gangart zu verhelfen, obwohl ihr zuvor durch die Bundesgesetzgebung Verzögerungen auferlegt worden sind. Die Hilflosigkeit der Staatsführung gegenüber von ihr selbst geschaffenen Situationen kann kaum deutlicher zum Ausdruck kommen.

Je mehr die Politik lenkend und steuernd gegenüber der Wirtschaft auftritt, desto mehr wächst eine vertikal verzweigte Behördenpyramide. Wie auf einen Frontsoldaten mit wachsender Industrialisierung und Verplanung des Krieges immer mehr lenkendes, planendes und versorgendes Etappenpersonal entfällt, so wächst auch innerhalb der modernen interventionistischen Staatsverwaltung der bürokratische Zwischenhandel immer mehr an, während die an der Front stehenden Beamten oft recht einsam sind. Übertriebene Lenkung und Lenkungsänderung überlastet nun die Bürokratie mit Regulierungsaufgaben, worauf diese mit Langsamkeit reagiert.[19] Die Etappenbeamten geben den auf sie ausgeübten Druck nach unten in Richtung auf die Frontbeamten weiter, die mit Hilfe neuer Regulationen behördeninterner Art zu Mehrleistungen aufgefordert werden. Unter der Pression solcher Überlastquoten entwickeln die Frontbeamten Gegenstrategien, indem sie sich zu Interessengruppen zusammenschließen oder den organisatorischen «slack» individuell durch «Dienst nach Vorschrift»[20] zu erweitern versuchen. Die Möglichkeiten hierzu bieten die immer komplexer werdenden Vorschriften, die eine arbeits-

---

[19] Vgl. *Niklas Luhmann,* Funktionen und Folgen formaler Organisation, Berlin 1964, S. 194.

[20] Die Tatsache, daß einerseits ständig neue Vorschriften mit dem angeblichen Zweck erlassen werden, über ihre Anwendung staatliche Ziele zu erreichen, andererseits aber die genaue Befolgung dieser Vorschriften den Verwaltungsablauf stört, ist in sich selbst schon merkwürdig. Anscheinend geht der Vorschriftengeber davon aus, daß seine Anweisungen von den Beamten mit einem mehr oder weniger großen Diskont angewendet, also nur teilweise ernst genommen werden. Selbstverständlich muß der Beamte in vielen Fällen einen Ermessensspielraum erhalten und kann ihn im bremsenden oder fördernden Sinne ausnutzen. Trotzdem ist es kurios, wenn ein Befolgen von Vorschriften sogar zu einem Dienstvergehen erklärt werden kann, sofern der Beamte die Vorschriften wörtlich nimmt. Es wäre eher angebracht, den Urheber unanwendbarer Vorschriften disziplinarisch zu verfolgen. Die amerikanische Zollbehörde verlangt z. B. bei der Einreise von ausländischen Besuchern heute (Dezember 1978) folgende Angaben (Wortlaut des amtlichen amerikanischen Textes in deutscher Sprache):
«... 9. Führen Sie oder jemand in Ihrer Begleitung irgendwelche Früchte, Pflanzen, Fleisch, pflanzliche oder tierische Produkte, Vögel, Schnecken oder andere lebendige Organismen bei sich? 10. Haben Sie oder jemand in Ihrer Begleitung innerhalb von 30 Tagen vor Ankunft in den USA einen Bauernhof oder eine Ranch im Ausland besucht? 11. Führen Sie oder jemand in Ihrer Begleitung mehr als $ 5000,00 in Zahlungsmitteln bei sich, z. B. Münzen, Banknoten, Reiseschecks, Zahlungsanweisungen oder begebbare Inhaberpapiere? (Wenn zutreffend, muß von Ihnen auf Vordruck 4790 eine Aufstellung gemacht werden.)» Es werden außerdem Angaben gefordert über «alle von Ihnen im Ausland erworbenen Artikel (ganz gleich ob sie getragen oder gebraucht sind, ob sie zollpflichtig sind oder nicht, ob durch Kauf, Geschenk oder sonstwie erworben), die zum Zeitpunkt Ihrer Einreise in Ihrem Besitz oder dem Ihrer Familie befinden». Nichtamerikaner dürfen diese Erklärung mündlich abgeben, Einwohner der USA müssen sie schriftlich einreichen, wobei für die Wertangabe maßgeblich ist «tatsächlich bezahlter Preis oder angemessener Einzelhandelspreis im Einkaufsland bei nicht gekauften Gegenständen». Man kann sich vorstellen, welches Chaos auf amerikanischen Flugplätzen entstünde, wenn auch nur der Versuch gemacht werden würde, von Nichtamerikanern die totale Vermögenserklärung mündlich einzufordern, die diese Vorschrift vorsieht. Allein die recht souveräne Nichtbeachtung dieser Anordnungen durch die amerikanischen Beamten hat das Einreiseverfahren funktionsfähig erhalten.

teilige, aber ungenügend koordinierte und immer mehr anwachsende Etappenbürokratie erläßt. Da die Etappe nicht genügend informiert ist und auch oft nur papierene statt tatsächlicher Informationen für wertvoll hält, gelingt die Gegenstrategie der Frontbeamten in mehr oder weniger unorganisierter und weder für den Staat noch für den Staatsbürger vorhersehbarer Form.

Bevor es soweit kommt, hat freilich die Staatsverwaltung zunächst kaum ein professionelles Interesse, der Ausweitung der Staatstätigkeit wesentlichen Widerstand entgegenzusetzen. Erhöhte Beförderungschancen, Aussichten auf Macht und Einfluß üben ihre verführerische Kraft aus. Nicht nur in einer Armee, deren Mannschaftsbestand vergrößert wird, sondern auch bei den Wucherungen einer Verwaltungsbürokratie gibt es eine für die Verwaltungsangehörigen angenehme Phase. Schon *Alexis de Tocqueville*[21] hat es betont und *Max Weber* hat es wiederholt, daß Staat und Bürokratie im übrigen durchaus geneigt sind, ihre «Verwaltungsaufgaben im Dienst der zu beglückenden Beherrschten»[22] wahrzunehmen. Allerdings wird hierzu ein ausgeweitetes Netz von neuen formalen bis formalistischen Reglements notwendig, die den tatsächlichen oder vermeintlichen Erfordernissen des Tages möglichst eng angepaßt sein sollen.

Mit diesem Sündenfall beginnt die Degeneration der Verwaltung, und zwar vor allem dann, wenn gleichzeitig die äußeren Formen des Rechtsstaates und der rechtsstaatlichen Kontrollen aufrecht erhalten bleiben. Die Verwaltung kann hier nicht einfach anordnen, was ihr gut dünkt, sondern muß darauf drängen, daß zum Zwecke der paternalistischen Fürsorge ständig neue Maßnahmengesetze und Verwaltungsvorschriften erlassen werden. Anders glaubt man die wohlfahrtsfördernde Feinsteuerung nicht erreichen zu können. Selbst die «fleißigste» Gesetzgebung gerät allerdings dabei in immer größere Atemnot. Das läßt sich an der geradezu exponentiell anwachsenden Verschlechterung von juristischer und sprachlicher Qualität der Gesetze ablesen. Die Gesetzesänderungen, Verordnungen und Satzungen oder Verordnungs- und Satzungsänderungen folgen einander inflationsartig, weil ein emsiges Streben einsetzt, veränderlichen Sachverhalten jeweils genau passende administrative Maßanzüge anzumessen. Selbst die kleinste Gemeinde fühlt sich verpflichtet, die Lokalzeitungen mit immer neuen Satzungen, Satzungsänderungen und Bekanntmachungen zu füllen. Satzungen allein genügen indessen nicht mehr, sie müssen mit Erläuterungen und Ausführungsbestimmungen versehen werden, die sich nicht nur die Bürokratie, sondern auch der Bürger nebst sämtlichen Änderungen immer wieder neu einzuprägen hätte, wenn alles seinen formal richtigen Gang gehen soll. Natürlich wird die Bürokratie des von ihr selbst geschaffenen formalen Gestrüpps schließlich nicht mehr Herr. Rührend ist etwa die Bekanntmachung einer kleinen westdeutschen Gemeinde vom 23. November 1978, Ehepaare, die im Jahre 1979 das 50-, 60-, 65- oder 70jährige Ehejubiläum begehen oder Personen, die 100 Jahre alt werden, möchten sich zwecks Einplanung einer Ehrengabe umgehend, spätestens bis zum 10. Dezember 1978, unter Vorlage der entsprechenden Urkunden im Rathaus melden, weil es der Verwaltung nicht immer möglich sei, sämtliche Jubiläen festzustellen.

Die Regierungsspitze verschafft sich bei diesen Vorgängen insoweit eine gewisse Erleichterung, als sie sich vom Parlament umfangreiche Ermächtigungen erteilen läßt, um das aufreibende Geschäft der parlamentarischen Behandlung und der damit verbundenen Öffentlichkeit zu vermeiden. Gelegentlich verlangt freilich ein von betroffenen Bürgern angerufenes Gericht, daß die Angelegenheit durch ein formales Gesetz zu regeln sei.

---

[21] *Alexis de Tocqueville,* Über die Demokratie in Amerika, 2. Bd., (zuerst Französisch 1840) Stuttgart 1962, S. 342.
[22] *Max Weber,* Wirtschaft und Gesellschaft, a.a.O., S. 130.

Seufzend muß sich dann das Parlament doch mit der Angelegenheit befassen. Materiell ändert sich dadurch so gut wie nichts. Der Charakter der Parlamentsarbeit hat sich nämlich gegenüber der liberalen Ära völlig gewandelt. Das Parlament ist von einem echten Gesetzgeber zu einer Verwaltungsbehörde besonderer Art geworden, die ihre Anordnungen und Einzelfallentscheidungen in die Form von Gesetzen gießt.[23] Mit stark ins einzelne gehenden Regelungen ist ein Parlament jedoch meist fachlich und physisch überfordert. Was soll ein normaler Abgeordneter gleichzeitig zur Änderung der Zuckermarktordnung, zum Gesetz über Konkursausfallgeld, zum Abfallbeseitigungsgesetz oder gar zu einem Vorschaltgesetz zum Hochschulgesetz sagen? Wird ihm Zeit gelassen, so kann er sich einarbeiten, aber die Häufung von Gesetzen läßt ihm keine Zeit. Infolgedessen macht sich das Prinzip der Arbeitsteilung bemerkbar: Jedes Gesetz wird kleinen Gruppen von spezialisierten Abgeordneten zur Bearbeitung zugeteilt, meist solchen, die aus interessenpolitischen oder beruflichen Gründen der Materie nahestehen oder auf einem bestimmten Gebiet Sendungsbewußtsein entwickeln. Die übrigen Abgeordneten stimmen jeweils ohne genaue Kenntnis des Sachstandes dem Votum ihrer Parteispezialisten zu, wenn sie nicht der Abstimmung überhaupt fernbleiben. Sie hüten sich vor Interventionen in die monarchischen Rechte anderer Abgeordneter, weil auch sie selbst ja auf einem allerdings anderen Gebiet Spezialisten[24] sind und ihrerseits dort möglichst ungestört operieren möchten. Nur so läßt sich ein verwaltendes Parlament organisieren, wenn es umfassend und doch mit Hilfe formaler Gesetze regieren will.

Kompliziert wird der Verwaltungsprozeß im modernen Interventionsstaat der Bundesrepublik Deutschland nun noch dadurch, daß man zwar obrigkeitsstaatlich in alle Wirtschafts- und Lebensbereiche eingreifen will, andererseits aber ob solchen autoritären Tuns ein schlechtes Gewissen hat, weil man den Freiheitsanspruch der Verfassung und des Rechtsstaates nicht aufgeben will und darf. Als Ausweg erscheint eine Akzentverschiebung bei den Verwaltungszuständigkeiten, indem die Oberbehörden zunächst eine Fülle von Kompetenzen, insbesondere solchen, die unangenehm zu exekutieren sind und mit denen kein massenpublizistischer Ruhm zu erwerben ist, nach unten an die Front- und Linienbehörden verlagern. Dadurch entsteht allerdings das Problem des Machtzuwachses der Unterbehörden und der Koordination zwischen den dezentralisierten Bürokratien. Als Gegenmittel erscheint den Politikern vielfach eine Destabilisierung der Unterbehörden zweckmäßig, mit deren Hilfe die Front- und Linienbeamten ausreichend eingeschüchtert werden können. Mit den Worten «Demokratisierung» und «Öffentlichkeit» ist diese Destabilisierung nur unvollkommen beschrieben. Die Entscheidungsbefugnis von Einzelbeamten wird zunächst eingeengt und in kollegiale Gremien eingebunden, wie es auch der merkantilistische Staat mit seinen überaus schwerfälligen Kollegien einst getan hatte. Was der große Liberale *John Stuart Mill* hierzu und überhaupt zur staatlichen Verwaltung bemerkt hat, gilt auch heute: «Was das Collegium tut, das tut niemand, und niemand kann dafür zur Verantwortung gezogen werden.»[25] Bei

---

[23] Auf diesen Sachverhalt hat vor allem *F. A. von Hayek,* Die Anschauungen der Mehrheit und die zeitgenössische Demokratie, Ordo Bd. XV/XVI (1965), S. 19–41; auch: ders., Freiburger Studien, Tübingen 1969, S. 56–74, hingewiesen.

[24] Auf die Verödung des parlamentarischen Lebens durch solche Spezialisierung hat kürzlich der SPD-Fraktionsvorsitzende *Wehner* aufmerksam gemacht. Er bemerkte, daß es eigentlich keine wirkliche allgemeine politische Debatte mehr gebe. Sehr viele, die sich in den Bundestag hätten wählen lassen, befaßten sich ausschließlich mit Spezialfragen. (Pressebericht über ein Interview im Norddeutschen Rundfunk, Walsroder Zeitung vom 27. 11. 1978).

[25] *John Stuart Mill,* a.a.O., S. 188.

Gremien befreit die Vertraulichkeit der Beratung von mancherlei Rücksichten, das Interesse des Beamten an sachgemäßer Entscheidung bleibt deswegen nur dann ungemindert, wenn er dem Gremium für lange Zeit angehört, während kurzfristige Mitgliedschaften die Verantwortungslosigkeit fördern. Im Zuge basisdemokratischer Vorstellungen werden jedoch Mandate kraft Amtes immer weniger geschätzt und eine von Wahlen ausgehende ständige Rotation verantwortlicher Personen wird bevorzugt.[26] Bis sie sich eingearbeitet haben und nach dem Vorbild amerikanischer Präsidenten aus eigenen Verwaltungsfehlern haben lernen können, ist ihr Mandat schon wieder abgelaufen. Die Versuchung liegt nahe, die persönliche Unbequemlichkeit der Einarbeitung gering zu halten, das Amt zur Förderung eigener Ziele auszunutzen und alle Folgen der später regierenden Nachwelt zu überlassen, einschließlich unerledigter Aktenberge. Um nun die persönliche Verhaltensweise des Einzelbeamten identifizieren zu können, wird schließlich «Öffentlichkeit» der kollegialen Beratungen verlangt und – wie etwa an den Universitäten – mehr oder weniger hergestellt.

Ist der Beamte in sein Amt nur vorübergehend eingewiesen, also von Wahlen abhängig, wird er sich als Politiker verhalten müssen, kann sich also nicht mehr von seiner lokalen oder nach Interessengruppen eingeteilten Wählerschaft emanzipieren. Ist er von seinen Kollegen und Untergebenen auf den Schild gehoben, kann er zum Gruppenvertreter werden; hat ihn eine lokale Wählerschaft in das Amt gebracht, wird er zuerst auf diese Rücksicht nehmen. Soweit die Behörde Aufgaben erfüllt, die in der Tat in erster Linie eine solche Wählerschaft angehen, wäre dagegen wenig einzuwenden. Die kommunale Selbstverwaltung hat einmal auf solchen Grundsätzen beruht und sich wenigstens auch insoweit bewährt, als sie den jeweiligen Amtsinhabern ausreichende Amtsautorität und genügende Frist des Mandats eingeräumt hat. Wie aber will man mit einer derartig konzipierten Verwaltung die Wirtschaft nach zentralen gesamtwirtschaftlichen Konzepten lenken? Diese Frage ist besonders eindringlich zu stellen, wenn außerdem die nach strengen fachlichen Auslesekriterien in ihr Amt berufenen Beamten in den administrativen Kollegien mit nach Proporzschlüsseln gewählten Dilettanten kooperieren sollen. Die Zentralbehörden werden sich für die Durchsetzung ihrer Aufträge an die Berufsbeamten halten, denen aber gleichzeitig durch Demokratisierung und Öffentlichkeit die Möglichkeit beschnitten ist, sich durchzusetzen. Spieltheoretisch gesprochen können die an der Front stehenden Berufsbeamten nunmehr sowohl gegen Kunden und gewählte Mitbestimmer als auch gegen die Oberbehörden spielen und als ein beweglicher Eckpunkt in diesem Viereck das eigene Optimum anstreben.

Die Reaktion der Zentrale ist abzusehen: Da sie sich an nur gewählte, aber sonst in keinem Anstellungsverhältnis zum Staate stehende Gruppenvertreter nicht halten kann, wird sie ihren disziplinarischen Druck auf die Berufsbeamten verstärken. Außerdem wird sie die aus der Hand gleitenden Unterbehörden durch ins letzte Detail gehende Verwaltungsvorschriften an die zentralen Ziele binden. Diese Vorschriften sind um so unsinniger, je mehr sie ins Detail gehen, weil die Oberbehörden weder die Informationen noch die Erfahrungen besitzen, um sachgemäße Regelungen zu treffen. Die altpreußische und durchaus lobenswerte Tradition, daß jeder Oberbeamte die Tätigkeiten der Unterbeamten aus eigener Erfahrung kennen muß, außerdem aber gehalten ist, sich durch regelmäßige Bereisungen vor Ort immer wieder mit den neuesten Veränderungen an der Front

---

[26] So hat zum Beispiel die demokratisierende Gleichstellung von Studenten, Assistenten und Professoren an deutschen Hochschulen die Zahl derjenigen Gremienmitglieder stark erhöht, die nicht dauernd an die Verwaltung der Hochschulen gebunden sind, also an der fachlichen Einarbeitung in Verwaltungsvorgänge nur begrenzt interessiert sind, weil sich Fehlentscheidungen für sie selbst nicht auswirken.

durch eigenen Augenschein vertraut zu machen hat, gehört längst der Vergangenheit an. Dieses Verfahren scheitert schon allein an der ins Ungemessene gewachsenen Fülle der Regierungsmaterien.

Außerdem dringen die rein politischen Oberbeamten immer mehr vor, die sich über Parlamente und Parteien ein Anrecht auf Einfluß und Versorgung im Staatsapparat erworben haben. Da die wirtschaftslenkende und politische Verwaltung gewollt ist, liegt dies in der Natur der Sache, führt aber wegen mangelnder administrativer Fachkunde der politischen Oberbeamten zu häufig absurden Ergebnissen. Man wende nicht ein, die Zentrale lasse ja die Frontbeamten regelmäßig zum Rapport erscheinen und erbitte Stellungnahmen zu geplanten Erlassen und Vorschriften, so daß der Sachverstand der Front in den Entscheidungsprozeß eingehe. Längst sind solche Anhörungen wie diejenigen der Parlamente zu einem Ritual entartet, das nur dazu dient, in einem oft sehr undurchsichtigen Prozeß bereits gefallene politische Entscheidungen mit einem pseudodemokratischen Mantel zu verhüllen.

Soweit Anhörungsrechte nicht nur für die Frontbehörden, sondern auch für wirtschaftliche Interessengruppen bestehen, hängt es von Größe, Art und Einfluß dieser Gruppen ab, inwieweit sie die Verwaltung formen können. Weil die neomerkantilistische Interventionsverwaltung einzelne Gruppen begünstigen und andere benachteiligen muß, wird Einflußnahme der Gruppen auf Verwaltungsentscheidungen zu einer privatwirtschaftlichen Notwendigkeit. Die Bürokratie ist sogar auf solche Einflüsse angewiesen, denn wie *Max Weber* bemerkt: «Überlegen ist der Bureaukratie an Wissen: Fachwissen und Tatsachenkenntnis, innerhalb seines Interessenbereichs, regelmäßig nur: der private Erwerbsinteressent.»[27] Die Staatsverwaltung, soweit sie die Wirtschaft en detail lenken will, muß hierfür spezialisierte Lenkungsbehörden entwickeln, deren Denkungsart sich derjenigen der zu lenkenden Wirtschaftszweige und Gruppierungen zu assimilieren pflegt, zumal den spezialisierten Beamten lohnende Positionen in der Wirtschaft geboten werden können. Die Wirtschaft muß gegen den lenkenden Staat spielen, was ihr um so eher gelingt, wenn sie aus dessen Generalstab qualifizierte Kräfte zur Entwicklung der eigenen Gegenstrategie abwerben kann. Es wäre ein Mißverständnis anzunehmen, daß deswegen alle Lenkungs- und Aufsichtsbehörden korrupt werden. Soweit interessengebundene Sachinformation richtig ist, wird die behördliche Entscheidung dadurch sogar verbessert. Auch entwickeln Aufsichtsbehörden gegenüber den zu Beaufsichtigenden durchaus Herrschaftsinstinkte. Hat aber einmal ein Branchenressort eine Branche nach eigenem Urteil korrigiert, so verteidigt es diese Entscheidung im Verein mit der Branche gegen Änderungen durch die Zentralbehörde, schon um sich nicht selbst mangelnden Sachverstand zu bescheinigen. Ein gleiches gilt für die entsprechenden Spezialisten der Parlamente, so daß ein «eisernes Dreieck» von Ressortpartikularisten in Wirtschaft, Verwaltung und Parlament zustande kommt[28].

Damit nicht genug: Solange der Rechtsstaat formell weiter besteht, unterliegen alle Verwaltungsakte der gerichtlichen Nachprüfung und können manchmal noch nach Jahren durch die Rechtsprechung wieder rückgängig gemacht werden. Die Zahl der zu entscheidenden Rechtsfälle nimmt parallel mit der Zahl der Verwaltungsfälle und Gesetze zu. Die Gerichte müssen vielfach als Gesetze drapierte Verwaltungsakte auf ihre Rechtmäßigkeit prüfen, womit die Rechtsprechung zu einer Nebenverwaltung wird. Man

---

[27] *Max Weber*, Wirtschaft und Gesellschaft, a.a.O., S. 129.
[28] Vgl. *Paul H. Weaver*, Regulation, Social Policy, and Class Conflict, in: Institute for Contemporary Studies (Herausgeber), Regulating Business: The Search for an Optimum, San Francisco 1978, S. 193 ff.

spricht davon, daß der Rechtsstaat zu einem Rechtswegstaat[29] degeneriere und fordert, der «Verwaltung als eigenständiger Staatsgewalt»[30] gegenüber dieser Vielfalt von rechtlichen Behinderungen wieder zu ihrem Recht zu verhelfen. Für den umfassend lenkenden Verwaltungsstaat ist der Widerspruch zwischen Rechtsstaat und Verwaltungseffizienz in der Tat nicht aufzulösen. Folgerichtig gibt es in den kommunistischen Staaten grundsätzlich keinen gerichtlichen Rechtsschutz gegen Maßnahmen der Verwaltungsbehörden[31], weil die zentrale Lenkung der Wirtschaft zusammenbrechen müßte, wenn Gerichte durch Einzelfallentscheidungen Teile aus dem zusammenhängenden Gesamtgebäude der staatlichen Planung herausnehmen würden.

Im übrigen wird der Degenerationsprozeß der Verwaltung von einem Qualitätswandel der Beamtenschaft begleitet. In der liberalen Ära begnügte sich der Staat mit einem beschränkten Beamtenapparat und konnte deswegen hohe Anforderungen stellen. Dies ändert sich mit der Ausweitung der Bürokratie. Zwar kann durch fachliche Spezialisierung und Arbeitsteilung auch mit weniger geeigneten Personen eine funktionsfähige Verwaltung aufrecht erhalten werden, es nimmt dann aber der Bedarf an Beamten zu, die den nötigen Horizont für Aufsichts- und Koordinationsaufgaben besitzen. Menschen, die insbesondere für leitende Positionen im Staatsdienst taugen, sind noch wesentlich knapper als die ohnehin schon knappen Unternehmertalente. Infolgedessen macht sich eine Art von personellem Ertragsgesetz bemerkbar. Der Staatsdienst muß bei seiner Ausweitung mit weniger guten Staatsdienern zufrieden sein. Wenn außerdem die Auslese noch herabgestuft wird, weil unsere Zeit keine Eliten mehr verträgt, ist mit einem personellen Qualitätsabfall eine verminderte Funktionsfähigkeit des Staatsdienstes verbunden.

Es kommt aber noch ein weiteres hinzu:

Der neumerkantilistische Interventionsstaat der Gegenwart bringt einen Beamtentyp neuer Prägung hervor. Es genügt nicht mehr, daß der neue Beamte sein Fach versteht, rechtlich denkt und eine charakterfeste Person ist. Vielmehr muß er die Fähigkeit besitzen, zwischen den verschiedenartigen, auf die Verwaltung einwirkenden Kräften zu lavieren. Er muß Kompromisse zwischen Gesetzestreue, Folgsamkeit gegenüber der politischen Führung, Einvernehmen mit Gruppeninteressen und günstiger Beurteilung durch die Öffentlichkeit herstellen. Da das politische System die Wahrnehmung von Gruppeninteressen legalisiert und institutionalisiert hat, kann auch das bürokratische Eigeninteresse ungeschminkter nach vorn rücken. Alles zusammengenommen ist kaum auf einen Nenner zu bringen. In einem solchen Kräftefeld führen Gaben zum Erfolg, die den machiavellistischen Politiker auszeichnen: Machtinstinkt, Beherrschen von Behinderungstechniken bei gleichzeitiger Fähigkeit zur wirksamen Selbstdarstellung, Fähigkeit, politische Koalitionen zu schließen und Vorstöße anderer Koalitionen abzuwehren und so fort.[32] Vor allem aber muß man einen Instinkt für die jeweilige politische Windrichtung

[29] *Hans Peters*, Die Verwaltung als eigenständige Staatsgewalt, Kölner Rektoratsrede, Krefeld 1965, S. 19.

[30] Dsgl.

[31] Art. Verwaltungsrechtsschutz (*Carl Hermann Ule*), Handwörterbuch der Sozialwissenschaften, Bd. 11 (1961), S. 281.

[32] Besonders bedenklich ist in diesem Zusammenhang, daß auch die Beamten nicht mehr in vollem Umfange vorschrifts- und gesetzestreu sein können, weil sie nicht alle Vorschriften und Gesetze auch des eigenen Sachgebietes, geschweige denn verwandter Gebiete, voll beherrschen können, vor allem, wenn sie nicht Juristen sind. Infolgedessen ist jedermann angreifbar und kann daher mit der Drohung einer genauen Überprüfung auf vorschriftengemäße Amtsführung erpreßt und gefügig gemacht werden. In Vorwegnahme solchen Druckes werden die Staatsdiener auch dort gefügig, wo sie im Interesse der Sache unnachgiebig sein müßten. Die Verletzung abwegiger Vorschriften ist aber im Interesse sachgerechter Amtsführung erforderlich.

entwickeln und sich frühzeitig auf sie einstellen. Denn im lenkenden Interventionsstaat wechseln die erwünschten Maßnahmen und Opportunitäten von Tag zu Tag. Soweit der Beamte noch sachbezogen denkt, und von einem großen Teil der Beamten kann dies angenommen werden, muß er sich ständig damit befassen, unsachlichen Einflüssen und Anforderungen zu begegnen. Vor allem aber wird nun die Organisationsstruktur der Behörden selber zu einem Gegenstand der Politik, so daß zwar nicht die Anstellung, wohl aber die Qualität des Arbeitsplatzes, den der Beamte einnimmt, ständig zur Disposition politischer Kräfte steht. Deswegen muß der Beamte diese ununterbrochenen Reorganisationen zum Gegenstand seiner eigenen Aktivitäten machen. Wen wundert es, daß er hierbei auch egoistische Techniken erlernt, die im liberalen Rechtsstaat mindestens zurückgedrängt waren?

Schließlich kommt hinzu, daß das neomerkantilistische politische Gesamtsystem wie einst das ançien régime immer mehr den Instinkt für Selbsterhaltung vermissen läßt, den die Systemtheoretiker von jedem funktionierenden System erwarten. Insgeheim und immer mehr auch öffentlich wollen politische Führungskräfte eigentlich einen fundamental anderen Staat, sie leiten aber noch einen Beamtenapparat, der auf die bisherigen Gesetze und die bestehende Verfassung vereidigt ist und dafür einstehen soll, im Falle von Polizisten und Soldaten sogar mit dem eigenen Leben. Dieser Widerspruch trägt seine Selbstaufhebung in sich: Der Stil des unehrlichen Lavierens und des doppelzüngigen Opportunismus wird sich nach unten ausbreiten, wenn nicht Einhalt geboten wird.

Was könnte geschehen, um die geschilderten Schwierigkeiten und Lähmungen der modernen Staatsverwaltung zu überwinden? Was die Identität der Beamtenschaft angeht, so kann entweder durch Übergang zum totalitären Einparteienstaat und entsprechende Auswechselung der Staatsdiener die Anpassung von Verwaltungsapparat und staatlicher Zielfunktion im Rahmen einer zentral geleiteten Wirtschaft bewirkt werden. Oder aber man zieht wieder eindeutiger ein marktwirtschaftliches und rechtsstaatliches System vor. Marktwirtschaftliche Systeme haben den Vorzug, die Staatsverwaltung auch dadurch zu verbessern, daß die Beamten ohne untragbares persönliches und wirtschaftliches Risiko abwandern oder widersprechen können. Die private Vermögensbildung ist ja als Rückhalt in erheblichem Maße zugelassen, außerdem ist der Staat nicht der einzige Arbeitgeber wie in der zentralgeleiteten Wirtschaft. Im ganzen aber gilt gleichwohl das, was *August Wilhelm Rehberg* zu Beginn des vorigen Jahrhunderts bemerkt hat: «Es ist alles vergeblich, was versucht werden mag, die öffentlichen Geschäfte zu vervollkommnen, wenn die Denkungsart verschwindet, die in ihnen, blos deswegen, weil sie Sache des gemeinen Wesens sind, etwas höheres erkennt, als in jeder Privat-Sache.»[33]

Was das Koordinationsproblem zwischen den vielfach aufgefächerten Interventionsbehörden der neomerkantilistischen Mischwirtschaft betrifft, so könnten als Gegenmittel gegen Ressortpartikularismus Seitenkontakte zu anderen Ressorts noch stärker vorgeschrieben werden, als das ohnehin der Fall ist. Ein gesamtwirtschaftlich effizientes Ergebnis ist damit keineswegs gesichert. Oft findet ein Kuhhandel zwischen den Ressorts statt, indem eine Handlung des anderen Ressorts, die gegen die eigenen Rationalitätsvorstellungen verstößt, dann hingenommen wird, wenn das andere Ressort im umgekehrten Fall zu Gegenkonzessionen bereit ist. Vor allem aber können niemals alle wirklich betroffenen Ressorts vor einem Verwaltungsakt miteinander Kontakt aufnehmen, weil man bei einer wirtschaftspolitischen Maßnahme nicht immer weiß, wie und auf wen sie sich auswirkt und welches Ressort infolgedessen hätte gefragt werden müssen. Im übrigen steht die Langatmigkeit solcher horizontalen Koordinationen in einem grotesken Mißverhält-

[33] A.a.O., S. 82.

nis zu dem Anspruch der Interventionsverwaltung, schlagkräftig und zeitgerecht marktwirtschaftliche Fehlentwicklungen zu kompensieren.

Ein anderes Gegenmittel ist die Verminderung von Komplexität, um es nach Art der modernen soziologischen Systemtheorie auszudrücken[34]. Diese Vereinfachung kann wieder auf zweierlei Weise geschehen: Einmal kann eine echte Zentralverwaltungswirtschaft eingeführt werden. Im Interesse effizienter staatlicher Verwaltung wird dann der Rechtsstaat aufgehoben. Die Mitbestimmung von Gruppen in der staatlichen Verwaltung kann mindestens rechtlich durch einfache hierarchische Beziehungen und Wiederherstellung amtsgebundener Befugnisse und Verantwortlichkeiten ersetzt werden, den Unternehmungen kann ihre Selbständigkeit genommen werden, so daß ihre Möglichkeit zu Gegenstrategien eingeschränkt sind: Sie werden zu weisungsgebundenen staatlichen Unterbehörden. Eine komplexe und sich überlagernde Doppelplanung[35] von privater Wirtschaft und staatlicher Bürokratie für ein und denselben wirtschaftlichen Vorgang wird dadurch weitgehend vermieden. Durch Zentralisierung und Standardisierung kann das System weiter vereinfacht werden, büßt dann aber an Flexibilität ein, weil auf verschiedenartige Sachverhalte stereotyp vereinheitlichte Antworten gegeben werden. Die organisatorischen Schwächen einer solchen Zentralverwaltungswirtschaft liegen auf der Hand, obwohl die Staatsverwaltung gegenüber dem merkantilistischen Mischsystem einige Rationalitätsvorteile durch größere Übersichtlichkeit, Dominanz des Gehorsamsprinzips und Alleinzuständigkeit des Staates für alle Vorgänge besitzt. Gewiß werden im idealen Fall die Beamten mit klaren Anweisungsbefugnissen ausgestattet, es wird von ihnen Plantreue erwartet, ihre Dispositionsspielräume sind auf den Rahmen beschränkt, der von den Oberbehörden festgelegt ist. Ein solches System neigt jedoch wie die friederizianische Staatsmaschine zur bürokratischen Erstarrung: Trifft ein Beamter eine unternehmerische Entscheidung, so werden die Vorgesetzten dazu neigen, einen Erfolg als eigene Leistung auszugeben, ein Mißlingen aber dem Untergebenen anzulasten. Experimente empfehlen sich daher nicht und können auch nicht nach Belieben gestattet werden, weil der Beamte mit Staatseigentum operiert.[36] Umwälzungen sind allein der Staatsführung erlaubt, die auf überlegenes Wissen Anspruch erhebt und oft ins Gigantische strebende Experimente mit übermäßigen Risiken anstellt. Diese Risiken sind nicht nur deshalb groß, weil einseitige Großexperimente nicht das gesamte Feld der Ungewißheit ausreichend abtasten. Es wird außerdem durch Verzicht auf ein marktwirtschaftliches Preissystem die Orientierung im Suchprozeß aufgehoben. Die Staatsverwaltung mag organisatorisch handlungsfähig sein, ohne ökonomisches Richtmaß schlägt sie vielfach blind um sich.

Der zweite Weg zur Verminderung von Komplexität für die Staatsverwaltung ist der liberale. Auch dabei dürfen elementare organisatorische Grundsätze nicht außer Betracht gelassen werden. Der Beamte ist an möglichst dauerhafte Gesetze und klare behördeninterne Vorschriften zu binden, die es ihm erlauben, auch den Sinn dieser Anwei-

34 Vgl. *E. K. Scheuch, Th. Kutsch,* Grundbegriffe der Soziologie 1, Grundlegung und Elementare Phänomene, 2. Aufl. Stuttgart 1975, S. 256.
35 *Alfred Müller-Armack,* Diskussionsbeitrag in: Planung ohne Planwirtschaft, herausgegeben von *Alfred Plitzko,* Basel und Tübingen 1964, S. 42.
36 Vgl. *Hans Willgerodt,* Regeln und Ausnahmen in der Nationalökonomie, in: Systeme und Methoden in den Wirtschafts- und Sozialwissenschaften, *Erwin von Beckerath* zum 75. Geburtstag, herausgegeben von *Norbert Kloten, Wilhelm Krelle, Heinz Müller, Fritz Neumark,* Tübingen 1964, S. 723. *Helmut Leipold,* Die Verwertung neuen Wissens bei alternativen Eigentumsordnungen, in: Ökonomische Verfügungsrechte und Allokationsmechanismen in Wirtschaftssystemen, herausgegeben von *Karl-Ernst Schenk,* Schriften des Vereins für Socialpolitik, N.F. Bd. 97, Berlin 1978, S. 89–122.

sungen zu erkennen und im Rahmen eines nicht zu eng gehaltenen Ermessensspielraumes entsprechend sinngemäß zu entscheiden. Dem sorgfältig auszuwählenden Beamten des liberalen Staates kann durchaus selbständiges Denken und Handeln erlaubt werden, weil der Handlungsraum, der vom Staat im ganzen in Anspruch genommen wird, begrenzt ist. In der Marktwirtschaft ist es auch möglich, Einzelbehörden ohne Schaden für den Systemzusammenhang zu verselbständigen und sie an Verhaltensregeln zu binden, die dauerhaft sind. Dies gilt etwa für Notenbanken, Sparkassen, Sozialversicherungseinrichtungen, Verkehrsunternehmungen, Forstbehörden, staatliche Hochschulen und – last not least: Gerichte. Solche Verselbständigungen der Verwaltung bedeuten nicht, daß diese Behörden einen Beliebigkeitsspielraum erhalten, sondern sie werden im Gegenteil an ordnungspolitisch durchdachte Gesetze und Verhaltensregeln gebunden und also dem politischen Tagesstreit entzogen. Es wäre irrig zu meinen, eine sich beschränkende und mehr an Regeln und Gesetze als an umfassende Zentralpläne gebundene Bürokratie sei notorisch einfallslos, unelastisch und verantwortungsscheu. Die Erfahrungen der liberalen Ära beweisen das Gegenteil.

Wenn die Staatsverwaltung funktionsfähig sein soll, ist der Versuch abwegig, zwischen den erwähnten Alternativen einen pragmatischen Kompromiß dauerhaft zu machen. Der vielregierende und einen Totalitätsanspruch erhebende, aber doch nicht entschlossen zu einer vollen Zentralverwaltungswirtschaft übergehende Interventionsstaat ruiniert nicht so sehr die Wirtschaft als vielmehr sich selbst und seine eigene Verwaltung.[37] Zuständigkeitserweiterungen für die Staatsverwaltung bedeuten eben nicht ohne weiteres auch eine größere Wirksamkeit der Staatsbürokratie. Wenn diese Bürokratie immer mehr damit beschäftigt ist, sich selbst zu verwalten und als unförmiger Dinosaurier mühselig aufrecht zu stehen, ist nicht nur die Wirtschaft in Gefahr, sondern auch der Staat.

Summary

The Economic Order as a Decisive Factor for the Efficiency of the Civil Service and the Administration of the State

According to the liberal tradition the competences of the government and public administration should be restricted and regulated according to the rule of law. The bureaucracy of the state is seen as a possible danger to private autonomy and economic efficiency in the private as well as the public sector. Contrary to some liberal attitudes the neomercantilistic state with its all-embracing competences to intervene and to control private activities is not only harmful to personal freedom and the functioning of the economy but also to the efficiency of its own administration. The interventionist «big state» is not strong, but weak, because in the mixed economy of double planning by private enterprise and households on the one side and the public administration on the other side,

---

[37] Vgl. *Carl Schmitt*, Weiterentwicklung des totalen Staats in Deutschland, (1933), in: ders., Verfassungsrechtliche Aufsätze aus den Jahren 1924–1954, Berlin 1958, S. 359–366, insbesondere S. 362: «Der heutige deutsche Staat ist total aus Schwäche und Widerstandslosigkeit, aus der Unfähigkeit heraus, dem Ansturm der Parteien und der organisierten Interessenten standzuhalten. Er muß jedem nachgeben, jeden zufriedenstellen, jeden subventionieren und den widersprechendsten Interessen gleichzeitig zu Gefallen sein. Seine Expansion ist die Folge, wie gesagt, nicht seiner Stärke, sondern seiner Schwäche.»

both dealing with the same problems without clear demarcation of competences, the civil service cannot retain a high standard for several reasons: It is open to the influences of private pressure groups, subject to unstable political influences, cannot act according to long-lasting and well-defined principles, is overloaded with unreasonable burdens of red-tape, and cannot fulfil the real duties of the state efficiently, because the multiplicity of changing orders given to the civil service destabilizes the public administration itself. The institution of a market economy within a well-defined framework of constitutional competences of the state is one way to establish or reestablish a public administration able to preserve internal and external peace, stability and justice of the legal framework of society and economy, efficient supply of other public goods and defence of the common interest against pressure groups. A centrally administered economy requires a strong state incompatible with the rule of law; its administration might be somewhat superior to that of a mixed neomercantilistic economy, but has organizational deficiencies nevertheless. It is a liberal myth that members of the civil services are always inclined to destroy the liberal system. Many of the successful liberal reforms were promoted by civil servants not only in the common interest but also in the interest of a well-functioning public administration itself.

IV. Meinungsfreiheit

Milton Friedman

The Economics of Free Speech*

The structure of law that is appropriate for the maintenance of a free society cannot be determined without examining its economic implications. They are intimately related. I am going to try to illustrate this connection for a particular problem in law, the maintenance of free speech; in some ways the most fundamental of all the freedoms in our society.

At the extreme, there is a clear and direct relationship between economic arrangements, on the one hand, and free speech, on the other. For example, the restrictions on *Alexander Solzhenitsyn*'s free speech when he was in the Soviet Union were significantly affected by the character of the economic system, and not merely by the particular way in which the Soviet Union chose to use that economic system. Suppose you could stretch your imagination so far as to suppose that a totalitarian centralized system such as the Soviet Union was by some miracle dedicated to trying to preserve free speech. Consider the economic problems that would be involved in doing so. The real test of free speech is the ability of a minority to express its view. Suppose a small group in the Soviet Union would like to propagandize for capitalism. In order to propagandize, it has to rent a hall. Whom can it rent a hall from? All halls are owned by the government. In order to propagandize by putting out leaflets, it has to get a printing press. Where does it get a printing press? They're all owned by the government. It has to buy paper from a government owned company. It has to have it printed by a government owned printing shop. It would take an extraordinary degree of dedication to the principle of free speech for each and every one of these people along the line to be willing to make their facilities available, but even suppose they were willing to do so. Where would the money come from to finance these activities in a society in which the major sources of funds are governmental? There are some wealthy people in Russia, but they are not wealthy in the sense in which they can provide out of their own resources substantial sums of money for campaigns. On the contrary, to finance such activities would require a government fund for the propagation of subversive doctrine. Suppose such a fund existed. It's clear that the demand would exceed the supply – that would be a pretty attractive way to make a living! So with the best of will it would be literally impossible to maintain free speech in a full-fledged collectivist, socialist state.

We seldom recognize the enormous importance of diversified sources of financial and economic support in making it possible for a «nut» to have his say. You know, today's nut may be tomorrow's prophet. The essence of free speech is to preserve the opportunity for nuts to turn into prophets.

The relation between economic arrangements and free speech is close long before you get to a full-fledged socialist state. I want to illustrate how close that relationship is in terms of the situation in this country, and in other countries in the west, which we would

©Milton Friedman, 1978.

* Based on a talk given at dedication of court room, University of San Diego Law School, San Diego, California, November 7, 1977.

say are predominantly free societies. Consider, for example, the restrictions that have been imposed in the United States particularly in the course of the past forty or fifty years on various groups in our society. One group in the United States that has been denied free speech in practice, not in principle, are businessmen. Recently, I received a letter from an executive vice-president of an oil and gas association. I won't mention the name of the person or of the oil and gas association but I will only read what she said:

«As you know, the real issue more so than price per thousand cubic feet [this was with respect to energy legislation] is the continuation of the First Amendment of the Constitution, the guarantee of freedom of speech. With increasing regulation, as big brother looks closer over our shoulder, we grow timid against speaking out for truth and our beliefs against falsehoods and wrongdoings. Fear of IRS audits, bureaucratic strangulation or government harassment is a powerful weapon against freedom of speech.

«In the October 31st edition of the U.S. News & World Report, the Washington Whisper section noted that, ‹Oil industry officials claim that they have received this ultimatum from Energy Secretary *James Schlesinger*: ‹Support the Administration's proposed tax on crude oil or else face tougher regulation and a possible drive to break up the oil companies.›»

Let me give you another, more subtle example of the restrictions on free speech imposed on businessmen. I am sure all of you, like me, have received from your banks a little piece of paper printed by the U.S. Department of the Treasury which urges you to buy U.S. Savings Bonds. If that piece of paper were published by a private commercial concern, the Federal Trade Commission might very well castigate it as misleading and inaccurate advertising. I have often said that the U.S. Savings Bond campaign has been one of the greatest bucket-shop operations in history. The government tells people, «You buy these bonds and it will assure your future. This is the way to save and to provide income for your children's education and your retirement.» Then it turns around and produces inflation that erodes the value of those bonds so that anybody who has bought a bond during the past fifteen or twenty years has ended up getting back a sum that has less purchasing power, that will buy fewer goods and services, than the amount he originally paid. And, to add insult to injury, he has had to pay taxes on the so-called interest, interest that doesn't even compensate for the inflation produced by the federal government that sells him the bonds and makes those promises.

You may not agree with me. You may think the bonds are a good investment, but I introduced this example for a very different purpose. Do you suppose the bankers who send you this piece of paper believe it? Do what I've done. I've asked quite a number of bankers, «Do you think that savings bonds are a good investment for your customers?» They uniformly answer, «No, it's a terrible investment.» I say to them, «Why do you send this piece of paper around to your customers? Why are you participating in what I believe is fundamentally a bucket-shop operation?» They all give me the same answer: «The Treasury would be very unhappy if we didn't. There's great pressure from the Treasury.»

Not long since I talked in Salt Lake City with a middle-management executive of a large enterprise who was telling me how terrible he thought the savings bond campaign was. In the next breath he told me how much time he had to spend promoting it among his employees because of pressure from higher-ups who in turn were reflecting pressure from the U.S. Treasury. Do those bankers, or these executives, have effective free speech?

Of course, occasionally there are courageous bankers, courageous businessmen who, despite the cost, express themselves freely. But the public statements of business leaders are almost always bland. They talk in general terms about the evils of government regulation and about the importance of free enterprise, but when it comes down to cases, they are very careful not to be too specific. Again there are some noble exceptions.

You may say, «That doesn't matter, those are only businessmen; after all, businessmen have enough to do making money, they don't have to worry about free speech.» Let's turn to my own field, to academics and ask, «What has happened to the freedom of speech of academics?» Consider my colleagues at the University of Chicago in the medical school, most of whom are supported in their research by grants from the National Institute of Health. Which of them wouldn't think three times before he made an impassioned speech against national health insurance? I don't blame them, don't misunderstand me. I'm not criticizing anybody. I'm only trying to discuss the relationship between the economic arrangements we adopt on the one hand and free speech on the other. People ought to bear a cost for free speech. However, the cost ought to be reasonable and not disproportionate. There ought not to be, in the words of a famous Supreme Court decision, «A chilling effect» on freedom of speech. Yet there is little doubt that the extent to which people in the academic world are being financed by government has a chilling effect on their freedom of speech.

What is true for the medical people is equally true for my own colleagues in economics departments who are receiving grants from the National Science Foundation. I happen to think that the National Science Foundation ought not to exist, that it is an inappropriate function of government. Not very many of my colleagues would be willing to endorse that statement in public, certainly not those who have grants from the NSF. In fact, I've often said that about the only academic who in this day and age has freedom of speech is a tenured professor at a private university who's on the verge of, or has already, retired. That's me.

Let's go from the academics and these chilling effects on freedom of speech and look at the relationship between economic arrangements and freedom of the press in a more direct and immediate fashion. There was a story some time back about the *London Times*, a great newspaper in Britain, «The Great Thunderer» as it used to be called. It was prevented from publishing one day by a union, I believe typographers, though it may have been another of the technical mechanical unions. Why did they close it down? Because *The Times* was scheduled to run an article about the union's attempt to influence what was printed in the paper. That's as clear and straightforward a violation of the freedom of press as you can think of. You may say, «Well, that one didn't involve government.» Of course it did! Because no union can gain so dominant a position without the aid and backing of the government.

Another example from Great Britain is equally pertinent. There is now a National Union of Journalists in Great Britain which is pushing for a closed shop of journalists writing in British papers – and there is a bill pending in Parliament to facilitate this outcome. The union is threatening to boycott papers that employ non-members of the National Union of Journalists who are not willing to join and accept their declaration of principles. And all this in Great Britain, the home of our liberties, from whence came the Magna Carta.

To turn more directly to the courts, judges, like intellectuals in general, have shown a kind of schizophrenia as between different areas of free speech. The courts have tended to draw a sharp line between what they designate as political or cultural speech on the one hand and what they designate as commercial speech on the other. Thanks to the tutoring that Professor *Bernard Siegan* has given me, I realize that the Supreme Court recently has taken some timid steps toward extending First Amendment rights to commercial speech. They have done so in connection with a Virginia law that would have prevented pharmacists from advertising, an Arizona law that would have prevented attorneys from advertising, and a New Jersey local law that would have prevented people from putting «For Sale» signs on their property. The Supreme Court has declared all these laws unconstitutional. But in each decision, they have been very timid and have continued to insist that there is a sharp line between the two kinds of speech and that the First Amendment gives absolute protection only to political speech, and not to commercial speech.

While I welcome these recent moves, the difference in attitude toward political and commercial speech is still extreme. For example, a court in Ohio threatened to close down a pornographic magazine, *The Hustler,* and sentenced the proprietor and publisher to jail. A prestigious list of intellectuals signed a petition objecting strenuously to what they interpreted as a violation of free speech and an act of censorship. Personally, I do not see much difference between *The Hustler* case, as a restriction of freedom of speech, and the legal prohibition of radio and TV advertising of cigarettes. Yet no distinguished, or for that matter undistinguished, intellectuals signed a petition in behalf of the freedom of enterprises to advertise cigarettes – though one, namely myself, did write a Newsweek column to that effect. In its decision on the Virginia advertising case, the Supreme Court explicitly said its decision did not render it invalid for the government to require advertising to bear a warning label such as the warning label on cigarettes, «The Surgeon General has determined that smoking may be bad for your health.» Congress has now passed a new law which is going to require all saccharin to bear a similar label. I have yet to see any intellectuals object to that infringement on free speech. Yet suppose a law were passed requiring *The Hustler* magazine to carry a warning: «Reading this magazine may be dangerous to the moral health of children, other immature people, and even some mature people.» Is there any doubt that such a law would produce an uproar, and that it would be overturned by the first court to hear the case? You cannot maintain that this difference in reaction is because somehow the contents of *The Hustler* are more noble or uplifting than the smoking of cigarettes or the use of saccharin. The difference simply reflects what is fundamentally an arbitrary distinction between certain kinds of speech.

To give an even more dramatic example, we have no hesitancy in saying that requiring tobacco companies to put a warning label on cigarettes doesn't infringe on their freedom of speech. There is little doubt that far more human lives have been lost over the past century as a result of *Karl Marx's Das Kapital* than from smoking cigarettes. Would it therefore be appropriate to require every copy of *Marx's Das Kapital* to carry a warning label saying, «Reading this book may be dangerous to social and personal health?»

Everyone would agree that's a violation of free speech. Why the one and not the other? Personally, I think it's terrible to smoke cigarettes. I quit twenty years ago and so obviously I want everybody else to quit. Personally, I think *Marx's Das Kapital* is a pernicious and dangerous book. But that does not mean that I believe it is desirable to restrict advertising for either cigarettes or *Das Kapital.* On the contrary, I favor the avoidance of legal restrictions on either the one or the other.

The schizophrenia of intellectuals in general, of courts in particular, extends far beyond regarding commercial speech as somehow very different from political speech. It goes to the whole problem of the supposed distinction between political freedom on the one hand and economic freedom on the other, to the difference in the way that the courts have interpreted the free speech clause and the due process clause. We've seen in the extreme case of Russia, and in less extreme cases as well, that you cannot have political freedom without a very large measure of economic freedom, A large measure of economic freedom is a necessary condition for political freedom – but more to the present point, there is no really sharp line between the two.

Economic and political freedom are not different in kind and it is frequently not easy to distinguish between them. Let me illustrate. Russia does not permit free speech. Everybody agrees that's a violation of political freedom. Russia does not permit emigration. Is that a violation of economic freedom or of political freedom? Russia does not permit those people it lets go out as emigrants to take more than their bare personal possessions with them. Is that a violation of economic freedom or is it a violation of political freedom? Great Britain permits its citizens to emigrate and it permits free speech but it does not permit emigrants to take their property out with them. Is that a violation of economic freedom or of political freedom?

Recently, as it happened, I received another letter that illustrates this relation. This was a letter from Pakistan. It was from an academic at a Pakistan university who had studied at the London School of Economics and who was now back in Pakistan. He wrote, «I have been delving into the political philosophy of liberalism and invididualism and have read whatever little on the subject is available in our libraries . . . It has been my great misfortune that your highly popular work, Capitalism and Freedom, is not present in the libraries of this country . . . Exchange control regulations in this country prevent me from buying it from a publisher in the U.S.» Is that a restriction of his economic freedom or of his political freedom or of his intellectual freedom?

Take something closer to home yet. Freedom of choice about where your live is surely more important to most people than free speech as it has been typically defined. Yet the courts have routinely upheld zoning and land-use legislation that seriously interfere with freedom. Not to mention the kind of emigration requirements that I was just speaking about, a recent article in the Los Angeles Times illustrates the difficulty in drawing the line between economic and political freedom. The story is about a student at a high school in Iowa who is from Nicaragua and who is living in this country on a visa to attend high school. Unfortunately for him, he wanted to be self-supporting so he got a paper route that pays him nine dollars a week. The immigration services found out about that and they now tell him that he will have to leave the country unless he quits his job. Are they interfering with his economic freedom? Or are they interfering with his human and political and personal freedom?

When a city legislates zoning ordinances that prevent people within that city from making voluntary transactions with people outside the city to buy or sell property imposing great costs on one or the other or both, are they interfering with economic freedom or human, political freedom?

The line is a difficult one to draw, all of these cases, particularly the housing and the zoning cases, raise third-party effects, neighborhood effects as they are sometime called. An agreement between two people to buy a piece of land or build a house affects neighbors who look on it. The point I want to emphasize is that those same effects are present in all the free speech cases. There's no distinction on that ground.

Consider, for example, the recent case in which an American Nazi group wanted to have a march in a mostly Jewish suburb of Chicago. That was a clear free speech case, yet there is no doubt that it involved serious third-party effects in the way of a possible riot, imposing costs on residents or bystanders not directly involved, let alone the police costs of enforcing order.

Take such a simple thing as permitting a parade down a main street of a city. That may impose heavy costs on businesses along the way through the loss of custom.

Consider still a different third-party effect. A political candidate campaigns for office by riding around in a truck with a loudspeaker on top, blaring into houses along the way. If a commercial truck advertising, let's say, soap or perfume or detergent, were to try to blare out its message on the same streets, at the same volume, there's little doubt that that would be regarded as a serious violation of the freedom of others. But is the message the one is delivering really more important, more reliable and more trustworthy than the message the other is imparting?

I am myself a liberal in the true original sense of the term, namely, belief in freedom. So

I favor both free speech and economic freedom. And I would lean over backwards very far indeed with respect to third-party effects in order to preserve both. But that is not my main point in the present context.

My main point is to demonstrate that there is a basic and fundamental inconsistency in the attitude of intellectuals in general, and the judiciary in particular, to the two areas of freedom. I can understand how someone would be willing, in order to protect third parties, to restrict both free speech and economic freedom. That's a consistent position. I obviously can understand how someone would take the position I do-that the social objective of maintaining a free society is so important that a very strong presumption must exist before freedom in either area is restricted to avoid third-party effects. What I cannot understand is the schizophrenic position that almost any costs may be imposed on third parties in order to protect one kind of freedom, namely freedom of speech, but that almost any third-party effect, however trivial, justifies restricting another kind of freedom, namely economic freedom. That seems to me to be a wholly inconsistent position which no reasonably logical, consistent man who understands what is involved can hold.

Summary

The Economics of Free Speech

The relation between economic arrangements and freedom of speech is clear in the extreme cases of totalitarian economic systems such as the Soviet system. But it is extremely close even in the modern mixed economies. Businessmen, heavily dependent on government for contracts, or subject to regulation by one or another government agency, or subject to investigation with respect to taxes, will individually be reluctant to exercise their right to free speech in ways that might bring down governmental retaliation or harassment. Academics, dependent on government finance for support of their research, will likewise experience «a chilling effect» on their freedom of speech. It is appropriate that individuals bear a cost for exercising free speech – but the cost should not be disproportionate.

Freedom of the press, like freedom of speech, is affected by economic arrangements. Strong unions, gaining their strength from government support, are in a position to affect what the newspapers, magazines, and other media will publish.

Judges, like intellectuals in general, have shown a kind of schizophrenia in drawing a sharp line between «political or cultural speech» and «commercial speech.» This distinction cannot be defended. Freedom to publish pornography is not fundamentally different from freedom to advertise cigarettes; requiring or using labels about health on cigarette packages is not fundamentally different from requiring or using a label on *Marx's Das Kapital* saying «Reading this book may be dangerous to social and personal health.»

The schizophrenia extends far beyond speech – to a supposed distinction between political freedom and economic freedom. They are not different in kind and it is not easy to distinguish between them. Are Russia's restrictions on emigration a restraint of political freedom but Britain's restrictions on the property an emigrant may take with him solely a restraint of economic freedom?

There is a basic inconsistency in the attitude of intellectuals in general to the two areas of freedom. I can understand how someone would be willing, in order to protect third parties, to restrict both free speech and economic freedom. I naturally understand my own position – that the social objective of maintaining a free society is so important that a very strong presumption must exist before freedom in either area is restricted to avoid third-party effects. I cannot understand the schizophrenic position that almost any costs may be imposed on third parties to protect one kind of freedom, freedom of speech, but that almost any third-party effect, however trivial, justifies restricting another kind of freedom, economic freedom.

Helmut Gröner

Meinungsfreiheit und Wettbewerb

I. Meinungsfreiheit und Meinungsbildung

Die Grundidee einer freiheitlich demokratischen Staatsordnung fußt auf der Überzeugung, daß die leitbildhaften Auffassungen der Regierung aus einem eigenständigen und spontanen Prozeß der Meinungsbildung hervorgehen. «Sie verlangt daher» – wie es *Hayek* präzise formulierte – «das Bestehen eines großen, nicht von den Ansichten der Mehrheit beherrschten Bereichs, in dem sich die Anschauungen der einzelnen bilden können. Es wird ziemlich übereinstimmend erkannt, daß aus diesem Grunde Demokratie und Rede- und Diskussionsfreiheit untrennbar zusammengehören.»[1] Für die Bundesrepublik Deutschland hob das Bundesverfassungsgericht diesen Grundsatz eindeutig heraus mit der Feststellung, für ein freiheitlich demokratisches Staatswesen sei das Grundrecht der freien Meinungsäußerung «schlechthin konstituierend», es ermöglicht erst die ständige geistige Auseinandersetzung, den Kampf der Meinungen, die ihr Lebenselement ist».[2] In der ursächlichen Verknüpfung jenes Grundrechts mit dem freiheitlichen Staatswesen selbst und den dazugehörigen Ordnungsbereichen ist die Funktionsbestimmung der Meinungsfreiheit zu erblicken.[3]

Es war *John Stuart Mill*, der schon frühzeitig die allgemeine Bedeutung der Meinungsfreiheit hervorhob. Vor allem mit vier Argumenten belegt er, warum sie unverzichtbarer Teil aller freiheitlichen Ordnungen ist[4]:

- Eine Meinung, die unterdrückt wird, kann nach aller Erfahrung gleichwohl wahr sein. Nur wer menschliche Unfehlbarkeit für möglich hält, wird dies leugnen.
- Auch wenn eine unterdrückte Meinung im wesentlichen auf Irrtum beruht, ist nicht auszuschließen, daß sie – und sei es in winzigen Spuren – Teilwahrheiten enthält. Doch auch sie sind geeignet, zur Überprüfung der vorherrschenden, aber selten die ganze Wahrheit einschließenden Ansichten wesentlich beizutragen. So können auch irrige Auffassungen dazu verhelfen, Erkenntnisse zu verbessern und fehlerhafte Komponenten aufzudecken.
- Selbst wenn eine Meinung nach dem jeweiligen Erkenntnisstand die ‹ganze Wahrheit› darstellt, so wird sie doch, wenn sie nicht kräftig und offen angefochten wird, sowohl von ihren Gegnern als auch sogar von ihren Anhängern nur noch als Vorurteil vertreten.

---

[1] *Friedrich A. von Hayek:* Die Verfassung der Freiheit. Tübingen 1971, S. 133.

[2] BVerfGE, Bd. 7, S. 208.

[3] *Walter Schmitt Glaeser:* Mißbrauch und Verwirkung von Grundrechten im politischen Meinungskampf. Bad Homburg v. d. H., Berlin und Zürich 1968, S. 106–114 mit weiteren Literaturnachweisen.

[4] *John Stuart Mill:* Die Freiheit. Übersetzt und mit Einleitung und Kommentar herausgegeben von *Adolf Grabowsky.* Zürich 1945, S. 138–186.

– Dadurch erlahmt völlig unnötig das Verständnis für die vernünftigen und stichhaltigen Gründe, durch welche die Meinung fundiert ist, und der Sinn einer Konzeption gerät in Gefahr, abgeschwächt zu werden oder zugrunde zu gehen. Damit büßt sie mehr oder weniger rasch an politischer Strahl- und Überzeugungskraft ein.

Wer freiheitlich gesinnt ist, wird diesen Einschätzungen lebhaft zustimmen und aus eigener Erfahrung die allgemein formulierten Erkenntnisse *Mills* mit einer Reihe von Beispielen auch konkret nachempfinden können. Dabei dürfte deutlich werden, daß der hohe Rang des Grundwertes Meinungsfreiheit nicht nur auf bestimmte Lebensbereiche oder auf Fachdisziplinen beschränkt bleibt, sondern sich klar und umfassend in breitestem Spektrum widerspiegelt. So ist auf der einen Seite die Meinungsfreiheit selber nur gewährleistet, wenn die wirtschaftlichen Voraussetzungen zur Beschaffung und Verbreitung von Informationen und Meinungen erfüllt sind. Die wirtschaftliche Betätigung ist auf der anderen Seite aber nur dann frei, wenn Meinungsfreiheit besteht und die Informationen über wirtschaftliche Möglichkeiten und Handlungen unbehindert weitergegeben werden können. Daher betrifft die Meinungsfreiheit nicht zuletzt auch die Ökonomie im allgemeinen und hat zudem für die Wirtschaftspolitik im speziellen erhebliche Bedeutung.

In den vorliegenden Erörterungen soll darum vor allem die ökonomische Seite hervorgehoben und beleuchtet werden.[5] Dabei ist zu fragen, was die spezifisch ökonomischen Aspekte der Meinungsfreiheit ausmacht und welche Konsequenzen daraus vor allem für die Wirtschaftspolitik erwachsen. Der Zugang zur wirtschaftspolitischen Bestimmungsfunktion dieser handlichen Formel, als welche ‹Meinungsfreiheit› in ihrer komplexen Vielfalt bezeichnet werden könnte, wird erleichtert, wenn man zunächst die Einzelkomponenten dieses ordnungspolitischen Grundwerts herausschält.[6]

Meinungsfreiheit zielt immer auf freie Meinungsbildung ab. Damit aber ist zwingend ausgeschlossen, daß der Prozeß freier Meinungsfindung zum Instrument werden kann – in wessen Hand auch immer –, ohne sein Wesen völlig einzubüßen. Vielmehr handelt es sich bei ihm um ein Verfahren ‹selbstorganisierender Systeme›, in denen sich die einzelnen Elemente durch negative Rückkopplung wechselseitig anpassen.[7] Voraussetzung eines solchen Prozesses ist das Recht zu freier Informationsbeschaffung ebenso wie dasjenige auf freie Meinungsäußerung und Informationsvermittlung. Beide gemeinsam bilden die tragenden Säulen der Meinungsfreiheit überhaupt, denn ohne die Freiheit zum Informationsbezug wäre das Recht auf freie Meinungsäußerung substanzarm und müßte kraftlos gleichsam zu einer leeren Hülse verkümmern. Umgekehrt würden mit dem Fehlen des Rechts auf freie Meinungsäußerung zugleich auch die Möglichkeiten der Informationsbeschaffung untergehen, weil die Meinungsäußerung des einen notwendigerweise die Informationsquelle des anderen darstellt. Freiheit von Information und Meinungsäußerung stehen also in untrennbarem Verbund und lassen sich nicht voneinander lösen.

---

[5] Nicht eingegangen wird in diesem Zusammenhang auf die Probleme der Werbung, bei der gleichfalls wichtige Beziehungen zur Informations- und Meinungsfreiheit bestehen.

[6] Siehe hierzu *Walter Schmitt Glaeser*: Die Meinungsfreiheit in der Rechtsprechung des Bundesverfassungsgerichts. Archiv des öffentlichen Rechts, 97. Bd. (1972), S. 60–123 und S. 276–298 und die dort zahlreich angeführten Nachweise.

[7] *Erich Hoppmann*: Das Schutzobjekt eines Gesetzes zur Sicherung der Pressefreiheit. In: *Hubert Armbruster, Helmut Arndt, Otto Bachof* u. a. (Hrsg.): Pressefreiheit. Neuwied 1970, S. 118–124. Wesentliche Einsichten zum Verständnis derartiger komplexer Systeme sind *von Hayek* zu verdanken. Siehe vor allem: *Friedrich A. von Hayek*: Die Theorie komplexer Phänomene. Tübingen 1972.

Als Informationen werden Aussagen über Tatsachen ebenso vermittelt wie Meinungen, gesicherte Erkenntnisse gleichermaßen wie vage Vermutungen oder auch gewagte Spekulationen. Sie sind teils entgeltlich zu erhalten, teils unentgeltlich; ihre Übermittlung geschieht sowohl öffentlich als auch nichtöffentlich. Auch mögen sie auf breite Sympathie stoßen oder auf schroffe Ablehnung; sie unterstützen die Regierenden oder lassen ihr Handeln fragwürdig scheinen: Informationsfreiheit ist nicht an Kriterien von Sympathie, Opportunität oder verordneter Richtigkeit zu messen. Es kommt vielmehr darauf an, daß dem Staatsbürger «alle allgemein zugänglichen Quellen offenstehen und die Entscheidung darüber, ob und welche dieser Informationsquellen er benützen will, allein seinem Gutdünken überlassen bleibt».[8] Die auch wirtschaftspolitisch zentrale Frage ist das Problem der Allgemeinzugänglichkeit einer Informationsquelle, für die in der Bundesrepublik klargestellt ist, daß sie staatlich nur im Rahmen von Art. 5 Abs. 2 GG zu beschränken ist und nicht durch Hoheitsmaßnahmen begrifflich verengt werden darf. Dieses Grundrecht der Informationsfreiheit besitzt einmal eine individualrechtliche Komponente, denn es wird als elementares menschliches Bedürfnis angesehen, sich möglichst umfassend zu unterrichten, und zum anderen eine demokratisch-funktionelle Komponente, weil die öffentliche Willensbildung eines demokratischen Staates eine freie und möglichst gut informierte ‹öffentliche Meinung› verlangt.[9] Auch in der Meinungsäußerungs- und -verbreitungsfreiheit sind die individuelle – was schließlich in der Natur des Grundrechts als solchem liegt – und die demokratische Komponente wiederzufinden. Die Bedeutung der Meinungsfreiheit als für eine freiheitlich demokratische Staatsordnung «schlechthin konstituierend» führt dann über die ‹öffentliche Meinung› zur ‹institutionellen› Seite dieses Grundrechts, mit dem die Meinungsfreiheit den Charakter einer ‹öffentlichen Aufgabe› erhält[10], an der alle Wirtschaftseinheiten des Medienbereichs ‹mitwirken›. Der Schutz der Medienfreiheit vor willkürlichen Behinderungen «dient jenem Bereich freier Meinungsbildung, der sich ‹in der Öffentlichkeit› vollzieht».[11]

Die öffentliche Meinung als Bindeglied zwischen individueller und institutioneller Seite der Meinungsfreiheit ist das Ergebnis der Prozesse freier Meinungsbildung analog den Marktergebnissen von Wettbewerbsprozessen, in denen sich die Informationen der einzelnen Teilnehmer ständig wechselseitig anpassen.[12] Wie Wettbewerbsprozesse, so stellt auch die freie Meinungsbildung ein Entdeckungsverfahren[13] dar, das sich dadurch selbst rechtfertigt, daß ohne diesen Meinungsfindungsprozeß den Wirtschaftseinheiten relevante Informationen unbekannt blieben oder wegen mangelhafter Ausbreitungseffekte allenfalls mäßig genutzt würden. Das Informationspotential ist dabei im vorhinein unbekannt, weil es sich ja gerade erst durch das Suchverfahren der freien Meinungsbildung erschließt, so daß auch sein Ergebnis ‹öffentliche Meinung› nicht im einzelnen vorhergesagt werden kann. Außerdem dient der freie Meinungsbildungsprozeß ohne konkreten Einzelzweck einer Vielzahl von unbekannten Individuen / Wirtschaftseinheiten sowie einer «Vielfalt von individuellen Zwecken, die in ihrer Gesamtheit niemand kennt».[14]

---

[8] *Walter Schmitt Glaeser:* Die Meinungsfreiheit . . ., a. a. O., S. 64.

[9] Ebenda, S. 65–67. Auf den Zusammenhang von freier Meinungsbildung und öffentlicher Meinung wird noch kurz einzugehen sein.

[10] Zu Einzelheiten siehe *Walter Schmitt Glaeser*: Die Meinungsfreiheit . . ., a. a. O., S. 81–123.

[11] *Erich Hoppmann:* a. a. O., S. 119.

[12] Zum Prozeß freier Meinungsbildung siehe ebenda, S. 118–119.

[13] Grundlegend hierzu: *Friedrich A. von Hayek*: Der Wettbewerb als Entdeckungsverfahren. Kiel 1968. Wiederabgedruckt in: Derselbe: Freiburger Studien. Tübingen 1969, S. 249–265.

[14] *Erich Hoppmann:* a. a. O., S. 119.

II. Marktprozesse und Meinungsbildung

Der große individuelle und demokratische Nutzeffekt der Meinungsfreiheit, der kurz skizziert wurde, begründet zu Recht den hohen allgemeinen ordnungspolitischen Stellenwert dieses Prinzips. Das aber läßt vermuten, daß Meinungsfreiheit und Meinungsfindungsprozeß auch für die Wirtschaftspolitik und ihre ordnungspolitischen Grundlagen nicht bedeutungslos sein können. Für den institutionellen Medienbereich im weitesten Sinne, auf den später noch eingegangen wird, leuchtet dies unmittelbar ein, wenn man nur an die wirtschaftspolitischen Kontroversen über die Pressekonzentration denkt. Darüber hinaus gibt es jedoch weitere, nicht weniger wichtige Nahtlinien zwischen freier Meinungsbildung und Ökonomie. Sie sind nicht auf den ersten Blick erkennbar und sollen daher hier zunächst nachgezogen und dann verfolgt werden.

Grundpfeiler jeder marktwirtschaftlich geordneten Volkswirtschaft ist das Koordinationsverfahren wettbewerblicher Marktprozesse, durch welches die unüberschaubar große Zahl wirtschaftlicher Einzelpläne aufeinander abgestimmt wird. Dabei wirkt – wie bereits erwähnt – der Wettbewerb nach allgemeiner Erfahrung als äußerst leistungsfähiges Such- und Entdeckungsverfahren, das «insoweit wichtig ist, als seine Ergebnisse unvoraussagbar und im ganzen verschieden von jenen sind, die irgend jemand bewußt hätte anstreben können».[15] Beileibe nicht bloß die Marktvorgänge im Mediensektor, wie man vielleicht vorschnell vermuten könnte, sondern alle in ihrer Fülle unüberschaubaren wettbewerblichen Marktprozesse schlechthin bringen sozusagen in komplementärer Funktion Informationen hervor, geben sie weiter, revidieren sie und lassen sie letztlich mit unterschiedlichen Wahrnehmbarkeitsgraden in die Meinungsbildung einfließen. «Als wesentliches, wenn auch nicht ausschließliches Informationssystem dient (hierbei, d. Verf.) das Gefüge freier Marktpreise.»[16] Daher ist das Ausmaß, in welchem das Informationspotential einer Volkswirtschaft ausgeschöpft wird, auch abhängig von den Wettbewerbsverhältnissen auf jedem einzelnen Markt, was grundsätzlich ebenfalls für jede Art grenzüberschreitender ökonomischer Transaktionen gilt. Während wettbewerbliche Marktprozesse dadurch gekennzeichnet sind, daß auf vorstoßende Marktaktionen einzelner gewöhnlich dynamischer Unternehmer mehr oder minder schnell die Reaktionen der übrigen Marktteilnehmer folgen, bedeuten Wettbewerbsbeschränkungen, daß vorstoßende oder nachfolgende Wettbewerbshandlungen wenigstens eines aktuellen oder potentiellen Konkurrenten erzwungenermaßen oder auch freiwillig unterbleiben. Wettbewerbsbeschränkungen besitzen demnach eine Tendenz, das Verhalten der Marktteilnehmer zu uniformieren und unbeweglich werden zu lassen. Insoweit besitzen auch Wettbewerbsbeschränkungen eine ‹meinungsbildende› Kraft, die allerdings einseitig und sich wiederholend lediglich zunehmend nutzlosere Informationen über wirtschaftliche Immobilität liefert. Infolgedessen nimmt auf Märkten, die mit Wettbewerbsbeschränkungen durchsetzt sind, die Ausschöpfung des Informationspotentials, und zwar vor allem des innovationsträchtigen Potentials, spürbar ab. Es entstehen gleichsam internalisierte Informationsprozesse mit wettbewerbsbeschränkender Kraft. Jede Internalisierung von Informationen bedeutet nun wiederum eine, andere Wirtschaftseinheiten ausschließende, Privatisierung von Teilen der öffentlichen Meinung, wodurch sie als Bindeglied zwischen individueller und institutioneller Seite der Meinungsfreiheit unausbleiblich geschwächt wird.

---

[15] *Friedrich A. von Hayek:* Der Wettbewerb . . ., a. a. O., S. 250.
[16] *Hans Willgerodt:* Diskretion als wirtschaftspolitisches Problem. Hamburger Jahrbuch für Wirtschafts- und Gesellschaftspolitik, 20. Jahrg. (1975), S. 129–142, Zitat: S. 136.

Solche ‹Informationsverluste› zeigen eine sich verstärkende Tendenz, je ausgeprägter Wettbewerbsbeschränkungen sind und je länger sie auf einem Markt andauern. Denn hiermit wächst die Gefahr, daß kreative und imitierende Unternehmer diese Wirtschaftssektoren verlassen und hauptsächlich konservative Unternehmer mit starren Verhaltensweisen und ausgeprägt zünftlerischem Denken zurückbleiben. Außerdem gedeihen Kreativität und Dynamik nur dann, wenn sie immer wieder neu herausgefordert werden, sich täglich beweisen müssen und hierfür auch Gelegenheit haben. Wettbewerbsbeschränkungen verführen nur allzu leicht dazu, daß sich auch solche unternehmerischen Persönlichkeiten zu einem gemächlichen Schlenderschritt bequemen, die im Grunde durchaus initiativ und aktiv veranlagt sind.

So wie unternehmerische Aktivität nur dort zu erwarten ist, wo ein «spirit of competition» herrscht und wo die Bereitschaft, Neuland zu erobern, durch Erfolgschancen gekrönt zu werden verspricht, so wird sich auch in einem Gemeinwesen das konstitutionelle Recht der Meinungsfreiheit nur dann entfalten können, wenn seine Bürger gelernt haben und bereit sind, auch unkonventionelle Gedankengänge aufzunehmen und sich kritisch mit ihnen zu beschäftigen. Wo das gesellschaftliche Umfeld nicht die Aufgeschlossenheit zur Auseinandersetzung mit Ideen bringt, die andere Wege als die bisher beschrittenen weisen, wird Meinungsfreiheit verkümmern. Wo unternehmerische Impulse in einem Geflecht von Wettbewerbsbeschränkungen ersticken, werden Innovationen rar und vorantreibende Imitationen sowie Lerneffekte kaum mehr gezielt möglich sein.

Die bewußte Nutzung und die pflegliche Bewahrung des Rechts auf Meinungsfreiheit gelingt nicht ohne gleichzeitigen Schutz wettbewerblicher Verhaltensweisen; denn beide Bereiche menschlichen Seins stehen in wechselseitiger Kommunikation: Wer gewohnt ist, in konformem Gleichschritt seine Meinung den jeweils vorherrschenden Strömungen anzupassen, wird kaum dazu fähig sein, als Wirtschaftssubjekt Initiativen zu entwickeln, und sich kaum dynamisch bemühen, etwas zu tun, was ihn von der großen Masse seiner Konkurrenten unterscheidet. Wer umgekehrt mit wachen Sinnen danach trachtet, durch Innovationen seine Marktchancen zu verbessern, sich dadurch gerade von den Mitbewerbern abhebend, wird in seinen übrigen Lebensbereichen kaum einem Meinungskonformismus huldigen können.

Dies alles bestätigt die Notwendigkeit der Informationsfreiheit als Funktionsbedingung einer marktwirtschaftlichen Ordnung, denn nur unter dieser Bedingung können sich die Ausbreitungseffekte dynamischer Marktkräfte voll auswirken. Gleichzeitig ist der marktwirtschaftliche Informationsprozeß wettbewerblich geordneter Märkte, der zudem für die individuellen Wirtschaftseinheiten einen diskreten Mechanismus der Meinungsäußerung darstellt, hinreichend effizient. Zum einen, weil bei funktionierender Konkurrenz mit Informationen weit weniger Marktstrategie zu treiben ist als bei Wettbewerbsbeschränkungen, und zum anderen, weil dann marktpolitische Motive zur Geheimhaltung der eigenen Leistungsfähigkeit entfallen.[17] Deshalb bedarf es auch keiner weiteren wirtschaftspolitischen Anstrengungen, um den produktions- und absatzorientierten Informationsgrad bestimmter Marktteilnehmer zu erhöhen, denn es ist nicht möglich, auf diesem Wege eine vorbestimmte Wettbewerbsintensität herbeizuführen.

---

[17] Ebenda, S. 136–140. Der Zusammenhang von Informationsfreiheit und Eigentumsrechten erfordert eine besondere Analyse, die hier nicht vorgenommen werden kann. Als Ansatzpunkt bietet sich hierfür die in letzter Zeit lebhaft diskutierte Konzeption der Property Rights an.

Vielmehr sind Programme, die angebliche Informationslücken schließen sollen, mit beträchtlichen wirtschaftspolitischen Nachteilen belastet.[18]

Es sind freilich nicht allein privatwirtschaftliche Beschränkungen, die wettbewerbliche Marktprozesse beeinträchtigen und verhindern, sondern ebensolche oder ähnliche Marktwirkungen gehen regelmäßig von staatlichen Marktinterventionen aus. Deshalb sinkt der Umfang, in dem Marktprozesse Informationen zutage fördern, auch mit wachsenden staatlichen Markteingriffen ganz merklich. Dieses Absinken der Informationslieferungen verstärkt sich noch, wenn der Wettbewerb sowohl privatwirtschaftlich als auch staatlich beschränkt wird, weil unter Konkurrenzbeschränkungen stehende Marktteilnehmer ein Interesse daran haben, Informationen über ihren Bereich zu filtern, zu steuern, ja möglichst zu monopolisieren. Privatwirtschaftliche Wettbewerbsbeschränkungen benötigen eine Informationskontrolle, um ihren Bestand auf Dauer zu sichern, wie vielfältige Erfahrungen mit der Kartellbildung beweisen. Unter diesem Gesichtswinkel sind auch die verschiedenartigen Informationssammelstellen zu sehen, zu deren Rechtfertigung zwar durchweg eine Intensivierung des Leistungswettbewerbs behauptet wird, die aber gleichwohl zum Zwecke der Wettbewerbsbeschränkung errichtet werden und auch entsprechende Wirkungen zeigten.[19] «Durch das Kartellverbot werden» – so läßt sich allgemein formulieren – «diejenigen Informationen erheblich, mit denen sich im Wettbewerb stehende Unternehmen gegenseitig über ihr Marktverhalten und über ihre individuellen Plandaten unterrichten».[20] Damit geht es über die Problematik von Preismeldestellen hinaus um die Grenzen der Informationsfreiheit zwischen privaten Wirtschaftseinheiten überhaupt, die im Parallelprozeß miteinander konkurrieren. Wettbewerbstheoretische Untersuchungen der Marktwirkungen von Konkurrenzinformationen haben gezeigt[21], daß es zu einer Behinderung und Dämpfung des Wettbewerbs durch den Preisgabeeffekt von Informationen kommen kann. Hierbei handelt es sich um einen Effekt, der die eigene Reaktion eines Marktteilnehmers auf die über ihn preisgegebenen Informationen beschreibt. Wir haben es also mit einem Sonderfall der Rückkopplung zu tun. Die durch die Information erzielte Transparenz des Handelns kann in diesem Falle dazu führen, daß oligopolistische Verhaltensmuster herbeigeführt und/oder verfestigt werden und daß der Anreiz für autonome Wettbewerbsaktionen spürbar gehemmt wird. Deshalb ist es eine unverzichtbare und wesentliche Aufgabe der Wirtschaftspolitik, identifizierende Konkurrenzinformationen zu unterbinden, um «die Anonymität von Wettbewerbshandlungen zu schützen».[22]

Solange dem keine gesetzlichen Vorschriften entgegenstehen, besteht auch bei wettbewerbsbehindernden staatlichen Markteingriffen ein starkes Interesse, den verbliebenen Informationsstrom zu überwachen und zu steuern, um den privatwirtschaftlichen Nutzen solcher Marktregulierungen nicht auszuhöhlen oder gar zu gefährden. Denn solche staatlichen Marktsteuerungen werden gewöhnlich vorgenommen – ob erfolgreich oder nicht, sei hier dahingestellt –, wenn die sektorale Einkommensverteilung zugunsten

---

[18] Zu einer eingehenden Untersuchung dieser Probleme siehe: *Alfred Schüller*: Ein staatlich verordneter «Nürnberger Trichter»? Die Informationslücke als Problem staatlicher Wirtschaftspolitik in der Bundesrepublik Deutschland. ORDO, Bd. 22 (1971), S. 181–215.

[19] Als zusammenfassende Darstellung hierzu siehe: *Artur Woll*: Zur wettbewerbspolitischen Bedeutung der Markttransparenz. In: Theoretische und institutionelle Grundlagen der Wirtschaftspolitik. Theodor Wessels zum 65. Geburtstag. Berlin 1967, S. 119–217.

[20] *Ernst-Joachim Mestmäcker*: Europäisches Wettbewerbsrecht. München 1974, S. 287.

[21] Siehe hierzu: *Otto Gandenberger*: Konkurrenzinformation und Wettbewerb. Jahrbücher für Nationalökonomie und Statistik, Bd. 188 (1973 / 75), S. 10–31 und die dort angeführte Literatur.

[22] Ebenda, S. 28.

einer Branche beeinflußt werden soll. Im Verein mit diesem Beweggrund sind es häufig meist vermeintliche sogenannte Branchenbesonderheiten, die staatliche Markteingriffe provozieren oder entscheidend mithelfen, solche Maßnahmen den politisch Verantwortlichen abzutrotzen.

Diese Sachverhalte lenken den Blick auf die Frage, welche Informationen des Marktes wirtschaftspolitische Entscheidungsinstanzen benötigen. Der hier zu bedenkende wirtschaftspolitische Informationsbedarf hängt in hohem Maße von den Aufgaben und Konzeptionen der Wettbewerbs- und Strukturpolitik ab. Für die Wettbewerbspolitik dürfte weithin unbestritten sein, daß die Wettbewerbsbehörden ausreichende Kenntnisse über konkrete Fälle von Wettbewerbsbeschränkungen und Marktversagen besitzen müssen. Hierdurch werden sie in die Lage versetzt, umfassend wettbewerbliche Marktprozesse zu schützen sowie gegebenenfalls, sollte dies unausweichlich sein, möglichst wettbewerbsfreundliche Marktregulierungen vorzunehmen. Der öffentliche Bedarf an Marktinformationen steigt jedoch sprunghaft an, wenn die Wettbewerbspolitik zwar einerseits Konkurrenzbeschränkungen verhindern und ausschalten soll, sich aber andererseits zunehmend den unterschiedlichsten wirtschaftspolitischen Zweckmäßigkeitserwägungen fügen muß. Diese ‹dienende› Funktion, durch die gewisse, – vorweg bestimmte –, manchmal nicht einmal über den Tag hinaus relevante wirtschaftspolitische Ergebnisse angestrebt werden, kann die Wettbewerbspolitik aber nur ausfüllen, wenn sie auf weitgehende Einzelinformationen über die Marktteilnehmer zurückgreifen kann. Die damit erforderliche Informationsbeschaffung gerät dann leicht mit individuellen Schutzrechten in Konflikt. Wirtschaftseinheiten, die sich von solchen wettbewerbspolitischen Mitteln einen Vorteil versprechen, mögen das hinnehmen; doch werden dies gewöhnlich nicht alle betroffenen Marktbeteiligten sein. Vielmehr ist zu befürchten, daß sich gerade die leistungsfähigen und initiativen Anbieter durch einen Zwang zur Informationslieferung in ihren Rechten und in ihrem Handlungsspielraum beschnitten fühlen. Das wirkt leistungsdämpfend und verstärkt somit die marktpolitischen Schwierigkeiten, die der eigentliche Anlaß für das wirtschaftspolitische Eingreifen waren. Ähnliche Aussagen gelten auch für die Strukturpolitik, wenn sie sich nicht mit allgemein wirkenden, wettbewerbserhaltenden Anpassungsmaßnahmen begnügt, sondern weitgesteckte Absichten der Strukturgestaltung und -erhaltung verfolgt.

Diese Lenkungseinflüsse und Sickerverluste beim Informationsstrom bis hin zu seiner Austrocknung oder Umleitung in Richtung auf einseitige Produzenteninteressen im Gefolge von privaten oder staatlichen Wettbewerbsbeeinträchtigungen beschwören nun nicht gering zu schätzende ordnungspolitische Gefahren herauf.[23] Grundsätzlich verbindet sich, wie deutlich gemacht wurde, mit jeder Marktregulierung unausweichlich ein Informationsverlust, der die Möglichkeiten der einzelnen Bürger beschneidet, sich umfassend und zuverlässig zu unterrichten, wenn das jeweilige Ausmaß auch unterschiedlich sein mag. Gewiß rechnet der größte Teil der hier angesprochenen Informationen nicht zu den Quellen, die man gewöhnlich unter der Rubrik «allgemein zugänglich» einordnet, so daß die Schlußfolgerung naheliegt, der Marktinterventionismus behindere die Informationsfreiheit nicht im geringsten. Doch ist eine solche Annahme voreilig, denn dabei wird vergessen, daß die Informationsminderungen auch und vor allem die Bedingungen des Mediensektors verschlechtern, die Öffentlichkeit mit Nachrichten und fundierten Meinungsäußerungen zu versorgen. Darüber hinaus führen diese interventionsinduzierten Informationsverstopfungen und -regulierungen dazu, daß das Wissen in der Gesellschaft nicht mehr voll genutzt werden kann und daß damit Entwicklungschancen für die Zu-

---

[23] Vgl. auch *Eberhard Wille*: Planung und Information. Berlin 1970. S. 207–221.

kunft vertan werden.[24] «Effiziente Ordnungsformen bedürfen informationsinduzierter Verhaltensverbesserungen ihrer Systemelemente (Entscheidungseinheiten); diese Entscheidungseinheiten ihrerseits können nur dann lernen, wenn das System sie informiert und ihnen Freiheit(sgrade) beläßt.»[25] Es ist schwer zu verstehen, daß man wirtschaftspolitisch häufig schnell bereit ist, dies für Realformen von Zentralverwaltungswirtschaften anzuerkennen, aber man nicht selten im gleichen Atemzug die zwar vom Ausmaß her geringeren, aber grundsätzlich immer noch bedrohlichen gleichartigen Gefahren zu verharmlosen sucht, wenn es darum geht – um eine treffende Charakterisierung *Tuchtfeldt*s aufzugreifen[26] –, den ‹Interventionskapitalismus› zu verteidigen. Gerade dabei wird häufig übersehen, daß selbst punktuelle Interventionen, wenn sie effizient sein sollen, einer sicheren Informationsbasis bedürfen, sie sich freilich bei wuchernden staatlichen Marktregulierungen allmählich selbst diesen Boden entziehen. Schon alleine von den Störungen des Informationsprozesses her, und zwar nicht zuletzt im Verein mit deren Rückwirkungen auf eine wirtschaftspolitisch freie Meinungsbildung kann es leicht passieren, daß eine Spirale zirkulär verursachter Verschlechterungen der Interventionsergebnisse in Gang gebracht wird, die die wirtschaftspolitische Gefahr zusätzlicher staatlicher Lenkungsmaßnahmen steigert. Will man die Effizienz wirtschaftlicher Ordnungsformen erhöhen, so muß ihre ordnungspolitische Struktur derart verändert werden, daß Informationsstand und Entscheidungsspielraum der Wirtschaftseinheiten zunehmen[27], was nichts anderes bedeutet, als daß es einer Rückbesinnung auf zentrale ordnungspolitische Grundsätze eines marktwirtschaftlichen Systems bedarf. Daran sollten sich alle erinnern, die dem Prinzip der Meinungsfreiheit völlig zu Recht einen unverkürzt hohen Stellenwert beimessen.

Man könnte nun meinen, das Bemühen, über Wettbewerbsordnung sowie wirtschaftspolitische Daten- und Entscheidungstransparenz das Informationsniveau der Wirtschaftseinheiten anzuheben, führe schließlich zu der Gefahr, in weitgehender Fremdbestimmung zu enden, weil Freiheit Ungewißheit voraussetzt.[28] Diese Gefahr besteht jedoch nicht, weil – wie *Wille* gezeigt hat – Schranken bei den Informationskosten, bei der Qualität der Informationen und bei der Bereitschaft und Fähigkeit, Informationen zu verbreiten und aufzunehmen, sowie die Anzahl der vorhandenen Variationsmöglichkeiten dafür sorgen, daß eine marktwirtschaftliche Ordnung nicht zu einem determinierten System denaturieren kann.[29] Vielmehr wird das marktwirtschaftliche Ordnungssystem um so leistungsfähiger sein und um so reibungsloser funktionieren, je mehr Informationen zu den Wirtschaftseinheiten durchdringen. Deshalb ist Informationsfreiheit, die von wettbewerblichen Marktprozessen abgestützt und untermauert wird, für den Bürger wie für jede Wirtschaftseinheit schlechthin ein Schutz gegen Leistungsverschlechterungen von Unternehmen und von Organisationen. Denn Abwanderung und/oder Widerspruch als Gegenwehr gegen Leistungsrückgang[30] können nur dann je

---

[24] Zur näheren Begründung siehe: *Friedrich A. von Hayek*: Die Verwertung des Wissens in der Gesellschaft. In: Derselbe: Individualismus und wirtschaftliche Ordnung. Erlenbach–Zürich 1952, S. 103–121.

[25] *Eberhard Wille:* a. a. O., S. 213.

[26] *Egon Tuchtfeldt:* Der «Interventionskapitalismus» – eine gemischte Wirtschaftsordnung. Wirtschaftspolitische Chronik, 25. Jahrg. (1976), Heft 2 / 3, S. 61–74.

[27] Vgl. auch: *Eberhard Wille*: a. a. O., S. 213.

[28] *Ernst Heuss:* Freiheit und Ungewißheit. ORDO, Bd. 15 / 16 (1965), S. 43–54.

[29] *Eberhard Wille:* Freiheit und Information. ORDO, Bd. 22 (1971), S. 159–179.

[30] Siehe hierzu die eingehende Erörterung bei: *Albert D. Hirschman*: Abwanderung und Widerspruch. Tübingen 1974.

für sich oder zusammen durchschlagend wirken, wenn der einzelne die Möglichkeit hat, sich uneingeschränkt und umfassend zu informieren.

Während die Abwanderung, die im allgemeinen als wirksamstes Druckmittel gegen Leistungsschwäche angesehen wird, nicht ohne einen mehr oder weniger großen, von Alternativen bestimmten Handlungssppielraum auskommt, ist die Reaktionsweise des Widerspruchs über den Zugang zu Informationen hinaus unumstößlich auf die Freiheit zur Meinungsäußerung und -verbreitung angewiesen. Hauptsächlich gegenüber einem Leistungsabfall bei staatlichen und nichtstaatlichen Institutionen der Wirtschaftspolitik, bei denen meistenteils keine jederzeitige Abwanderung möglich ist, sondern gewöhnlich nur zu den im mehrjährigen Abstand stattfindenden Wahlen, ist die Reaktionsweise Widerspruch manchmal die einzig mögliche Gegenmaßnahme.[31] Der wirtschaftspolitische Widerspruch im Zuge einer freien Meinungsbildung zielt darauf, Widersprüche im Zielkatalog aufzudecken sowie die Tauglichkeit und die Nebenwirkungen von verwirklichten, beschlossenen oder geplanten wirtschaftspolitischen Maßnahmen nachzuweisen, was als ein leistungsminderndes Versäumnis der Träger der wirtschaftspolitischen Verantwortung zu betrachten ist. Freilich sind die hier aufgeworfenen Fragen bei weitem nicht immer so einfach zu beantworten, wie sich das auf den ersten Blick vermuten läßt, denn nicht wenige wirtschaftspolitische Instrumente sind in ihren gesamten Auswirkungen theoretisch umstritten, so daß sich in der öffentlichen Meinung kontroverse wissenschaftliche Positionen widerspiegeln.

Es ist allerdings nicht auszuschließen, daß Widerspruch in der wirtschaftspolitischen Meinungsfindung destruktiv und nicht wie erhofft konstruktiv wirkt, so daß sich die eigentlich beabsichtigte Leistungsverbesserung nicht einstellt. So kann ein ständiger lautstarker Widerspruch die sich anbahnenden wirtschaftspolitischen Leistungssteigerungen eher behindern als fördern, weil wirtschaftspolitische Kursänderungen aufgrund der sich stets rührenden Widerstände[32] und wegen der Wirkungsverzögerungen nicht selten einen erheblichen zusätzlichen Zeitbedarf benötigen, um überhaupt zum Tragen zu kommen. Daß die produzierenden und die konsumierenden Wirtschaftseinheiten ihrer Meinung mehr oder weniger erfolgreich Ausdruck verleihen können und es auch tun[33], ist im wirtschaftspolitischen Entscheidungsprozeß zwingend notwendig. Nur so erhalten die wirtschaftspolitisch Verantwortlichen die erforderlichen Signale, die sie für die Bestimmung des Kurses ihrer Wirtschaftspolitik benötigen. Indes haben sie in gleicher Weise auch einen Anspruch darauf, unter Bedingungen tätig zu werden, die es erlauben, möglichst abgewogene Entscheidungen zu treffen. «Der Bürger muß daher abwechselnd einflußreich und fügsam sein.»[34] Nun verursacht die Reaktionsweise des Widerspruchs im allgemeinen einen Aufwand an Zeit und an sonstigen Kosten. Das schränkt eine übertriebene Neigung ein, allem und jedem zu widersprechen, und hilft mit, sich auf bedeutsame wirtschaftspolitische Belange zu konzentrieren. Je intensiver und je umfangreicher allerdings die wirtschaftspolitischen Steuerungsmaßnahmen der öffentlichen Verbände sind, desto mehr Widerspruch wird laut werden und um so länger wird er anhalten. Gewiß ist die öffentliche Meinung als Ergebnis einer freien Meinungsbildung ein kaum zu unterschätzender Integrationsfaktor.[35] Das ist ganz besonders für die Diskussion über höherrangige

---

[31] Zu Einzelheiten siehe ebenda, S. 25–36.
[32] Siehe hierzu: *Egon Tuchtfeldt*: Widerstände gegen wirtschaftspolitische Maßnahmen. Jahrbücher für Nationalökonomie und Statistik, Bd. 184 (1970), S. 366–380.
[33] Auf die Probleme des wirtschaftspolitischen Einflusses von Verbänden auf die Meinungsbildung wird hier nicht eingegangen.
[34] *Albert D. Hirschman*: a. a. O., S. 27.
[35] *Walter Schmitt Glaeser*: Mißbrauch ..., a. a. O., S. 111–112.

wirtschaftspolitische Ziele und ordnungspolitische Grundprobleme hervorzuheben. Doch auch eine «pluralistische Gesellschaft benötigt ein Mindestmaß an Identitätsbewußtsein»[36], wenn der gesellschaftliche Zusammenhalt dauerhaft bewahrt werden soll. Für die wirtschaftspolitische Meinungsfindung ist es deshalb wichtig, daß die Marktwirtschaft als freiheitliche Ordnungsform auf einem breiten und stabilen Grundkonsens fußt.[37] An der öffentlichen Meinung gerade der jüngeren Vergangenheit läßt sich jedoch unschwer ablesen, daß die Prinzipien dieser Wirtschaftsordnung heftig umstritten sind.[38] Von entscheidender Bedeutung ist dabei, wie die Funktionsweise einer marktwirtschaftlichen Ordnung im Prozeß der freien Meinungsbildung interpretiert wird. Hier läßt sich erkennen, daß sowohl bei Theoretikern und Praktikern der Wirtschaftspolitik als auch bei Meinungsmittlern Unsicherheiten bestehen, weil weder ein einzelner noch eine Arbeitsgruppe eine komplexe Ordnung wie die Marktwirtschaft und deren feinverästelte Abläufe als Ganzes hinreichend überblicken und erkennen kann.[39] Insofern gibt es immer eine Kluft im Grad der Information über das ungewöhnlich komplexe System einer marktwirtschaftlichen Ordnung einerseits und über die scheinbar viel leichter determinier- und steuerbaren wirtschaftspolitischen Interventionssysteme andererseits.

Dieser uneinholbare Informationslag verlangt von allen theoretisch oder praktisch an der Wirtschaftspolitik Beteiligten, zweifellos aber ganz besonders von den Meinungsmittlern, ein außergewöhnlich hohes Maß an Verantwortung.[40] Das Verantwortungsbewußtsein wird in unserer modernen Gesellschaft allerdings nur zu häufig von einem starken Hang zur Verhinderung fruchtbarer Diskussion ausgehöhlt.[41] Gerade bei ordnungspolitischen Erörterungen wird so das Vordringen zu den entscheidenden Kernfragen vereitelt.

Nur zu häufig werden die an Interventionen geknüpften wirtschaftspolitischen Wünsche und Ziele mit ihrer Verwirklichung verwechselt. Und zu oft wird über den großen Schwierigkeiten, die äußerst verwickelten Zusammenhänge von Wirtschaftsprozessen marktwirtschaftlicher Systeme überschaubar zu machen und adäquat zu interpretieren, vergessen und verkannt, daß die Funktionstüchtigkeit des Marktes nicht durch Grenzen in der Auffassungsgabe bei einigen Wirtschaftsführern oder von Institutionen limitiert wird, selbst wenn deren Qualität beträchtlich sei mag.

Die weitverbreitete Hochachtung vor der «Machbarkeit» im Bereich der Wirtschaft, verbunden mit einem geheimen Grauen vor dem stillen, friktionsarmen Ablaufen von Prozessen, die nicht «mit großer Hand» zu steuern sind, dürften es sein, die «ein Einfalls-

---

[36] *Dieter Stammler:* Die Presse als soziale und verfassungsrechtliche Institution. Berlin 1971, S. 207.

[37] Siehe: *Christian Watrin:* Wie gefährdet ist die marktwirtschaftliche Ordnung? Wirtschaftspolitische Chronik, 27. Jg. (1978), Heft 1, S. 55–69, hier: S. 62–67.

[38] Dabei geht es nicht um die berechtigte Kritik an Verstößen gegen das marktwirtschaftliche Ordnungsprinzip, die die ordnungspolitische Glaubwürdigkeit unterminieren, zumal wenn sie engstirnig mit fadenscheinigen wirtschaftspolitischen Argumenten verteidigt werden.

[39] *Christian Watrin:* a. a. O., S. 64–65.

[40] Auf den Zusammenhang von Verantwortung und öffentlicher Meinung hat *Popper* vor längerem bereits aufmerksam gemacht, als er vielleicht etwas überspitzt formulierte: Die öffentliche Meinung «ist zwar oft aufgeklärter und weiser als die Regierungen, bedeutet aber ohne die Zügel einer starken liberalen Tradition eine Gefahr für die Freiheit». Karl R. *Popper:* Die öffentliche Meinung im Lichte der Grundsätze des Liberalismus. ORDO, Bd. 8 (1956), S. 7–17, Zitat: S. 16.

[41] Siehe: *Eric Voegelin:* Diskussionsbereitschaft. In: *Albert Hunold* (Hrsg.): Erziehung zur Freiheit. Erlenbach – Zürich und Stuttgart 1959, S. 355–372, hier: S. 366–370.

tor ideologischer Deutungen»[42] eröffnen. Hier gilt es, in breiten Kreisen ein Verständnis zu wecken für Grundprinzipien dezentraler Wirtschaftslenkung, eine Aufgabe, die der Entwicklung eines Volkes aus autoritärer zu demokratischer Regierungsform nicht nur in Scheinparallelen vergleichbar ist. Darüber hinaus läßt sich der Gefahr, daß ordnungspolitische Fehleinschätzungen in der öffentlichen Meinung aufgrund unzureichenden Wissens zu eigentlich unerwünschten wirtschaftspolitischen Orientierungen führen, am wirkungsvollsten dadurch begegnen, daß der autonome wirtschaftspolitische Interventionsspielraum der öffentlichen Entscheidungsträger möglichst gering gehalten wird.[43] Dadurch wird zumindest die gängige Vorstellung reduziert, als genüge es, administrativen Stellen genügend Detailvollmachten zu geben, um effiziente Wirtschaftsprozesse zu garantieren.

III. Mediensektor und Wettbewerb

Bisher wurden Probleme der freien Meinungsbildung betrachtet, wie sie weithin abseits der institutionellen Meinungsmärkte anzutreffen sind. Fraglos wird jedoch die öffentliche Meinung von den Marktprozessen dominiert, in denen Presse, Rundfunk und Fernsehen als wichtigste Anbieter von Nachrichten und Meinungen auftreten. Die hier bestehenden Marktverhältnisse sind durch Wettbewerbsbeschränkungen der unterschiedlichsten Art gekennzeichnet; sie können an dieser Stelle nicht im einzelnen erörtert werden.[44] Der Strukturwandel in den Medientechnologien[45] bietet allerdings Chancen, Wettbewerbsbeschränkungen abzubauen und für die Zukunft auszuschalten. Hierauf gerichtete Bestrebungen treffen jedoch auf den erbitterten Widerstand von Verfechtern staatlich gestalteter und geregelter Medienbereiche, die eine privatwirtschaftliche Struktur des Mediensektors, vor allem auch der Presse, im Blick auf die öffentliche Aufgabe ‹Meinungsfreiheit› für nicht angemessen halten.[46] Demgegenüber wird zu Recht betont, daß die Wettbewerbspolitik einen Beitrag zur Meinungsvielfalt zu leisten imstande ist. Jedoch nur unter der – wenngleich realitätsnahen – Annahme, «daß die Vielfalt wirtschaftlich selbständiger Verlage und anderer Medieneinheiten eine gesteigerte Wahrscheinlichkeit für die Meinungsvielfalt begründet».[47] Wirtschaftliche Maßnahmen gegen Wettbewerbsbeschränkungen und Konzentrationsprozesse im Mediensektor[48] hätten

---

[42] *Christian Watrin:* a. a. O., S. 64. Zur Ideologiebildung auch im Zusammenhang mit dem Prozeß der Meinungsfindung siehe die ausführliche Analyse bei: *Gérard Gäfgen:* Zur Ökonomie der Ideologiebildung. In: *Heinz Sauermann* und *Ernst-Joachim Mestmäcker* (Hrsg.): Wirtschaftsordnung und Staatsverfassung. Festschrift für Franz Böhm zum 80. Geburtstag. Tübingen 1975, S. 163–182.

[43] Vgl. auch: *Karl R. Popper:* a. a. O., S. 15–16.

[44] Siehe hierzu: *Ernst-Joachim Mestmäcker:* Medienkonzentration und Medienvielfalt. Baden-Baden 1978; *Bruce M. Owen:* Economics and Freedom of Expression. Cambridge, Mass., 1975, und die von diesen Autoren angeführte Literatur.

[45] Zu einem kurzen Überblick siehe: *Eberhard Witte:* Strukturwandel des Kommunikationssystems der Bundesrepublik Deutschland. Hamburger Jahrbuch für Wirtschafts- und Gesellschaftspolitik, 23. Jahrg. (1978), S. 167–180.

[46] Siehe: *Ernst-Joachim Mestmäcker:* Medienkonzentration . . ., a. a. O., S. 13–32.

[47] Ebenda, S. 30.

[48] Ausführlich diskutiert wurde in letzter Zeit die Frage der Pressekonzentration. Die Literatur hierzu ist kaum noch zu übersehen. Zur wettbewerbspolitischen Problematik siehe: *Matthias F. Steinmann* und *Egon Tuchtfeldt:* Über Maßnahmen gegen Pressekonzentration. In: *Hugo Sieber*

dann den Charakter von medienpolitischen Vorbeugungsmaßnahmen, denn bei einer Vielzahl von «wirtschaftlich selbständigen Einheiten [am Markt, d. Verf.] ist die Gefahr der Gleichschaltung geringer als bei abhängigen Einheiten».[49]

Es wird immer wieder der Schutz der Meinungsfreiheit als Argument gegen wettbewerbsfördernde Auflockerungen des Medienbereichs bemüht. «Die Vorstellung, daß die Anbieter am Markt der Meinungen in erster Linie an der Aufrechterhaltung eines möglichst freien Wettbewerbs interessiert seien, um so die Chancen des eigenen Wortes nicht zu gefährden, ist leider nicht zutreffend.»[50] Dabei überrascht, daß gerade diejenigen, die auf der einen Seite lautstark weitestgehende Interventionen auf den Gütermärkten fordern, andererseits für die Medienmärkte – ganz in der Tradition altliberaler Vorstellungen – jegliche staatliche Ordnungspolitik für die Marktprozesse bei der freien Meinungsbildung als verderblich ablehnen. Sie übersehen freilich geflissentlich, daß auf den Meinungsmärkten eine erhebliche Konzentration, Tendenzen zur politischen Marktschließung und andere Wettbewerbsbeschränkungen zu beobachten sind, die in völliger Analogie zu den Verhältnissen auf Gütermärkten stehen.[51] Da diese Wettbewerbsbeschränkungen sowie die jetzige wirtschaftspolitische Sonderstellung und das für die Zukunft anvisierte Eigendasein von Massenmedien die Meinungsvielfalt nicht nur nicht erhöhen, sondern sogar wesentlich behindern, kann ein einfacher Hinweis auf das Prinzip der Meinungsfreiheit den Fortbestand dieser Marktverhältnisse nicht rechtfertigen.

Außerdem wird das Argument vorgetragen, im Medienbereich liege ein grundsätzliches Marktversagen vor.[52] Es zwinge dazu, den Angebotsprozeß im Rahmen einer freien Meinungsbildung einer staatlichen Regulierung zu unterwerfen. Als Beleg wird zunächst angeführt, Wettbewerbsprozesse führten im Medienbereich wegen kommunikationssoziologischer und -psychologischer Bedingungen zu Konformismus und zur Überbetonung der Kategorie ‹Unterhaltung› gegenüber der freien Meinungsbildung. Das mag so sein, ist jedoch mit ökonomischen Kriterien nicht zu überprüfen. Wenn man aber eine solche Entwicklung mit wirtschaftspolitischen Mitteln aufhalten will, so sind die Konsequenzen leicht abzusehen: Denn es wäre erforderlich, den Marktzugang zu beschränken, Subventionen zu gewähren oder gar zu Verstaatlichungen zu greifen. Welches Mittel man auch einsetzen mag, die Maßnahmen verlangen unumgänglich Vorkehrungen zum Schutz der Meinungsfreiheit, um vor allem die Unabhängigkeit vom Staat zu sichern. Es wird nun angenommen, daß das ‹Modell der gesellschaftlich relevanten Gruppen› dies

---

und *Egon Tuchtfeldt* (Hrsg.): Wettbewerbspolitik in der Schweiz. Festgabe zum 80. Geburtstag von *Fritz Marbach*. Bern 1972, S. 205–225; *Ernst-Joachim Mestmäcker*: Medienkonzentration . . ., a. a. O., S. 33–43 und S. 69–105.

[49] *Ernst-Joachim Mestmäcker*: Medienkonzentration . . ., a. a. O., S. 30.

[50] *Christian Watrin*: a. a. O., S. 65.

[51] Siehe auch *R. H. Coase*: The Market for Goods and the Market for Ideas. The American Economic Review, Papers and Proceedings, Bd. 64 (1974), S. 384–391; derselbe: Advertising and Free Speech. The Journal of Legal Studies, Bd. 6 (1977), S. 1–34, hier besonders: S. 1–8; *Gérard Gäfgen*: a. a. O., S. 175–182.

[52] Siehe: *Jochen Röpke*: Zur politischen Ökonomie von Hörfunk und Fernsehen. Publizistik, 15. Jahrg. (1970), S. 98–113; derselbe: Wettbewerb, Pressefreiheit und öffentliche Meinung. Schmollers Jahrbuch, 90. Jahrg., I. Halbbd. (1970), S. 171–191. Diese Behauptung ist, allerdings ohne markttheoretisch fundiert begründet zu sein, auch anzutreffen bei: *Herbert Krüger*: Über die Eignung des Modells «Wettbewerb» zur Sicherung des angebotenen Leistungsstandes der Massenkommunikationsmittel. Archiv für Urheber-, Film-, Funk- und Theaterrecht, Bd. 38 (1962), S. 129–144; derselbe: Die öffentlichen Massenmedien als notwendige Ergänzung der privaten Massenmedien. Frankfurt am Main und Berlin 1965.

politisch gewährleisten könne.[53] Die gegenwärtigen Konflikte zwischen Rundfunkanstalten und politischen Parteien bestätigen jedoch die Funktionsfähigkeit dieses Modells in keiner Weise, denn die institutionalisierte Repräsentation in den Rundfunkorganen, die eine Ausgewogenheit der Meinungen gewährleisten soll, kann die Staatsunabhängigkeit nicht verbürgen. Denn wie «im wirtschaftlichen Bereich die Eigengesetzlichkeit des Marktes, so setzt sich im politischen Bereich die Eigengesetzlichkeit des Kampfes um politische Mehrheiten durch»[54], der sich in den Aufsichtsorganen der Medien fortsetzt. Einmal gehören nämlich Parteienvertreter diesen Gremien an und zum anderen neigen die gesellschaftlich relevanten Gruppen in ihren Verhaltensweisen den ihnen nahestehenden Parteien zu, so daß eine Oligopolisierung der Kontrollkompetenz eintritt. Außerdem setzt eine Repräsentation gesellschaftlicher Meinungen immer auch Kriterien zur Abgrenzung der relevanten Gruppen und zur Festsetzung der Zahl ihrer Vertreter voraus. Es ist jedoch ein Irrglaube, anzunehmen, man könne in einer pluralistischen Gesellschaft hierfür jemals einen zuverlässigen Schlüssel finden, so daß auf diesem Wege keineswegs Meinungsvielfalt zu garantieren ist. Bedenkt man noch, daß die zum Zuge kommenden Gruppen selbst der Kontrolle durch die öffentliche Meinung zu unterwerfen sind, weil sie über eine große Autonomie und über beträchtliches politisches Gewicht verfügen, dann ist es sicherlich zweifelhaft, ob gerade sie für die Aufgabe besonders qualifiziert sind, eine ausgewogene öffentliche Meinung zu garantieren.

Ferner wird argumentiert, die öffentliche Meinung sei ein soziales Gut, für das in wettbewerblichen Marktprozessen nur eine suboptimale Versorgung zu erzielen sei.[55] Bei einem öffentlichen Gut funktioniert bekanntlich nicht das bei privaten Gütern über den Preis wirkende Ausschlußprinzip. Deshalb wirft *Jochen Röpke* die Frage auf, ob die Staatsbürger als Nutznießer des sozialen Gutes öffentliche Meinung bereit wären, die Produktionskosten zu tragen, «wenn ihnen gleichzeitig verfassungsrechtlich garantiert ist, daß sie vom ‹Gebrauch› des Gutes nicht ausgeschlossen werden können».[56] Nimmt man das Ausschlußkriterium als Anhaltspunkt für eine wirklich scharfe Grenzziehung zwischen den einzelnen Güterkategorien, so gibt es in der Realität wenig eindeutig private und ebensowenig eindeutig öffentliche Güter. Gewöhnlich treten Mischformen auf, die jeweils mehr zur einen oder anderen Seite hin tendieren. Von der öffentlichen Aufgabe der Sicherung von Meinungsfreiheit her gesehen, sind der öffentlichen Meinung Elemente eines Kollektivgutes eigen, so vor allem Nichttrivialität beim Verbrauch, die privatwirtschaftlich-wettbewerbliche Marktprozesse stören kann. Freilich darf man aber auch nicht die Gegengewichte übersehen, die geeignet sind, diese Störfaktoren abzumildern.[57] So ist das ‹Meinungsangebot› aus der Natur der Sache heraus durch eine ungeheure Produktdifferenzierung gekennzeichnet, die zugleich noch durch das Urheberrecht abgesichert wird. Zwar wird man für diesen Fall einer eigentlich ‹übermäßigen› Produktdifferenzierung in einer Marktanalyse Wettbewerbsbeschränkungen nachweisen können, doch solange eine hinreichend große Zahl selbständiger Unternehmen die Angebotsseite besetzt, wäre die Meinungsvielfalt nicht in Gefahr, zumal die einzelnen Anbieter bei einer derartigen Marktsituation gewöhnlich auch hinreichend hohe Gewinne erzielen. Darüber hinaus sind weitere marktpolitische Datensetzungen durch den Staat er-

---

[53] Zur Kritik an diesem Modell siehe *Ernst-Joachim Mestmäcker*: Medienkonzentration . . ., a. a. O., S. 17–21.

[54] Ebenda, S. 20.

[55] Neben den angeführten Arbeiten von *Jochen Röpke* vgl. auch: *Egon Sohmen*: Marktwirtschaft, Presse und Werbung. Tübingen 1971, S. 6–8.

[56] *Jochen Röpke:* Wettbewerb . . ., a. a. O., S. 185.

[57] Siehe: *Bruce M. Owen*: a. a. O., S. 18–20.

forderlich, um eine dezentrale privatwirtschaftliche Funktionsweise von Meinungsmärkten zu verbessern und zu verankern, was im einzelnen markttheoretisch noch nicht untersucht ist. Die Grundsätze einer freiheitlichen Ordnung gebieten es, diesen Weg einzuschlagen, denn die Alternative hieße staatliche Regulierung mit der Gefahr obrigkeitlicher Bevormundung der Meinungsbildung, die damit wohl ihre Freiheit einbüßen müßte.

Summary

Freedom of Opinion and Competition

According to *Hayek*, freedom of speech and liberty of discussion are inseparably related to a free democratic order. The precondition for free formation of opinion is the right to acquire information as well as the right to freely express one's opinion and to exchange information.

‹Public opinion› as the link between the individual and the institutional side of freedom of speech is the result of the process of free formation of opinion analogous to market results stemming from competition, in which the information of the individual participants are countinuously mutually adjusted. Free formation of opinion therefore represents, like competition, a process of discovery, providing economic participants with all the necessary information. The information potential is unknown in advance since it only starts with the process of the free formation of opinion, so that the result, ‹public opinion›, cannot be foreseen in detail.

Freedom of speech is also of importance to economic policy and its fundamentals in shaping the economic order. The keystone of every market economy is the co-ordination principle of competitive market processes by which a variety of single economic plans is automatically coordinated. Therefore, the extent, to which the information is exploited, depends on the circumstances of competition in every single market. In markets, where restraints of competition exist, the exploitation of possible sources of information decreases significantly. These restraints can be of private origin and / or caused by official market interventions. If, however, the possibility exists for producers and consumers to express their opinion, there will be the necessary signals guiding the economic agent in their economic actions.

Public opinion is dominated, without question, by those market processes in which the Press, Radio, and Television act as the most important suppliers of news and opinions. There, the market circumstances are characterised by restraints of competition of all kinds. But the change in media technology could make it possible – if this chance is taken – to reduce restraints of competition and to eliminate them for the future, because only the variety of mass-media makes freedom of speech possible.

V. Wettbewerb

Israel M. Kirzner

Entrepreneurship, Choice, and Freedom

The concept of freedom is a notoriously difficult one to pin down. Philosophers and social scientists have exercised extraordinary ingenuity and subtlety in order to identify the slight variations in shades of meaning separating the many writers who have attempted to define freedom. In this paper it will be argued that economists, perhaps more than others, have been subject to strong temptation altogether to overlook what should surely be considered an important, if not the essential, aspect of human freedom. The task of pointing out the source of this possible confusion presents, it will turn out, an opportunity worthwhile not only for its own sake, but also for the help it can provide in understanding the role of freedom in achieving social efficiency, and in assessing the consequences for society of its curtailment. Professor *Stigler* has recently challenged those who see the growth of the modern state as a danger to liberty, to specify concretely the liberties that have been in fact impaired by this growth.[1] I shall argue that a proper understanding of liberty suggests that, in the very nature of things, such specification cannot be expected; moreover such proper understanding, it can be shown, reveals the loss of liberty that results from the growth of government, in a manner sufficiently convincing to render such specification hardly necessary.

I. Freedom, Choice, and Economics

Among the multitude of meanings attached to the notion of freedom, it is widely held to pertain to some or other aspect of choice. And it is this circumstance that seems responsible for what we shall argue to be the overly narrow perception of individual freedom which holds peculiar temptation for economists. Choice is, after all, very much a matter of concern to the economist. Efficiency – the norm for economic discussion – has everything to do with correct choice; rationality in choice is the assumption basic to the main body of economic theory; and economics itself is defined in terms of the choices men make concerning the allocation of scarce means to satisfy multiple competing ends. But this preoccupation by the economist with choice, it may be argued, is responsible for the incomplete appreciation of freedom which seems to pervade much economic literature.

The problem is easily presented. Choice, for the economist, has come to mean the solution of a maximization problem. The economist sees the decision-maker, whether consumer, producer, or resource-owner, as allocating given means in such a way as to maximize the value of ends attained, (with the relative rankings of the various ends seen as given). Freedom of choice refers to the liberty enjoyed by the agent of selecting those courses of action which he himself sees as maximizing his utility (or profit, or whatever

[1] G. J. *Stigler*, «Reflections on Liberty», in: The Citizen and the State (Chicago 1975), p. 14.

else is seen as being maximized). Limitations on freedom take the form of prohibitions or constraints which prevent the attainment of goals that might otherwise be selected.

Basic to choice for the economist, then, is the given character of both ends and means.[2] The hierarchy of ends worthy of attainment is a given one; the constellation of means capable of achieving the various ends is also given. The act of choice is seen as occurring within the framework of this given ranking of ends and constellation of means. Freedom of choice, as well limitations on such freedom, are, then, viewed only as they impinge on the situation of the economizing individual facing his given ends-means framework. No matter what constraints, limitations, or prohibitions may be imposed on the economizing individual, they touch his freedom of choice not at all, for the economist, so long as they do not affect the individual's ability to achieve the optimum position relevant to (and implicit in) the given ends-means environment.

And it is here that scope for confusion is to be found. No matter how important the problem of efficient decision-making, against the background of given ends and means may be, it represents only one narrow aspect of the human condition. As Mises[3], Shackle[4], and Lachmann[5], have again and again reminded us, the economist's view of the decision abstracts from elements that are crucial to the true character of human choice. The notion of given ends and means may be a useful one for certain purposes, but it does serious violence to the full reality of choice. Acting man never does approach the moment of decision already equipped with a clear, «given», picture of the relevant ends and means. It is only at the moment of decision itself that man is compelled to bring to some kind of focus all his doubts and conjectures concerning what goals are worthwhile pursuing and what resources and technologies are available. The choices of men subject to unexplainable whims and taste-changes – operating in a world the realities of which are by no means immediately apparent, and which moreover are themselves characterized by continuous, kaleidic change – can hardly be subsumed, without serious strain, under the heading of maximizing calculations.

Once this broader view of choice is recognized, the notion of freedom of choice is surely seen to mean far more than the ability to realize a calculated optimum position. Freedom of choice can now be seen to encompass the liberty to make up one's own mind as to the ranking of the ends to be pursued, and concerning the means to be judged available for the purpose. Once a given ends-means framework has been adopted, freedom can only mean the freedom to achieve that which one has already announced that one wishes to achieve. It is apparently this narrow view of freedom which many economists seem to have adopted. But, with acting man seen as approaching choice with no one framework of ends and means having been yet firmly adopted, freedom in choice is at once seen as freedom to announce (i. e. to choose) what it is that one wishes to achieve.

We may, to put it more bluntly, say that the «narrow» view of freedom which we have attributed to the standard economist's conception of choice, turns out to involve no choice at all. One has, in this conception of choice, in effect already chosen before the

---

[2] This was very clearly recognized in the earliest writings in which the economist's view of choice was spelled out. See L. *Robbins*, The Nature and Significance of Economic Science (2nd Edition, London 1935), pp. 12, 24, 33, 46; F. H. *Knight*, «The Nature of Economic Science in Some Recent Discussion», American Economic Review, 24, June 1934, p. 229.

[3] See on this *I. M. Kirzner*, The Economic Point of View (Van Nostrand, 1960), pp. 161f., Competition and Entrepreneurship (Chicago 1973), pp. 33f.

[4] See e. g. *G. L. S. Shackle*, Epistemics and Economics, A Critique of Economic Doctrines (Cambridge 1972), for countless observations on this matter, (many of them indexed under «choice»).

[5] *L. M. Lachmann*, «From Mises to Shackle; An Essay on Austrian Economics and the Kaleidic Society», Journal of Economic Literature, 14, March 1976.

moment of decision. With given ranking of ends and with given means, the optimum position is fully implied in the data. Freedom, as well as its curtailment, can under such assumed circumstances, refer only to the ability (or its curtailment) to achieve a given goal.[6] On the other hand the wider view of freedom recognizes that when men refer to the freedom to choose they have in mind liberty to select among a wide range of moral and value frameworks, of ethical systems, of tastes; they have in mind liberty to make their own guesses concerning present realities and future uncertainties; they have in mind liberty to determine for themselves what opportunities they are in fact confronted with.

The above discussion can be stated concisely, using the contrast which the writer has elsewhere drawn between the «Robbinsian», allocation, maximizing, view of the economizing decision, and the «Misesian», entrepreneurial view of human action.[7] For the Robbinsian decision-maker freedom means freedom to proceed to where one (already) wishes to be; for the Misesian entrepreneurial human agent, freedom means freedom to discover and to determine for oneself where it is that one wishes to be.[8]

II. Freedom and Power

The foregoing may throw light on the much discussed confusions surrounding the distinction between freedom and power. Economists have tended to succumb to the temptation to define freedom in such a way as to make it indistinguishable from power. For

---

[6] It is true that the given framework of ends and means is seen as that of the decision-maker himself – the goal referred to in the text is the agent's «own» goal – but freedom is not, in the narrow view, referred back to the choice process by which that framework came to have been adopted as the relevant one.

[7] See: Competition and Entrepreneurship, pp. 33f.

[8] The distinction drawn here between the narrow, «economist's» view on freedom, and the broader «entrepreneurial» view, has not, to the writer's knowledge, been made in the literature. In the philosophical literature, it seems rather clear, many writers had the broader view in mind – apparently without dreaming of the possibility of the narrower view. Many of the writers cited by *Mortimer J. Adler* in Chapter 24 of his The Idea of Freedom (Garden City 1958), «Creativity Through Choice as an Element in the Meaning of Self-Determination» – appear to fall into this class. Among economists F. H. *Knight*, whose writings on freedom have been the most voluminous, complex, and difficult, appeared possibly to have at least glimpsed the broader view in a number of passages. «In economic discussion liberty means the right of the individual to choose his own ends and the means or procedure most effective for realizing them.» F. H. *Knight*, Freedom and Reform, (New York 1947, p. 377). «In practical application, the doctrine of maximum individual freedom necessitates . . . that the individual is the final judge of the means to his own happiness, as well as of the result.» (Ibid. p. 2.) *Isaiah Berlin* has explored *J. S. Mill's* views on human freedom in terms which perhaps suggest the importance of the distinction argued in this paper, *Berlin* attributes to *Mill* a view of freedom which sees man as «The seeker of ends, . . . with the corollary that . . . the larger the field of interplay between individuals, the greater the opportunities of the new and the unexpected; the more numerous the possibilities for altering his own character in some fresh or unexplored direction . . .» (*I. Berlin*, «John Stuart Mill and the Ends of Life», in: Four Essays on Liberty (Oxford University Press, 1969), p. 178. «Mill believes», *Berlin* maintains, «that man is spontaneous, that he has freedom of choice, that he moulds his own character . . . *Mill's* entire view of human nature turns out to rest not on the notion of the repetition of an identical pattern, but on his perception of human lives as subject to perpetual incompleteness, self-transformation, and novelty . . .» (Ibid. p. 189).

these writers freedom means simply the ability to attain what one wishes to attain.[9] A small number of writers, notable among economists being Professor *Hayek*[10] and Professor *Machlup*[11], have emphatically denounced the confusion involved in blurring the distinction between freedom and power. A number of writers (perhaps *Knight* should be listed as the most notable among these[12]) have, while recognizing that freedom is not the same as power, somehow offered formulations of the concept of freedom which turn out to involve substantial identification of it with power, after all. Our earlier discussion can be helpful in clarifying the issues. Let us consider what has changed when a particular option, hitherto available to a decision-maker, is somehow removed from the list of possibilities. In particular let us ask what this change may possibly be considered to have done to the «freedom of choice» of that decision-maker.

Now, from a Robbinsian point of view (seeing the decision-maker as having already, before the act of choice, become fully aware of the options available to him, and having already determined his ranking of conceivable outcomes), it should be apparent that the removal of an option that had hitherto been available may mean one of two things. If the option in question was one which the Robbinsian decision-maker would not have adopted, then its removal has no effect whatsoever. Since, even before his moment of decision, the decision-maker had already adopted a well-defined ends-means framework, courses of action that are dominated by the optimal solution, are simply irrelevant – they have been inexorably declared to be irrelevant by the structure of the ends-means framework taken as a datum. On the other hand, should the option that has been removed have been the optimal one, then of course its removal affects our decision-maker in a very significant way. But it is important for us not to misinterpret in what this effect consists. What has occurred is that there was a course of action which the decision-maker wished to adopt, that has been denied to him. He may well be bitterly disappointed at having an anticipated desirable experience pulled out of his reach. If the removal of this option was brought about by human design, he may well be outraged by its loss. He may denounce the loss as a violation of a commitment made to him, or he may denounce it as a violation of a right which he possessed, or as sheer robbery, but he will not be able to describe it as having affected his freedom to choose. To be sure his maximizing decision must now be recalculated, from among those other courses of action which had hitherto been rejected as suboptimal. The second-best solution now steps up into first place. But this does constitute a restriction on freedom of choice. (If there is a line of standby passengers – standing in order of priority – hoping to get on to a particular flight, and there is only one seat available, the person standing at the head of the line will get on the plane. If, just before being permitted to enter the aircraft this individual is suddenly removed from the line – for whatever reason – the passenger second-in-line now steps up to the head of the line.

---

[9] A clear example is that offered by *T. G. Moore*'s interesting suggestion for measuring the degree of freedom in a society. *Moore*'s thesis is «that freedom can be defined in terms of welfare. A change in the cost of action . . . can be considered to be a movement toward freedom if it increases welfare . . . If the cost to the individual of performing some action is lowered without affecting the cost to others, then we will consider that a movement toward a freer society.» (*T. G. Moore*, «An Economic Analysis of the Concept of Freedom.» Journal of Political Economy, 77, July / August, 1969, pp. 532f.)

[10] *F. A. Hayek*, The Constitution of Liberty (Chicago 1960), pp. 16ff.

[11] *F. Machlup*, «Liberalism and the Choice of Freedoms», in *E. Streissler* (ed.), Roads to Freedom, Essays in Honor of Friedrich A. von Hayek (London 1969), pp. 124ff.

[12] On some of the difficulties in *Knight*'s discussions of freedom, see *Machlup*, op. cit. pp. 129f.; *F. A. Hayek*, The Constitution of Liberty, loc. cit., p. 422, n. 7.

The relative positions of the individuals in line has already marked out the priority rank-ing, no selection needs to be made as to who is to be admitted. The removal of the first passenger does not, therefore, create any new need to choose. It would not be correct to say that the removal of the first passenger has restricted freedom of choice with respect to who is to be permitted on the plane, because the line of waiting hopeful passengers is a shorter one.) So that, for Robbinsian decision making, the removal of a preferred option does not interfere with the decision-maker's «freedom of choice». In fact, as was pointed out in the preceding section, the Robbinsian decision-maker never does have to choose – in the true sense of the word. If, nonetheless, the removal of a preferred option does, in some crude use of language, come to be described as somehow cramping the freedom of choice of the decision-maker, then this can be understood only as consisting in the restric-tion imposed on the decision-maker's ability to achieve definite goals. Freedom has, in the Robbinsian framework, come inevitably to be merged with the concept of power to achieve goals.

On the other hand, from the perspective of acting man as an entrepreneur for whom the task of deciding embraces the very identification and ranking of ends, and recognition of means, the matter seems altogether different. From this perspective the removal of an option does indeed interfere with the decision-maker's freedom of choice. For the human agent, seen as entrepreneur, each available course of action is, quite possibly, the optimal one. In fact, it is the essence of choice, in this context, to choose the optimal course of ac-tion – not in the sense of figuring out the solution to a maximization problem (where the solution is already determined by the rankings assumed in the data), but in the sense of choosing the ranking itself. So that the removal of an option does indeed affect freedom of choice. This is so not because its removal denies the decision-maker something he wi-shes to attain; (before the act of choice it has not yet been determined which option he does in fact wish to attain). The removal of an option restrictively alters the range from which choice may be made. Even if the lost option would – in some not well-defined sense – have been a rejected course of action, its removal nonetheless still constitutes an interference with freedom of choice. At the moment of choice this option was a possible option, it had not yet been rejected either explicitly (through choice) or implicitly (through the given structure of some already-adopted ends-means framework.)

III. Freedom and the Range of Alternatives

Is freedom increased by the addition of options which the decision-maker will not adopt (because he prefers one of the existing options)? Is freedom restricted by the remov-al of options which the decision-maker would anyway have rejected? The discussion in the preceding section can throw light on these questions, which have been raised from time to time in the literature of freedom.

Locke maintained that even if a prisoner does not wish to leave his cell, he is nonethe-less not a free man because the option of leaving his cell is not available to him. If the ac-tion voluntarily taken by a man is the only one available to him, «he is not free, though perhaps the action is voluntary».[13] *Knight,* on the other hand, argued that a fence along the edge of a ravine does not restrict the freedom of hikers, since they would not wish to

---

[13] *J. Locke,* Essay Concerning Human Understanding, Vol. I Book II, Chapter 21, Sect. 8. See the discussion of *Locke*'s view in *M. J. Adler,* The Idea of Freedom, p. 115f.

fall over the edge anyway.[14] As we have seen, the issue appears to revolve round the distinction between Robbinsian «maximizing» decisions, and Misesian «entrepreneurial» choice.

If *Locke's* prisoner, who loves his cell beyond any other place he can imagine, is to be seen as not free, this can only mean that one considers the possibility of what the prisoner would be at liberty to do were he to change his mind. Clearly this is relevant only if one admits the possibility of escaping from a given Robbinsian framework in which one has one's mind already fully made up (except for the chore of calculation). *Knight's* fence may be declared innocent of interfering with the freedom of hikers only because one views them as having already adopted a framework of ends which, however tentative and fluid, is yet seen as definitely ranking suicide below all other conceivable options.

Professor *Machlup*, who insists strongly on maintaining the sharp distinction between freedom and power, has drawn attention to the possibility that an increment of freedom may itself inspire the acquisition of power. «In other words, certain freedoms may be of great importance for individuals and for society when no knowledge, no opportunity, and no power exist as yet to make use of presumably ‹empty› freedoms. Their importance lies in the aspirations and ambitions which they arouse and which may lead to the search for the knowledge, opportunity, and power that are required to exercise the previously unused freedoms..»[15] *Machlup* has in mind a potential option for the attainment of which the decision-maker lacks the physical power. So long as he is debarred by human restrictions from exercising this option (even if he had the physical power to do so), he will not expend the effort or search for the knowledge required to win this physical power. The acquisition of freedom from human restrictions may inspire the discovery of ways of overcoming the physical obstacles to exercising the option. This very interesting possibility raised by *Machlup* provides an excellent example to illustrate our position.

On the face of it *Machlup*'s case appears difficult to understand. There is, we take it, some course of action for which certain inputs are required in order for it to be implemented. These inputs may be physical in character, or they may take the form of knowledge, services of various kinds, and the like. Now either the individual under consideration already has these inputs (or other inputs able to produce these inputs) available to him, or he does not. If he does already have them available to him, then it is not clear how the acquisition of the freedom to pursue this particular course of action can be credited with inspiring the power to do so; this power was already possessed. On the other hand, if the inputs were not available up until the moment when this freedom was acquired, then it is not clear how, merely through acquiring this freedom, our individual suddenly becomes endowed with inputs previously unavailable to him. *Machlup* uses the example of a bicycle-rider able to pedal at no more than 20 m. p. h. who did not find it worthwhile to work harder to earn money to buy a car because of a law limiting all vehicles to a maximum of 25 m. p. h. The abolition now of the legal speed limit increases his desire for a car, and he works harder to earn the money to buy it. Thus the freedom to drive at 60 m. p. h., while ineffective to one not owning a car, is effective, nonetheless, in arousing the ambition to achieve the power to exercise the previously unused freedom (to acquire a car).

But surely this example is one in which the power to acquire a car (and to drive at 60 m. p. h.) was possessed all the time. This individual always had open to him, physically,

[14] F. H. *Knight*, «The Meaning of Freedom», in C. M. *Perry*, (ed.), The Philosophy of American Democracy (Chicago 1943), p. 65.
[15] *Machlup*, op. cit. p. 130.

the option of working harder to earn money to buy the car; he did not exercise this option because of the existence of the speed limit, which made this option not worthwhile. *Machlup* uses this example to show that «actual capacity» may be «created only after the freedom is established». It is true that the individual, up until the lifting of the speed limit, had no car and thus lacked the «actual capacity» to drive at 60 m. p. h. immediately; but he certainly did not lack the actual capacity to acquire the car, and thus, indirectly, to drive at 60 m. p. h. It is true that the freedom acquired to drive at 60 m. p. h. converted the «potential» of owning a car, into a «reality». It is not, however, clear how this constitutes an expansion of «power» in any sense relevant to economic discussion.

What *Machlup* has noticed for us, it appears, is something highly significant (although *Machlup*'s example, or his exposition of it, does not seem to be sufficiently clear). The point concerns the acquisition of freedom to pursue a particular course of action for which the individual indeed possessed the necessary inputs – but the very possibility of which has escaped his entrepreneurial attention. So long as the law limits all vehicles to 25 m. p. h., a worker may not see the acquisition of a car as being within his reach at all. Opportunities of which one is prohibited to take advantage, tend not to be noticed at all. It is only when the speed limit has been lifted that an already feasible course of action comes into the decision-maker's field of vision. The acquisition of freedom may indeed be credited with inspiring the determination to achieve a specific goal. As *Machlup* has noticed, freedom is fertile in the creation of actual (i. e. perceived) opportunities. A potential opportunity not yet noticed, may, through the addition of an increment of freedom, become an actual one. The process by which potential opportunities can, in this sense, be converted into actual ones, is certainly of utmost importance for economists.

What it is wished to point out here is that this fertility of freedom, to which *Machlup* has so valuably drawn our attention, can be discussed only within the context of what we have called the broader, «entrepreneurial» concept of freedom. An increment of freedom, in this sense, may be responsible for the identification by a decision-maker of a perceived ends-means framework otherwise hidden from him. This fertility of freedom is completely excluded from the purview of the narrower, «Robbinsian» conception of freedom. Within the Robbinsian given ends-means framework, freedom means the freedom to pursue perceived, chosen courses of action. It is of the essence to this concept of freedom that all opportunities have already been given to the decision-maker in a manner that ensures his awareness of them. Under such circumstances an increment of freedom can hardly inspire new opportunities. Opportunities which may be physically possible with this increment of freedom, are opportunities which would have been equally physically feasible without it. All opportunities of which the decision-maker will be aware after the acquisition of an increment of freedom, were opportunities of which (by the rules of the Robbinsian framework) he was aware already before the increment of freedom was acquired. There is no room, within this framework, for any fertility in freedom.

IV. On Not Knowing What One Lacks

So long as freedom is perceived from what we have called the Robbinsian perspective, it becomes, we found in an earlier section, inevitable for it to become identified with the power to achieve chosen goals. Loss of freedom, quite similarly, comes to be identified with thwarted desires. Freedom comes, from such a perspective, to be something the curtailment of which triggers immediate pain. One cannot lose freedom, in this view, without feeling its loss. The matter is seen quite differently from the «entrepreneurial» perspective on freedom.

As was learned from Professor *Machlup* in the preceding section, the entrepreneurial view on freedom permits us to see how freedom to choose may inspire the discovery of opportunities that may be invisible to those from whom the freedom to choose is denied. Those from whom the freedom to choose has been denied, will, in such cases, have no inkling that they are being denied any otherwise attainable goal. One denied the right to choose to enter college may never realize that he possesses the intellectual potential to be admitted to college. Denial of freedom to choose, from this perspective, does not at all necessarily inflict the pain of thwarted desires. In fact one may lack freedom, and be convinced that one's well-being is wholly unaffected by its lack.

All this appears to be directly relevant to the challenge of Professor *Stigler* cited at the outset of this paper. *Stigler* asked for concrete specification of what liberties have in fact been impaired by the growth of the modern state. If «we canvass the population»,

Stigler claims, «we shall find few people who feel that their range of actions is seriously curtailed by the state».[16] Such a challenge takes it for granted that each impairment of liberty removes out of reach of the relevant individual or individuals some perceived and desired opportunity. To speak vaguely about loss of liberty without being able to specify precisely what opportunities have been closed off, would, on such an understanding, indeed raise serious questions concerning the reality of the loss. But, as we have seen, a broader understanding of the meaning of freedom, and of its loss, makes it entirely plausible that abrogations of freedom may indeed affect individuals without their being aware (or for that matter without the awareness of anyone else – observing social scientists included) that their welfare has been damaged by this abrogation. It is no longer a necessary condition for the existence of loss of freedom, that the loss be a felt one. It is true that *Stigler* himself seems not entirely unaware of the point here being made. He recognizes that «the most exploited of individuals probably does not feel the least bit exploited» – citing the example of the complaisant slave. But the point as seen by *Stigler* appears to rest on naive ignorance concerning the very existence of limitations of freedom, – and clearly assumes only the slightest importance in *Stigler*'s view. For us the point arises peculiarly from the entrepreneurial perspective on freedom – and is of much greater significance. We shall return later in this paper to discuss further implications of this insight.

V. The Paradox of Freedom

Our discussion of the «entrepreneurial» view on the nature of freedom can throw some light, perhaps, on the riddle to which philosophers have drawn our attention in their discussions of the relation between freedom and reason. On the one hand human choice is declared to be «free» – at least in the sense that man feels free to choose what he may. On the other hand, in the very exercise of his free choice, man discovers himself to be searching for the «correct» course of action, – so that in fact his choice is in some sense dictated by that «correct» option. From this perspective «when people . . . understand that in moral questions they are free to form their own opinions, they feel this freedom not as an emancipation but as a burden».[17] At least some philosophers have argued that no inconsistency is

---

[16] *Stigler*, ibid.
[17] R. M. *Hare*, Freedom and Reason (Oxford 1963), p. 3.

involved in this apparent paradox. «For a moral agent to choose that good which in the light of reflection approves itself as intrinsically greatest is to exercise the only freedom worth having... To choose most responsibly is to see alternative goods with full clearness and to find the greatest of them tipping the beam.»[18] No doubt these classic philosophic issues entail considerations far more profound than those raised in this paper. Nonetheless our discussion does appear to hold some relevance for these issues.

In the course of arriving at a decision on any question, man simultaneously (i) «fixes» the ends-means framework relevant to his situation, and (ii) calculates the optimal course of action relevant to that framework. The latter task is one to which freedom of choice is, in a definite sense, irrelevant; the correct answer is given, one is merely searching for it. Freedom to choose, at this level, consists entirely of the burden of calculating correctly, of avoiding mistakes. Nonetheless, because, as discussed earlier, this second task of calculation is never in fact divorced from the first step, – that of identifying the ends-means framework itself – acts of choice are never possible without a genuine sense of freedom, i. e. the unconstrained freedom to select whatever ranking of ends one may wish to uphold, or whatever set of means one may wish to recognize as being available. Now there may well be deeper levels of rationality which moral philosophers may wish to consider relevant to the very selection of a ranking of ends, but, at least at the superficial level appropriate to the economist, one source of the apparent paradox between one's sense of freedom and one's sense of the burden imposed by the rationality postulate, seems to be illuminated by the discussion in this paper.

What we now realize is that in the course of the act of choice man «freely» identifies the criteria for what will now be considered to be «correct» calculation of the optimal course of action. Ex post, one understands the course of action chosen by an individual as having been constrained by these criteria. In the calculations that are part of his actions, the individual seeks the answer dictated by these criteria. But, at the same time, the very act of choice which encompasses these calculations, encompasses also the free, undictated identification of what criteria are to be considered the relevant ones. The sense of emancipation and the sense of burden and responsibility thus both simultaneously have their places in free choice.

VI. The Social Importance of Freedom

The insights provided by the «entrepreneurial» view of freedom, enable us to understand the social implications of individual freedom, in a manner more profound than otherwise possible. Moreover these insights enable us to understand how so unnecessarily limited a view of the social significance of freedom has in fact come to be adopted by so many economists.

For most economists, individual freedom is held to carry social significance – if indeed it is so held at all – only insofar as it permits the simultaneous achievement by each market participant of an optimal course of action within a framework of given ends and means. With given technological opportunity sets, with given resource endowments, with given consumer preference functions, individual freedom allows market participants (under specified assumptions) to achieve the Paretian optimum embodied in the relevant general equilibrium solution. Restrictions on freedom by the state are therefore seen as bringing

---

[18] B. *Blanshard,* Reason and Analysis (LaSalle, Ill. 1973), p. 493.

about sub-optimal market outcomes, as viewed from the standpoint of the data. A free market in housing, it is understood, generates an equilibrium configuration of construction and of housing prices which may be in some sense optimal. Rent control, it is therefore shown, by restricting individual choices, generates sub-optimal levels of prices and production. And so forth.

All this is no doubt correct and important. But it should be clear from our earlier discussion, that it fails entirely to exhaust the full significance for society of an environment of freedom. This above view rests entirely on the assumption that available opportunities are somehow instantaneously and costlessly known to market participants. In the real world this is, however, not the case. It is here that the full significance of freedom can be glimpsed. A free society is one in which individuals are free to discover for themselves what the available range of alternatives in fact is. In his masterful critiques of the theory of central planning, *Hayek* directed attention to the circumstance that the imformation available in an economy is always scattered among countless individuals, never concentrated in the mind of a single central planner. *Hayek* pointed the need for a social institutional structure capable of organizing the scattered available scraps of information in a way capable of being brought to bear for the efficient allocation of society's resources.[19] The competitive market, *Hayek* showed us, is in fact a discovery process, one in which society discovers what options are feasible and how important they are. Freedom, *Hayek* has shown in his more recent works, is of social significance precisely because no single mind can know in advance what will be discovered by social cooperation within a free environment. The «case for freedom», *Hayek* pointed out, «rests chiefly on the recognition of the inevitable ignorance of all of us concerning a great many of the factors on which the achievement of our ends and welfare depends ... Liberty is essential in order to leave room for the unforseeable and unpredictable ... It is ... because we rarely know which of us knows best that we trust the independent and competitive efforts of many to induce the emergence of what we shall want when we see it ...[20] If we know how freedom would be used, the case for it would largely disappear.»[21] Our discussion approaches very similar conclusions from a somewhat different angle.

For us, individual freedom emerges as significant for society because it inspires each individual to discover what opportunities in fact confront him. It is not only the case, that is, that «society» – or its central planners – do not «know» all the scattered information known by individuals in a society. At any given moment each individual does not know the information in fact costlessly available to him. An environment of freedom encourages the discovery by individuals of what opportunities each of them in fact faces. If a market economy is believed to possess powerful equilibrating tendencies, these tendencies depend on freedom not only to permit – as *Hayek* showed – the social deployment of existing information; these tendencies depend on freedom also to permit (through the very same Hayekian market processes) the discovery by individuals of those opportunities (made available by the attitudes and the knowledge of fellow market participants as well as by the technological possibilities existing in nature), the grasping of which constitutes the steps in the equilibrating process.

Restrictions on economic freedom hurt society, therefore, in ways far more serious than recognized by most economists. We have drawn attention to the circumstance that, from the «entrepreneurial» view on freedom, an individual may suffer loss of freedom

---

[19] F. A. *Hayek*, «The Use of Knowledge in Society», American Economic Review, 35, September 1945.
[20] Constitution of Liberty, p. 29.
[21] Ibid. p. 31.

without realizing any loss in his welfare. We now see that an analogous situation pertains to society as a whole. Restriction of economic freedom restrains society from reaching what would have been Pareto-optimal equilibrium situations. As *Hayek* showed, this in effect means that society would not know what losses in «social welfare» have been suffered as a result of the restricted freedom – since no one can know what the market might have discovered. Our own discussion shows us that restriction of economic freedom restrains society from achieving its full potential in yet another sense – again a sense in which it may never be known that any loss of welfare has occurred at all. As we have seen in our discussion (following *Machlup*) of the «fertility of freedom» the restriction of economic freedom may inhibit individuals from discovering opportunities which they might have noticed had they been free to exploit them. Loss of freedom may thus lower individual and social achievement without anyone realizing what has been lost or what has failed to be achieved. A free society is fertile and creative in the sense that its freedom generates alertness to possibilities that may be of use to society; a restriction on the freedom of a society numbs such alertness – it blinds society to possibilities of social improvement. By the very nature of the damage that such restriction wreaks, its harmful effects on social welfare may not be able to be noticed, or measured, or specified. For the understanding of these profoundly important social consequences of economic freedom, it has been argued in this paper, economists must, in turn, deepen their understanding of the nature of freedom itself.

Summary

Entrepreneurship, Choice, and Freedom

Following *Robbins*, economists have concentrated on the analysis of decision-making in the context of given frameworks of ends and means. They have, as a result, come to treat the notion of «freedom of choice» in an unhelpfully restricted way. Freedom has come to mean the freedom to select the optimum course of action consistent with the given ends-means framework. It is argued here that a fuller notion of freedom emerges when attention is focussed on the identification and adoption of the ends-means framework to be held relevant to decision-making.

It appears that the overly restricted concept of freedom (that relevant to choice within a given ends-means framework) is responsible for the tendency among economists – a tendency deplored by Professors *Hayek* and *Machlup* – to identify freedom with power. To remove a preferred option from a decision-maker's range of choice, is, after all, to diminish his power to fulfil his goals. On the other hand, in the broader view of freedom, removal of any option – even that which will in fact not be preferred – genuinely restricts freedom of choice (since, prior to the adoption of an ends-means framework, that option might, after all, have turned out to be the preferred one).

The broader notion of freedom directs our attention to what *Machlup* has called the «fertility of freedom». Freedom encourages the discovery of opportunities as yet not noticed. The restricted view of freedom, confined to choice among given, perceived, opportunities, is unable to notice this important consequence of freedom.

For the restricted view of freedom, its curtailment necessarily means the blocking of a perceived and preferred course of action. Claims that freedom has, in a particular context, been curtailed may then properly be expected to be able to identify exactly what has been blocked. But, in the broader view on freedom, loss of freedom could well consist entirely in the loss of options as yet unperceived. One lacking freedom may in fact be entirely unaware of what he hås lost. In this broader view, therefore, to expect the consequences of loss of liberty to be listed concretely, is to display misunderstanding of the very nature of the loss.

The dual aspect to the notion of freedom identified in the paper, it is suggested, can perhaps throw light on a paradox concerning freedom that has been raised by philosophers. To be free, while generating a sense of liberation (insofar as freedom permits one to choose without constraint), nonetheless may also generate a sense of burden (insofar as a freely chosen ends-means framework then «imposes» the «obligation» to calculate the «correct» optimum relevant to that framework).

The paper concludes by drawing attention to the significance for social well-being, of the broader notion of individual freedom, and of the fertility of freedom which it makes possible.

Klaus Stern

Unternehmensphilosophie und Verfassungsordnung – die Auswirkungen der grundgesetzlichen Wirtschaftsverfassung auf die Formulierung einer Unternehmensphilosophie

In der Einleitung zu seiner grundlegenden Schrift «Die Verfassung der Freiheit», die er selbst als umfassende «Neudarstellung einer Philosophie des menschlichen Zusammenlebens» verstand[1], beklagte *Friedrich A. von Hayek* zu Recht, die Grundlagen unserer Zivilisation seien immer mehr in Vergessenheit und Mißachtung geraten, und das Interesse der Zeitgenossen richte sich viel mehr auf die Grundlagen einer Neuordnung der Gesellschaft als auf die Prinzipien, auf denen die bestehende Gesellschaftsordnung aufgebaut ist. In der Tat bedarf es gerade heute mehr denn je vielfältiger und ständig zu wiederholender Bemühungen, um deutlich zu machen, welches die fundamentalen Grundsätze und Normen sind, die unserer freiheitlichen Ordnung zugrunde liegen. Dieser Aufgabe hat sich der Jubilar in unermüdlicher Weise, zuletzt wieder in seinen drei Vorlesungen über Demokratie, Gerechtigkeit und Sozialismus[2] mit unbestechlicher Prägnanz unterzogen. Diesem Ziel wollen auch die folgenden Betrachtungen dienen, die einem der hervorragendsten Nationalökonomen unserer Zeit, dem Nobelpreisträger für Wirtschaftswissenschaften des Jahres 1974, gewidmet sind.

I. Wirtschaftsverfassung und Unternehmensphilosophie in staatsrechtlicher Betrachtungsweise

Zwei Begriffe sind in dem gewählten Thema zentral: grundgesetzliche Wirtschaftsverfassung und Unternehmensphilosophie. Beide könnten – und werden es verschiedentlich auch – mit einem Fragezeichen versehen werden, z.B. deshalb, weil «so etwas» gar nicht existiere; zu Unrecht, wie zu zeigen sein wird. Eingeräumt sei allerdings, daß beide Begriffe Kennzeichnungen für höchst komplexe Tatbestände und komplizierte Zusammenhänge sind, die einer Präzisierung und genauerer Erläuterung bedürfen.

Beide Begriffe führen offensichtlich Staatsrechtswissenschaft, Philosophie und Wirtschaftswissenschaft zusammen – Wissenschaftsdisziplinen, die aus *einer* wissenschaftlichen Kompetenz kaum bewältigt werden können. Wenn der Staatsrechtswissenschaftler zu diesem Thema Stellung nimmt, so wird er naturgemäß bestimmte juristische Akzente hervorheben. Gerade dies scheint mir in besonderem Maße geboten zu sein, weil die sich aus dem Verfassungsrecht ergebenden Konsequenzen für ökonomische Themata derzeit

---

[1] Tübingen 1971, S. 2 (engl. Originalausgabe: The Constitution of Liberty, London 1960). Vgl. auch *E. Grabitz,* Freiheit und Verfassungsrecht, Tübingen 1976.
[2] Heft 63 der Vorträge und Aufsätze des Walter Eucken Instituts, Tübingen 1977.

häufig nicht nur vernachlässigt, sondern geradezu mit Vorbedacht, gelegentlich sogar mit deutlicher politischer Absicht, beiseite geschoben werden. In ähnlicher Weise beklagte *H. P. Ipsen* in seiner Schrift zur kartellrechtlichen Preiskontrolle unlängst, Privatrechtswissenschaftler und Ökonomen pflegten die Existenz und Relevanz des Verfassungsrahmens, in den auch das Kartellrecht gestellt ist, nicht zu erörtern, beide operierten vielmehr durchweg «im praesumierten verfassungsrechtlichen Niemandsland».[3]. Indessen bedarf es angesichts der Allgegenwärtigkeit des Verfassungsrechts offenkundig erhöhter Sensibilität für die verfassungsrechtliche Dimension zahlreicher die Wirtschaft betreffender gesellschafts-, sozial- und wirtschaftspolitischer Vorhaben. Daraus sind intensive Bemühungen um die Interpretation des Geflechts der Verfassungsaussagen für die Wirtschaft abzuleiten. Ihnen dienten beispielsweise Referate und Diskussionen der Vereinigung der Deutschen Staatsrechtslehrer zum Thema «Unternehmen und Unternehmer in der verfassungsrechtlichen Ordnung der Wirtschaft»[4].

Einen zweiten Grund für die Berechtigung, die ökonomische Realität Unternehmen aus staatsrechtlicher Warte zu betrachten, möchte ich – wenn ich die wirtschaftswissenschaftliche Literatur zum Unternehmen[5] richtig einschätze – in der Isolierung der Betrachtung auf die unternehmerische Binnenorganisation, auf Managementprobleme und die rechtsformale Gestalt unter Hintansetzung der Standort- und Positionsbestimmung des Unternehmens in unserer Staats- und Gesellschaftsordnung sehen. Jene Probleme sind gewiß wichtig, aber solche Introvertiertheit hat wesentliche Bereiche des Unternehmensumfeldes unberücksichtigt gelassen. Gewiß ist nicht zu verkennen, daß neuerdings ein Wandel eingetreten ist. So hat z. B. *Horst Albach* in seinen einleitenden Bemerkungen zur Tagung der Gesellschaft für Wirtschafts- und Sozialwissenschaften, des Vereins für Socialpolitik, 1975 in Aachen über «Die Bedeutung gesellschaftlicher Veränderungen für die Willensbildung im Unternehmen» die Untersuchung der Wechselwirkung zwischen Gesellschaft und Unternehmen als ein Forschungsobjekt betrachtet, «das der gemeinsamen Anstrengung von Betriebswirten, Volkswirten, Soziologen und Politologen bedürfte». Der später vorgelegte gedruckte Text erwähnt glücklicherweise auch den Juristen[6]. Dazu ließe sich bemerken, daß sich der Soziologe prinzipiell jedes Themas annimmt ohne Rücksicht auf seine Kompetenz. Der Beitrag der Politologie scheint mir eher schmal zu sein; die deutsche Politische Wissenschaft hat andere Sorgen und macht andere Sorgen[7]. Daß jedoch das Unternehmen in starkem Maße Daten und Bedingungen vom Staate, besonders seinen Gesetzen und seiner Politik, erhält, bedarf deutlicher Betonung. Die folgenden Ausführungen können nur einige wesentliche Zusammenhänge aufzeigen; sie erschöpfen das Thema gewiß nicht. Zu groß ist die in Kauf genommene Verlustliste, wie sie etwa durch die Fragenkreise Selbstverwaltung, d. h. vorzugsweise Verbandsverwaltung der Wirtschaft, Einfluß des Rechts der Europäischen Gemeinschaften und damit die gesamte unternehmerische «Außenpolitik» einschließlich der Kooperation des Unternehmens mit dem Staat[8] gekennzeichnet wäre.

---

[3] Kartellrechtliche Preiskontrolle als Verfassungsfrage, Baden-Baden 1976, S. 27.
[4] Referate von *P. Saladin* und *H. J. Papier*, VVDStRL Heft 35, Berlin, New York, 1977, S. 7 ff., 55 ff. mit anschließender Diskussion; siehe dazu weiterhin *G. Püttner*, DÖV 1976, 433 ff.; *K. Wenger*, DÖV 1976, 437 ff.; *K. H. Friauf*, DÖV 1976, 624 ff.; *W. Rüfner*, DVBl 1976, 689 ff.
[5] Neueste ausführliche Nachweise im Handwörterbuch der Wirtschaftswissenschaften (HdWW) zum Stichwort Unternehmen (1978).
[6] *H. Albach – D. Sadowski* (Hrsg.), Schriften des Vereins für Socialpolitik, Bd. 88 (Berlin 1976), S. 5.
[7] Vgl. etwa *K. Stern*, Das Staatsrecht der Bundesrepublik Deutschland, Bd. I, München 1977, § 2 IV 4, 5.
[8] Dazu insbes. *H. Krüger*, Das Wirtschaftspolitische Mitwirkungsverhältnis, Frankfurt/M., Berlin 1974.

II. Der Begriff der Unternehmensphilosophie

Vorab bedarf es der Klärung dessen, was unter Unternehmensphilosophie zu verstehen ist. Hierbei geht es selbstredend nicht um die Philosophie als Wissenschaftsdisziplin, eher schon um die angelsächsische philosophy, und zwar nicht die des Unternehmensträgers oder des individuellen Unternehmers, die höchst subjektiv sein mag, sondern um die des Unternehmens, also um eine eher objektivierte Erscheinung.

Unternehmen wird dabei verstanden als jene Institution, in der Produktionsfaktoren zur Herstellung von Gütern oder Leistungen durch einen unternehmerischen Willen unter dem Gesichtspunkt ökonomischer Rationalität kombiniert werden[9]. Im hier zu untersuchenden Zusammenhang kann die Frage seines Verhältnisses zum Betrieb vernachlässigt werden[10]. Wohl aber bedarf es der Klarstellung, daß ein Unternehmen im soeben definierten Sinne Klein-, Mittel- oder Großunternehmen, daß der Unternehmensträger eine Einzelperson, eine Gesellschaft mit oder ohne eigene Rechtspersönlichkeit sein kann, daß also eine Vielfalt von Rechtsformen denkbar ist. Betrachtet man das Großunternehmen – in der Regel eine Aktiengesellschaft, als sog. Publikumsgesellschaft organisiert –, so ist dieses heute vorzugsweise Manager-, nicht mehr Eigentümerunternehmen, d. h. in ihm prägt in starkem Maße das Management den unternehmerischen Willen, nicht die Vielzahl der Eigentümer. Gerade dieses Unternehmen findet in mannigfacher Hinsicht das Interesse wirtschaftsverfassungsrechtlich relevanter Gesetzgebung. Es genügt eine kurze Nachkriegschronologie mit den Stichworten: Montanmitbestimmungsgesetz 1951, Betriebsverfassungsgesetz 1952, Mitbestimmungsergänzungsgesetz 1956, Gesetz gegen Wettbewerbsbeschränkungen 1957 mit mehreren Novellen, Aktiengesetz 1965, Publizitätsgesetz 1969, Betriebsverfassungsgesetz 1972, Mitbestimmungsgesetz 1976. Dieses große Unternehmen ist es auch, das weithin die Aufmerksamkeit einer zunehmend kritischen Öffentlichkeit auf sich zieht. In weiten Teilen steht es auch im Mittelpunkt meiner Betrachtungen.

Die Verwendung des Begriffs Unternehmens*philosophie* könnte den Eindruck erwecken, daß es hierbei – der Wissenschaft von der Philosophie entsprechend – um eine «metaphysische Letztdeutung» des Unternehmens geht. So hoch ist der Anspruch nicht gesteckt, ganz abgesehen davon, ob sich diese bei einem Gebilde von solch praller ökonomischer Realität, das höchst verschiedene Leistungen hervorbringt, die von trivialster Bedürfnisbefriedigung bis zu höheren geistigen und kulturellen Werten reichen, realisieren ließe. Unternehmensphilosophie ist in der jüngeren betriebswirtschaftlichen Fachlite-

[9] Zum rechtlichen Verständnis des Unternehmensbegriffs, der in den diversen einschlägigen Regelungsbereichen (insbesondere Wettbewerbsrecht, Arbeitsrecht, Steuerrecht) keineswegs identisch ist, vgl. BGHZ 31,105 (108 f.); *F. Brecher,* Das Unternehmen als Rechtsgegenstand, Bonn 1953; *F. Rittner,* Unternehmen und freier Beruf als Rechtsbegriffe, Tübingen 1962; *Th. Raiser,* Das Unternehmen als Organisation, Berlin 1969; *V. Emmerich,* Das Wirtschaftsrecht der öffentlichen Unternehmen, Bad Homburg 1969; *K. Wenger,* Die öffentliche Unternehmung, Wien, New York 1969, insbes. S. 259 ff.; *G. Püttner,* DÖV 1976, 433 f., *K. Tipke,* Steuerrecht, 5. Aufl. Köln 1978, S. 384 f. – Nachweise zur volks- und betriebswirtschaftlichen Terminologie bei *P. Saladin,* VVDStRL Heft 35 (1977), S. 8 f. (mit Fn. 2 und 3) und *R. Kolbeck,* HdWW 14. Lfg. 1978, S. 65 ff.

[10] Dazu zuletzt *E. Grochla,* Art. Betrieb, Betriebswirtschaft und Unternehmung, in: Handwörterbuch der Betriebswirtschaft, 4. Aufl. 1974/76, Sp. 541 ff. m.w.Nachw.; *R. Kolbeck,* HdWW, aaO, S. 65 ff.

ratur vor allem als das Phänomen verstanden, das die Stellung des Unternehmens zu der ihn umgebenden Umwelt kennzeichnet. In diesem Sinne ist zwar nicht der Begriff, aber der Sachverhalt alt; denn kein von Menschen geschaffenes Gebilde ist in einer Welt, die von jeher durch menschliche Gemeinschaften geprägt ist, seien sie nun Dörfer, Stämme, die antike Polis, der Fürstenstaat des Mittelalters oder der moderne Staat der Industriegesellschaft von heute, ohne sein soziales Umfeld faßbar und erfaßbar. Danach ist Unternehmensphilosophie definiert worden:

- als der Verhaltensrahmen, durch den die Unternehmung ihren Standort in der Umwelt findet und beibehält;
- als ethische, moralische oder kulturelle Norm;
- als Grundeinstellung des Unternehmers zu seiner Umwelt;
- als die allgemeinen Zielvorstellungen, die einerseits auf Wertvorstellungen und Motivationen der zur Willensbildung gehörenden Personen, andererseits auf deren Einschätzung von Gegebenheiten und Entwicklungstendenzen der Unternehmungen und ihrer Umwelt beruhen[11].

Zuletzt haben W. *Busse v. Colbe* und M. *Perlitz* unter Unternehmensphilosophie «die Gesamtheit der grundsätzlichen, ökonomischen, gesellschaftlichen und ethischen Wert- und Zielvorstellungen der Unternehmensleitung bezüglich des Unternehmens und seiner Stellung in der Umwelt» verstanden.[12] In diesen Definitionen steckt viel Gemeinsames; doch sind begriffliche Nuancierungen unverkennbar – bei der Spannweite von Unternehmen und Philosophie offenbar unvermeidlich. Interessant ist, daß alle Definitionen teils subjektive, teils objektive Kriterien einfließen lassen, wobei einmal diese, das andere Mal jene betont werden.

Zu Beginn habe ich hervorgehoben, das subjektive Moment, die philosophy des individuellen Unternehmers, aus meinen Ausführungen heraushalten zu wollen und auf das Unternehmen als solches abzustellen. Gewiß ist dies nur bis zu einem gewissen Grade möglich; denn das Unternehmen ohne Unternehmer ist ein Unding[13]. Im Lichte einer Unternehmensphilosophie sind es namentlich die folgenden individuellen unternehmerischen Entscheidungen:

- Einstellung zur sozialen Verantwortung,
- Einstellung zu Gewinn und Wachstum,
- Einstellung zum ökonomisch-technischen Fortschritt,
- Einstellung zum Risiko,
- Präferenz für bestimmte Produktarten, Märkte oder Technologien[14],

die entscheidend das Unternehmen determinieren. In dieser Aufzählung nehmen jedoch die unternehmensendogenen Elemente ein zu starkes Gewicht ein. Die exogenen Faktoren dürfen nicht vernachlässigt werden. Sie spielen heute angesichts der Einbettung des

---

[11] Nachweise bei R.-B. *Schmidt*, Unternehmungsphilosophie und Umweltschutz, in: Jürgen Wild (Hrsg.), Unternehmungsführung, Festschrift für E. Kosiol, Berlin 1974, S. 133 f.; siehe ferner H. *Ulrich*, Die Unternehmung als produktives soziales System, 2. Aufl. Bern, Stuttgart 1970, S. 317 ff.

[12] Art. Unternehmenspolitik, in: HdWW, 14. Lfg. 1978, S. 146, unter Bezugnahme auf G. A. *Steiner*, Top Management Planning, New York 1969.

[13] Zum Gedanken der Verselbständigung des Unternehmens *Badura-Rittner-Rüthers*, Mitbestimmungsgesetz 1976 und Grundgesetz, München 1977, S. 191 (mit Fn. 20). – Unter verfassungsrechtlichem Aspekt bedenklich erscheint allerdings eine daran orientierte bloß funktional-deskriptive Definition der Unternehmer als der «für die Geschicke der Unternehmung verantwortlichen Personen» (so aber P. *Saladin*, aaO, S. 9), da auf diese Weise das personale Eigengewicht des Unternehmers verschleiert wird.

[14] So W. *Busse von Colbe* und M. *Perlitz*, aaO, S. 146.

Unternehmens in einen vielfältigen staatlich-gesellschaftlichen Interdependenzzusammenhang eine nicht zu unterschätzende Rolle. Eine Unternehmensphilosophie muß daher Rücksicht nehmen auf die dem Unternehmen vor- und aufgegebenen staatlichen und gesellschaftlichen Grundbedingungen seiner Existenz, jene Daten und Ordnungen, die da sind, in die es hineingestellt ist, und die vorzugsweise von anderen Kräften geschaffen und geändert werden. In einem solchen Kranz von Daten, Ordnungen, Wertvorstellungen ist jedes Unternehmen eingebunden, ohne Rücksicht darauf, was es produziert oder wie groß es ist oder in welcher Rechtsform es betrieben wird. Das eine Unternehmen wird von diesen Faktoren mehr, das andere weniger berührt.

Nun liegt es auf der Hand, daß das Großunternehmen, in dem ein sehr großer Teil des Sozialprodukts erwirtschaftet wird, nicht nur in der Öffentlichkeit weitaus größeres Gewicht besitzt als das kleinere Unternehmen, sondern auch für die staatliche Wirtschaftsverfassung zentrale Bedeutung erlangt hat. Die Unternehmensgeschichte beweist dies seit der industriellen Revolution. Damit tritt unweigerlich die Frage in den Blickpunkt, was denn nun diese grundgesetzliche Wirtschaftsverfassung ist und wie sie auf die Formulierung der Unternehmensphilosophie einwirkt.

III. Die Wirtschaftsverfassung des Grundgesetzes

Die Frage nach der grundgesetzlichen Wirtschaftsverfassung bewegt die deutsche Staatsrechtswissenschaft seit den 50er Jahren[15]. Sie ist nicht damit beantwortet, daß das Grundgesetz im Gegensatz zur Weimarer Reichsverfassung einen Abschnitt «Das Wirtschaftsleben», in dem sich ein Konglomerat von liberalen, sozialen und sozialistischen Gedanken fand, nicht kennt. Sie ist auch nicht damit beantwortet, daß man das Bundesverfassungsgericht zitiert, das in seiner Entscheidung vom 20. 7. 1954[16] ausgeführt hat: «Das Grundgesetz garantiert weder die wirtschaftspolitische Neutralität der Regierungs- und Gesetzgebungsgewalt noch eine nur mit marktkonformen Mitteln zu steuernde ‹soziale Marktwirtschaft›. Die ‹wirtschaftspolitische Neutralität› des Grundgesetzes besteht lediglich darin, daß sich der Verfassungsgeber nicht ausdrücklich für ein bestimmtes Wirtschaftssystem entschieden hat. Dies ermöglicht dem Gesetzgeber die ihm jeweils

---

[15] Vgl. statt vieler *L. Raiser,* in: Festschrift für J. von Gierke, Berlin 1950, S. 181 ff.; *H. C. Nipperdey,* Soziale Marktwirtschaft und Grundgesetz, 3. Aufl. Köln 1965; *H. Krüger,* Allgemeine Staatslehre, 2. Aufl. Stuttgart 1966, S. 575 ff.; *E. R. Huber,* DÖV 1956, 97 ff., 172 ff. und 200 ff.; *K. Ballerstedt,* in: Die Grundrechte, Bd. III/1, Berlin 1958, S. 1 ff.; *H. Ehmke,* Wirtschaft und Verfassung, Karlsruhe 1961, S. 7 ff.; *H. F. Zacher,* Festschrift für F. Böhm, Karlsruhe 1965, S. 63 ff.; *H. P. Christen,* Die Wirtschaftsverfassung des Interventionismus, Zürich, St. Gallen 1970; *R. Schmidt,* Wirtschaftspolitik und Verfassung, Baden-Baden 1971, S. 135 ff.; *H. H. Rupp,* Grundgesetz und «Wirtschaftsverfassung», Tübingen 1974; *R. Scholz,* Paritätische Mitbestimmung und Grundgesetz, Berlin 1974, S. 32 ff.; *E. J. Mestmäcker,* Festschrift für F. Böhm, Tübingen 1975, S. 383 ff.; *P. Badura,* JuS 1976, 205 ff.; *M. Schmidt-Preuß,* Verfassungsrechtliche Zentralfragen staatlicher Lohn- und Preisdirigismen, Baden-Baden 1977, S. 81 ff.; *H. C. F. Liesegang,* Die verfassungsrechtliche Ordnung der Wirtschaft, Hamburg 1977; *P. J. Tettinger,* BB 1977, 1617 ff. m.w.N.; eine Zusammenschau bietet der von *U. Scheuner* herausgegebene Sammelband «Die staatliche Einwirkung auf die Wirtschaft», Frankfurt 1970. Repräsentativ für die Schweiz etwa *F. Gygi,* Die schweizerische Wirtschaftsverfassung, 2. Aufl. Basel 1978; für Österreich die Beiträge in der Festgabe für F. Korinek, Wien 1972.

[16] BVerfGE 4, 7 ff. (17 f.).

sachgemäß erscheinende Wirtschaftspolitik zu verfolgen, sofern er dabei das Grundgesetz beachtet.» Der letzte Satzteil ist nach denWorten des derzeitigen Präsidenten des Bundesverfassungsgerichts «die gewichtigste Aussage des Urteils»[17]. Man mißversteht das Bundesverfassungsgericht, wenn man daraus schließt, das Gericht würde eine grundgesetzliche Wirtschaftsverfassung schlechthin verneinen. Was es ablehnt, ist die Existenz eines «Systems», eines «Modells» (etwa im Sinne *Euckens*), einer Theorie, kurz: es votiert für eine «Modellneutralität» (*E. Grabitz*). Insofern bedarf der Begriff der Wirtschaftsverfassung aus der Sicht juristischen Begriffsverständnisses einer Präzisierung.

Im rechtswissenschaftlichen Sinne ist Wirtschaftsverfassung die Summe der verfassungsrechtlichen Normen und Prinzipien für die Ordnung der Wirtschaft.[18] Danach erweist sich eine Abschichtung gegenüber nationalökonomisch orientierten Deutungen als geboten. Sie verstehen diesen Terminus entweder als bloß faktischen Zustand einer Volkswirtschaft oder weitergehend als die Gesamtheit aller Vorschriften und Institutionen in bezug auf die Wirtschaft, als die Wirtschafsordnung[19]. Zur Wirtschaftsverfassung gehören – soll der Begriff eine heuristische Funktion erfüllen – mithin allein die im Grundgesetz niedergelegten Aussagen. Dieses aber enthält sehr wohl wirtschaftsverfassungsrechtlich relevante Vorschriften, Festlegungen für die wirtschaftliche Ordnung. Diese als Wirtschaftsverfassung zusammenzufassen ist ebenso berechtigt wie wir von Wehrverfassung, Arbeitsverfassung, Notstandsverfassung usw. sprechen. Sozialbereiche sind daher ebensowenig wie staatliche Bereiche verfassungsfrei, sondern «verfassungsdurchwirkt». In welchem Umfang dies der Fall ist, ist eine andere Frage. Jedenfalls kann die Existenz einer Wirtschaftsverfassung nicht geleugnet werden. Wenn *H. Krüger*[20] von einer Mehrzahl subkonstitutioneller Verfassungen spricht, aber nur eine Verfassung mit Verfassungsrang anerkennen will, die Staatsverfassung, so ist dies unvollständig, solange er nicht sagt, was für ihn den Staat und seine Verfassung ausmacht. Zu einer Staatsverfassung gehören jedenfalls auch die Grundlagen des Verhältnisses des Staates zu den sich nachhaltig mit dem Wirtschaften beschäftigenden Bürgern.

Natürlich ist die Wirtschaft nicht selbst Verfassungsgeber, sondern das Volk in seiner Gesamtheit. Wirtschaftsverfassung ist die Summe jener vom pouvoir constituant erlassenen Verfassungsrechtsnormen, in denen die Grundlagen für die wirtschaftliche Ordnung, das wirtschaftliche Geschehen und die staatliche Wirtschaftspolitik festgelegt sind. Nur auf dieser Basis ist es verständlich, daß das Bundesverfassungsgericht wiederholt wirtschaftspolitische Gesetze und Exekutivmaßnahmen am Maßstab des Grundgesetzes auf ihre Verfassungsmäßigkeit überprüft hat[21], wobei es an dieser Stelle nicht auf das Ergebnis ankommt, sondern die Kontrolle an sich. Ein anderer verfassungsrechtlicher

---

[17] Vgl. *E. Benda,* in: B. Gemper (Hrsg.), Marktwirtschaft und soziale Verantwortung, Köln 1973, S. 189.

[18] *K. Stern,* FamRZ 1976, 130; *R. Schmidt,* aaO, S. 98 ff., 128; *K. Korinek,* in: Wirtschaft und Verfassung in Österreich, Festgabe für F. Korinek, Wien 1972, S. 35; *M. Schmidt-Preuß,* aaO, S. 86; *J. Isensee,* Der Staat Bd. 17 (1978), S. 161 ff., 165.

[19] Siehe dazu *D. Karsten,* Schmollers Jahrbuch für Wirtschafts- und Sozialwissenschaften, Bd. 88 (1968), S. 129 ff.; *H. Lampert,* Art. Wirtschaftsordnung, Evang. Staatslex., 2. Aufl. 1975, Sp. 2934 f.; *P. J. Tettinger,* BB 1977, 1618.

[20] DÖV 1976, 618.

[21] Vgl. etwa BVerfGE 4,7 – Investitionshilfegesetz; 7, 377 – Apothekenurteil; 10,89 – Erftverband; 13,97 – Handwerk; 15,235 – Pflichtzugehörigkeit zur IHK; 16,147 – Werkfernverkehr; 19,119 – Kuponsteuer; 21,150 – Weinwirtschaftsgesetz; 23,50 – Nachtbackverbot; 29,402 – Konjunkturzuschlag; 30,250 – Absicherungsgesetz; 30,292 – Erdölbevorratung; 36,66 – Stabilitätszuschlag; 36,321 – Besteuerung des Schallplattenumsatzes; 37,1 – Weinwirtschaftsabgabe; 38,61 – Leberpfennig; 40,371 – Verbot von Werbefahrten.

Standpunkt wäre in sich fragwürdig; denn niemand kann bestreiten, daß eine Verfassung an einem inneren Widerspruch litte, wenn einer freiheitlichen, auf Parteienkonkurrenz freier Wahl, freiem Mandat, freier Presse, freier Meinung und Information basierenden Staatsverfassung nicht eine gesellschaftliche und ökonomische Verfassung entspräche, die nicht ebenso frei durch Eigentums-, Vertrags-, Koalitions-, Wettbewerbs-, Investitions-, Konsum- und Arbeitsplatzfreiheit strukturiert wäre. Es kann in *dieser* Hinsicht – was nicht heißt in jeder, wie manche sog. «Demokratisierer» meinen[22] –, nur *konstitutionelle Gleichartigkeit, strukturelle Gemeinsamkeit*, also grundsätzliche Entsprechung, geben. Die Gesamtverfassung ist wesensprägend für die Teilbereiche, wie die Teile die Gesamtverfassung gestalten. In diesem Sinne verfaßt das Grundgesetz das Gemeinwesen und in ihm auch die Wirtschaft. Das Problem der Wirtschaftsverfassung im Sinne einer Grundentscheidung der Verfassung für die in der Wirtschaft geltenden Ordnungsprinzipien besteht daher nicht in der Suche nach diesem Prinzip, sondern in der Frage nach den Grenzen, die dem Gesetzgeber und der Regierung in der Modifizierung dieses Prinzips gesetzt sind. Vergegenwärtigt man sich diesen Grundtatbestand, so ist klar, daß zentrale Planwirtschaft und Freiheit einander ausschließen, daß Lenkungs- und Kommandowirtschaft – ganz gleich, wer das Kommando führt – zu mehr Herrschaft über den Menschen führen und Freiheit negieren. Diese ordnungspolitische Differenzierung, die universale Dimension besitzt, darf nicht vernebelt werden. Besonders deutlich wird sie in ihrem Gegenbild, wenn man nämlich die Ordnung des Ostens heranzieht: Zentralverwaltungswirtschaft und politische wie bürgerliche Unfreiheit nach dem Verfassungstext und in der Verfassungwirklichkeit. So heißt es z. B. in Art 9 III der Verfassung der DDR von 1968 (i.d.F. v. 1974) lapidar: «Die Volkswirtschaft der DDR ist sozialistische Planwirtschaft». Man sollte deshalb klar erkennen, daß der Streit um die Wirtschaftsverfassung heute auch und vielleicht sogar vornehmlich Kampf um die freiheitliche Lebensordnung schlechthin ist, also um die Verfassung der Freiheit im Sinne *Hayeks*.

Die Grundentscheidung über die Wirtschaft ist nur einer Summe von Einzelentscheidungen zu entnehmen, die aber ihrerseits wieder zu einer Prinzipienentscheidung zusammengefügt werden können. Wie aus dem Bundesstaatsprinzip die ungeschriebene Bundestreue abgeleitet wird, ist aus dem Freiheitscharakter der Grundrechte ein ökonomisches Grundprinzip deduzierbar. Eine freiheitliche Verfassung kann ökonomisch ihrem Typus nach nicht *ordnungsneutral* sein; sie würde sonst das Wesen der Freiheit, die unteilbar ist, verfehlen[23].

Welche Vorschriften des Grundgesetzes sind es nun, die diese Wirtschaftsverfassung ausmachen und die vor allem[24] für das Unternehmen maßgeblich sind:
– Es ist die allgemeine Handlungsfreiheit des Art. 2 I, die auch in ökonomischer Hinsicht besteht, wie das Bundesverfassungsgericht wiederholt betont hat;[25]

[22] Vgl. insoweit *K. Stern*, Staatsrecht, § 18 III; *H. Krüger*, DÖV 1976, 619; *L. Fröhler*, in: Wirtschaft und Verfassung in Österreich, Festgabe F. Korinek, aaO, S. 99; *J. Isensee*, aaO, S. 166 ff.
[23] Vgl. *K. Wenger*, Wirtschaftspolitische Blätter 1974, 133 ff. (136 ff.) – Gegen die Neutralität zuletzt auch *H. H. Rupp*, Archiv für öffentliches Recht Bd. 101 (1976), S. 174; *K. H. Friauf*, DÖV 1976, 625; *K. H. Friauf/R. Wendt*, Eigentum am Unternehmen, Köln 1977, S. 10; *H. J. Papier*, Zeitschrift für das gesamte Handelsrecht und Wirtschaftsrecht (ZHR) 1978, S. 78; *ders.*, VVDStRL Heft 35 (1977), S. 77. – Grundlegend hierzu *F. A. von Hayek*, Die Verfassung der Freiheit, Tübingen 1971, insbes. im XV. Kapitel und im Dritten Teil.
[24] Natürlich sind auch noch andere Grundrechte als die nachstehend genannten wirtschaftsrelevant, doch nicht in gleich spezifischer Weise.
[25] Siehe BVerfGE 8,274 (328); 9,3 (11); 10,89 (99); 12,341 (347 f.); 21,87 (90 f.); 27,375 (384 f.); 29,260 (266 f.); *R. Scholz*, Archiv des öffentlichen Rechts, Bd. 100 (1975), S. 274 ff.; *Badura-Rittner-Rüthers*, aaO, S. 232 f.

- es ist die Vereinigungsfreiheit des Art. 9 I;
- es ist die Berufs- und Gewerbefreiheit des Art. 12 I;
- es ist die Eigentumsfreiheit des Art. 14 I;
- es ist die Freizügigkeit des Art. 11 I;
- es ist das System von Macht und Gegenmacht der tariflichen Koalitionen des Art. 9 III;
- es ist die Idee des sozialen Rechtsstaats der Art. 20, 28 mit ihren vielfältigen Ableitungen[26];
- es ist schließlich die Verpflichtung von Bund und Ländern auf das gesamtwirtschaftliche Gleichgewicht in Art. 109 II.[27]

Dies zusammengenommen macht die Idee einer *gesamtverfassungsrechtlichen* Freiheitsentscheidung aus, wie ich es im Mitbestimmungshearing des Deutschen Bundestags vom 19. 12. 1974[28] genannt habe.

Natürlich ist diese Freiheitsentscheidung nicht schrankenlos. Das war Freiheit im verfaßten Staat niemals. Dementsprechend kennen die vorgenannten Grundrechte Einschränkungen durch Gesetzesvorbehalte; doch sichert Art. 19 Abs. 2 GG die Präponderanz der Freiheit. Ferner gibt das Sozialstaatsprinzip der Art. 20, 28 GG dem Staat ein Mandat zu sozialpolitischem Handeln und zur Sozialbindung ökonomischen Handelns[29]. Wirtschaftspolitisches Handeln ist durch diese Verfassungsentscheidungen zwar nicht exakt festgelegt, aber vorgeformt und begrenzt, eingeordnet in ein «Koordinatensystem»[30], das den Gestaltungsspielraum der Staatsorgane einschränkt, wie es der Sinn einer Verfassung ist.

IV. Die verfassungsrechtlichen Konsequenzen für die Formulierung einer Unternehmensphilosophie, dargestellt vor allem am Beispiel der Mitbestimmungsgesetzgebung

Überträgt man dieses Geflecht wirtschaftsverfassungsrechtlicher Normen und der zu seiner Konkretisierung erlassenen Gesetze auf die Formulierung einer Unternehmensphilosophie, so wird man vorab den makroökonomischen und den mikroökonomischen Bereich zu unterscheiden haben. Zwischen beiden besteht indessen Interdependenz: Lenkungsmaßnahmen in einem Sektor färben auch auf den anderen ab. Oder anders formu-

---

[26] Vgl. dazu *K. Stern,* Das Staatsrecht, aaO, § 20 und § 21.

[27] Während die Zuordnung der vorgenannten Verfassungsrechtsnormen zur Wirtschaftsverfassung unstreitig ist, ist die Einordnung des Art. 109 Abs. 2 GG nicht zweifelsfrei; vgl. *K. Stern,* in: Stern-Münch-Hansmeyer, Gesetz zur Förderung der Stabilität und des Wachstums der Wirtschaft, Komm. 2. Aufl. Stuttgart, Berlin, Köln, Mainz 1972, S. 115; *U. Scheuner,* Die Erhaltung des gesamtwirtschaftlichen Gleichgewichts. Der verfassungsrechtliche Auftrag zur aktiven Konjunkturpolitik, in: Verfassung, Verwaltung, Finanzkontrolle, Festschrift für Hans Schäfer, Köln 1975, S. 109 ff., 112 ff.; *H. Fischer-Menshausen,* in: v. Münch, Kommentar zum Grundgesetz, Bd. III, München 1978, Art. 109 Rdnr. 8 ff.; *H. C. F. Liesegang,* aaO, S. 56 ff.; *K. Vogel/M. Wiebel,* Bonner Kommentar, Zweitbearbeitung, Art 109 Rdnr. 100; *P. Badura,* Wachstumsvorsorge und Wirtschaftsfreiheit, in: Hamburg-Deutschland-Europa, Festschrift für H. P. Ipsen, Tübingen 1977, S. 367 ff.; *G. Nicolaysen,* Wohlstandsvorsorge, ebda, S. 485 ff., 494 ff.

[28] Vgl. das Protokoll des Bundestagsausschusses für Arbeit und Sozialordnung Nr. 62 vom 19. 12. 1974, S. 122.

[29] Dazu ausführlich *K. Stern,* Staatsrecht, § 21 I 4 und III.

[30] *K. H. Friauf,* DÖV 1976, 625.

liert: Unternehmerische Freiheit im mikroökonomischen Bereich ist nicht zu verwirklichen in einem System makroökonomischer Zentralplanung. Der Blick in die Verwaltungswirtschaften des Ostens zeigt, daß nur in einem ganz begrenzten Maße Freiheit im mikroökonomischen Verhalten eingeräumt und überhaupt verwirklichungsfähig ist. Im Prinzipiellen kann es nur Homogenität geben. Das hat z.B. der Gesetzgeber des Stabilitäts- und Wachstumsförderungsgesetzes vom 8.6.1967 (BGBl. I S. 582) klar erkannt, wenn er wirtschafts- und finanzpolitische Maßnahmen zur Erhaltung des gesamtwirtschaftlichen Gleichgewichts nur «im Rahmen der marktwirtschaftlichen Ordnung» zuläßt.[31] Nicht zu verkennen ist allerdings, daß in diesem Bereich der sog. Globalsteuerung, also jener Lenkungsmaßnahmen, die gesamtwirtschaftliche Größen beeinflussen, im Gegensatz zum mikroökonomischen Interventionismus, der zielgerichtet und direkt das unternehmerische Handeln beeinflußt, etwa durch Subventionen, Abschöpfungen und sonstige Eingriffe, eine erhebliche Großzügigkeit sowohl in rechtlicher als auch in ökonomisch-systemkonformer Hinsicht angenommen wird. Erst in jüngster Zeit scheinen auf Grund einiger Realitäten (Staatsverschuldung, Anwachsen des Staatssektors) und bestimmter Forderungen, wie Investitionslenkung, Steuerung der Notenbank, «Demokratisierung» der Wirtschaft oder doch wenigstens stärkere Planification der Wirtschaft, die Sinne geschärft für die daraus sich ergebenden grundsätzlichen Ordnungsprobleme.

Die soeben genannten Postulate sind unzweifelhaft auch von wirtschaftsverfassungsrechtlicher Relevanz; sie stoßen auf grundgesetzliche Schranken, was nur beispielhaft verdeutlicht werden kann.

Die genannten grundrechtlichen Freiheitsrechte und die dem Strukturprinzip des sozialen Rechtsstaats immanenten Grundsätze enthalten im Kern die Entscheidung zugunsten einer Markt- und Wettbewerbswirtschaft, ein System der Dezentralisation und Pluralität von Entscheidungsbefugnissen, freilich auch der Verantwortlichkeiten und Risiken. Es besteht die Dominanz privatautonomer Führung der Wirtschaft bei nicht unerheblicher Teilhabe der öffentlichen Hand. Im sog. Feldmühle-Urteil vom 7.8.1962 hat das Bundesverfassungsgericht ausdrücklich von der «freien wirtschaftlichen Betätigung des Unternehmens» gesprochen[32]. Dieses unternehmerische Handeln fällt je nach seiner Ausprägung in den Schutzbereich verschiedener Grundrechte, der Berufs- und allgemeinen Handlungsfreiheit sowie namentlich in den des Eigentums.[33]

Hierauf ist etwas näher einzugehen, weil zwei neuere Fragenkreise dazu Anlaß geben. Es ist einmal die Diskussion um die paritätische Mitbestimmung in größeren Unternehmen[34], zum zweiten der verfassungsrechtlich eng damit verbundene Ansatz, das unter-

---

[31] Vgl. *Stern-Münch-Hansmeyer*, Komm., aaO, § 1 Anm. VI; *A. Möller*, StabG., Komm., 2. Aufl. Hannover 1969, § 1 Anm. 7.

[32] BVerfGE 14,263 (281).

[33] Zur Interpretation dieses Grundrechts siehe insbes. die aktuellen Darstellungen von *O. Kimminich*, Bonner Kommentar, Drittbearbeitung 1976; *P. Badura*, Eigentum im Verfassungsrecht der Gegenwart, 49. DJT 1972, Teil T; *W. Leisner*, Sozialbindung des Eigentums, Berlin 1972, jeweils m.w.N.; weiterhin auch *O. Issing/W. Leisner*, Kleineres Eigentum, Göttingen 1976; *E. Grabitz*, VVDStRL Heft 35 (1977), S. 151; *K. H. Friauf/R. Wendt*, Eigentum am Unternehmen, Köln 1977; *E. J. Mestmäcker*, Festschrift H. Westermann, Karlsruhe 1974, S. 414; zur Rspr. des Bundesverfassungsgerichts im Überblick zuletzt *A. Krämer*, NJW 1977, 1426 ff.

[34] Aus einem breiten Schrifttum hierzu seien an dieser Stelle nur genannt: *Badura-Rittner-Rüthers*, Mitbestimmungsgesetz 1976 und Grundgesetz, München 1977; *K. Doehring*, BB 1978, 265 ff.; *H. J. Papier*, ZHR 142 (1978), S. 71 ff.; *H. Wiedemann*, BB 1978, 5 ff.; *P. Hanau*, Zeitschrift für Unternehmens- und Gesellschaftsrecht (ZGR) 1977, 397 ff.; *M. Lieb*, Aktuelle Probleme der Mitbestimmung, in: Lernen und Entscheiden, Festschrift zum 50jährigen Bestehen des Lehrinstituts für das kommunale Sparkassen- und Kreditwesen, Stuttgart 1978, S. 125 ff.; *Th. Raiser*,

nehmerische Eigentum, wie überhaupt das Produktiveigentum aus der Schutzgarantie des Art. 14 auszuklammern und diese nur noch auf das Privateigentum des persönlichen Bedarfs zu reduzieren[35]. So wird etwa die These aufgestellt: «Unternehmen, die von der Beschäftigungsseite oder durch ihre Produktion öffentliche Bedeutung erlangen, können im Hinblick auf verfassungskräftige Rechte der Beschäftigten und der Allgemeinheit nicht Privateigentum eines beliebigen Inhabers sein»[36]. Wäre diese Behauptung richtig, so läge auf der Hand, daß damit die Entscheidungsstruktur der Wirtschaft fundamental verändert würde; denn das Unternehmen funktioniert vornehmlich auf der Grundlage des Privateigentums und der daraus sich ergebenden unternehmerischen Dispositionsfreiheit. Eigentum impliziert nicht nur die Möglichkeit wirtschaftlicher Nutzung, sondern gewährt zugleich die Berechtigung, über die in ihm inkorporierten Vermögensrechte durch Planung und zweckgerichtete Verfügung zu bestimmen[37]. Die Eigentumsgarantie gewährleistet in den Worten des Bundesverfassungsgerichts ein Ensemble von «Herrschafts-, Nutzungs- und Verfügungsrechten».[38] Wenngleich das Unternehmenseigentum funktionale Besonderheiten aufweist und nicht schlankweg pauschal mit anderen Eigentumskategorien wie Grundeigentum, Urheberrechten, Eigentum an Sachgütern hinsichtlich seiner inhaltlichen Ausformung und Eingrenzung gleichgesetzt werden kann, sondern – wie diese jeweils – in seiner konkreten rechtlichen Ausprägung von strukturgerechter gesetzgeberischer Gestaltung im Sinne von Art. 14 Abs. 1 Satz 2 GG abhängt, ist eine totale Freistellung oder partielle Abkoppelung dieser Eigentumskategorie vom Grundrechtsschutz unzulässig[39]. Mit Recht hat *Rupp*[40] betont, eine Unternehmens- und Wirtschaftsverfassung vertrage sich nicht schon dann mit dem Grundgesetz, wenn bestandsverändernde Eingriffe in individuelle Eigentümerpositionen quantitativ in der Minderheit blieben oder sich nur auf bestimmte Eigentumsformen bezögen, sondern erst dann, wenn das verfassungsrechtliche Eigentumsprinzip auch individuell gelebte konkrete Wirklichkeit bleibe. Das Eigentum schlechthin ist es, das unternehmerische Lei-

---

Grundgesetz und paritätische Mitbestimmung, Berlin 1975; *R. Scholz*, Paritätische Mitbestimmung und Grundgesetz, Berlin 1974; *P. Lerche*, Festschrift H. P. Ipsen, Tübingen 1977, S. 437 ff.; *J. Isensee*, Der Staat Bd. 17 (1978), S. 161 ff.; *K. H. Friauf/R. Wendt*, aaO, S. 76 ff. – Umfassende Literaturnachweise zur verfassungsrechtlichen, arbeitsrechtlichen und gesellschaftsrechtlichen Problematik der Mitbestimmungsgesetzgebung bei *Th. Raiser*, Mitbestimmungsgesetz, Komm., Berlin-New York 1977, Einl. S. 48 ff., 57 f. und 62; *D. Hoffmann/J. Lehmann/H. Weinmann*, Mitbestimmungsgesetz, Komm., München 1978; *K. Fitting/O. Wlotzke/H. Wißmann*, Mitbestimmungsgesetz, Komm., München 1976; *F. Fabricius* (Hrsg.,) Gemeinschaftskommentar zum Mitbestimmungsgesetz, Neuwied, Berlin 1976; *F. Kübler/W. Schmidt/S. Simitis*, Mitbestimmung als gesetzgebungspolitische Aufgabe, Baden-Baden 1978.

[35] So *H. Rittstieg*, Eigentum als Verfassungsproblem, Darmstadt 1975, S. 361.

[36] *Ders.*, aaO. – Auf dieser Linie liegt auch die Argumentation, das Eigentum könne «keinen Rechtstitel über Menschen» geben; so etwa *R. Richardi*, in: Das Arbeitsrecht der Gegenwart, Bd. 13 (1976), S. 27; *E. Stein*, Staatsrecht, 6. Aufl. Tübingen 1978, S. 163 und 189; *A. Podlech*, Der Staat 15 (1976), S. 46. Dazu bereits *Badura-Rittner-Rüthers*, aaO, S. 214 f.; *H. H. Rupp*, Grundgesetz und «Wirtschaftsverfassung», Tübingen 1974, S. 30; *H. J. Papier*, aaO, S. 75.

[37] So zu Recht *U. Scheuner*, Die staatliche Einwirkung auf die Wirtschaft, Frankfurt 1971, S. 49 f.; siehe auch *H. J. Papier*, ZHR 142 (1978), S. 76 f.; *J. Isensee*, aaO, S. 174; *F. Böhm*, in: Das Unternehmen in der Rechtsordnung, Festgabe H. Kronstein, Karlsruhe 1967, S. 11 ff.; *H. J. Wipfelder*, in: Recht und Staat, Festschrift G. Küchenhoff, Berlin 1972, S. 747 ff. (761): Art. 14 GG schützt «die unternehmerische Eigeninitiative auf der Grundlage des Privateigentums».

[38] BVerfGE 31, 229 (239).

[39] Vgl. *K. H. Friauf*, DÖV 1976, 626 f.; *ders.* mit *R. Wendt*, Eigentum am Unternehmen, Köln 1977.

[40] Grundgesetz und «Wirtschaftsverfassung», S. 25.

tungsmacht legitimiert, in der Sprache des Bundesverfassungsgerichts «die freie wirtschaftliche Betätigung des Unternehmens in der Richtung auf einen gemeinsamen Gesellschaftszweck der Aktionäre und die Konkretisierung dieses Zwecks auf Grund eines den Aktionären letzten Endes gemeinsamen Interesses»[41]. Es ist mithin ein entscheidendes Datum jeder Unternehmensphilosophie.

Auch das Managerunternehmen ist nicht «Unternehmen an sich», nicht aus der Eigentums- und Vereinigungsfreiheit dergestalt entlassen, daß der Aktionär sein Eigentum etwa einem «Sozialverband» überlassen hätte, der dann als solcher abgelöst vom Eigentumsrecht geformt werden könnte[42]. Das Recht des Anteilseigners lebt in der Delegation seiner Eigentümerposition auf Leute seines Vertrauens in der Nutzbarmachung seines Eigentums fort. Ihm verbleibt auch das Risiko. Das Bundesverfassungsgericht sah in der Aktie ausdrücklich «gesellschaftsrechtlich vermitteltes Eigentum»[43]. In ihr verkörpern sich zugleich Vermögenswerte wie auch Mitgliedschaftsrechte[44]. Diese essentiellen Komponenten der Privatnützigkeit[45] des Aktionärseigentums dürfen nicht aus gesellschaftspolitischen Motiven heraus schlichtweg auseinanderdividiert werden. Es wäre verfehlt, die Augen davor zu verschließen, daß diese Kategorie des Privateigentums, wie sie uns heute im Rahmen der Organisationsform des Großunternehmens begegnet, ein arbeitsteiliges, durch Delegation und Zusammenfassung wirksames Eigentumsgefüge darstellt, das vielfache moderne wirtschaftliche und funktionale Anforderungen erfüllt. Auch im Großunternehmen beruhen die wesentlichen Aufgaben der Kapitallenkung, der Personalauswahl und der wirtschaftlichen Leitung letztlich auf Entscheidungen der Aktionärs-Eigentümer[46]. Gewiß ist in der großen Publikumsgesellschaft die «Legitimationsbasis atomisiert»[47]; sie ist es aber nicht minder, eher noch stärker bei der Legitimationskette für die Staatsgewalt. Wer hier die «Mündigkeit» betont, darf sie dort nicht aus dem Auge verlieren.

In der Mitbestimmungsgesetzgebung geht es in verfassungsrechtlicher Hinsicht um zwei Grundfragen:

Erstens: Verliert der Inhaber des unternehmensrechtlichen Eigentums den ausschlaggebenden, maßgeblichen Einfluß in der Leitung und Ausrichtung des Unternehmens durch ihn selbst oder durch von ihm legitimierte Vertrauenspersonen? Jedenfalls für die strikt paritätische Mitbestimmung des ersten Entwurfs der Bundesregierung war das zu bejahen[48]. Sehr viel schwieriger wird die Frage für die wohl nur funktionell paritätische Regelung des Mitbestimmungsgesetzes 1976 zu beantworten sein. Der sog. Stichentscheid darf jedenfalls nicht überschätzt werden.

Zweitens: Wird durch die Mitbestimmung die Unternehmensverfassung aus der we-

---

[41] BVerfGE 14,263 (281); zu Recht spricht es daher von einer «Wirtschaft freier Unternehmer auf der Grundlage des Privateigentums und freier Kapitaldisposition» (aaO, S. 282); siehe auch *U. Scheuner,* aaO, S. 50 f.

[42] Dazu *Badura-Rittner-Rüthers,* aaO, S. 211 (mit Fn. 84).

[43] BVerfGE 14,263 (276); 25, 371 (407).

[44] BVerfGE 14,263 (285); 25,371 (407); vgl. auch *Badura-Rittner-Rüthers,* aaO, S. 202 f.; *Friauf/Wendt,* aaO, S. 53 ff.

[45] Zu dieser wesensbestimmenden Funktion des Eigentums BVerfGE 31,229 (240) mit 24,367 (389 f.), 26,215 (222); *R. Reinhardt,* in: Reinhardt/Scheuner, Verfassungsschutz des Eigentums, Tübingen 1954, S. 14 ff.; *Badura/Rittner/Rüthers,* aaO, S. 225 f.; *W. Leisner,* BB 1978, 102.

[46] *U. Scheuner,* Die staatliche Einwirkung auf die Wirtschaft, Frankfurt 1971, S. 53, unter Hinweis auf *F. Rittner,* in: Marburger Gespräche über Eigentum-Gesellschaftsrecht-Mitbestimmung, Marburg 1967, S. 68 ff.; zustimmend *Friauf/Wendt,* aaO, S. 58 f.

[47] *K. H. Friauf,* DÖV 1976, 628.

[48] Vgl. meine Stellungnahme beim Mitbestimmungs-Hearing, Prot. aaO, S. 18 ff., 121 ff.

sentlich privatrechtlich vermittelten Prävalenz der Unternehmensentscheidungsorgane in eine stärker öffentlich-rechtlich begründete, andersartig legitimierte Entscheidungsstruktur überführt, in der ein Kondominium mit den Repräsentanten der Arbeitnehmer, vornehmlich den Gewerkschaften, besteht? Auch dies war für eine strikt paritätische Mitbestimmung zu bejahen. Dahinter hätte eine Ordnungsentscheidung von erheblicher verfassungsrechtlicher Tragweite gelegen, die nicht nur die Unternehmens-, sondern auch die Sozialstruktur gewandelt, namentlich das Tarifvertragssystem, das auf gleichgewichtiger Macht und Gegenmacht beruht, aus den Angeln gehoben hätte.

Daß durch einen solchen Schritt die Unternehmensphilosophie nachhaltig beeinflußt worden wäre, ist offenkundig. Es bleibt abzuwarten, wie sie durch die knapp unter der Parität liegende Gesetz gewordene Regelung betroffen wird[49]. Das Bundesverfassungsgericht ist hier zur Klärung aufgerufen, nachdem der Vorprüfungsausschuß mit Beschluß vom 20. 1. 1977 eine Verfassungsbeschwerde von Anteilseignern einer Gesellschaft mit Rücksicht auf das zuvor einzuhaltende Verfahren nach § 98 AktG zunächst nicht zur Entscheidung angenommen hatte[50]. Inzwischen haben einige Zivilgerichte die Auffassung vertreten, die Bestimmungen des Mitbestimmungsgesetzes über die Bildung und Zusammensetzung der Aufsichtsräte von Aktiengesellschaften verstießen nicht gegen das Grundgesetz[51]. Demgegenüber hält das Landgericht Hamburg die Regelungen in § 7 Abs. 1 und 2 i. V. mit § 31 MitbestG für mit Art. 9 Abs. 3 GG unvereinbar, da hierdurch die Arbeitnehmer auf den die Funktion des Arbeitgebers wahrnehmenden Vorstand einen solchen Einfluß gewännen, daß von einer Gegnerunabhängigkeit der Arbeitgeberseite nicht mehr gesprochen werden könne[52], und hat einen Vorlagebeschluß nach Art. 100 Abs. 1 GG gefaßt. Hierüber und über die Verfassungsbeschwerden betroffener Gesellschaften und der Arbeitgeberverbände wird das Bundesverfassungsgericht nunmehr zu entscheiden haben. Bei der verfassungsrechtlichen Würdigung wird auch zu bedenken sein, daß die Unternehmensmitbestimmung bereits auf ein System stark ausgebauter betrieblicher Mitbestimmung stößt, die in gewissem Umfang bereits auch wirtschaftliche Angelegenheiten erfaßt[53], so daß sich die Mitbestimmungsrechte kumulieren.

Betriebsverfassungsgesetz und Mitbestimmungsgesetz sind heute erkennbar Teil des unternehmerischen Ordnungsrahmens. Der Pflichtenkatalog des Unternehmens wird indessen noch von einer Reihe weiterer Gesetze bestimmt, von denen einige bedeutsame hier genannt sein sollen.

Das Aktiengesetz 1937 hat den Vorstand bei seiner Unternehmenspolitik in § 70 an «das Wohl des Betriebs und seiner Gefolgschaft und den gemeinen Nutzen von Volk und Reich» gebunden. Was immer damit gemeint war, es war eine umfassende generalklauselartige Sozialbindung, die der Sozialpflichtigkeit des Eigentums in Art. 14 II GG ähnlich ist. Das Aktiengesetz 1965 hat diese Formel nicht übernommen. In der Begründung

[49] Dazu umfassend *Badura-Rittner-Rüthers,* aaO; siehe auch *H. J. Papier,* ZHR 142 (1978), S. 71 ff.; *J. Isensee,* aaO, S. 161 ff.

[50] BVerfG, NJW 1977, 529.

[51] So OLG Düsseldorf, BB 1978, 466; LG Stuttgart, NJW 1977, 535; LG Mannheim, NJW 1977, 1971.

[52] DB 1978, 990; siehe auch *Badura-Rittner-Rüthers,* aaO, S. 137 ff. und 234 ff.; *H. J. Papier,* ZHR 142 (1978), S. 83 f.; *J. Isensee,* aaO, S. 177 f.

[53] §§ 106 ff. BetrVG 1972; vgl. dazu *Badura-Rittner-Rüthers,* aaO, S. 125 f.; *H. J. Papier,* aaO, S. 73 f.; *P. Hanau,* aaO, S. 406 ff. Wer das Ganze freilich als Ausfluß sog. «Arbeitnehmergrundrechte» erblickt, (die sich freilich im Grundgesetz nicht finden lassen), für den ist Mitbestimmung natürlich nur am Rande ein Verfassungsproblem (so etwa *P. H. Naendrup,* in: Fabricius (Hrsg.), Gemeinschaftskommentar zum Mitbestimmungsgesetz, Neuwied, Berlin 1976, Einl. II Rdnr. 106).

des Regierungsentwurfs wurde ausgeführt, die Berücksichtigung der Belange der Arbeitnehmer und der Allgemeinheit verstehe sich von selbst. Die Kommentarliteratur zum Aktiengesetz läßt offen, ob diese Bindung dem Gesetz immanent sei[54]. Man wird wohl der Mitbestimmungskommission der Bundesregierung folgen können, wenn sie betont: Ungeachtet der sozialen und sozialpolitischen Bindungen des Unternehmens muß sich die Unternehmenspolitik an der Rentabilität als der primären unternehmerischen Zielfunktion orientieren[55]. Indes hat die Ablösung der «großen Bindung» eine Reihe kleiner Bindungen aufleben lassen, die sehr weit gehen können. Man denke etwa an die Aufsichtsbefugnisse, die die Wirtschaftsaufsicht über Unternehmen des Kredit-, des Versicherungs-, des Energieoder des Personenbeförderungssektors besitzt[56]. Sie alle sind wegen ihrer besonderen Bedeutung in spezifischer Weise in Pflicht und Dienst der Allgemeinheit genommen. Rechnet man dazu die Unternehmen, die allein oder mehrheitlich im Besitz der öffentlichen Hand sind, so fragt sich, ob denn die traditionelle Funktionenteilung zwischen Staat und freier Wirtschaft nicht schon einer Art Mischsystem gewichen ist, in dem der öffentlichrechtliche Anteil nach österreichischem, italienischem oder britischem Muster immer weiter wächst. Einige Stimmen fordern sogar, man möge endlich von der sog. Sozialisierungskompetenz des Art. 15 GG Gebrauch machen, um dem Großunternehmen, namentlich wenn es multinational verflochten sei, seine «Macht» zu nehmen[57]. Daß es hierzu horrender Entschädigungssummen bedürfte, wird meist großzügig verschwiegen. Die Idee der «Vergesellschaftung» fasziniert, obschon niemand bisher je klargelegt hat, wie denn die Trägerschaft, die Leitung und Organisation des sozialisierten Unternehmens tatsächlich aussehen soll. Nur so viel sei festgestellt, eine Umsetzung der Ermächtigung des Art. 15 in die Tat würde das bestehende Wirtschaftssystem erheblich umgestalten. Wichtige Teile der Wirtschaft würden nicht mehr dem Prinzip privatautonomer Gestaltung unterliegen. Die Beispiele der Welt um uns haben nicht gerade den Beweis des Besseren dieser Wirtschaftsform erbracht.

Es überrascht darum nicht, wenn stattdessen der Ruf nach weniger rigorosen Steuerungsinstrumenten erklingt, etwa nach Preis- und Investitionskontrollen unterschiedlicher Intensität[58]. Eine allgemeine Preis- und Investitionssteuerung bedeutet eine weitgе-

---

[54] Vgl. zum Diskussionsstand *J. Meyer-Landrut*, in: Aktiengesetz, Großkommentar, 3. Aufl., Bd. I/2, Berlin, New York 1973, § 76 Anm. 9; *Godin-Wilhelmi*, AktG, Komm., 4. Aufl., Berlin 1971, § 76 Anm. 5; *P. Hanau*, BB 1969, 761; *V. Emmerich*, Das Wirtschaftsrecht der öffentlichen Unternehmen, Bad Homburg 1969, S. 235 ff.; *U. Huber*, in: H. Albach – D. Sadowski (Hrsg.), Die Bedeutung gesellschaftlicher Veränderungen für die Willensbildung im Unternehmen, Schriften des Vereins für Socialpolitik, Bd. 88 (Berlin 1976), S. 153 f. (mit Fn. 36).

[55] BTags-Drucks. VI/334, S. 102.

[56] Im Überblick *P. Badura*, in: I. v. Münch, Besonderes Verwaltungsrecht, 4. Aufl. Berlin, New York 1976, S. 307 f. m.w.N. – Zur Wirtschaftsaufsicht allgemein *M. Bullinger*, VVDStRL Heft 22 (1965), S. 264 ff.; *E. Stein*, Die Wirtschaftsaufsicht, Tübingen 1967; *R. Scholz*, Wirtschaftsaufsicht und subjektiver Konkurrentenschutz, Berlin 1971.

[57] Vgl. diesbezüglich etwa *H. Ridder*, Die soziale Ordnung des Grundgesetzes, Opladen 1975, S. 100 ff.; *H. H. Hartwich*, Sozialstaatspostulat und gesellschaftlicher status quo, Köln, Opladen 1970, insbes. S. 344 ff. Zu Art. 15 GG zuletzt *H. J. Papier*, VVDStRL Heft 35 (1977), S. 84 ff. Das Problem unternehmerischer Macht wird m. E. weitgehend überbetont (so etwa *P. Saladin*, aaO, S. 40). Der Kompetenztitel des Art 74 Nr. 16 GG lautet: «Mißbrauch wirtschaftlicher Machtstellung».

[58] Siehe nur *N. Reich*, ZRP 1976, 67 ff.; *T. Sarrazin* (Hrsg.). Investitionslenkung, «Spielwiese» oder «vorausschauende Industriepolitik»?, Bonn-Bad Godesberg 1976; *V. Helms*, Investitionsfonds und Lenkung privater Investitionen, Darmstadt 1976; *K. G. Zinn*, Investitionslenkung – Traditionelles Konzept für die traditionelle Krise, in: Politik und Wirtschaft, Festschrift für G. von Ey-

hende Außerkraftsetzung des Marktmechanismus. Sie würde jene unternehmerischen Freiheiten, die aus den Grundrechten abzuleiten sind, antasten; sie ist daher verfassungswidrig.[59]

Dem Großunternehmen von heute ist nicht selten die Stellung der «pouvoirs intermédiaires» von gestern zugeschrieben worden; deren Macht habe der Staat – ebenso wie im 17. Jahrhundert der Absolutismus die der Feudalmächte – zu brechen, zumindest habe er Gegenkräfte aufzubauen[60]. Ich zweifle, ob diese Parallele berechtigt ist[61]. Unternehmerische Macht – wenn überhaupt diese Bezeichnung am Platze ist – ist heute vielfältig eingebunden: durch die Rechtsordnung des Staates, durch das Gegengewicht gewerkschaftlicher Macht, von der *Hans F. Zacher* meinte, sie sei «allgegenwärtig»[62], unkontrolliert[63] und gegen sie sei «offenbar nicht mehr zu regieren»[64], und schließlich durch eine harte Konkurrenz, der sich nur ganz wenige Monopol- oder marktbeherrschende Unternehmen entziehen können.

Das Gesetz gegen Wettbewerbsbeschränkungen hat durch Kartellverbot, durch Mißbrauchsaufsicht über marktbeherrschende Unternehmen und durch Fusionskontrolle Dämme gegen die Entstehung von Marktmacht errichtet und zur Sicherung des Wettbewerbs beigetragen. Ob dem Trend zum Großunternehmen damit hinreichend gegengesteuert ist, muß offen bleiben. Eine gute Durchmischung von Klein-, Mittel- und Großunternehmen scheint mir ein wesentlicher Faktor für die Erhaltung einer Marktwirtschaft zu sein.

V. Die «gesellschaftspolitische» Dimension der Unternehmensphilosophie

Das Unternehmen gerät in jüngster Zeit zunehmend in das sog. «gesellschaftspolitische» Blickfeld; ja gerade dieses ist es, das dem Begriff Unternehmensphilosophie eine neue Dimension verleiht. *Kurt H. Biedenkopf* hat dies in einem Vortrag anläßlich der Jahrestagung des Verbandes der Chemischen Industrie 1974 folgendermaßen umschrieben: «Vor allem wird die Tendenz zunehmen, das Unternehmen nicht als eine privatrechtliche, sondern als eine gesellschaftliche Veranstaltung zu sehen, an deren Organisation und Durchführung ein Allgemeininteresse besteht. Sie kommt in den politischen Ansprüchen zum Ausdruck, die an das Unternehmen gestellt werden»[65]. Als Stichwort für

nern, Opladen 1977, S. 98 ff. – Vgl. in diesem Zusammenhang auch *M. Schmidt-Preuß*, Verfassungsrechtliche Zentralfragen staatlicher Lohn- und Preisdirigismen, Baden-Baden 1977; *K. A. Schachtschneider*, Der Staat Bd. 16 (1977), S. 493 ff.

[59] Vgl. *R. Scholz*, Grenzen staatlicher Aktivität unter der grundgesetzlichen Wirtschaftsverfassung, in: Der Staatssektor in der sozialen Marktwirtschaft, Schriftenreihe der Hochschule Speyer, Bd. 59, Berlin 1976, S. 130; *Friauf/Wendt*, Eigentum am Unternehmen, Köln 1977, S. 92 ff.

[60] Vgl. *P. Saladin*, VVDStRL Heft 35 (1977), S. 34 ff. m.w.N.

[61] Ablehnend auch *Friauf/Wendt*, aaO, S. 74 f.

[62] Festschrift für F. Berber, München 1973, S. 554. Die Gewerkschaften haben nur ca. 7 Millionen Mitglieder bei ca. 25 Millionen Arbeitnehmern.

[63] AaO, S. 567 f.; siehe auch *J. Isensee*, aaO, S. 179.

[64] AaO, S. 572. Man vergleiche die Zahl der Gewerkschaftsmitglieder in Parlamenten und Regierungen mit derjenigen von Unternehmern und Unternehmensmanagern!

[65] Über den Wandel der Gesellschaft. Am Beispiel des Unternehmensrechts, Düsseldorf, Wien 1975, S. 22 f.; vgl. diesbezüglich etwa *P. Ulrich*, Die Großunternehmung als quasi-öffentliche Institution, Stuttgart 1977.

diese soziale Funktion[66] des Unternehmens genügen: Umweltschutz, Vermögensbildung, Sozialverantwortlichkeit des Unternehmens und des Unternehmers. Diesen von der Politik gestellten Fragen können Unternehmen, Unternehmer und ihre Verbände nicht ausweichen. Sie sind zuvörderst konzeptionell zu bewältigen, will sagen, daß für die Lösung dieser Probleme Konzeptionen zu erarbeiten sind, die nicht auf Flickschusterei oder dem Blick auf den nächsten Wahltermin beruhen. Die Politik muß sich bei diesen Zukunftsaufgaben von der Lösung nach dem Modell massenpsychologisch größter Wirksamkeit freimachen, etwa der Devise: Die Unternehmer können es schon bezahlen. Unternehmerisches Denken muß sich andererseits von einem rein defensiven Konzept lösen; es muß selbst Impulsgeber werden. Nicht wenige deutsche Unternehmungen und ihre Verbände haben dies erkannt, und in der Lösung vieler sozialer Fragen waren gerade deutsche Unternehmen Vorbild für eine spätere Gesetzgebung. Die grundgesetzliche Wirtschaftsverfassung hat hier keine Patentrezepte zu bieten. Sie hat nur Aussagen von grundsätzlichem Gehalt parat. Die außenpolitische Potenz wie innenpolitische Handlungsfähigkeit unseres Staates beruhen auf der Leistungskraft unserer Wirtschaft. Sie wird getragen von der Funktionstüchtigkeit der Unternehmen und diese wiederum basiert auf Kreativität und freier unternehmerischer Gestaltung ebenso wie auf Fleiß und Tüchtigkeit aller im Unternehmen Tätigen. Diesen Elan freizusetzen, war Sinn und Ziel der freiheitlichen grundgesetzlichen Wirtschaftsverfassungsentscheidung, die ihren Vollzug in der Schaffung marktwirtschaftlicher Strukturen verbunden mit dem richtigen Maß an Sozialverpflichtung fand. Das System der Markt- und Wettbewerbswirtschaft, der individuellen Leistung und Entscheidung, ist nicht nur ein System der Güterproduktion und Bedarfsdeckung oder ökonomisch eingerichteter Kalkulation, sondern auch eine Rechtfertigung der Vorrangstellung des einzelnen und seiner autonomen Entscheidungsfreiheit. Zugleich hat es eine strategische Funktion zur Verwirklichung der freiheitlichen Ordnung im Ganzen, weil es ein hohes Maß an politischer wie bürgerlicher Freiheit verbürgt[67]. Mit der Verankerung verfassungsrechtlicher und ordnungspolitischer Grundentscheidungen allein ist unsere Freiheit aber nicht gesichert. Man muß auch nach ihnen handeln. Eine freiheitliche Ordnung kann nur funktionieren, wenn ein Grundbestand an gemeinsamen Wertüberzeugungen besteht und beachtet wird. Die Fähigkeit, der Wille und das Bewußtsein, sein Handlungsprogramm von freiheitlichen Prinzipien leiten zu lassen, hängen vom Vorhandensein und der Wirkkraft eines bestimmten gesetzlichen und institutionellen Rahmens ab, genauer von der Existenz von freiheitlichen Instituten zur Konkretisierung der vorgezeichneten Grundordnung. Werden uns diese Überzeugungen als «Roads to Freedom»[68] auch in der Zukunft leiten in der Staats- wie in der Unternehmens-

---

[66] Vgl. dazu *P. Saladin*, aaO, S. 15 ff. mit zahlr. Nachw.: corporate social responsibility. Seine Zusammenfassung: «Der Verfassungsstatus der Unternehmung und des Unternehmers ist bereits heute nicht nur ein Status der Freiheit, sondern auch ein Status beträchtlicher Verantwortung. Freilich ermangelt diese Pflichtstellung in ihrer verfassungsmäßigen Ausformung der Eindeutigkeit und in ihrer gesetzlichen Konkretisierung der Kohärenz» (S. 26) ist zutreffend.

[67] Zum Zusammenhang zwischen Marktwirtschaft und freiheitlicher Demokratie jetzt auch *G. Gutmann*, Art. Marktwirtschaft, HdWW, S. 151 f. Über die Verbindung von Rechtsstaat und Sozialstaat zum Modell der Sozialen Marktwirtschaft vgl. *K. Stern*, Das Staatsrecht, aaO, § 20 V 2. Zu wenig werden die stilbildenden Elemente des Grundgesetzes für die Konzeption der Sozialen Marktwirtschaft bei *R. Blum*, Art. Marktwirtschaft, soziale, HdWW, S. 156 f., deutlich. Die Aufdeckung der Zusammenhänge der Entstehung der Staatsverfassung 1948/49 und der Konzipierung der Idee der Sozialen Marktwirtschaft harrt erstaunlicherweise der wissenschaftlichen Erforschung in Rechts- und Wirtschaftswissenschaft.

[68] So der Titel der von *E. Streissler* u. a. herausgegebenen Festschrift für F. A. von Hayek aus dem Jahre 1969.

führung, dann besitzen wir nicht nur die richtige Unternehmensphilosophie zur Bewältigung der Zukunftsaufgaben, sondern zugleich auch die bessere Staatsphilosophie[69].

Summary

Company Philosophy and the Constitution – The Effects of the Constitutional Framework of the Economy on the Formulation of a Company Philosophy

In a legal sense the constitutional framework of the economic order means the total of all individual constitutional rules and principles concerning the economy. The fundamental principle behind the Basic Law of the Federal Republic of Germany is the constitutional guaranty of free decision, especially with respect to property, profession, place of employment, competition, investment, consumption, and the ability to enter into contracts and to form coalitions. The Basic Law is not indifferent to the economic order in that it provides for a constitutional framework of the economy, which is structurally in harmony with the political framework.

It is this set of rights that in principle guaranties the free economic activity of the enterprise – also of the large company, organized as a Public Limited Liability Company – thus providing decisive data for the formulation of a company philosophy. In view of the contemporary socio-political environment, the development of convincing, actively advocated entrepreneurial concepts is required to realize the constitutionally guarantied predominance of freedom in the economic sphere as well, i. e. in theory and practice.

---

[69] Diese Einsicht wurde vornehmlich *F. A. von Hayek* nicht müde zu betonen; vgl. Der Weg zur Knechtschaft (Neudruck München 1971 der deutschen Ausgabe 1945; engl.: The Road to Serfdom, 1944); *ders.*, Die Verfassung der Freiheit, Tübingen 1971; *ders.*, Individualismus und wirtschaftliche Ordnung, 2. Aufl. Salzburg 1976; *ders.*, Demokratie, Gerechtigkeit und Sozialismus, Tübingen 1977.

Dieter Schmidtchen

Ausbeutung aufgrund einer Wettbewerbsbeschränkung durch Zustand? Kritische Analyse der theoretischen Grundlagen einer freiheitsgefährdenden Wettbewerbspolitik*

I. Vorbemerkungen

«Das Leben in der Gesellschaft bedeutet notwendig, daß wir für die Befriedigung der meisten Bedürfnisse von den Dienstleistungen anderer abhängig sind; in einer freien Gesellschaft sind diese Dienstleistungen freiwillig, und jeder kann bestimmen, wem er Dienste leisten will und welches seine Bedingungen sind.»[1] Dieses Selbstbestimmungsrecht kann nicht schrankenlos sein, wenn man ein System allgemeiner Freiheit vor Augen hat. Denn es ist nicht auszuschließen, daß Situationen existieren, in denen eine Person (oder Personengruppe) einer anderen Person (oder Personengruppe) die Bedingungen diktiert, zu denen sie bereit ist, Leistungen zu erbringen. Die Zustimmung zu diesen Bedingungen erfolgt dann nicht freiwillig, sondern aufgrund des Zwangs der besonderen Umstände. In solchen Fällen, die etwa in der Theorie des natürlichen Monopols analysiert werden, hat der Staat – auch nach liberaler Überzeugung – die Pflicht, einzugreifen, notfalls, indem er einem Unternehmen Preise vorschreibt.

Eine derartige Politik muß nicht per se freiheitsgefährdend sein. Sie ist jedoch in den Fällen als freiheitsgefährdend zu klassifizieren, in denen überhaupt kein Diktat der Austauschbedingungen seitens eines Marktteilnehmers erfolgt, sondern diese freiwillig akzeptiert werden. (Wobei als Indizien für die Freiwilligkeit das Vorhandensein von Ausweichmöglichkeiten und das Fehlen willkürlich gesetzter «Wanderungshemmnisse» angesehen werden können.) Das Leitprinzip einer freiheitsorientierten Wettbewerbspolitik lautet demgemäß: Ergreife erst dann Maßnahmen zur Einschränkung des Rechts, die Austauschbedingungen autonom festzusetzen, wenn feststeht oder (mit hoher Wahrscheinlichkeit) zu vermuten ist, daß eine Situation vorliegt, in der diese Bedingungen nicht freiwillig akzeptiert werden. Man kann dieses Prinzip auf die Kurzformel bringen: soviel Selbstbestimmung der Austauschbedingungen wie möglich, soviel Eingriffe in dieses Selbstbestimmungsrecht wie unbedingt nötig.

Legt man dieses Prinzip zugrunde, dann hat – so lautet die These – die deutsche Wettbewerbspolitik gegenüber marktbeherrschenden Unternehmen einen Weg beschritten, der als mit einer freien Gesellschaft und einer freiheitlichen Marktordnung unvereinbar bezeichnet werden muß. Einige Beispiele mögen dies verdeutlichen:

---

* Aus Zeitgründen kann die vorgesehene Erwiderung zu dem nachfolgend abgedruckten Beitrag erst im nächsten Band erscheinen.

[1] *Von Hayek, F. A.:* Die Verfassung der Freiheit, Tübingen 1971, S. 164.

– Im Herbst 1973 wurde vom Bundeskartellamt ein Verfahren gegen einen Trocken-rasiererhersteller *(Braun)* wegen mißbräuchlicher Preis- und Rabattgestaltung mit dem Zweck eingeleitet, dessen Werksabgabepreise für inländische Händler zu senken.

– Im April 1974 erhielten mehrere Unternehmen der Mineralölindustrie vom Bundeskartellamt Preisherabsetzungsverfügungen, nach denen die Benzinpreise auf den Stand vor der Erhöhung am 9. April 1974 zu senken waren.

– Ebenfalls im Frühjahr 1974 wurde ein Arzneimittelhersteller *(Merck)* vom Bundeskartellamt aufgefordert, die Preise für Vitamin-B-12-Präparate um 60 bis 70 Prozent zu senken.

– Aufgrund eines Beschlusses vom 16. Oktober 1974 erging an einen anderen Arzneimittelhersteller *(Hoffmann-La-Roche)* die Aufforderung, die Herstellerabgabepreise um 40 % *(Valium)* bzw. 35 % *(Librium)* zu senken.

– Im Mai 1974 versuchte das Bundeskartellamt durch eine einstweilige Anordnung, die zweite Preiserhöhung innerhalb weniger Monate von einem Automobilhersteller (VW) zu verhindern.

– Seit Jahren droht das Bundeskartellamt den Autobahntankstellen die Einleitung von Mißbrauchsverfahren und Preisherabsetzungsverfügungen an, wenn deren Preise um einen bestimmten Betrag (neuerdings 0,02 DM) höher sind als diejenigen benachbarter Straßentankstellen.

– Anfang Mai 1974 tauchte schließlich auch noch die Idee einer vorbeugenden Mißbrauchskontrolle auf: Marktbeherrschende Unternehmen hätten danach Preiserhöhungsabsichten dem Bundeskartellamt anzumelden und sich die Preiserhöhungen genehmigen zu lassen.

Das Recht zu all diesen Eingriffen in das vom Standpunkt der Funktionsweise einer marktwirtschaftlichen Ordnung zentrale unternehmerische Recht, die Absatzpreise autonom festzusetzen[2], leitete das Bundeskartellamt von seinem gesetzlichen Auftrag ab, die Ausnutzung von vom Wettbewerb nicht kontrollierten Handlungsspielräumen marktbeherrschender Unternehmen zu Lasten Dritter – und dazu gehören auch die Konsumenten – zu verhindern. Es sah sich gleichsam in der Position eines Hüters der freiheitlichen Marktordnung, als Gegenkraft und Stellvertreter der «unsichtbaren Hand» in all den Fällen, wo diese vermeintlich kraftlos geworden war (marktbeherrschende Stellung).

Wenn die Politik des Kartellamts hier gleichwohl als freiheitsgefährdend bezeichnet wird, dann deshalb, weil mit dem Argument, das unternehmerische «Diktat» der Austauschbedingungen bekämpfen zu müssen, ein staatliches Diktat der Austauschbedingungen erfolgt ist – ohne daß ein im Sinne der liberalen Theorie definierter Notfall vorgelegen hat. Das oben formulierte Leitprinzip wurde also verletzt. Aus diesem Grunde ist es auch nicht verwunderlich, daß kritische Beobachter der wettbewerbspolitischen Praxis in der Bundesrepublik das Bundeskartellamt mit einem Preiskommissar verglichen haben, dessen Markteingriffe zur Systemveränderung führten[3] und letztlich einen Mißbrauch der Mißbrauchsaufsicht darstellten.[4]

---

[2] Es ist wichtig, zu erkennen, daß Eingriffe in die Preissetzungsautonomie nicht nur eine freiheitsbeschränkende Dimension aufweisen. Insoweit der Preisparameter von staatlichen Interventionen betroffen ist, muß notwendigerweise auch die Frage der Beeinträchtigung der Effizienz des Preissystems in bezug auf den Informations-, Entdeckungs- und Koordinationszusammenhang aufgeworfen werden. (Zu diesen Funktionen des Preissystems siehe *Röpke, J.*: Die Strategie der Innovation, Tübingen 1977, S. 355 ff.)

[3] Siehe *Hoppmann, E.*: Kartellamt als Preiskommissar? Preiskontrolle – Mittel zur Systemveränderung, in: Wirtschaftsdienst, 8/1974, S. 389 ff.

[4] Siehe *Hoppmann, E.*: Mißbrauch der Mißbrauchsaufsicht – Die Einführung des Ausbeutungsmißbrauchs in die deutsche Wettbewerbspolitik, in: Mitteilungen der List-Gesellschaft, Mai 1976, S. 155 ff.

Die Ansicht des Bundeskartellamtes ist mittlerweile höchstrichterlich bestätigt worden. Der Bundesgerichtshof hat im Rechtsbeschwerdeverfahren des Unternehmens *Hoffmann-La-Roche* gegen das Bundeskartellamt entschieden, daß es grundsätzlich mit dem Schutzzweck des Gesetzes gegen Wettbewerbsbeschränkungen (GWB) vereinbar sei, wenn das Kartellamt marktbeherrschenden Unternehmen Höchstpreise vorschreibe.[5] Wenngleich damit auch die Frage der Zulässigkeit von direkten Preisinterventionen im Rahmen der praktischen Wettbewerbspolitik geklärt ist, kann die wissenschaftliche Wettbewerbspolitik, auch wenn sie von einer gewissen «Fremddefinition» ihrer Arbeitsschwerpunkte *(K. Borchardt)* lebt, doch nicht einfach zur Tagesordnung übergehen. Dies gilt um so mehr, wenn zu vermuten ist, daß den eigentlichen Ursachen, die zur wirtschaftslenkenden, freiheitsgefährdenden und willkürlichen[6] Wettbewerbspolitik geführt haben, noch nicht genügend nachgespürt wurde.[7]

Im folgenden sollen deshalb die theoretischen Grundlagen dieser Wettbewerbspolitik einer kritischen Analyse unterzogen werden. Dies geschieht im Lichte neuerer markttheoretischer Erkenntnisse und in der Hoffnung, einen Beitrag zu leisten zu dem die liberale Wettbewerbspolitik immer wieder bewegenden Thema, wo die Grenze liegt, von der ab staatliche Eingriffe freiheitsgefährdend werden.

Da sich Wettbewerbspolitik in einem Rechtsstaat in der Form der Anwendung von Gesetzen vollzieht, sei von den Regelungen im Gesetz gegen Wettbewerbsbeschränkungen (GWB) ausgegangen.

II. Zur rechtlichen Lage

Gemäß § 22, V GWB kann die Kartellbehörde einem marktbeherrschenden Unternehmen ein mißbräuchliches Verhalten untersagen und Verträge für unwirksam erklären. Zweck dieser Regelung ist es, die Ausnutzung unternehmerischer Handlungsspielräume (= Unternehmensmacht), die nicht oder nicht in ausreichendem Maße dem «Wettbewerb als Kontrollregulans» *(W. Möschel)* unterliegen, zu Lasten Dritter zu verhindern.

Die erwähnten machtbedingten Handlungsspielräume können nach herrschender Ansicht von einem marktbeherrschenden Unternehmen auf zweierlei Weise mißbräuchlich ausgenutzt werden. Die erste Möglichkeit – der sogenannte Behinderungsmißbrauch – ist dadurch gekennzeichnet, daß das marktbeherrschende Unternehmen behindernde oder diskriminierende Praktiken anwendet: etwa Kopplungen, Ausschließlichkeitsklauseln oder diskriminierende Preisdifferenzierungen. Mit Hilfe dieser «leistungsfremden» Mittel ist es in der Lage, vorhandene Machtpositionen auszubauen oder diese abzusichern, an sich leistungsfähige Unternehmen vom Markt zu verdrängen oder «unangemessene» Schranken für Newcomer zu errichten.[8] Das marktbeherrschende Unternehmen legt hier also ein wettbewerbsbeschränkendes Verhalten[9] an den Tag und verschlechtert absichtlich die Wettbewerbsbedingungen für die anderen Marktteilnehmer.

[5] Siehe dazu BGH, Beschluß v. 16. 12. 1976 (Valium / Librium).
[6] Siehe zu diesem Punkt insbesondere die kritische Analyse von *Hoppmann, E.*: Mißbrauch der Mißbrauchsaufsicht, S. 178ff.
[7] Das ist um so bedauerlicher, als nur eine exakte Ursachenanalyse die Faktoren ermitteln kann, an denen man ansetzen muß, wenn man Verbesserungen erzielen will.
[8] Siehe Tätigkeitsbericht des Bundeskartellamts 1977, Bundestagsdrucksache 8/703, S. 25.
[9] Die Monopolkommission spricht von «wettbewerbswidrigen Verhaltensweisen». (Siehe Sondergutachten I, Anwendung und Möglichkeiten der Mißbrauchsaufsicht über marktbeherr-

Da diese Wettbewerbsbeschränkungen eine Folge unternehmerischer Maßnahmen sind, hat man dafür den Ausdruck «Wettbewerbsbeschränkung durch Maßnahme» geprägt.[10]

Während sich die Maßnahmen des Behinderungsmißbrauchs sowohl gegen Angehörige der gleichen Marktseite wie gegen solche vor- und nachgelagerter Wirtschaftsstufen sowie von Drittmärkten richten, vollzieht sich die zweite Form des Mißbrauchs – der sogenannte Ausbeutungsmißbrauch – (in erster Linie) gegenüber Marktteilnehmern der vor- oder nachgelagerten Wirtschaftsstufe.

Bei der Frage, ob eine Ausbeutung vorliegt, geht es darum, ob Leistung und Gegenleistung angemessen sind.[11] Stehen Leistung und Gegenleistung in einem Mißverhältnis, dann ist nach Ansicht des Bundeskartellamtes der Tatbestand der Ausbeutung erfüllt.

Ausbeutung wird vollzogen durch einseitige inhaltliche Ausgestaltung der Austauschbedingungen, also durch einen machtbedingten Einsatz von Aktionsparametern gegenüber der vor- oder nachgelagerten Wirtschaftsstufe. Der in der bisherigen Praxis im Vordergrund des Interesses stehende Aktionsparameter war der Preis. Allerdings läßt sich nach Ansicht des Kartellamtes auch mit anderen Aktionsparametern Ausbeutung betreiben.

Die soeben gegebene Interpretation der Struktur der Mißbrauchsaufsicht im Rahmen des § 22 GWB entspricht der offiziellen Lesart. Verhinderung des Behinderungsmißbrauchs und Verhinderung des Ausbeutungsmißbrauchs erscheinen hier als «zwei große, inhaltlich verschiedene Aufgabenbereiche».[12] Ausbeutung einerseits und Behinderung andererseits verkörpern in dieser Sicht zwei eigenständige rechtliche Mißbrauchstatbestände.

Diese Lesart ist jedoch nicht die einzig mögliche. Für *Hoppmann*, einen der entschiedensten Kritiker des Vorgehens des Kartellamtes, sind nämlich Ausbeutung und Behinderung nicht unabhängig voneinander: Bei Fällen der Behinderung «wendet die marktbeherrschende Unternehmung ein wettbewerbswidriges Verhalten an; etwa durch Kopplungen, diskriminierende Preisdifferenzierungen, Ausschließlichkeitsklauseln, wettbewerbswidrige Preissysteme und anderes mehr. Dabei ergeben sich auch ‹unangemessene›, nämlich wettbewerbswidrige Preise, und man hatte bisher die Ausnutzung einer marktbeherrschenden Stellung durch unangemessene Preise immer als Begleiterscheinung bzw. als Reflex eines wettbewerbswidrigen Verhaltens (Behinderung, Diskriminierung, usw.) angesehen, so daß die beiden Aufgabenbereiche, von denen das Kartellamt spricht, inhaltlich nicht verschieden sind».[13] Nach dieser «Reflextheorie» ist Ausbeutung also nur möglich, wenn das marktbeherrschende Unternehmen vorher einen Behinderungsmißbrauch begangen hat. Mit anderen Worten: Ausbeutung setzt ein zeitlich vorhergehendes

---

schende Unternehmen seit Inkrafttreten der Kartellgesetznovelle, Baden-Baden 1975, S. 29.) Diese Wortwahl erscheint dann nicht besonders glücklich, wenn unter diesen Begriff auch die Setzung überhöhter Preise subsumiert wird – eine Maßnahme, die nicht notwendig wettbewerbsbeschränkend zu sein braucht.

[10] Siehe dazu *Borchardt, K., Fikentscher, W.*: Wettbewerb, Wettbewerbsbeschränkung, Marktbeherrschung, Stuttgart 1957.

[11] Siehe *Markert, K.*: Kostenkontrolle bei der Mißbrauchsaufsicht über marktbeherrschende Unternehmen, in: Der Betriebsberater, Heft 13, Mai 1975, S. 581. Siehe auch *Gabriel, S.*: Preiskontrolle im Rahmen der Wettbewerbspolitik, Tübingen 1976, S. 39f.

[12] Entscheidung des Bundeskartellamts vom 21. 3. 1974, in: Wirtschaft und Wettbewerb, Entscheidungssammlung, S. 1483f.

[13] *Hoppmann, E.*: Mißbrauch der Mißbrauchsaufsicht, S. 164.

aktives, wettbewerbsbeschränkendes Verhalten voraus, also eine Wettbewerbsbeschränkung durch Maßnahme. Es ist demgemäß ein zusätzliches, den Wettbewerb beschränkendes Element, das erst die Voraussetzungen schafft, die eine Ausbeutung ermöglichen (These des «additiven Elements»).

Geht man – wie das Kartellamt – davon aus, daß in der dem § 22 GWB zugrunde liegenden Vorstellungswelt zwei unabhängige (eigenständige) rechtliche Mißbrauchstatbestände existieren, dann wird damit zugleich unterstellt, daß eine Ausbeutung möglich sei auch ohne ein zusätzliches wettbewerbsbeschränkendes Verhalten. Das Bundeskartellamt braucht demgemäß bei Mißbrauchsverfahren nicht erst eine die Ausbeutung ermöglichende wettbewerbsbeschränkende Maßnahme zu suchen und nachzuweisen: «Auf Märkten, die aufgrund struktureller Beschränkungen nicht der Kontrolle durch den Wettbewerb unterliegen, stellt das Fordern eines überhöhten Preises als solches einen Mißbrauch dar. Es ist die Wettbewerbsbeschränkung durch Zustand, die bereits den Mißbrauch ermöglicht.»[14] Während die Reflextheorie auf der Idee einer «Ausbeutung aufgrund wettbewerbsbeschränkenden Verhaltens» beruht, wird hier die Möglichkeit einer «Ausbeutung ohne wettbewerbsbeschränkendes Verhalten», also lediglich als Konsequenz einer «Wettbewerbsbeschränkung durch Zustand», unterstellt.[15] Diese Variante nennt man deshalb auch «reinen» Ausbeutungsmißbrauch.

III. Marktbeherrschung und Wettbewerbsbeschränkung durch Zustand

Nach dem Gesetz ist ein Unternehmen marktbeherrschend, «soweit es als Anbieter oder Nachfrager einer bestimmten Art von Waren oder gewerblichen Leistungen ... ohne Wettbewerber ist oder keinem wesentlichen Wettbewerb ausgesetzt ist ...»[16] Fragt man nach den Ursachen dieser Situation, so stößt man auf die Wettbewerbsbeschränkung durch Zustand: Der Umstand, daß ein Unternehmen ohne Wettbewerber ist oder keinem wesentlichen Wettbewerb ausgesetzt ist, ist die Wirkung (Folge) einer Wettbewerbsbeschränkung, die ihrerseits auf einen bestimmten Zustand eines Marktes zurückzuführen ist. So kann beispielsweise der Wettbewerb beschränkt sein, weil die Möglichkeit des Marktzutritts gesetzlich ausgeschlossen ist oder weil ein Unternehmen A ein abhängiges Unternehmen B veranlaßt, einem Konkurrenten von A den Absatzweg oder die Bezugsquellen zu versperren. Die Beziehung zwischen marktbeherrschender Stellung einerseits und Wettbewerbsbeschränkung durch Zustand andererseits wird hier also im Sinne einer Ursache-Wirkung-Beziehung interpretiert: Weil der Wettbewerb durch einen bestimmten Zustand des Marktes beschränkt ist, ergibt sich die Marktbeherrschung und eröffnen sich die anfänglich erwähnten Handlungsspielräume. Es ist zu vermuten, daß nach der Logik des Gesetzes die Wettbewerbsbeschränkung durch Zustand einzige Ursache für die Marktbeherrschung ist und daß demgemäß die Idee einer Wettbewerbsbeschränkung durch Zustand notwendigerweise bei der Anwendung des Gesetzes eine Rolle spielen muß. Aus diesen Überlegungen folgt dreierlei:

---

[14] Schmidt, M.: Zur Kontrolle wirtschaftlicher Macht. Aufgabe und Befugnisse der Kartellbehörde nach § 22 GWB, in: WiST, 6/1975, S. 269.

[15] Siehe dazu auch Hoppmann, E.: Mißbrauch der Mißbrauchsaufsicht, S. 164, der von «Ausbeutung ohne wettbewerbswidriges Verhalten» spricht.

[16] Von dem 1973 hinzugefügten Tatbestand der überragenden Marktstellung sei einmal abgesehen.

Erstens: Wettbewerbsbeschränkung durch Maßnahme (Behinderungsmißbrauch) und Wettbewerbsbeschränkung durch Zustand sind aus der Sicht des Gesetzes nicht gleichgeordnet, sondern die Wettbewerbsbeschränkung durch Zustand ist – via Marktbeherrschung – eine Voraussetzung für das Ergreifen wettbewerbsbeschränkender Maßnahmen.

Zweitens: Das Gesetz impliziert die Möglichkeit einer Ausbeutung ohne vorheriges wettbewerbsbeschränkendes Verhalten.[17]

Drittens: Das Bundeskartellamt war aufgrund der Logik des Gesetzes gezwungen, die Konzeption einer Ausbeutung ohne wettbewerbsbeschränkendes Verhalten zu entwickeln. Wenn dies aber richtig ist, dann konnte es nicht umhin, zu den oben erwähnten direkten Preisinterventionen zu greifen, denn es gibt nur eine einzige Möglichkeit, die Ausbeutung ohne wettbewerbsbeschränkendes Verhalten zu bekämpfen, nämlich die direkte Preisintervention.[18]

Damit wird deutlich, daß die Schlüsselvariable für das Eindringen interventionistischer Tendenzen in die deutsche Wettbewerbspolitik die Idee von der Wettbewerbsbeschränkung durch Zustand darstellt.[19]

Im folgenden wird versucht, diese Idee einer kritischen Analyse zu unterziehen. Dazu ist zunächst die Frage zu stellen, was man sich eigentlich unter einer solchen Wettbewerbsbeschränkung durch Zustand vorzustellen hat und welche Faktoren eine solche Wettbewerbsbeschränkung bewirken.[20]

[17] Verwunderlich ist nur, daß diese Implikation erst relativ spät vom Bundeskartellamt aufgedeckt wurde.

[18] Das Argument, daß das Kartellamt ja auch noch den Zugang zum Markt erleichtern könne, impliziert die Existenz durch private Maßnahmen errichteter Zugangsschranken, die durch kartellbehördlichen Beschluß beseitigt werden könnten. Es erscheint fraglich, ob in diesem Falle noch von «reinem» Ausbeutungsmißbrauch gesprochen werden kann. Andere denkbare Maßnahmen zur Erleichterung des Marktzugangs fallen nicht in den Kompetenzbereich des Amtes. Im übrigen wäre auch zu fragen, ob sie mit den Prinzipien einer freiheitlichen Ordnung vereinbar sind. In den Fällen, die durch die Reflextheorie erfaßt werden, ergibt sich ein anderes Bild. Hier ist man nicht genötigt, zum Mittel der Preisintervention zu greifen, wenn man Ausbeutungsmißbrauch bekämpfen will: Ist Ausbeutung nämlich lediglich ein Reflex wettbewerbsbeschränkenden Verhaltens, dann verschwindet der Sachverhalt der Ausbeutung in dem Augenblick, in dem das wettbewerbsbeschränkende Verhalten bekämpft wird. Und dies ist durch mit einem freiheitlichen System konforme Verhaltensverbote möglich. Dazu benötigt man keine systeminkonformen Maßnahmen wie die staatlichen Zwangseingriffe in die Preissetzungsautonomie der Unternehmen. – Hingewiesen sei auch noch auf den Sachverhalt, daß die marktbeherrschende Stellung als solche nicht verboten ist, und daß das deutsche Wettbewerbsrecht die Möglichkeit einer Entflechtung nicht vorsieht.

[19] Das eigentliche Problem der Bekämpfung des «reinen» Ausbeutungsmißbrauchs wird also hier – entgegen der vorherrschenden Meinung – nicht in der Bestimmung des mißbräuchlichen Verhaltens gesehen, sondern in der Bestimmung der marktbeherrschenden Stellung.

[20] Diese Frage hat nicht nur Bedeutung für den Fall des Ausbeutungsmißbrauchs, sondern auch für den des Behinderungsmißbrauchs, denn auch dieser setzt ja – gemäß der Logik des Gesetzes – eine Wettbewerbsbeschränkung durch Zustand voraus, die erst eine marktbeherrschende Stellung ermöglicht. (Und das Bundeskartellamt muß erst das Vorliegen einer solchen Stellung nachweisen, bevor es gegen Mißbräuche vorgehen darf.) Letztere wird – und das muß man beachten – nach der Idee des Gesetzes durch keinerlei wettbewerbswidriges Verhalten geschaffen – was nicht ausschließt, daß sie de facto durchaus auch auf diese Weise entstehen kann. Das wettbewerbswidrige Verhalten – der Behinderungsmißbrauch – begründet nach dem Gesetz nicht die marktbeherrschende Stellung, sondern setzt diese – und damit die Wettbewerbsbeschränkung durch Zustand – als bereits vorhanden voraus. Die Wettbewerbsbeschränkung durch Zustand ermöglicht also erst die wettbewerbsbeschränkenden Praktiken genauso, wie sie die Ausbeutung ermöglicht.

IV. Wettbewerbsbeschränkung und die Heterogenität des Marktes

Um herauszufinden, was Wettbewerbsbeschränkung durch Zustand meint und wodurch sie bewirkt wird, erscheint es angebracht, an einer Aussage des Bundeskartellamtes über den Zweck der Mißbrauchsaufsicht anzusetzen: Danach hat diese «insbesondere die Aufgabe, das Fordern unangemessener Preise zu verhindern, soweit solche Forderungen dadurch möglich sind, daß Unternehmen die Preise ohne oder weitgehend ohne gegenseitige Rücksichtnahme oder ohne Rücksichtnahme auf andere Wettbewerber festlegen können und dadurch nicht gezwungen sind, in einer gegenseitigen Kontrolle die Preise jeweils möglichst niedrig festzusetzen, um am Markt bestehen zu können».[21] Das Bundeskartellamt unterstellt hier offensichtlich eine Situation, in der das Unternehmensverhalten hinsichtlich des Aktionsparameters Preis nicht der Kontrolle durch Wettbewerb unterliegt (= Marktbeherrschung).[22] Das Unternehmen muß also über einen wettbewerblich nicht kontrollierten Bereich autonomer Preissetzung verfügen.[23] Dieser resultiert aus der Marktbeherrschung bzw. der dieser zugrundeliegenden Wettbewerbsbeschränkung durch Zustand. Insoweit die Preise in diesem Bereich gesetzt werden, handelt es sich nach Ansicht des Kartellamtes nicht um wettbewerblich zustande gekommene Preise. Sie werden deshalb als unangemessen bezeichnet.

Sieht man in der Existenz eines Spielraums autonomer Preissetzung den Reflex einer Wettbewerbsbeschränkung durch Zustand und unterstellt, daß solche Zustände mit Hilfe des Marktstrukturansatzes beschrieben werden können, dann stellt sich die Frage nach den Marktstrukturen, bei denen die Sätze der Markttheorie Preissetzungsspielräume voraussagen.

Die Marktstruktur bildet bekanntlich einen Komplex aus verschiedenen Marktstrukturkomponenten. Ein Preissetzungsspielraum muß demgemäß ursächlich auf eine bestimmte Ausgestaltung von Marktstrukturkomponenten zurückgeführt werden. An solchen Marktstrukturkomponenten sind aus der Markttheorie unter anderem bekannt:
– Verschiedenheit der Produkte (sachliche, örtliche, persönliche, zeitliche Präferenzen)
– Unvollkommenheit des Wissens und unvollständige Markttransparenz
– Marktzugangsbarrieren.

In der Preistheorie werden diese Faktoren als Marktunvollkommenheitsfaktoren oder Monopolelemente bezeichnet. Liegt zumindest einer dieser Unvollkommenheitsfaktoren vor, dann spricht man normalerweise von einem heterogenen Markt. Markttheoretisch gesehen unterstellt die These von der Ausbeutung aufgrund einer Wettbewerbsbeschränkung durch Zustand also die Existenz eines heterogenen Marktes. Im heterogenen Markt ist der Wettbewerb beschränkt, und es existieren vom Wettbewerb nicht kontrollierte Preissetzungsspielräume (= Preissetzungsmacht), deren Ausnutzung als mißbräuchliches Verhalten klassifiziert und dem Tatbestand der Ausbeutung subsumiert wird. Ursa-

---

[21] Entscheidung des Bundeskartellamts vom 16. 10. 1974, a. a. O., S. 1532.
[22] «Der Tatbestand der Marktbeherrschung kann ... bereits gegeben sein, wenn die betreffenden Unternehmen nur hinsichtlich der oder des für das mißbräuchliche Verhalten maßgeblichen Wettbewerbsmittels nicht vom Wettbewerb kontrolliert werden.» (Ebenda, S. 1532.)
[23] Das Bundeskartellamt spricht von «Preisbildungsspielräumen» (ebenda, S. 1528.). Der BGH vom «überragenden, einseitigen Verhaltensspielraum» (Urteil des BGH vom 3.7. 1976, a. a. O., S. 1442).

che dieser Wettbewerbsbeschränkungen sind die Marktunvollkommenheitsfaktoren.[24] Daß diese Interpretation nicht fehlgeht, zeigt die oben zitierte Ansicht von *M. Schmidt*, einem Mitglied des Bundeskartellamts, der für solche Märkte eine Wettbewerbsbeschränkung durch Zustand unterstellt, «die aufgrund struktureller Beschränkungen nicht der Kontrolle durch den Wettbewerb unterliegen».

Um die folgende Diskussion der Hauptthese des Bundeskartellamtes, aber auch des Kammergerichts und des BGH, die sich diese Ansicht des Kartellamtes zu eigen gemacht haben, zu erleichtern und um Mißverständnisse zu vermeiden, sei der Grundgedanke der soeben vorgenommenen Interpretation in das exakte begriffliche Instrumentarium der Markttheorie übersetzt. Dabei wird die Verschiedenartigkeit der Produkte als Ursache für die Heterogenität eines Marktes angesehen, was den in den anfänglich erwähnten spektakulären Mißbrauchsfällen zum Ausdruck kommenden Vorstellungen der Kartellbehörde entspricht.[25]

Unterstellt seien 2 heterogene Produkte (x_1, x_2), die in substitutiver Beziehung stehen. Die Produktnachfragefunktionen lauten: $x_1 = f_1 (p_1, p_2)$ und $x_2 = f_2 (p_1, p_2)$. Die Heterogenität dieser Produkte zeigt sich darin, daß bei Konstanz von p_1 und Sinken von p_2 die Menge x_1 nicht Null wird und daß bei Konstanz von p_2 und bei Sinken von p_1 die Menge x_2 einen positiven Wert behält.[26] Als Maß für die Preissetzungsautonomie kann die Kreuzpreisabhängigkeit der Konkurrenznachfrage[27] dienen, also $dx_1 : dp_2$ bzw. $dx_2 : dp_1$. Je geringer der Wert der Kreuzpreisabhängigkeit ist, um so höher ist die Preissetzungsautonomie[28], also die Preissetzungsmacht. Oder mit anderen Worten: Je geringer die Kreuzpreisabhängigkeit ist, um so weniger ist die Höhe des einen Preises durch die jeweilige Höhe des anderen bestimmt.

Aber, so ist sofort zu fragen, ist dies Folge einer Wettbewerbsbeschränkung? Beschränkt der Zustand der Heterogenität eines Marktes, also die Existenz von Marktunvollkommenheitsfaktoren, bereits den Wettbewerb?

---

[24] Eben diese Monopolelemente werden in der Tat als Ursache dafür angeführt, daß in der pharmazeutischen Industrie der Wettbewerb beschränkt sei, echter (wirksamer) Preiswettbewerb fehle und demgemäß eine Ausbeutung durch Setzen mißbräuchlich überhöhter Preise stattfinden könne. So wird darauf verwiesen, daß die Markttransparenz gering sei, suggestive Werbung Meinungsmonopole schaffe und eine monopolistische Produktdifferenzierung stattfinde. Ferner sei auch die Preiselastizität der Nachfrage – gemeint ist die Firmennachfrage – gering. (Siehe Entscheidung des Bundeskartellamts vom 16.10. 1974, a. a.O., S. 1533; Urteil des OLG vom 5.1. 1976, a. a.O., S. 1651; Urteil des BGH vom 14.10. 1976, a. a.O., S. 1459.) Siehe auch *Hoppmann, E.*: Das Konzept des wirksamen Preiswettbewerbs, Tübingen 1978, S. 5.)

[25] Damit soll nicht geleugnet werden, daß es auch andere Faktoren gibt, die einen Spielraum autonomer Preissetzung begründen können, etwa die räumliche Verteilung von Anbietern eines physisch identischen Produkts. Allerdings wären dann diese Produkte «ökonomisch» nicht identisch.

[26] Dies liegt an der Existenz einer Kernnachfragefunktion, in der der Sachverhalt der Heterogenität letztlich zum Ausdruck kommt. (Zum Begriff der Kernnachfrage siehe *Fehl, U., Oberender, P.*: Grundlagen der Mikroökonomie, München 1976, S. 191ff.)

[27] Zu diesem Begriff siehe *Heuß, E.*: Allgemeine Markttheorie, Tübingen, Zürich 1965, S. 146ff.

[28] Es kommt bei der Frage der Preissetzungsautonomie also nicht darauf an, ob und wie z.B. x_1 auf Veränderungen von p_1 reagiert, sondern darauf, ob und inwieweit die Konkurrenznachfragefunktion $x_1 = f_1 (p_1, p_2)$ auf Veränderungen von p_2 reagiert, wenngleich auch die zuerst genannte Beziehung nicht unabhängig von der zuletzt genannten ist. (Siehe dazu *Heuß, E.*, a. a. O., S. 148.)

V. Die Kriterien zur Indikation einer Wettbewerbsbeschränkung durch Zustand

1. Der Gleichgewichtszustand bei vollkommener Konkurrenz

Betrachtet man einmal die Marktunvollkommenheitsfaktoren, die vom Bundeskartellamt als für die pharmazeutische Industrie typisch angeführt werden und die eine Wettbewerbsbeschränkung bewirken sollen, dann zeigt sich, daß sie ohne Ausnahme Abweichungen darstellen, und zwar Abweichungen von einem Zustand, der unter anderem durch folgende Merkmale gekennzeichnet ist: vollständige Markttransparenz, fehlende Produktdifferenzierung (identische Produkte), Fehlen subjektiver Präferenzen, Preiselastizität der individuellen Preis-Absatz-Funktion im Wert von unendlich. All dies sind Eigenschaften des Gleichgewichtszustandes bei vollkommener Konkurrenz. Der Markt ist homogen, Marktunvollkommenheitsfaktoren fehlen und damit auch Bereiche autonomer Preissetzung. Vielmehr wird der Preis vom Markt als Datum genommen; niemand erwartet, ihn durch seine Handlungen zu seinem Vorteil beeinflussen zu können.[29] Es existiert keine Preissetzungsautonomie und keine (partielle) Unabhängigkeit von den Preisen der Mitanbieter. Die jeweiligen Preise sind in höchstmöglichem Maße vom Wettbewerb kontrolliert.[30] Alle Marktteilnehmer sind gleich – auch in bezug auf ihre absolute Machtlosigkeit.[31] Es herrscht Preiseinheitlichkeit.

Wenn man diesen «Ideal»-Zustand des Gleichgewichts bei vollkommener Konkurrenz als Kriterium für unbeschränkten Wettbewerb verwendet, dann sind alle davon abweichenden Eigenschaften Indizien für Wettbewerbsbeschränkungen, und die diese Abweichungen verursachenden Faktoren – also die Monopolelemente – die Ursachen dieser Wettbewerbsbeschränkungen. Denn eben diese Monopolelemente schaffen die monopolistischen Bereiche in den Preis-Absatz-Funktionen und entziehen demgemäß – zumindest partiell – die Preissetzung der Kontrolle durch die Mitanbieter. Heterogenität eines Marktes bedeutet dann per se Wettbewerbsbeschränkung.

Wer das Modell des Gleichgewichts bei vollkommener Konkurrenz als normativen Maßstab in der Wettbewerbspolitik verwendet[32], legt jedoch eine Situation zugrunde,

---

[29] Zur Kritik an diesem Modell siehe *Fehl, U., Oberender, P.*, a. a. O., S. 29ff.

[30] Das Angebot ist auch nicht «oligopolistisch», und die Gewinne und Kosten sind auch nicht monopolistisch überhöht, wie dies als für die pharmazeutische Industrie typisch bezeichnet wird. (Siehe *Hoppmann, E.*: Das Konzept des wirksamen Preiswettbewerbs, S. 5.)

[31] Und wenn man im Wettbewerb ein Instrument zur Machtkontrolle sieht, ist es vielleicht gar nicht einmal so verkehrt, diesen Zustand «vollkommen» zu nennen. Die Machtlosigkeit ist vollkommen. Private Willkür ist nicht möglich.

[32] Und das wird tatsächlich getan. *K. E. Schmidt*, ein Angehöriger des Kartellamtes, schreibt in der Festschrift für *Eberhard Günther*, daß das «Wettbewerbsgleichgewicht im Sinne der Preistheorie» die Beurteilungsnorm sei, und daß ein wirksamer Preiswettbewerb Preise und Gewinne auf das Niveau des Wettbewerbsgleichgewichts herabdrücke. (*Schmidt, K. E.*: Die Bedeutung des Preiswettbewerbs im Begriff des wesentlichen Wettbewerbs im Sinne von § 22 GWB, in: Festschrift für E. Günther, Wettbewerb im Wandel, Hrsg.: E. Gutzler u. a., Baden-Baden 1976, S. 311f.) *Hoppmann* kommentiert dieses Vorgehen so: «Obwohl man in thesi oft erklärt, daß man diesen Zustand (gemeint ist das Gleichgewicht bei vollkommener Konkurrenz, D. S.) nicht als Maßstab verwenden wolle, wendet man ihn in praxi dann aber implizit doch an ... Proklamierte und praktizierte Methode decken sich dann nicht.» (*Hoppmann E.*: Das Konzept des wirksamen Preiswettbewerbs, S. 8.)

die erstens niemals existiert und niemals existieren kann; in der zweitens der wettbewerbliche Marktprozeß erloschen ist (Nirwana-These)[33]; vor deren Hintergrund drittens Wettbewerbsbeschränkungen zur Ubiquität werden und die viertens in ihren konkreten Eigenschaften mangels ausreichender Informationen niemals willkürfrei beschrieben werden könnte.[34]

Zum ersten Teil dieser These braucht nichts weiter gesagt zu werden. Die restriktiven und unrealistischen Bedingungen, unter denen ein solches Gleichgewicht besteht, sind allgemein bekannt.[35]

Zum zweiten Teil – der Nirwana-These: Bekanntlich bezeichnet Nirwana einen Zustand völliger und seliger Ruhe. In einem Gleichgewicht der vollkommenen Konkurrenz ist das auch der Fall. Die Pläne der Wirtschaftssubjekte sind total koordiniert. Der Marktprozeß verläuft stationär, und es gibt keine Neuerungen und Veränderungen. Versteht man unter Wettbewerb einen evolutorischen, Strukturen umgestaltenden Prozeß, wie die neuere Wettbewerbstheorie und der Koordinationsansatz[36] das tun, dann wird man einen solchen Wettbewerb hier vergeblich suchen. Während für einen Buddhisten

---

[33] Siehe dazu *Hoppmann, E.*: Das Konzept des wirksamen Preiswettbewerbs, S. 11, der diesen Begriff einer Arbeit von *H. Demsetz* entnommen hat.

[34] Zu diesen Punkten siehe *Hoppmann, E.*: Das Konzept des wirksamen Preiswettbewerbs, S. 11ff.

[35] Zur Kritik siehe auch *v. Hayek, F. A.*: Der Sinn des Wettbewerbs, in: derselbe: Individualismus und wirtschaftliche Ordnung, Erlenbach – Zürich 1952, S. 122ff.

Man könnte den Einwand erheben, daß die Maßstabsfunktion des Gleichgewichtszustands bei vollkommener Konkurrenz (Allokationsoptimum) nicht dadurch aufgehoben wird, daß in der Dynamik einer realen Wirtschaft dieser Zustand nicht erreicht wird oder daß er gar nicht erreicht werden soll. Denn um überhaupt Marktprozesse beurteilen zu können, benötige man irgendeine Optimalvorstellung darüber, wohin sie führen können, sonst hinge die «Prozeßkritik» orientierungslos in der Luft. Was z. B. eine bessere Versorgung sei, könne nicht durch den Prozeß allein, sondern nur durch das Ergebnis des Prozesses beurteilt werden, das sich vom Ausgangszustand positiv unterscheiden müsse. In diesem Sinne hätte die Wettbewerbspolitik die Aufgabe, solche Prozesse zu bekämpfen, die die in Richtung auf das Allokationsoptimum wirkenden Kräfte behindern. Wettbewerbspolitisch unbedenklich wären in dieser Sicht Abweichungen vom Optimum, die auf der Setzung neuer Leistungsdaten beruhen. Wettbewerbspolitisch zu bekämpfen hätte man dagegen Maßnahmen, die das Ziel verfolgten, eine Anpassung der Wirtschaft an die neuen Daten (Imitationsprozeß) zu verhindern.

Diese Vorstellung ist in mehrerlei Hinsicht problematisch: Zunächst geht es in der Wettbewerbspolitik darum, zu entscheiden, ob ein wettbewerblicher Marktprozeß vorliegt oder nicht. Diese Frage kann jedoch mit einem reinen Prozeßkriterium beurteilt werden. «Prozeßkritik» hängt auch durchaus nicht orientierungslos in der Luft, wenn sie nicht auf Optimalzustände Bezug nimmt. Denn die Kriterien zur Beurteilung eines Marktprozesses müssen theoretisch fundiert sein. Dazu benötigt man jedoch nicht die Vorstellung eines Allokationsoptimums. Ob in einem konkreten Fall eine Beschränkung der Innovationsfreiheit oder der Imitationsfreiheit vorliegt, läßt sich allein anhand eines Prozeßkriteriums beurteilen. Dazu ist es nicht notwendig zu wissen, wie das Ergebnis der Innovation bzw. der Imitation im Lichte eines Optimalzustandes einzuschätzen ist. Schließlich ist auch zu fragen, ob es möglich ist, einen Optimalzustand zur wettbewerbspolitischen Norm zu erheben und zugleich die Meinung zu vertreten, er sei gar nicht erstrebenswert. Warum normiert man ihn dann?

[36] Nach dem Koordinationsansatz gibt es evolutorischen Wettbewerb nur im ökonomischen Ungleichgewicht. Wettbewerb ist danach ein Ergebnis des Versuchs, noch nicht koordinierte Pläne aneinander anzupassen. (Siehe dazu *Hoppmann, E.*: Das Konzept des wirksamen Preiswettbewerbs, S. 15ff.; *Schmidtchen, D.*: Methodologische und systemtheoretische Grundsätze der Wettbewerbspolitik, in: Wirtschaftsdienst 9/1978; derselbe: Wettbewerbspolitik als Aufgabe, Baden-Baden 1978, S. 111ff.)

das Nirwana als erhoffter Endzustand gilt, ist zu bezweifeln, ob ähnliches auch für den Wettbewerbspolitiker gesagt werden kann.

Zum dritten Punkt: Die Bedingungen des Gleichgewichts sind derart idealistisch, daß kein realer Markt ihnen genügen wird. In jedem Markt existieren dann Wettbewerbsbeschränkungen durch Zustand. Wettbewerbsbeschränkungen durch Zustand werden also zur Ubiquität.[37] Die Paradoxie liegt auf der Hand: Wenn man einen im Sinne der neueren Wettbewerbstheorie wettbewerbslosen Zustand als Norm verwendet, dann sind die «Wettbewerbsbeschränkungen» der Realität gerade darin begründet, daß in der Realität Wettbewerb vorhanden ist.

Viertens schließlich müßte dieser Maßstab, um angewendet werden zu können, konkretisiert werden. Die Kartellbehörden müßten in einer konkreten Wirtschaft in bezug auf konkrete Marktprozesse angeben, welche Preise, Kosten und Marktstrukturen sich ergäben, wenn der Zustand vollkommenen Konkurrenzgleichgewichts realisiert wäre. Diese Präzisierungen setzen jedoch ein Wissen voraus, das kein Mensch besitzen kann. Wird dieser Zustand dennoch von irgend jemandem in allen wettbewerbspolitisch relevanten Einzelheiten beschrieben, dann liegt das vor, was *F. A. von Hayek* die «Anmaßung von Wissen» genannt hat.[38]

2. Der Zustand unvollkommener Konkurrenz

Wenngleich auch vieles für die These spricht, daß sich das Kartellamt dem Modell des vollkommenen Konkurrenzgleichgewichts verpflichtet fühlt, so wird man ihm allein mit dieser Interpretation wohl doch nicht ganz gerecht. Das Modell der vollkommenen Konkurrenz als Muster für einen Zustand unbeschränkten Wettbewerbs zu verwenden hat nämlich zur Folge, daß bereits bei einer geringfügigen Heterogenität des Marktes und darauf beruhenden geringfügigen Verhaltensspielräumen der Unternehmen die Diagnose auf Wettbewerbsbeschränkung und Vorliegen einer marktbeherrschenden Stellung lauten müßte. Das ist ein Ergebnis, dem nicht von allen zugestimmt werden dürfte und das auch den an anderer Stelle mehrfach geäußerten Ansichten des Bundeskartellamts wider-

[37] Man könnte einwenden, daß die normative Verwendung des Modells des Gleichgewichtszustands bei vollkommener Konkurrenz nicht dazu zwinge, alle Abweichungen von diesem Zustand mit Wettbewerbsbeschränkungen in Verbindung zu bringen. (Allerdings werden in der theoretischen Welt, in der dieses Modell als Norm entwickelt wurde, alle Abweichungen davon auf Wettbewerbsbeschränkungen zurückgeführt. Welchen Sinn hätte es sonst, von «monopoly elements» zu sprechen? Natürlich ist man an diesen Sprachgebrauch nicht gebunden.) Nur erhebt sich dann die Frage, wie man mit Hilfe dieses Modells Wettbewerbsbeschränkungen theoretisch und in der Realität diagnostizieren und Hinweise für die wettbewerbspolitische Therapie gewinnen will? (Auf einige Probleme, die entstehen, wenn man dieses Modell als Norm «aufweicht», wird im folgenden Abschnitt eingegangen.)

[38] Siehe *v. Hayek, F. A.*: Die Anmaßung von Wissen, in: ORDO, Band 26 (1975), S. 12ff. Noch eine Anmerkung zu der Vorstellung, das mit dem Modell des Gleichgewichtszustands beschriebene Allokationsoptimum als wettbewerbspolitische Norm ungeachtet der Tatsache zu verwenden, daß es nicht realisierbar ist: Selbst wenn man dieser Idee zustimmt, muß man das Optimum als mögliche Norm verwerfen, weil es nicht praktikabel definiert werden kann. Um als Norm zu dienen, muß das Optimum konkretisiert sein. Denn das praktische wettbewerbspolitische Problem besteht immer darin, in einem konkreten Fall anzugeben, ob eine Handlung zum Optimum hinführt oder nicht. Ist kein eindeutiger, empirisch überprüfbarer Maßstab vorhanden, dann ist der Willkür Tor und Tür geöffnet. Man kann dem Problem dadurch auszuweichen versuchen, daß man postuliert, jede Neuerung und jede Imitation stelle einen Schritt hin zum Optimum dar. Wozu benötigte man dann aber noch ein solches Optimum?

spricht. Denn danach ist ein Unternehmen nicht schon dann marktbeherrschend, wenn es irgendeinen heterogenitätsbedingten Verhaltensspielraum besitzt, sondern erst dann, wenn dieser Spielraum im Verhältnis zu seinen Wettbewerbern überragend ist. Das Kartellamt spricht manchmal auch von einem Mißverhältnis zwischen dem Freiheitsbereich des marktbeherrschenden Unternehmens und den Freiheitsbereichen der übrigen Marktteilnehmer oder von einer Ungleichverteilung der Macht.

Diese differenzierte Sicht des Amtes hat nun zur Folge, daß nicht jeder «Satz» von Marktunvollkommenheitsfaktoren Wettbewerbsbeschränkungen bewirkt und nicht jeder Verhaltensspielraum Marktbeherrschung bedeutet. Anders als bei Verwendung der soeben dargestellten Norm des Gleichgewichts bei vollkommener Konkurrenz führt nun die Heterogenität als solche nicht mehr notwendigerweise – also per se – zu einer Wettbewerbsbeschränkung. Erst wenn eine bestimmte Schwelle der Heterogenität überschritten ist, von der an Verhaltensspielräume überragend werden, hätte man von Wettbewerbsbeschränkung und Marktbeherrschung zu sprechen. Unterhalb dieser Schwelle liegende Heterogenitätsgrade des Marktes wären dagegen mit unbeschränktem Wettbewerb kompatibel.

Kennzeichnet man diese Vorstellung mit Hilfe der Kategorie der Kreuzpreisabhängigkeit, dann ist der Verhaltensspielraum des Unternehmens 1 im Vergleich zu dem des Unternehmens 2 überragend, wenn a) $dx_1 : dp_2 < dx_2 : dp_1$ und b) diese Ungleichheit ein bestimmtes Maß überschreitet. Gleichheit der Kreuzpreisabhängigkeiten oder geringfügige Ungleichheit wären vereinbar mit unbeschränktem Wettbewerb.

Im Gegensatz zum Modell des vollkommenen Konkurrenzgleichgewichts sind in dieser Konzeption unternehmerische Verhaltensspielräume auch bei unbeschränktem Wettbewerb vorhanden. Dies entspricht der Sicht der neueren Wettbewerbstheorie, die den Wettbewerb als dynamischen Prozeß von Vorstoß und Nachfolge interpretiert, in dem ständig Verhaltensspielräume aufgebaut und wieder erodiert werden. Die in diesen Verhaltensspielräumen zum Ausdruck kommende Macht ist kompetitive Macht und konstitutiv für Wettbewerb. Da es im Wettbewerbsprozeß stets Machtvorsprünge gibt, ist die kompetitive Macht ungleichmäßig verteilt. Mißt man diese kompetitive Macht mit Hilfe der Kreuzpreisabhängigkeit, dann bedeutet dies, daß die Kreuzpreisabhängigkeiten bei Wettbewerb unterschiedlich groß sind und sich vor allem im Zeitablauf ständig ändern werden. Welches konkrete Machtverteilungsmuster sich bei unbeschränktem Wettbewerb ergeben und wie es sich im Zeitablauf verändern wird, ist jedoch prinzipiell offen. Und es existiert keine ökonomische Theorie, mit deren Hilfe für einen Markt das wettbewerbliche Verteilungsmuster der Macht konkret inhaltlich bestimmt werden könnte. Da aber eben diese Festsetzung notwendig ist, um eine Wettbewerbsbeschränkung durch Zustand und einen überragenden Verhaltensspielraum zu diagnostizieren, bedeutet ein Festhalten an dieser Norm, der Willkür in der Wettbewerbspolitik Tor und Tür zu öffnen. Die Aussage, der Wettbewerb sei beschränkt, wenn und insofern die Heterogenität des Marktes und die Ungleichverteilung der Verhaltensspielräume ein bestimmtes Maß überschreiten, ist Ergebnis einer privaten und persönlichen Bewertung, die sich nicht auf empirisch abgestützte Erkenntnisse der Nationalökonomie berufen kann. Eine solche Wettbewerbspolitik kann demgemäß nicht den Anspruch erheben, rational genannt zu werden.[39]

---

[39] Siehe auch *Hoppmann, E.*: Das Konzept des wirksamen Preiswettbewerbs, S. 14.

VI. Eröffnung versus Beschränkung von Verhaltensspielräumen

Beide angeführten Maßstäbe zur Diagnose einer Wettbewerbsbeschränkung durch Zustand weisen einen gemeinsamen Mangel auf: Sie sind allein auf die Eröffnung (Existenz) von Verhaltensspielräumen fixiert, die mit der Heterogenität eines Marktes verbunden sind. Die wettbewerbspolitisch entscheidende Frage lautet jedoch nicht, ob die Heterogenität als solche bzw. die Heterogenität jenseits einer gewissen Schwelle Handlungsspielräume eröffnet, sondern ob sie Handlungsspielräume (wettbewerbliche Entfaltungsmöglichkeiten) beschränkt und ob der Handlungsspielraum eines Unternehmens durch Beschränkung des Handlungsspielraums eines anderen Unternehmens gewonnen wird. Versteht man unter Wettbewerb nämlich eine Verhaltensweise im Zeitablauf[40], dann kann man eine Wettbewerbsbeschränkung nur als Verhaltensbeschränkung interpretieren. Damit ergibt sich die Frage: Kann der Zustand eines Marktes – hier seine Heterogenität – das Verhalten von Wettbewerbern beschränken? Diese für die Beurteilung der «Ausbeutungsfälle» entscheidende Frage ist weder vom Bundeskartellamt noch von den Gerichten in ihrer Bedeutung erkannt worden.

Verhaltensbeschränkung kann in diesem Zusammenhang nur bedeuten, daß ein Wettbewerber durch die Heterogenität gezwungen wird, erstens ein Handeln (oder ein Geflecht von Handlungen) zu unterlassen, das von ihm selbst als für sich vorteilhaft eingeschätzt wird, und zweitens eine Handlung (oder einen Handlungskomplex) zu ergreifen, die (der) gemessen an der (dem) unterlassenen als suboptimal zu bezeichnen ist. Wettbewerbsbeschränkung heißt also Einschränkung des Handlungsfeldes von Wettbewerbern oder anders: der Wettbewerbsfreiheit. Damit lautet die Frage: Beschränkt die Heterogenität eines Marktes die Wettbewerbsfreiheit?

Die Heterogenität eines Marktes bewirkt, daß die Nachfragebeweglichkeit (partiell) eingeschränkt wird. Die Nachfrager empfinden eine Präferenz für einen bestimmten Anbieter mit der Folge, daß die Preishöhe nicht mehr das allein ausschlaggebende Kriterium für ihre Wahlentscheidung darstellt. Obwohl der Preis eines Gutes 1 höher ist als der eines Substitutionsproduktes 2, wandern die Nachfrager von Produkt 1 nicht oder nicht fühlbar zum Produkt 2 ab.

Hat diese Bindung der Nachfrage an ein Produkt aber eine Wettbewerbsbeschränkung zur Folge? Keineswegs. Der Produzent von Gut 2 wird durch diese Tatsache nämlich nicht daran gehindert, seine Leistung, also das Aggregat aus Produktqualität, Werbung, Konditionen und Preis, seiner Zielsetzung gemäß auszugestalten. Ob er allerdings sein Ziel – etwa Nachfrager von Gut 1 für sich zu gewinnen – erreicht, steht auf einem anderen Blatt. Hierfür ist maßgebend seine in der Marktleistung zum Ausdruck kommende Kompetenz relativ zu der des Produzenten von Gut 1, so wie sie in der Sicht der Nachfrager erscheint. Besitzen die Nachfrager Entscheidungs- und Handlungsfreiheit, dann kann der Umstand, daß die Nachfragebeweglichkeit eingeschränkt ist, keine Beschränkung der Wettbewerbsfreiheit des Produzenten von Gut 2 bewirken. Dieser Umstand hindert ihn nämlich nicht daran, alles, was in seinen Möglichkeiten steht, zu mobilisieren und zu aktivieren, um seine Zielsetzung zu erreichen.

Wollte man von Wettbewerbsbeschränkung immer schon dann sprechen, wenn ein Unternehmen seine Ziele nicht erreicht, weil die Nachfrager freiwillig bei einem Konkurrenten kaufen, so hätte dies absurde Konsequenzen. Denn die Diagnose einer Wettbe-

---

[40] Siehe Tätigkeitsbericht des Kartellamtes 1963, BT-Drucksache IV–2370, S. 10.

werbsbeschränkung hinge von dem rein subjektiven Faktor ab, wie anspruchsvoll und ehrgeizig ein Unternehmen seine Ziele formuliert. Eine solche Vorstellung impliziert letztlich, daß eine Wettbewerbsbeschränkung dann nicht vorliegt, wenn ein Unternehmen allmächtig ist, also in der Lage ist, die Umwelt nach seinem Bilde zu formen. Logischerweise kann dies jedoch nicht für alle Unternehmen zugleich gelten. Man muß also Kompetenzbeschränkungen als mit unbeschränktem Wettbewerb kompatibel ansehen und damit die Möglichkeit akzeptieren, daß bei unbeschränktem Wettbewerb Unternehmen aufgrund eines Kompetenzgefälles ihre Ziele nicht realisieren können. Sie sind dann gezwungen, in der Folge entweder die Ziele bescheidener zu formulieren oder aber nach anderen Wegen zu suchen. Dieser Zwang ist ein in natürlichen Umständen begründeter Zwang[41]; er beschränkt nicht die Wettbewerbsfreiheit. Einem solchen Zwang unterworfene Unternehmen handeln freiwillig.

Man kann diese für die Wettbewerbspolitik zentralen Zusammenhänge auch noch unter einem anderen Aspekt betrachten. Der Umstand, daß Unternehmen 2 aufgrund nicht ausreichender Kompetenz seine Ziele nicht erreichen kann, mag dazu führen, daß Unternehmen 2 gemessen an der von ihm gewünschten Situation einen Schaden erleidet, etwa in Form eines Betriebsverlustes. Ursache mag eine Qualitätsverbesserung bei dem Produkt des Unternehmens 1 gewesen sein. Die Handlungsmöglichkeiten von Unternehmen 2 sind durch diese Qualitätsverbesserung bei Produkt 1 beschränkt worden[42], aber: Solange «die Handlung, die seine Schwierigkeiten verursacht, nicht bezweckte, (es) . . . zu bestimmten Handlungen oder Unterlassungen zu zwingen, solange die Absicht der Handlung, die schädigt, nicht ist, . . . (es) in den Dienst der Ziele eines anderen zu stellen, ist ihre Wirkung auf seine Freiheit keine andere als die einer Naturkatastrophe – eines Feuers oder einer Überschwemmung, die . . . (ein) Heim zerstören, oder eines Unfalls, der . . . (jemandes) Gesundheit schädigt».[43] Den Ansichten *v. Hayeks* folgend sollte man in diesen Fällen nicht von Beschränkungen der Freiheit sprechen, denn es fehlt hier das Element des willkürlichen Zwangs.[44] Die Handlungen, die die Menschen bei ihrer Reaktion auf diese «natürlichen Umstände» ergreifen, sind freiwillig. Das gilt auch für die Handlungen des Unternehmens 2.

Da dieser Aspekt der Freiwilligkeit von Handlungen von zentraler Bedeutung für die Wettbewerbspolitik ist, sei noch die Ansicht von *Nozick* wiedergegeben, der sich in jüngster Zeit mit diesem Problem befaßt hat: «Ob die Handlungen eines Menschen freiwillig sind, hängt . . . davon ab, wodurch seine Möglichkeiten beschränkt sind. Wenn es Naturtatsachen sind, so sind seine Handlungen freiwillig. (Ich kann freiwillig an einen Ort gehen, an den ich lieber aus eigener Kraft fliegen würde.) Auch die Handlungen anderer Menschen schränken meine Möglichkeiten ein. Ob deshalb meine Handlungen nicht mehr freiwillig sind, hängt davon ab, ob die anderen zu ihren Handlungen berechtigt waren.»[45]

---

[41] Unterstellt ist, das sei noch einmal betont, daß die durch eine geringe Kreuzpreisabhängigkeit bedingten Verhaltensspielräume bei Entscheidungs- und Handlungsfreiheit der Nachfrager zustande kommen. Die Nachfrager kaufen freiwillig bei dem teureren Unternehmen.

[42] Diese Beschränkung zeigt sich hier darin, daß Unternehmen 2 keinen kostendeckenden Preis durchsetzen kann und in der Folge sein Aktionspotential verringert wird.

[43] *Von Hayek, F. A.:* Die Verfassung der Freiheit, S. 166.

[44] Siehe ebenda, S. 13ff.

[45] *Nozick, R.:* Anarchie, Staat, Utopia, München o. J., S. 240. «Wenn B und B' heiraten, so wird ihre Entscheidung nicht einfach dadurch zu einer nicht mehr freiwilligen, daß sie etwas anderes noch lieber getan hätten. Diese andere, am stärksten bevorzugte Möglichkeit, würde die Mitwirkung anderer erfordern, die aber, wie es ihr gutes Recht ist, etwas anderes vorgezogen haben.» (Ebenda, S. 240.) «Die Tatsache, daß ihre einzige andere Möglichkeit (in ihren Augen) viel

Einschränkungen der Handlungsmöglichkeiten eines Unternehmens durch die Handlungen anderer sind in diesem Sinne keine Wettbewerbsbeschränkungen, wenn die anderen zu ihren Handlungen berechtigt waren. Die Nutzung einer überlegenen Kompetenz seitens des Unternehmens 1, die zu einer Verbesserung der Marktleistung führt und die Handlungsmöglichkeiten eines Unternehmens 2 beschränken, wird man nicht als unberechtigt bezeichnen können.[46] Anders ist jedoch in den folgenden Fällen zu urteilen. Unberechtigt ist die Einschränkung einmal dann, wenn jemand die Kompetenz zu einer Handlungsalternative besitzt, diese aber deshalb nicht ergreifen kann, weil ihm die zur Realisierung dieser Alternative notwendigen Ressourcen nicht zur Verfügung stehen, da sein Konkurrent mit dem Ziel der Behinderung deren Quellen monopolisiert hat.[47] Die

schlechter ist, und die Tatsache, daß andere ihre Rechte in bestimmter Weise ausgeübt und damit die Wahlmöglichkeit für Z und Z' beeinflußt haben, bedeutet nicht, daß sie nicht freiwillig geheiratet haben.» «Die Entscheidung eines Menschen zwischen verschiedenen unangenehmen Möglichkeiten wird nicht dadurch zu einer nicht mehr freiwilligen, daß andere im Rahmen ihrer Rechte freiwillige Entscheidungen trafen und freiwillig handelten, derart, daß dem betreffenden keine bessere Möglichkeit übrig blieb.» (Ebenda, S. 241.)

Man darf natürlich nicht so naiv sein, das Problem des «freiwilligen Zwangs» zu leugnen. Es gibt sicher Fälle, in denen Auswahlmöglichkeiten fehlen, so daß sich jemand nur scheinbar freiwillig für die Wahl der noch verfügbaren Alternative entscheiden kann. Die wettbewerbspolitische Beurteilung dieses Sachverhalts hängt davon ab, welche Mittel zur Herbeiführung dieser Situation angewandt worden sind.

Instruktiv dürfte in diesem Zusammenhang auch der Fall sein, in dem ein Unternehmen ohne willkürliche Wettbewerbsbeschränkungen in den Besitz von für ein anderes Unternehmen unentbehrlichen Ressourcen gekommen ist. Das Entstehen einer solchen Situation ist dann vom Standpunkt einer wettbewerblichen Ordnung hinzunehmen. Das bedeutet jedoch nicht, daß der berechtigte Erwerb des Eigentums an diesen Ressourcen das Recht verleiht, sich zukünftig in wettbewerbsbeschränkender Weise zu verhalten.

[46] Die Frage, ob Handlungen berechtigt sind oder nicht, kann nur anhand einer Norm entschieden werden. Vermittels dieser Norm ist die Menge der möglichen Handlungen in berechtigte und unberechtigte aufzuteilen. Soll eine Wettbewerbsordnung errichtet werden, dann sind wettbewerbsbeschränkende Handlungen «unberechtigt». Sie werden als unberechtigt bezeichnet, weil sie wettbewerbsbeschränkend sind. Diese Argumentation ist nicht tautologisch, denn Handlungen werden nur dann als wettbewerbsbeschränkend klassifiziert, wenn sie mit dem Ziel in Konflikt stehen, die Wettbewerblichkeit von Marktprozessen zu sichern. Der Einteilung von Handlungen in wettbewerbliche und wettbewerbsbeschränkende liegt also ein materielles Kriterium zugrunde.
Es ist natürlich niemals ausgeschlossen, daß auf der rechtlichen Ebene Handlungen als nicht wettbewerbsbeschränkend (und demgemäß berechtigt) erscheinen, die tatsächlich – gemessen an der wettbewerbspolitischen Zielsetzung – nicht berechtigt sein dürften. Dann ist die Rechtsordnung unvollkommen und entsprechend zu ergänzen. Es könnte natürlich auch ein Zielkonflikt vorliegen, der zu Lasten des Zieles «Sicherung der Wettbewerblichkeit von Marktprozessen» entschieden wurde. In einer vollkommenen Rechtsordnung wären alle wettbewerbsbeschränkenden Handlungen als unberechtigt erfaßt.

[47] Man wird an dieser Stelle die Frage nach dem staatlich garantierten Patentschutz aufwerfen müssen. Wenn die Rechtsordnung das Institut des Patents zur Verfügung stellt, dann sind alle Handlungen von Unternehmen, die die Nutzung dieses Instituts zum Zweck haben, berechtigt, wenn und insofern sie den Rechtsrahmen beachten. Berechtigt sind also die Handlungen, die die Rechtsordnung nicht verbietet bzw. ausdrücklich erlaubt. Erlaubt die Rechtsordnung Handlungen (etwa Sperrpatente), die aus wettbewerbspolitischen Gründen nicht gewünscht werden, dann muß man die Gesetze derart ändern, daß diese Handlungen nicht mehr berechtigt sind. Ein freiheitliches System ist gerade dadurch gekennzeichnet, daß in ihm das Prinzip der «Herrschaft des Gesetzes» gilt. «Die Freiheit ist das Recht, alles tun zu dürfen, was die Gesetze erlauben.» (Montesquieu)

andere Möglichkeit besteht darin, daß ein Konkurrent Maßnahmen mit dem Ziel ergreift, die Kompetenz des anderen zu verschlechtern oder aber eine an sich mögliche Nutzung zu verhindern. Jedesmal liegt eine Wettbewerbsbeschränkung vor. Hinter beiden Formen von Wettbewerbsbeschränkungen stehen unternehmerische Maßnahmen behindernder Art. Natürlich ist das Ergebnis dieser Maßnahmen ein Zustand, der die Wettbewerbsfreiheit beschränkt. Ob ein Zustand als wettbewerbsbeschränkend angesehen werden muß, hängt jedoch allein davon ab, wie er entstanden ist. Beschneidung von Handlungsmöglichkeiten ist zwar eine notwendige Bedingung für eine Wettbewerbsbeschränkung, aber noch nicht hinreichend. Nicht jede (objektive) Beschränkung der Handlungsmöglichkeiten von Akteuren ist demgemäß als eine Wettbewerbsbeschränkung zu klassifizieren.[48] Die Schaffung und Einführung eines neuartigen Produkts wird man wohl kaum – jedenfalls nicht per se – als ein Mittel zur Monopolisierung notwendiger Ressourcen oder zur Behinderung von Konkurrenten ansehen können. Vielmehr ist sie ein Ausdruck von «Leistungswettbewerb», der eine Verbesserung der Marktversorgung zur Folge hat.[49]

[48] Diese Aussage ist von besonderer Bedeutung, wenn man Probleme des Markteintritts vor sich hat. Es ist z. B. möglich, daß ein Anbieter nicht in den Markt eintritt, weil er meint, er könne gegen den bereits Etablierten nicht bestehen. Hier liegt ebenfalls keine Wettbewerbsbeschränkung durch Zustand vor. Wenn von einem Marktzutritt Abstand genommen wird, dann zeigt dies entweder, daß die subjektive Kompetenz als nicht hinreichend eingeschätzt wird, um erfolgreiche Leistungen gegen die Konkurrenz des bereits im Markt befindlichen Unternehmens zu erbringen. Die Wettbewerbsfreiheit ist nicht beschränkt. Der potentielle Newcomer könnte seine Kompetenz voll entfalten, aber er schätzt die Erfolgsaussichten – angesichts der am Markt vorhandenen Kompetenz – gering ein. Er verzichtet freiwillig auf den Marktzutritt. Deshalb wird durch den bereits Etablierten auch seine Wettbewerbsfreiheit nicht beschränkt. Es sei denn, dieser verhält sich in einer Weise, zu der er nicht berechtigt ist (z. B. abschreckende Preissetzung). Dann liegt aber Wettbewerbsbeschränkung durch Maßnahme vor. Denn ohne dieses Verhalten würde der Newcomer in den Markt eintreten. Oder aber, der potentielle Newcomer rechnet mit zukünftigen unberechtigten Verhaltensweisen des bereits im Markt befindlichen Unternehmens (z. B. ruinöse Konkurrenz). Dann aber befürchtet er Wettbewerbsbeschränkung durch Maßnahme und bleibt deshalb dem Markte fern. Seine Entscheidung wird maßgeblich davon geprägt sein, wie er die Kompetenz der Kartellbehörden einschätzt, eine Wettbewerbsbeschränkung durch Maßnahme zu bekämpfen. – Auch der «Zustand», daß ein Unternehmen einen überragenden Preissetzungsspielraum besitzt, kann die Wettbewerbsfreiheit nicht beschränken. Denn einmal ist dieser Zustand nichts anderes als ein Reflex der Heterogenität des Marktes und zum anderen hindert dieser Bereich die Mitanbieter nicht daran, ihre (heterogenen) Produkte auf den Markt zu bringen und vermittels des Einsatzes verschiedener Aktionsparameter dafür Nachfrage zu schaffen. – Auch hohe Risiken eines Markteintritts beschränken die Wettbewerbsfreiheit nicht. Ähnliches gilt für den Fall, daß die Nachfrage preisunelastisch ist. (Zur Kritik siehe *Hoppmann, E.*: Marktmacht und Wettbewerb, S. 16f.; sowie derselbe: Preisunelastizität der Nachfrage als Quelle von Marktbeherrschung, in: Wettbewerb im Wandel, Festschrift für E. Günther, Hrsg.: *Gutzler, E. u. a.*, Baden-Baden 1977, S. 283ff.)

[49] Betrachtet man unter diesem Aspekt einmal die Argumentation der Kartellbehörde und der Gerichte in den «Pharma-Fällen», dann wird deutlich, daß es sich bei den «Pharma-Fällen» um wettbewerbspolitische Irrläufer handelt. So wird *Roche-Grenzach* als marktbeherrschend bezeichnet, weil es bei *Valium* und *Librium* keinem wesentlichen Wettbewerb ausgesetzt sei. Zugleich wird darauf hingewiesen, daß neue Anbieter mit heterogenen Produkten – und zum Teil höheren Preisen – am Markt aufgetreten seien und daß diese «nicht nur keine Marktanteilsverluste erlitten, sondern zu ungunsten von *Valium* und *Librium* noch beträchtliche Marktanteilsgewinne erzielt» hätten. (Entscheidung des Bundeskartellamts vom 16.10. 74, a. a. O., S. 1527.) Nachstoßender Wettbewerb war also möglich, und er erfolgte auch. (Ebenda, S. 1528.) Die nachfolgenden Unternehmen besaßen Handlungsspielräume und nutzten sie, und zwar – wie das meist der Fall sein wird – bei der Erschließung und Ausschöpfung zusätzlicher Nachfrage. Der

VII. Endzustands-Grundsätze und historische Grundsätze

Wie bereits erwähnt, geht es bei dem Ausbeutungsmißbrauch um die Frage, ob Leistung und Gegenleistung angemessen sind. Um die Angemessenheit – etwa eines Preises – beurteilen zu können, benötigt man einen normativen Maßstab oder Grundsatz. Im Prinzip sind zwei Arten von Grundsätzen denkbar [50]: Endzustands- oder Endergebnisgrundsätze und historische Grundsätze.

Endzustands-Grundsätze sind statischer Natur. Sie orientieren sich am gegenwärtigen Zeitquerschnitt des Wertes ökonomischer oder anderer Variablen. Man kann sie deshalb auch als strukturelle Grundsätze bezeichnen.[51] Wendet man die Idee vom Endzustands-Grundsatz auf das Ausbeutungsproblem in einem einzelnen Markt an, dann zielt dieser Grundsatz auf ein ideales Marktverhältnis, bei dem Ausbeutung fehlt – mit anderen Worten: Er gibt an, welches der angemessene Preis bzw. die angemessene Preisstruktur ist. Konfrontation des real sich ergebenden Preises bzw. der tatsächlichen Preisstruktur mit diesem angemessenen Preis bzw. der angemessenen Preisstruktur ermöglicht die Diagnose, ob Ausbeutung vorliegt oder nicht. Alle Konzepte, die sich auf wettbewerbsanaloge Preise oder Preisstrukturen oder «Als-ob»-Überlegungen stützen, wollen solche Endzustands-Grundsätze ermitteln.[52]

Historische Grundsätze[53] enthalten keine Beschreibung einer idealen Konstellation, in der Angemessenheit von Leistung und Gegenleistung gewahrt ist, sondern sie beziehen sich darauf, wie eine reale Austauschkonstellation zustande kommen muß, damit die in

Markt expandierte nämlich – ein Sachverhalt, dessen Konsequenzen völlig übersehen wurden, wie das folgende Zitat zeigt: «Unter den Bedingungen wirksamen Preiswettbewerbs hätte das Auftreten nachstoßender Wettbewerber mit therapeutisch weitgehend austauschbaren Präparaten und die damit verbundene Beseitigung einer weitgehenden Alleinstellung auf dem Markt zu einem Wettbewerbsprozeß durch Preissenkungen durch *Roche-Grenzach* und Preisunterbietungen durch die nachstoßenden Wettbewerber führen müssen» (ebenda, 1528). Warum die Preise gesenkt werden sollten, wenn die Nachfrage expandiert und lediglich der Marktanteil zurückgeht, bleibt das Geheimnis des Bundeskartellamtes. – Im *Merck*-Fall schreibt der BGH (Urteil des BGH vom 3.7. 1976, a. a. O., S. 1442): «Aufgrund des Auftretens von Wettbewerbern mit teilweise erheblich niedrigeren Preisen ist ihr (nämlich die Unternehmung *Merck*, die vom Kartellamt und Kammergericht als mit einem überragenden allseitigen Handlungsspielraum versehen bezeichnet wurde) mengenmäßiger Marktanteil in den Jahren seit 1956 stetig zurückgegangen.» Einige Vitamin-B-12-Produzenten ragen «durch ihre niedrige Preisgestaltung heraus; sie haben ihren Markterfolg weitgehend ihrer niedrigen Preisgestaltung zu verdanken» (ebenda, S. 1442). Auch hier ist zu fragen, warum *Merck* die Preise hätte senken sollen, wenn die Firmennachfrage, was bei sinkendem Marktanteil der Fall sein kann, sich noch nach rechts verschoben haben sollte. Lag eine Linksverschiebung vor, dann wäre eine Preissenkung ebenfalls nicht notwendig gewesen. Denn einmal hängt es vom Unternehmensziel ab, wie man sich im Markt verhält. So hätte *Merck* zum Beispiel einen Rückgang der Preis-Absatz-Funktion als zielkonform betrachten können. Wenn nicht, wäre zu prüfen, ob eine Preissenkung überhaupt in der Lage ist, eine Linksverschiebung der Preis-Absatz-Funktion zu kompensieren. Der einzige Effekt kann unter Umständen aufgrund der niedrigen direkten Nachfrageelastizität darin bestehen, daß der Umsatz sinkt.

[50] Diese Zweiteilung greift einen Gedanken auf, den *Robert Nozick* im Zusammenhang mit seiner Theorie der Verteilungsgerechtigkeit entwickelt hat. (Siehe *Nozick, R.*: Anarchie, Staat, Utopia, a. a. O., S. 143ff.)

[51] Siehe ebenda, S. 146.

[52] Auch die Festlegung von mit unbeschränktem Wettbewerb kompatiblen Mustern von Verhaltensspielräumen (Gleichgewichtszustand der vollkommenen Konkurrenz, Zustand unvollkommener Konkurrenz) läuft auf die Formulierung eines solchen Grundsatzes hinaus.

[53] Siehe ebenda, S. 146ff.

ihr implizierten Bedingungen des Austauschs als angemessen gelten können. Historische Grundsätze finden ihren Ausdruck in Spielregeln, nicht jedoch in der Struktur von Spielergebnissen. Ein Preis z. B. gilt dann als angemessen, wenn er auf eine den Spielregeln gemäße Weise zustande gekommen ist, von der man unterstellt, daß sie zu angemessenen Preisen führt. Das konkrete Spielergebnis ist ex ante prinzipiell unbekannt, und die jeweiligen sich im Verlauf des Spiels herausbildenden Ergebnisse erhalten ihren Gütestempel und ihre Unbedenklichkeitsbescheinigung allein aufgrund der Art und Weise, wie sie zustande gekommen sind.

Ein Prinzip, das sich auf die Art und Weise des Zustandekommens von Preisen bezieht, die als angemessen gelten sollen, ist der Wettbewerb. An ihn knüpft man die Hoffnung, daß er aufgrund seiner machtausgleichenden Wirkungen einen «gerechten» Interessenausgleich schafft. Da Wettbewerb die Freiwilligkeit des Austausches sichert, kann man mit einiger Plausibilität davon ausgehen, daß derjenige, der eine wettbewerbliche Austauschbedingung akzeptiert, diese als angemessen betrachtet.

Der Grundgedanke des historischen Grundsatzes, die Angemessenheit des Preises durch ein wettbewerbliches Entdeckungsverfahren zu ermitteln, in dem Anbieter und Nachfrager frei entscheiden können, läßt sich folgendermaßen verdeutlichen:

Bekanntlich «bildet» sich der Preis bei vollkommener Konkurrenzpreisbildung im Schnittpunkt der Angebotsfunktion mit der Nachfragefunktion. Der Austausch erfolgt zu diesem Preis freiwillig. Er gilt deshalb als angemessen. Verringert sich nun das Angebot bei gegebener Nachfragefunktion, dann steigt der Preis des Gutes an. Ist dieser höhere Preis nun angemessen oder nicht? Trotz gleichgebliebener Qualität des Produktes gilt der nunmehr höhere Preis ebenfalls als angemessen, und zwar deshalb, weil er sich im freien Wettbewerb – der hier allerdings annahmegemäß nur den Preisparameter kennt – gebildet hat.

Analoge Überlegungen gelten für den Fall heterogener Konkurrenz, bei dem die Unternehmen über Preissetzungsspielräume in ihren individuellen Preis-Absatz-Funktionen verfügen. Angenommen, die Heterogenität eines Marktes sei Ausdruck wettbewerblichen Handelns, sie sei den wettbewerblichen Spielregeln gemäß, durch die Nutzung der Wettbewerbsfreiheit, entstanden.[54] Dann sind die jeweiligen Preissetzungsspielräume in den Preis-Absatz-Funktionen (und die diesen Funktionen entsprechenden Marktanteile) Ergebnisse eines wettbewerblichen Marktprozesses. Die Spielräume autonomer Preissetzung sind wettbewerblich begründet (kompetitive Macht). Die im Rahmen dieser Autonomie gesetzten Preise sind wettbewerblich zustandegekommene Preise, und sie gelten deswegen nicht als ausbeuterisch. Wesentlich ist, zu erkennen, daß das «Ausnutzen» dieser wettbewerblich bedingten Preissetzungsmöglichkeit keinen Verstoß gegen das wettbewerbliche Preisbildungsprinzip darstellt. Daraus folgt, daß es unzutreffend ist, von einem wettbewerblich nicht kontrollierten Preissetzungsspielraum bei freier heterogener Konkurrenz zu sprechen, wie es das Bundeskartellamt mehrfach getan hat. Wenn der Preissetzungsspielraum das Ergebnis eines wettbewerblichen Prozesses ist, dann ist seine Ausnutzung durch entsprechende Preissetzung damit zugleich wettbewerblich legitimiert. Die sich herausbildende Preisstruktur ist demgemäß ebenfalls eine wettbewerbli-

---

[54] Dieser Aspekt der Genese der Heterogenität eines Marktes kann naturgemäß von Wettbewerbskonzepten, die sich einem statischen Wettbewerbsbegriff verpflichtet fühlen, nicht erfaßt werden. Jenen ist es damit auch verwehrt, den wesentlichen Unterschied zwischen restriktiver und kompetitiver Marktmacht zu erkennen. Nur Preissetzungsspielräume, die durch Einsatz restriktiver Marktmacht und das heißt hier: bei Vorliegen von Mißbräuchen durch Maßnahme entstanden sind, stellen wettbewerbspolitisch ein Problem dar. Wettbewerblich entstandene dagegen nicht.

che. (Es sei denn, die Erosion der Preissetzungsspielräume werde mit wettbewerbsbeschränkenden Mitteln verhindert!) Während sich bei homogener Konkurrenz tendenziell einheitliche Preise herausbilden, ergibt sich bei heterogener Konkurrenz eine Preismarge. Darin kommt gewissermaßen das Spezifikum heterogener Konkurrenz zum Ausdruck.

Diese Überlegung leitet über zu der folgenden These: Solange die Wettbewerbsfreiheit nicht beschränkt ist und solange die Nachfrager frei entscheiden können, welches Produkt sie kaufen wollen – beide Bedingungen, die notwendig und hinreichend sind, kennzeichnen die freie heterogene Konkurrenz –, kann es niemals zu einer Ausbeutung kommen. Der sich bildende Preis ist immer Ergebnis eines «gerechten» Interessenausgleichs – und demgemäß «angemessen».

Dies läßt sich noch unter einem anderen Aspekt verdeutlichen. Angenommen, ein Unternehmen besitze einen wettbewerblich zustandegekommenen Preissetzungsspielraum. Es nutze diesen vollständig aus, mit der Folge, daß der von ihm geforderte Preis weit über denen der Konkurrenzprodukte liegt. Die Nachfrager könnten zwar auf ein billigeres Konkurrenzprodukt abwandern, aber sie tun es nicht. Die Tatsache, daß sie nicht abwandern, obwohl sie es könnten, ist ein Indiz dafür, daß in der Sicht der Käufer – und nur diese kann entscheidend sein – dem höheren Preis auch eine höhere Gegenleistung entspricht.[55] Genau dies aber ist die Bedingung, die erfüllt sein muß, wenn keine Ausbeutung vorliegen soll. Denn Ausbeutung ist ja immer durch eine Nicht-Äquivalenz von Leistung und Gegenleistung definiert.[56]

Freie heterogene Konkurrenz führt also immer zu angemessenen Preisen – die Preisstruktur zwischen den heterogenen Produkten ist eine durch Wettbewerb bestimmte Struktur.[57] Das bedeutet, daß die Preisunterschiede zwischen heterogenen Produkten – so groß sie auch im Einzelfall sein mögen – keinen Anlaß zu direkten Preisinterventionen geben, wenn und insofern erstens die sie ermöglichenden Preisbildungsspielräume den wettbewerblichen Prinzipien gemäß entstanden sind und zweitens diese nicht mit wettbewerbswidrigen Mitteln gegen eine Erosion verteidigt werden.[58]

[55] Höhere Gegenleistung ist dabei umfassend zu definieren. Dazu gehört auch die Einsparung von Informationskosten.

[56] Diese Bedingung ist sicherlich auch im Falle des reinen Angebotsmonopols erfüllt. Deshalb ist sie nicht hinreichend für das Verneinen von Ausbeutung. Die hinreichende Bedingung lautet, daß sich die Austauschbeziehungen ohne Beschränkungen der Wettbewerbsfreiheit und der Nachfragefreiheit bilden müssen.

[57] Daran wird noch einmal deutlich, daß die Ansicht des Kartellamtes, die Setzung der Preise innerhalb eines wettbewerblich zustandegekommenen Preissetzungsspielraums erfolge nicht unter wettbewerblicher Kontrolle, darauf beruht, daß es sich an den Preisbildungsprinzipien der homogenen Konkurrenz orientiert.

[58] In dieser Argumentation ist eine sogenannte formale Nachfragefreiheit impliziert. Wenn die Nachfrager nicht zu bestimmten Handlungen gezwungen werden und die Konkurrenten unbehindert ihre Waren anpreisen können, dann gilt die Entscheidung der Nachfrager zum Beispiel für das teuerste Produkt als eine freiwillige Entscheidung. Außerdem ist zu beachten, daß jedes heterogene Produkt irgendwann einmal eine Innovation darstellte und sich gegen andere Produkte durchsetzen mußte. Kam die Nachfrage freiwillig zu ihm? Auch wenn ein Konkurrent das Zwanzigfache an Werbemitteln aufwendet und demzufolge den höchsten Preis setzen kann, hat das als wettbewerbspolitisch unbeachtlich zu gelten, wenn die dazu notwendigen finanziellen Mittel wettbewerbskonform erworben und wettbewerbskonform, also ohne Verstoß gegen die Spielregeln, verwendet werden. Akzeptiert man dieses Prinzip nicht und lehnt man ferner das Prinzip der formalen Nachfragefreiheit ab, dann bewegt man sich notwendigerweise außerhalb des Rahmens einer freiheitlichen Ordnung und landet in letzter Konsequenz im totalen Interventionismus.

VIII. Abschließende Bemerkungen

Die oben vorgetragenen Gedanken kreisen um die im Zentrum jeder Wettbewerbspolitik stehende Frage, was man unter Wettbewerbsbeschränkung verstehen und wie man sie erfassen und bekämpfen sollte. Im Prinzip bieten sich zwei Wege an, die mit den Begriffen «historischer Grundsatz» und «Endzustands-Grundsatz» umschrieben werden können. Beide Wege führen zu völlig konträren wettbewerbspolitischen Konzeptionen.

Eine an historischen Grundsätzen orientierte Wettbewerbspolitik fragt stets: Wie sind unternehmerische Handlungsspielräume, konkret: Preissetzungsspielräume, entstanden, und mit welchen Mitteln werden sie verteidigt? Sind die praktizierten Handlungen gerechtfertigt, dann sind es auch die Preissetzungsspielräume und die gesetzten Preise. Welche Handlungen gerechtfertigt sind, entscheiden die Spielregeln, die sich in einem langwierigen Erfahrungsprozeß herauskristallisieren und ständiger Überprüfung bedürfen. Grundidee einer derart orientierten Wettbewerbspolitik ist es, daß Zustände wettbewerbsbeschränkender Art und daraus resultierende Preissetzungsspielräume durch bestimmte unternehmerische Maßnahmen herbeigeführt werden. Unterbindet man diese behindernden Maßnahmen, dann bekämpft man damit auch zugleich die Möglichkeiten, ausbeuterische Preise zu setzen. Schutz der Wettbewerbsfreiheit vor Beschränkungen, so lautet das Ziel. Da solche Beschränkungen immer Handlungen von Personen voraussetzen[59], kann eine derartige Wettbewerbspolitik mit gesetzlichen Handlungsverboten arbeiten. Handlungsverbote lassen sich justitiabel formulieren. Sie haben allgemein, voraussehbar und bestimmt zu sein, so daß die Wirtschaftssubjekte sich in ihrem Verhalten an sie anpassen können, und behördliche Willkür eine Schranke an ihnen findet.[60] Da diese Form der Wettbewerbspolitik die Spielregeln einer marktwirtschaftlichen Ordnung gestaltet, genügt sie auch den Prinzipien einer Wirtschaftspolitik im Rechtsstaat.[61] Konkret bedeutet dies, daß man den Problemen privater wirtschaftlicher Macht mit einer genauen Fixierung allgemeiner Rechtsregeln beizukommen versucht, die es erlauben, wettbewerbsbeschränkende Handlungen zu spezifizieren, zu diagnostizieren und zu bekämpfen. Die Ansicht, daß die Probleme des Ausbeutungsmißbrauchs über die Setzung und Anwendung derartiger Rechtsregeln nicht lösbar seien und daß deshalb Kartellbehörden im Wege des Ermessens entscheiden müßten, läuft auf die Behauptung hinaus, daß bei den Problemen des «reinen» Ausbeutungsmißbrauchs die Grenzen der Leistungsfähigkeit eines rechtlich ausgeprägten Spielregelsystems erreicht sind.

Man kann die direkten Preisinterventionen des Kartellamtes natürlich auch als ultima ratio ansehen, wenn alle anderen Möglichkeiten versagen. Liberalen Prinzipien entspräche es dann aber, den Notfall in allgemeiner Weise zu definieren, so daß jedermann nachprüfen kann, ob ein solcher vorliegt. Auch Regelungen der Notfälle müssen in eine allgemeine gesetzliche Form gebracht werden.

Als Notfälle hat man bisher die natürlichen Monopole angesehen. Sind die Fälle des Ausbeutungsmißbrauchs hier zu subsumieren? Das würde zu einer starken Erweiterung

---

[59] Das können auch staatliche Instanzen sein, wie die Pharma-Märkte zeigen. Staatlich geschaffene Regelungen verhindern hier, daß eine preisausgleichende Arbitrage auftritt. (Zu diesem Problem siehe *Hamm, W.*: Wettbewerbspolitische Fragen der Pharmaindustrie, in: pharma dialog, 38 / 1975.)

[60] Zum Charakter dieser Regelungen siehe *von Hayek, F. A.*: Die Verfassung der Freiheit, S. 178ff. Eine solche Politik müßte Regeln aufstellen, denen zu entnehmen ist, wann und wie sich Handlungsspielräume legal bilden.

[61] Zu diesen Prinzipien siehe ebenda, S. 285ff.

des Begriffs des natürlichen Monopols führen und damit zu einer Inflation der Bereichsausnahmen. Im Weltbild des § 22 GWB erscheinen marktbeherrschende Unternehmen nicht als natürliche Monopole; sie sind und bleiben vielmehr in eine marktrationale Ordnung eingebunden. Darf man sie dann jedoch wie ein natürliches Monopol behandeln?

Eine an historischen Grundsätzen ausgerichtete Wettbewerbspolitik kann sich keine konkreten Marktergebnisse zum Ziel setzen, denn die Spielregeln prägen nur den allgemeinen Charakter der Ergebnisse (Muster im Sinne *v. Hayeks*). Das ist anders bei einer Wettbewerbspolitik, die Endzustands-Grundsätze verfolgt. Hier werden wettbewerbliche Marktergebnisse normiert, wodurch Wettbewerbspolitik eine ganz andere Qualität erhält. Verfolgt die Wettbewerbspolitik Endzustands-Grundsätze, dann werden Wettbewerbsbeschränkungen diagnostiziert, indem man tatsächliche Handlungsspielräume von Unternehmen an einer von wettbewerbspolitischen Instanzen normierten Struktur wettbewerbspolitisch unbedenklicher Handlungsspielräume mißt. Ausnutzung eines derart diagnostizierten überragenden Handlungsspielraums durch entsprechende Preissetzung führt dann zur Ausbeutung. Da bei einer Ausbeutung aufgrund einer Wettbewerbsbeschränkung durch Zustand definitionsgemäß eine wettbewerbsbeschränkende Verhaltensweise fehlt, entfällt die Möglichkeit, durch ein Verbot der letzteren zugleich die Ausbeutung zu verhindern. Man kann nur eines tun, nämlich gegen die vermeintliche Ausbeutung mit einer punktuell-interventionistischen Politik vorzugehen. Es bleibt keine andere Wahl. Damit aber setzt die Wettbewerbspolitik nicht an der Gestaltung der Spielregeln an, sondern sie greift direkt ins Spiel ein und gibt die Spielergebnisse vor.

Die Praktizierung von Endzustands-Grundsätzen ist unvereinbar mit einer freiheitlichen Wirtschaftsordnung. Weil eine freiheitliche Wirtschaftsordnung ein offenes System darstellt, sind die sich wettbewerblich herausbildenden Strukturen der Preissetzungsspielräume sowie die Preisstrukturen selbst grundsätzlich unbekannt; vor allem aber kommt es ständig zu Umstrukturierungen. Die Freiheit sprengt Strukturen. Will man gleichwohl eine Endzustandsstruktur durchsetzen, kommt man nicht umhin, den Wirtschaftssubjekten bestimmte Verhaltensweisen vorzuschreiben. An die Stelle einer Ordnung durch Gesetze tritt die Ordnung durch Befehl.[62]

---

[62] Man könnte einwenden, daß zur Realisierung einer Endzustandsstruktur lediglich ein Verbieten genüge, ein Gebieten also nicht nötig sei. Das Argument übersieht, daß man eine Endzustandsstruktur im Wege des Verbietens nur ansteuern kann, wenn das Verbieten materiell dem Gebieten gleichkommt. Ein Befehl kann in der Form eines Verbietens erteilt werden. – Zu der Unterscheidung von Gesetz und Befehl siehe *v. Hayek, F. A.*: Die Verfassung der Freiheit, S. 178ff. «Freies Handeln, in dem ein Mensch seine eigenen Ziele mit den Mitteln verfolgt, die ihm sein eigenes Wissen anzeigt, muß sich auf Umstände gründen, die nicht von einem anderen willkürlich geändert werden können. Es setzt das Bestehen eines bekannten Bereichs voraus, in dem die Umstände nicht von einem anderen Willen so gestaltet werden können, daß sie dem Handelnden keine andere Wahl lassen als die, die der andere vorschreibt. Zwang kann jedoch nicht völlig vermieden werden, weil die einzige Methode, ihn zu verhindern, die Androhung von Zwang ist. Eine freie Gesellschaft hat dieses Problem gelöst, indem sie dem Staat das Monopol der Zwangsausübung überträgt und versucht, diese Gewalt des Staates auf jene Fälle zu beschränken, in denen sie zur Vermeidung von Zwang durch private Personen erforderlich ist. Das ist nur dadurch möglich, daß der Staat bekannte private Bereiche der einzelnen gegen Eingriffe von anderen schützt und diese Bereiche nicht durch spezielle Zuweisung, sondern durch Setzung von Bedingungen abgrenzt, unter denen der einzelne seinen eigenen Bereich bestimmen kann, indem er auf Regeln vertraut, die ihm sagen, was die Regierung in verschiedenen Situationstypen tun wird.» (Ebenda, S. 28.) Diese staatlichen Regeln müssen allgemein, gewiß und voraussehbar sein, damit vermieden wird, daß die Willkür privaten Zwangs nicht lediglich durch die Willkür staatlichen Zwangs ersetzt wird. Dies jedoch wird nur erreicht, wenn diese Regeln Gesetze im «echten» Sinne sind und nicht etwa Befehle.

Summary

Exploitation through Restraints of Competition due to the State of a Market? A Critical Analysis of the Theoretical Basis of a Competition Policy Harmful to Freedom

If the right of the enterprise to autonomously determine its conditions of exchange is considered an essential characteristic of a free economic order, the competition policy as pursued in the Federal Republic of Germany must be regarded as a danger to this order. To prevent exploitation by excessive prices, the Federal Cartel Authority (Bundeskartellamt) has on various occasions tried to prescribe maximum prices to companies, which – according to its standards – are holding dominant positions in the market. While in the past restrictive business practices (Wettbewerbsbeschränkung durch Maßnahme) were considered the only reason for exploitation, the Federal Cartel Authority has now adopted the diverging and most controversial view that, irrespective of any active practices, the possibility of exploitation also exists in cases of restraints of competition resulting from the state of a market (Wettbewerbsbeschränkung durch Zustand).

This article deals with the interpretation of «Wettbewerbsbeschränkung durch Zustand» and its identification in practice on the part of the Federal Cartel Authority. The thesis is advocated that «Wettbewerbsbeschränkungen durch Zustand» result from the heterogeneity of markets, which implies areas of indeterminacy in pricing. There are two criteria to identify areas of indeterminacy; the model of static equilibrium with perfect competition and models of monopolistic competition. The weak points of these concepts are expounded. Subsequently the characteristic common to both models is examined, i.e. that market imperfections as such or over and above a certain degree result in restraints of competition. If, however, competition means a complex of free actions, restraints of competition are nothing but restraints of freedom. Examples are given to demonstrate that the heterogeneity of a market does not limit this freedom of competition.

Finally, some consequences of an idea, developed by *Robert Nozick* in his book «Anarchy, State, and Utopia» are stated. *Nozick* distinguishes historical and structural principles of justice. It appears that a competition policy compatible with a free economic order should follow historical principles.

Wernhard Möschel

Die Idee der rule of law und das Kartellrecht heute

Am Beispiel der gezielten Kampfpreisunterbietung

I. Einleitung

Das wissenschaftliche Werk *Friedrich August von Hayeks* ist in Gegenstand und Methode dadurch gekennzeichnet, daß es beinahe durchgängig jene Grenzen überschreitet, welche der Spezialisierungsprozeß der einzelnen Sozialwissenschaften während des 19. Jahrhunderts zwischen diesen ausgebildet hat. Umfassender Bezugspunkt seiner erkenntnistheoretischen, nationalökonomischen, juristischen, soziologischen wie politikwissenschaftlichen Fragestellungen sind die Bedingungen von Freiheit im Sinne eines Zustandes, in welchem Zwang auf Menschen von seiten anderer Menschen so weit herabgemindert ist, als dies im Gesellschaftsleben möglich ist.[1] *Von Hayek* weiß sich dabei von einer geisteswissenschaftlichen Tradition geprägt, die wesentlich im England des 17. und 18. Jahrhunderts ausgebildet und über den Konstitutionalismus der Vereinigten Staaten historisch wahrscheinlich am stärksten befördert wurde.

Im Bereich der deutschen Rechtswissenschaft haben die staats- wie gesellschaftstheoretischen Arbeiten *von Hayeks* bis heute keine große Resonanz gefunden. Umso nachhaltiger ist der Einfluß seines Denkens auf die Grundlagendiskussion innerhalb des speziellen Sektors des Kartellrechts bzw. des Rechts der Wettbewerbsbeschränkungen, wie man heute allgemeiner formuliert. Seine Charakterisierung des Wettbewerbs als Entdeckungsverfahren[2] mit Folgewirkungen bis in die feinsten Verästelungen des geltenden Rechts hinein ist mittlerweile Allgemeingut geworden. Die Überwindung jenes «Neuen Leitbildes der Wettbewerbspolitik»[3] mit ihrer Orientierung an ökonomischen performance-Vorstellungen gründet sich auf seine gedankliche Vorarbeit.[4] Dies ist in gewisser

---

[1] Vgl. *F. A. von Hayek*, Die Verfassung der Freiheit, Tübingen 1971, S. 13.

[2] So der Titel eines Vortrags aus dem Jahre 1968, veröffentlicht in: Kieler Vorträge, Neue Folge 56, Hrsg. *E. Schneider*, Kiel 1968. Wieder abgedruckt in: *F. A. v. Hayek*, Freiburger Studien, Tübingen 1969, S. 249 ff.; vgl. früher schon die Aufsätze: Die Verwertung des Wissens in der Gesellschaft, Der Sinn des Wettbewerbs, «Freie Wirtschaft» und Wettbewerbsordnung, in: Individualismus und wirtschaftliche Ordnung, Erlenbach-Zürich 1952, S. 103 ff., 122 ff., 141 ff.

[3] So der Titel einer Veröffentlichung von *W. Kartte* aus dem Jahre 1969 mit Bericht über eine entsprechende Meinungsbildung innerhalb einer Arbeitsgruppe des Bundesministeriums für Wirtschaft. Erscheinungsort: Köln, Berlin, Bonn, München.

[4] Sie wurde besonders wirksam über die wettbewerbstheoretischen Arbeiten *E. Hoppmanns*, z.B. Das Konzept der optimalen Wettbewerbsintensität, JbNSt 179 (1966), 287 ff.; *ders.*, Die Funktionsfähigkeit des Wettbewerbs, JbNSt 181 (1967), 251 ff.; *ders.*, Zum Problem einer wirtschaftspolitisch praktikablen Definition des Wettbewerbs, in: Grundlagen der Wettbewerbspoli-

Weise paradox, da *F. A. von Hayek* dem Regelungsanliegen des Rechts der Wettbewerbsbeschränkungen eine verhältnismäßig periphere Bedeutung beimißt. In seinem Werk «Die Verfassung der Freiheit», welches die Summe seines Denkens zieht und auch dieser Festschrift den Namen gegeben hat, widmet er jener Frage nur einige wenige, von deutlicher Skepsis gegenüber der Praxis des amerikanischen Antitrustrechts geprägte Zeilen.[5] Der tiefere Grund dafür liegt in der Auffassung *von Hayeks* begründet, daß in diesem Bereich das Ausmaß an Regelungs- oder Eingriffswillkür zu groß und die Idee der rule of law als eines stetigen Ordnungsrahmens für Entdeckungsprozesse, die aus freien Interaktionen erwachsen, zu wenig realisiert ist. Meine These lautet, daß hier im Regelungsgegenstand selbst ein Zielkonflikt zwischen Regelungsnotwendigkeit und Regelungsmöglichkeit angelegt ist. Gerade von den Wertvorstellungen *von Hayeks* her, die Zwangsunterworfenheit von Menschen unter den Willen anderer Menschen[6] auf ein Minimum zu reduzieren, sollte dieser Konflikt nicht im Sinne einer tendenziellen Abstinenz des regelnden Staates gelöst werden. Im folgenden wird nicht versucht, eine Theorie der unvollkommenen Gesetzgebung zu formulieren. Vielmehr soll den angedeuteten Fragen an Hand eines Sachverhaltes nachgegangen werden, der im Recht der Wettbewerbsbeschränkungen erheblich geworden ist. Vorweg ist das spezifische Verständnis der rule of law bei *von Hayek* skizziert.

II. Die rule of law bei F. A. von Hayek

Die Herrschaft des Gesetzes über Menschen im Gegensatz zu einer Herrschaft von Menschen über Menschen ist eine Schlüsselkategorie im Freiheitsdenken *F. A. von Hayeks*. Er erkennt darin nicht eine Regel des Rechts, sondern ein politisches Ideal, ein metagesetzliches Prinzip, welches die Staatsgewalt bei den mit Zwang verbundenen Tätigkeiten beschränken sollte.[7] Die wichtigste Konsequenz daraus ist, daß sich damit eine bestimmte *inhaltliche* Vorstellung von dem verknüpft, was mit «Gesetz» gemeint ist. Es bedarf kaum der Erwähnung, daß *von Hayek* hierbei keine allgemeine Theorie des Rechtssatzes entwickelt oder gar eine Stellungnahme zu einem positivrechtlichen Gesetzesbegriff innerhalb einer historischen Rechtsordnung abgibt.[8] Sein klassisch-liberaler, in der Neuzeit wesentlich auf *J. Locke*[9] rückführbarer Ansatz bringt *von Hayek* dazu, in der Unterscheidung von förmlichem und materiellem Gesetz, die sich z. B. in der deutschen

tik, Hrsg. *H. K. Schneider,* Berlin 1968, S. 9 ff. ; *ders.,* «Neue Wettbewerbspolitik» : Vom Wettbewerb zur staatlichen Mikro-Steuerung, ZHR 184 (1970), 397 ff.; *ders.,* Fusionskontrolle, Tübingen 1972; *ders.,* Marktmacht und Wettbewerb, Tübingen 1977; zuletzt *ders.,* Das Konzept des wirksamen Preiswettbewerbs, Tübingen 1978.

[5] AaO (Fußn. 1), S. 336–338.

[6] *Von Hayek* versteht unter «Zwang» solche Veränderung der Umgebung oder der Umstände eines Menschen durch jemand anderen, daß dieser, um größere Übel zu vermeiden, nicht nach seinem eigenen zusammenhängenden Plan, sondern im Dienst der Zwecke des anderen handeln muß; siehe: Die Verfassung der Freiheit, (Fußn. 1), S. 27, 161 ff.

[7] Die Verfassung der Freiheit, (Fußn. 1), S. 266 ff.

[8] Entwicklungsgeschichtlicher Überblick z. B. bei *R. Grawert,* Artikel Gesetz, in: Geschichtliche Grundbegriffe, Bd. 2, Stuttgart 1975, S. 863–922.

[9] Zwei Abhandlungen über die Regierung, deutsch von *H. J. Hoffmann,* Frankfurt 1967, Buch II, § 22, S. 215, 284 ff.

Staatsrechtslehre seit *P. Laband*[10] durchgesetzt hat, eine gefährliche Abirrung von seinem Postulat zu sehen: «Die Bezeichnung ‹Gesetz› für all das, was die gewählten Volksvertreter beschließen und für jede Anordnung, die sie als Regierung unter dem Gesetz treffen..., ist aber nicht viel besser als ein schlechter Witz. Das ist in Wahrheit einfach gesetzlose Ausübung der Regierungsgewalt.»[11]

Gesetze, die den Anforderungen der rule of law genügen, sind vielmehr solche «Verhaltensregeln, die nicht nur für alle Staatsbürger, sondern auch für den Staat gleichermaßen gelten. Sie sind generell und abstrakt in dem Sinne, daß sie weder bestimmte Personen noch bestimmte Zeitpunkte oder Orte nennen und daß es tatsächlich nicht voraussehbar ist, welche Wirkungen sie auf bestimmte bekannte Personen haben werden. Sie beziehen sich nur auf das Verhalten der Menschen zueinander – und zum Staat –, aber nicht auf ihre private Sphäre.»[12] Es handele sich im wesentlichen um langfristige Maßnahmen, in ihrer Wirkung immer nur für die Zukunft bestimmt, als Regel indes bekannt und gewiß.[13] Erfaßt sei in etwa das, was man als Zivil- und Strafrecht kenne, ausgeschlossen das ganze übrige öffentliche Recht, insbesondere das Staats- und Verwaltungsrecht und auch das Verfahrensrecht.[12]

Die geistesgeschichtliche Nähe dieser Auffassung zum historisch-konventionellen Rechtssatzbegriff, wie er sich in Deutschland innerhalb der spätkonstitutionellen Staatslehre entwickelt hatte – danach diente das Recht entweder der Abgrenzung der Rechte und Pflichten der einzelnen Rechtssubjekte gegeneinander und damit der sozialen Schrankenziehung oder der Regelung von staatlichen Eingriffen in Freiheit und Eigentum der Bürger[14] – ist evident.

Dieses klassische Ideal der rule of law oder des government under the law wird nun von *von Hayek* in unerbittlicher intellektueller Strenge und Folgerichtigkeit in vielfältigen Problemzusammenhängen als Bewertungsmaßstab herangezogen: Innerhalb der Organisation staatlicher Willensbildung tritt er für eine Zweiteilung des demokratischen Repräsentativorgans ein. Der Erlaß «echter Gesetze» im eben skizzierten Sinne sollte einer auf lange Frist gewählten und ausschließlich auf diese Aufgabe beschränkten Versammlung vorbehalten sein. Alle übrigen Aufgaben sollten von einer Regierungsversammlung, im wesentlichen organisiert wie die Parlamente westlicher Demokratien, wahrgenommen werden: «Das Ideal des government under the law kann nur erreicht werden, wenn auch die Volksvertretung, die die Regierungstätigkeit dirigiert, unter Regeln steht, die sie selbst nicht ändern kann, sondern die von einer anderen demokratischen Körperschaft

---

[10] Zusammenfassend *P. Laband*, Das Staatsrecht des Deutschen Reiches, Bd. 2, 5. Aufl. Tübingen 1911, S. 61 ff.; dazu z. B. *E. W. Böckenförde*, Gesetz und gesetzgebende Gewalt. Von den Anfängen der deutschen Staatsrechtslehre bis zur Höhe des staatsrechtlichen Positivismus, Berlin 1958, S. 226 ff.

[11] *Von Hayek*, Drei Vorlesungen über Demokratie, Gerechtigkeit und Sozialismus, Tübingen 1977, S. 9; vgl. auch *ders.*, Die Verfassung der Freiheit, (Fußn. 1), S. 187: «Ein ‹Gesetz›, das ein spezieller Befehl ist und nur ‹Gesetz› genannt wird, weil es von einer gesetzgebenden Behörde ausgeht, ist das Hauptinstrument der Unterdrückung.»

[12] *Von Hayek*, Recht, Gesetz und Wirtschaftsfreiheit, in: Freiburger Studien, Tübingen 1969, S. 47, 49.

[13] Die Verfassung der Freiheit, (Fußn. 1), S. 270 ff.; dort auch weitere Ausdifferenzierungen.

[14] Siehe dazu z. B. *P. Laband*, aaO (Fußn. 10), S. 73; *G. Jellinek*, Gesetz und Verordnung, Freiburg i. Br. 1887 (Neudruck 1919), S. 240; *G. Anschütz*, in *K. von Stengel/M. Fleischmann*, Wörterbuch des deutschen Staats- und Verwaltungsrechts, Bd. 2, 2. Aufl., Tübingen 1913, S. 214; *G. Meyer/G. Anschütz*, Lehrbuch des deutschen Staatsrechts, 7. Aufl. München und Leipzig 1917, S. 639 ff., 655 ff.; vgl. als Überblick *E. W. Böckenförde*, aaO (Fußn. 10), S. 132 ff., 266 ff.; *D. Jesch*, Gesetz und Verwaltung, Tübingen 1961, S. 15 ff.

bestimmt werden, die gewissermaßen die langfristigen Prinzipien festlegt.»[15] Es ist selbstverständlich, daß eine solche Gesellschaftsordnung keinen vorgegebenen, kollektiven Zwecken dienen kann, sondern nur als spontane, offene, auf freiem Austausch beruhende Gesellschaft konzipierbar ist; wohlfahrtstheoretische Vorstellungen sind darin schon im Denkansatz notwendig dysfunktional.[16] Umverteilende soziale Gerechtigkeit ist in solcher spontanen Ordnung «sinnlos»; für die Erhaltung einer friedlichen Gesellschaft freier Menschen seien zwar Regeln gerechten Verhaltens der einzelnen unabdingbar, Versuche aber, soziale Gerechtigkeit herzustellen, mit dieser nicht vereinbar.[17] Eng damit zusammen hängt das Verdikt über eine allgemeine Progression der steuerlichen Belastung der einzelnen.[18]

Dies sind nur einige Beispiele für Schlußfolgerungen, welche *von Hayek* aus seinem Postulat ableitet. Es trägt indes nicht die formulierte Skepsis im Hinblick auf einen legislativen wie jurisdiktionellen Kampf gegen Wettbewerbsbeschränkungen. Dies soll am Tatbestand der gezielten Kampfpreisunterbietung im einzelnen dargetan werden.

III. Zur gezielten Kampfpreisunterbietung

Die gezielte Kampfpreisunterbietung bezeichnet den Sachverhalt, daß ein – in der Regel marktmächtiges – Unternehmen die Preise eines Konkurrenten in der Absicht unterbietet, diesen zum Ausscheiden aus dem Markt zu zwingen, um sodann freie Bahn für den eigenen Absatz und die künftige Preisbestimmung zu haben.[19] Dies ist zunächst nur eine grobe Umschreibung, die – wie sich zeigen wird – zu differenzieren ist. Ein solcher Sachverhalt wird im deutschen Recht seit dem Benrather-Tankstellen-Urteil des Reichsgerichts[20] schon von § 1 UWG erfaßt. Er ist auch ein unbestrittener Anwendungsfall des § 22 GWB (Mißbrauch einer marktbeherrschenden Stellung) sowie des § 26 Abs. 2 GWB (Verbot unbilliger Behinderung). Im amerikanischen Recht spricht man von predatory pricing. Es ist über die spezielle Strafvorschrift des Sec. 3 Robinson-Patman Act, das Monopolisierungsverbot und das Verbot der versuchten Monopolisierung nach Sec. 2 Sherman Act sowie – im Falle einer Diskriminierung – über Sec. 2 Clayton Act in der Fassung des Robinson-Patman Act faßbar. Hinzu tritt wie immer die Generalklausel des Sec. 5 FTC-Act.

---

[15] Vgl. Recht, Gesetz und Wirtschaftsfreiheit, in: Freiburger Studien, S. 47, 53 ff.; *ders.*, Die Anschauungen der Mehrheit und die zeitgenössische Demokratie, ebenda, S. 56, 72 ff. ; *ders.*, Drei Vorlesungen, (Fußn. 11), S. 17 ff.

[16] Z. B. Grundsätze einer liberalen Gesellschaftsordnung, in: Freiburger Studien, S. 108, 121; *ders.*, Rechtsordnung und Handelnsordnung, ebenda, S. 160, 168 ff.

[17] Grundsätze einer liberalen Gesellschaftsordnung, (Fußn. 16), S. 114/115; *ders.*, Drei Vorlesungen, (Fußn. 11), S. 24 ff.; *ders.*, Law, Legislation and Liberty, 2. Bd., London 1976, S. 62 ff.

[18] Grundsätze einer liberalen Gesellschaftsordnung, (Fußn. 16), S. 123; eingehender in: Die Verfassung der Freiheit, (Fußn. 1), S. 387 ff.

[19] Vgl. für alle A. *Baumbach/W. Hefermehl*, Wettbewerbs- und Warenzeichenrecht, 12. Aufl. München 1978, § 1 UWG Anm. 206; unverändert grundlegend *F. Böhm*, Wettbewerb und Monopolkampf, Berlin 1933.

[20] RGZ 134, 342.

1. Die Gespensterthese

In amerikanischen Untersuchungen hat man Sachverhalte dieser Art aus theoretischen wie empirischen Gründen als eher imaginär bezeichnet, da solche Preispolitik als Mittel der Monopolisierung nachgerade «foolish» wäre.[21] Für eine an der rule of law ausgerichtete Wettbewerbspolitik bedeutete dies, daß solche Verhaltensweisen kein Gegenstand rechtlicher Regelung zu sein brauchten. Solche These gründet indessen auf irrigen Feststellungen. Es ist richtig, daß eine Kampfpreisunterbietung zu Lasten von Konkurrenten insofern nicht eine einseitige Maßnahme ist, als das unterbietende Unternehmen Nachfrager finden muß, die bereit sind, zu diesen Preisen abzuschließen.[22] Unter der Prämisse, daß diese den Charakter des Kampfpreises erkennen und daß sie ihr langfristiges eigenes Interesse an einer preisgünstigen Versorgung höher bewerten als eher kurzfristige Kostenvorteile, ist die Schlußfolgerung denkmöglich, daß das unterbietende Unternehmen gar keine Abnehmer findet. Irgendeine Realität ist damit nicht beschrieben. Die Abgrenzung einer Kampfpreisunterbietung gegenüber dem erfolgreichen Einsatz des Preises als Wettbewerbsparameter ist so schwierig, daß die implizierte Voraussetzung vollständiger Information bei den Abnehmern häufig nicht erfüllt sein wird. Dahinstehen mag, ob die weiter zugrunde gelegte Extremform eines homo oeconomicus nicht bereits zum homunculus geworden ist. Schließlich ist nicht bedacht, daß ein Weiterbezug von dem bekämpften Außenseiter (oder den Außenseitern) zum höheren Preis dann nicht durchzuhalten ist, wenn die billigere Versorgung der Konkurrenten beim unterbietenden Unternehmen die Wettbewerbslage entsprechend beeinflußt. Das wäre nur wieder anders unter der in der Regel theoretisch bleibenden Prämisse, daß der bekämpfte Außenseiter jetzt die gesamte Nachfrage (trotz seines höheren Preises) auf sich ziehen könnte und zu ihrer Befriedigung auch in der Lage wäre.

Ebensowenig überzeugt der Gedankengang, Kampfpreisunterbietungen seien schon deshalb irrational, weil ein Aufkauf des zu verdrängenden Konkurrenten regelmäßig billiger sei. Dies ist nicht schlüssig auf der jedenfalls heute sowohl für die USA wie die Bundesrepublik zutreffenden Prämisse, daß ein in eine Monopolisierung mündender Zusammenschlußvorgang grundsätzlich unzulässig ist. Während ein Zusammenschluß sich schwerlich verbergen läßt, ist dies für die Kampfpreisunterbietung dagegen möglich. Zu beachten ist auch, daß eine auf Verdrängung zielende Preispolitik nicht notwendig impliziert, daß das unterbietende Unternehmen dabei keine Kostendeckung erreicht (sog. soft predation).[23] Selbst auf der Basis eines billigeren Aufkaufs ist die erforderliche Willenseinigung zwischen den Beteiligten nur im theoretischen Modell problemlos. Die Wirklichkeit kann sehr verschieden sein. Auch wäre zu bedenken, daß predatory pricing durchaus

[21] Grundlegend *J. McGee*, Predatory Price Cutting: The Standard Oil (N. J.) Case 1, J. Law & Econ. 137 (1958) = 6 J. of Reprints for Antitrust L. & Econ. 279 (1975); siehe weiter *L. Telser*, Abusive Trade Practices: An Economic Analysis, 30 Law & Contemp. Prob. 488 (1965); *ders.*, Cutthroat Competition and the Long Purse, 9 J. Law & Econ. 259 (1966); *R. Zerbe*, The American Sugar Refinery Company, 1887–1914: The Story of a Monopoly, 12 J. Law & Econ. 339 (1969); *D. Dewey*, The Theory of Imperfect Competition: A Radical Reconstruction, New York und London 1969, 7. Kap.; *K. Elzinga*, Predatory Pricing: The Case of the Gunpowder Trust, 13 J. Law & Econ. 223 (1970); *R. Bork*, The Antitrust Paradox, New York 1978, S. 155.

[22] Zu dieser Überlegung *R. Posner*, Antitrust Law. An Economic Perspective, Chicago u. London 1976, S. 184.

[23] *B. S. Yamey*, Predatory Price Cutting: Notes and Comments, 15 J. Law & Econ. 129, 133 (1972) = 6 J. of Reprints for Antitrust L. & Econ. 587, 593 (1975); dagegen *R. Koller II*, On the Definition of Predatory Pricing, 20 Antitrust Bull. 329 (1975) = 6 J. of Reprints for Antitrust L. & Econ. 577 (1975).

einen Einfluß auf die Höhe des erzielbaren Erlöses haben kann.[24] Schließlich fällt ins Gewicht, daß Kampfpreisunterbietungen als Marktzutrittsschranken gegenüber potentiellen Konkurrenten einen Sinn haben können. Das gilt nicht nur auf dem Markt, auf welchem der Preiskampf ausgelöst wird. Dies kann in der Realität des diversifizierten, auf vielen Märkten zugleich tätigen Unternehmens auf Grund seiner Abschreckungswirkung auch auf anderen Märkten wirksam werden. An der hier zurückgewiesenen Kritik ist richtig nur, daß solche gezielten Preisunterbietungen in der Regel weniger zu Verdrängungs- als zu Disziplinierungszwecken eingesetzt werden. Das heißt, es werden Marktverhältnisse angestrebt, in welchen Preiswettbewerb zum Erliegen kommt und durch eine Preisführerschaft des dominierenden Unternehmens ersetzt ist.

Letzteres leitet zum empirischen Aspekt der Frage über. In Deutschland sind Sachverhalte dieser Art kaum vor die Gerichte gekommen.[25] Doch bedeutet dies nicht, daß sie nicht existent sind. Dies belegen Erfahrungen in den USA. Zwar ist auch dort die Bewertung dieser Frage kontrovers. Doch zeigt genauer differenzierende Analyse dies: Die Vorschrift des Sec. 3 Robinson-Patman Act, welche Rabattdiskriminierungen, regionale Preisdifferenzierungen und Verkäufe zu «unreasonably low prices» unter Strafe stellt, wenn sie zu Vernichtungszwecken erfolgen[26], ist in der Praxis obsolet geblieben.[27] Richtig ist auch, daß in den großen, von der Antitrust Division des Department of Justice geführten Verfahren predatory pricing zwar vorkam, aber eher eine periphere Rolle spielte.[28] Doch liegt dies wesentlich daran, daß die Sachverhalte auf einer weniger problematischen Basis aufgegriffen wurden. Dies relativiert z. B. die Grundlagenuntersuchung von *McGee*[29], der im klassischen Fall der Monopolisierung des Petroleummarktes durch die Standard Oil Company of New Jersey aus dem Jahre 1911[30] keine Anzeichen für predatory pricing entdeckt: Juristisch im Vordergrund standen die Unternehmenszusammenschlüsse durch Standard Oil. Predatory pricing wird in der amerikanischen Praxis überwiegend von der Federal Trade Commission verfolgt und erscheint hier schwer-

---

[24] Das wäre nur wieder anders auf der Basis eines mehr oder minder vollkommenen Marktes für Unternehmen bzw. bei entsprechend niedrigen Marktzutrittsschranken; in dieser Richtung argumentiert z. B. *R. Koller II*, aaO (Fußn. 23).

[25] Neben RGZ 134, 342 Benrather Tankstelle ist auf LG Frankfurt BB 1960, 228 zu verweisen (mit zutreffender Kritik von *A. Baumbach/W. Hefermehl*, 12 Aufl., § 1 UWG Anm. 211); *M. Kisseler*, Die Vernichtung des Gegners als Zweck des Wettbewerbs?, WRP 1978, 81, 83 ff., berichtet von einem nicht veröffentlichten Urteil des LG Aschaffenburg; in der Praxis des BKartA ist auf Tätigkeitsbericht 1975, BT-Drucks. 7/5390, S. 76/77 zu verweisen (Ischia-Reisen und Terramar).

[26] Sie ist nicht Antitrust Law im Sinne des Clayton Act und gibt deshalb keine Basis für private Schadensersatzklagen und einstweiligen Rechtsschutz ab, Nashville Milk Co. v. Carnation Co., 355 U.S. 373 (1958). Zu beachten ist, daß die Gesetze zahlreicher Einzelstaaten gegen solche Praktiken auch zivilrechtliche Rechtsbehelfe gewähren, dazu 2 CCH Trade Regulation Reporter, §§ 6801 ff.

[27] Von 1936 bis 1975 hat das Department of Justice nur sieben Verfahren eingeleitet; keines hatte Erfolg; vgl. *American Bar Association*, Antitrust Law Developments, 1975, S. 162, 163.

[28] Hierzu *R. Koller II*, The Myth of Predatory Pricing: An Empirical Study, 4 Antitrust L. & Econ. Rev. 105 (Summer 1971); jüngere Rechtsprechungsnachweise bei *Ph. Areeda/D. Turner*, Predatory Pricing and Related Practices Under Sec. 2 of the Sherman Act, 88 Harv. L. Rev. 697 ff. (1975); *O. Williamson*, Predatory Pricing: A Strategic and Welfare Analysis, 87 Yale L. J. 284 ff. (1977); siehe auch die Nachweise bei *E. Cooper*, Attempts and Monopolization: A Mildly Expansionary Answer to the Prophylactic Riddle of Section Two, 72 Mich. L. Rev. 375, 454 (1974) in Fußn. 232.

[29] AaO (Fußn. 21).

[30] 221 U.S. 1 (1911).

punktmäßig in der Spielart der regionalen Preisdiskriminierung. Die FTC hat zwischen 1914, dem Jahr ihrer Errichtung, und 1970 über 1300 Verfahren solcher und verwandter Art durchgeführt.[31]

Wer Vertrauen in die Selbstheilungskräfte des Wettbewerbs setzt – sie dürften noch immer der ärgste Feind von Wettbewerbsbeschränkungen sein – und überdies die Schutzzwecke einschlägigen Rechts nach Kriterien wohlfahrtstheoretisch verankerter Nutzen-Kosten-Überlegungen relativiert[32], mag gleichwohl dieser Erscheinungsform des Wirtschaftskampfes keine legislative Aufmerksamkeit zuwenden wollen. Von den so dezidiert an einer freien Handelnsordnung ausgerichteten Wertvorstellungen *von Hayeks* her wäre freilich die gegenteilige Schlußfolgerung angezeigt: Eine eliminierende oder disziplinierende Kampfpreisunterbietung macht die Gewerbefreiheit Privater zum Ermessensgegenstand anderer Privater. Dies wäre eine Erscheinungsform unerträglichen Zwanges in seinem Sinne. Von daher hat *von Hayek* in der Tat auch empfohlen, daß «alle diskriminierenden oder andere gezielte Aktionen gegen einen tatsächlichen oder potentiellen Konkurrenten, die ihm ein bestimmtes Marktverhalten aufzwingen sollen»,[33] mit Sanktionen bedroht werden sollten. Auf dieser Basis erwächst indes das Problem, die Vernichtungsunterbietung abzugrenzen gegenüber Unterbietungen als Ausdrucksform erwünschten lebhaften Wettbewerbs. Es wird sich zeigen, daß die Abgrenzungskriterien seinem hohen Ideal der rule of law schwerlich genügen können.

2. Das Abgrenzungsproblem

Die Denkansätze sind vielgestaltig.

a) Die Vernichtungsabsicht

Eine Anknüpfung an dieses subjektive Element ist verbreitet. In Deutschland gilt eine Wettbewerbshandlung, die nicht auf Förderung der eigenen Absatztätigkeit zielt, sondern auf rein Destruktives, angesichts ihres Zweckes als unlauter.[34] Sie wird nachgerade zum Urfall des Nichtleistungswettbewerbs. Im amerikanischen Recht wird das Erfordernis der Vernichtungsabsicht zur Abgrenzung zwischen Monopolisierungshandlung und noch zulässigem Wettbewerb herangezogen, ebenso zur Ermittlung des specific intent, der beim Versuch der Monopolisierung erforderlich ist. Bei Diskriminierungssachverhalten verwendet die Rechtsprechung die Feststellung eines predatory intent als Mittel, um die Feststellung der nach dem Gesetz erheblichen Auswirkungen auf den Wettbewerb[35]

---

[31] Vgl. *J. Blair*, Economic Concentration. Structure, Behavior & Public Policy, New York 1972, S. 341; dort auch weitere Nachweise zum einschlägigen Schrifttum.

[32] Exemplarisch *R. Posner*, aaO (Fußn. 22), S. 187, 188.

[33] Grundsätze einer liberalen Gesellschaftsordnung, (Fußn. 16), S. 124; *von Hayek* hält es für am sinnvollsten, wenn diese Verhaltensweisen mit mehrfachem Schadensersatz bedroht würden.

[34] Vgl. für alle *A. Baumbach / W. Hefermehl*, 12 Aufl., UWG § 1 Anm. 206.

[35] «... where the effect of such discrimination may be substantially to lessen competition or tend to create a monopoly in any line of commerce, or to injure, destroy or prevent competition with any person who either grants or knowingly receives the benefit of such discrimination, or with customers of either of them ...».

ohne eingehende Marktanalyse treffen zu können. Aus der Vernichtungsabsicht wird auf eine mögliche Beeinträchtigung des Wettbewerbs selbst geschlossen.[36]

Als genereller Maßstab müßte solche subjektive Anknüpfung auf Skepsis stoßen. Motivation und innere Einstellung allein bewirken für sich noch nichts. Eine Verkehrswirtschaft ist gerade dadurch gekennzeichnet, daß sie keinem konkreten, kollektiv vorgegebenen Zweck unterworfen ist, die daran teilnehmenden Menschen vielmehr beliebige Ziele verfolgen können, ohne daß ihre Gesinnung erheblich wird. Der geringere Bedarf an Moral ist bekanntlich einer der wesentlichen Vorzüge einer marktwirtschaftlichen Ordnung.[37] Entscheidend sind vielmehr die intendierten oder jedenfalls möglichen Wirkungen auf die Freiheit der Wettbewerbsprozesse selbst, «weil man erfahrungsgemäß davon ausgehen kann, daß Unternehmen, die dieses Ziel in ihre Geschäftspolitik aufgenommen haben, auch die Mittel haben, es zu realisieren, oder doch jedenfalls bis zu einem Punkt vordringen können, der unter Wettbewerbsgesichtspunkten ein Einschreiten erfordert.»[38] Im Grunde handelt es sich um den Versuch, über die Wirtschaftspläne eines Unternehmens zur Wettbewerbssituation selbst vorzustoßen. Wenn dem so ist, wird freilich zweifelhaft, welcher rechtserhebliche Unterschied zu Sachverhalten besteht, in denen preispolitische Maßnahmen «sehenden Auges» zur Elimination von Wettbewerbern führen, ohne daß dem unterbietenden Unternehmen unbedingt daran liegt. Als Beispiel sei hingewiesen auf Lockvogelangebote mit Dauercharakter[39], etwa wenn ein Supermarkt Benzin unter Einstandspreisen anbietet. Für dieses Unternehmen handelt es sich um eine Maßnahme der Werbepolitik, welche auf Grund seiner Mischkalkulation nicht nur möglich, sondern sinnvoll wird. An den Wettbewerbsverhältnissen auf dem lokalen Benzinmarkt liegt ihm gar nichts. Dennoch ist in solchen Fällen absehbar, wann ein benachbartes Tankstellenunternehmen aus dem Markt scheiden muß. Ein aufschlußreicher Sachverhalt liegt auch einer amerikanischen Entscheidung aus jüngster Zeit zugrunde:[40] AMPOT, ein größeres, diversifiziertes Unternehmen, und PE, ein schwach kapitalisiertes Einproduktunternehmen, waren die einzigen Anbieter eines chemischen Stoffes, der zur Herstellung von Treibsätzen für Raketen Verwendung fand. Nachfrager war (mittelbar) fast ausschließlich der amerikanische Staat. Angesichts zurückgehender Nachfrage waren beide Anbieter in der Lage, mit ihrer jeweiligen Kapazität den gesamten Bedarf zu decken. Die Kostendegression bei steigender Auslastung war gewaltig. Ein niedrigeres Angebot konnte angesichts der (später korrigierten) Vergabepraktiken dazu führen, daß ein Anbieter sämtliche Aufträge erhielt. AMPOT entschloß sich angesichts dieser Lage zu Preiswettbewerb und bot den chemischen Stoff zu Preisen an, welche zwar unter den Ge-

---

[36] National Dairy Prods. Corp. v. FTC, 412 F. 2d 605, 618 (7th Cir. 1969); Cornwell Quality Tools Co. v. C.T.S. Co., 446 F. 2d 825 (9th Cir. 1971); Continental Baking Co. v. Old Homestead Bread Co., 476 F. 2d 97 (10th Cir. 1973); im deutschen Schrifttum siehe hierzu etwa W. H. *Roth*, Das amerikanische Diskriminierungsverbot, in Für und Wider ein allgemeines Diskriminierungsverbot, Köln, Berlin, Bonn, München 1976, S. 1, 10. Auch die Rechtfertigungsmöglichkeiten des meeting competition, der cost justification und der changing market conditions entfallen dann.

[37] Vgl. dazu O. *von Nell-Breuning*, Können Neoliberalismus und katholische Soziallehre sich verständigen? in 2. Festschrift für F. Böhm, Tübingen 1975, S. 459, 469/470.

[38] Vgl. W. *Möschel*, Der Oligopolmißbrauch im Recht der Wettbewerbsbeschränkungen. Eine vergleichende Untersuchung zum Recht der USA, Großbritanniens, der EWG und der Bundesrepublik Deutschland, Tübingen 1974, S. 193.

[39] Vgl. P. *Ulmer*, Der Begriff «Leistungswettbewerb» und seine Bedeutung für die Anwendung von GWB- und UWG-Tatbeständen, GRUR 1977, 565, 572.

[40] Pacific Engineering & Production Co. of Nevada v. Kerr-McGee Corp. and Kerr-McGee Chemical Corp., 551 F. 2d 790 (10th Cir. 1977), cert. denied, 54 L Ed 2d 160 (1977).

samtkosten lagen, aber immerhin noch einen Deckungsbeitrag erbrachten. Es war AM-POT klar, daß PE hierbei keine Überlebenschance besaß. Das Gericht wies die Klage von PE auf dreifachen Schadensersatz ab. Predatory pricing liege nicht vor. «We realize that our ruling leads to the somewhat untoward result that the larger of two competitors will survive while the smaller may expire. Bigness, however, is not a disqualification to compete.»[41]

Neben diesen wettbewerbspolitischen Abgrenzungszweifel treten praktische Schwierigkeiten, solche Vernichtungsabsicht festzustellen: Motivationslagen sind vielfach sehr komplex. Ihr Nachweis ist überdies nur schwer möglich. Die Zeiten des Benrather-Tankstellenfalles, zu denen die beteiligten Unternehmen an ihrer Disziplinierungsabsicht keinerlei Unklarheiten aufkommen ließen[42], sind vorbei. In der amerikanischen Praxis konnte ein «direct intent» zwar an Hand von unternehmensinternen Unterlagen und dergleichen in einer Reihe von Fällen nachgewiesen werden.[43] Regelmäßig sind die Gerichte indes auf Indizien angewiesen (sog. inferential predatory intent). Es ist nicht überraschend, daß dann subjektive und objektivierende Kriterien tendenziell miteinander austauschbar werden.[44]

b) Das Kostenkriterium

Das Kriterium eines Verkaufs unter (verschieden definierten) Selbstkosten wird in diesem Zusammenhang vielfach herangezogen. Es kann dies als ein Element innerhalb der Gesamtwürdigung des Verhaltens eines Wettbewerbers verstanden werden. Es kann weiter im Sinne eines «double inference test» ein Weg zur Feststellung einer Vernichtungsabsicht sein: Aus den Unterkostenverkäufen schließt man auf den predatory intent, von diesem auf die Beeinträchtigung des Wettbewerbs.[45] Schließlich kann das Kriterium aus sich heraus ausschlaggebende Bedeutung haben. Bezüglich letzterem hat sich in den Vereinigten Staaten in jüngster Zeit eine eingehende Diskussion entfaltet. *Areeda/Turner*[46] meinen, daß Preise eines Unternehmens mit Monopolmacht, welche unter den kurzfristigen

---

[41] AaO, S. 799.

[42] RGZ 134, 342, 344.

[43] Siehe dazu die Note: Unlawful Primary Line Price Discriminations: Predatory Intent and Competitive Injury, 69 Col. L. Rev. 137, 142 (1968); aus der Rspr. Porto Rican American Tobacco Co. v. American Tobacco Co., 30 F. 2 d 234 (2d Cir. 1929), cert. denied, 279 U.S. 858 (1929); E. B. Muller & Co. v. FTC, 142 F. 2d 511 (6th Cir. 1944); Utah Pie Co. v. Continental Baking Co., 386 U.S. 685 (1967).

[44] Vgl. dazu W. *Möschel*, Pressekonzentration und Wettbewerbsgesetz. Marktbeherrschung, unlauterer Wettbewerb und Sanierungsfusionen im Pressebereich, Tübingen 1978, S. 105 ff.

[45] Vgl. International Air Indus., Inc. v. American Excelsior Co., 517 F. 2d 714, 723 (5th Cir. 1975), cert. denied, 424 U.S. 943 (1975); Pacific Engineering & Production Co. v. Kerr-McGee Corp., 551 F. 2d 790 (10th Cir. 1977). F. *Böhm*, Wettbewerb und Monopolkampf (Fußn. 19) sah wegen langfristig schädlicher Auswirkungen in Unterkostenverkäufen grundsätzlich Nichtleistungswettbewerb (S. 227 ff.), der nur ausnahmsweise zu rechtfertigen sei (defensive Preise u. ä., S. 304 ff.); im Falle eines marktbeherrschenden Unternehmens sollte nach Grundsätzen des prima facie-Beweises diesem der Nachweis obliegen, daß seine Preise – allgemein gefordert – über den Kosten lägen (S. 312 ff.). F. *Böhm* hielt Formen der Mischkalkulation für nicht mehr von der Gewerbefreiheit gedeckt (S. 300). Doch sind dann erforderliche Tätigkeitsabgrenzungen – sie entfielen nur bei Einproduktunternehmen – notwendig willkürlich.

[46] Predatory Pricing and Related Practices Under Section 2 of the Sherman Act, 88 Harv. L. Rev. 697 (1975), geringfügig geändert auch in *Ph. Areeda/D. Turner*, Antitrust Law, Boston 1978, §§ 711–722.

Grenzkosten liegen, immer als predatory gelten sollten[47], Preise, die darüber liegen, dagegen nie. Aus Gründen der Praktikabilität schlagen sie vor, als Annäherungswerte für die in der Regel nicht feststellbaren Grenzkosten die in vernünftiger Weise vorweggenommenen durchschnittlichen variablen Kosten zu nehmen. Der Gedankengang ist orientiert an Effizienzvorstellungen, die aus statischen Modellen der Preistheorie abgeleitet sind. Ihr Bemühen ist es, einerseits auch einem marktmächtigen Unternehmen noch Preiswettbewerb zu ermöglichen, andererseits Anforderungen der Rechtsanwendung zu genügen. Auf einer ähnlichen wohlfahrtstheoretischen Grundlage definiert *Posner* als predatory pricing so kalkulierte Preise, daß ein gleich oder in höherem Maße effizienter Wettbewerber vom Markt ausgeschlossen wird.[48] Neben dem Fall, daß die kurzfristigen Grenzkosten unterschritten und ein Nichtverkauf damit billiger wäre als die Aktion selbst, sieht er dies auch dann verwirklicht, wenn (hier mit Verdrängungsabsicht) unter den langfristigen Grenzkosten verkauft wird.[49] Aus Gründen leichterer Meßbarkeit hält er hierbei einen Rückgriff auf die Durchschnittskosten, wie sie sich nach der historischen Kostenrechnung des Unternehmens ergeben, für geboten («average balance sheet costs»). *Scherer* hält den Ansatz von *Areeda/Turner* für zu eng: Er befürchtet, daß dieser wettbewerbswidriges Verhalten zuläßt, welches mit langfristiger Wohlfahrtsmaximierung nicht vereinbar sei, und empfiehlt eine Beibehaltung der in der Rechtsprechung überwiegend praktizierten Gesamtanalyse.[50] *Areeda/Turner* halten letzteres für zu unbestimmt und spekulativ.[51] *Williamson*[52], ähnlich orientiert an Kriterien von welfare superiority und von administrability, will Kostenkriterien auf Preiskämpfe innerhalb eines weiten Oligopols etablierter Firmen beschränken, wohingegen er im Hinblick auf die Abschreckung von Newcomern auf Kriterien der Produktionsausweitung abstellt.[53] Innerhalb der Diskussion um eine Reform des Robinson-Patman Act schließlich hatte die Antitrust Division zwei Gesetzesvorschläge eingereicht, wonach es ungesetzlich sein sollte, «knowingly to sell on a sustained basis at a price below the reasonably anticipated average direct operating expense incurred in supplying the commodity.»[54] Gemeint waren

---

[47] Sie machen eine Ausnahme für den wenig praktischen Fall, daß die Preise zwar unter den Grenzkosten, aber über den Durchschnittskosten liegen, dagegen aber z.B. nicht für Sachverhalte sog. promotional pricing oder des meeting competition, aaO, S. 713 ff.

[48] AaO (Fußn. 22), S. 188 ff.

[49] Das Argument ist, daß ein Unternehmen, das aus dem Markt ausscheidet, weil es zu Preisen unter seinen langfristigen Grenzkosten nicht anbieten will, leistungsfähiger als das unterbietende Unternehmen sein kann, aaO (Fußn. 22), S. 191, 192.

[50] *F. Scherer*, Predatory Pricing and the Sherman Act: A Comment, 89 Harv. L. Rev. 869 (1976); dazu *Ph. Areeda/D. Turner*, Scherer on Predatory Pricing: A Reply, ebenda S. 891 und *F. Scherer*, Some Last Words on Predatory Pricing, ebenda, S. 901.

[51] 89 Harv. L. Rev. 891, 897 (1976).

[52] Predatory Pricing: A Strategic and Welfare Analysis, 87 Yale L. J. 284 (1977); dazu *Ph. Areeda/D. Turner*, Williamson on Predatory Pricing, 87 Yale L. J. 1337 (1978), und *O. Williamson*, A Preliminary Response, ebenda. S. 1353.

[53] «Short Run: Dominant firms that expand their (demand adjusted) output in the face of new entry will be deemed to be engaged in predatory behavior – even if the resulting market price exceeds the dominant firm's average variable costs.
Long Run: Sustained production by dominant firms or successful entrants shall be deemed predatory if revenues are not fully cost recovering with respect to an appropriate assignment of all expenses incurred during the long-run interval,» 87 Yale L. J. 284, 334 (1977).

[54] Report of the Department of Justice, Antitrust Division, Reform of the Robinson-Patman Act, vom 9. Juli 1975; der Vorschlag ist abgedruckt auch bei *Cr. Campbell/St. Emanuel*, A Proposal for a Revised Price Discrimination and Predatory Pricing Statute, 13 Harv. J. on Legislation 125, 218 ff. (1975) oder in Recent Efforts to Amend or Repeal the Robinson-Patman Act – Part 1,

damit die unmittelbar zuzurechnenden Produktions- und Vertriebskosten für die betreffende Ware sowie jene anteiligen Abschreibungen, Zinskosten, Miet- und Pachtkosten, Gemeinkosten, Werbungskosten, welche direkt mit der Menge der hergestellten Ware variieren.[55] Vier Ausnahmen waren vorgesehen (Eintritt in einen Konkurrenzpreis «in good faith», Newcomer mit einem Marktanteil unter 10 %, besondere Umstände wie Verderblichkeit, Saisoncharakter der Ware und dergleichen, keine klare Gefährdung für einen Wettbewerber).

So sehr Verlustpreisverkäufe im Einzelfall ein Indiz für Verdrängungsabsicht oder ein Faktor im Rahmen einer wettbewerblichen Gesamtanalyse sein können, so zweifelhaft bleiben die Versuche, starre, an Kostenkriterien anknüpfende Regeln zu entwickeln. Zwischen der Justiziabilität i. S. der rule of law und der wettbewerbspolitischen Plausibilität solcher Regeln entsteht ein Zielkonflikt[56], der hier zu Lasten der materiellen Einsehbarkeit dieser Regeln entschieden wäre. Areeda/Turner weisen zur Rechtfertigung ihres short-run marginal cost-Ansatzes (SRMC) unter anderem auf diese beiden Gesichtspunkte hin:[57] SRMC-Preise seien das Ergebnis in wettbewerblichen Märkten und hätten den sozialen Vorteil, daß Ressourcenfehlleitungen vermieden seien. Regeln, welche einen Preisschirm über SRMC's erfordern, also Preise, die wesentlich über den kurzfristigen Grenzkosten liegen und nicht unterschritten werden dürften, tendierten notwendig dazu, nicht effiziente Konkurrenten zu protegieren bzw. solche auf den Markt zu locken. Hierzu bleibt zweierlei anzumerken: Eine Orientierung an ökonomischen Effizienzvorstellungen ist unbefriedigend, wenn ein Recht, welches Wettbewerbsbeschränkungen unterbindet, in erster Linie auf den Schutz individueller Handlungsfreiheiten, auf die Beseitigung von Zwang im Sinne von Hayeks zielt. Referenzsystem ist überdies ein Modell mehr oder weniger vollkommener Konkurrenz. Dieses vermag freilich lediglich einen Zustand zu beschreiben, in welchem Ressourcen optimal oder suboptimal alloziert sind. Wettbewerb ist bei dieser Gleichgewichtsanalyse definitionsgemäß zum Erliegen gekommen, so daß daraus über wettbewerbliche Handlungen selbst, die treibenden Kräfte, die zu diesem Gleichgewichtszustand und zu seiner Veränderung führen, nichts gesagt ist.[58] Im Grunde handelt es sich um Als-ob-Konzeptionen, bei denen ein Mengenanpasserverhalten zum Maßstab genommen wird, obwohl ein marktmächtiges Unternehmen gerade nicht mit einer horizontalen Nachfragekurve konfrontiert ist, sondern die Preise mit seinem Marktverhalten beeinflussen kann.

Diese Schwäche in der wettbewerbstheoretischen Basis schlägt auch auf das Problem der Kostenmeßbarkeit durch. Dies beginnt mit der Frage, welche Elemente überhaupt zu den Kosten gerechnet werden können, führt über das unvermeidliche Ermessen bei der Ermittlung von Mengen- und Wertkomponenten bis hin zur Zurechnung der Gemeinko-

---

Hearings before the Ad Hoc Subcommittee on Antitrust, the Robinson-Patman Act, and Related Matters of the Committee on Small Business, House of Representatives, 94th Cong., 1st Sess. 1975, S. 590–593; im deutschen Schrifttum dazu z. B. H. Hölzler/K. Stockmann, Robinson-Patman Act. Mehr Wettbewerb durch Entschärfung des Preisdiskriminierungsverbots? RIW 1976, 628 ff.; R. Schulte-Braucks, Die Diskussion um die Reform des Robinson-Patman Act in den USA, WRP 1977, 473 mit Abdruck des Reform Statute.

[55] Sec. 5 (e) Predatory Practices Act of 1975 bzw. Sec. 13 (e) Robinson-Patman Reform Statute of 1975.

[56] Grundsätzliches bei W. Möschel, Der Oligopolmißbrauch, (Fußn. 38), S. 7 ff.

[57] Besonders klar in 87 Yale L. J. 1337, 1339 (1978).

[58] Vgl. dazu zuletzt E. Hoppmann, Das Konzept des wirksamen Preiswettbewerbs, 1978, S. 10; W. Möschel, Wettbewerb im Schnittfeld von Rechtswissenschaft und Nationalökonomie, in Festschrift zum 500jährigen Bestehen der Tübinger Juristenfakultät, Tübingen 1977, S. 333 ff., auch abgedruckt in WiSt 1978, 351 ff.

sten auf die einzelnen Produkte. Dafür gibt es bekanntlich kein logisch begründbares Verfahren. Die Praxis verteilt sie in der Regel in dem Ausmaß, als die einzelnen Produkte dies marktmäßig verkraften können.[59] Nun wäre es zwar möglich, in dieser Hinsicht kraft Konvention oder Setzung ein für allemal bestimmte Kalkulationsrichtlinien zu fixieren. Für den Zweck, wettbewerbliches Preisverhalten von monopolisierendem abzugrenzen, wäre dies indes ein ganz untaugliches Verfahren. Solche Festsetzung bliebe willkürlich, wenn sie der besonderen Situation einer Branche oder auch eines Unternehmens nicht Rechnung trüge. Tut sie dies, gerät ihr Zweck der Verfahrenssicherheit ins Wanken. Wettbewerbspolitisch würden über solche Gleichschaltungen eher unerwünschte Wirkungen ausgelöst, nämlich Tendenzen zu einer Art Zwangskartellierung. Die Fixierung auf den Aktionsparameter Preis läßt im übrigen die anderen Aktionsvariablen außer Betracht (Produktdifferenzierung, Qualitätswettbewerb udgl.), über welche ein Unternehmen verfügen kann. Werden sie berücksichtigt, läuft das Ganze auf eine nicht vollziehbare Kontrolle einer Unternehmenspolitik insgesamt bis hin zu Investitionsentscheidungen hinaus. Auch ist zu bedenken, daß keine Produktion leichter ist als die von Kosten.

Wichtiger ist noch, daß eine Preisuntergrenze für eine Leistungseinheit nicht nur von den Kosten bestimmt wird, sondern auch von liquiditäts- und sicherheitsorientierten Überlegungen sowie von Rentabilitätsfaktoren. Ausschlaggebend ist dabei das Interesse eines Unternehmens an der Erwirtschaftung eines möglichst großen Gewinns für das Gesamtunternehmen und nicht bei jeder einzelnen Leistung. Besonders deutlich ist dieser Zusammenhang, ohne darauf beschränkt zu sein, bei der Herstellung absatzmäßig miteinander verbundener Güter (Extremfall Kuppelprodukte), wie sie für Mehrproduktunternehmen verbreitet sind. Starre Kalkulationsrichtlinien würden hier eine wettbewerbspolitisch erwünschte Flexibilität und Reagibilität von Unternehmen nachgerade behindern.

Im Kern operieren solche Kostenanknüpfungen unter Bedingungen der Gewißheit, wie sie in der Wirklichkeit der Absatzmärkte – jedenfalls für generelle Regeln – nicht unterstellt werden können. Es werden bekanntlich ja nicht nur die Preise eines Gutes von seinen Kosten, sondern wegen der damit regelmäßig verbundenen Kostenstreuung umgekehrt ebenso die Kosten vom Preis bzw. Absatz eines Gutes her bestimmt. Dies erfordert ständige Prognosen und Anpassungen unter sich verändernden Bedingungen, die nicht in starren Regeln festlegbar sind. So hängen z.B. bei vorhandenen fixen Gemeinkosten die Kosten nur eines einzigen Gutes von den Annahmen über den Absatz sämtlicher anderer Güter ab. Der Hinweis, daß man sich hier mit einer reasonable expectation behelfe, beseitigt dieses Problem nicht, sondern benennt es nur.

Hiermit soll nicht in Frage gestellt werden, daß Kostenanknüpfungen in diesem Zusammenhang einen Erkenntniswert haben können; dies gilt insbesondere für die Frage, ob ein Unternehmen bei zeitlich zurückliegenden Preisen sich von sachgemäßen wirtschaftlichen Überlegungen hat leiten lassen. Sie öffnen aber keinen Weg, der den Anforderungen einer rule of law nach dem *Hayekschen* Ideal genügen könnte.

c) Marktpreis als Vergleichsgröße

Im deutschen Schrifttum hat man vorgeschlagen, zur Abgrenzung zwischen leistungsgerechter und leistungsfremder Preisunterbietung auf ein Vergleichsmarktkonzept zurückzugreifen: Nicht zu beanstanden sei ein Preis, «der sich in einem im übrigen ver-

---

[59] Zu diesen Fragen z.B. *H. D. Deppe*, «Selbstkosten» – eine betriebswirtschaftlich gerechtfertigte Preisuntergrenze? in *W. Eikentscher*, Die Preisunterbietung im Wettbewerbsrecht, 2. Aufl. Heidelberg 1962, S. 85 ff. mit umfänglichen Nachweisen.

gleichbaren Wettbewerbsmarkt unter Bedingungen des Leistungswettbewerbs herausgebildet hat.»[60] Dies lag hier deshalb nahe, weil die Rechtsprechung jedenfalls in Extremfällen eine Preisüberhöhungskontrolle bei marktmächtigen Unternehmen bejaht und dabei auf Vergleichsmärkte rekurriert.[61] Im amerikanischen Antitrustrecht sind solche Preiskontrollen dagegen nur in peripheren Zusammenhängen erheblich, und zwar im wesentlichen als flankierende Maßnahmen für Strukturgestaltungen.[62] Aber auch bei solcher Momentaufnahme eines anderen historischen Marktes mit höherer Wettbewerbsintensität bleibt es unausweichlich, dem dynamischen Charakter des Wettbewerbsgeschehens Rechnung zu tragen: So sei die Unterbietung eines solchen Vergleichspreises nicht leistungsfremd, wenn sie durch besondere Umstände (u. a. auch Einführungspreis) oder durch die Effizienz des Preisunterbieters veranlaßt sei.[63] Doch damit wird das Anliegen, stärker generalisierende, Rechtssicherheit verbürgende Kriterien zu entwickeln, in seinem Kern getroffen:[64] Ein Unternehmen, das durch Unterbietung des «Marktpreises» seinen Absatz zu steigern hofft, befindet sich ständig in der Situation eines Einführungspreises, mit dem es neue Nachfrage für sich zu erschließen sucht. Der Hinweis auf die höhere Leistungsfähigkeit des Preisunterbieters ist als Rechtskriterium nicht vollziehbar, wenn damit die gesamte Effizienz eines (Mehrprodukt-)Unternehmens der Realität gemeint sein sollte. Bedeutung hätte es allenfalls bei sog. Schleuderverkäufen kurz vor einem Konkurs. Ist damit die Effizienz auf einem jeweiligen Einzelmarkt gemeint, wird ein solches Unternehmen nicht nur in eine Addition von nichtexistenten Einproduktunternehmen zerlegt, sondern jetzt bedarf es wieder Richtlinien zur Feststellung «angemessenen» Aufwands und «angemessener» Erlöse, welche schnurstracks zu den oben behandelten Kostenkriterien zurückführen. Wer diese verwirft, da sie «aus marktwirtschaftlicher Sicht... kein relevanter Bezugspunkt» sein können[63], müßte dieses Verdikt folgerichtig auch auf die Marktpreisvariante erstrecken.

d) Der Mißbrauchstransfer

Dieser Sachverhalt, der sich an die im deutschen Recht grundsätzlich anerkannte Möglichkeit einer Preisüberhöhungskontrolle anschließt, wird hier nur abgrenzend erwähnt. Er ist dadurch gekennzeichnet, daß ein marktbeherrschendes Unternehmen mißbräuchlich überhöhte Gewinne aus einem sachlich oder geographisch unterschiedenen Markt auf anderen Märkten in der Weise einsetzt, daß dort die Wettbewerbslage «spürbar beeinflußt»[65] wird. Auf eine Verdrängungsabsicht auf dem Drittmarkt kommt es dabei

---

[60] Grundlegend *P. Ulmer,* Der Begriff «Leistungswettbewerb» und seine Bedeutung für die Anwendung von GWB und UWG-Tatbeständen, GRUR 1977, 565, 572; *ders.,* Mehr Wettbewerb?, WuW 1978, 330, 335 ff.; siehe auch *ders.,* Wettbewerbs- und kartellrechtliche Grenzen der Preisunterbietung im Pressewesen, AfP 1975, 870 ff. und *ders.,* Schranken zulässigen Wettbewerbs marktbeherrschender Unternehmen, Baden-Baden 1977, S. 98 ff.

[61] BGHZ 68, 23 = WuW/E BGH 1435 Vitamin B 12; aus dem abundanten Schrifttum siehe nur *W. Möschel,* Wettbewerb im Schnittfeld, (Fußn. 58), S. 351 ff. mit weiteren Nachweisen und zuletzt *R. Fischer,* Der Mißbrauch einer marktbeherrschenden Stellung (§ 22 GWB) in der Rechtsprechung des Bundesgerichtshofes, ZGR 1978, 235 ff. sowie *Monopolkommission,* Fortschreitende Konzentration bei Großunternehmen. Zweites Hauptgutachten Baden-Baden 1976/1977, Tz. 376 ff.; zum Recht der EG siehe EuGH, Urteil v. 14. 2. 1978 (Rs 27/76), WuW/E EWG/MuV 425 Chiquita-Bananen.

[62] Im einzelnen *W. Möschel,* Rechtsordnung zwischen Plan und Markt, Tübingen 1975, S. 40 ff.

[63] *P. Ulmer,* GRUR 1977, 565, 572.

[64] Hierzu auch *W. Möschel,* Pressekonzentration, (Fußn. 44), S. 106 ff.

[65] Vgl. (zu einem Koppelungstatbestand) WuW/E OLG 995, 999 Handpreisauszeicher.

nicht an. Auch entscheiden nicht allein die wettbewerblichen Auswirkungen; von daher wäre es völlig gleichgültig, aus welchen Quellen sich die Subventionierung bei Niedrigpreisangeboten speist. Maßgeblicher Bezugspunkt bleiben die mißbräuchlich überhöhten Preise. Ihr Unrechtsstigma verliert sich nicht, wenn damit verbundene Gewinne auf andere Märkte mit dort wettbewerbsbeeinträchtigenden Konsequenzen transferiert werden. Doch ist für die Praxis hier auf Grund des ausgesprochenen Notbehelfscharakters solcher Preiskontrolle und der Beweisanforderungen, welche der BGH dabei stellt, im Grunde nichts zu erwarten.[66]

e) Marktstrukturverantwortung

Eine besonders weitgreifende Konzeption läßt sich mit dem Stichwort Marktstrukturverantwortung benennen. Dahinter steht die Vorstellung, ein Unternehmen müsse ab einem bestimmten Grade von Marktmacht bei seinem Verhalten auf die kompetitive Struktur des Marktes Rücksicht nehmen und sich – etwa bei Maßnahmen der Preispolitik – konkurrentenverdrängender Niedrigpreise enthalten: Ein kurzfristiges Abnehmerinteresse wird zurückgestellt gegenüber dem langfristigen Interesse an einer Aufrechterhaltung stärker wettbewerblicher Märkte, in der Regel in dem schlichten Sinne einer größeren Zahl von Anbietern. Die Handhabung des Diskriminierungsverbots im amerikanischen Recht tendiert z. T. in diese Richtung.[67] Zu nennen wäre auch die berühmte Alcoa-Entscheidung.[68] Gestützt auf den rechtssystematischen Zusammenhang zwischen dem per se-Verbot von Preiskartellen und der Innehabung von Monopolmacht als power to fix prices – «that distinction is nevertheless purely formal»[69] – brachte sie eine Gleichstellung von Monopolisierungshandlung und Innehabung bzw. Aufrechterhaltung von Monopolmacht. Der Kern des Monopolisierungsvorwurfs betraf in diesem Sachverhalt den Umstand, daß *Alcoa* es immer verstanden hatte, durch rechtzeitige kapazitätserweiternde Investitionen jeder Nachfragesteigerung gegenüber gewappnet zu sein und gleichzeitig damit unausweichlich den Marktzutritt für Newcomer zu behindern. Für Maßnahmen der Preispolitik könnte dies, zu Ende gedacht, bedeuten, daß ein Monopolunternehmen jener Art die Entwicklung konkurrierender Außenseiter nicht behindern darf, sie sozusagen unter einer Art Preisschirm zu nähren habe. Doch bereits die Alcoa-Entscheidung selbst berücksichtigte thrust upon-Ausnahmen[70] und die spätere Entwicklung hat gezeigt, daß auch ein Monopolunternehmen i. S. von Sec. 2 Sherman Act nicht sehenden

---

[66] Siehe im einzelnen *W. Möschel*, Pressekonzentration, (Fußn. 44), S. 92 ff.; *K. Markert*, Mißbrauchsaufsicht nach §§ 22, 26 Abs. 2 GWB, in Schwerpunkte des Kartellrechts 1976/77 Köln, Berlin, 1978, S. 27 ff.; *Monopolkommission*, Zweites Hauptgutachten Baden-Baden 1976/77 Bonn, München, Tz. 377 ff.

[67] Vgl. z. B. die heftig kritisierte Utah Pie-Entscheidung des Supreme Court, Utah Pie Co. v. Continental Baking Co., 386 U.S. 685 (1967); dazu z. B. *W. Bowman*, Restraint of Trade by the Supreme Court: The Utah Pie Case, 74 Yale L. J. 70 (1967) = 6 J. of Reprints for Antitrust L. & Econ. 259 ff. (1975); im dt. Recht z. B. *W. H. Roth*, aaO (Fußn. 36).

[68] United States v. Aluminum Co. of America, 148 F. 2d 416 (1945).

[69] AaO, S. 428.

[70] Erklärung der Innehabung der Monopolmacht im wesentlichen auf Grund höherer wirtschaftlicher Effizienz: «Superior skill, superior products, natural advantages, (including accessibility to raw materials or markets), economic or technological efficiency, (including scientific research), low margins of profits maintained permanently and without discrimination, or licenses conferred by, and used within, the limits of law», vgl. United States v. United Shoe Machinery Corp., 110 F. Supp. 295, 342 (D. Mass. 1953); weitere Nachweise bei *J. von Kalinowski*, Antitrust Laws and Trade Regulation, Bd. 2, New York 1971, § 9.03.

Auges dulden muß, wie Außenseiterunternehmen seine Marktanteile durch günstigere Preise erodieren.[71] Im deutschen Schrifttum stehen dem Denkansatz der Marktstrukturverantwortung Auffassungen nahe, welche die Preispolitik marktbeherrschender Unternehmen ausschließlich an Hand ihrer Wirkungen auf den Restwettbewerb beurteilen wollen.[72]

In der Tat empfiehlt es sich nicht, marktbeherrschenden Unternehmen eine generelle Verantwortung für die Marktstruktur bzw. die Lebensfähigkeit ihrer Konkurrenten aufzuerlegen.

– In einer Rechtsordnung wie der deutschen, welche im Unterschied zur amerikanischen kein Monopolisierungsverbot kennt, wäre es sinnwidrig, das Entstehen solcher Marktstellungen zuzulassen, aber ihre Innehabung zu sanktionieren.

– Marktstellungen dieser Art können Resultante nicht beherrschbarer Entwicklungen (historische Zufälle, Rückzug Dritter aus dem Markt und dergleichen) oder gerade wirksamen Wettbewerbs sein (höhere Leistung im allgemeinsten Sinne). Läßt man deshalb Ausnahmen etwa nach Art des thrust upon-defense zu, so werden detaillierte Einzelfallanalysen doch wieder unausweichlich.

– Entscheidend ist, daß eine solche «marktstrukturelle Vorauskalkulation» des Preisverhaltens nicht mehr eine einzelne, ggfl. isoliert abstellbare Verhaltensweise zum Gegenstand hätte, sondern das Angebot einer Unternehmensleistung als solche, die dann ihrerseits wegen der bekannten Interdependenzen mit der Gesamtpolitik eines Unternehmens zusammenhängt.[73] Definiert man deren Inhalte von Rechts wegen, so ist der Boden einer auf freien Interaktionen beruhenden Wirtschaftsordnung notwendig verlassen.

– Im Kern liegt diesen Denkansätzen eine verhältnismäßig grobschlächtige, statisch marktformenorientierte Wettbewerbsvorstellung zugrunde («vier Wettbewerber sind besser als drei»). Eine Anknüpfung daran wie z.B. im Rahmen einer marktanteilsorientierten Zusammenschlußkontrolle mag – faute de mieux – i.S. eines Gefährdungstatbestandes so lange tolerabel sein, als den betroffenen Unternehmen andere Verhaltensalternativen offen bleiben, im Falle einer unzulässigen Fusion z.B. internes Unternehmenswachstum. Wenn Preisverhalten marktbeherrschender Unternehmen generell die Lebensfähigkeit anderer Konkurrenten zum Maßstab nehmen müßte, wäre das eine Daumenregel ohne jedes wettbewerbspolitische Sicherheitsnetz.[74]

Damit ist nicht ausgeschlossen, daß eine solche Marktstrukturverantwortung auf Grund einer Interessenabwägung im Einzelfall[75] zu bejahen ist. Ein Beispiel dafür mag etwa ein auf Dauer abgesicherter absoluter Nachfragemonopolist (Fernmeldeverkehr

---

[71] Siehe dazu das spektakuläre Verfahren Telex Corp. v. IBM Corp. 367 F. Supp. 258 (N. D. Okla. 1973), aufgehoben 510, F. 2d 894 (19th Cir. 1975); cert. dismissed, 423, U.S. 802 (1975); siehe auch oben zu Fußn. 40, 41.

[72] Vgl. J. Baur, Der Mißbrauch im deutschen Kartellrecht, Tübingen 1972, S. 221 ff.

[73] Vgl. hierzu auch E. J. Mestmäcker, Medienkonzentration und Meinungsvielfalt, Baden-Baden 1978, S. 114 ff.; Ansätze in dieser Richtung finden sich in BGH NJW 1977, 1060 Feld und Wald II (ständige Gratislieferung eines Auflagenteils einer Fachzeitschrift als Verstoß gegen § 1 UWG); doch enthält die Entscheidung keine generellen Aussagen über die Zulässigkeit von Mischkalkulationen; siehe zu diesen Fragen auch A. Baumbach/ W. Hefermehl, 12. Aufl., § 1 UWG Anm. 207 ff. und zuletzt BGH WRP 1978, 656 mini-Preis, 658 Elbe-Markt und BGH NJW 1978, 2598 Tierbuch.

[74] Vgl. dazu in anderem Zusammenhang W. Möschel, Preiskontrollen über marktbeherrschende Unternehmen, JZ 1975, 393, 398; H. Schmidbauer, Allokation, technischer Fortschritt und Wettbewerbspolitik, Tübingen 1974, S. 253.

[75] Im einzelnen siehe unten Abschnitt f.

der Post auf Grund Gesetzes) sein, der durch das Erfordernis einer Einheitstechnik unter Systemträgerschaft eines marktmächtigen Anbieters Wettbewerb auch auf der Marktgegenseite in wesentlichen Bezügen unmöglich macht. Hier obliegt dem Unternehmen eine solche Verantwortung im Hinblick auf die kleineren Anbieter. Auch im militärischen Beschaffungswesen z. B. sind Sachverhalte dieser Art nicht selten.

Überwiegend wird heute die Konzeption einer Marktstrukturverantwortung wegen der implizierten Schwächen in einer modifizierten Form vertreten:[76] Die Strukturverschlechterung werde als Mißbrauch einer marktbeherrschenden Stellung dann erheblich, wenn das zu überprüfende Verhalten «leistungsfremd» sei. Das Kammergericht ist in zwei Fällen des Behinderungswettbewerbs von diesen Kriterien ausgegangen.[77]

Ein substantieller Generalisierungsgewinn im Sinne der rule of law ist auch damit indes nicht erreicht. Die Formeln vom Leistungs- bzw. Nichtleistungswettbewerb weisen im kritischen Bereich auf das Referenzsystem freien Wettbewerbs selbst zurück, so daß auch hier das Abgrenzungsproblem im Grunde nur einen neuen Namen und keine Antwort gefunden hat. Wettbewerbstheoretisch ist namentlich die Ambivalenz der zu beurteilenden Verhaltensweisen je nach den Marktumständen nicht hinreichend berücksichtigt. So können – um nur ein Beispiel zu nennen – Preisdiskriminierungen Elemente einer Verdrängungsstrategie sowie Ausdruck wirksamen Wettbewerbs sein, etwa in der Form stillschweigender Nachlässe auf Märkten, in denen Preiswettbewerb erstarrt ist.[78] Diesem Gesichtspunkt kommt im deutschen Recht angesichts der Relativität des Marktbeherrschungsbegriffs besonderes Gewicht zu. So kann die Eingriffsschwelle des § 22 Abs. 1 Nr. 2 GWB («überragende Marktstellung») auch dann überschritten sein, wenn ein Unternehmen noch wesentlichem Wettbewerb ausgesetzt ist.[79] Die Vermutung des § 22 Abs. 3 S. 1 Nr. 1 GWB ist für Einzelunternehmen schon bei einem Marktanteil von $1/3$ erfüllt, wohingegen z. B. beim Monopolisierungsverbot des Sec. 2 Sherman Act eine Marktanteilsbetrachtung sich an Größenordnungen zwischen 68 % und 90 % zu orientieren pflegt.

f) Theorie der beweglichen Schranken

Nach all dem drängt sich die Schlußfolgerung auf, daß es jedenfalls im Bereich der Preispolitik marktbeherrschender Unternehmen keine Alternative gibt zu jener von § 26 Abs. 2 GWB her geläufigen Praxis, die «Interessen der Beteiligten unter Berücksichtigung der auf die Freiheit des Wettbewerbs gerichteten Zielsetzung des Gesetzes gegeneinander abzuwägen.»[80] Man kann dies eine Theorie der beweglichen Schranken nennen. In den Denkkategorien des amerikanischen Antitrustrechts würde man sagen, daß hier keine per se-Regel besteht, sondern eine Gesamtanalyse im Sinne der rule of reason erforderlich wird. Dieses Anliegen wurde bereits vor 60 Jahren von Justice *Brandeis* auf eine klassische Formel gebracht:

[76] Grundlegend P. *Ulmer*, Schranken zulässigen Wettbewerbs, (Fußn. 60), S. 58 ff.; *ders.*, GRUR 1977, 565, 572, 576; ähnlich jetzt A. *Baumbach/W. Hefermehl*, 12. Aufl., § 1 UWG Anm. 710.

[77] WuW/E OLG 1767 Kombinationstarif; WuW/E OLG 1983 Rama-Mädchen; in der erstgenannten Entscheidung forderte das Gericht eine «schwerwiegende Verschlechterung» der Marktstruktur, in der zweiten ist etwas abgeschwächt von der «Gefahr einer nicht unerheblichen und nicht nur vorübergehenden Verschlechterung der Marktstruktur» die Rede. Zur Kritik siehe P. *Ulmer*, GRUR 1977, 565, 576; W. *Möschel*, Pressekonzentration, (Fußn. 44), S. 19 ff.; E. J. *Mestmäcker*, Medienkonzentration, (Fußn. 73), S. 126 ff.

[78] Vgl. für alle W. *Möschel*, Der Oligopolmißbrauch, (Fußn. 38), S. 40 ff. mit weiteren Nachweisen.

[79] BGHZ 68, 23 Librium/Valium.

[80] Vgl. BGHZ 38, 90, 102 Grote-Revers; WuW/E BGH 1027, 1029 Sportartikelmesse II, st. Rspr.

«Der wahre Test der Rechtmäßigkeit ist derjenige, ob die auferlegte Beschränkung den Wettbewerb regelt und dadurch möglicherweise fördert, oder ob sie den Wettbewerb unterdrücken oder sogar zerstören kann. Um diese Frage zu beantworten, muß das Gericht in der Regel die besonderen Umstände des Geschäftszweiges berücksichtigen, auf den sich die Beschränkung bezieht; seinen Zustand vor und nach der Auferlegung der Beschränkung; die Art der Beschränkung und ihre tatsächliche oder wahrscheinliche Auswirkung. Die Geschichte der Beschränkung, das in der Vorstellung bestehende Übel, den Grund für die Auswahl der besonderen Abhilfe, den Zweck oder das Ziel, das erreicht werden soll, all dies sind relevante Tatsachen. Dies ist nicht deshalb so, weil eine gute Absicht eine im übrigen zu beanstandende Regelung rechtfertigt oder umgekehrt, sondern deshalb, weil die Kenntnis der Absicht dem Gericht dabei helfen kann, die Tatsachen auszulegen und Folgen vorherzusagen.»[81]

Von daher wird auch der Stellenwert eines Vernichtungszweckes im Zusammenhang der Preisunterbietung klarer: Es ist nicht der einzige hier erhebliche Tatbestand, sondern bezeichnet nur jenen Ausschnitt, bei welchem ein Werturteil über den Monopolisierungscharakter einer Handlung unschwer möglich ist.

Insgesamt führen die hier angestellten Überlegungen zu einem Ergebnis, das aus der Sicht einer *Hayek*schen rule of law eher als resignativ zu bezeichnen ist. Doch kann ein Gewinn auch darin liegen, daß man sich der inhärenten Grenzen eines Wettbewerbsrechts bewußt bleibt.

Summary

The Concept of the ‹Rule of Law› and the Antitrust Law Today. The Example of Predatory Pricing

On German legal doctrine, the influence of *von Hayek's* scholarly work has been strongest in the legislation to counter restraints of trade. Somehow this is paradoxical since *von Hayek* takes rather a sceptical position with respect to the regulatory objectives in this field. For him rulemaking on competition remains too arbitrary, the political ideal of the rule of law too far from being reached. As against this the author of this article puts forward his thesis that a conflict of goals regarding the necessity and possibility of regulation lies in the subject-matter of such regulation itself which, however, should not be solved in favor of complete regulatory abstinence of the government. After an outline of *von Hayek's* rule of law conception, the author sets forth his thesis by analyzing the treatment of predatory pricing in U.S.-American and German antitrust law.

At first he rejects, for empirical and theoretical reasons, the frequently expressed view that predatory pricing is too exceptional a case to deserve the legislator's attention. What is true about it is that, as a rule, predatory pricing is not so often applied to drive competitors out of business but rather to discipline them. For a legislator committed to freedom, a need for regulating arises from the fact that the freedom of private persons to do business is left to the discretion of other private persons. However the criteria distinguishing predatory pricing from pricing due to vigorous competition hardly live up to the ideal of a

[81] Chicago Board of Trade v. United States, 246 U.S. 231, 238 (1918); aus jüngster Zeit im Zusammenhang vertikaler Vertriebsbeschränkungen dazu Continental T.V. v. GTE Sylvania, 433 U.S. 36 (1977), dt. Übersetzung in GRUR 1978, 300; im Schrifttum dazu *R. Pitofski,* The Sylvania Case: Antitrust Analysis of Non-price Vertical Restrictions, 78 Col.L.Rev. 1 ff. (1978).

rule of law as *von Hayek* understands it. The author critically analyzes several approaches (predatory intent, cost criteria, market prices as comparative data, abusive transfer of market power, theory of the responsibility for the market structure). He comes to the conclusion that there exists – as it often is the case in the law to counter restraints of trade – no alternative to a rule of reason in the sense of a thorough examination of the facts of each particular case. From the standpoint of the rule of law concept as advocated by *von Hayek,* this is rather a resigning view. Yet, it may be positive already not to lose sight of the limits inherent in antitrust law.

Norbert Horn

Aktienrecht und Entwicklung der Großunternehmen (1860–1920)

Über Zusammenhänge rechtlicher und wirtschaftlicher Entwicklungen beim Übergang zum modernen Industriestaat

Die Rechtsordnung des bürgerlichen Rechtsstaates gehört zu den wesentlichen Funktionsbedingungen der Marktwirtschaft. Die ständig neue Ordnungsaufgabe des Rechts, diese Funktionsbedingungen als Grundlage persönlicher Freiheit und allgemeiner Wohlfahrt zu erhalten, ist ein Hauptproblem der modernen Industriegesellschaft, in der einerseits die ökonomischen und sozialen Möglichkeiten der Marktwirtschaft ständig erweitert wurden, zugleich aber auch ständig Kräfte zu ihrer Beseitigung entstehen. Dem bereits von *Adam Smith* betonten Zusammenhang von Rechtsordnung und Marktwirtschaft hat *Friedrich A. v. Hayek* in seinem wissenschaftlichen Werk stets große Aufmerksamkeit gewidmet.[1] Im folgenden sollen einige Aspekte dieses Zusammenhangs in historisch vergleichender Perspektive skizziert werden.[2]

Der Übergang zur modernen Industriewirtschaft ist eng verknüpft mit der Entwicklung von Großunternehmen als Strukturelementen des sozioökonomischen Systems. Dieser Vorgang ist historisch relativ jung; er vollzog sich in den westlichen Industrieländern Deutschland, England, Frankreich und den USA ungefähr zwischen 1860 und 1920 in Fortsetzung früherer, nach der Jahrhundertmitte allmählich beschleunigter Industrialisierungsprozesse.[3] Zu Beginn dieses Zeitraums sind Großunternehmen mit, sagen wir

---

[1] Nur als Beispiel, das allerdings zum Folgenden in enger sachlicher Beziehung steht, sei *v. Hayeks* Plädoyer für eine Stärkung der Rechtstellung der Aktionäre im Interesse einer volkswirtschaftlich richtigen (marktförmigen) Kapitalallokation genannt; ders., The Corporation in a Democratic Society, in: Management and Corporations 1985 ed. *Ashen/Bach*, 1960, S. 99 ff. Dieses Argument war etwa in der deutschen Aktienrechtsreform 1965 von Bedeutung.

[2] Der folgende Text wurde am 29. 9. 1978 auf dem Deutschen Rechtshistorikertag in Berlin vorgetragen und um Fußnoten ergänzt. – Weiterführende Untersuchungen zum Thema finden sich in dem demnächst erscheinenden Sammelband: *Horn/Kocka* (Hg.), Recht und Entwicklung der Großunternehmen 1860–1920. Kritische Studien zur Geschichte, Göttingen 1979.

[3] Vgl. allg. *W. G. Hoffmann*, Das Wachstum der deutschen Wirtschaft seit der Mitte des 19. Jahrhunderts, Berlin 1965, insbes. S. 62 ff., *K. Borchardt*, Die industrielle Revolution in Deutschland, München 1972; *J. Kocka*, Unternehmer in der deutschen Industriegesellschaft, Göttingen 1975, S. 88 ff.; *M. Hacker*, The Course of American Economic Growth and Development, New York 1970, S. 172 ff.; *S. Landes*, Technological Change and Development in Western Europe, 1750–1914, in: The Cambridge Economic History of Europe VI/I, Cambridge 1966, S. 421 ff., *D. North*, Industrialisation in the United States, ebenda VI/II, S. 693–705. – Die Periodisierung dient primär als zeitliches Raster der Betrachtung. Sie erscheint auch sachlich vertretbar, begegnet allerdings zwei Einwänden: erstens hat sich die Zunahme von Anzahl und Größe der Unter-

über 1000 Arbeitnehmern die seltene Ausnahme, die nur in wenigen Wirtschaftszweigen zu finden ist, wie in der eisenverarbeitenden Industrie (Borsig, Krupp). Am Ende des Zeitraums sind industrielle Großproduktion, Großunternehmen und Unternehmensverbindungen prägende Elemente der Volkswirtschaft.

Zur typischen und vorherrschenden Organisationsform der Großunternehmen wird die Kapitalgesellschaft in Form der AG, société anonyme, stock company, corporation. Zum Beispiel waren unter den hundert größten Unternehmen in Deutschland 1887 und 1907 rd. 90% als Kapitalgesellschaft organisiert, zumeist als AG, weniger häufig als Gewerkschaft, Kommanditgesellschaft aA oder GmbH.[4] Die AG weist hier nach der Jahrhundertwende die größten Betriebseinheiten auf. Das eingezahlte Kapital aller AGs, das 1873 rd. 1,2 Milliarden Mark betrug, war 1913 rd. zehnmal so hoch. Auch in den USA wurde die corporation zur dominierenden Rechtsform der sich ab 1880 entwickelnden Großunternehmen; in England wurde die stock company zu dieser Zeit namentlich für Unternehmenszusammenschlüsse genutzt.[5]

Der Anteil des Rechts an der Entwicklung der Großunternehmen soll in drei Schritten thesenartig skizziert werden: (I) durch eine rechtsvergleichende Charakterisierung der Aktienrechte in der Ausgangslage des Zeitabschnitts; (II) durch Fragen nach der gesamtwirtschaftlichen Funktion des Aktienrechts im Hinblick auf neuere Theorien zum Verhältnis von Wirtschaft und Recht; (III) durch die rechtshistorische Kommentierung spezieller wirtschaftshistorischer Theorien der Entwicklung der Großunternehmen.

I.

Die Aktienrechte der vier betrachteten Länder unterliegen namentlich in der Anfangsphase des hier betrachteten Zeitraums (also ca. 1860–1875) ganz gleichartigen Entwicklungstendenzen. Überall schuf eine neue Aktiengesetzgebung die Grundlage für die freie Verfügbarkeit der AG als Organisationsinstrument für Unternehmen: in England die umfassende Regelung des Companies Act von 1862 (unter Einbeziehung gesetzgeberischer Schritte seit 1844[6]); in Frankreich nach halbherzigen Gesetzen von 1856 und 1863 die loi sur les sociétés von 1867 als ausführliche Ergänzung der rudimentären Regelung im Code de Commerce[7]; in Deutschland die erste einheitliche Regelung des Aktienwesens im ADHGB (1861) und seine Liberalisierung durch die Novelle von 1870[8]; in den

---

nehmen in fließenden Übergängen vollzogen, nur undeutlich akzentuiert durch Gründungs- und später Konzentrationswellen; zweitens ist die wirtschaftliche Ausgangslage der vier betrachteten Länder zunächst noch unterschiedlich; dazu auch i. F.

[4] Nach neueren Untersuchungen von *Kocka* und *Siegrist*, in: *Horn/Kocka* a.a.O. Vgl. zum Folgenden auch R. *Passow*, Die Aktiengesellschaft, Jena 1922², S. 29.

[5] Vgl. für die USA z.B. A. A. *Berle*/G. C. *Means*, The Modern Corporation and Private Property, New York 1933; für England B. C. *Hunt*, The Development of the Business Corporation in England 1800–1867, Harvard 1936; L. *Hannah*, Mergers in British Manufactoring Industry 1880–1918, in: Oxford Economic Papers 26/1, 1974, S. 1–20.

[6] v. 7. 8. 1862, 25 & 26 Vic., c. 89. Vgl. auch Fußnoten 11 u. 12.

[7] Gesetz No. 15.328 v. 24.7. 1867, Bulletin des Lois No. 1513, tome 30 (1867), S. 95. Vorausgegangen war die Regelung im Code de Commerce (Art. 29–40), ein Gesetz über Kommanditgesellschaften auf Aktien v. 1856 und ein Gesetz über die freie Gründung kleiner Aktiengesellschaften von 1863.

[8] Novelle v. 11.6.1870, Bundesgesetzblatt des Norddeutschen Bundes Nr. 21, S. 376–386.

USA die etwa 1875 abgeschlossene liberalisierende Aktiengesetzgebung der Einzelstaaten «to incorporate for any lawful purpose».[9]

Fast gleichzeitig beendete die Gründungsfreiheit die in allen vier Ländern geführte Jahrhundertdebatte um die freie Zulassung der juristischen Person für wirtschaftliche Zwecke. Dieses Ergebnis wurde auf durchaus unterschiedlichen Wegen erreicht. Auf dem Kontinent wurde das in den sechziger Jahren gelockerte System staatlicher Konzessionierung abgelöst. A l'avenir, les sociétés anonymes pourront se former sans l'autorisation du gouvernement.[10]

In England und den USA war das System der Einzelverleihung (octroi) seit den vierziger Jahren zurückgedrängt worden.[11] Haupthindernis der Gründungsfreiheit in England blieb die abschreckende unbeschränkte Haftung der Aktionäre. Diese wurde bereits durch Gesetze von 1855 bis 1857 beseitigt; der Companies Act von 1862 registriert nur dieses Ergebnis, gepriesen als «a masterpiece of legislation … to throw open to all the coveted privilege of carrying on business with limited liability».[12] Auf dem Kontinent war umgekehrt die beschränkte Haftung der Aktionäre seit dem Code de Commerce kein rechtstechnisches Problem des Aktienrechts, wenngleich sie lange Zeit Gegenstand wirtschaftspolitischer Bedenken und damit Rechtfertigung des Konzessionssystems geblieben war.

Die neuen Aktienrechte stimmen ferner in der Tendenz überein, das Organisationsrecht der AG stärker durch objektive Normen zu regeln, während es zuvor weithin der Satzung oder dem Einzelverleihungsakt vorbehalten war. Der Aktienrechtler *Klein* hat daher einmal die neuen Aktienrechte als «nachklassisches Aktienrecht» bezeichnet.[13] Unter Organisationsrecht i.e.S. sind dabei die Normen zu verstehen, welche die für die Kapitalgesellschaft handelnden Personen und deren Rechtsmacht und Verantwortlichkeit festlegten. Das kontinentale Recht geht in dieser Tendenz allerdings deutlich weiter als das angelsächsische Recht. Der Companies Act von 1862 etwa gibt für viele dieser Fragen nur eine dispositive Regelung im Gesetzesanhang (Table A).

Schließlich liegt den Aktienrechten trotz aller rechtstechnischen Unterschiede ein im ganzen ähnliches Organisationsmodell zugrunde. Danach hat die AG erstens ein zentrales, regelmäßig kollegiales Geschäftsführungsorgan: Vorstand, conseil d'administration, board of directors. Zweitens sollen die Mitglieder dieses Organs im Interesse der Gesellschaft und ihrer Aktionäre handeln: als «mandataires», als «Organ» oder als «trustee». Der Versammlung der Aktionäre schließlich sind bestimmte grundsätzliche Entscheidungen vorbehalten. In Deutschland führt dies zur Betonung der Generalversammlung als oberstes Willensorgan der AG in der Novelle von 1884[14], während im Bereich des

---

[9] Überblick bei *Brandeis*, Dissenting Opinion in: Liggett Co. v. Lee, 288 US 516, 548 ff. (555).

[10] Art. 21, Lois sur les sociétés v. 1867. In Deutschland Änderung von Art. 208 ADHGB durch die Novelle von 1870.

[11] England: Joint Stock Companies Act 1844 (7 & 8 Vic., c. 110); USA: die einzelstaatlichen Verfassungen begannen ab 1846 das octroi-System zu verbieten; *G. H. Evans*, Business incorporation in the US 1800–1943, New York, 1948, S. 11.

[12] *S. B. Palmer*, Company Law, London 1898[2], S. 8. Haftungsbeschränkung brachte bereits der Limited Liability Act v. 14.8.1855 (18 & 19 Vic., c. 193) und die Joint Companies Acts von 1856 und 1857 (19 & 20 Vic., c. 47; 20 & 21 Vic., c. 17).

[13] *F. Klein*, Die neueren Entwicklungen in Verfassung und Recht der Aktiengesellschaft, Wien 1904, S. 15.

[14] Allg. Begründung zur Aktiennovelle 1884 in: Anlagen zu den Verhandlungen des Reichstags Band 78, 1884, S. 233 ff. (293).

common law eine Kompetenzteilung mit originären Verwaltungsrechten des board of directors anerkannt blieb.[15]

Die hier skizzierten gleichartigen Entwicklungstendenzen der Aktienrechte in den vier betrachteten Ländern spiegeln ähnliche Industrialisierungsprozesse mit gleichartigen Organisationsbedürfnissen, den allgemeinen Sieg des wirtschaftspolitischen Liberalismus und schließlich rechtsvergleichende Lernprozesse.[16] Andererseits traf diese ähnliche Gesetzgebung auf durchaus noch unterschiedliche wirtschaftliche Entwicklungsgrade: in den sechziger Jahren besaß England noch immer einen beträchtlichen Vorsprung im Industrialisierungsgrad und in industriewirtschaftlicher Erfahrung; auf dem Kontinent führt dahinter Frankreich; die USA und Deutschland beginnen aber aufzuholen und überflügeln im gesamten Betrachtungszeitraum die anderen Staaten sowohl in den gesamtwirtschaftlichen Zuwachsraten wie in den Industrialisierungsfortschritten.[17]

II.

Die Frage nach den unmittelbaren wirtschaftlichen Vorbedingungen und Auswirkungen der neuen Aktiengesetze, insbesondere der Gründungsfreiheit, führt zu der grundsätzlichen Frage nach dem Verhältnis von Wirtschaftsentwicklung und Bildung von Wirtschaftsrecht. Diese wird von einer neueren Schule der Wirtschafts- und Sozialgeschichte, die unter dem Stichwort «property rights theory» bekannt geworden ist, neu formuliert.[18] Im Gegensatz zum herkömmlichen marxistischen Ansatz, der die Rechtsentwicklung als reine Funktion der Wirtschaftsentwicklung ansieht, betont sie die selbständige Bedeutung der institutionellen Vorgaben, die (auch) das Recht für Wirtschaftsabläufe liefert, und spricht ihnen eine entscheidende Rolle zu. In der Betonung des institutionellen Ansatzes berührt sie sich teilweise mit der historischen Schule der Nationalökonomie, übertrifft diese allerdings in der Betonung der Rolle des Rechts.

Die Verifizierung dieses Ansatzes durch Detailanalysen von Gesetzgebungsvorgängen und Gerichtsurteilen steht noch aus. Auch ein Blick auf Wirtschaftsentwicklungen im zeitlichen Zusammenhang mit den Gesetzgebungsvorgängen führt nicht zu einer eindeutigen Antwort i.S. eines Kausalnexus auf die Frage, ob Recht Wirtschaftsabläufe hervorbringt oder umgekehrt Wirtschaftsabläufe sich ihr Recht schaffen.[19] Der Companies Act 1862 war von einem Gründungsboom bis 1866 gefolgt[20], die deutsche Aktiennovelle von 1870 bekanntlich vom Gründungsfieber und anschließendem Gründungskrach von 1873.[21] Gründungsboom und anschließende Krise sind jedoch nur z.T. durch die Si-

---

[15] Automatic Self-Cleansing Filter Syndicate Company v. Cunninghame (1906), 2 Ch. 34, C. A.: «the directors alone shall manage!» Schon in Foss v. Harbottle ist die Verantwortlichkeit der von der Aktienmehrheit gestützten directors gegenüber einzelnen Aktionären verneint.

[16] Zu letzterem demnächst H. *Coing*, Rechtsvergleichung als Grundlage von Gesetzgebung im 19. Jahrhundert, in: Jus commune VI (1979).

[17] Allg. Nachweise dazu oben Fußnote 3.

[18] D. C. *North/R. P. Thomas*, The Rise of the Western World. A New Economic History, Cambridge (Mass.) 1973; K. *Borchardt,* Der «Property Rights-Ansatz» in der Wirtschaftsgeschichte, in: J. *Kocka* (Hg.), Theorien in der Praxis des Historikers, Göttingen 1977, S. 140 ff.

[19] Zum Zusammenhang von wirtschaftlicher Entwicklung und Spekulation mit der Rechtsentwicklung vgl. schon R. *Ehrenberg*, Die Fondsspekulation und die Gesetzgebung, Berlin 1883, S. 127 und passim.

[20] B. C. *Hunt*, a.a.O., S. 144 ff.

[21] Vgl. Allg. Begründung zur Novelle 1884 a.a.O.

gnalwirkung der Novelle von 1870 und ihre unzureichenden Gründungsvorschriften zu erklären. Allgemeiner Wirtschaftsboom und der Sieg von 1871 als politische Mitursache sind einzurechnen und immerhin verläuft in Österreich Gründungsboom und Krise zeitlich parallel trotz fortbestehenden Konzessionssystems.[22] Umgekehrt geht bereits dem ADHGB eine in den fünfziger Jahren deutlich verstärkte Gründungstätigkeit von Aktiengesellschaften voraus. In den USA schließlich sind die Gründungs- und Expansionswellen der sechziger und frühen siebziger Jahre wohl aus selbständigen wirtschaftlichen Ursachen zu erklären und daneben im Zusammenhang mit dem Bürgerkrieg zu sehen; Gründungsfreiheit und Entwicklung der Aktienrechte erscheinen also eher als Folge denn als Startsignal wirtschaftlicher Entwicklungen. Ähnliches gilt wohl für Frankreich im Hinblick auf das Gesetz von 1867.

Der «property rights-Ansatz» scheint leichter diskutierbar und erfolgversprechender, wenn man statt der Rechtsbildungsvorgänge die Rechtsinhalte und damit die Institutionen analysiert. Relativ leicht lassen sich eine Reihe institutioneller Vorteile der AG feststellen: die Finanzierung risikoreicher Großinvestitionen durch Kapitalzusammenfassung namentlich bei unentwickelten Kapitalmärkten (was schon im Eisenbahnbau von großer Bedeutung war), die Dauerhaftigkeit und differenzierte Organisation der AG, der Zugang zu den sich entwickelnden Kapitalmärkten, die Erleichterung externen Unternehmenswachstums durch Beteiligungserwerb, Konzernierung und Fusion. Andererseits paßt die AG nicht ohne weiteres in das Erklärungsmodell der property rights theory. Danach ist der wirtschaftliche Erfolg der sich entwickelnden liberalen Marktwirtschaft maßgeblich durch seine rechtlichen Grundlagen bedingt, nämlich die Garantie von Privateigentum und die Gewerbefreiheit, die das Innovationspotential und die Risikobereitschaft der Privatwirtschaftssubjekte freisetzte und durch den Markt koordinierte. Dabei kombinierte das Privateigentum Entscheidungskompetenz, Gewinnchancen und Verlustrisiko im individuellen Unternehmer. Gerade dieser durch die property rights theory betonte Internalisierungseffekt durch Verlust- und Haftungsrisiko aufgrund Privateigentums ist jedoch bei der Aktiengesellschaft durch die teilweise und fortschreitende Trennung von Herrschaft und Haftung reduziert.

Diese Trennung zeigt sich einmal darin, daß die Kapitalverwendungsentscheidungen in immer stärkerem Umfang vom Management getroffen wurden, ihre Folgen aber die Aktionäre trafen.[23] Sie zeigt sich ferner in der Möglichkeit zu aktienrechtlicher Beherrschung von Unternehmen durch Mehrheitsaktionäre oder sogar gegen die Mehrheit bei gestaffelter Beteiligung und bei Streubesitz.[24] Die leichte Übertragbarkeit der Aktie erlaubte schließlich, daß die Gründer oder sonstigen Eigenkapitalgeber ihre persönlichen Gewinninteressen keineswegs mit langfristigen Kapitalerhaltungsinteressen i.S. der property rights theory zu verbinden brauchten, weil sie kurzfristige Spekulations- und Veräußerungsgewinne realisieren konnten. Die Gründungsbooms bieten dafür in allen Ländern reiches Anschauungsmaterial. Die Geschichte z.B. der amerikanischen Eisenbahngesellschaften ist zugleich eine Geschichte des Gründungsschwindels, vor allem durch Überkapitalisierung und Aktienverwässerung, sowie des kurzfristigen Aussaugens von Unternehmen, des «wrecking the company» unter Ruinierung des Anlagevermögens durch Großaktionäre, die anschließend ihre Aktien wieder abstießen.[25] Volkswirtschaft-

[22] *Ehrenberg* a.a.O., S. 143 ff.
[23] Dazu auch i. F. III.
[24] Allg. dazu *L. D. Brandeis*, Other People's Money and How the Bankers Use it, New York 1914; *Berle/Means* a.a.O.; *R. Liefmann*, Beteiligungs- und Finanzierungsgesellschaften. Eine Studie über den Effektenkapitalismus, Jena 1923.
[25] Vgl. *W. W. Cook*, The Corporation Problem, New York 1891.

lich entstanden dadurch beträchtliche externe Kosten: geprellte Kleinaktionäre, heruntergewirtschaftete Unternehmen, Vertrauenskrisen auf den Kapitalmärkten, Kapitalzerstörung.

Gleichwohl hat sich allenthalben die in Kapitalgesellschaften organisierte Industriewirtschaft über Rückschläge und Krisen hinweg kräftig fortentwickelt. Man kann dies teils mit unabweisbaren organisatorischen Bedürfnissen erklären, teils mit der Professionalisierung der Führungskräfte[26], schließlich damit, daß insgesamt die wirtschaftlichen Vorteile der AG die genannten Nachteile überwogen. Daneben ist die selbständige institutionelle Bedeutung der weiteren Aktienrechtsentwicklung in Rechnung zu stellen. In der Aktienrechtsgesetzgebung von den siebziger Jahren an zeigt sich die Bereitschaft und Fähigkeit der Gesetzgeber, in Revision liberaler Vorstellungen Probleme des Schutzes der Anleger und Kleinaktionäre rechtlich zu lösen und damit die geschwächten Internalisierungsmechanismen des Aktieneigentums zu kompensieren.

In Deutschland und England ist diese Bereitschaft am stärksten. Die Aktiennovelle von 1884 suchte die Rechte der Aktionäre und die Verantwortlichkeit der handelnden Organe zu stärken und verschärfte die Gründungsvorschriften erheblich: Gebot der Vollzeichnung, Teileinzahlung, Verbot der Unterpariemission und des Erwerbs eigener Aktien, Gründungsprüfung, Gründerhaftung.[27] In England werden nach 1862 unter anderem die Gründungsvorschriften verschärft: der Directors' Liabilities Act von 1890 z. B. verschärfte die Haftung für Prospektangaben, der Companies Act von 1900 schrieb einen Emissionsprospekt bestimmten Inhalts vor.[28] In Frankreich blieb die Aktienrechtsgesetzgebung zunächst auf marginale Korrekturen beschränkt, griff aber einzelne Schutzprobleme auf, so in dem kurzlebigen Gesetz von 1893 über die beschränkte Marktfähigkeit von Aktien gegen Sacheinlagen (action d'apport) und im Gesetz von 1907 über die Publizität von Aktienemissionen, ferner in der Sicherung der Aktionärsstimmrechte durch die Gesetzgebung von 1913.[29] Eine gegenläufige Bewegung ist in den USA festzustellen. Dort ging die einzelstaatliche Gesetzgebung dazu über, im Wettstreit um die Einwerbung von Neugründungen in fiskalischem Interesse die Gründungsvorschriften zu verwässern, wobei New Jersey und Delaware unrühmliche Vorkämpfer waren.[30] Bei dieser negativen Entwicklung ist die bundesstaatliche Rechtszersplitterung und allgemein die schwächere staatliche Infrastruktur in Rechnung zu stellen; als bundesstaatliche Reaktion ist die Antitrustgesetzgebung ab 1890 zu nennen. Zugleich entwickelte sich die externe Unternehmenskontrolle durch Rechnungslegung, Publizität und allmählich funktionsfähige Kapitalmärkte. Es scheint, daß im internationalen Vergleich diesem externen Kontrollmechanismus des Kapitalmarktes in den USA und wohl auch in England mehr zugetraut wurde als dem Aktienrecht und seiner Anwendung in den Gerichten.

---

[26] *J. Kocka*, Unternehmer in der deutschen Industrialisierung, a.a.O., S. 110 ff., 115 ff.

[27] Vgl. die Allg. Begründung zur Novelle 1884 a.a.O.

[28] Überblick über die zahlreichen Änderungen des Companies Act 1862 bei *L. C. B. Gower*, The Principles of Modern Company Law. London 1957², S. 34 ff. Der Act von 1890 (53 & 54 Vic., c. 64) und der Act von 1900 (63 & 64 Vic., c. 26) sind in den Companies Act 1908 (c. 80, 84) aufgenommen. Die Publizitätsanforderungen führten allerdings z. T. zum Ausweichen auf die (im Companies Act 1908 anerkannte) private company.

[29] Überblick bei *J. Hamel / G. Lagarde*, Traité de droit commercial, Paris 1954, S. 1133 ff.

[30] *Brandeis* a.a.O. (wie Fußnote 9).

III.

Der Beitrag des Aktienrechts speziell zur Ausbildung und Organisation von Großunternehmen kann anhand einiger neuerer wirtschaftshistorischer Erklärungsmodelle diskutiert werden.

1. Das bekannteste Erklärungsmodell ist die These von der Entwicklung des Managerkapitalismus. Sie ist neuformuliert von *Chandler* und *Daems*[31], die in zeitlicher Abfolge drei Typen der Beziehung der Eigenkapitalgeber zur Unternehmensfunktion, also zur Kapitalverwendungsentscheidung, unterscheiden: (a) Im Typ des «Eigentümerkapitalismus» übte der (wichtigste) Eigenkapitalgeber selbst die Unternehmerfunktion aus; (b) in einem Zwischentyp beschränkten sich die einflußreichen Kapitalgeber, neben die die Banken traten, auf Grundsatzentscheidungen und delegierten die laufenden Entscheidungen an die angestellte Geschäftsleitung; (c) im «Managerkapitalismus» schließlich hat die angestellte Geschäftsleitung alle Unternehmerfunktionen an sich gezogen. Die Rechtsform der AG erlaubte die Verwirklichung aller drei genannten Typen und wurde auch tatsächlich so verwendet. Zugleich aber spiegelt die Aktienrechtsentwicklung die Tendenz zum Managerkapitalismus. Dies läßt sich im Recht der Geschäftsleitung deutlich erkennen.

Langfristig konnten Großunternehmen nicht in der ursprünglichen, klassischen Form des Eigentümerkapitalismus geführt werden. Dies lag nicht nur an Finanzierungsproblemen, sondern auch in Geschäftsführungsproblemen begründet. Dazu zunächst ein nichtaktienrechtliches Beispiel. 1872 richtete Krupp als oberstes kollegiales Vertretungs- und Entscheidungsorgan seiner Werke die sog. «Procura» ein.[32] Krupp selbst behielt sich Grundsatzentscheidungen und Weisungsrecht vor. Seine Werke hatten zu dieser Zeit rd. 17 000 Arbeitnehmer. Das Beispiel Krupp zeigt Probleme der Organisation der Geschäftsleitung, die in allen Großunternehmen auftraten, ähnliche rechtliche Lösungen verlangten und sich im Ergebnis auch trotz aktienrechtlicher Unterschiede durchsetzten. Erstens ergab sich das Bedürfnis nach Einrichtung eines obersten Kollegialorgans der Geschäftsleitung mit gesammelter Fachkompetenz und entsprechend größerer Kapazität zur Informationsverarbeitung und Kontrolle. Dieses Bedürfnis wurde in allen Aktienrechten befriedigt. Zweitens zwang die Unternehmensgröße und die zunehmende Komplexität und Akzeleration der Wirtschaftsabläufe dazu, den Personen, die mit den täglichen Geschäften des Unternehmens befaßt waren, wichtige Entscheidungsbefugnisse zu überlassen, gleichgültig ob sie de iure die oberste Geschäftsleitung innehatten. Es ergab sich also die Notwendigkeit der Delegation von Entscheidungsbefugnissen von den Kapitaleigentümern oder deren Vertretern auf das top management. Da man diesem nicht die ganze Unternehmerfunktion überlassen wollte, mußte man es materiell kontrollieren und Grundsatzentscheidungen zurückbehalten. Es entstand das Problem zweier Entscheidungsebenen und deren Koordination, wie es im Beispiel Krupp sinnfällig wird und typisch ist für die erwähnte Zwischenform des «Kapitalismus». Die Konzeption der Aktienrechte zu diesem Punkt ist unterschiedlich, die tatsächlichen Ergebnisse sind ähnlich.

Nur im deutschen Recht wurde im Doppelsystem von Vorstand und Aufsichtsrat das Modell zweier Entscheidungsebenen rechtlich abgebildet. Man überschätzte jedoch die Möglichkeit klarer Funktionstrennung und vor allem die Kontrollkapazitäten des Aufsichtsrates. Die Einführung des Vorstandes im ADHGB zunächst spiegelt die tatsächlich

---

[31] A. D. *Chandler*/H. *Daems*, Introduction, in: *H. Daems*/H. *van der Wee*, The Rise of Managerial Capitalism, Den Haag 1974, S. 1–34.

[32] Text bei *R. Passow*, Die Aktiengesellschaft, a.a.O., S. 512.

eingetretene Delegation von Kompetenzen an die obersten Betriebsbeamten. Daneben behielt der alte Verwaltungsrat Unternehmerfunktionen und als 1870 der Aufsichtsrat als Überwachungsorgan zum Ersatz der weggefallenen Staatsaufsicht eingeführt wurde, behielt er zugleich Geschäftsleitungsfunktionen des alten Verwaltungsrates bei. Damit war die Funktionstrennung unklar.[33] Zahlreiche Statuten sahen ein Instruktionsrecht des Aufsichtsrates an den Vorstand vor. Die preußische Denkschrift von 1877 zur Aktienreform wies darauf hin, daß der Aufsichtsrat teils untätig bleibe, teils selbst als Vorstand fungiere.[34] Die Novelle von 1884 betonte daher die Überwachungsfunktion des Aufsichtsrats (Art. 225) und die Rechtsprechung drängte z. T. Eingriffe in die Geschäftsführung des Vorstandes zurück. – Mit der gesetzlichen Aufgabe der umfassenden Kontrolle der Geschäftsleitung war der Aufsichtsrat vollständig überfordert; es fehlten intime Kenntnisse der Betriebsabläufe, laufende Information und Fachkompetenz. Hinzu trat die Häufung von Aufsichtsratsmandaten – 1901 hatten 70 Personen 1184 Aufsichtsratssitze inne[35] – persönliche Abhängigkeit von Vorstand oder von Großaktionären, starker Einfluß der Banken, Mißachtung der Interessen von Kleinaktionären. Dies zeigt die im Anschluß an die Wirtschaftskrise ab 1901 geführte heftige Aufsichtsratsdebatte.[36] Deren Ergebnislosigkeit mag nicht zuletzt darauf beruhen, daß die Reduzierung der Funktionen des Vorstandes, also des tatsächlichen Managements, faktisch nicht möglich war. *Rathenau* bezeichnet 1917 die Restfunktionen des Aufsichtsrates: ein gewisses Gegengewicht gegen die Geschäftsleitung als potentielle Kontrollinstanz («fleet in being»), Beratungstätigkeit, Krisenmanagement und Selektion des Führungsnachwuchses.[37] Ergänzend ist hinzuweisen auf die Funktion des Aufsichtsrates, gerade durch Mandatshäufung übergreifende Informationsnetze namentlich der Bankenvertreter auszubilden. Die Unternehmenspolitik wurde dadurch nach Kapitalmarktgesichtspunkten beeinflußt, die Selbstrekrutierung des Managements gefördert.

Die Aktienrechte der drei *anderen* Länder kannten nur ein *einheitliches* Geschäftsführungsorgan. Gleichwohl zeigt die Rechtsentwicklung auch hier zunächst die Tendenz zur Ausbildung zweier Entscheidungsebenen, anschließend zur Kompetenzhäufung bei der faktischen Geschäftsleitung, dem Management. In Frankreich war der Verwaltungsrat insgesamt weder bereit noch in der Lage, die Geschäftsführung selbst zu übernehmen. Das erforderliche top management wurde aus dem Verwaltungsrat rekrutiert, etwa dessen président oder einem anderen Mitglied als «administrateur délégué», der die Gesellschaft laufend vertrat.[38] Ausnahmsweise bildeten Großunternehmen wie die Compagnie des Chemin de fer du Nord sogar aus den Reihen des Verwaltungsrates einen conseil de direction, der dem deutschen Vorstand genau entsprach. Häufiger aber wurde ein Dritter durch die im Gesetz selbst vorgesehene (unklare) «substitution de mandat» (Art. 22) als ein mit allen Vollmachten ausgestatteter directeur général durch den Verwaltungsrat oder die Aktionärsversammlung bestellt, unterstützt von anderen, angestellten Führungskräften (directeurs techniques). Man war sich um die Jahrhundertwende einig, daß diese eingesetzte Führungskraft, also der administrateur délégué oder der directeur général, die eigentliche unternehmerische Funktion ausübte: «il est lui, dans les sociétés sé-

---

[33] Vgl. Darstellung und Kritik der Gesetzgebung bei *Passow*, S. 392 ff.

[34] Drucksachen zu den Verhandlungen des Bundesrats des Deutschen Reichs, Session 1876, Nr. 89 insbes. S. 68.

[35] *F. Stier-Somlo*, Die Reform des Aufsichtsrats der Aktiengesellschaft, ZHR 53 (1903), S. 20–27.

[36] Vgl. Fn. 35. Neuere Zusammenfassung bei *R. Wiethölter*, Interessen und Organisation der Aktiengesellschaft, Karlsruhe 1961, S. 288.

[37] *W. Rathenau*, Vom Aktienwesen, Berlin 1917, S. 15 ff.

[38] Vgl. zum folgenden *E. Thaller/P. Pic*, Traité Général Théorique et Pratique de Droit Commercial, 3 Bde., Paris 1907/1924, no. 1122 ff.

rieuses, l'homme méritant et la cheville ouvrière de l'entreprise».[39] Die Funktionstrennung zwischen beiden Ebenen war durchaus unklar und man beklagte in der juristischen Literatur das Fehlen einer «théorie générale de la gestion de l'entreprise». Entsprechend verläuft die Entwicklung im Bereich des common law. Nur indirekt zeichnet sich das zunehmende Gewicht der unterhalb der Ebene des board tätigen tatsächlichen Geschäftsleitung darin ab, daß etwa die amerikanische Rechtsprechung zunehmend Regeln für typische Rechte und Pflichten der corporate officers ausbildete. Das Problem der Koordinierung beider Entscheidungsebenen wurde faktisch durch Personalunion gelöst, und auf die Dauer behielten nur die managing directors innerhalb des board die eigentlichen Entscheidungsfunktionen. Die outside directors wurden funktionsarm wie viele Aufsichtsratsmitglieder.[40]

Dieses Bild wäre zu ergänzen durch eine Analyse der Entwicklung der Aktionärsrechte gegenüber der Verwaltung (Geschäftsleitung). Hier sei nur vermerkt, daß in allen Ländern die Rekrutierung der Geschäftsleitung zwar nicht dem Willen der Großaktionäre, wohl aber den Entscheidungen der Aktionärsversammlungen teilweise entrückt wurde, in Deutschland durch den Aufsichtsrat unter Bankeneinfluß, in den USA namentlich durch die Kontrolle des Abstimmungsmechanismus aufgrund Stimmrechtsmandats (proxy) an den board selbst. Die Entkoppelung des Managements vom Aktionärswillen ist im Bereich des common law relativ stärker ausgeprägt durch weitgehende Disposition des board über nachgeordnete Satzungsbestimmungen (articles, bylaws) und die damit verbundenen Finanzierungsentscheidungen wie Aktienemission, Schaffung neuer Aktiengattungen usw., was auf dem Kontinent der Generalversammlung vorbehalten war.

Abschließend sei nach der Rolle des Aktienrechts in der starken Unternehmenskonzentrationsbewegung gefragt, die von den achtziger Jahren an namentlich in den USA und in Deutschland zu verzeichnen ist.[41] Man hat vermutet, die freie Zulässigkeit der Kartellbildung in Deutschland habe hier die Unternehmenskonzentration verlangsamt. Tatsächlich ist nach neueren Forschungen von *Kocka* die Konzentrationsbewegung in Deutschland relativ stark. Rathenau rühmt den Aufbau von Großunternehmen geradezu als spezifische deutsche Leistung.[42] Mannigfache Konzentrationsursachen sind bekannt und werden erörtert: technologische Bedürfnisse nach größeren Unternehmenseinheiten, Kostenvorteile der Großproduktion, der Wunsch oder Zwang, in unübersichtlichen und expandierenden Märkten, bei schärfster Konkurrenz und Preisverfall, die Marktabläufe monopolistisch zu kontrollieren. Auch der Einfluß des Bankensystems auf das Industriesystem namentlich in Deutschland und den USA sowie die Entfaltung der Kapitalmärkte ist zu beachten.

Übersehen wird häufig die Bedeutung des Aktienrechts als Konzentrationsmitursache. Die durch Aktienrecht und die sich entwickelnden Kapitalmärkte gegebene bloße Möglichkeit, Unternehmensbeteiligungen rasch zu erwerben und zusammenzufassen, zusammen mit Wettbewerbsfurcht und Wettbewerbsdruck waren wohl die stärksten Mo-

---

[39] E. *Thaller*, Traité élémentaire de droit commercial à l'exclusion du droit maritime, Paris 1904[3], no. 655 bis.

[40] Einzelheiten zum Vorstehenden und Folgenden bei D. *Karjala* und N. *Horn*, in: Horn/Kocka, a.a.O., (wie Fußnote 2).

[41] Allgemein dazu die Nachweise in Fußnote 3 und F. *Blaich*, Kartell- und Monopolpolitik im Kaiserlichen Deutschland, Düsseldorf 1973, *Hans Pohl*, Die Konzentration in der deutschen Wirtschaft vom ausgehenden 19. Jahrhundert bis 1945, Z. f. Unternehmensgeschichte Beiheft 11 (1978), S. 4–44; A. S. *Dewing*, The Financial Policy of Corporations, Bd. 4, 1920, S. 34 ff., abgedruckt bei R. E. *Curtis*, The Trusts and Economic Control, New York 1931; L. *Hannah*, Mergers in British Manufacturing Industry 1880–1918, a.a.O.

[42] Vom Aktienwesen, a.a.O.

tive zur Konzentration überhaupt; deren Dynamik und Ausmaß wäre ohne die aktien-
rechtlichen Instrumente nicht denkbar.

Konzernbildung durch Beteiligung einer Kapitalgesellschaft an einer anderen Kapitalgesellschaft ging auf dem Kontinent ohne rechtliche Einwände vonstatten. In den USA
wurde sie durch die Holding-Gesetzgebung ab 1888 gegen den Widerstand der Gerichte
erkämpft.[43] Häufig wurde bereits die Neugründung einer Kapitalgesellschaft als erster
Schritt in diese Rechtsform für den Zusammenschluß zahlreicher kleinerer Einzelunternehmen genutzt: z. B. wurde 1888 in England die Salt Union aus 63 Einzelfirmen gebildet.[44] – Für die Bündelung von Beteiligungsrechten wurden besondere Rechtsformen benutzt, so der trust in den USA, der trotz seiner Kurzlebigkeit berühmt-berüchtigt wurde
wegen der beispiellosen Machtzusammenballung des Standard Oil Trust von 1882, ferner die allgemein verbreitete Form der Interessengemeinschaft. Der Standard Oil Trust
stellte zwischen der Auflösung des Trust und der Bildung der Holding eine Bündelung bereits vorhandener gleichgerichteter Aktionärsinteressen dar, eine «community of interests».[45] Wettbewerbsbeschränkende Absprachen («Monopole») wurden häufig in
Frankreich und Deutschland durch Aktientausch, also wechselseitige Beteiligung, untermauert, so die 1904 geschlossene Interessengemeinschaft zwischen den Hoechster
Farbwerken und der Firma Casella.[46] Zu nennen ist schließlich die Gründung von Ge-
meinschaftsunternehmen in den USA seit den achtziger Jahren, in Deutschland wenig
später (Beispiel: Duisburger Kupferhütte), meist in Form der Kapitalgesellschaft. Ihre typische Funktion war die gemeinsame Verkaufsorganisation (Syndikat); ein Beispiel bietet die Gründung des Rheinisch-Westfälischen Kohlesyndikats 1893. Schließlich sind die
besonderen Finanzierungsmöglichkeiten auch der einfachen AG in ihrer Bedeutung für
internes Unternehmenswachstum zu beachten.

Man muß das aktienrechtliche Instrumentarium für die Konzentration im Zusammenhang mit anderen, namentlich ökonomischen Faktoren sehen. Vor dem Hintergrund
zahlloser Zusammenbrüche und mißlungener Zusammenschlüsse hat nun die wirtschaftshistorische Forschung nach positiven ökonomischen Faktoren für Unternehmenswachstum gefragt und dabei namentlich spezifische Unternehmensstrategien analysiert, nämlich neben dem allgemeinen Streben nach Expansion von Absatz und Marktanteil die Strategie der Integration vor- und nachgelagerter Marktstufen (also Rohstoffe
oder Weiterverarbeitung) und die Produktdiversifikation.[47] Diese Unternehmensstrategien konnten insbesondere für die USA und Deutschland, wohl auch für England verifi-
ziert werden[48], Untersuchungen zu Frankreich stehen noch aus. Namentlich für die Inte-

[43] Die Rechtsprechung lehnte zunächst die Aktienbeteiligung einer corporation an einer anderen
corporation als «ultra vires» ab. Dagegen eröffnete die einzelstaatliche Gesetzgebung diese Möglichkeit, zuerst in New Jersey (1888) und New York (1890). Überblick bei *Curtis* a.a.O. (wie
Fußnote 41).

[44] *L. Hannah*, a.a.O. (Wie Fußnote 5), S. 6 f.

[45] *Curtis*, The Trusts and Economic Control, a.a.O., S. 32 f.

[46] *R. Liefmann*, Kartelle und Trusts und die Weiterbildung der volkswirtschaftlichen Organisation,
Stuttgart 1922⁵, S. 203 f.

[47] *J. Kocka*, Expansion – Integration – Diversifikation. Wachstumsstrategien industrieller Großunternehmen in Deutschland, in *H. Winkel* (Hg), Vom Kleingewerbe zur Großindustrie, Schriften
des Vereins für Socialpolitik, NF Bd. 83, Berlin 1975, S. 203–226.

[48] Zu Deutschland *Kocka* a.a.O. (wie Fußnote 47) und in: *Horn/Kocka*, a.a.O. (Wie Fußnote 2); zu
den USA vor allem die Untersuchungen von *Chandler* (Wie Fußnote 31 u. 49); zu England *P. L.
Payne*, The emergence of the large-scale company in Great Britain, 1870–1914, EHR 20, 1967,
531 ff.; *L. Hannah*, a.a.O. (wie Fußnote 5); ders., The rise of the corporate economy, London
1976.

gration war der Beteiligungserwerb naheliegend, der Aktienerwerb seine bequemste Form. Aktienrechtsgeschichte und Unternehmensgeschichte ergänzen sich insoweit zu einem deutlicheren Bild.

Darüber hinausgehend hat *Alfred Chandler* kürzlich die These aufgestellt, daß die ökonomische Hauptursache für das Wachstum erfolgreicher Großunternehmen der Umstand sei, daß die Koordination von Wirtschaftsabläufen durch unternehmerische Organisation sich der Koordination dieser Abläufe durch Marktprozesse als überlegen erwiesen habe.[49] Die These ist als Erklärungsversuch für den faktischen Erfolg bestimmter Großunternehmen und Unternehmenskonzentrationen faszinierend. Als allgemeine Konzentrationstheorie erscheint sie jedoch sehr unvollständig; sie kann zudem als Rechtfertigungstheorie für Monopole mißverstanden werden. Die Geschichte des Aktienrechts und seiner Praxis zeigt, daß bei der Bildung und Behauptung von Großunternehmen und Unternehmenszusammenschlüssen nicht nur ökonomische Rationalität am Werk war, sondern ein mächtiger Antriebsfaktor in den bloßen und handgreiflichen Möglichkeiten rascher Kapitalmobilisierung, Beteiligungsumschichtung und Machtzusammenballung lag, die das aktienrechtliche Instrumentarium und die Kapitalmärkte boten. Die wirtschaftshistorische Konzentrationstheorie kann in diesem Punkt durch die Geschichte des Aktienrechts relativiert und korrigiert werden.

Summary

Company Law and the Development of the Big Enterprise (1860–1920)

On Some Relations between the Legal and the Economic Development in the Period of Transition to the Modern Industrial State.

From the development of company law and the growth of business enterprises during the period between 1860 and 1920, one can learn something about law as a basic condition for market economy and the interplay between law and economy. In Western industrialized countries such as Germany, France, Great Britain and the USA, the rise of the big enterprise took place rather simultaneously during that period, particularly after 1880. These enterprises were organized for the most part as companies (corporations). This article describes the history of company law on a comparative basis and considers with it some theories of economic history on the development of big enterprises. (I) A comparative review reveals striking similarities of the company laws of these four countries, particularly for the earlier period of 1860–1875, despite fundamental differences in their legal traditions and in the level of industrialization. In all four nations, the freedom to incorporate for any legal purpose and limited liability of shareholders made the company a readily available tool for business organization. The company laws followed roughly the same organizational pattern. All this indicates the victory of economic liberalism, similar industrialization processes with similar organizational needs and, finally, the mutual learning of comparative legal experiences. (II) Whether this legislation was the effect of or the cause for concurrent economic developments cannot be determined merely by an examination of the boom periods which partly preceded and partly followed the enact-

---

[49] A. D. *Chandler*, The Visible Hand. The Rise of Modern Business Enterprise in the United States, Cambridge (Mass.), 1977.

ments of the various company laws. A certain answer can, however, be expected from the «property rights theory» which maintains that law is an important institutional factor for economic development and that the market economy could develop in the 19th century only because private property allowed private investment and combined its opportunities and its risks in the entrepreneur. The company offered several undeniable institutional advantages over the individual entrepreneur: the accumulation of large amounts of capital from many small contributions; the spread of investment risks; the differentiated organization; access to developing capital markets; and external growth potential through acquisitions and mergers. On the other hand, the company does not perfectly fit the explanatory model of the property rights theory because of the partial separation of ownership and control and of opportunities and risks. Company legislation in Europe after 1875 can partly be explained as a response to these institutional disadvantages and as an effort to compensate the external effects by law. In the USA, the competition of the states so attract incorporators prevented the development of such a policy. (III. 1.) Economic history offers several theories on the formation of big enterprises which can be tested in the light of the history of company law. The theory that, in the large company, the function of the entrepreneur shifted from the capital owner to the managers (managerial capitalism) can be confirmed to a large extent by the development of the company law rules on management. In all countries, the organizational needs of the big enterprises required, in the first instance, the formation of boards of several directors (instead of one single director), and secondly, a certain separation of daily business decisions and basic policy determinations by capital owners and, finally, an increased delegation of responsibilities to the managers in charge of daily decisions. Only German company law developed a «two-tiers» system of managing and supervisory boards; but the possibility in such a system of making a clear distinction of functions and responsibilities was overestimated and it became a source of continuing debate. In the other countries, company law provided only one board in which, however, a separation of functions and responsibilities between outside directors and managing directors took place. The growing power of managing directors and highranking corporate officers (together with the similar position of the German managing board of directors) confirm the description of managerial capitalism. (III.2.) Theories regarding the strategies of growing enterprises (which normally followed a policy of diversification of products and of backward and forward integration) also can be confirmed by studying the various legal tools for external growth provided by company law. (III.3.) Recently, *Alfred Chandler* has put forward a new theory on the growth of enterprises as a result of the economic advantages of coordination by management over coordination by the market. This theory of economic rationality can be challenged by the legal historian who can demonstrate that company law, together with the developing capital markets, offered legal tools for the build-up of economic power during the late 19th century, regardless of its economic rationality.

Alfred Schüller

Eigentumsrechte, Unternehmenskontrollen und Wettbewerbsordnung

> «The interest of a management striving for control of more resources will be to maximize aggregate profits of the corporation, not profits per unit of capital invested. It is the latter, however, which should be maximized if the best use of the resources is to be secured.» *Friedrich A. von Hayek* [*]

Die *von Hayeksche* Leitidee einer primär von den Gewinninteressen der Anteilseigner bestimmten Verfassung der Unternehmen, insonderheit der Aktiengesellschaft, impliziert eine für viele Zeitgenossen provozierende Feststellung: Eine konsequent eigentumsbestimmte Unternehmensverfassung bringt unmittelbar jene wohltätigen gesamtwirtschaftlichen Wirkungen hervor, die freie Märkte mit hoher Wettbewerblichkeit auszeichnen. Im folgenden soll mit Hilfe des Erklärungsansatzes der «Ökonomischen Theorie der Eigentumsrechte», häufig auch Property Rights-Theorie genannt [1], gezeigt werden, daß schwere Gefährdungen der Wettbewerbsfreiheit aus Verstößen gegen die zitierte Handlungsmaxime resultieren, insbesondere aus rechtlich verursachten Eigentumsaushöhlungen, die eine Gewinnmaximierung je Kapitalanteil ausschließen.

I. Eigentumsrechte als wettbewerblicher Allokationsmechanismus

Im Anschluß an *H. Demsetz* [2] kann man vier Aufgaben unterscheiden, die jeder akzeptable Allokationsmechanismus zu leisten hat: Erstens müssen Informationen über Möglichkeiten und Vorteile aus dem Einsatz von Ressourcen in alternativen Verwendungen erzeugt werden, zweitens sind Personen mit Handlungs- und Entscheidungskompetenz auszustatten, drittens sind diese Personen zur Nutzung dieser Kenntnisse und Kompetenzen zu motivieren und viertens sind ihre Leistungen positiv oder negativ zu sanktionieren. Als wirksamstes Mittel zur Lösung dieser Aufgaben gelten in der Property Rights-Theo-

---

[*] *F. A. von Hayek*, The Corporation in a Democratic Society: In whose Interest ought it to and will it be run? In: Derselbe, Studies in Philosophy, Politics and Economics, Chicago 1967, S. 308.

[1] Vergleiche *E. G. Furubotn* und *S. Pejovich*, Property Rights and Economic Theory: A Survey of Recent Literature, Journal of Economic Literature, Vol. 10, 1972, S. 1137–1162; dieselben (Hrsg.), The Economics of Property Rights, Cambridge / Mass. 1974; *H. G. Manne*, The Economics of Legal Relationships. Readings in the Theory of Property Rights, St. Paul, New York, Boston, Los Angeles, San Francisco 1975.

[2] *H. Demsetz*, The Exchange and Enforcement of Property Rights, Journal of Law and Economics Vol. 7, 1964, S. 16.

rie private Eigentumsrechte im Sinne von Vermögens- oder Verfügungsrechten. Diese nach *H. Demsetz* durch «Internalisierung von Externalitäten»[3] entstehenden Ausschlußrechte werden in einem weit über den juristischen Begriff des Eigentums hinausgehenden Sinn als individuelle Handlungsmöglichkeiten oder Entscheidungskompetenzen rechtlicher oder tatsächlicher Art aufgefaßt. Auf die ökonomische Relevanz dieses sehr weit gefaßten Eigentumsbegriffs hat *F. A. von Hayek* mit dem Hinweis aufmerksam gemacht, daß das sich aus Verträgen ergebende große Netzwerk von Rechten «ein ebenso wichtiger Teil unseres geschützten Bereichs und ebensosehr die Grundlage unserer Pläne (ist) wie ein eigener Besitz».[4]

Tatsächlich sind Eigentums-, Vermögens- oder Verfügungsrechte die Grundlage jedes Wirtschaftsverkehrs. Mit ihrer Hilfe werden mehr oder weniger weitgehende individuelle Zuständigkeitsbereiche für die Nutzung von Gütern, sei es in der Form der Produktion, des Verbrauchs oder des Sparens, abgegrenzt. In der Ausgestaltung von Eigentumsrechten sieht die Property Rights-Theorie den wichtigsten X-Effizienz-Faktor im Sinne jener Einflußgröße, die nach *Harvey Leibenstein*[5] als Ursache dafür anzusehen ist, daß wirtschaftliche Leistungen (outputs) nicht nur von eindeutig erkennbaren Inputfaktoren und Produktionsfunktionen abhängen, sondern in ganz besonderer Weise auch von (Ordnungs-)Bedingungen, wie zum Beispiel vom Anreiz- und Kontrollsystem, unter dem das Management in Abhängigkeit von bestimmten rechtlich-institutionellen Gegebenheiten, etwa dem Aktienrecht, arbeitet. Hinsichtlich des Anspruchs, die Wirkungsweise von Eigentumsrechten ursächlich als *wettbewerblichem* X-Effizienz-Faktor erfahrungswissenschaftlich zu erklären, steht man nun vor der Schwierigkeit, daß nicht alle einflußbestimmenden Umstände und Daten im Wechselspiel von Eigentumsrechten und Wettbewerbsordnung bekannt sind. Wissenschaftlich vertretbare Voraussagen von Einzelergebnissen dürften so gut wie ausgeschlossen sein. In diesen für die Wirtschafts- und Sozialwissenschaften typischen Fällen eines begrenzten Tatsachenwissens sollten wir, so meint *F. A. von Hayek*[6], unsere Unwissenheit ernster nehmen und uns bei hinreichender Kenntnis der allgemeinen Bedingungen für das Entstehen eines bestimmten Einflußfaktors, hier von Eigentumsrechten, auf «Muster-Voraussagen» oder «Erklärungen des Prinzips» beschränken. Mit dieser Methode läßt sich nun zur Wirkungsweise von Eigentumsrechten folgendes prognostizieren:

> In dem Maße, in dem inhaltlich zweifelsfrei bestimmte, von jedem respektierte und frei transferierbare Eigentumsrechte begründet werden können, entstehen nicht nur Vorteile für die Eigentümer, sondern auch für die Gesellschaft. Denn es darf erwartet werden, daß individuelle Vermögensrechte – wegen ihrer aus dem Eigeninteresse und der Haftung erwachsenden Anreiz- und Kontrollwirkung – die Nutzung von knappen Gütern auf bestmögliche Weise gewährleisten.

Tatsächlich können wir ständig beobachten und erfahren: Je exklusiver Eigentumsrechte ausgestattet sind und je freizügiger über sie verfügt werden kann, desto größer ist der Anreiz, mehr Wissen über gewinntragende Möglichkeiten des Eigentumserwerbs und der Eigentumsnutzung zu erlangen und auf dieser Grundlage das in die Produktion, Nutzung und Kontrolle von knappen Gütern zu investieren[7], was die besten Aussichten hat,

---

[3] Zur Entstehung von Verfügungsrechten kommt es, wenn die Kosten der privaten Aneignung (Internalisierung) geringer sind als der davon erwartete Nutzen. Vergleiche *H. Demsetz*, Toward a Theory of Property Rights, The American Economic Review, Vol. 57, 1967, S. 347ff.

[4] *F. A. von Hayek*, Die Verfassung der Freiheit, Tübingen 1971, S. 170.

[5] Vergleiche *H. Leibenstein*, Beyond Economic Man. A New Foundation for Microeconomics, Cambridge / Mass. und London 1976.

[6] *F. A. von Hayek*, Die Theorie komplexer Phänomene, Tübingen 1972, S. 33ff.

[7] Vergleiche *R. A. Posner*, Economic Analysis of Law, Boston und Toronto 1973, S. 12. *F. A. von Hayek* hat diese wie andere Muster-Aussagen der neuen ökonomischen Theorie der Eigentums-

sich als «richtig» zu erweisen. Eigentümer haben, so kann man auch sagen, eine vom Eigeninteresse bestimmte und kontrollierte Kompetenz, die es ihnen erlaubt, ihre Aktivitäten sachlich, räumlich und zeitlich nach Gesichtspunkten einer strengen Kosten- und Nutzenrechnung zu wählen. Sie werden deshalb bei entsprechendem Spielraum der Rechtsordnung ihre Bemühungen zum günstigsten Erwerb und zur bestmöglichen Nutzung von Eigentumsrechten, also ihre «Internalisierungsanstrengungen», verstärken.

Da hierbei alternative Verwendungen wiederum in räumlicher, zeitlicher und sachlicher Hinsicht unter Einschluß der Vorteile der Arbeitsteilung und Spezialisierung zu bedenken sind, also dem Kalkül der Opportunitätskosten umfassend zu genügen ist, wird der im System von Eigentumsrechten freigesetzte Eigennutz ungewollt eine wettbewerbliche Lösung der eingangs genannten vier Allokationsaufgaben hervorbringen. Das Ergebnis dieser vielfältigen individuellen Internalisierungsbemühungen ist nicht in demselben Sinne ein bewußt gestaltbares Allokationssystem wie die rechtliche Eigentumsordnung, sondern eine davon sich wesentlich unterscheidende spontane «Handelnsordnung».[8] Diese besteht in einem marktmäßigen Wirtschaftsprozeß und wird hier in Verbindung mit allen diese Ordnung regelnden Maßnahmen des Staates Wettbewerbsordnung genannt.

Die Wettbewerbsordnung wird also durch die Art der Eigentumsordnung konstituiert. Demnach würde zwischen den angeführten Bezugskomplexen Eigentumsrechte, Unternehmenskontrollen und Wettbewerbsordnung eine Kausalbeziehung in der genannten Reihenfolge bestehen, die jedoch – einmal entstanden – über Rückkoppelungseffekte eine zirkuläre Verknüpfung aufweist und sich dadurch in ein sich selbst organisierendes dynamisches Marktsystem verwandelt. Dabei ist umstritten, in welchem Ausmaß diese Ordnung des Schutzes durch rechtsstaatliche Vorkehrungen, zum Beispiel gegen wettbewerbsbehindernde Formen des Erwerbs oder der Nutzung von Eigentumsrechten, bedarf, damit im Prozeß der marktwirtschaftlichen Koordinierung von Eigentumsrechten jene Informationen, Kompetenzen, Motivationen und Sanktionen entstehen können, die die Voraussetzung für wirtschaftlichen Wohlstand und die Freiheit der Menschen in einer Volkswirtschaft sind.

Die keineswegs neue Erkenntnis, daß das Privateigentum und die Regeln des Rechts, die es zur Sicherung freier wettbewerblicher Märkte begrenzen, einen originären Allokationsmechanismus verkörpern, wird in der praktischen Wettbewerbspolitik immer weniger beachtet. Dies ist eigentlich erstaunlich. Wenn nämlich private Eigentumsrechte die Wurzel der marktwirtschaftlichen Wettbewerbsordnung sind[9], dann müßte folgerichtig

rechte bereits früher mit einer zeitlosen Aussage wie folgt formuliert: «Das Bestreben, den Beitrag der einzelnen Menschen, die ihre eigenen Interessen verfolgen, zur Bedürfnisbefriedigung der anderen möglichst groß werden zu lassen, führt nicht bloß zum allgemeinen Prinzip des ‹Privateigentums›, es hilft uns auch bei der Bestimmung des Inhalts der Eigentumsrechte im Hinblick auf verschiedene Arten von Dingen. Damit der Einzelne bei seinen Entscheidungen alle physischen Wirkungen, die diese Entscheidungen zur Folge haben, in Rechnung zieht, ist es notwendig, daß der Verantwortlichkeitsbereich ... alle unmittelbaren Wirkungen möglichst vollständig einschließt, die seine Handlungen auf die Befriedigung haben, die andere aus den Dingen seines Wirkungsbereichs ziehen.» *F. A. von Hayek*, Wahrer und falscher Individualismus, in: Derselbe, Individualismus und wirtschaftliche Ordnung, erste Auflage, Erlenbach-Zürich 1952; zitiert nach der zweiten, erweiterten Auflage, Salzburg 1976, S. 33.

[8] *F. A. von Hayek*, Rechtsordnung und Handelsordnung, in: Freiburger Studien. Gesammelte Aufsätze von *F. A. von Hayek*, Tübingen 1969, S. 161ff.

[9] Vergleiche *F. A. von Hayek*, Die Verfassung der Freiheit, a.a.O., S. 150f. und passim; *W. Eucken*, Grundsätze der Wirtschaftspolitik, vierte, unveränderte Auflage, Tübingen und Zürich 1968, S. 254–291; *F. Böhm*, Der Zusammenhang zwischen Eigentum, Arbeitskraft und dem Betreiben eines Unternehmens, in: *K. H. Biedenkopf, H. Coing* und *E.-J. Mestmäcker* (Hrsg.), Das

bei der Untersuchung der Bedingungen für eine marktwirtschaftliche Wettbewerbsordnung intensiver danach gefragt werden, was die gesetzlichen Regelungen über das Eigentum beinhalten müssen, damit Muster der gewünschten Art, nämlich wettbewerbliche Märkte, entstehen können.

Tatsächlich ist immer häufiger die Rede von einer ausweglosen Legitimationskrise des Privateigentums als marktwirtschaftlicher Ordnungsfaktor. Zur Begründung wird insbesondere auf das Problem der Unternehmenskontrolle verwiesen. Für die Aktiengesellschaft, die heutzutage dominierende Form der Großunternehmung, habe, so wird gesagt, die Trennung zwischen Rechtsinhaberschaft und tatsächlicher Verfügung über Eigentum zu einer unüberbrückbaren Entfremdung zwischen Aktionären und angestellten Managern geführt. In solchen, die heutige Wirtschaftsstruktur prägenden Unternehmen könne der interne Entscheidungs- und Handlungsprozeß nicht mehr von einem einzigen Ziel her gesteuert werden, etwa dem im Interesse der Eigentümer liegenden Ziel der freien Verfügung über das Gewinnmaximum je Kapitalanteil. Es müsse vielmehr mit dem konkurrierenden Streben des Managements und anderer Unternehmensgruppen nach Maximierung ihres eigenen Nutzens gerechnet werden, was von den rechtlichen Eigentümern nicht mehr kontrollierbar sei. Verhindern lasse sich diese Eigentumsverdünnung, so wird weiter gefolgert, durch Maßnahmen der inneren und äußeren Kontrolle seitens der Aktionäre allenfalls graduell; denn die als Transaktionskosten bezeichneten Kontrollaufwendungen, die die Eigentümer zur Wahrnehmung und zum Schutz ihrer Rechte aufzuwenden hätten, seien größer als die davon zu erwartenden Vorteile. Besonders verbreitet ist die Meinung, daß die Höhe der Kontrollkosten der Aktionäre mit dem Ausmaß der Streuung der Anteilsrechte positiv korreliere und daß in dem Maße, in dem das Aktionärseigentum durch die Nicht-Eigentümer in den Unternehmen, insbesondere durch die angestellten Manager, ausgehöhlt werde, das Privateigentum seine konstitutive Bedeutung für die Wettbewerbsordnung einbüße.

Weiter wird gefolgert: Je mehr Kleinaktionäre, desto größer die Unabhängigkeit der Unternehmensleitung von der Willensbildung und Entscheidung der Eigentümer. Demgemäß würde eine erfolgreiche Politik der breiten Streuung des Aktienbesitzes den Prozeß der Funktionsentleerung des Privateigentums nur noch beschleunigen. Als Ausweg wird von mancher Seite empfohlen, die Allokationsaufgabe anderen, nicht primär eigentumsbestimmten Instanzen unter Einschluß staatlicher Aufsichts- und Lenkungsverfahren zu überantworten:

Durch eine konstruktivistisch-interventionistische Wettbewerbspolitik[10], durch Formen interner und externer Mitbestimmung am unternehmerischen Entscheidungsprozeß durch Nichteigentümer, durch ein System von sogenannten demokratisch organisierten Wirtschafts- und Sozialräten und durch staatliche Investitionslenkung oder strukturbestimmende Programmierung des Wirtschaftsgeschehens (Rahmenplanung) mit dem Ziel, die Produktion am «gesellschaftlichen Bedarf» zu orientieren.

Im folgenden wird die Ansicht vertreten, daß die für die Großaktiengesellschaft konstatierte Trennung von juristischem Eigentum und ökonomischer Verfügung nicht das Ergebnis einer unvermeidlichen oder gar gesetzmäßigen Entwicklung der Marktwirtschaft ist, sondern die Folge von volkswirtschaftlich unbedachten gesetzgeberischen Regelungen, die die allokative Leistungsfähigkeit des Aktieneigentums und damit die Ent-

---

Unternehmen in der Rechtsordnung. Festgabe für Heinrich Kronstein aus Anlaß seines 70. Geburtstages, Karlsruhe 1967, S. 11–45; E.-J. *Mestmäcker*, Verwaltung, Konzerngewalt und Rechte der Aktionäre, Karlsruhe 1958, S. 20ff.

[10] Vergleiche hierzu E. *Hoppmann*, Soziale Marktwirtschaft oder konstruktivistischer Interventionismus, in: E. *Tuchtfeldt* (Hrsg.), Soziale Marktwirtschaft im Wandel, Freiburg 1973, S. 27–68.

stehung von eigentumsinduzierten Wettbewerbswirkungen mehr und mehr behindern. Die entsprechenden Maßnahmen der Wirtschaftspolitik werden vielfach als Übergang von der «interessenmonistischen» (kapitalorientierten) zur «interessenpluralistischen» (gesellschafts- oder sozialorientierten) Unternehmungsverfassung bezeichnet. Zumindest für die Wettbewerbsordnung, so soll hier gezeigt werden, bedeutet diese Entwicklung tatsächlich eine weitgehende Umkehrung des Verhältnisses von Gewünschtem und Bewirktem, wobei manches darauf hindeutet, daß man sich der bewußten Begriffsverdrehung bedient, um die Durchsetzung von einseitigen Produzenteninteressen besser verschleiern zu können oder um die für die Durchsetzung anderer Interessen notwendige Funktionsunfähigkeit des Privateigentums als konstitutiven Ordnungsfaktors der Marktwirtschaft nachweisen zu können.

II. Kapitalmarkt und eigentumsinduzierte Wettbewerbseffekte

Die Organisationsform der Kapitalgesellschaft verdankt ihre Entstehung der Sammlung und der Zusammenfassung vieler verstreuter Kapitalien.[11] Das Engagement der Eigner solcher Unternehmen beruht in der überwiegenden Zahl der Fälle eindeutig mehr auf finanziellen als auf manageriellen Interessen.[12] Die Trennung von Eigentum und tatsächlicher Verfügungsmacht in der Kapitalgesellschaft folgt dem Interesse der meisten Aktionäre an einer ihren Fähigkeiten und Risikoneigungen entsprechenden Funktionenspaltung des Eigentums. Ohnehin ist für die Mehrzahl der Aktionäre, bedingt durch ihre «unternehmerische» Inkompetenz in Fragen der Unternehmensleitung, eine aktive Teilnahme an der Unternehmensführung ausgeschlossen. Folglich ist das, was im Interesse der Aktionäre liegt, nicht dasselbe, was den klassischen Eigentümerunternehmer interessiert. Den Aktionären genügen geeignete Verfahren und Rechtsregeln, um kompetente Unternehmensführer auswählen und so kontrollieren zu können, daß diese eine vergleichsweise günstige Rendite erwirtschaften. In den dominierend an Renditeerwartungen orientierten Anlageentscheidungen der Aktionäre manifestiert sich ein «unternehmerisches» Verhalten, in dem eine Quelle für eigentumsinduzierte Wettbewerbseffekte liegt. Diese kann durch bewußte rechtliche Ausformung des Kapitalmarktes[13] in den Dienst der Wettbewerbspolitik gestellt werden. Voraussetzung dafür ist vor allem, daß die von der Aktie vermittelten Eigentumsrechte jenen Anreiz zur Suche und zur Nutzung der jeweils günstigsten Anlageart bieten, der dazu führt, daß der entsprechende Teil des Kapitalmarktes gleichsam eine integrierende und dominierende Steuerungs- und Kontrollfunktion im Gesamtsystem der Faktor- und Produktmärkte ausüben kann.

Der Kapitalmarkt müßte dann für die nach Anlagemöglichkeiten suchenden Aktionäre zu der Instanz werden, die bestmögliche Antworten auf die Frage gibt, welche beste-

---

[11] Aus der Fülle der hierzu vorliegenden Schriften vergleiche *P. C. Martin*, Die Entstehung des preußischen Aktiengesetzes von 1843, Vierteljahresschrift zur Wirtschaftsgeschichte, Band 56, 1969, S. 499–542.

[12] Vergleiche auch *H. G. Manne*, Our two Corporation Systems: Law and Economics, in: Derselbe (Hrsg.), The Economics of Legal Relationships, a. a. O., S. 512. Siehe auch *R. A. Posner*, a. a. O., S. 179.

[13] Vergleiche *K. Hopt*, Vom Aktien- und Börsenrecht zum Kapitalmarktrecht? Teil 1: Der international erreichte Stand des Kapitalmarktrechts, Zeitschrift für das gesamte Handelsrecht und Wirtschaftsrecht, 140. Band, 1976, S. 201–235. Teil 2: Die deutsche Entwicklung im internationalen Vergleich, a. a. O., 141. Band, 1977, S. 389–441.

henden oder neu zu gründenden Unternehmen unter Berücksichtigung des Strukturwandels und des Wachstums der Wirtschaft für die Zukunft besonders gute Anlagechancen erwarten lassen. Da es sich in der Regel um konkurrierende Einschätzungen unter Unsicherheit handelt, entstehen auf diesem Wege zugleich günstige Voraussetzungen für eine vielfältige wettbewerbliche Unternehmensstruktur. Insoweit liegt es nahe, das Geschehen in den Unternehmungen als ein Abbild des (Kapital-)Marktgeschehens zu analysieren und dabei einzelwirtschaftlich organisierte (Unternehmens-)Märkte (Intrafirm Markets) von Märkten im üblichen Sinne (Interfirm Markets) zu unterscheiden. Wegen der komplexen Interdependenz beider Markttypen ist es auch so schwierig, einzelne Erscheinungsformen und Ergebnisse dieses ganzen Marktsystems ursächlich exakt dem Einfluß der externen Marktkräfte oder der internen Unternehmensorganisation zuzuordnen. Deshalb sind auch manche der in jüngster Zeit publizierten empirischen Untersuchungen, die der Art der Unternehmenskontrolle (manager-controlled oder owner-controlled firms) ursächlich ganz bestimmte Marktergebnisse zuzuschreiben und daraus allgemeine Maßstäbe für die Effizienzbeurteilung alternativer Kontrollformen abzuleiten versuchen[14], eher im Sinne *von Hayeks* als Ausdruck einer unzulässigen «Anmaßung von Wissen» zu werten.[15]

In Anknüpfung an die Prognose der Wirkungsweise von Eigentumsrechten läßt sich für die Wirkungsweise des Aktieneigentums folgende Musteraussage formulieren:

Nur dann, wenn alle Teilungen des Eigentums freiwillig eingegangen und wieder aufgelöst werden können[16], sind Wahl und Kontrolle der günstigsten Verwendungsart auf dem Kapitalmarkt möglich. Es müßte demnach zur Hervorbringung dieses Ergebnisses und der daraus folgenden oben beschriebenen Kapitalmarkteffekte offenbleiben, welchen inhaltlichen Gebrauch die Eigentümer konkret von ihren Rechten machen.

Diesen Bedingungen entspricht nun aber das Aktieneigentum nach der in der Bundesrepublik Deutschland geltenden Rechtsordnung nicht, wenn man sich die Ausgestaltung wichtiger Rechte aus dem bekannten Katalog von Einzelrechten[17] des Aktieneigentums ansieht. So ist zum einen das Verfahren der Gewinnverteilung nach dem Mehrheitsprinzip durch die Hauptversammlung eine Ursache dafür, daß über die dadurch begünstigte Selbstfinanzierung gleichsam «internalisierte» Kapitalmärkte[18] der Unternehmen (Intrafirm Markets) entstehen, die der wettbewerbsfördernden Kontrolle des allgemeinen Kapitalmarktes entzogen sind. Zum anderen sind die genannten Einzelrechte der Aktie vom vermeintlichen Anspruch der Aktionäre auf ein unteilbares unternehmerisches Anteilseigentum bestimmt. Demzufolge bilden die wichtigen Funktionen des Aktieneigentums,

---

[14] Vergleiche etwa *W. A. McEachern*, Corporate Control and Growth: An Alternative Approach, Journal of Industrial Economics, Vol. XXVI, 1978, S. 257–266.

[15] *F. A. von Hayek,* Die Anmaßung von Wissen, ORDO, Band 26, 1975, S. 12ff.

[16] Vergleiche hierzu *E. Streissler*, Privates Produktiveigentum – Stand und Entwicklungstrends der Auffassungen in kapitalistischen Ländern, in: Eigentum, Wirtschaft, Fortschritt. Zur Ordnungsfunktion des privaten Produktiveigentums. Band 12 der Veröffentlichungen der Walter Raymond-Stiftung, Köln 1970, S. 101.

[17] Dazu gehören:
1. Das Recht auf die Beteiligung am Gesellschaftsgewinn (Dividendenbezugsrecht).
2. Das Recht auf den anteiligen Liquidationserlös (Liquidationsanteil).
3. Das Recht des Aktienverkaufs.
4. Das Vorrecht auf den Bezug junger Aktien bei Kapitalerhöhungen.
5. Die Mitverwaltungsrechte, insbesondere in Form des Stimmrechts.

[18] Vergleiche *O. E. Williamson*, Managerial Discretion, Organization Form, and the Multi-Division Hypothesis, in: *R. Marris* und *A. Wood* (Hrsg.), The Corporate Economy: Growth, Competition, and Innovative Potential, London und Basingstoke 1971, S. 343–386.

vor allem die verschiedenen Vermögensrechte und das Stimmrecht, eine untrennbare Einheit. Abweichende individuelle Gestaltungsmöglichkeiten im Sinne einer Aufspaltung der Einzelrechte werden mit der Begründung abgelehnt, nur ungespaltenes (integrales) Aktionärseigentum mache Eigentum zu einer gesellschaftlich nutzbringenden Institution.[19]

III. Aktienrecht und eigentumsinduzierte wettbewerbliche Unternehmenskontrolle

Das geltende Aktienrecht weist der Gesamtheit der Aktionäre, die die Hauptversammlung bilden, die Rolle eines natürlichen Eigentümers zu. Diese Fiktion des «Als-Ob-Unternehmereigentums» stellt die Aktionäre nach innen wie nach außen so, als würde ein jeder in seiner Person wirklich Eigentum und Verfügungsgewalt vereinen wollen und können. In Verfolg dieser offensichtlich mit den tatsächlichen Interessen der Aktionäre nicht in Einklang stehenden Theorie des umfassenden Eigentümerunternehmers wurden im Aktienrecht die Vermögensinteressen, von denen eher angenommen werden darf, daß die Aktionäre sie wahrnehmen können und wollen, nur unzureichend berücksichtigt. Dies sei an den folgenden drei mir besonders wichtig erscheinenden Aspekten des Aktieneigentums beispielhaft erläutert, ohne daß hier auf alle ökonomischen und juristischen Implikationen und Konsequenzen eingegangen werden könnte.

1. Das wettbewerbsbehindernde Prinzip «demokratischer» Gewinnverwendungsbeschlüsse

Laut Aktienrecht entscheidet die Hauptversammlung über die Verwendung des Bilanzgewinns durch Mehrheitsbeschluß. Dabei ist zu berücksichtigen, daß ein erheblicher Teil der Gewinne vorab in Form von gesetzlich begünstigten, erlaubten oder gebotenen Zuführungen zu den offenen oder stillen Rücklagen einbehalten werden kann beziehungsweise muß, ohne daß für dieses Risikokapital Zug um Zug Eigentumsrechte begründet werden. Aus der Sicht der ökonomischen Theorie der Eigentumsrechte ergeben sich folgende Einwände gegen die Majoritätsregel bei der Gewinnverteilung:
a. Man darf wohl ausschließen, daß die Aktionäre hinsichtlich ihrer Vorstellungen über die bestmögliche Gewinnverwendung tatsächlich einer einheitlichen Beurteilungsnorm unterliegen.[20]
b. Das Ergebnis des mehrheitlichen Gewinnverteilungsbeschlusses vermittelt nach außen die für eine freie Eigentümergesellschaft eigentlich widersprüchliche Vorstellung eines monolithischen Stimmblocks «des» Kapitals. Dieser Eindruck verleitet dann, wie die Diskussion um die paritätische Mitbestimmung erkennen läßt, leicht zu dem weitergehenden Fehlschluß, die aktienrechtliche Unternehmensverfassung sei, weil sie einer kol-

---

[19] Vergleiche hierzu K. *Schredelseker*, Eigentümerkontrolle in der großen Aktiengesellschaft. Ein Beitrag zur Diskussion um ein Unternehmensverfassungsrecht, Frankfurt/Main 1975, S. 106ff.
[20] Inzwischen wird dieses im völligen Widerspruch zu einer Gesellschaft von Eigentümern stehende Verfahren der mehrheitlichen Gewinndisposition von ganzen Branchen, z. B. von der chemischen Industrie, als «Prinzip der Einheitsdividende» praktiziert. Vergleiche Frankfurter Allgemeine Zeitung, Nr. 97 vom 12. 5. 1978, S. 19.

lektiven Entscheidungsregel der rechtsfähigen Institution «des» Kapitals – eben der Hauptversammlung – folgt, interessenmonistisch und genüge nicht den interessenpluralistischen Ansprüchen innerhalb und im Umkreis der Unternehmen. Vielmehr erfordere das Prinzip einer symmetrischen Interessenwahrung, daß zumindest auch die Arbeitnehmerschaft «als Ganzes» eine der Institution der Anteilseignerversammlung adäquate (Teil-)Rechtsfähigkeit zugebilligt werde, damit die Arbeitnehmerseite ihre Einkommensziele gleichfalls «wie mit einer Stimme» verfolgen könne.

c. Empirische Untersuchungen zeigen, daß Hauptversammlungen bei der Abstimmung über die Gewinnverwendung dazu neigen, weitgehend den vom Gewinnthesaurierungsinteresse bestimmten Vorschlägen des Vorstands zu folgen.[21] Über die dadurch begünstigte Selbstfinanzierung entstehen gleichsam «internalisierte» firmenspezifische Kapitalmärkte, die der Eigentümerkontrolle und der Kontrolle des öffentlichen Kapitalmarktes entzogen sind. Damit werden die unter Wettbewerbsgesichtspunkten wichtigen Allokations- und Reallokationsfunktionen des Kapitalmarktes behindert, und zwar zugunsten der von den Unternehmensleitungen favorisierten Anlageentscheidungen.[22] Die Wettbewerbsordnung ist davon mindestens in zweifacher Hinsicht tangiert: Erstens durch eine Erhöhung der Marktzutrittsschranken für alle diejenigen Newcomer, die sich der strengen Prüfung des öffentlichen Kapitalmarktes nicht entziehen können; zweitens durch die Behinderung des für eine dynamische Struktur des volkswirtschaftlichen Wettbewerbsprozesses wichtigen Vorgangs einer reibungslosen, wenn möglich präventiven Reallokation der Ressourcen zwischen schrumpfenden und expandierenden Märkten und Branchen. Fehlleitungen des Kapitals drohen dabei vor allem dann, wenn sich in den späteren Phasen der Marktentwicklung die unternehmerischen Expansionsspielräume immer mehr verengen und immobile Unternehmensleiter vorherrschen. Diese werden in dem Maße vom Druck befreit, sich neuen entwicklungsgünstigeren Märkten zuzuwenden, in dem sie die Hauptversammlung zu einem weitgehenden Dividendenverzicht im Interesse vermeintlich lebenswichtiger Investitionen im «eigenen» Unternehmen veranlassen oder durch gesetzliche Gewinnverwendungsvorschriften (Rücklagen) zwingen können. Die Bedingungen für eine automatisch wirksame prophylaktische Wettbewerbspolitik werden dadurch verschlechtert. So muß man sich ernsthaft einmal fragen, ob es in der Werft- oder Stahlindustrie der Bundesrepublik Deutschland zu Strukturkrisen gekommen wäre, wenn die privaten Aktionäre in höherem Maße über die Investitionspolitik dieser Branchen zu entscheiden gehabt hätten?!

d. Die durch den Entzug der vollständigen individuellen Gewinnverfügungskompetenz begünstigte Selbstfinanzierung wirkt sich verstärkt bei Gesellschaften mit Großaktionären aus, die bekanntlich nicht nur aus aktuellen steuerlichen Erwägungen an einer weitgehenden Einbehaltung der Gewinne im «eigenen» Unternehmen interessiert sind.

Soweit die thesaurierten Gewinne die produktivitätsbedingte Lohnzahlungsfähigkeit erhöhen und diese tatsächlich von Arbeitnehmerseite voll ausgeschöpft wird[23], können besonders die Eigentumsrechte der kleineren Aktionäre zugunsten von Einkommensin-

---

21 Vergleiche *G. H. Roth*, Die Herrschaft der Aktionäre in der Publikums-AG als Gegenstand rechtssoziologischer Betrachtung, in: *H. W. Kruse* (Hrsg.), Festschrift für Heinz Paulick zum 65. Geburtstag, Köln-Marienburg 1973, S. 94ff.

22 Zu den Wettbewerbswirkungen vergleiche eingehender *H. O. Lenel*, Ursachen der Konzentration, 2., neubearbeitete Auflage, Tübingen 1968, S. 303.

23 Vergleiche *H. Willgerodt*, Von der Macht des Kapitals – Mythen und Wirklichkeit, in: *Chr. Watrin* und *H. Willgerodt* (Hrsg.), Widersprüche der Kapitalismuskritik. Festgabe für Alfred Müller-Armack zum 75. Geburtstag, Wirtschaftspolitische Chronik des Instituts für Wirtschaftspolitik an der Universität zu Köln, 25. Jahrgang, Heft 2/3, 1976, S. 45.

teressen der Nichteigentümer ausgehöhlt werden.[24] Im Umfang dieses Zwangssparprozesses werden alternative externe Anlage- und Entwicklungsmöglichkeiten behindert, insbesondere aber wird die für eine wettbewerbliche Marktstruktur wichtige Reallokation entsprechend dem tatsächlichen Produktivitätsgefälle zwischen den Unternehmen und Branchen verzögert. Insgesamt werden damit Chancen für entwicklungsträchtige Investitionen, für entsprechende Arbeitsplätze und für eine bessere und billigere Güterversorgung vertan.

e. Dem unverdünnten individuellen Gewinndispositionsanspruch der Aktionäre kommt unter wettbewerbspolitischen Gesichtspunkten auch deshalb eine besondere Bedeutung zu, weil das geltende Aktienrecht ohnehin den wirkungsvollsten Kontrollhebel der Aktionäre, das Austrittsrecht und in seinem Gefolge den Abfindungsanspruch ausschließt. Fehlt den Aktionären die Entscheidungsfreiheit über den gesamten auf ihren Kapitalanteil entfallenden Gewinn, so entsteht also eine Sanktionslücke in doppelter Hinsicht; sie wird durch die Möglichkeit des Aktienverkaufs über die Börse nur zu einem geringen Teil geschlossen.

Nun ist mit folgendem Gegeneinwand zu rechnen: Ähnlich wie die Arbeiter in den sogenannten Selbstverwaltungsunternehmen jugoslawischen Typs an maximalen Einkommensaneignungen interessiert sind, strebten vor allem die Kleinaktionäre nach einer kurzfristigen Dividendenmaximierung zu Lasten langfristiger Investitionsinteressen der Unternehmen. Dieses Argument – häufig von betriebswirtschaftlicher Seite vorgebracht – scheint mir aus folgenden Gründen nicht überzeugend zu sein:

a. Die Unternehmensleiter könnten sich auf das Aktionärsverhalten präventiv einstellen und durch ihre Unternehmenspolitik langfristige Gewinnerwartungen begründen, die die Aktionäre zu einem dauerhafteren Engagement am Unternehmen veranlassen.

b. Der Anreiz für einen Aktionär, am selben Unternehmen beteiligt zu bleiben und erzielte Gewinne zu thesaurieren, ist schon wegen der Informationskosten für einen Anlagewechsel gegeben.

c. Dieser Anreiz dürfte wesentlich größer sein, wenn Gewinnrückführungen Zug um Zug in Beteiligungen mit Stimmrecht verwandelt werden und den Aktionären dadurch Vermögens- und Kontrollrechte nach Maßgabe ihrer tatsächlichen Risikobeteiligung zuwachsen. Dies würde die aus Gründen der Verlustvorkehrung zu rechtfertigende Reservebildung der Unternehmen auch bei fehlenden gesetzlichen Reservebildungsvorschriften nicht ausschließen, nur mit dem Unterschied, daß die Vorstände einem stärkeren Begründungs- und Informationszwang einerseits und einer geringeren Erfolgssicherheit bei ihren Thesaurierungsbestrebungen andererseits ausgesetzt wären.

d. Um hinsichtlich der unternehmerischen Politik der Verlustvorkehrung auch bei den Aktionären keine Sanktionslücke entstehen zu lassen, sollten sie bei Verweigerung einer ausreichenden betrieblichen Reservebildung im Verlustfall mit einer anteiligen Herabsetzung ihrer Aktiennennwerte rechnen müssen.

Hätte das Management die Aktionäre im Direktkontakt von der Zweckmäßigkeit ei-

---

[24] Der Zwangssparprozeß, der den Kleinaktionären von den Großaktionären in der beschriebenen Weise abgenötigt werden kann, wird durch die dividendenminimierende Strategie der sogenannten «Mitbestimmungsträger» (also der Gewerkschaften) verstärkt: «Bei rationalem Verhalten der Großaktionäre und bei entsprechender Aufklärung der Kleinaktionäre mit einem Grenzsteuersatz von ca. 35% müßten» – so heißt es in einer einschlägigen Analyse – «durch einen Dividendenstopp die Aktienkurse eher steigen als fallen. Die Konsuminteressen (der Kleinaktionäre, A. Sch.) wären dann über teilweise Verkäufe der im Kurs gestiegenen Aktie zu befriedigen». Dies läuft offensichtlich auf die Empfehlung einer weiteren Konzentration des Aktienbesitzes hinaus. Vergleiche «Das Mitbestimmungsgespräch», 24. Jahrgang, Heft 7/8, 1978, S. 175.

ner mehr oder weniger weitgehenden Gewinnthesaurierung zu überzeugen, müßten also nicht mehr wie heute die Kleinaktionäre nach Bittstellermanier dem Vorstand Dividendenzugeständnisse abringen, wäre wohl die These von der Ohnmacht der Aktionäre in einem entscheidenden Punkt nicht länger aufrechtzuerhalten.[25]

Es ist unter den heutigen Bedingungen des Kapitalmarktes nicht einzusehen, warum es den Unternehmen nicht möglich sein sollte, ihren Eigenkapitalbedarf ausschließlich durch Aktienemission im Wege der Kapitalerhöhung zu decken.

Insgesamt kommt es also über die Einschränkung des Gewinnverfügungsrechts der Aktionäre zu einer Inhibierung von eigentumsinduzierten Wettbewerbs- und Wachstumseffekten, zumal die vom Management favorisierte Selbstfinanzierung in Verbindung mit der kartellartigen Bildung und Sicherung von gleichfalls risikofreien bzw. risikofrei gehaltenen Sonderrechten der Arbeitnehmer am Eigentum der Aktionäre durch das Mitbestimmungsgesetz wettbewerbsbehindernde Formen des externen Unternehmenswachstums und der Marktschließung begünstigt. Soweit die Selbstfinanzierung zugleich der Umsatzmaximierung dient, steht dieses Unternehmensziel, wie manchmal angenommen wird, nicht im Widerspruch zur Gewinnmaximierung der Gesamtunternehmung, wohl aber zur Gewinnmaximierung je Kapitalanteil der Aktionäre und damit zur bestmöglichen Lösung der eingangs genannten Allokationsaufgaben. Fehlt nämlich den Aktionären die Entscheidungsfreiheit über den gesamten auf ihren Kapitalanteil entfallenden Gewinn, so haben sie auch keinen so großen Anreiz, jene umfassenden Kenntnisse zu erlangen oder zu verwerten, die den volkswirtschaftlich größten Nutzen ihrer Eigentumsrechte sicherstellen könnten. Hätten sie diesen Handlungsspielraum, so könnten die daraus folgenden Entscheidungen selbstverständlich den Interessen der Unternehmensleitungen zuwiderlaufen. Von der Möglichkeit enttäuschter Erwartungen und der ihr zu verdankenden Eigenkontrolle der Manager sind aber in Verbindung mit der wettbewerblichen Kontrolle des öffentlichen Kapitalmarktes die Allokations- und Wohlfahrtswirkungen aus der eingangs zitierten Handlungsmaxime *F. A. von Hayeks* in hohem Maße abhängig.

2. Zur Frage einer separaten Stimmrechtsnutzung

Bekanntlich schließt das Aktiengesetz die Möglichkeit der Funktionenspaltung zwischen Vermögens- und Stimmrecht, also auch die separate kommerzielle Nutzung von Stimmrechten aus. Das Stimmrecht darf nur durch schriftliche Bevollmächtigung von anderen ausgeübt werden, und zwar jederzeit widerruflich und mit einer ziemlich konkreten inhaltlichen Weisung. Über die volkswirtschaftliche Zweckmäßigkeit einer davon abweichenden Freiheit der Stimmrechtsverwertung lohnt es sich einmal nachzudenken:

a. Das Stimmrecht wird nach den Aktiennennbeträgen bemessen und ist nach Mestmäcker[26] allein aus den der Beteiligung entsprechenden Vermögensrisiken zu erklären, nicht aber aus einem demokratischen Prinzip. Dies meinen die Vertreter der Idee der Aktionärsdemokratie. Deshalb versuchen sie, aus der Vorstellung «Stimmrecht ist Stimmpflicht» über die vom Gesetz vorgeschriebene gemeinsame Ausübung des Vermögens- und des Stimmrechts eine möglichst umfassende Entscheidungs- und Kontrollpartizipation der Aktionäre in der Hauptversammlung zu begründen. Die Erfahrung zeigt nun aber, daß sehr viele Aktionäre dieser Vorstellung nicht Folge leisten.

[25] Vergleiche auch *F. A. von Hayek*, The Corporation in a Democratic Society, a. a. O., S. 307. Siehe auch schon *E. Schmalenbach*, Die Aktiengesellschaft, 7. Auflage, Köln und Opladen 1950, S. 33.
[26] Vergleiche *E.-J. Mestmäcker*, a. a. O., S. 11.

Auch zeigt die Möglichkeit, nach §§ 139ff. Aktiengesetz stimmrechtslose Vorzugsaktien auszugeben, daß in Höhe der Differenz zwischen der Mindestdividende für die Vorzugsaktien und der niedrigeren Normaldividende für die Stimmrechtsaktien eine separate Stimmrechtsbewertung bereits heute möglich ist.

b. Im Verhältnis von Stimmrechtswert und Vermögenswert der Aktie können Spielräume für unternehmerische Arbitragemöglichkeiten bestehen, die gerade unter Gesichtspunkten der Wettbewerbsordnung interessant erscheinen. In systematischer Weise hat sich hierzu wohl als erster *H. G. Manne*[27] geäußert, allerdings – wie mir scheint – weniger konsequent unter wettbewerbspolitischen Gesichtspunkten. Manne sieht im Stimmrecht vor allem aus folgenden Gründen ein wichtiges Instrument der Unternehmenskontrolle (corporate control):

Erstens, weil über das Stimmrecht Konkurrenten beherrscht werden können; zweitens, weil auf diese Weise sonst nicht zugängliches kostensparendes technisches Wissen und ökonomische Größenvorteile erworben werden können und drittens, weil sich der Vermögenswert der Aktienanlage steigern läßt, wenn eine Gesellschaft über die Stimmrechtsausübung ein besseres Management erhält.

Aus den ersten beiden Gründen, so folgert *Manne*, wird der Stimmrechtspreis tendenziell mit dem Vermögenswert der Aktie steigen; eine separate Stimmrechtsverwertung wird den Aktionären weniger interessant erscheinen. Dagegen wird sich im Falle erwarteter Vermögenswertzuwächse durch Einsatz eines qualifizierteren Managements das Preisverhältnis zwischen beiden Rechten anders gestalten. Allgemein läßt sich sagen, daß der Preis des Stimmrechts größtenteils von der Einschätzung des Spielraums für weitere Vermögenswert- oder Dividendensteigerungen abhängt. Je besser das etablierte Management arbeitet, desto vollständiger werden die möglichen Erhöhungen des Vermögenswertes beziehungsweise der Dividende realisiert, desto mehr tendiert der Stimmrechtspreis nach Null. Die Preisentwicklung für Stimmrechte informiert also im dritten Fall darüber, in welchem Umfang vermutlich Spielräume für eine bessere Nutzung des X-Effizienz-Faktors bestehen. Über die wettbewerbspolitischen Implikationen einer separaten Stimmrechtsnutzung ist damit noch nichts ausgesagt.

c. Hinsichtlich der potentiellen Nachfrager für Stimmrechte drängt sich aus dem gleich noch eingehender zu erörternden Grunde die Empfehlung auf, nur wirklich stimmrechtsfähige natürliche Personen zuzulassen.[28] Über den Erwerb von separaten Stimmrechten dürften wohl vor allem die besonders renditeinteressierten «unternehmerischen» Anteilseigner stärkeren Einfluß als heute auf die interne Unternehmenspolitik gewinnen; auch könnte der manchmal als «Berufsopponent» bezeichnete initiative Typ des Kleinaktionärs mit einer größeren Zahl von separaten Stimmrechten dem Interesse der Kleinaktionäre an einer ungeschmälerten Gewinnverteilungspolitik stärkeres Gewicht verleihen; Großaktionäre als Stimmrechtsnachfrager wären wohl für die Kleinaktionäre in dieser und anderer Hinsicht weniger zuverlässige Interessenvertreter. Allgemein ist bei den Stimmrechtsanbietern soviel Eigeninteresse vorauszusetzen, daß sie mit der Übertragung, in welcher Form dies auch immer geschehen mag, unter keinen Umständen den Vermögenswert der Aktie gefährden wollen. Als Nachfrager wären auch Privatbankiers vorstellbar, die sich auf die Möglichkeit einer effektiven Stimmrechtsnutzung spezialisieren und auf diese Weise im Wettbewerb mit den großen Universalbanken gestärkt werden könnten. Diese und andere Stimmrechtsnachfrager könnten das Angebot eines Stimmrechtspreises an eine vertraglich zu fixierende eigene Erfolgsbeteiligung im Falle

---

[27] *H. G. Manne*, Some Theoretical Aspects of Share Voting. An Essay in Honor of Adolf R. Berle, in: *H. G. Manne* (Hrsg.), The Economics of Legal Relationships, a. a. O., S. 537.

[28] Vergleiche hierzu den folgenden Abschnitt 3.

von Vermögenswert- oder Dividendensteigerungen in einem bestimmten Zeitraum knüpfen. Aber schon die glaubwürdige Zusicherung separater Stimmrechtsverwerter, auf die Unternehmenspolitik wirksamen Einfluß im Interesse einer günstigen Entwicklung des Vermögenswertes und der Gewinne ausüben zu wollen, kann insbesondere Kleinaktionäre dazu veranlassen, das Stimmrecht auch kostenlos zu übertragen. Dabei ist zu berücksichtigen, daß bei Gesellschaften mit weitgestreutem Aktienbesitz schon ein Stimmrechtserwerb von weniger als 10% für eine starke Kontrollausübung ausreichen kann. Zu prüfen wäre, ob nicht auch die Manager selbst als Nachfrager von Stimmrechten zugelassen werden könnten, wenn sie meinen, dadurch erfolgreichere Wirtschaftspläne realisieren zu können. In diesem Zusammenhang müßte allerdings die Frage der Erfolgshaftung des Vorstands sorgfältig überdacht werden.[29]

d. Die Möglichkeit, das Stimmrecht separat vom Vermögenswert nach eigenem Gutdünken an geeignet erscheinende Sachwalter übertragen zu können[30], hätte für viele Anteilseigner den Vorteil, daß ihnen nicht – wie heute – nur Kosten der Stimmrechtsnutzung entstehen, sondern auch ein Gegenwert nach Maßgabe der eigenen Entscheidung und Risikobereitschaft winkt. Dies könnte für Kleinaktionäre besonders interessant sein, weil die Koalitionsbildung als deren einzige Möglichkeit der Durchsetzung von Stimmrechtsinteressen heute mit so hohen Kosten verbunden ist, daß solche Aktivitäten in der Regel zugunsten der «kostenlosen» Depotstimmrechtsverwertung durch die Banken unterbleiben.

e. Es ist nicht auszuschließen, daß die im Zusammenhang mit der separaten Stimmrechtsnutzung begründeten Entgelte oder Erwartungen das Interesse der Kleinaktionäre an «ihren» Unternehmen eher und nachhaltiger zu wecken vermögen als noch so gute Informationen über das, was in den Hauptversammlungen zur Diskussion und Abstimmung steht. Und in den Stimmrechtspreisen könnten sich die Einfluß- und Kontrollmöglichkeiten der Aktionäre auf ihre Unternehmungen genauer widerspiegeln als in noch so hohen Anwesenheitsziffern bei Sitzungen von Hauptversammlungen der heutigen Art. Die separate Verwertung des Stimmrechts könnte zugleich das Depotstimmrecht der Banken in seiner heutigen überwiegend wettbewerbsfeindlichen Form in Frage stellen. Jedenfalls ließe sich die bisherige kostenlose Stimmrechtsnutzung durch die Depotbanken nicht länger mit dem Argument verteidigen, andernfalls wäre es schwierig, das zur qualifizierten Beschlußfassung nötige Quorum zu erreichen.

---

[29] Siehe hierzu die Überlegungen von *W. Eucken*, a.a.O., S. 279ff. Zu den privatrechtlichen Problemen einer Erfolgshaftung des Vorstandes vergleiche *E.-J. Mestmäcker*, Zum Verhältnis der Wirtschaftswissenschaft und Rechtswissenschaft im Aktienrecht, in: *L. Raiser, H. Sauermann* und *E. Schneider* (Hrsg.), Das Verhältnis der Wirtschaftswissenschaft zur Rechtswissenschaft, Soziologie und Statistik, Schriften des Vereins für Socialpolitik, N. F. Band 33, Berlin 1964, S. 114.

[30] Eine zeitliche Limitierung, zum Beispiel nach dem Muster der für 15 Monate erteilbaren Vollmacht zur Ausübung des Stimmrechts durch Banken (Depotstimmrecht) oder durch andere geschäftsmäßige Stimmrechtsausüber, die auch nach dem heutigen Aktienrecht, allerdings ohne Entgelt für die Aktionäre, tätig sein können, könnte im Interesse der Revidierbarkeit der Verkaufsentscheidung und der davon ausgehenden zusätzlichen Selbstkontrolle der Stimmrechtserwerber nützlich sein. Bei den Stimmrechtsanbietern wiederum ist soviel Eigeninteresse vorauszusetzen, daß sie mit dem Verkauf unter keinen Umständen den Vermögenswert der Aktie gefährden wollen.

3. Die wettbewerbsfeindliche Stimmrechtsfähigkeit der Aktiengesellschaft

Die wettbewerbsbehindernden Konsequenzen des Aktienrechts resultieren vor allem daraus, daß die Institution des Eigentumsrechts natürlicher Personen mechanistisch auf Kapitalgesellschaften übertragen wurde. Das Rechtsinstitut der juristischen Person, die über unbeschränkte Rechtsfähigkeit verfügt, erlaubt es den Aktiengesellschaften nämlich, Anteils- und Stimmrechte an anderen Gesellschaften zu begründen und zu nutzen. Auf diese Weise wird eine von den Verfügungsrechten der Anteilseigner faktisch weitgehend losgelöste und von Managerinteressen bestimmte Konzentration von unternehmerischen Kontrollrechten ermöglicht. Für die Wettbewerbsordnung interessiert vor allem die Möglichkeit der Konzentration durch Konzernierung, die zur Folge hat, daß die abhängigen Gesellschaften aufhören, als wirtschaftlich selbständige Anbieter und Wettbewerber am Markt aufzutreten.[31] Die Entwicklung der externen Unternehmenskonzentration läßt immer deutlicher erkennen, daß die eigentumsrechtlichen Erfordernisse einer liberalen Wettbewerbsordnung bei der Gestaltung des Aktienrechts nicht angemessen beachtet worden sind.[32,33] Die Vermutung, daß die notwendigen Änderungen derzeit politisch nicht durchsetzbar sind, kann nicht als Beweis dafür angesehen werden, daß die privatrechtlichen Möglichkeiten zur Förderung einer wettbewerblichen Unternehmensstruktur nicht mehr gegeben seien.[34] So könnte man sich vorstellen, daß Art und Umfang der Rechtsfähigkeit der juristischen Person «Aktiengesellschaft» und damit ihre Konzernierungsfähigkeit, losgelöst von den individuellen Entscheidungen der Aktionäre, begrenzt werden, indem ihr das Privileg der Stimmrechtsfähigkeit vorenthalten wird. Andere Vorschläge einer wettbewerbskonformen Bestimmung der Rechte von Aktiengesellschaften wurden von liberalen Politikern bereits während der Entstehungszeit des deutschen Aktienrechts im vorigen Jahrhundert gemacht.[35]
Mit dem preußischen Aktiengesetz von 1843 wurde schließlich jedoch ein Weg beschritten, auf dem man sich unter Vernachlässigung der von Eigentumsregelungen ausgehenden Wettbewerbseffekte überwiegend vom Gläubigerschutz sowie von den Interessen der Unternehmensleitung und der übrigen Belegschaft an der Arbeitsplatz- und Ein-

[31] Vergleiche hierzu *F. A. von Hayek*, «Freie Wirtschaft» und Wettbewerbsordnung, in: Derselbe, Individualismus und wirtschaftliche Ordnung, a. a. O., S. 150ff. Ausführlich hierzu auch *H. O. Lenel*, Ursachen der Konzentration, a. a. O., S. 361ff.

[32] *Franz Böhm* hat die antimarktwirtschaftliche Konsequenz der Stimmrechtsfähigkeit von Aktiengesellschaften einmal wie folgt charakterisiert: «Wer aus irgendwelchen Gründen dem Abschluß von Verträgen mit seinesgleichen aus dem Weg gehen will, der findet im Recht der Kapitalgesellschaft die Möglichkeit, sich an seinesgleichen zu beteiligen, sei es durch Erwerb eines Pakets, d. h. eines Stücks von ihm, sei es mittels der Methode der «Verflechtung der Directorate» – etwa nach dem Prinzip: jeder des anderen Geschäftsführer». *F. Böhm*, Das Recht der internationalen Kartelle. Zu dem Buch von Heinrich Kronstein mit dem gleichen Titel, ORDO, Band 20, 1969, S. 306f.

[33] «The Corporation (allowing to have voting rights, A. Sch.) thereby becomes, instead of an association of partners with a common interest, an association of groups whose interests may be in strong conflict; and the possibility appears that a group which directly owns assets amounting only to a small fraction of those of the corporation, may, through a pyramiding of holdings, acquire control of assets amounting to a multiple of what they owns themselves. By owning a controlling interest in another corporation and so on, a comparatively small amount owned by a person or groups may control a very much bigger aggregative of capital». *F. A. von Hayek*, The Corporation in a Democratic Society, a. a. O., S. 309.

[34] Vergleiche zu dieser Ansicht *K. Schredelseker*, a. a. O., S. 267.

[35] Vergleiche *P. C. Martin*, Die Entstehung des preußischen Aktiengesetzes von 1943, a. a. O., S. 539f. Vergleiche auch *H. C. Simons*, Economic Policy for a free Society, Chicago 1948, S. 58ff.

kommenssicherung in «ihren» Betrieben leiten ließ und dabei eine Einschränkung der Aktionärsrechte in Kauf nahm. Mit dem Inkrafttreten des Mitbestimmungsgesetzes wurde diese Praxis der Aushöhlung von Aktionärsrechten systematisch verstärkt. Im Gegensatz zu der überwiegend den Interessen der Nichteigentümer dienenden Aktienrechtsordnung im weitesten Sinne müßte ein privates Gesellschaftsrecht, das wettbewerblichen Unternehmensstrukturen förderlich sein soll, stärker auf die Anreicherung der Verfügungsrechte der Anteilseigner bedacht sein.

Die Auffassung, nach der das Aktiengesetz die Unternehmensverbindungen unter gesellschaftsrechtlichen Aspekten und das Gesetz gegen Wettbewerbsbeschränkungen unter wettbewerbspolitischen Gesichtspunkten zu regeln und zu beurteilen habe[36], mag heute zwar weit verbreitet sein, sie steht aber nicht in Übereinstimmung mit der Erfahrung, daß Versäumnisse im ersten Bereich nicht oder nur mit unverhältnismäßig großem Aufwand, wie er bekanntlich mit effektiven Fusionskontrollen und Dekonzentrationsregelungen verbunden ist, im zweiten Bereich auszugleichen sind. Seit sich die Politik der Unternehmensverfassung quasi als autonomer Bereich der Privatrechtspolitik von der Politik der Wettbewerbsordnung gelöst hat, ist die Aufgabe, wettbewerbliche Märkte zu sichern, unnötig erschwert.

IV. Zur Frage der Entstehung wettbewerbsfördernder Märkte für unternehmerische Kontrollrechte in der Bundesrepublik Deutschland

Für die Frage, wie die Eigentumsrechte der Aktionäre durch gesetzliche Vorkehrungen in den Dienst der Wettbewerbspolitik gestellt werden könnten, ist es wichtig zu wissen, daß vom Prinzip der marktwirtschaftlichen Zu- und Abwanderung – vor allem durch Aktienkäufe und -verkäufe sowie durch ungeschmälerten Gewinnabzug – eine größere Kontrollwirkung zu erwarten ist als vom Prinzip des Widerspruchs.[37] Vor allem entsteht für das Management ein positionsgefährdender Konkurrenzdruck, wenn Außenseiter über die Börse versuchen, durch Aktienkauf einen bestimmenden Kontrolleinfluß zu erlangen. Allerdings hat diese Kontrollform den Nachteil, daß der an der Börse zu zahlende Preis nachfragebedingt in einem Umfang ansteigen kann, der den erwarteten Gewinn aus dem Kontrollerwerb übersteigt. Dies kann für die oben im Anschluß an *H. G. Manne* genannten Fälle zutreffen, soweit über die Börse Stimmrecht und Vermögenswert gemeinsam gekauft werden müssen.

1. Übernahmeangebote (Take-over-bids) und Unternehmenskontrolle

Eine sehr viel intensivere Kontrollbeziehung zwischen Eignern und Managern läßt sich nach dem Aktienrecht einiger westlicher Länder, vor allem Englands, Belgiens, Frankreichs und der USA, durch das Verfahren des Übernahmeangebots (take-over bid, tender

---

[36] Vergleiche *H. Würdinger*, Aktien- und Konzernrecht, dritte, völlig neubearbeitete Auflage, Karlsruhe 1973, S. 247.

[37] Zu den beiden Kontrollprinzipien «Abwanderung» und «Widerspruch» vergleiche *H. O. Hirschman*, Abwanderung und Widerspruch, Tübingen 1974.

offer, tender bid usw.) herbeiführen.[38] Es handelt sich dem Prinzip nach um einen Vorgang, bei dem den Aktionären unmittelbar, zeitlich befristet und unwiderruflich ein Verkaufsangebot zu einem meist über dem Börsenkurs liegenden Preis unterbreitet wird. Dieses Verfahren ist grundsätzlich auch auf den separaten Stimmrechtserwerb beschränkt vorstellbar, soweit es dabei darum geht, den X-Effizienz-Faktor im Interesse der Eigner zu verbessern oder ein unfähiges Management aus dem Sattel zu heben. Man kann in den Übernahmeangeboten auch ein Verfahren sehen, mit dessen Hilfe Arbitragemöglichkeiten zwischen dem Markt für Vermögenswerte und dem Markt für unternehmerische Kontrollrechte genutzt werden können. Da sich alle Beteiligten um einen bestmöglichen Informationsstand bemühen werden, ist damit zu rechnen, daß im Verlauf des Verfahrens Kenntnisse zutage gefördert werden, die die Entscheidungsfindung aller wesentlich erleichtern. Volkswirtschaftlich wichtig ist, daß alle so entstehenden Informationen letztlich der «Kritik des Kapitalmarktes»[39] unterworfen sind und daß die Kaufentscheidungen über diesen zugleich an der Rentabilität der Faktor- und Gütermärkte orientiert sind. Auf die Frage der zweckmäßigsten Ausgestaltung von Übernahmeverfahren unter Wettbewerbsaspekten kann hier nicht näher eingegangen werden. Für die Aktionäre liegen die Vorteile, allgemein ausgedrückt, darin, daß die Durchsetzungskosten (Transaktionskosten) wirtschaftlicher Eigentumsrechte gesenkt werden. Dies sei an folgenden Ergebnisvorhersagen dem Prinzip nach verdeutlicht:

a. Die Beziehung, die durch die latente Gefahr des Übernahmeangebots zwischen Eignern und Managern entsteht, unterscheidet sich in ihrer unvorhersehbaren Entwicklung wesentlich von den externen Kontrollverfahren herkömmlicher Art, wie Börsenkursentwicklung, Aktienankäufe über die Börse[40], Fusionen oder Konzernierungen. Diese Kontrollen bedrohen die Existenz des Managements in der Regel nicht unmittelbar. Zudem gibt das Übernahmeangebot den Aktionären Gelegenheit, alternative Bewertungen ihrer Beteiligung unter Einschluß des Stimmrechts zu erfahren, was vor allem dann erleichtert wird, wenn es zu Parallelangeboten und Gegenangeboten der gefährdeten Manager kommt und wenn das Stimmrecht separat gehandelt werden kann. Auf diese Weise können die Stimmrechte zu denjenigen gelangen, die sie am vorteilhaftesten zu nutzen verstehen.[41]

b. Die Möglichkeit, die Kontrolle über eine Zielgesellschaft zu erlangen, verspricht unter wettbewerbspolitischen Gesichtspunkten besonders vorteilhafte Wirkungen gegenüber Managern von Gesellschaften mit weitgestreutem Aktienbesitz. Schon die latente Übernahmedrohung kann in dieser Situation ein wirksames Mittel sein, um erstens die Aktivitäten des Managements wie von selbst stärker an den Interessen der Anteilseigner auszurichten oder um zweitens die Manager zur Vermeidung ihrer Ablösung als Team zu veranlassen, sich rechtzeitig von leistungsschwächeren Kollegen zu trennen. Dieser, einer möglichen Übernahme vorgelagerte Herausforderungsdruck ist nicht nur geeignet, den

---

[38] Vergleiche im einzelnen H. *Dietrich*, Die Tender Offer im Bundesrecht der Vereinigten Staaten, Frankfurt / Main 1975; U. *Immenga*, Der Preis der Konzernierung, in: H. *Sauermann* und E.-J. *Mestmäcker* (Hrsg.), Wirtschaftsordnung und Staatsverfassung. Festschrift für Franz Böhm zum 80. Geburtstag, Tübingen 1975, S. 264ff.; derselbe, Aktiengesellschaft, Aktionärsinteressen und institutionelle Anleger, Tübingen 1971, S. 30ff.; A. *Singh*, Take-Overs. Their Relevance to the Stock Market and the Theory of the Firm, Cambridge 1971.

[39] Zu dieser Formulierung vergleiche H. O. *Lenel*, a. a. O., S. 305.

[40] Die schockartige Übernahmedrohung verleiht den Bewegungen auf den Aktienmärkten eine zusätzliche Kontrollwirkung.

[41] Vergleiche H. G. *Manne*, Some Theoretical Aspects of Share Voting, in: Derselbe (Hrsg.), The Economics of Legal Relationships, a. a. O., S. 534–554; derselbe, Mergers and the Market for Corporate Control, Journal of Political Economy, Vol. 73, 1965, S. 110ff.

wettbewerblichen Prozeß der Kontrolle und Auslese unter den Managern in Gang zu halten und zu verschärfen, sondern auch die von den Börsenkursen ausgehenden Informationen unmittelbar in interne leistungssteigernde Verhaltensänderungen der Unternehmensleitung zu transformieren. Ohne Zweifel wird durch die latente Gefahr der Übernahme das Selbsterhaltungsinteresse des etablierten Managements bei sinkenden Börsenkursen in starkem Maße herausgefordert. Der Informationsgehalt der Börsenkurse wird größer. Börsenkurse werden damit zu einer wichtigen strategischen Variablen der Unternehmenspolitik. Die häufig als ohnmächtig und desinteressiert bezeichneten Kleinaktionäre können auf diesem Weg, auf dem sie direkt zum Verkauf ihrer Beteiligung aufgefordert werden, ihre Eigentumsrechte am Unternehmen in einer für das Management unbequemen Form der Kontrolle zur Geltung bringen.[42] Seine präventive Anpassungsbeweglichkeit wird stärker herausgefordert.

c. Indem sich das bedrohte Management zur Vermeidung seiner Ablösung gezwungen sieht, sein Leistungsvermögen offenzulegen und zum Zweck einer realistischen Neubewertung des Aktienkurses bisher vielleicht versteckte Gewinne und Leistungsreserven der Gesellschaft zu enthüllen, erhalten die Aktionäre eine Alternative zur Offerte des Übernahmeanbieters. Dadurch wird das Risiko der Fehlentscheidung weiter gemindert.

Insgesamt werden alle an diesem Verfahren Beteiligten veranlaßt, das günstigste Verhältnis von Leistung und Gegenleistung auszuloten und die so zustandekommenden Ergebnisse in Form von Eigentumsrechten zu internalisieren. Darin sind die mit diesem Kontrollverfahren verbundenen gesamtwirtschaftlichen Allokationsvorteile zu sehen.

2. Bedingungen für eine wettbewerbskonforme Anwendung des Übernahmeverfahrens in der Bundesrepublik Deutschland

a. Für die Funktionsfähigkeit von Märkten für unternehmerische Kontrollrechte ist eine hohe Bedingungstransparenz förderlich, dagegen ist eine weitgehende Erwartungstransparenz[43], herbeigeführt etwa durch genaue Offenlegungs- oder Weisungspflichten der einen oder anderen Seite, hinderlich. Denn der Übernahmeanbieter kann den über dem Börsenkurs liegenden Kaufpreis der Aktie in der Regel nur erwirtschaften, wenn die wesentlichen Einzelheiten seiner Strategie für eine erfolgreiche Unternehmenspolitik nicht vorher offengelegt werden müssen: «Clearly», so bemerkt *Manne*[44], «the market for corporate control relies heavily on the production, not on the wide dissemination of information about corporations». Tatsächlich ist die detaillierte Aufdeckung der Übernahmepläne durch den Offerenten – das Gleiche gilt für den separaten Stimmrechtserwerb – keine notwendige Bedingung für die Aktionärsentscheidung. Für den Eigner ist vielmehr ausschlaggebend, daß ihm durch freien Wettbewerb um das Kontrollrecht ein

---

[42] «Without the market, many small shareholders could not have any idea of what the vote itself was actually worth to them. Thus, the corporate system of allowing the sale of votes guarantees an electorate that is both relatively well-informed and more intensely interested in the outcome of the election than would be the case if votes were not transferable. And it does this with no harm to the interests of anyone associated with or affected by the corporation». H. G. *Manne*, Some Theoretical Aspects of Share Voting, a. a. O., S. 548.

[43] Zu diesen Begriffen vergleiche A. *Woll*, Zur wettbewerbspolitischen Bedeutung der Markttransparenz, in: Theoretische und institutionelle Grundlagen der Wirtschaftspolitik. Theodor Wessels zum 65. Geburtstag, Berlin 1967, S. 199–218.

[44] H. G. *Manne*, Cash Tender Offers: A Reply to Chairman Cohen, Duke Law Journal, 1967, S. 239.

ausreichender Eigentumsschutz geboten wird. Hier wie auch sonst ist die Marktgarantie ausreichend für die angemessene Sicherung von Eigentumsrechten.[45]

b. Die Frage ist, ob Märkte der beschriebenen Art in der Bundesrepublik Deutschland entstehen können und wie sie gegebenenfalls zu ordnen sind, damit sie im Sinne der beschriebenen Allokationswirkungen funktionsfähig bleiben. Diese Allokationseffekte könnten z. B. dadurch gefährdet werden, daß der beim Übernahmeverfahren zustandekommende Aktienhandel als Einfallstor für Fusionen mit einer den Wettbewerb beschränkenden konzentrationsfördernden Wirkung mißbraucht wird.

Zunächst einmal hat es den Anschein, daß die Übernahmedrohung das Management um so mehr zu besseren Leistungen herausfordert, je weniger Fusionshindernisse der staatlichen Wirtschaftspolitik bestehen. So könnten zum Beispiel auf wettbewerbsschwachen Produktmärkten jene Anbieter in den Genuß von Marktmachtgewinnen gelangen, die im Wege eines Übernahmeangebots die Unternehmenskontrolle erwerben, so daß über den Wettbewerb auf dem Kapitalmarkt die Vorteile aus vermachteten Produktmärkten denjenigen zugeordnet werden, die sie am besten zu nutzen verstehen.[46] Deshalb meint *Manne*[47], eine staatliche Fusionsbehinderung auf wettbewerbsschwachen Märkten begünstige die Fehlallokation von Ressourcen und erschwere den Prozeß der Auslese unter den Unternehmensleitern. Damit werde die auf solchen Märkten einzige Möglichkeit einer erfolgreichen Effizienzkontrolle der Anteilseigner gegenüber dem Management ausgeschlossen. Dies treffe vor allem auf Gesellschaften mit weitgestreutem Aktienbesitz zu.

Bei der Beurteilung dieses Arguments ist zunächst zu bedenken, daß die rechtlichen Ursachen, die die Vermachtung von Produktmärkten zur Folge haben, die gleichen sein können, die auch für Beschränkungen der Funktionsfähigkeit des Kapitalmarktes verantwortlich zu machen sind. Weiterhin gilt es im Einzelfall zu prüfen, ob nicht der Monopolisierungstatbestand Folge einer unbeschränkten Fusionspolitik in einer Phase der Marktentwicklung ist, in der eine fortschreitende Monopolisierung durch eine wirksame Antikonzentrationspolitik leicht hätte verhindert werden können.[48] Hier wird deutlich, daß der Aktienhandel in der beschriebenen Form eine präventive Fusionskontrolle nicht überflüssig, wohl aber vielleicht weniger dringlich in der praktischen Anwendung machen kann. Dies gilt in dem Maße, in dem der Kapitalmarkt die finanziellen Entscheidungen der Unternehmen koordiniert und Wettbewerb auf den Produktmärkten herrscht. Damit der Kapitalmarkt diese seine volkswirtschaftlich vorrangige Aufgabe bestmöglich erfüllen kann, sind vor allem folgende Voraussetzungen notwendig:

(1) Ein den Eigentumsinteressen der Aktionäre dienendes Aktienrecht mit ungeschmä-

---

[45] Vergleiche hierzu allgemein W. *Leisner*, Privateigentum ohne privaten Markt? Gibt es eine verfassungsrechtliche Garantie «des Marktes»? Betriebs-Berater, 30. Jahrgang, Heft 1, 1975, S. 1–6.

[46] Vergleiche A. A. *Alchian* und R. A. *Kessel*, Competition, Monopoly, and the Pursuit of Pecuniary Gain. Aspects of Labour Economics, Conference of the Universities National Bureau Committee for Economic Research, Princeton N. J. 1962, S. 160.

[47] H. G. *Manne*, a. a. O., S. 239.

[48] Vergleiche E. *Heuß*, Allgemeine Markttheorie, Tübingen 1965, S. 265ff. und W. *Möschel*, Das Oligopolproblem als Glaubwürdigkeitstest des Antitrustrechts, in: H. *Sauermann* und E.-J. *Mestmäcker* (Hrsg.). Wirtschaftsordnung und Staatsverfassung, a. a. O., S. 421–448. Zur Widerlegung der These, Wettbewerb auf Märkten für Unternehmenskontrolle könne fehlende Konkurrenz auf den Produktmärkten kompensieren; vergleiche auch J. *Röpke*, Die Strategie der Innovation. Eine systemtheoretische Untersuchung der Interaktion von Individuen, Organisation und Markt im Neuerungsprozeß, Tübingen 1977, S. 400ff.

lertem Dividendenrechtsanspruch bei Verzicht auf die konzentrationsfördernde Stimmrechtsfähigkeit von juristischen Personen (vergleiche Kapitel III.).

Damit würden aus dem Kreis potentieller Nachfrager von unternehmerischen Kontrollrechten jene ausscheiden, die – wie Körperschaften des privaten oder öffentlichen
Rechts – bekanntlich am stärksten zur wettbewerbsbeschränkenden Konzentration neigen und die Möglichkeit eines separaten Stimmrechtserwerbs für diesen Zweck am ehesten zu mißbrauchen versucht sind.

(2) Verzicht des Staates auf Maßnahmen, durch die große Unternehmen prinzipiell
konkursunfähig gemacht werden.

Gegenüber solchen quasi nationalisierten Unternehmen greift die Kapitalmarktkon-
trolle im hier verstandenen Sinne ins Leere.[49]

(3) Ein möglichst weitgestreuter Aktienbesitz[50] und die Beseitigung des Depotstimm-
rechts in seiner heutigen Form.

Dem steht in der Bundesrepublik Deutschland gegenwärtig vor allem ein vergleichsweise zu anderen Ländern hochkonzentrierter Daueraktienbesitz der Banken und eine
hohe Repräsentanz von Bankenvertretern in den Aufsichtsräten von Aktiengesellschaften entgegen. Diese Konzentration von unternehmerischen Kontrollrechten bei den Banken, verstärkt durch das diesen wegen des Fehlens separater Märkte für Stimmrechte kostenlos und tatsächlich weitgehend zur freien Disposition zufallende Depotstimmrecht,
entzieht dem Kapitalmarkt einen wesentlichen Teil jener eigentumsinduzierten Wettbewerbseffekte, die von einem freien Markt für «corporate control» erwartet werden können.

Welchen Widerspruch eine Reform der jetzigen Regelung auslösen dürfte, läßt sich
zum einen daraus ableiten, daß jedes Management das größte Interesse hat, Bankenvertreter im Aufsichtsrat zu haben, die der Unternehmensleitung einen von den Aktionären
unabhängigen finanziellen Rückhalt verschaffen und die über einen Sonderzugang zum
Kredit- und Kapitalmarkt die wirksamste Abwehr einer drohenden Ablösung des Managements sicherstellen können. Zum anderen gibt es Hinweise dafür, daß die Banken das
Stimmrecht der Aktionäre in fast 100% der Fälle nach ihren eigenen Vorstellungen, die
sich regelmäßig mit den Vorschlägen der Verwaltung decken, ausüben, und daß solche
Entscheidungen nur zu einem geringen Teil von den Kleinaktionären gewollt sind.[51]

Solange die Banken mit ihrem beträchtlichen Beteiligungsbesitz an Aktiengesellschaften im Dienst der Aufrechterhaltung etablierter Kontrollverhältnisse stehen, kann sich in
der Bundesrepublik Deutschland kein leistungsfähiger Markt für unternehmerische Kon-

---

[49] Bei der offensichtlichen Neigung des Staates, gegenüber großen Unternehmen in Notfällen stets
mit einer gesamtschuldnerischen Bürgschaft einzuspringen, verwundert es nicht, wenn in empirischen Untersuchungen festgestellt wird (z. B. von A. *Singh*, Take-overs, Economic Natural Selection, and the Theory of the Firm: Evidence from the Post War United Kingdom Experience The
Economic Journal, Vol. 85, 1975, S. 497–515), daß take-over bids für Großunternehmen eine
sehr viel geringere Gefahr darstellen als für kleinere Gesellschaften. Deshalb liegt es auch für die
Unternehmensleitungen großer Aktiengesellschaften nahe, der Übernahmedrohung bevorzugt
durch Maßnahmen der Konzentration zu begegnen, nicht aber primär durch höhere Gewinnan-
strengungen wie für kleinere Unternehmen unausweichlich ist. Auch werden mit zunehmender
Unternehmensgröße die Finanzierungsschranken für Übernahmeangebote immer höher.

[50] Insoweit ist die herrschende Meinung, ein breit gestreuter Aktienbesitz erleichtere die Entstehung
einer von den Interessen der Anteilseigner unabhängigen Managermacht, in Zweifel zu ziehen.

[51] Vergleiche *G. H. Roth*, Die Herrschaft der Aktionäre in der Publikums-AG als Gegenstand
rechtssoziologischer Betrachtung, a. a. O., S. 94ff.

trollrechte bilden. Dieser Zustand läßt sich vielleicht am ehesten in Verbindung mit dem Entzug jener Stimmrechtsfähigkeit ändern, die juristischen Körperschaften wie natürlichen Personen entgegen den Ordnungsprinzipien einer Eigentümergesellschaft verliehen worden ist.[52]

V. Folgerungen

Die heute bestehenden Möglichkeiten interner Aktionärskontrollen, die auf dem Kontrollprinzip des Widerspruchs beruhen (über die Hauptversammlung, über Aufsichts- und Sonderprüfungsrechte sowie Publizitätsvorschriften und Maßnahmen des Minderheitenschutzes), scheinen in einem beachtlichen Ausmaß einer Theorie des Aktieneigentums zu entsprechen, die nicht nur unrealistisch ist, sondern auch die Bedingungen für ein wettbewerbliches Marktsystem verschlechtert[53]:
– Unrealistisch ist diese Theorie deshalb, weil das ihr folgende Aktiengesetz den Aktionären in wichtigen Verfügungsrechten die Möglichkeit zu einem wirklich unternehmerischen Eigentümerverhalten vorenthält, während es ihnen zugleich Rechte verleiht, die – und dies gilt vor allem für Kleinaktionäre – keine besonderen Internalisierungsanstrengungen sinnvoll erscheinen lassen.
– Die Bedingungen der Wettbewerbsordnung werden verschlechtert, weil das bestehende Aktienrecht die allokative Leistungsfähigkeit des Aktieneigentums beeinträchtigt.
Angesichts der vielfältigen Schwächen des Widerspruchs als Kontrollprinzip wäre zu prüfen, ob die sogenannten externen Kontrollen – die geschilderten Möglichkeiten der Abwanderung – nicht die für ein wettbewerbliches Marktsystem wirksameren Kontrollmöglichkeiten der Aktionäre sind und deshalb ihre Effektuierung als Form einer präventiven Wettbewerbspolitik angestrebt werden sollte.
Die sich in den hier angeführten externen Kontrollformen äußernden individuellen Vermögensinteressen mit ihren unbeabsichtigten Wettbewerbswirkungen aufzuspüren, heißt das Aktieneigentum als ökonomischen Ordnungsfaktor ersten Ranges zu entdecken. Zugleich ist damit die Aufgabe verbunden, die als wettbewerbskonform erkannte allokative Leistungsfähigkeit von privaten Eigentumsrechten mit den Mitteln des Rechts zu sichern. In diesem Sinne kann man mit *Posner*[54] von einer spezifisch ökonomischen

---

[52] An diesem Lösungsvorschlag gemessen ist die Empfehlung der Monopolkommission, den Kreditinstituten den Eigenerwerb von Anteilen an Nichtbanken zu untersagen, sofern mehr als 5 % der Summe der Kapitalanteile erworben werden, als weniger weitgehend im Sinne des Leitsatzes «Mehr Wettbewerb ist möglich» zu bezeichnen. Vergleiche Monopolkommission (Hrsg.), Hauptgutachten 1973 / 1975: Mehr Wettbewerb ist möglich, 2. Auflage, Baden-Baden 1977, S. 296.

[53] Die Aktienrechtsreform von 1965 bildet in dieser Hinsicht keine Ausnahme, weil die vorgeblich im Interesse der Aktionäre vorgenommene Neugestaltung der Rechnungslegung, des Auskunftsrechts, des Minderheitenschutzes und anderer Maßnahmen nicht bis zum Kern der ökonomischen Eigentumsrechte im hier verstandenen privatrechtlichen Sinne vorgedrungen ist. Auch in der Aktienrechtsneuregelung von 1965 steht die gesellschaftsrechtliche Betrachtung im Mittelpunkt aller Problemlösungen. Vergleiche hierzu K. *Ballerstedt*, Gesellschafts- und unternehmensrechtliche Probleme der Unternehmenskonzentration, in: *H. Arndt* (Hrsg.), Die Konzentration in der Wirtschaft, Schriften des Vereins für Socialpolitik, Band 20/I, zweite Auflage, Berlin 1971, S. 603–644.

[54] *R. A. Posner*, a. a. O., S. 12.

Allokationsleistung des Rechtswesens sprechen, ohne daß man dabei in eine vordergründig radikale Erklärung der Rechtsordnung aus «rein» wirtschaftlichen Interessen und Problemstellungen verfallen müßte.[55]

Diese sicher noch sehr viel sorgfältiger auch um betriebswirtschaftliche und juristische Aspekte zu erweiternde Betrachtung des Verhältnisses von Aktieneigentum und Wettbewerbsordnung ist nicht nur wissenschaftlich reizvoll. Sie verdient auch aus naheliegenden wirtschaftspolitischen Gründen Beachtung:

Die Gewerkschaften versuchen als sogenannte «Mitbestimmungsträger», Eigentumsrechte ihrer Mitglieder an den Unternehmen in konzentrierter antikompetitiver Form zu begründen. So besteht ohne Zweifel ein wichtiger Zweck der Mitbestimmung darin, über eine Einschränkung der unternehmerischen Dispositionsfreiheit ein, wie *Franz Böhm* es genannt hat, «Stillhaltekartell»[56] zur Sicherung von «angestammten» Arbeitsplätzen und Einkommenschancen zu etablieren. Soweit es auf diesem Wege zu einer dem Mindestlohneffekt entsprechenden Arbeitslosigkeit kommt und soweit versucht wird, ihr durch Inflation zu begegnen, wird das Beschäftigungsproblem aus der privatwirtschaftlichen Zuständigkeit von freien Vertragspartnern herausgenommen und zu einer mit öffentlichen Mitteln zu finanzierenden Staatsangelegenheit erhoben, ohne daß erkennbar wäre, wie die Mitbestimmungsregelung die ihr häufig nachgesagten wettbewerbsfördernden Effekte hervorbringen könnte. Der für die marktwirtschaftliche Wettbewerbsordnung so überaus wichtige Markt der Führungskräfte beispielsweise wird wesentlich beschränkt, wenn «überbetriebliche Kontakte auf der Arbeitnehmerseite die Berufung eines Vorstandsmitgliedes in gleichwertige Stellungen in andere Unternehmen erschweren».[57] Aber nicht nur die gewerkschaftlich organisierte Arbeitnehmerseite, auch die Unternehmensleiter sind bestrebt, negative Sanktionswirkungen des Wettbewerbs auszuschalten. Auf beiden Seiten ist deshalb mit einem Sonderinteresse an der Bildung internalisierter bzw. überbetrieblicher Sonder-Kapitalmärkte durch Aushöhlung und Immobilisierung des Aktieneigentums zu rechnen, an Finanzierungsmöglichkeiten also, die der strengen wettbewerblichen Kontrolle des Kapitalmarktes entzogen sind.

Wird gleichwohl ein wettbewerbliches Marktsystem gewünscht, könnten die hier zur Diskussion gestellten Möglichkeiten in Verbindung mit einer verstärkten betrieblichen Vermögensbildung in Form von Aktien ein Gegengewicht bilden, wobei die Belegschaftsaktionäre über die Nutzung der hier diskutierten Aktienrechte eine Form der Mitbestimmung praktizieren könnten, die diesem Begriff einen adäquaten Inhalt zuzuordnen vermag. Anderenfalls besteht folgende Gefahr:

In dem Maße, in dem den Aktiengesellschaften immer mehr sogenannte gesellschaftliche, staatliche und politische Aufgaben und Verantwortlichkeiten aufgezwungen wer-

---

[55] Vergleiche hierzu kritisch N. *Horn*, Zur ökonomischen Rationalität des Privatrechts – Die privatrechtstheoretische Verwertbarkeit der «Economic Analysis of Law», Archiv für civilistische Praxis, 176. Band, Tübingen 1976, S. 310. Gleichwohl ist es nicht zu bestreiten, daß zahlreiche rechtliche Regelungen ihren Ursprung in wirtschaftlichen Entwicklungen und Zweckmäßigkeiten haben. Vergleiche hierzu H.-G. *Krüsselberg*, Wirtschaftswissenschaft und Rechtswissenschaft, in: D. *Grimm* (Hrsg.), Rechtswissenschaft und Nachbarwissenschaften. Erster Band: Soziologie, Politik, Verwaltung, Wirtschaft, Psychologie, Kriminologie, zweite, unveränderte Auflage, München 1976, S. 168–192.

[56] *F. Böhm*, Das wirtschaftliche Mitbestimmungsrecht der Arbeiter im Betrieb, ORDO, Band 4, 1951, S. 153 und passim.

[57] Mitbestimmung im Unternehmen. Bericht der Sachverständigenkommission zur Auswertung der bisherigen Erfahrungen bei der Mitbestimmung, Stuttgart, Berlin, Köln, Mainz 1970, Ziff. 58/59.

den, wird – gewollt oder ungewollt, sei dahingestellt – die staatssozialistische Weiterbildung der Aktiengesellschaft betrieben. Sie aber führt

– entweder zur Syndikalisierung der Volkswirtschaft mit einer Gruppeneigentümerverfassung, die eher zu einer kartellartigen als zu einer offenen wettbewerblichen Marktkontrolle führen dürfte, oder sie
– ebnet – wie *Walther Rathenau* es formuliert hat – der Verstaatlichung unmittelbar den Weg.[58]

Summary

Property Rights, Corporate Control and Competition Order

The article shows that the liberal competition order is particularly in danger of being undermined by legal restrictions on property rights. Thus, in the Federal Republic of Germany, laws pertaining to the operation of joint-stock companies prevent the stockholder from obtaining a maximum profit per share. According to *Friedrich A. von Hayek*, this principle of profit distribution is a prerequisite for the optimum utilization of scarce goods.

The present article examines this opinion from the point of view of the new «Economic Theory of Property Rights». It is shown that private property and the legal regulations limiting it can embody an original allocation mechanism of a competitive nature. The allocative performance of private property rights is recognized as being a stimulus to competition; however, it requires deliberate legal safeguards. This is overlooked by those who consider that private property is in a hopeless crisis as a factor regulating the free-market economy, and who, for example, maintain, with reference to modern joint-stock companies, that the separation between legal ownership and actual power of disposal in regard to property in present corporate law has led to an unbridgeable alienation between stock-owners and managers. In fact, the extensive separation of legal ownership and actual economic control as assumed particularly for large joint-stock companies is not the result of an inevitable or even organic development of the free-market economy, but the consequence of economically ill-conceived regulations of the laws pertaining to the operation of joint-stock companies:

1. The procedure for profit-distribution prescribed by these laws on the basis of the majority principle at the shareholders' general meeting means that, as it were, «internalized» capital markets originate for companies via the possibility of self-financing provided by this procedure, and that these capital markets are beyond the control of the capital market in general. Thus, the managers, although not the owners, gain, at practically no expense, a free hand in regard to risk capital that is independent of the capital market. The possibility of investing private capital in enterprises of fundamental importance for the total economy is necessary, if the competition order of the free

---

[58] *W. Rathenau,* Vom Aktienwesen. Eine geschäftliche Betrachtung, Berlin 1917, S. 41. *K. Marx* erblickte gar in der Aktiengesellschaft und ihrer eigentumsfeindlichen Ausformung und der daraus gefolgerten Vermachtung der Wirtschaft die allerunmittelbarste Vorbereitung des Sozialismus. *K. Marx,* Das Kapital. Kritik der politischen Ökonomie. Dritter Band, Buch III: Der Gesamtprozeß der kapitalistischen Produktion, in der Reihe: Marx-Engels-Werke, Band 25, Berlin (Ost) 1964, S. 451 ff. und passim.

market is to function. However, this ability is hampered by the managers' preference for the above-mentioned «internalized» capital markets, whenever investment capital is needed.

2. These laws also preclude the possibility of the splitting of functions between the property rights and the voting rights of the stockholders, and thus also preclude the separate sale of voting rights. The legalizing of a free sale of voting rights could pave the way for an efficient utilization of stock-property which in turn would strengthen the competition order.

3. However, these laws endanger the competition order, especially because joint-stock companies as «legal persons» may enjoy the same property rights as natural persons. This unrestricted legal status permits joint-stock companies to obtain shareholding and voting rights in other companies, and exploit them for forms of concentration which are in restraint of competition.

The task of securing competitive markets could be considerably lightened if voting rights were restricted to natural persons.

That the stockholders' property rights can be put to the service of economic policies for encouraging competition very effectively has been shown in certain Western nations, where take-over bids are permitted, leading to markets for corporate control. A number of legal measures are needed in order to ensure that these procedures will stimulate competition and lead to the development of effective markets for corporate control. In essence, the goal of all these procedures should be to protect stock-property from being economically undermined and immobilized.

VI. Besteuerung

James M. Buchanan

Constitutional Constraints on Governmental Taxing Power*

«To distinguish effectively the legislation on general rules by which the tax burden is to be apportioned among the individuals from the determination of the total sums to be raised, would require such a complete re-thinking of all the principles of public finance that the first reaction of those familiar with the existing institutions will probably be to regard such a scheme as wholly impracticable. Yet nothing short of such a complete reconsideration of the institutional setting of financial legislation can probably stop the trend towards a continuing and progressive rise of that share of the income of society which is controlled by government. This trend, if allowed to continue, would before long swallow up the whole of society in the organization of government.»

F. A. *Hayek*, Law, Legislation and Liberty, Vol. III, The Political Order of a Society of Free Men (Chicago: University of Chicago Press, forthcoming), Chapter 16.

I. Introduction

In the passage cited above, Professor *Hayek* has pointed to the necessary distinction between the structure of taxation and the level of taxation. Implicit in the *Hayek* position, in the citation and elsewhere, is the belief that effective control over the structure, by which *Hayek* means the allocation or distribution of tax shares among persons, will insure adequate control over the level of taxation. That is to say, *Hayek* suggests that if the powers of governments to modify tax-share distribution through ordinary legislation are appropriately restricted, there should be no need to limit the powers of legislative-parliamentary majorities in setting the overall level of public outlays, and, hence, of taxes.

Hayek's belief in the overall efficacy of democratic processes within the constraints imposed by general tax rules may not be shared by every observer of the fiscal Leviathan, and, in any case, it should be evident that *Hayek's* proposal is only one among a set of possible «fiscal or tax constitutions» that might be suggested. My purpose in this paper is to discuss, in very broad terms, the possible set of rules and arrangements that may be introduced to define the limits on the taxing powers of governments in modern Western democracies. The «tax constitution» may include constraints on the level as well as the structure of taxation. I shall explore questions that arise in any attempt to lay down some preferred set of tax rules.

* I am indebted to my colleague, *Geoffrey Brennan,* for helpful suggestions.

II. Why Are Fiscal Constraints Desired?

The first step in any discussion of fiscal constraints involves the basic reasons for imposing any restrictions of the power of governments to tax. At the practical level, and as indicated in the citation from *Hayek* above, mere observation of the rates at which governments have grown, and notably in the decades since World War II, is perhaps sufficient to justify examination of the prospects for fiscal constraints. At the analytical level,
the logic of fiscal constraint is relatively straightforward. If government should match the
image of the benevolent despot that informs so many of the normative policy models used
by modern economists, constitutional constraints on governmental behavior, in taxation
or in any other respect, might not be necessary. Even under such an extreme assumption,
however, the mere fact that separate persons have separate utility functions would insure
that any governmental decision-process is necessarily inconsistent and unstable. A «social welfare function» cannot logically exist, given a set of reasonably desired properties
for such a function. All of this is quite apart from the recognition that any governmental
decision-makers must be assumed to have proclivities to act in accordance with their
own, rather than some vaguely defined general or public interest. For both of these basic
reasons, it is within any person's interest to impose some limits on the taxing power of
governmental decision-making coalitions, regardless of how «democratically» such a
coalition might be organized, and how inclusive the voting rule might be. The normative
foundations for a tax constitution emerge directly from the utility-maximizing behavior
of any, and hence all, persons in the polity.

The logical argument for tax constraints does not depend on the supposition that dem-
ocratically-selected ruling coalitions or legislative majorities will, in each and every
budgetary period, raise the levels of taxing and spending beyond those deemed to be
desirable or efficient by the average citizen. To the extent that checks imposed by competitive electoral politics hold taxing and spending within «reasonable» limits, the constitutional constraints may not become binding. But this is no argument against the existence
of such constraints, which may well be designed to offer protection against undue fiscal
exploitation in precisely those situations where the competition among politicians and
parties fail to control tax-spending explosion. The internal controls of democratic politics and the constitutional controls imposed external to the ordinary legislative process
are complements rather than substitutes.

III. Existing Tax Constitutions

It is important to recognize that constitutional constraints on governmental powers to
tax do exist in Western democratic societies, even if these constraints have been almost
totally neglected by economists. In the United States Constitution there is a provision that
requires that federal direct taxes shall be uniformly apportioned among the separate
states, and this constitutional proviso was interpreted by the courts in such a way as to
prohibit the levy of progressive income taxes throughout the first century and one-half of
the national experience. In order for the Federal government to secure the power to levy
progressive taxes on personal incomes, the United States Constitution was specifically
amended in 1913. The uniformity requirement would still prohibit federal government
taxation of residents of specific geographic areas on any discriminatory bases. Further,

and quite apart from the formal provisions in the written constitution, the more general requirements for due process would prohibit the levy of overtly discriminatory taxes of many varieties, on the part of either the federal or the state-local governments. Much the same conclusion would probably apply to almost all of the Western democracies, although I am not personally familiar with the constitutional law on taxation in countries other than the United States.

There are constitutional-legal restrictions on governmental powers to tax persons differentially. That is to say, a person is, to a degree, legally protected from the arbitrary fiscal exactions of government which might set him up as against equal treatment of his fellows. The more general principle of «equality before the law» extends in this respect to taxation.

Such legal constraints against arbitrary or discriminatory treatment are to be contrasted with the almost total absence of constraints on the level of taxation that may be imposed on the body of taxpayers, on the overall share in total income or product that may be exacted by the fisc. Both formal constitutional law and the tradition of the common law are silent on the second type of constraint, which the accumulating evidence on the rapid growth in the governmental share in national incomes makes clear.

There is also an asymmetry between the legal-constitutional constraints on taxation and those on public outlays. Although no constraints on the overall levels of taxation exist, there are legal restrictions, as noted, on the differential tax treatment of persons and groups. No such constraints exist on the spending side of the fiscal account. Governments can, and do, discriminate in the pattern of outlays, proffering benefits to specifically chosen groups, whether these be classified geographically, occupationally, demographically, or otherwise. The general principle of «equality before the law» has never been applied to the distribution of governmental benefits among citizens. This asymmetric treatment of benefits tends, of course, to undermine the restricting influence of any tax-side constraints against overall fiscal discrimination by governments. General taxes that are used to finance discriminatory benefits can produce distributional results that are almost equivalent to those produced by the use of discriminatory taxes.

While it is necessary to recognize that some constitutional-legal constraints on governmental fiscal powers do exist, and notably on the powers to impose discriminatory taxes, it is also essential to avoid attributing efficiency to the existing legal structure in these respects. As suggested, the evidence of this century implies that existing legal rules have not been effective in curbing the fiscal appetites of governments. In this setting, it becomes appropriate to raise questions about additional and/or alternative tax rules and arrangements that might serve the long-term interests of taxpayers better than those interests seem to have been served by the legal institutions in being. The existing structure possesses little or no normative standing in such an evaluation sense; there is no basis for an argument to the effect that elements of such a structure are somehow the most desirable because they are observed to exist.

The existing structure does have methodological standing in that any improvement or suggestions for improvement must take that which exists as the starting point for change, the position upon which and from which any changes must be made.

IV. What is a «Good» Tax Constitution?

Before alternative suggestions for reform in the fiscal or tax constitution are examined, it is necessary to discuss the issue of normative criteria for judgment. We need some basis on which to argue that one proposed set of fiscal or tax constraints is better or worse than another. There may exist widespread agreement on the desirability for reform, on the need for some change in that which exists, but until and unless some criterion for evaluation is discussed, differing personal preferences may characterize the discourse.

Care is required at precisely this point, however, lest we impose too readily a strictly teleological straightjacket on the argument, a straightjacket that is not at all appropriate. In order to define a «good» set of tax rules, a «good» tax constitution, it is not necessary to have in mind, or even to postulate for purposes of argument, specific end-states that governmental decision-taking under such rules must produce. The appropriate criterion for «goodness» is to be found in the process of agreement on potential change among potential taxpayers rather than in the end-state that such change is intended to insure.[1] A change is defined to be «good» because it is agreed to by members of the community; members do not agree because a change is somehow independently «good».

If, however, the test is agreement, how can a whole group of potential taxpayer-beneficiaries, even conceptually, be expected to agree on anything? The assignment of tax shares is a zero-sum game; agreement seems impossible on its face. It is here that a constitutional perspective becomes imperative. If tax rules, rather than the in-period distribution or assignment of tax shares, are discussed, it is possible to conceive of general agreement among all potential taxpayers. If a person is uncertain about his own economic position in a sequence of future fiscal periods, when the rules to be chosen are anticipated to remain in effect, he will be led, via his own self-interest, to opt for rules that seem «fair» in the sense that they offer plausibly acceptable or tolerable results regardless of economic position in the community.

In its extreme or limiting variant, the setting for individual choice postulated here is that made familiar by *John Rawls*.[2] Behind a genuine «veil of ignorance» and in some «original position», the individual knows nothing at all about his own role or position. In less extreme variants, such as that postulated by *Gordon Tullock* and myself in The Calculus of Consent,[3] the individual need only be assumed to be highly uncertain about his own future prospects. In any such choice settings, the only relevant choice is among rules that are expected to remain in effect over a sequence of periods.

Agreement among all persons will not necessarily emerge in such constitutional choice settings, even at some conceptual level. This much must be acknowledged. But the range for disagreement is necessarily narrowed, and dramatically so by comparison with that which characterizes the zero-sum struggle over in-period tax shares. Disagreement at the level of constitutional choice is not disagreement derived from divergencies of personal economic interests of the standard sort, at least in the limit. Disagreement may emerge as a result of differing assessments of the predicted working properties of alternative institutional arrangements. A «bargaining range» of sorts may exist, even in idealized constitu-

---

[1] For perhaps the best treatment of the distinction between process and end-state criteria, see, *Robert Nozick,* Anarchy, State and Utopia (New York 1974).
[2] *John Rawls,* A Theory of Justice (Cambridge: Harvard University Press, 1971).
[3] *Ann Arbor:* University of Michigan Press, 1962.

tional choice.[4] From this it follows that there may be several possible sets of arrangements or institutions that might emerge, even from the most severely constrained contractual setting. For purposes of discussion, therefore, we must look to fiscal and tax constraints that may possibly satisfy the contractarian criterion while continuing to acknowledge that there may exist other sets of constraints which might equally qualify and which could, in whole or in part, substitute for the particular set under examination.

In the following sections of the paper, I shall examine alternative sets of constitutional constraints on the fiscal powers of government. In any normative evaluation of these constraints, the criterion should be the possible derivation from a genuine constitutional choice-contractarian calculus. Could this set of proposals have emerged from a contractual agreement among persons in the community, each one of whom is, at the moment of choice, uncertain about his own economic position during the sequence of periods in which the constraints are to be operative?

V. The Generality of Fiscal Rules

The discussion in all of the preceding sections is, in one sense, preliminary to an examination of alternative institutional schemes or arrangements that have roughly the same objective, that of keeping governmental fiscal activities within some proximate relationship to the desires of taxpayers-beneficiaries. In this section, I shall discuss *Hayek's* proposal for the generality of fiscal rules. Following this, I shall examine proposals for modifying the political decision structure, notably those of *Knut Wicksell*, proposals that indirectly affect fiscal outcomes. Beyond these proposals, which may be classified as political, I shall then examine more explicit fiscal constraints. These may take several forms. Constitutional limits may be placed on the allowable rate structure of specific tax instruments. The total tax revenue, or level of public outlay, may be restricted to a defined maximum share or proportion of national income or product. Yet another variant involves constitutional restriction on the allowable bases of taxation. Finally, the political competition inherent in fiscal federalism may accomplish indirectly what explicit fiscal constraints are aimed for directly. Each of these alternatives will be examined in concluding parts of this paper.

As noted in the Introduction, *Hayek* has stressed the importance of generality in fiscal as well as other aspects of law. If the government is required to levy taxes in accordance with «general rules», protection against arbitrary fiscal exploitation may seem to be provided. But what does taxation in accordance with general rules mean in this context?

As I have suggested above in the discussion of existing fiscal constraints, the requirement for generality in taxation has little or no effect unless it is somehow accompanied by a like requirement with respect to the spending or outlay side of the governmental fiscal account. Generality in spending is perhaps easier to define than generality in taxation, even though real-world applications of the generality precept are much less prevalent. To say that government spending must be general would imply that all members of the political community, including the members of decision makers for government itself, either secure or have access to the same level of publicly-financed or publicly-supplied goods

---

[4] For a discussion of this bargaining range and the predicted results of contractual agreement, see, *James M. Buchanan* and *Roger Faith*, «Subjective Elements in Rawlsian Contractual Agreement on Distributional Rules» (Working Paper CE 78-6-3, June 1978).

and services. A restriction to the effect that government could finance only purely public or purely collective goods and services, defined technologically in the Samuelsonian sense of nonexcludability and nonrivalry in consumption, would meet such a requirement. Operationally, however, there is not and could not be any categorical distinction drawn between such goods and services, if indeed they exist, and other goods and services that government might finance or provide. The generality precept might still be satisfied, however, even with impure and partially or fully partitionable goods and services, if provision is such as to insure that each person, each member of the polity, receives an equal share. For example, government could, conceptually, finance the purchase and provision of, say, milk, which is clearly a partitionable «private» good. But the generality requirement would still be met if everyone in the community should be given an equal quantity.

Direct grants of money might even satisfy the generality criterion provided again that all persons get equal payments. Such equal-share grants may seem to negate the very purpose of most fiscal transfer programs, but such grants may, nonetheless, qualify under the Hayekian rule of general law.

The problems that arise with such grants are directly related to those that arise in any attempt to define generality in taxation. Let us suppose that the generality requirement is met on the spending side of the budget. What allocations of tax shares are permissible under the generality precept? Especially in The Constitution of Liberty,[5] Hayek argued in favor of proportional taxation and in opposition to progressive taxation. He implied that proportionality in rates would meet the generality criterion. So long as those who take decisions on behalf of government should, themselves, be subjected to fiscal-tax costs in the same relation to personal incomes as others in the community, there would be some clearly felt restricting influence on expansive outlays, an influence that need not be present under a progressive rate structure.

If governmental outlays should be restricted to the purchase and provision of purely public goods and services, the Hayek argument would be valid. The argument would also hold for «private» or partitionable goods and services that are not retradable because of technological reasons (e. g., haircuts), provided that such goods and services are made available equally to all persons. However, if direct money transfers and/or spending on retradable private goods is allowed, even if such spending is general, proportionality in taxation is not sufficient to exert any constraining influence. Consider a very simple example where direct but general pecuniary transfers are financed through proportional income taxation. Suppose there is a three-person community, with pre-tax incomes of $ 1000, $ 100, $ 100. Constitutionally, transfers must be made equally per head and taxes must be proportional. The two-person majority can, in this setting, fully equalize post-tax, post-transfer incomes by levying a 100 per cent tax and transferring $ 400 to each of the three persons. (I neglect incentives in this example.) Much the same result could be accomplished even if direct cash transfers should be prohibited, while governmental outlays on partitionable and retradable goods and services are retained as permissible. The proportionality criterion for taxation, in and of itself, may do little or nothing to constrain the fiscal appetites of government, even in those settings where governmental decision-makers pay taxes like everyone else and secure nothing more than their pro-rata shares of governmentally financed benefits.

---

[5] Chicago 1960. Chapter 20, pp. 306–323.

VI. The Political Decision Structure

In Law, Legislation, and Liberty, and notably in the third and concluding volume,[6] Hayek discusses changes in the basic institutions of political decision-making that might insure adherence to the general rule of law. With respect to fiscal decisions, and as indicated in the citation at the start of this paper, Hayek suggests that the structure of tax rates be set by a separate and distinct «law-making» body, members of which are selected for longer terms and from persons with more restrictive qualifications, while decisions on the levels of taxation (and spending) would remain with ordinary legislative or parliamentary bodies. As the simple numerical example above suggest, however, constraints on the rate structure, even if these should prove highly effective in preventing arbitrary manipulation of tax rates for partisan or short-term political advantage, may not be sufficient to insure against fiscal exploitation. It may be necessary to constrain both the rate structure and the level of taxes.

Constraints may, however, be indirectly exerted through changes in the political decision structure, in the rules for making fiscal decisions for the polity. It is at this point that Knut Wicksell assumes a position of special significance. He is unique among pre-modern economists in recognizing the proclivities of parliamentary majorities to thwart rather than to promote the desires of taxpayers. Wicksell did not, however, propose direct constraints on the taxing powers of government; indeed, he suggested that taxes should be even more flexible than those observed in his time. He sought to reform the rules for political decision making by replacing majority voting in legislatures with a rule of unanimity. Wicksell recognized that only with an effective unanimity rule could there be any guarantee that governmental spending projects would return expected benefits in excess of costs, would be «efficient» in the standard sense. In order to implement a unanimity rule, to widen potential areas of agreement among all groups of taxpayers, tax-share distributions were to be left as wide open and as flexible as possible.[7]

There can be no quarrel with the claim that the Wicksellian constitution would constrain government's fiscal appetites. We need only to ask: «How much public spending could be observed if all taxes had to be approved unanimously in the legislature?» to get a feel for the answer. The problems with the Wicksellian reforms are the opposite of those suggested with the generality criterion. Governments may be so constrained as to prevent them from financing goods and services that may be desired by the citizenry and which only governments can provide. Wicksell himself recognized the overly restrictive nature of the strict unanimity rule, and he proposed departure from the extreme version when he came to practical implementation. He replaced strict unanimity with a qualified voting rule of something on the order of a five-sixths vote of the members of a legislative assembly.

Any shift away from the extremum of unanimity toward less inclusive voting rules, however, must allow for the prospect of fiscal exploitation of persons and groups who do not accede to the decisions made. A five-sixths decision rule, standing alone as the only constitutional requirement, would not prevent the excluded one-sixth from suffering arbitrary taxation at the expense of the dominant or ruling five-sixths. There is a necessary trade-off between less inclusive rules which allow for expanded fiscal activities by governments and the prospects for fiscal exploitation of groups that remain outside the rul-

---

[6] F. A. Hayek, Law, Legislation and Liberty, Volume III The Political Order of a Society of Free Men (Chicago [forthcoming]).

[7] Knut Wicksell, Finanztheoretische Untersuchungen (Jena 1896).

ing coalition. In any constitutional choice calculus, this trade-off must be explored and analyzed, but the predicted results in terms of taxing and spending levels predicted vary within wide limits.[8]

VII. Tax Rate Limits

In modern Western democracies, little or nothing has been done toward moving toward the achievement of Wicksellian-type reforms in constitutional structure. Further, the fiscal experience of the twentieth century has exacerbated rather than resolved the problems that prompted *Wicksell* to advance his proposals. Simple majority voting continues to occupy a sacrosanct role in both the theory and the practice of modern politics, for the general electorate as well as in legislative assemblies and in committees. The constraints on fiscal outcomes that are exercised by the existing political decision procedures and/or by the existing legal rules are minimal. In the setting that we observe, therefore, more explicit constraints on governmental taxing and spending powers would seem to be dictated.

These explicit constraints may take any one of several forms. I shall first examine very briefly the possible efficacy of imposing maximum rate limits on specific taxes. Suppose, for example, the existence of a constitutional provision that restricts the taxation of personal income to some maximum average rate, say, one-third. Such a provision would clearly constrain government's ability to raise revenues from this single source or base. Unless, however, such a restriction should be accompanied by bounds on the allowable bases for taxation generally, the net impact of the restriction on income-tax rate might be minimal. Faced with a maximum-rate limit on one taxable base, a revenue-seeking government could simply shift to alternative bases. Specific rate limits would not be wholly ineffective, and especially as applied to major revenue producers in modern fiscal systems, but such limits would have to be supplemented by other controls. On balance, specific tax rate limits are probably dominated by other forms of fiscal constraint when viewed from the perspective of a potential taxpayer's constitutional choice calculus.

VIII. Tax Revenues and Total Spending as Shares in National Product or Income

Partly in recognition of the difficulties of constraining government effectively by maximum-rate limits, practical attention shifts to proposals for restricting the size of the government budget, measured either in terms of revenue intake or spending outlay. Absolute limits on total revenues or on total outlay are, of course, conceptually possible, but most proposals here take the form of allowable shares or proportions of the income or product generated in the community. Such ratio or share proposals reflect the view that the primary concern arises with respect to the proportionate rather than with the absolute size of the governmental sector in the economy. Under the ratio-type constraints, tax

---

[8] The analysis in The Calculus of Consent was largely concentrated on this trade-off. See, *James M. Buchanan* and *Gordon Tullock,* The Calculus of Consent (Ann Arbor 1962).

revenues and total outlays are allowed to increase, but only in line with general economic growth.

The imposition of this sort of fiscal constraint at some constitutional stage requires the substantive determination of a desired relative size of the governmental sector. Such a determination is not necessary in either of the first two constitutional reforms discussed, both of which are purely procedural. The difficulties in settling on an appropriate governmental share, even in terms of some maximal limit, are manifold. The preferred size of the governmental sector, as measured by either revenues or outlays, will vary over time as technology changes, as economic and social characteristics of the political community change, as the efficiency of government itself changes. And unless nonfiscal constraints on governmental activity are also present, the imposition of a binding revenue or spending constraint may do little more than shift the structure of government toward direct regulation and away from taxation.

A second major criticism of ratio or share-type constraints on revenues or outlays arises from the tendency for maximal limits to become minimal. This feature can be illustrated by the ratio-type proposals that were widely discussed in the United States in 1978. Widespread frustration with the observed explosive growth in taxation and in public spending, and at all levels of government, provoked a varied set of proposals aimed at slowing down the relative increase in government's share in the economy. However, in order to reduce the disruption that might be threatened by overt reductions in budgets, proponents of constitutional ratio-type limits tended to settle on roughly status quo shares as those that would be maximally allowable. But, of course, if such constraints should be constitutionally implemented, any prospects for reducing government's share below status quo levels become very remote.

A further problem with ratio-type fiscal constraints lies in the economic sophistication required on the part of citizens and politicians whose support must be organized to implement any constitutional change. Taxpayers think in terms of specific levies, and of their own treatment under such levies by the taxing authorities. They do not think in terms of such abstractions as total tax revenues or total spending, and surely not in terms of the ratio between two abstract entities, total budgets and total product or income. As best, and even ignoring the difficulties noted above, ratio-type constraints seem much more congenial to the professional economist consultants than to the practicing politicians or to the average taxpayer.

IX. Limits on Tax Bases

A more suitable approach may be some constitutional control over the bases upon which taxes may be livied, rather than control over either the specific rates of tax on the one hand or over total revenues on the other. Such control over the bases for taxation retains the advantage of the procedural limits in that no constitutionalstage determination of the preferred governmental share in the economy is required, at least in the precise sense. To the extent that government is constitutionally precluded from levying taxation on more than a limited number of activities, its revenue share is necessarily restricted, and especially so as the activities excluded from taxation are substitutable for those upon which taxes may be levied.

Consider an apparently extreme, but still relevant, example. Suppose that government is allowed to levy personal taxes on money incomes but that it is constitutionally prohibited from taxing income-in-kind. In such a setting, as income tax rates increase, taxpayers will, of course, shift toward income-in-kind. This shift generates an excess burden, familiar from analyses of welfare economics. What economists have overlooked, however, is the constraining influence that such potential shifts can exert on government's fiscal appetites. Faced with the prospect that taxpayers can, and will, shift to non-taxable options, even if at some cost, governments will find that maximal-revenue limits are attained at much lower budgetary levels than would be the case if the tax base should be fully «comprehensive».

Consideration of the possible efficacy of base constraints in imposing genuine fiscal controls on government tends to turn upside down precepts drawn from traditional normative theories of taxation, those which emphasize excess burden under equi-revenue models of analysis. «Noncomprehensiveness» rather than «comprehensiveness» becomes a possibly desirable attribute of a tax structure.[9]

Properly chosen tax-base constraints may also be effective in providing incentives for governments or governmental agencies to provide the goods and services valued by the taxpayers themselves rather than prerequisites of bureaucratic office. If the constitutionally allowable bases for taxation are chosen so as to be strongly complementary to the public goods to be provided, governments will find it necessary to perform with tolerable efficiency in order to collect tax revenues. A highway agency charged with producing and maintaining roads will be motivated to fulfill its assigned function if its revenue base is restricted to gasoline and vehicle levies.[10]

As noted with respect to overall constraints on revenues or on spending, tax-base constraints could not, in themselves, be effective in controlling governmental intrusions into the economy until and unless these are accompanied by constraints on governmental regulatory powers. The latter can always substitute for fiscal powers; this is a simple fact that must be reckoned with in any discussions of constitutional reform.

X. Geographic Limits on Tax Bases: Fiscal Federalism and Voting with the Feet

Political federalism offers a means of limiting tax bases, tax rates, total budgets, as well as the range and scope of governmental regulatory activity. To the extent that fiscal and regulatory powers can be lodged in governmental units smaller in geographic extent than the effective size of the interdependent economy, and with some minimal number of political units, competition among such political units will insure against undue exploitation of citizens, and without explicit constitutional controls. The rights of citizens to migrate freely, to vote with their feet or with their mobile resources, will limit the extent to which their demands for governmentally provided goods and services can be ignored by governmental units, regardless of the personal proclivities of the politicians.

If the central government, the political entity that is coincident in area with the econ-

---

[9] For a more formal analysis of constraints on bases of tax, see *Geoffrey Brennan* and *James M. Buchanan*, «Towards a Tax Constitution for Leviathan», Journal of Public Economics, 8 (December 1977), 255–273.

[10] For a detailed analysis of this usage of tax-base constraints, see *Geoffrey Brennan* and *James M. Buchanan*, «Tax Instruments as Constraints on the Disposition of Public Revenues», Journal of Public Economics, 9 (June 1978), 301–318.

omy (and which because of this coincidence assume some role in policing the economy itself such as insuring free trade and migration among subunits), can be restricted constitutionally in its range of functions, explicit fiscal constraints may not be needed. And, indeed, the federal structure of the United States which vested residual fiscal as well as regulatory powers with the separate states throughout the early part of the nation's history, may have rendered additional constitutional constraints on government's fiscal proclivities unnecessary. As the central government has come to be more dominant, however, and notably during the middle years of the twentieth century, the need for additional constraints has clearly emerged. The devolution or decentralization of fiscal and regulatory powers, once these have been seized by the central government, may prove more difficult to achieve than the more direct constraints on the central government's exercise of such powers, in any of the forms examined above.

XI. Conclusions

The formal analysis of such controls on government has scarcely commenced. Political economists must forgo their temptations to tell governments what they «should do», and spend more time predicting what governments «will do» under varying forms of constraint. Only on such analysis can solid proposals for constitutional reform be based. *Wicksell* led the way; both his and *Hayek's* proposals deserve a better hearing than they have got. Normative discourse must shift to the stage of constitutional reform.

The proposals for constitutional reform aimed at curbing the fiscal powers of modern Leviathan are not, of course, mutually exclusive. All of the proposals discussed in this paper, and others, deserve attention, analysis, discussion, and serious consideration as means toward accomplishing what should be accepted as a legitimate objective. Modern public choice, which has only been developed within the decades since World War II, now allows us to understand more about the way governments work. This understanding in turn suggests that governments, like markets, work effectively only if they are constrained by constitutional rules, by «laws and institutions» that serve to keep various natural proclivities to excess within bounds or limits.

Summary

Constitutional Constraints on Governmental Taxing Power

Hayek has suggested basic change in the fiscal constitution. He proposes to separate the collective decision concerning the allocation of tax shares and the collective decision concerning the overall level of taxation, assigning these decisions to different bodies. *Hayek's* proposal is only one among many possible changes in the fiscal constitution of democratic government, all of which may be aimed at limiting the abuse of the taxing power.

This paper examines, in broad and general terms, alternative constitutional means of limiting the taxing power of government. Limits on tax rates, on tax bases, and on total taxes as shares in income are evaluated against criteria for a «good» fiscal constitution.

Gilbert Tixier

Justice de l'impôt et égalité devant l'impôt

Le point de départ de la théorie de l'égalité devant l'impôt se trouve dans l'article 13 de la Déclaration des droits de l'homme et du citoyen. Ce texte dispose: «pour l'entretien de la force publique et pour les dépenses d'administration, une contribution commune est indispensable: elle doit être également répartie». Cette formule, assez vague, a été l'objet de diverses interprétations. On y a vu d'abord la référence à l'impôt proportionnel. Puis, à la fin du 19° siècle, sous la pression des idées socialistes et de la théorie marginaliste, on y a substitué le concept de la progressivité de l'impôt[1]. En 1901, fut institué en France un droit progressif de 1 à 18 % sur les successions et surtout des lois de 1914 et 1917 établirent l'impôt sur le revenu.

A partir de 1938, en s'appuyant sur la théorie Keynésienne, certains économistes affirmèrent que la progressivité fiscale représentait une condition nécessaire pour la réalisation du plein emploi. «Le renforcement de la progressivité de l'impôt direct et l'allégement des taxes sur la consommation suscitent un affaiblissement de la propension à l'épargne des classes riches et un encouragement à la consommation des grandes masses de la population, d'où il résulte une reprise de l'activité économique»[2]. Ces idées ont été largement diffusées en France par les partis de gauche et le programme commun (de la gauche) préconisait l'institution d'un impôt sur le capital à partir d'un million de francs. Cette mesure s'insérait dans un cadre plus vaste visant à promouvoir un changement de société.

Cependant, si l'on se réfère à un sondage récent de la *Sofres*, établi pour le compte de l'hebdomadaire «Le Nouvel Observateur» en 1975, 65 % des Français trouvent que le système français des impôts n'est «pas très juste» ou «pas du tout juste».

I. Les impôts indirects et la justice de l'impôt

Il semble que nos compatriotes, en formulant cette opinion, pensent surtout à l'impôt sur le revenu. Or, le rendement de celui-ci n'est de l'ordre que de 20 % des recettes fiscales globales et l'impôt sur les sociétés ne fournit que 12 %. La T.V.A. et les droits indirects représentent 66 %[3]. A cet égard, des études successives menées par le C.R.E.D.O.C. et la

---

[1] Cf. sur ce point *J. Lecaillon*: «Le problème de l'impôt progressif dans les pays occidentaux.» R.S.L.F. 1957, p. 296.

[2] Cf. *Lecaillon*, op. cit., p. 298. Cette analyse apparait aujourd'hui comme dépassée. Le schéma Keynésien n'avait pas prévu l'hypothèse de la «stagflation», c'est à dire l'existence simultanée de la stagnation et de l'inflation.

[3] Comme nous le soulignons dans notre ouvrage (*Tixier-Gest* Droit fiscal LGDJ 1978, p. 284), le rapport fait par *Necker* aux Etats Généraux de 1789 montre que la fiscalité indirecte fournissait à la fin de l'Ancien Régime les deux tiers des ressources fiscales.

Direction de la Prévision du Ministère des Finances (en 1973) montrent une très faible progressivité de la charge de la T.V.A. par rapport aux dépenses de consommation, en dépit des écarts considérables qui existent entre les différents taux (le taux réduit est de 7 %, le taux majoré de $33^1/_3$ %, le taux normal de 17,6 %).

Le rapport T.V.A./dépenses de consommation en pourcentage est de 10,7 pour la tranche de revenu de 3000 à 10000, de 11,5 pour la tranche supérieure à 50000 F (dans l'ensemble 11,3).

Il est vrai que l'existence de fortes accises frappant un certain nombre de biens dont la consommation augmente à mesure que le revenu s'élève (alcool, tabac, carburant) améliore quelque peu la progressivité de l'impôt indirect par rapport à la dépense (*Cf. P. Kende:* Etudes des effets différentiels des impôts sur la consommation: Revue consommation CREDOC n° 2, Avril-Juin 1971).

Dans l'ensemble, la T.V.A. marque un progrès par rapport aux impôts cumulatifs: *M. Lauré,* dans son Traité de politique fiscale, a établi dès 1956 que la T.V.A. est un impôt neutre frappant le produit final d'une même charge fiscale, quelle que soit la longueur du circuit économique.

L'impôt sur le chiffre d'affaires cumulatif, au contraire favorisait indûment les circuits courts au détriment des circuits longs. D'autre part, dans le cadre d'un marché commun où la taxe sur le chiffre d'affaires était payée dans le pays de destination du produit, ce type d'impôt favorisait les pays pratiquant la technique des remboursement forfaitaires de taxe (par exemple l'Italie avant l'introduction de la T.V.A.) au détriment de ceux qui avaient déjà mis en place un système de T.V.A.[4]. Une directive de 1967 a donc préconisé l'adoption de la T.V.A. dans tous les Etats de la Communauté. La 6° Directive, qui entre en vigueur en France le 1° janvier 1979, doit harmoniser l'assiette (extension de la T.V.A. aux professions libérales).

Mais ce système n'est pas aussi idéal qu'on veut bien l'affirmer: les achats et ventes sans factures permettent d'éluder l'impôt: c'est la raison pour laquelle on a institué des bons de remis, c'est à dire des titres de transport authentifiés, dans certains circuits de production et de distribution (chaussures, farines, fruits et légumes). Et puis, il y a la pratique plus sophistiquée des factures sans ventes. Il s'agit d'une fraude par comptabilisation d'opérations fictives qui permet aux fraudeurs de présenter aux vérificateurs fiscaux une comptabilité apparemment irréprochable. Grâce à cette technique, certaines entreprises se constituent des caisses noires (remise ultérieure de commissions occultes). Certains spécialistes évaluent la fraude en matière de T.V.A. à 50 milliards de francs. En réalité, il est très difficile de donner des chiffres même approximatifs.

II. La justice de l'impôt et les impôts directs

A la justice dans l'impôt qui suppose une certaine neutralité, on oppose parfois le concept de justice par l'impôt. Les Gouvernements socialistes en Suède, au Royaume-Uni à partir de 1945 en ont fait un instrument de nivellement des classes sociales. Malheureusement, dans le même temps, l'esprit d'initiative, la volonté d'entreprendre sont lourdement pénalisés. Les revenus non gagnés en Angleterre subissent un taux maximum d'im-

---

[4] La raison en est simple dans les pays comme l'Italie, le remboursement étant forfaitaire (on ne pouvait par définition connaître le poids exact de taxes cumulatives ayant frappé tel ou tel produit) les produits ayant suivi un cycle de fabrication intégré (exemple Fiat) étaient avantagés.

pôt de 98 %, les revenus gagnés un taux de 83 %. Les droits de succession sont également très élevés.

En France, la fiscalité directe, tout en étant lourde, n'a pas connu encore de tels excès. Mais son poids relatif a tendance à augmenter.

L'impôt sur le revenu est fortement progressiv (de 0 à 60 %) et surtout le glissement des tranches, déterminé chaque année par le législateur, ne suit pas exactement l'érosion monétaire. En d'autres termes, le taux maximum de 60 % est plus rapidement atteint en 1978 qu'en 1975 en francs constants.

Malgré un certain nombre de déclarations d'intention, le concept d'égalité devant l'impôt n'est pas toujours respecté.

1°) Au niveau de chaque catégorie de contribuables, le fisc entend favoriser le petit ou le moyen contribuable au détriment du «gros»[5]. Il existe en France un véritable mythe du «petit», petit artisan, petit commerçant, petit paysan. Sans doute la menace du recours à la taxation d'office d'après les signes extérieurs (article 168 C.G.I.) explique le désir de passer inaperçu du fisc. Mais trop d'agriculteurs moyens et connaissant une réelle aisance sont imposés d'après le forfait (bénéfice forfaitaire à l'hectare). Ils sont ainsi imposés sur un bénéfice très inférieur[6] au bénéfice réel. Il est vrai que, même au Royaume Uni, les autorités fiscales connaissent mal les revenus des «farmers». Seuls les exploitants agricoles disposant de plus de 500 000 F. de recettes brutes annuelles sont imposés en France d'après le bénéfice réel.

Il existe une réelle disparité de traitement fiscal au sein de la même catégorie de revenus. Cette constatation peut être aussi faite, dans une moindre mesure, au niveau des bénéfices industriels et commerciaux, des bénéfices non commerciaux (B.N.C.).

Aux concepts ambigus de justice de l'impôt et d'égalité devant l'impôt, il est préférable de substituer la notion d'équité de l'impôt.

Ce terme suppose l'existence d'une certaine neutralité de l'impôt et même un souci de favoriser les éléments les plus dynamiques, l'entrepreneur au sens large du terme. Le profit devrait être stimulé puisqu'il est à la fois le guide de l'activité économique, le moyen de financement de la croissance et un indicateur d'efficacité.

Cette notion de profit correspond pour *Schumpeter* à une fonction propre à l'entrepreneur qui est la fonction d'innovation, pour *Knight* à la rémunération de celui qui assume les risques de l'incertitude, pour M. *Barre* au fruit d'une dialectique de l'entrepreneur et du milieu.

Ce concept de profit reste la pierre angulaire de l'économie de marché. Elle n'est pas suffisamment reconnue par le législateur. Certes, les actionnaires domiciliés en France des sociétés françaises ont été, dans une certaine mesure, favorisés par l'institution d'un avoir fiscal de 50 %, aux termes de la loi du 12 juillet 1965. La loi Monory a édicté pour 1978 une exemption à concurrence de 5000 F. des sommes investies dans l'acquisition

---

[5] On parle périodiquement d'un impôt sur les grosses fortunes mais à partir de quel seuil cet impôt sera-t-il assis? Une commission d'études a été récemment nommée. Par ailleurs une décision du Conseil Constitutionnel de 1973, saisi par le Président du Sénat, a annulé une disposition d'une loi votée par le Parlement. Ce texte établissait une discrimination entre les contribuables faisant l'objet d'une taxation d'office en vertu de l'art. 180 imposant d'après les dépenses personnelles ostensibles ou notoires. Les gros contribuables ne pouvaient apporter la preuve du caractère exagéré des bases d'imposition. Le Conseil Constitutionnel a considéré cette disposition comme contraire au principe d'égalité des citoyens devant la loi.

[6] Le taux de sous estimation des bénéfices de l'exploitation agricole avait été évalué en 1972 par le Conseil des Impôts à 77 %. Cela signifiait que, sur un revenu de 100 F. 77 F. restent inconnus au fisc. Il est probable que des progrès ont été accomplis depuis cette date.

d'actions de sociétés françaises. Mais ces avantages fiscaux sont contrecarrés par l'imposition, à compter du 1° janvier 1979, des plus values mobilières.

De même, si la loi de finances pour 1979 accorde l'exemption d'impôt sur les sociétés à certains bénéfices réinvestis dans les P.M.E. (petites et moyennes entreprises), les dirigeants salariés de sociétés qui détiennent plus de 35 % des droits sociaux ne bénéficient que d'une réfaction de 10 % pour la fraction supérieure à 150 000 F des salaires (nets de frais professionnels). Cette mesure apparait d'autant plus inopportune qu'une telle catégorie de chefs d'entreprises assure des risques que ne courent pas les dirigeants salariés d'importantes sociétés anonymes qui sont simplement des gestionnaires et ne détiennent le plus souvent qu'un nombre infime d'actions de ces sociétés . . .

La notion d'égalité devant l'impôt est aussi violée par la nouvelle législation accordant des faveurs fiscales (réfaction de 20 %, égale à celle dont bénéficient les salariés) aux membres des professions libérales assujetties au régime du bénéfice réel dont les recettes brutes sont inférieures à 605 000 F. Si ce chiffre est dépassé, aucune réfaction n'est octroyée[7].

2°) Ces efforts de rapprochement du régime fiscal des salariés et de celui des non salariés – souhaités par la loi Royer du 27 décembre 1973 – butent toujours sur le même obstacle: la connaissance exacte des revenus non salariaux. *M. Giscard d'Estaing* avait déjà posé en 1970 le principe: «à revenu connu égal, impôt égal». Le maintien de la réfaction de 20 % au profit des salariés et des quelques titulaires de B.I.C. ou des B.N.C. tenant une comptabilité précise déterminant leur bénéfice réel et ayant adhéré à ces centres de gestion agréés apparait comme justifié à deux points de vue.

D'une part, le Conseil des Impôts, dans un rapport de 1977 (p. 119), estime toujours que les bénéfices industriels et commerciaux perçus par les entrepreneurs individuels sont sous estimés.

D'autre part, la réfaction de 20 % devrait bénéficier à toute personne qui se procure un revenu en mettant en jeu sa force personnelle de travail (salarié, travailleur individuel, chef d'entreprise pour la partie de sa rémunération qui correspondrait à un salaire fiscal).

Surtout, il faudrait revoir l'échelle des taux de l'impôt sur le revenu dont la progressivité est trop rapide eu égard au pouvoir d'achat réel. L'opinion publique commence seulement à prendre conscience de ce qu'ou delà du prélèvement fiscal, il existe un prélèvement parafiscal beaucoup trop lourd[8], et surtout un prélèvement insidieux qui résulte d'un taux d'inflation annuel proche de 10 %.

En présence d'un Etat qui maîtrise mal son budget, le contribuable a des réactions certes malsaines pour l'économie du pays (fuite des capitaux ou recherche de valeurs refuge: achats de lingots ou de pièces d'or, acquisition de tableaux, de bijoux, d'objets d'art ou de meubles anciens) mais finalement rationnels.

Si l'on compare le comportement d'un épargnant qui aurait investi en 1972 300 000 F. en valeurs mobilières (et qui aurait donc favorisé l'activité économique) et celui d'un autre qui aurait acheté des lingots, ce dernier a effectué le meilleur placement.

Il faudrait avoir le courage de prendre des mesures extrêmement novatrices pour

---

[7] Nous connaissons le cas d'un avocat qui a fait inscrire son épouse au barreau, a conclu un contrat d'association avec elle: chacun des avocats peut désormais bénéficier de la réfaction si les recettes brutes de chacun d'eux demeurent inférieures à 605 000 F. Ainsi la loi est tournée dans son esprit, mais non dans sa teneur. Cet exemple réel montre l'inconvénient des régimes dérogatoires.

[8] Le Ministre de la Santé publique a brusquement «découvert» en décembre 1978 que la Sécurité Sociale connaîtrait en 1979 un déficit de 17 milliards de francs. Il a été décidé d'augmenter les cotisations patronales et ouvrières. Mais il n'a guère été question de réduire le montant des dépenses ou de diminuer le taux de couverture du «petit risque».

mettre un terme à ces pratiques malthusiennes. Assorti d'une exemption à la base des revenus les plus faibles, un impôt proportionnel ou très faiblement progressif serait un élément décisif d'une nouvelle politique fiscale. Seule celle-ci serait susceptible de transformer les mentalités, de redonner le goût d'entreprendre et de réaliser des profits.

L'égalité devant l'impôt serait plus pleinement assurée et le dogme dépassé de la justice par l'impôt (qui a ruiné l'économie britannique et provoqué la fuite des cerveaux, brain drain) serait définitivement abandonné.

Mais quel Gouvernement oserait en France prendre un tel risque? Le nivellement dans la médiocrité est une solution, hélas, plus vraisemblable.

Summary

Fiscal Justice and Fiscal Equality

The claim that taxation should follow the principle of equality has been quite differently interpreted in the course of the years. It first meant that tax rates should be proportional, later on progressive tax rates were considered to favour equality.

Under the influence of the Keynesian theory – it also affected French fiscal policy – a progressive income tax in combination with moderate indirect taxes was supposed to be particularly suited to promote economic activities. However, recent inquiries revealed that the French are not altogether satisfied with their fiscal system, they do not judge it to be just especially with respect to direct taxes.

As to the justice of indirect taxes, the introduction of the value-added-tax system represented some progress though this system too leaves quite a few loopholes for tax evasion and fraud. It is not only the high and rising burden of direct taxation that causes discontent in France: the same kind of income is subjected to different ways of assessment and tax rates; moreover, the French fiscal system is felt to be detrimental to economic growth. It seems not to sufficiently take into consideration the importance of profits for the economy. Various examples of the most recent tax legislation are given to illustrate this reproach. Well aware of the difficulties involved, the author recommends a reform of the French fiscal system. A reformed system ought to renounce the dogma of equality via taxes, ought to guarantee more fiscal equality and to provide new incentives to the economy and the spirit of entrepreneurship.

VII. Internationale Ordnung

Lucas Beltrán

Collectivism and the International Order

I. Socialism and Foreign Trade

In the second half of the nineteenth century and the first decades of the twentieth century, socialists considered themselves internationalist. Many people also considered them internationalist. The declared goal of socialists was then the abolition of national States and the creation of a World State. Their organizations were called *Worker's Internationals*. It was a commonly held view then that socialism and internationalism went together, and that capitalism and nationalism also went together. Socialism meant the brotherhood of all men, while capitalism implied domination of governments by plutocratic forces and the unavoidable confrontation of the interests of different countries, that is, of different capitalist groups.

The situation changed during the first seventy five years of the present century. The Worker's Internationals have survived; however they now look like thin ghosts, devoid of intellectual background and emotional appeal. Communist and socialist parties concentrate their attention on their own national economies. Socialism and internationalism have increasingly divorced from each other.

How can this change be explained? Is present nationalism a temporary deviation from the international outlook inherent to the nature of socialism? A historical survey does not seem to confirm this hypothesis. On the contrary: it suggests that collectivism is essentially nationalist and that the internationalism of the last century and the beginning of the present century was a passing mood.

Early socialist writers advocated closed economies. They either reserved foreign trade to the State or omitted to deal with it. In the latter case, the context of their reasonings revealed that freedom of foreign trade was excluded. If the State had to direct the economic processes, individuals could not be free to import or export goods. The logic of the system does not admit this sort of freedom. This is the case of *Plato, Morus, Saint-Simon, Owen* and *Fourier. Fichte* gave to his book the unequivocal title *Der geschlossene Handelsstaat*[1] *(The Closed Commercial State)*.

Socialist parties were never in office in the nineteenth century (except for short periods in exceptional circumstances) and so they were able to preach inconsistent doctrines. Free trade did not go along with the rest of their programmes although it attracted them for several reasons. One of these was the defence of the consumption of the poor – «your food will cost you more» was a free trade slogan which found an easy echo in socialist organizations.

But the main attraction was probably the high esteem in which internationalism was held in the eighteenth and nineteenth centuries, due to the work of liberal authors.

---

[1] *J. G. Fichte,* Der geschlossene Handelsstaat, Tübingen 1800; reprint Jena 1920.

II. The Era of Internationalism

In the sixteenth and seventeenth centuries, the attitude of independent states to one another was that of competition and hostility. Even in the eighteenth century, Voltaire wrote: «Human condition is such that to wish the greatness of one's country is to wish evil to its neighbours . . . It is clear that a country cannot win if another country does not lose».*(Dictionnaire philosophique, article Patrie)*.[2]

In the eighteenth century this conception was attacked. *David Hume* expressed the opposite view in a forcible manner: «In opposition to this narrow and malignant opinion, I will venture to assert that the increase of riches and commerce in any one nation, instead of hurting, commonly promotes the riches and commerce of all its neighbours; and that a State can scarcely carry its trade and industry very far, where all the surrounding States are buried in ignorance, sloth and barbarism . . . Were our narrow and malignant politics to meet with success, we should reduce all our neighbouring nations to the same state of sloth and ignorance that prevails in Morocco and the Coast of Barbary. But what would be the consequence? They could send us no commodities. They could take none from us: our domestic commerce itself would languish for want of emulation, example and instruction! And we ourselves should soon fall into the same abject condition to which we had reduced them. I shall therefore venture to acknowledge that, not only as a man, but as a British subject, I pray for the flourishing commerce of Germany, Spain, Italy and even France itself.» *(Of the Jealousy of Trade)*.[3]

There were several schools and currents of opinion which advocated the solidarity of all peoples. The most prominent among them were the liberal economists, the most distinguished economist being of course *Adam Smith,* who proclaimed «the obvious and simple system of natural liberty».[4] His opinion conquered men's minds more completely than he himself had hoped. He wrote: «To expect indeed that the freedom of trade should ever be entirely restored in Great Britain is as absurd as to expect that an Oceana or Utopia should ever be established in it.»[5]

But thanks to his ideas, obstacles to foreign trade were gradually eliminated. In 1846 the great decision to suppress the Corn Laws was taken. In 1860 the remaining protective duties were removed. From this date onwards Great Britain became a free trade country.

Although other European nations did not go as far as Great Britain, they all made similar progress. In 1860 the French and British governments signed the treaty commonly known as the *Cobden–Chevalier* Treaty which marked the highest point reached by France in her freedom of international trade. Germany's first *Zollverein*, formed in 1834, widened its boundaries in the following years. In Spain as a consequence of the liberal revolution of 1868, import duties were drastically reduced in 1869 and foreign economic relations liberalized in every sense.

The freeing of trade produced the benefits which classical economists had expected. The international division of labour was established and countries began to specialize in the industries for which nature or history had endowed them. Freedom and specialization determined a rapid growth of wealth. Many authors have analyzed this development. One of these is *Simon Kuznets* who, in a work comprising several volumes, tried to

---

[2] F. M. A. *Voltaire,* Dictionnaire philosophique, article «Patrie», Paris 1961.
[3] D. *Hume,* Of the Jealousy of Trade, in: D. *Hume,* Writings on Economics, edited and introduced by E. Rotwein, Edinburgh 1955, pp. 78 and 81–82.
[4] A. *Smith,* Wealth of Nations, Vol. II, (Edwin-Cannan's edition) London 1930, p. 184.
[5] A. *Smith,* Wealth of Nations, Vol. I, (Edwin-Cannan's edition) London 1930, p. 435.

measure growth from the beginning of the nineteenth century until the present time, in terms of total product and *per capita* product.[6] Economists like *Schumpeter* and *Werner Sombart*, with socialist tendencies, celebrated this growth in glowing terms. Even *Marx* sang to the glories of freedom of international trade in a certain sense. In his *Communist Manifesto* he wrote: «The bourgeoisie, by the rapid improvement of all instruments of production, by the immensely facilitated means of communication, draws all nations, even the most barbarian, into civilization. The cheap prices of its commodities are the heavy artillery with which it batters down all Chinese walls, with which it forces the barbarians' intensely obstinate hatred of foreigners to capitulate. It compels all nations, on pain of extinction, to adopt the bourgeois mode of production, it compels them to introduce what it calls civilization into their midst, i.e. to become bourgeois themselves... The bourgeoisie, during its rule of scarce one hundred years, has created more massive and more colossal productive forces than have all the preceding generations together».

Freedom of trade – national and international – also gave peace, order and dignity to human life. Governments respected foreign people and foreign property more and more, even in case of war. International travel became freer than it had ever been so far. Money was convertible everywhere. With the international division of labour, national economies became really integrated, the term integration being never used.

All this had an influence on socialist thought, or at least on socialist tactics. In the atmosphere of enthusiasm for freedom of trade, to preach national isolation would have seemed to betray the cause of progress and would have been akin to political suicide. So socialist parties declared themselves in favour of free trade.

Even some of the most utopian collectivists made statements to this effect. In France, during the last years of the July Monarchy and the first years after the 1848 revolution, the disciples of *Charles Fourier* joined forces with the liberals in the fight for free trade.

III. The Protectionist Reaction

In the eighteen eighties a new protectionist movement started in Germany and began to spread, with more or less strength, to other countries including France, Italy and Spain. The new movement gave additional reasons to the socialists to advocate free trade. The political parties which favoured this new protectionism were conservative. Liberals continued to defend free trade, and socialists sided with them.

From 1848, when the German liberal revolution failed, until the end of the First World War the main German party which fought the nationalist policy of *Bismarck* and Kaiser *Wilhelm II*. was the Social Democratic party. As they were always in opposition, the German Social Democrats could combat the capitalism, protectionism and militarism of governments; and promise, for the day when they would be in office, a totally contrary policy, namely a socialist, free trade and pacifist policy. The influence which German Social Democracy exerted on other socialist parties and on general public opinion convinced many people that socialism and international harmony were the same thing.

---

[6] *S. Kuznets,* Modern Economic Growth: Rate, Structure and Spread, New Haven 1966; Economic Growth of Nations: Total Output and Production Structure, Cambridge, Mass. 1971.

IV. Pierson's Article

The first scientific analysis of the relations between socialism and foreign trade was *The problem of value in the socialist economy* (1902), an article written by the eminent Dutch scholar and politician *N. G. Pierson*.[7] The occasion of its publication was as follows.

Pierson had made a general statement concerning the impracticability of socialism which in April 1902, caused *Karl Kautsky*, the then leader of Marxism, to give a lecture on the probable working of socialism. (In 1907, an English translation of this lecture and of a previous one was published under the title *The social revolution and On the morrow of the social revolution*).[8] With his lecture *Kautsky* broke the Marxist injunction not to waste time thinking about what would happen after the big social change, though he showed that he was not aware of the problems which an economist could see; for instance, he said nothing about foreign trade under socialism. This moved *Pierson* to write his article, which appeared in Dutch and was subsequently translated into several languages. In 1935 an English version was included in the book *Collectivist economic planning*, edited by *F. A. Hayek*.

Some of the ideas in the article may seem obvious now. However, at the beginning of the century they were scientific novelties, since it was widely believed then that economic problems were peculiar to capitalism and that, under socialism, everything would be different. *Pierson* showed that in a socialist community the question of value would not be eliminated: market economies solve automatically many problems which include this question; if economic freedom were replaced by orders of governments, the latter ought to supply deliberate solutions.

This would happen in problems of foreign trade which are analyzed at some length in the article. One of these problems refers to the needed capital. «If the Netherlands send manufactured goods to Java, and receive in exchange coffee and rice, this business can be transacted in three ways: (1) Java first sends us the coffee and rice, and only when these goods have been received, perhaps only when they have been partly consumed, do we consign the equivalent. (2) The Netherlands first export manufactured goods to Java and await the arrival of the equivalent. (3) Both countries ship their products at approximately the same time, so that they meet half-way. In the first case Java furnishes the capital, in the second the Netherlands, while in the third each does its share».

Under market economy conditions, the country with a lower interest rate provides the capital. This is scarce in general and a low interest rate is an indication of relative abundance; so the supply of capital for foreign trade falls on the country which is better able to bear its burden. If foreign trade were carried on by governments, how would it be decided which country would furnish the capital?

A similar problem is posed by the transport of the goods, specially by sea. Among market economies this task is fulfilled by the people of nations who have differential advantages for shipping. The shipping is done by countries with an abundance of capital or with easy access to other countries' capital and which enjoy certain conditions in the fields of labour and organization. If foreign trade passed to be a State enterprise, how would it be decided who would perform this important task?

---

[7] N. G. Pierson, The Problem of Value in the Socialist Society, reprint in: *F. A. v. Hayek* (Ed.), Collectivist Economic Planning, London 1935, pp. 41–85. (Dutch original: Het waardeproblem in een socialistische Maatschappij, in: De Economist, Vol. 41 (1902), pp. 423–56).

[8] K. Kautsky, The Social Revolution and On the Morrow of the Social Revolution, London 1907.

Another problem is foreign investment. With free markets, the investment of capital by rich countries in underdeveloped nations is determined by private advantage. This process is profitable to everybody, specially to the poor nations which thanks to it can rapidly have railways and industrial plants. If a change in the social structure of the world caused the profit incentive of foreign investment to disappear, it would be necessary to devise other mechanisms to bring capital from the rich nations to the poor.

Experience proved the wisdom of *Pierson's* assertions. In the seventy five years since he wrote his article, communism in a part of our planet and State intervention in the rest of it have rendered non-operative the old apparatus of foreign investment moved by private advantage. Can anybody doubt that the result has been most unhappy? Today there are rich countries with lots of capital and poor countries with very little. To transfer capital from the former to the latter would be beneficial to all. However, the authorities of socialist and non-socialist economies have not been able to develop a method of transfer which might have replaced the old one.

And now the representatives of the different shades of anti-capitalist mentality who have brought about the present state of affairs complain bitterly.

Finally *Pierson* comes to the more general question: which commodities will be traded among independent socialist countries? At which prices? Or what quantities of one good will be exchanged for given quantities of another? A little reflection shows that the amount of labour expended on each product cannot provide a formula which will be accepted gladly by every country. A country could not be obliged to part with goods it produced and in return receive goods produced by another country which had embodied in them the same amount of work. It seems that even among socialist countries two principles which govern international trade between free market countries ought to be maintained: (1) Recognition of the freedom of every country to exchange or not to exchange at her own discretion (2) Exchange on a basis of equivalent services.

A fact which makes the problem more difficult still is that foreign trade is not limited to trade between two countries alone. To begin with, we can imagine triangular trade: country A could sell to country B and buy nothing from it; country B could sell to country C and not buy from it; and country C could sell to country A and buy nothing from it. Then B would pay A with the proceeds of its exports to C; C would pay B with the proceeds of its sales to A; and A would pay C with the proceeds of its sales to B. In practice international trade is more complicated than this, it is multilateral. Many nations buy from and sell to other nations variable amounts of goods, and only some general balance of the accounts of each of them with the rest is necessary.

Pierson suggests that socialist countries would be obliged to create an international market which would determine the prices of goods and even the interest of money for foreign transactions.

V. The Twentieth Century

Until 1914 the attitude of socialists in favour of free trade continued. The protectionist movement went on in most countries. In Great Britain, after 1903, *Joseph Chamberlain* succeeded in converting the Conservative party to protectionism. But the Labour party and general opinion remained faithful to free trade.

In 1917 the communists conquered power in Russia and in 1918 the Social Democrats formed a government in Germany. Soon after, several European countries had governments which were more or less strongly influenced by socialists. Coming to power revealed to socialists the internal contradictions of their nineteenth century programmes, which combined State control of the economy with free trade. Their ultimate goal of a World State was not denied but receded in their perspective. It is obvious to say that the Russian communists established an almost autarkic regime, with only a trickle of foreign trade in the hands of the government.

The socialist parties which gained influence in market economy countries after 1918 had insufficient power to make them socialist at once. So they tried to introduce measures which would bring socialism gradually. In doing this, they could not maintain their free trade traditions, which they quickly forgot and adopted the protectionist policies then in vogue. When the great depression (1929–1939) came, the socialists did not differ from the other parties in their foreign trade policies which consisted generally in restricting imports.

The British Labour party persisted longer than others in its free trade ideas. The *McKenna* duties on imports of clocks, watches, bicycles and motor cars, imposed during the First World War and retained after it, were abolished in 1924 by a short-lived Labour government (and restored in 1925 by the conservatives). *Philip Snowden,* the Labour Chancellor of the Exchequer in the Government formed in 1929, was until 1932 an uncompromising free trader. When in 1932 and the following years the British National government abandoned free trade and built a growing system of protection, the members of the Labour party who had refused to join it, railed at the new policy and condemned it as reactionary and contrary to popular interests.

VI. Some Theoretical Considerations

Pierson's article did not stimulate socialist authors to work on the problems of foreign trade. It is astonishing how little thought they have given to them. Even *Schumpeter,* in his widely read book *Capitalism, Socialism and Democracy*[9], where he tries to foresee in some detail what will happen after the advent of socialism, does not face these problems and scarcely mentions them. A socialist theory of international trade does not exist.

When we analyzed *Pierson's* article, we indicated a reason which helps to explain this lack of interest: socialists tend to believe that in a collectivist community no problems would emerge which have not been present in market economies. This expectation is unfounded.

Market economies solve most economic problems automatically. We mentioned some relating to foreign trade where this happens. This happens also in other fields of our economic life: the problem of how a community should divide its current production between consumption goods and investment goods is solved through the rate of interest; the problem of which consumption goods should be produced is decided by the demand of consumers; the problem of who is going to be a entrepreneur is decided by competition among the people who wish to be so; and so on and so forth.

As these problems are solved automatically and with little friction, superficial observers do not notice them. If apparently they do not exist in our world, socialists have no fear of their presence in another sort of world, e. g. in a socialist system. But this system would

---

[9] *J. Schumpeter,* Capitalism, Socialism and Democracy, New York 1942.

have no automatic resorts to solve problems of this kind, so that they would need the conscious analysis and decisions by the authorities.

In a sense the authorities can *solve* any difficulty relating to the internal life of a country. The solution may be dear in terms of human dignity and happiness lost or of pain and dishonour inflicted, but any question can be settled by a political authority endowed with coercive powers.

However, questions relating to international trade cannot be solved in the same way because they affect at least two countries and there is not a political authority with power over all the people involved.

Socialism cannot be associated with freedom to buy and sell in international markets. The theory of free trade, as formulated by *Adam Smith,* perfected by *David Ricardo* and developed by other authors, presupposes a market economy in different countries as well as free prices in all of them. It also advocates non-interference of the authorities, so that individuals may take advantage of international differences of prices and tend to eliminate them. Nothing of this can be practicable in an economy in which production of goods and their internal distribution is in the hands of the government. It is not possible to run a socialist economy and maintain the doctrine of free trade. If socialist parties did abandon it as soon as they came to power, this did not happen by chance, nor was it a betrayal of principle – they could not have done otherwise.

A completely socialised economy cannot even organize foreign trade in a rational way. (As *Mises* proved, it cannot organize rationally internal processes either). Socialism means public ownership of all production goods, as well as the production and distribution of consumption goods by the political authorities which up to now have power in national states. A government which plans the economy of its country does not take into consideration the plans of other governments for their respective countries. But there is little probability that the different national plans (even when they ran smoothly, which is improbable, nay impossible) will dovetail and engender international harmony. Discrepancies will produce international frictions more serious than those among free economy States.

If production goods belong to the State, they do not change hands and are not valued. Hence the cost of the goods they help to produce cannot be calculated. Therefore it is not possible for a socialist government to decide rationally which of the commodities produced should be destined for home consumption or use, and which for export. And it is not possible for two socialist governments to find a criterion for fixing the terms under which the exchange of the goods is to be made from one country to the other. Only if socialist countries coexist with non socialist countries can they utilize the prices ruling in the latter to value the traded goods. If now communist nations can undertake foreign trade with no more difficulties than they encounter, it is because market economies supply them with information about prices. *Mises* was not joking when he suggested that a socialist world would do well to allow the market economy to survive in one country: this would provide the others with precious information which they could not easily obtain otherwise.

Modern economies which are not completely socialized, are far from free. They are what has come to be called mixed economies. Free trade is difficult for them. Economies powerfully influenced by socialist ideas, with some (or many) nationalized sectors, high taxation, full employment at every cost, and trades unions with monopoly power, have an inherent inflationary bias which engenders periodical «balance of payments crises». The right remedy would be to change the general policy mentioned. As this is not «politically possible», the second best would be a devaluation now and then. But devaluations if frequent, are also objectionable from a political point of view. So, in practice, recourse is taken to protectionism, and these countries restrict imports through taxes and quotas, pay differential subsidies to exports, make bilateral accords, control foreign exchange and manipulate it, etc.

The imagination of experts and officials is always working to discover new forms of protectionism which have the least offensive appearance possible. They are also working to find new names for protectionism. The latest discovery has been to call it «organized free trade».

The word «integration», as applied to countries in regard to international trade, is modern. But when it was invented, the possibility of its becoming a reality had waned. A necessary condition for international integration is the right economic order within each country: socialist or interventionist states cannot be integrated.

All projects of regional integration have failed in the sense that the national economies which they tried to integrate have remained more separated than nations were in the nineteenth century, when these apparently ambitious projects did not exist. The European Common Market had probably some favourable effects, at least in comparison with feasible alternatives, but the movements of people, commodities and capital between member states and between them and third countries are less free than in the nineteenth century. And the discrepancies between the national policies of the member states frequently put the Common Market on the brink of dissolution.

VII. Colonialism

Until the First World War, socialists not only believed that their system was consistent with free trade and international harmony, they also held that capitalism had a necessary consequence – imperialism or colonialism – and that this could not exist without capitalism. But history shows many examples of imperialism before capitalism was born. And in several countries – Switzerland, Sweden, Norway, Denmark – capitalism has existed for many years without a shadow of imperialism.

Yet socialists succeeded in infiltrating their ideas into public opinion: capitalism was full of contradictions which excluded peaceful economic cooperation between nations; industrial states needed growing markets for their output, if overproduction had to be avoided; at the same time, it was necessary for them to be sure of their supply of raw materials. A colonial empire solved both difficulties: an abundance of natural resources and low wages in the colonies produced raw materials at cheap prices; at the same time, tariff preferences gave an easy outlet to metropolitan industrial goods.

With small differences of shade, this was the approach to the problem of *Lenin* and *Rosa Luxemburg*, of *Cecil Rhodes* and Marshall *Lyautey*. Socialists also spread the idea that colonial campaigns and wars were always promoted, in the last resort, by the representatives of high economic interests, the notorious «industrial and banking circles». They gave the orders; the politicians and generals obeyed them.

If such interpretation had been correct, it would have been sensible to foresee *a priori* that Europe, where most of the colonial powers were located, would be impoverished after the loss of their colonies in the years following the Second World War. But when the war ended Europe experienced one of its most intense periods of economic development. If we look at the question with more detail, we observe facts which are more surprising still for those who accepted the socialist view of colonialism. According to this view, the prosperity of the Netherlands and Japan was closely dependent on their large colonial empires. Both these countries were small, overpopulated and endowed with few natural resources. How could they survive or maintain their standards of life without their extensive and rich colonies? In fact, after losing them, the Netherlands now enjoy a much higher standard of life, while Japan has in the last decades had a quicker growth than any other country in the world. It is due to this, that the poverty of the majority of Japan's population in the days of her imperial splendour, has been replaced by universal welfare.

There is an even clearer example, that of Germany. The need for colonies was an element of national-socialist propaganda: closely confined by her frontiers, Germany could not live without colonies. Now the Federal Republic of Germany, with frontiers still more close, separated from the Eastern territories which supplied her with farm products, has a higher standard of life than Imperial Germany, the Weimar Republic and the Third Reich ever had, and she continues to watch the incessant rise of her standard.

The socialist view on colonialism is proof of the inability to understand the functions of foreign trade. It is a fallacy grounded on the assumption that two territories must be under the same political authority if they are to be able to trade with advantage. But if there are no artificial obstacles, trade is as profitable to two independent nations as to two provinces of the same state.

Colonial history is complex. It was influenced by economic factors, but other factors – political, military, religious, etc. – had a still stronger influence. The incentives to form colonial empires were sometimes noble and sometimes mean; the results of these formations were sometimes good and sometimes bad. But colonial expeditions planned by «financial capitalism» are a myth. Colonies meant economic advantages for some people; every fact is beneficial to somebody. But as a whole, they were not profitable, and their independence was an economic gain for the home countries.

There are two sorts of colonialism: political and economic. The first implies legal and military dominion, but not discrimination of production or trade. There is economic colonialism, when besides political domination such discrimination is imposed.

Political colonialism means no economic advantage for the metropolis: she must finance «the savage wars of peace» to keep the colony quiet and to defend it against other powers. For the rest, her citizens trade with the colony's citizens as if they belonged to an independent nation.

Economic colonialism consisted usually in a structure of the metropolis' and of the colony's tariffs which tried to stimulate commerce between them. This is a distortion of business and the theory of international trade shows that practically always it hurts the metropolis, the colony, and the rest of the world.

Economic colonialism may also consist in forcing the colonial population to sell their goods or their work at prices lower than those ruling in the free markets. There is a theoretical possibility that this kind of economic colonialism might be profitable to the metropolis: through monopolistic organizations or through sheer force, the metropolis might «exploit» the colony in the literal sense of that word. But the probability of a successful exploitation is small: most often, practical difficulties and the resistence of the native population will provoke such high police expenses that the net result of this policy will be unfavourable.

Political colonialism was an extensive phenomenon in modern history, but economic colonialism was not. In the nineteenth and twentieth centuries up to 1929, colonies traded almost freely with every country on equal or similar terms. It was only during the years 1929–1939 that colonial powers sometimes tried to extract advantages from their colonies. Tried, but very seldom succeeded.

Imperialism and colonialism were not an essential part of the liberal order, but rather a foreign body inlaid in it. As long as the liberal mentality prevailed, the economic importance of colonialism was small. Only when socialist and interventionist ideas gained influence did economic colonialism become somewhat more significant.

VIII. Communist Countries – The Comecon

While Russia was the only communist state in the world, self-sufficiency was more or less the official policy. However, the advantages of foreign trade are so great that she acceded to import and export certain commodities. The particular specification of these commodities was based on complex criteria in which economic, political, diplomatic and strategic considerations all had an influential part to play.

After the Second World War communism was adopted by other countries. The rulers of some of these countries had a vague conception of autarky and favoured the creation of all types of industries. But soon contrary ideas prevailed; the economists in the new communist nations knew about the advantages of the international division of labour. The conception developed that these nations had to stimulate foreign trade, especially with other communist countries. But to what extent old autarkic programmes should be maintained, to what extent trade with other communist countries should go, to what extent trade with noncommunist nations should be allowed remained unclear.

The integration plans in the free economy world had an influence on the communist block. In 1947, Great Britain, France and Russia discussed Marshall Aid. Russia decided not to accept it, and in 1948 the O. E. E. C. (later called the O. E. C. D.) was created without the communist countries. The latter the following year set up the Council for mutual economic assistance or Comecon.

In 1957 the Treaty of Rome gave birth to the European Common Market, which was attacked in the communist press and gave added impetus to the activities of the Comecon.

The Comecon was born at a Moscow conference in January 1949. Its original members were the Soviet Union, Poland, Rumania, Bulgaria, Czechoslovakia and Hungary. Albania joined in February of the same year, East Germany in September 1950, and Mongolia in June 1962. Albania withdrew from the Comecon in 1962. Yugoslavia, China, North Korea, North Vietnam and Cuba have attended meetings of the Comecon as observers.

Economic integration does not mean the same thing to communist countries and market economies. In the latter it consists essentially in eliminating the obstacles which governments have placed in the way of foreign trade undertaken by private enterprises. In communist countries, foreign trade is carried on by governments, and integration consists in coordinating various national economic plans in order to achieve specialization of production, international division of labour, and prosperity (which in free economies are brought about automatically by competition).

Which criteria should direct these processes? The Comecon is not a supranational authority which can issue orders to national governments. For a free and spontaneous coordination, communist countries lack the guide which only a system of market prices, national and international, can supply; within each country prices are largely an administrative affair, so prices in one communist country are different from those in other communist countries and from the free prices prevailing in international markets.

The idea of using these free prices for trade between the Comecon States was put forward, but was attacked on the grounds that it implied subordination of socialist economies to «capitalist world monopolies». In the end, it was accepted because it would have been difficult to do otherwise: the Comecon meeting of June 1958 declared that prices for international trade between communist countries should be established «on the basis of average world market prices on the principal market for the commodity in a clearly defined period».

However, at the Comecon meetings, delegations often demand higher prices for their countries' exports, which they sometimes obtain.

At the meeting of the Comecon in December 1961, a resolution was adopted under the title *Basic Principles of International Socialist Division of Labour*[10], in which socialism and international trade of communist nations with both communist and non-communist countries were praised. However the text said nothing about the criteria and methods needed for organizing these trade exchanges, and is yet another proof that socialism lacks a doctrine of international trade.

The Comecon has tried to bring about the sort of integration that seems practicable under socialism. Until its creation, trade between communist nations (and between them and free market nations) was on a bilateral basis, i. e. the government of each country negotiated its international exchanges with each of the other governments. The Comecon tried to introduce multilateralism. It also tried to convince communist governments of the need to coordinate their economic plans.

The difficulties of reaching these goals are expressed in the following statements by communist officials and economists, quoted in *Michael Kaser's* book *Comecon, Integration Problems of the Planned Economies.*[11]

«We said long ago that a better cooperation should be established between our countries. It is impossible to develop everything everywhere simultaneously. Unfortunately we have often spoken in vain. Hungarians, Poles, Rumanians, and the others have tried to build up everything by themselves. Perhaps it is only little Albania which has not attempted this ... In the Soviet Union this naturally is not the same problem as elsewhere, since Soviet industry produces for a vast demand. The same applies to China with its immense population. But for small countries this creates very great problems, for which solutions cannot be found within national boundaries.

As regards tractor or motor vehicle production, for example, the situation today is that tractors and motor vehicles are produced not only in the Soviet Union but by Poland, Czechoslovakia, Hungary, and Rumania. Thus production is not always profitable. The sooner and the better we develop the division of labour between our countries, the stronger will our economies be».[12]

«If the answer to what are the main criteria for the economic efficacity of the international socialist division of labour has already been given in the *Basic principles*, the other, more important question – how practically to apply these criteria – is for the present still unelucidated. Of course, this is far from being accidental. The economists of socialist countries have failed to solve many major problems of determining the economic efficiency of production even at the national level, let alone at the scale of the world socialist economic system.»[13]

The authors of the following quotation observed that although it was government policy «to turn to account the advantages arising from an international division of labour ... we have not yet succeeded in switching over ... The theory of autarky still survives in our Party teaching, our periodicals, our planning methods and in the minds of certain of our economic leaders ... While the production plan, it is true, is supposed to

---

[10] The Basic Principles of International Socialist Division of Labour, adopted by Comecon in December 1961, reprint in: M. *Kaser,* Comecon, Integration Problems of the Planned Economies, London 1965, pp. 190–195.

[11] M. *Kaser,* Comecon, Integration Problems of the Planned Economies, London 1965.

[12] *Khruschev's* remarks to a party of Hungarian journalists. Quoted by *Kaser,* op. cit., p. 59.

[13] O. *Bogomolow,* Voprosy economiki, n° II, 1963, pp. 5–6. Quoted by *Kaser,* op. cit., pp. 37–38.

take into account the international division of labour, no calculations have been made for this purpose».[14]

«Is it possible to suggest to a people's democracy, which has more favourable conditions of raw material production, that it should develop only its heavy industry, while we develop only light industry and agriculture? It is known that the development of heavy industry is much more costly than that of light industry. Can we demand of a friendly country that it should have a substantial part of its national income invested in coal mining, metal production and other branches of heavy industry, and leave us to develop only the cheap branches of the national economy?»[15]

In spite of all these difficulties, trade between the Comecon countries has increased and may increase further in the future. But it remains inadequately small. In his book, published in 1965, *Michael Kaser* remarked that the industrial output of the Comecon group is as large as that of the European Common Market and the British Commonwealth put together, but its trade – both among its members and with the rest of the world – amounts to only a quarter of theirs. In the years elapsed since 1965 the position has not changed fundamentally.

IX. The Problem today

In the free market world, no influential political party advocates international freedom of trade. The arguments in favour of it, which a century ago were widely understood by the electorate, have been much forgotten and now can be defended only by minorities.

Conservative parties have no longer articulate programmes. They are usually pressure groups which uphold the interests of the people who finance them. If these people are entrepreneurs who believe they will benefit by some protectionist measure, the party generally supports it; so, to-day, most conservative parties are protectionist.

The same thing may be said of many so-called liberal parties. Often they are less liberal – in the original sense of the word – than the conservatives. This is the case of the Liberal parties of Great Britain and the Federal Republic of Germany.

But as a rule socialists surpass all other parties in their efforts to restrict foreign trade. They know from experience that their founding fathers, from *Plato* downwards, were right in thinking that a socialist community should try to be as autarkic as possible, and commit to its government the country's little foreign trade. They have realized that socialism means, in the last resort, the fusion of politics and economics, the granting of economic power to political authority. Nowadays, even in a mixed economy, the government can take almost any measure which it thinks conducive to the welfare of the citizens or to the winning of votes in the next election. If a measure has bad consequences, or if anything goes awry, the government can take other measures to try to correct the situation. And the socialists wish to suppress all limits to this power of governments.

From this wish derives their position in relation to the Common Market. This is not a liberal institution, but membership of it sets limits to economic nationalism. This explains why European socialist and communist parties, lukewarm at the beginning towards it, have become more and more hostile with the passing of time.

[14] *T. Liska and A. Marias,* Optimum Returns and the International Division of Labour, in: the Hungarian paper Kozgazdasagi Szemle number I, 1954, pp. 75–94. Quoted by *Kaser*, op. cit., p. 54.
[15] Hungarian Paper Szabad Nep, 31 July 1955. Quoted by *Kaser*, op. cit., p. 52.

Besides this, the socialist – like the conservative and liberal parties – are today pressure groups defending the interests of the people who finance them. In recent months, socialist and communist parties in the Common Market countries have opposed the entry of Portugal, Spain and Greece into the E. E. C. Their main reason is that this entry would, in the first instance at least, damage the agricultural interests of the Common Market nations with which the socialist parties have close connections and with which they wish to have closer connections still.

The free trade traditions of the British Labour party lasted a long time. Even after the Second World War they had a representative in *Ernest Bevin*. In a statement to the House of Commons he said that he longed for the time when the only necessary things to travel abroad would be to walk to Victoria Station, to buy a ticket, and to sit in the train with a few pounds in one's pocket. But the logical consequences of socialist policies in the long years the party has been in office compelled it to adopt more and more anti-liberal measures in matters relating to foreign trade. And the left wing of the Labour party advocates further measures still, including quantitative restrictions of imports.

It was through a Labour government that Britain officially applied for membership of the Common Market. However when this was achieved, subsequent labour governments have resented the ties which membership has imposed on their power to curtail the economic freedom of their subjects. The left wing of the Labour party has actually called for the abandonment of the Common Market. The more moderate elements of Labour, where liberal traditions linger, are trying to preserve membership and to make it consistent with the radical socialist measures asked for by the left.

In the last four or five years the United States has introduced measures to keep out imports. Both the Republican and the Democratic parties are responsible for this. But the Democratic party, which used to be the free trade party, is now more inspired by socialist ideas and is probably more prone to protectionism as a consequence. In South America, Canada and Australia, the parties with stronger socialist influence are more inclined to protectionism.

Although the course of events has been not exactly the same in every country, in general it may be said that in the middle of the nineteenth century freedom for the internal economy of most countries was greater than ever before or afterwards. Correspondingly, the decade of the eighteen sixties was the time of maximum freedom for international trade. At the beginning of the second half of the century, State intervention of internal economies increased. With some ups and downs, this has been increasing until now. Around 1880 a protectionist movement started which has not yet ceased. There have been free trade reactions, such as after the Second World War, when the G. A. T. T. was created. However there seems to have been a long term trend since the middle of the nineteenth century towards intervention and socialism within countries, and another long term trend since 1880 towards foreign trade protectionism. The parallelism, with a lag, of these two tendencies does not appear to be a matter of chance.

Summary

Collectivism and the International Order

In the nineteenth century socialists were often considered internationalist by themselves and by others. Now communist and socialist governments and parties concentrate their attention on their own national economies; international ideals and programmes have receded in their perspective. What are the reasons for this change?

Collectivism is essentially nationalist. Early socialist writers (*Plato, Morus, Saint-Simon, Fichte*) described autarkic communities. – But in the nineteenth century liberal thinkers (*Hume, Adam Smith*, etc.) convinced the enlightened opinion of the advantages of internationalism. Great Britain adopted free trade and other countries liberalized their foreign economic policies. Internal and external economic freedom produced growth and welfare. To preach national isolation in such an atmosphere would have been political suicide for the socialists; so they declared themselves in favour of free trade. But they never formulated a doctrine which could reconcile internal control of the economy with external freedom.

In 1902 N. G. *Pierson* published an article which contains the first scientific analysis of the relations between socialism and foreign trade. He suggested that countries which might adopt socialism would be obliged to create an international market to determine the prices of goods for foreign transactions.

In 1917 communists came to power in Russia, and soon after socialist parties participated in European governments. These facts revealed to them the internal contradictions of their nineteenth century programmes. They quickly forgot their free trade tradition and adopted autarky in Russia and protectionist policies elsewhere. The British Labour Party persisted longer in its free trade ideas than other socialist parties, but once it had abandoned them, it became one of the most protectionist.

Socialists argued that colonialism was a necessary consequence of capitalism. But they never could prove that, and the loss of colonies was accompanied by prosperity in the former metropoles: Japan, the Netherlands, the Federal Republic of Germany.

In the communist countries, the difficulties to organize foreign trade and its smallness are further proofs of the lack of a socialist doctrine of international economic relations.

From the middle of the nineteenth century until now, State intervention in the economic life has been increasing (with some ups and downs), and foreign trade has been less and less free (with ups and downs, too). The parallelism of these two tendencies is not due to chance.

Gerard Curzon and Victoria Curzon Price

The Undermining of the World Trade Order

I. Introduction: The deteriorating trade scene

In December 1971 the representatives of the principal industrialized countries met in Washington to perform an emergency operation on a dying patient – the Bretton Woods fixed exchange-rate system. On this occasion they also agreed to hold a new round of GATT trade negotiations, which would open as soon as the United States had passed the appropriate trade legislation enabling the President to negotiate with foreign powers on behalf of the US Congress. This legislation was long in coming. In the meantime the Bretton Woods system died and OPEC raised the price of oil. When the US Trade Bill of 1974 was finally passed, the world was a different place. The GATT trade negotiations in fact openend officially in Tokyo in September 1973, slightly ahead of the US trade legislation and just before the upheavals of the Yom Kippur war and have been with us for the last five years. They have gone through various titular mutations and have been known successively as the Nixon Round, the Tokyo Round and finally as the Multilateral Trade Negotiations – a safe title which has proved longer-lived than the other two. At the time of writing it is still not clear what the outcome of five and a half years of trade negotiations will be. A conclusion there must be, however, because the US Trade Legislation expires in 1979 and the US Congress must be given time to ratify the agreements – if any – that have been negotiated in Geneva. Whatever the outcome – and opinions range from the deeply pessimistic to the cautiously optimistic – the world trade order that will emerge will be both less secure and less universal than that which governed inter-state trade relations from 1958 to 1971.

It is always difficult to put precise dates to epochs, but 1958–1971 was the period during which convertibility and fixed exchange rates under IMF rules were applied by most developed countries. Under this system the world trade order was particulary favoured, but the very expansion of trade and productivity that it helped to create sowed some of the seeds of the disequilibria that were to affect the 1970s. However, there is an important organic link between international trade and international monetary systems. Under fixed exchange rates and exchange control, a trade system based on market forces cannot survive; under fixed exchange rates and convertibility, it flourishes, but such a monetary system is not viable over the longer term: from time to time exchange rates have to change to reflect changes in countries' underlying competitive positions and different rates of inflation. Under flexible exchange rates and convertibility, a trade system can flourish too, but the extra element of constant change and uncertainty introduced by daily exchange rate variations seems to have a dampening effect compared with the apparently more perfect but in the long run equally unstable fixed exchange rate system.

The point to remember is that the present rather chaotic appearance of the international monetary scene should not be confused with the absence of order. As long as currencies remain freely convertible, at least for the purpose of financing current transactions, we are in a very orderly system, fully compatible with a trade system based on market rather than governmental decisions. There is no denying, however, that the instability in currency markets, due mainly to short-term capital account transactions, has been in part transmitted to international trade, which in turn has raised a number of issues for the international trade order.

The GATT Multilateral Trade Negotiations (MTNs) have been conducted in a flexible exchange rate environment. Far from making agreements based on reciprocity and mutual advantage easier to achieve, however, governments are as anxious as ever to ensure that they do not «give away» in terms of import access as much as they «gain» in terms of new export opportunities. This might seem surprising, in as much as governments no longer have to fulfil strict parity obligations, but as *Harry Johnson* has pointed out, flexible exchange rates remove the external (balance-of-payments) rationale for reciprocity, but not the internal justification, that is, the need to balance the losses experienced in the import-competing sector with gains in the export sector. Indeed, he argues that floating rates may make it more difficult to reduce tariffs on the basis of reciprocity because «the rest of the economic population . . . instead of being probably favourably inclined, in view of the net benefits to them as consumers . . . are faced with general uncertainty about the effects of trade liberalization on their own economic welfare», due to exchange rate fluctuations.[1]

In addition, most European governments have spent the last five years fighting inflation with conservative economic policies, while in the United States organized labour, traditionally a supporter of liberal trade policies, has turned protectionist because several developing countries joined Japan as efficient producers of manufactured goods which unsurprisingly happened to threaten a maximum of jobs.

As a result of all these various factors, the principal negotiating countries entered the arena with a marked lack of enthusiasm. And while they played out the leisurely game of diplomatic bargaining, the trade order upon which they were building began to crumble. A paradoxical situation developed whereby one set of government officials was given the task of reducing barriers to trade and improving the world trade order, while another set was required to devise subtle new barriers to trade and undermine the existing trade order. That this should happen is in itself not surprising: governments pursue so many different objectives that conflicts and contradictions are bound to appear sooner rather than later.[2] But in fact, the paradox is more apparent than real. The efforts directed towards freer trade are aimed mainly at manufactured goods traded between developed countries with similar relative prices (North-North trade), while the process of trade restriction applies mainly to trade in manufactured goods between countries with very dissimilar relative prices, that is, between the North Atlantic countries on the one hand, and Japan and certain advanced developing countries on the other (North-South and North-East trade). Such a hybrid combination of liberalism and protection is a familiar feature of customs union theory and it could be argued that a North Atlantic preferential trading zon is in the process of being created. This is the antithesis of the GATT, whose objective is to establish a universal, non-discriminatory trading order.

Although the growing trade restraints take many forms — ranging from the abuse of anti-dumping duties and emergency import quotas to volontary export restraints, export quotas and cartels — we shall concentrate on two forms of protection, namely, export restraints and industrial policies.

---

[1] *Harry G. Johnson*, «Trade Negotiations and the New International Monetary System», Commercial Policy Issues, Graduate Institute of International Studies, Geneva, 1976, p. 24.

[2] *J. Tumlir*, «The Economic and Trade Policy Problems of the 1980s», mimeo, 13/4/1978, p. 2.

These exemplify the increased use of discretionary power by the state in areas of micro-economic decision-making formerly left to market forces. We shall show, firstly, that they are used with growing frequency, secondly that because they are often used together, their impact is greatly magnified, and, finally, that they are symptomatic of a collective rejection of the market as an allocator of resources stemming from a craving for security. The idea that mankind can bend natural forces to its will is deeply embedded in occidental thought, and economics is no exception. In this domain, however, it is not the ecology of the Nile basin, or marine life in the North Sea that is at stake, but the very keystone of our social structure – individual liberty.

II. Export restraints

Export restraints can be divided into three broad categories. First there are fully recognized export restrictions which enjoy the sanctity of multilateral treaty law – restrictions on textile exports from developing countries being for the time being the only case in point. Secondly, there are export restrictions agreed upon bilaterally by developing country governments at the request of developed country governments, which usually take the form of an informal exchange of diplomatic notes but may also be included in a formal document. Such ad hoc arrangements cover a mixed bag of goods and are usually supposed to be temporary. Despite their informal nature, however, they do constitute treaties and create international rights and obligations. As *Jackson* points out: «International agreements are not limited to those embodied in formal documents, authenticated with ceremony, but include . . . the specifying of an arrangement, together with mutual assurances and understandings as to how all parities will behave in response».[3] According to this view there is no difference in law between a «voluntary» export restraint entered into by one country at the request of another, and an «orderly marketing arrangement» between two countries. Finally, arrangements may be concluded between private producers in the exporting and importing countries to limit trade. Such arrangements tend to be illegal in terms of domestic law, but are frequently encouraged by governments, because the second type of arrangements (ad hoc inter-governmental agreements) conflict with the General Agreement of Tariffs and Trade, to which most governments have subscribed and which constitutes the theoretical basis of the current international legal trade order.

1. Multilateral export restrictions

The current problem of export restraints is linked to that of «market disruption», the earliest post-war manifestation of which occurred in the 1950s and 1960s, when Japan emerged from its post-war reconstruction phase as an efficient exporter of manufactured products especially textiles. When Japan acceded to GATT in 1955, fourteen countries, including France, Britain and the Benelux, invoked Article XXXV, which absolved them of the need to grant full, non-discriminatory treatment to Japan for as long as they wished. Other members of GATT simply invoked balance-of-payments difficulties and

---

[3] *John H. Jackson*, Legal problems of International Economic Relations, American Casebook Series, West Publishing Co., St. Paul, Minn. 1977, p. 105.

their right to exercise «some degree of discrimination as between sources of supply» (Article XIV of GATT and VIII of the IMF) by virtue of the «scarce currency» clause – and no currency was scarcer than the yen. Even after 1958, by which time most western European countries had made their currencies convertible on current account, many of them continued to discriminate against Japanese exports on balance-of-payments grounds.

The GATT set up a working party on the «Avoidance of Market Disruption» in December 1959 to study the problem of Japan and how to integrate it more fully into the trading system while guaranteeing the interests of existing members. It was, «of course, recognized that sharp increases in imports, over a brief period of time and in a narrow range of commodities, can have serious economic, political and social repercussions in the importing countries»,[4] and it can be seen from the working party's report that Japan was prepared to deal with the matter «by friendly consultation under Article XXII or by voluntary export control»[5]. The working party's investigations in fact revealed that this was exactly how the problem of market disruption was being dealt with in Europe and the United States[6]. In the end, Japan succeeded in persuading its developed-country trade partners to withdraw their reservations under Article XXXV and to give Japan the nominal legal right to full, non-discriminatory treatment, on the understanding that Japan would cooperate over the problem of market disruption and exercise, if necessary, voluntary export controls. The legal form of Japan's accession to GATT had altered, but the underlying reality had not.

While ad hoc governmental or private export restraints can be applied from time to time on a few well-defined products here and there, without raising the embarrassing question of their legality, it is quite another matter when such restraints become semipermanent and cover a wide range of goods. It then becomes necessary to clothe them in a general mantle of legal respectability.

This, in effect, has happened to trade in textiles. In July 1961 the United States called a meeting of countries involved in trade in cotton textiles, whose outcome was an agreement according to which any importing country could «request any participating country to restrain, at a specified level not lower than the level prevailing for the (previous) twelve-month period», its exports of cotton textiles causing or threatening to cause market disruption.[7] The Short-Term Arrangement Regarding Cotton Textiles entered into force for a year in October 1961 and on its expiration it was replaced by the Long-Term Arrangement Regarding International Trade in Cotton Textiles (LTA). It is significant that the term «arrangement» was used rather than «agreement»: it suggests that the cotton exporting countries did not agree to see their rights under GATT diminished, but reluctantly submitted to pressure put upon them by more powerful importing countries. It is also highly interesting, in view of the subsequent extension of the LTA to cover all branches of the textile and clothing industries, to note that the signatories also «recognize that, since these measures are intended to deal with the special problems of cotton textiles, they are not to be considered as lending themselves to application in other fields.» (LTA, Article 1).

Briefly, the Long-Term Arrangement legitimized bilateral agreements to restrain exports. The only limitation placed on such agreements was that the existence of market disruption should be acknowledged by both parties and that provision be made for growth in trade of at least 5 per cent per annum. Exporters, however, simply switched to

[4] GATT, Doc Spec. (59) 222 p. 5.
[5] GATT, Doc. SR 15/17 p. 153.
[6] GATT, Doc. L/1164.
[7] GATT Secretariat, BISD 10/S p. 19.

textiles other than cotton and continued to expand production and trade. The problem of market disruption for import-competing firms was thus not solved, but shifted to other sectors, and in 1973 the arrangement was broadened. The word «cotton» was dropped from the title, as was all reference to the time-frame involved: the «Arrangement Regarding International Trade in Textiles», known as the Multifibre Agreement or MFA entered into force on 1 January 1974 for four years[8]. All forms of textiles and clothing were now brought into the legalized system of export restraint, and an institutional improvement could be discerned in the shape of the Textiles Surveillance Body which was to supervise and monitor the bilateral agreements negotiated within its framework. A growth rate of 6 per cent per annum (as opposed to 5) was provided for in the event that restrictions lasted over a year.

The MFA was carefully worded so as not to conflict too openly with GATT – indeed, the parties stated clearly in the preamble that they were «determined» to have full regard to the «principles and objectives» of GATT.

The MFA nevertheless departs from GATT in two respects. First, it permits the use of export or import quotas to cope with cases of severe market disruption, whereas one of the important general principles of the GATT system is to forbid the use of quantitative trade controls (except in a few specified situations which do not include market disruption). The original reason behind this distinction was a general understanding that protection by means of tariffs was compatible with an international trade system based on market principles, since it worked impartially through the price mechanism, whereas protection by means of quotas was not, since it worked through direct government intervention. More specifically, Article XI of GATT states quite clearly that:

«No prohibitions or restrictions other than duties, taxes or other charges, whether made effective through quotas, import or export licences, or other measures, shall be instituted or maintained by any contracting party on the importation of any product of the territory of any other contracting party or on the exportation or sale for export of any product destined for the territory of any other contracting party.»

From this it is clear that the categoric prohibition of quotas extends to export as well as to import restraint, and therefore covers the comparatively recent innovation in protection constituted by quantitative export restraints as opposed to import controls. Secondly, the MFA departs from another, equally fundamental, GATT rule of nondiscrimination in the application of trade restrictions. Whereas Article XIX of the General Agreement, dealing with safeguards in cases of market disruption, permits the use of non-discriminatory trade restraints (unilaterally imposed by the importing country), the MFA states that restrictions on trade in textiles must be agreed upon bilaterally and «shall be limited to the precise products and to countries whose exports of such products are causing market disruption» (MFA, Article 3.2).

GATT's rule of non-discrimination is to be found repeated several times throughout the General Agreement. It expresses the view that while it is acceptable for a country to favour its national producers over foreign sources of supply, it is not done to grant a more favourable treatment to one set of foreigners than to another. This principle is well founded both in law and economics. In economics it ensures that the lowest-cost foreign supplier will expand at the expense of higher-cost foreign suppliers, which leads to the second-best optimum (given that the first-best optimum of free trade is not attainable). In law, the principle of non-discrimination guarantees the trading rights of smaller and weaker countries, whose ability to bargain for conditions of equal access to markets is, in the absence of law, inferior to that of larger and stronger ones. Lately this legal protection

---

[8] GATT Secretariat, BISD, 21/S pp. 3–19 contains the text of the MFA.

has been sacrificed by the principal beneficiaries (the small, the weak, the poor) in exchange for tariff preferences, granted to them by developed countries. By dint of uniting their forces, and in the teeth of strong opposition on the part of the strong and the rich, developing countries succeeded in obtaining a waiver from the principle of non-discrimination for the General System of Preferences in 1971.[9] Without wishing to enter into the debate as to how much, if at all, developing countries have gained from this system, it is noteworthy that the MFA, permitting discriminatory trade controls on developing countries' textile exports, followed in within a year. Having derided the principle of non-discrimination for so long, developing countries were in no position to invoke it when it came to measures introduced by the rich and the strong to cope with market disruption. They had to take the good with the bad, and learn within the space of a few months that discriminination cuts both ways. In a global sense the benefits of GSP are probably fully offset by the losses due to the MFA, but they are distributed unevenly across the developing world, with the most efficient bearing the losses and the least efficient reaping most of the gains. That this reduces income for everybody in the long run is surely obvious.

Be this as it may, there is no doubt that the MFA, with its 40-odd signatories, its published text and its official status within the GATT system, constitutes international trade law. The hurdle of incompatibility with the basic GATT law is cleared by various injunctions to use trade restraints «sparingly», to «endeavour to avoid discriminatory measures» (Article 3.2) and to limit their duration to «periods not exceeding one year, subject to renewal or extension for additional periods of one year» (Article 3.8). This in practice means indefinitely, because of the plural form of the word «periods» but at first glance, it looks as though such restrictions are intended to be strictly temporary.

Indeed, it is a recognized principle of international law that one may depart from existing legal obligations if circumstances change fundamentally, and great emphasis is placed on the exceptional nature of the MFA. Thus it is mentioned that «since measures taken under this Arrangement are intended to deal with the special problems of textile products, such measures should be considered as exceptional and not lending themselves to application to other fields» (Article 1.7). The similarity of this phrase compared with the one used in the LTA is striking. It was obviously lifted straight out of the Cotton Textile Arrangement and inserted in the Multifibre Arrangement, this action in itself giving the lie to the statement that «such measures should be considered as exceptional and not lending themselves to application to other fields». One could not hope to find a better documented example of *George Orwell*'s «Double talk».

In fact, the MFA does constitute a precedent in the sense that it provides a model of what general principles of trade law to apply in cases of severe market disruption: namely discriminatory import or export quotas. Whether the legal experts like it or not, this is precisely how developed countries have coped with market disruption in a host of industries since 1973.

Furthermore, just as the Long-Term Cotton Textile Arrangement was succeeded by the more comprehensive MFA, so the latter has become more restrictive with time. Developing countries' exports of textiles in fact grew faster than 6 per cent per annum from 1973–1978, and according to the EEC at least, the Arrangement needed «tightening up». In the course of the negotiations leading to its renewal in December 1977, the EEC offered «firm guarantees of access» in exchange for a commitment on the part of less-developed exporting countries «to limit their supplies to levels which the Community can bear

---

[9] GATT Secretariat, BISD, 18/S, p. 24–26.

and to accept orderly growth of these exports in the future»[10]. In effect, what happened was that the MFA was renewed without change, but the thirty-two bilateral agreements which the EEC negotiated in 1977–78 under its auspices became stricter. The growth in EEC imports was linked to growth in total domestic consumption in the Common Market, which is likely to be well under 6 per cent per annum for the eight sensitive product categories involved. The problem of the compatibility of these agreements with the basic MFA text has been neatly dealt with as follows: reference is made in the Protocol extending the MFA for another four years to «certain understandings» according to which «it is clearly understood that reasonable departures from certain provisions of the MFA will be jointly agreed in particular cases».[11]

This innocent-sounding phrase introduces an entirely new principle into North-South trade relations, namely that while developing countries may strive to capture a certain share of developed countries' markets, the latter may, at their own discretion, set limits both as to the absolute size of that market share and as to its growth, if any.

We are now a considerable distance from basic GATT principles, but since we have covered it in two separate steps, to the accompaniment of ritual incantations on the theme of «the reduction of trade barriers and the liberalization of world trade in textile products», the event has passed virtually unnoticed.

So much for orderly marketing arrangements which have been given the cloak of respectability in the form of an official «arrangement» like the one regarding international trade in textiles. But at least this arrangement is out in the open. At least the bilateral «agreements» that are negotiated within its frame of reference are recorded and discussed in the Textiles Surveillance Body. At least we know where we are.

2. Informal export restrictions

What is one to think, on the other hand, of all the other inter-governmental arrangements to restrict exports that we know are in operation? There is no GATT «arrangement» concerning international trade in steel products, yet it is a publicly recorded fact[12] that the EEC has negotiated agreements with several steel-producing countries according to which the latter have agreed to respect the EEC's minimum steel price. It is equally well known that Japan restricts the export of (inter alia) sewing machines, ball bearings, electronic apparatus and automobiles[13] (although it is not always clear exactly who does the restricting – the government or the industry). It is also known that the United States has over 200 bilateral agreements with exporting countries to restrict exports «voluntarily», only 70 of which concern textiles. The remainder cover steel, automobiles, TV sets, shoes, leather handbags and meat[14].

Although most developed countries respect their GATT obligations under Article X to publish their trade laws, regulations, juridical decisions and administrative rulings of general application, there is no comprehensive obligation to notify them to the GATT Secretariat. They therefore lie buried in the mountains of regulations issued daily by the modern state, and to extract them from the surrounding mass poses a familiar economic

---

[10] Bulletin of the European Communities, No. 12, 1977, pp. 9–10.
[11] Idem, p. 10.
[12] Bulletin of the European Communities, various issues, 1978.
[13] IMF, Annual Report of Exchange Restrictions, 1977, p. 271.
[14] Neue Zürcher Zeitung, «Gefahrvoller Protektionismus nach Maß», Fernausgabe Nr. 97, 28. April 1978.

and engineering problem: will the value of the final product justify the cost of extracting it from what is undoubtedly very low-grade ore? The answer, until recently, was no, but in March 1978 the GATT Secretariat began to issue on a «restricted» basis a bi-yearly document entitled «Survey of Developments in Commercial Policy». This is a welcome and courageous initiative, of which probably not all the contracting parties will approve.

In the meantime, contracting parties do have obligations to notify the GATT Secretariat of a number of trade measures, especially those which involve some departure from general GATT rules, inter alia, balance of payments restrictions (Article XII), quotas (Article XIII), subsidies (Article XVI), state trading enterprises (Article XVII) and emergency measures (Article XIX), not to mention agricultural regulations, customs unions and free trade areas, anti-dumping and countervailing duties and many more that need not detain us here.

Since «voluntary» export restraints and orderly marketing arrangements are trade restrictions of a quantitative nature, they fall within the terms of Article XIII, according to which contracting parties must «promptly inform all other contracting parties having an interest in supplying the product concerned» and «shall give public notice thereof» (Article XIII, 3(c)). Although the article is written mainly in terms of import quotas, the final paragraph adds, as if by afterthought «the principles of this Article shall also extend to export restrictions» (Article XIII, 5).

This, however, does not amount to an obligation to inform the GATT Secretariat regularly, so that it can centralize and process all the relevant data, and the uncertainty at present surrounding trade regulations constitutes a considerable barrier to trade in its own right.

The International Monetary Fund, by virtue of its yearly review of its members' currency controls, monitors developments in the field of trade regulation as well, and probably has more information on such matters at its disposal than does the GATT Secretariat. Not all of it is published, however. Table 1 is gleaned from the last two issues of the IMF's Annual Report on Exchange restrictions and undoubtedly constitutes the mere tip of the iceberg as far as export restrictions are concerned. Only eleven countries are expressly listed as using export restrictions on trade, and not all of them are directly related to the problem of market disruption. For instance, the purpose of the Australian restrictions on the export of primary products is not to forestall market disruption in consuming countries, but to raise the export price of Australian primary products and encourage their further processing locally. However, the export restrictions listed for Taiwan, Hong Kong, India, Japan and others in the table are of the type being discussed.

Countries using export restrictions, as listed in IMF's Annual Report on Exchange Restrictions, 1976, 1977.

Country	Products (if mentioned)	Reference
Australia	«to assist in the orderly marketing of primary products».	IMF/76/p. 48
Taiwan	Export quotas on canned mushrooms and asparagus. Restrictions on textiles and stainless steel flatware.	IMF/77/p. 125
Hong Kong	Export licences required for textiles, foodstuffs and electrical products.	IMF/77/p. 218
India	Exports subject to minimum prices: mica, tobacco, handwoven woolen carpets.	IMF/77/p. 227
Jamaica	Export licences for ready-made garments.	IMF/77/p. 266

Country	Products (if mentioned)	Reference
Japan	Export licences on textiles and sewing machines, mentioned as examples only.	IMF/77/p. 270
Korea	«Certain exports on a restricted list require individual licenses».	IMF/77/p. 282
Malaysia	Subject to export licensing: all textiles, certain confectionery, tiles, fish meal, bricks and so-called «dollar-area goods».	IMF/77/p. 301
New Zealand	Export quotas on beef and veal to the US and cheddar-type cheese to the UK. Export controls on tallow and mutton.	IMF/77/p. 308
Pakistan	Licences needed for 24 items as well as for sports goods; minimum prices maintained for unspecified «other» goods and for textile products for export to the EEC.	IMF/77/p. 356
Singapore	«Exports of certain textiles to: Austria, Belgium, Denmark, France, the FRG, Ireland, Italy, Luxemburg, the Netherlands, Norway, Sweden, the UK and the US are subject to quantitative restriction».	IMF/77/p. 397

Although only nine of the countries listed in Table 1 are expressly mentioned as exercizing export controls to forestall the imposition of import restrictions by other countries, the vast majority of developing countries practise export licensing as a matter of course. There are three reasons for this. Firstly they often wish to guarantee adequate supplies to domestic consumers or domestic industries of essential products and to prevent their export in an unprocessed state. Secondly, they wish to ensure that the foreign exchange proceeds from exports duly turn up in the central bank at the official exchange rate, and will only grant an export licence if the exporter undertakes to deposit his export earnings with the exchange control authorities within a specified period of time. Thirdly, governments wish to ensure that the stated export price corresponds to the market value of the exported goods, and is not an under-stated intra-firm transfer price, and will frequently only deliver an export licence if the declared price is equal or superior to a set «reference» price. Since the administrative machinery is already in existence, it is all too easy for such countries to add a fourth objective to the export control apparatus – that of restricting exports to developed countries in order to forestall import restrictions. Oil exporting countries aside, there are only ten developing countries that do not operate a fully fledged export licensing system[15]. On the other hand, most developed countries have dismantled the administrative apparatus for the quantitative control of trade and there might even be a public outcry if it were reinstated. In these circumstances it is not surprising that modern protection takes the form of export rather than import restriction.

More detailed information concerning export restrictions operated by South Korea, Taiwan, Colombia and Singapore has been published by the IMF in a booklet entitled «The Rise in Protectionism»[16] from which it is apparent that trade restrictions of all kinds have increased significantly in number since 1973. It is frequently (and correctly) noted that the level of protection in the trade system at any one time cannot be determined in an absolute sense. It is less frequently pointed out, however, that such pre-

---

[15] Bahamas, Grenada, Guatemala, Haiti, Honduras, Hong Kong, Israel, Mexico, Nicaragua and Panama. IMF, Annual Report on Exchange Restrictions, op. cit.

[16] *Bahram Nowzad,* The Rise in Protectionism, IMF Pamphlet Series, No. 24, Washington, D.C., 1978.

cise information is not strictly necessary. It is quite enough for most purposes to know in which direction one is going, and the available evidence is sufficiently detailed to provide a fairly clear picture. If one takes the three countries for which the IMF provides information in numerial form (Taiwan, Colombia and South Korea) the number of restrictive measures affecting their exports rose from an insignificant level in 1971–1973, to 16 in 1974 and 1975, 22 in 1976 and 42 in 1977.

Number of measures affecting exports

	1971	1972	1973	1974	1975	1976	1977	cumulative total
Taiwan	–	–	–	–	1	6	19	26
Colombia	–	–	–	2	1	1	1	5
South Korea	3	–	1	14	14	15	22	69
Total by year	3	–	1	16	16	22	42	

Source: *Bahram Nowzad*, The Rise in Protectionism, IMF, Washington D.C., 1978

3. Private arrangements to restrict exports

However informal these arrangements may be, they nevertheless represent inter-governmental arrangements. They may be in breach of GATT, but they follow the basic lines laid down in the Multifibre Arrangement. What is one to think, on the other hand, of private arrangements to restrict exports? What is one to think of the arrangement between the British Society of Motor Manufacturers and Traders (SMMT) and the Japanese Automobile Manufacturers Association (JAMA) according to which the latter has promised to take a «prudent» approach to the UK market?[17]

If inter-governmental agreements are but incompletely recorded, and of doubtful legality, private arrangements to achieve the same purpose are even more phantasmic and beyond the reach of the all-too-short arm of the law. One only gets to know of their existence by accident, when an anti-trust authority clumsily stumbles into one, or when they have been in existence so long that no one really bothers to hide them any more.

The EEC anti-trust authorities proclaimed in 1972[18] that they would prosecute any private arrangements to restrict imports into the Common Market whether engaged in by member or by non-member firms. The occasion for this pronouncement was a growing awareness of the fact that many Japanese products were not entering the EEC as freely as they might[19]. After this statement, a number of self-limitation agreements were notified to the Commission, only two of which, however, gave rise to published decisions. One concerned an agreement between two French ball-bearing manufacturers (SKF Compagnie d'Applications Méchaniques and Société Nouvelle de Roulements) and four Japanese firms (Nippon Seiko Kaisha, Koyo Seiko Ltd., Fujikoshi Ltd., and NTN Toyo Bearing Ltd.) according to which the latter had agreed to raise their prices to French levels. The other involved an agreement between five French mushroom packers and the

---

[17] Financial Times, 9 November 1978, p. 7.
[18] EEC Commission, Journal Officiel, No. C. 111, 21 October 1972, p. 13.
[19] Questions were also being raised in the European Parliament as to the legal status of such private restrictive arrangements: see Questions écrites, Nos. 192 and 299 (1972).

Taiwan Mushroom Packers United Export Corporation which divided up the German market for tinned mushrooms by means of agreed prices and export quotas[20].

In both cases, the parties were ordered to discontinue their arrangements, though only the French mushroom packers were actually fined. A great many more such arrangements are obviously in existence some of which have presumably been notified to the Commission (this protects the parties from possible fines). But it is noteworthy that no public action against private voluntary export restraints has been undertaken by the EC Commission since January–February 1975.

This is partly because the Commission has elevated such private auto-limitation arrangements to the status of public restraints, either in the shape of anti-dumping duties (the case of ball bearings) or of inter-governmental treaties permitting the use of quotas (the case of man-made fibres) or of minimum prices (the case of steel). On the other hand, private agreements restricting the import of automobiles, television sets and other relatively sophisticated apparatus appear to exist (if newspaper reports are to be believed) yet do not seem to be prosecuted. While one can understand why this might be so – the recession of course multiplies the «need» for private voluntary restraints and makes prosecution thereof under anti-trust legislation distinctly unpopular – it is nevertheless disturbing that the application of the law should seem so flexible.

The frontier between private and public arrangements is sometimes difficult to discern. For instance, when developed countries start anti-dumping investigations, they may end up negotiating more or less directly with the relevant industrial groups in third-world exporting countries, where the mere threat of an official anti-dumping investigation is often quite enough to persuade exporters to promise to raise their prices. In the case of such «out of court» settlements, it is impossible to tell whether dumping really occurred and whether or not anti-dumping duties would have been justified.

Irrespective of the legal merits, it is for instance interesting to note that when the EEC Commission began an anti-dumping investigation on haematite pig-iron from Brazil, Brazilian exporters (not the Brazilian government) «gave undertakings» that satisfied the Commission that the introduction of protective measures was «unnecessary at present».[21] Similar «undertakings» have been reported for quartz crystals, kraft liner, wire rod, steel angles and shapes, steel bars, rods, and sheets from the EFTA countries, Japan, Canada and South Africa.

The enforcement of such semi-private, semi-public hybrid agreements of course presents few problems, for the Commission is free to resume anti-dumping investigations whenever it pleases.

4. Some Normative Questions

Are minimum price arrangements to be preferred to export quotas?

Export restraints tend to be classifiable into two broad categories: either the exporting country promises to «respect» the price level of the importing country, or it undertakes to keep shipments within a pre-determined ceiling, or it occasionally promises to do both. One might be tempted to argue, by analogy with the well-known distinction between tariffs and import quotas, that an export restraint which operated through minimum prices might be preferable to one which worked with outright controls, and in some instances

[20] EEC Commission, Fourth Report on Competition Policy, April 1975, p. pp. 50–51.
[21] EEC Commission, Journal Officiel, No. C. 187, 5 August 1977.

one might be right. But it should not be overlooked that an undertaking to respect the importing country's price level is the equivalent of a variable import levy: it neutralizes all price competition. There is therefore not much to choose between minimum price arrangements and export quotas: they are both very effective methods of restricting trade.

Are export restraints to be preferred to import restrictions?

It is frequently said that orderly marketing arrangements are admittedly restrictive, but that in a distinctly second-best world, they are preferable to outright import controls, which are their only realistic alternative.

One argument is that if the exporting country is responsible for the administration of the trade restraint, it will be able to give it as wide an interpretation as possible, while if the administration were entrusted to the importing country, the latter would give it as narrow an interpretation as possible. There is some merit to this argument. Japanese exporters became past masters at devising ways to fill their quotas with higher value-added goods, and switching to products not covered by the quotas (switching from restricted passenger cars to unrestricted light commercial vans in the UK, which in turn have just become restricted, thus encouraging Japanese producers to turn to unrestricted heavy vehicles, is a good current example). Indeed, one could hypothesize that selective trade restraints on labour-intensive products caused Japanese firms to climb up the ladder of economic development unusually quickly and, if so, this would be a strong argument in their favour. But when market disruption becomes really acute, as is now the case of textiles in Europe, a quota system is devised which leaves practically no scope for enterprising intra-sectoral shifts.

Another argument is that since the exporting countries are the ones to suffer from trade restrictions, and since they also tend to be much poorer than the importing countries, it constitutes a sort of rough justice that they should, by means of exercizing export restraints, be allowed to collect the rents associated with trade control. However, sweetening the pill in this way is dangerous. In countries where political and economic power is exercised by a small elite, the latter will be able to appropriate the quasi-rents of export restraints, and will end up supporting rather than opposing the system. The tale is told – and can well be believed – that when a representative from a certain developed country went to negotiate an «orderly marketing» arrangement in a developing country, he was approached by the secretary of a local business association and asked how to get one's products included in the list of restricted items. A further drawback to voluntary export restraints is that they practically imply the cartellisation of the export industry. How else would one expect local industrialists to divide the spoils of trade restraint?[22]

On the other hand, an argument in favour of using import quotas to cope with market disruption would be that here, at least, no one denies the existence of an obligation to notify and justify such action to other GATT members. Furthermore, consumers in importing countries might become more aware of the extra tax on their incomes that they are paying, if trade restrictions were imposed at home, rather than by countries on the other side of the world. As it is, perhaps the most important single reason why governments in importing countries are so willing to let exporters in developing countries enjoy the quasi-rents of protection is precisely because they do not want their consuming, voting and tax-paying public to be alerted to the extent of present levels of protection.

---

[22] *Jan Tumlir*, «Comment», in: *Gerard Curzon* and *Victoria Curzon* (eds.), The Multinational Enterprise in a Hostile World, London, 1977, p. 103, draws attention to this point.

In most Western countries, after all, the tariff is a matter of intense political debate in parliament and in the press during which some of the more obvious costs of protection are given a public airing, and protected interests have to explain why they deserve to be singled out for especially favourable treatment. By persuading exporting countries to do the job for them, governments of importing countries neatly avoid the entire public discussion of their trade policies.

On balance, therefore, we consider that import controls, even of a quantitative nature, are preferable to export restraints, however flexible. The long-run cost of allowing exporting countries to administer our import restrictions is to smother the old debate between free trade and protection.

Is public recognition of export restrictions, as for instance under the Multifibre Arrangement, to be preferred to under-cover proliferation?

Put this way, the answer can only be in the affirmative. Since the uncertainty surrounding voluntary export restraints is a trade barrier in its own right, one can only approve of an international aggreement which brings them out into the open. In the same breath, however, one must deplore the fact that a system such as that operated under the protective wing of the MFA should have become part of international trade law. It is a general principle of law that a contract entered into under threat or duress is unenforceable in the courts. The Multifibre Arrangement however, provides a legal framework within which export restraint agreements are entered into under the implicit threat of anti-dumping investigations at best or import controls at worst. Take the uncomfortable position of Hong Kong, which depends on the EEC for about a quarter of its total exports, and on the United States for another quarter. On the other hand, Hong Kong is totally insignificant for either of these two trading mammoths: the EEC depends on the Crown Colony for 0.5 per cent of its exports, and the United States for 0.8 per cent.

Even a giant like India is in very much the same position. While the EEC takes 20 per cent of its exports, India takes only 0.8 per cent of the EEC's exports, and the ratios for the United States are respectively 10 and 1.2 per cent.

In these circumstances, neither Hong Kong nor India is in a position to wield the threat of retaliation provided in Article XXIII of GATT, and which is supposed to protect members from the unilateral confiscation of markets, with which competitive suppliers are often rewarded fot their efforts.

For this reason alone, one should not confuse the legalization of «voluntary» export restraints, even if they are paraded under the blander title of «orderly marketing arrangements» and even if they are embodied in formal instruments indisputably part of international law, with order in the world trade system. To the extent that they represent clearly unequal bargains, extracted by means of explicit or implicit threats, they express the most profound disorder in the world trade system and a retreat from a system based on a balance of rights and obligations to one based on duties and privileges.

Painting the lily, or the urge to improve

No one would dispute the need for constant adaptation and improvement of the rules guiding human conduct, nor – since such rules must reflect the complex and diverse needs of society – the need for some exceptions to the law in particular and well-defined cases. However, if, in the process of adaptation, the exceptions become too numerous, they «eat up» the law, and one enters, imperceptibly, a state of anarchy. There is an analogy here with economics, where policies based on partial equilibrium analysis often turn out to be wrong in practice because one has ignored their impact on other things. Thus with the growing number of exceptions to GATT. Each one, taken singly, has its rationale – and its beneficiaries. But each one helps to erode the basic rule.

For example, one of the «achievements» of the Tokyo Round may well be the legalization of selective safeguards under Article XIX. Briefly, such a reform would release countries from the obligation to apply emergency import restrictions in a non-discriminatory manner. In exchange, they would have to submit to collective surveillance of their selective (i. e. discriminatory) trade controls. This development stems from the fact that Article XIX, which permits the use of emergency tariffs in case of «serious» injury to domestic producers, has in practice been by-passed by the proliferation of «voluntary» export restraints. It is hoped that by permitting a more flexible application of Article XIX, one will tempt governments back into the legal fold.

Quite apart from the doubtful economics of selective safeguards, which penalize the most efficient producer and freeze existing producers into current patterns of trade and production, how is the principle of selectivity, if agreed upon by a significant number of countries, though not by all, to be grafted onto Article XIX of GATT? The principle of non-discrimination will be violated twice over: a knotty legal problem.

More generally, we are told that a great deal of effort in the Tokyo Round has gone into drafting a number of non-tariff barrier «codes». Yet they can only apply as between signatories, wounding yet again GATT's principle of non-discrimination.[23] Thus the negative side-effects of these much-heralded remedies arguably outweigh their (debatable) benefits, and progress on this front may well represent a net loss for world trade order as a whole.

III. Industrial Policy

The economic attributes of government have expanded steadily from the simple provision of public goods and services and the regulation of monopolies (as recognized by the classical school) to encompass macro-economic full-employment policies (as propounded by *Keynes* and his followers) and the redistribution of wealth (as put forward by social market philosophers as different as *Erhard* on the one hand and *Beveridge* on the other).

Lately, people have argued increasingly in favour of adding a fifth economic attribute of government, namely, industrial policy. It is felt that governments should have an industrial «strategy» – a set of long term industrial goals – to guide all-too haphazard market forces through the troubled waters of the daily struggle for survival to some desirable destination. To some extent, governments have had implicit industrial policies for a very long time, since the very act of erecting a tariff establishes a system of incentives and disincentives which affects the pattern of industrial production and the allocation of resources. But tariffs are now thoroughly played out as instruments of industrial strategy. Most industrialized members of GATT have bound the majority of their tariffs, and cannot change them and as for members of the European Economic Community, they have even relinquished sovereignty over their tariffs to the EEC Commission. Non-tariff barriers are increasingly scrutinized and criticized, so direct and indirect subsidies remain the

---

[23] *Gerard and Victoria Curzon,* «The Multi-Tier GATT System», in: *Otto Hieronymi* (ed.), The New Economic Nationalism, Battelle Geneva Research Centre, London, 1979.

last instrument unquestionably still in government hands to direct the economy towards a pre-conceived set of objectives. General subsidies, like tariffs in the past, alter basic market signals, but let individual market operators take the micro-economic decisions which actually lead to the desired allocation of resources.

But modern industrial policy aims at more than merely setting a general framework in this way. It descends increasingly into the micro-economic sphere of economic decision taking, formerly reserved to private decision takers. Industrial policy is therefore gradually encroaching on the market system and replacing it in several areas. Since such decisions are no longer taken on the basis of commercial considerations, a serious question of compatibility with the entire GATT system arises.

For example, President *Kennedy's* aim, stated in 1961, to put a man on the moon within ten years is a good instance of a «macro» strategic objective set by government. Within that general framework, the vast majority of the micro-economic actions which actually put Messrs *Armstrong* and *Aldrin* there in July 1969 was left to the private firms which produced all the elements that went into the project, some of which were imported from foreign firms when they happened to be more competitive or had a unique product.

By way of contrast, when the British government decided to save British Leyland, or the French government decided which of two firms should take over the failing Boussac textile empire, or the Italian government decided to merge Motta and Alemagnia into one huge icecream monopoly, they all took microeconomic industrial policy action, thereby short-circuiting market forces which would otherwise have had unpalatable results – bankruptcy, loss of jobs, loss of output, unwanted foreign take-overs, and so forth. Extensive industrial policies of a micro type are now prevalent in the developed world and constitute, if not a new, at least an enhanced threat to the world trade system.

1. Industrial Policy and the GATT

We shall start with a brief review of GATT rules with regard to industrial policy. The term itself, of course, does not appear in the General Agreement, but the principal instruments of industrial policy are direct subsidies of various kinds, government procurement and (less frequently) outright nationalization, and GATT has fairly clear provisions regarding each of these. As far as subsidies are concerned (Article XVI) a country may grant them on condition that, if they operate «directly or indirectly to increase exports of any product from, or to reduce imports of any product into» its territory, such a country must (a) notify GATT of the extent and nature of the subsidy and (b) should it cause or threaten to cause «serious prejudice» to any other member, the latter may request discussions with a view to «the possibility of limiting the subsidization».

By comparsion with obligations regarding tariffs, for which subsidies are a direct and in many ways superior substitute, these provisions are strict. GATT itself places no restrictions on the use of tariffs as instruments of government policy apart from the obligation to apply them in a non-discriminatory fashion to foreign trade. Nowhere is it expressly stated in GATT, for instance, that if one country's tariff policy causes «serious prejudice» to another contracting party's interests, must there be consultation. Only if a country changes a bound tariff would there be a clear breach of a GATT obligation.

By any other standard of comparison, however, GATT's provisions regarding subsidies are weak in that if a subsidy policy harms another country, all that is required of the government guaranting such aids is to consult on the «possibility» of limiting its impact (it goes without saying that we are discussing here the effect of general subsidies, and not export subsidies, which are clearly prohibited in Article XVI, Section B).

The importing country, however, is free to act unilaterally to protect its interests. Under Article VI, it may introduce a countervailing duty on subsidized imports provided (a) the offsetting duty does not exceed the margin of subsidization and (b) local producers are suffering or are likely to suffer «material injury». Besides giving rise to debates of almost theological intensity on the difference between «serious prejudice» and «material injury», Article VI constitutes a curb on the proliferation of excessive subsidization, or would do so if used more freely. As it is, until now, one of the most effective brakes on the proliferation of subsidies has lain in domestic US trade law, which specifies that imports bearing any subsidy must be taxed by a corresponding countervailing duty, irrespective of whether or not any domestic US producer is being (or is likely to be) injured. This has meant that a great many European exports to the United States could have been subject to countervailing duties, had the application of the law not been temporarily waived during the Tokyo Round negotiations. It also meant that one of the EEC's principal negotiating objectives was to persuade the United States to adopt an «injury criterion» before applying countervailing duties, in line with GATT's Article VI. This is part of the final Tokyo Round package, and if the US Congress accepts it (which is by no means self evident) the world trade system will lose the principal disciplinary measure which dissuades governments from over-subsidizing infant or geriatric industries.

As far as state enterprises are concerned, GATT's Article XVII requires that they should act as though they were privately owned – «solely in accordance with commercial considerations». Thus, governments are not supposed to use nationalization as a hidden method of promoting or protecting this or that industry. The fact that the British coal, steel and shipbuilding industries are nationalized is not, in itself, in breach of GATT but the fact that they do not obey normal commercial criteria, and have to have their chronic losses covered by direct government grants presumably is, because part of their turnover is generated through foreign trade.

If subsidies and state enterprises come within the scope of GATT's provisions, government procurement «for immediate or ultimate consumption in governmental use» is expressly excluded. (Article XVII. 2). Thus it is perfectly in order in terms of international law for governments to «buy national» for their own consumption. The only obligation is not to discriminate between different foreign suppliers in the event that a local supplier should not be forthcoming. The parallel with rules concerning tariffs is clear.

Finally, although these provisions help us to understand the spirit (and the letter) of GATT law, they pale almost to insignificance before the most amazing and far-reaching of GATT's provisions, contained in Article XXIII. This article, entitled «Nullification or Impairment», states that if any member of GATT should consider «that any benefit accruing to it directly or indirectly under this Agreement is being nullified or impaired . . . as the result of

(a) the failure of another contracting party to carry out its obligations under this Agreement, or

(b) the application by another contracting party of any measures, whether or not it conflicts with the provisions of this Agreement, or

(c) the existence of any other situation»

it may approach the offending government and ask for consultation. Should the talks fail, the matter may be referred to the *contracting parties* who, acting collectively, may authorize the injured party to withdraw such concessions as they deem «appropriate in the circumstances».

The important point to note is that Article XXIII can be invoked by any GATT member, even in the absence of any breach of a GATT obligation. Thus any instrument of industrial policy, whether it is mentioned in GATT or not, if it is prejudicial to other countries' trade interests, can, if bilateral talks fail, be subjected to international scrutiny and, ultimately, sanctioned. The problem thus lies not in the inadequacy of the law, which is exceptionally comprehensive, but in a collective conspiracy not to apply it: it is the old problem of people in glass houses not throwing stones.

2. Subsidies and the disruption of trade

From the economic point of view, it is not so much the form which a subsidy takes – direct grants, indirect support through government procurement, or even more remote encouragement through a protective tariff or a tax on other goods – they all have much the same effect in the end. They expand the production of some goods at the expense of others, and thus alter a country's demand for, and supply of, all tradable and traded goods. Other countries' patterns of trade are therefore bound to be affected by them. The question in practice is by how much? And the answer depends partly on the size of the country, or group of countries, applying the subsidy and partly on the size òf the subsidy. Thus, a small country could apply a small subsidy without disrupting other countries' trade patterns. A small country applying a large subsidy, or a large country applying a small subsidy, might be another matter, and of course, a large country applying a large subsidy would be extremely disruptive of international trade. This is why the growth of subsidization in Western Europe and especially the EEC is a matter of considerable concern for the future stability of the trading order.

3. Subsidies and subsidies

Within the broad basket category of subsidies one can establish various sub-categories according to the extent of trade disruption they are likely to cause. The EEC Commission, for instance, in applying Article 93 of the Rome Treaty, makes a clear distinction between investment subsidies, which are deemed to encourage firms to adapt to changing circumstances, and employment subsidies or stop-gap loans to cover operating losses, which are considered to discourage firms from adjusting. Within the generally approved category of investment subsidies, moreover, the ECC Commission (a) limits their intensity (to prevent «des surenchères stériles») and (b) has expressed its disapproval of «certaines activités de prestige dont l'avenir industriel est problématique».[24] We ourselves are not sure that useful distinctions between various subsidies can be drawn along these functional lines because of the «shifting» effect. A firm receiving an investment grant might be able to use some of its own resources to keep on redundant labour or avoid closing down an inefficient plant, while a firm receiving an employment grant might be able to spend some of its own resources on new investment, so it is by no means clear that an investment grant necessarily helps the adjustment process while an employment subsidy does not.

We therefore prefer a classification system based on the level of generality of the aids, whatever shape they may take. There are notable differences between (a) general subsidies available to all firms anywhere and producing any product, (b) aids to all firms producing any product but operating in a specified area (e.g. regional grants), (c) aids to all firms operating anywhere but producing a specified product (e.g. infant or geriatric

---

[24] EEC Commission, Second Report on Competition Policy, April, 1973, p. 90.

industry grants) and (d) aids to specific firms (for reasons of nationalism, prestige, sentimentality or simply employment).

Type (a) subsidies do not distort the allocation of resources directly, but attempt to alter the supply of factors of production, usually capital. The impact of such factor subsidies on the structure of industry is only indirect, in that if they succeed, they will broadly favour the development of capital-intensive industries to the determent of labour-intensive activities. Some general subsidies are designed to reduce the cost of labour (for instance, the British temporary employment subsidy), which encourages the development of labour-intensive manufactures. Such general subsidies will have a minimal impact on other countries' patterns of trade. They will reduce the need to import capital-intensive products generally (in the case of investment subsidies) or labour-intensive products (in the case of employment grants) but they will not affect the allocation of resources within these broad categories. (Countries which do both at once, like the United Kingdom, Sweden and the Netherlands, of course, pursue self-defeating policies). The disrupting effect of such general subsidies is usually small also because governments, if they offer general subsidies, have to spread their resources thinly over the whole range of new and past investments, and their final impact will be almost imperceptible.

This is, indeed one reason why subsidy policies are generally selective. Another reason is that if all industries are encouraged indiscriminatorily, one will emerge with a pattern of production very close to what market forces would have produced anyway – and governments are not prepared to call this an «industrial strategy», since the whole point of having one is to improve on market forces.

Type (b) industrial policies aim at altering the geographical allocation of resources, but are indiscriminate as to industries. They will therefore not affect a country's industrial product mix, unless there are industries which would have invested in the depressed region anyway, in which case they will cause over-investment in this branch and sow problems for the future (the fate of the British shipbuilding industry is a case in point). On the whole, however, given that most modern industries are footloose and not tied down to a particular geographic location, if regional grants are designed merely to offset the disadvantages of location in a depressed region, their impact on trade patterns will be minimal, although their impact on the balance of payments and/or exchange rates might be discernible if the subsidies more than offset the disadvantages of the location.

Type (c) industrial policies – aids to specific industries – will, by their very nature, have a direct impact on the structure of production and, hence, trade. If a government is selective in its choice of industries to promote, as for instance the French government is, its impact on other countries' trade will be far from negligible. If most of its resources, on the other hand, are devoted to regional development, as is the case in the UK, then the chances of causing other countries substantial injury are more remote.

Finally, type (d) subsidies are aimed at helping individual firms, usually to save them from suffering the death penalty under market laws, but also to promote mergers or to encourage a promising company. These also tend to be disruptive of trade because a relatively small sum can make a very big difference to their ability to compete and grow.

The extent of the disruption in either case obviously depends on the size of the firm or industry and the amount of aid it succeeds in obtaining. When the British government puts £ 1.4 billion into British Leyland, or £ 400 million into promoting micro-processors,[25] or the French government pours an estimated 5 billion francs into computers[26] it

---

[25] EEC Commission, Fifth Report on Competition Policy, April, 1976, p. 84, and Financial Times, 7 December 1978, p. 1.

[26] *Jacques Jublin* and *Jean-Michel Quatrepoint,* French Ordinateurs: de l'affaire Bull à l'assassinat du Plan Calcul, eds. *Alain Moreau,* Paris, 1976, p. 272–273.

clearly has more of an effect on other countries' trade patterns than when the UK government props up the Meriden Motor Cycle Company or the French government lengthens Lip's credit facilities. It is therefore the sheer size of the resources at the disposal of governments and their will to use them selectively rather than generally, which constitutes the new element in the trading system, rather than the fact that such a time-honoured practice as subsidization should occur.

For the moment, governments cling to the idea that they should be free to use these vast resources in any way they deem fit. It has not yet become clear that other governments can take similar action, by subsidizing the very same industries, and thus offset the effects of the first government's policies. The end result of a subsidy war is not different from that of a tariff war: a minimum of trade and a maximum of self-sufficiency. For this reason it has become urgent to set a limit to the escalation of selective subsidies, by agreeing to a binding of levels, or at least an upper limit, and this holds as much for the preservation of dying firms as for the promotion of new ones. However, although the Tokyo Round has devoted considerable time to discussing the subsidy question, it seems highly unlikely at the present time that such limits will be set in the near future.

4. Infant versus geriatric industry protection

Industry-specific or firm-specific subsidies can be further divided into two broad types: those whose aim is to encourage the «industries of the future» and those which attempt to support industries in decline. Without exception, the long-term objective of European governments' industrial strategies is to «achieve desirable targets such as higher profitability, increased investment and a greater ability to compete in world markets»[27]. In other words, the principal intention is to support industries of the future, and as no one can object to such a worthy aim, governments command wide respect for having stated it. It also gives them an alibi when, for unavoidable short-term social (read political) reasons, they reluctantly come to the rescue of industries or firms in decline. What is frequently overlooked however, is that governments face a problem of choice like any other economic agent, and the more they allocate to preserving the past for short-term political reasons, the less they can devote to their stated long-term objective. Furthermore, as time goes by, the short term very quickly becomes the medium term, and the medium term the long: and the economy, instead of being closer to the long term objective, ends up in fact considerably further away from it than when it was originally defined. That governments which pursue such policies should enjoy the confidence of their electorates and be re-elected is of course wonderous, but then so is the fact that many people readily support protection as a remedy to combat economic ills.

Even if governments were true to their stated long-term objectives, it should of course be understood that infant industry protection is a gamble. From the international trade point of view, if it succeeds, and the infant grows into a strong, viable new industry, then everybody gains, including consumers in the rest of the world. If it fails, everybody loses, including people in the subsidizing country. People like to quote the United States, Japan and Germany as successful examples of infant industry protection but one has a sneaking suspicion that protection was not the most important or even a modest factor in the history of their industrial development, and other countries would do well to study the genus before attempting to transplant it.

[27] *D. L. Hodgson,* Government Industrial Policy, National Westminster Bank, Quarterly Review, August 1977, p. 6.

5. Adjustment assistance versus adjustment resistance

Even when government is momentarily side-tracked from its long-term objective of raising productivity and international competitiveness, and flies to the rescue of a firm or sector in distress, it will of course be stated that such aid as it can spare will be strictly temporary. It must be used to buy time so that the firm can adjust to change, either by improving its efficiency, or by fading gracefully away. Seen in this light, «adjustment assistance» as it is usually called, is often depicted as a useful ally of the world trade order.

Like the infant industry argument, the adjustment assistance argument while theoretically plausible, is open to doubt in practice. Since its purpose is to place a veil between market forces and the firm in distress, in order to slow down the pace of adjustment to a socially acceptable speed, the chances are that the firm will no longer perceive the need to adjust at all. Thus adjustment assistance has a built-in tendency to become adjustment resistance. One has only to cite the case of shipbuilding and textiles in the EEC at the present time. Many years ago, these important industries were granted temporary protection, during which they were supposed to shed labour at a fast enough rate to be able in due course to confront their Japanese competitors. Europe's clothing industry has been «adjusting» for over seventeen years[28], and its shipbuilding yards have been subsidized for about as long. However, as mentioned above, in 1977 instead of reducing the level of textile protection and subsidization, as one might have expected after a generation or so of adjustment assistance, the EEC raised it substantially. The EEC's steel policy, composed of both internal production «discipline» and protection from outside suppliers, is also intended to promote adjustment. Yet there is no denying that if the net result is to raise steel prices in the EEC by 50 per cent, the incentive to adjust is correspondingly reduced.

In other words, there is a contradiction between adjustment assistance and its supposedly temporary, not to say short-term nature. Or, to put the same point in another way, if the only socially acceptable pace of adjustment is one that is so slow as to be imperceptible to the workers, it may be imperceptible to the management as well.

6. Subsidies and export restraints – a powerful combination

From the official Multifibre Arrangement to the subtlest and humblest export restraints, the explosive growth of protection and the total disregard for legal obligations by a great number of developed countries are, in themselves, extremely worrying. Used in combination with selective subsidies they become a recipe for total protection at best and for possible trade war at worst. Their ultimate intention and effect is to enlarge the share of the domestic market reserved to local producers and to reduce trade to a minimum.

There seem to be two routes by which industries may enjoy the benefit of this dual protection. In one, the process starts with an identifiable «import problem» – generally competition from Japan or an advanced developing country. The industry as a whole, that is, workers and management together, ask their government to negotiate an export restraint. After a time, since their problems are likely to persist, they return with a request for a subsidy. This the government may or may not grant, depending on the size of the industry and the number of jobs involved: the larger the industry and the greater the number of jobs at stake, the more likely it is that a state subsidy of one sort or another will be provided. The government will make a laudable attempt to link the offer of aid with an

---

[28] *Richard Blackhurst,* «Reluctance to Adjust and Economic Nationalism» in: *Otto Hieronymi* (ed.), The New Economic Nationalism, Battelle Geneva Research Centre, London 1979.

obligation, on the part of the stricken industry, to «restructure». But since no one is anxious to see unemployment figures swell, great store is placed on industry's ability to raise productivity without firing workers. This implies increasing production, which in turn means either increasing exports or reducing imports, or both. This appears to be an excellent strategy to the short-sighted, who fail to see that other countries are bound to take offsetting measures at best, or start a subsidy-countervailing-duty war at worst. The international political implications of protective industrial policies, adopted on the basis of simplistic partial-equilibrium analysis and assuming that «other things» remain equal, are therefore serious.

The second route by which a combination of trade restraints and subsidies can occur is via «industrial strategy» per se. Here the trigger mechanism is not an «import problem» but any other challenge or opportunity perceived either by an industry or, spontaneously, by the state. Together, they devise a «strategy»: the French government's computer policy or the British Sector Working Parties programme are cases in point. But no matter how close the links may be between business and the state, or how cordially they may together determine various strategic objectives by sector, they will inevitably come up against a third party who cannot be so easily coopted: the foreign producer. The latter can upset the most careful of plans. Luckily for the strategic planners, however, modern trade practices provide the ideal solution: voluntary export restraints. Thus one is not surprised to find industrial strategies going hand in hand with trade restrictions: steel, shipbuilding and textiles are all cases in point.

IV. Concluding remarks

We have dealt in this paper with two of several threats to the liberal trading order. They are, however, only facets of a general problem which has implications going far beyond the preservation of cordial international relations or even base material considerations, such as how to maintain and if possible improve our present standard of living, and that of others less fortunate than ourselves.

The great scholar to whom this volume of Essays is dedicated, has analysed the problem many years ago, and although the context has changed, the issues have not.

The craving for security, which is alive in each and every one of us, causes groups of individuals to attempt to protect themselves against threats to their incomes due to market fluctuations by enlisting the support of the state. This is perfectly understandable. What is more mysterious is why such interest groups frequently succeed in obtaining the protection they seek from the rest of society.

As Professor *Hayek* has said, in a passage which could have been written today:

«That anybody should suffer a great diminution of his income and bitter disappointment of all his hopes through no fault of his own, and despite hard work and exceptional skill, undoubtedly offends our sense of justice. The demands of those who suffer in this way, for state interference on their behalf to safeguard their legitimate expectations, are certain to receive popular sympathy and support. The general approval of these demands has had the effect that governments everywhere have taken action, not merely to protect the people so threatened from severe hardship and privation, but to secure to them the continued receipt of their former income and to shelter them from fluctuations of the market».[29]

[29] F. A. *Hayek,* The Road of Serfdom, Routledge & Sons Ltd, London, 1946, (Abridged Edition), p. 63.

This passage, we believe, helps to explain better than any other, why there should be widespread public support for protecting Europe's textile and clothing industries, its steel mills, its shipyards and soon, perhaps, its mass-produced electrical appliances, electronic goods and automobiles.

It is not enough for the state to provide collective insurance against unemployment, to protect people from «severe hardship and privation», for this is done, and fairly generously, throughout industrial Western Europe. What is being asked for is shelter from the fluctuations of the market (since these offend our sense of justice) – in a word, not unemployment insurance, but job and income insurance.[30]

Let us analyse this thought more closely.

To the extent that people in other walks of life do not understand that they have to pay for protecting others from market risk, their outraged sense of justice comes very cheap. They need to be informed of the costs to themselves and to the community at large which would result from protecting weak sectors, before they can take an informed and responsible view of the issue.

To the extent that people in other walks of life understand that policies to protect other people's jobs and incomes represent a loss of income for themselves and ultimately a net reduction of income for all concerned, their sympathy and support for protection does more credit to their heart than to their head. If they are prepared to sacrifice part of their present and future wealth in a spirit of solidarity with those, who through no fault of their own, are threatened with a loss of income, it is doubtless because the absolute amounts appear small in relation to the current social harmony that they appear to buy. But this position is untenable in the long run. Demands for protection will inevitably build up over time, since market fluctuations themselves cannot be prevented. If it becomes an accepted general principle that anyone suffering a reversal of fortune may claim protection therefrom, the efficient sectors will very soon end up paying amounts that are large both in relation to their own incomes and in relation to the social harmony that they are supposed to buy, since the latter will disintegrate once national income begins to fall, and will require ever larger sums to maintain itself at previous levels. Moreover, quite apart from random market fluctuations, protection feeds upon itself, not only through the demonstration effect, but also through the innumerable linkages throughout the economy, between the protected and the unprotected sectors. Its ultimate cost is therefore very high, however insignificant its short-term cost may appear to be.

Finally, it is possible that people in other walks of life, while not at present threatened by market fluctuations, live in fear of a future change in their luck, and therefore tend to support policies to help those suffering now, even if they have to pay for it. They are, in effect, taking out an insurance policy against the risks of the market system, but perhaps without realizing the high long-run cost of such an insurance scheme.

Although it would be useful to have an idea, however imperfect, of how high the cost of protection really is, this is not the most important issue. The spirit of national solidarity, the offended sense of justice and the concern for one's future security are all very human motivations, and it little behoves a proponent of the «dismal science» to criticize them on material grounds alone. In fact, it is not enough to demonstrate that sheltering large sectors of the economy from the risks of the market ultimately reduces everybody's incomes: it is a sacrifice that people seem to be prepared to make in the name of the three human motives discussed above. It is not even enough to demonstrate that by accepting the risks and profits of the market, everybody's incomes will ultimately rise: man does not live by

---

[30] *Jan Tumlir,* «National Interest and International Order», International Issues, No 4, Trade Policy Research Centre, London, 1978, p. 6.

bread alone, and an appeal to his material instincts is unlikely to succeed – it has failed to do so for the last two hundred years, and one sees no reason why this should change.

The clinching argument against protecting people from the risks of the market system in fact lies beyond economics, and it is Professor *Hayek's* vital contribution to have pointed out that individual freedom and economic security are incompatible with each other: «either the choice and the risk rest with the individual or he is relieved of both».[31]

If economic security becomes a privilege for all, derived from the state, then ultimately the state, and not the individual, must decide what economic tasks people should undertake, since the state and not the individual bears the risk.

This trade-off might be thought exaggerated. After all, one could argue that it might be very sensible to sacrifice a little bit of freedom for a lot more security, and one would certainly stop before the threat to freedom became substantial. In concrete terms, this view represents the compromise between the market and the state as allocators of the nation's resources known as the «mixed economy». As long as the frontier between the state and the market was clearly defined, and the market sector was large enough to constitute a counterweight to the state sector, the mixed economy compromise seemed a viable, though not necessarily optimal, form of social organization. The present policy of providing automatic guarantees to threatened jobs and incomes in the market sector, however, goes well beyond the normal definition of the mixed economy. It strikes at the mainspring of what is left of the market system, since it deprives it of its role as allocator of resources.

This fundamental revolution in our economic system is taking place almost unnoticed for two reasons. First, the transfer of the role of resource allocator from market to state is, paradoxically, being made at the request of the principal market operators themselves. Management and labour join forces when it comes to preserving their present (or future) incomes, and either do not see, or do not wish to see, that they are cutting the branch on which they sit. Secondly, the transfer of responsibility for allocating the nation's resources is being made without altering the ownership structure of those resources. Shareholders continue to «own» certain assets, and of course, people continue to «own» their labour-power. But the decision-making power over the allocation of those resources is slipping steadily away into the hands of a body of people who, though perhaps competent, are not subject to the discipline of the market and may one day abuse their power.

Even if, under the kindest and most unrealistic of interpretations, they do not abuse their power, they will occasionally have to take decisions to alter the allocation of the nation's resources. Managers and employees will therefore have to learn to accept change at least as much under economic dictatorship as under the market system. In other words, economic security is a chimera that mankind can pursue to the end of time, but which no economic system can provide for long. We are thus forced to conclude that large numbers of people in mature industrial countries are sacrificing their freedom of individual choice and action for the mere illusion of economic security, because they neither understand the nature of economic dictatorship, nor the nature and need for change under any system, nor, most important of all, the vital link between individual liberty and the market system.

---

[31] *F. A. Hayek,* The Road to Serfdom, op. cit., p. 64.

Summary

The Undermining of the World Trade Order

During the Tokyo Round of GATT negotiations, whose purpose has been to liberalize trade and improve the legal framework for world trade, various forces have been at work to produce the opposite result. This paradox is explained by the fact that liberalizing efforts concern essentially intra-developed country trade, while protectionist measures, taking the form of «voluntary» export restraints and «orderly» marketing arrangements, are aimed at developing countries and Japan. Such a hybrid combination of liberalism and protection is a familiar feature of customs union theory and it could be argued that a North Atlantic preferential trading zone is in the process of being created. This is the antithesis of the GATT, whose objective is to establish a universal, non-discriminatory trading order.

Such a trading order is well-founded in both law and economics. In law, non-discrimination ensures that the weak enjoy the same treatment as the strong. In economics, non-discrimination ensures that the efficient are promoted and the inefficient penalized, which ensures an efficient use of the world's scarce resources.

A second threat to the GATT system stems from the increased use of discretionary power by the state in areas of micro-economic decision-making, formerly left to market forces. It is a fundamental unwritten rule of the GATT game that most of the decisions concerning what goods countries should produce and trade, in what quantities and at what prices, should be left to the market. The GATT sets limits to government policies affecting private decisions, but pre-supposes that the state will not assume direct responsibility for them.

Several developed western European countries, however, have adopted wideranging selective subsidies to industry whose objective is to short-circuit market forces which would otherwise have had politically undesirable results – bankruptcy, unemployment, loss of production, foreign take-overs, excessive dependence on foreign technology, increased imports, and so forth. By doing so, they distort the pattern of production and trade and alter the unwritten rules of the game. Until now, one of the most effective brakes on the proliferation of subsidies has lain in domestic US trade law, which specifies that imports bearing any «bounty or grant» must be taxed by a countervailing duty, which offsets the aid as exactly as possible. This brake may be lifted in the future as part of the Tokyo Round.

When orderly marketing arrangements and selective industrial policies are used together, they constitute a recipe for total protection.

The deterioration of the world trading system is part of a wider problem: the rejection by a growing number of people of market forces as the principal allocator of resources. Clearly, those suffering the risks of market forces are the first to reject the system. However, they are supported by those enjoying its benefits through a combination of national solidarity, an offended sense of justice and concern for future security. Since these are very human emotions, it is not enough to demonstrate that by rejecting the risks (and benefits) of the market everybody's income will ultimately fall – man does not live by bread alone. No indeed. In fact, the clinching argument in favour of the market system has been provided by Professor *Hayek* himself: «either the choice and the risk rest with the individual or he is relieved of both». In the long run, the opportunity cost of economic security is the loss of individual liberty, beside which the loss of real income pales to insignificance.

To judge from economic policies at present in force in many mature industrial nations, large numbers of people are prepared to sacrifice their freedom of choice for economic security, because they neither understand the nature of economic dictatorship, nor the need for change, nor the vital link between liberty and the market system.

VIII. Einzelfragen

Artur Woll

Das Währungssystem einer freiheitlichen Ordnung

I. Zur Bedeutung des Währungssystems für eine freiheitliche Ordnung

1. Die Einschätzung durch Gegner und Anhänger einer freiheitlichen Ordnung

Zu den fundamentalen Erfahrungen unseres Jahrhunderts gehört: Das Währungssystem und die freiheitliche Ordnung in Staat, Gesellschaft und Wirtschaft sind untrennbar verbunden. Wir haben gelernt, daß monetäre Störungen eine Demokratie oder staatliche Instabilitäten hochentwickelte Geldwirtschaften ruinieren können – und oft dürfte schwer auszumachen sein, was Ursache oder Folge unhaltbarer Zustände gewesen ist. Einige Gelehrte haben viel Scharfsinn darauf verwendet, die theoretischen Bedingungen für eine Entkoppelung von Währungssystem und Wirtschaftsablauf – ein Teilproblem des Themas – zu beschreiben. Bekannt dürfte das Konzept des «neutralen» Geldes sein, das nach Ansicht eines maßgeblichen Analytikers dem wohlverstandenen laissez-faire erst seine faire Chance geben würde.[1] Neutrales Geld, so erwünscht es auch scheinen mag, ist eine theoretische Konstruktion[2], die für die Realität wohl eine Illusion bleibt. Mit anderen Worten: Maßnahmen der Geldpolitik schlagen empirisch nachweisbar stets auf Preise und Produktion durch, auch wenn sich ihre Wirkungen zeitlich unterscheiden.[3]

Die Zusammenhänge zwischen dem Währungssystem und der freiheitlichen Ordnung haben die Gegner der Freiheit frühzeitig, ihre Anhänger oft – wenn überhaupt – nur unzulänglich erkannt. Ein «klassischer» – zugleich kommentierter – Beleg für die gegnerische Auffassung stammt von *Keynes*, der im Jahr 1919 schrieb: «*Lenin* is said to have declared that the best way to destroy the capitalist system was to debauch the currency ... *Lenin* was certainly right. There is no subtler, no surer means of overturning the existing basis of society than to debauch the currency.»[4] Es kann dahingestellt bleiben, ob *Lenin* diese Äußerung, die in seinen Schriften meines Wissens nicht auffindbar ist, wirklich von

---

[1] *J. G. Koopmans*, Zum Problem des «Neutralen» Geldes, in: *F. A. von Hayek* (Hrsg.), Beiträge zur Geldtheorie, Wien 1933, S. 234.

[2] Vgl.: *F. A. von Hayek*, Über «neutrales» Geld, in: Zeitschrift für Nationalökonomie, Bd. 4 (1933), S. 658 ff.

[3] Beiläufig sei angemerkt, daß neuerdings Anhänger von *Keynes* versuchen, ihren neoklassischen Gegnern in der monetären Debatte das Stigma «Geldneutralität» aufzudrücken. Würden diese *Keynesianer* die Publikationen ihrer Kontrahenten kennen, wüßten sie, daß zahlreiche Neoklassiker das Konzept der Geldneutralität für irreal halten.

[4] *J. M. Keynes*, The Economic Consequences of the Peace, in: The Collected Writings of *John Maynard Keynes*, Vol. II, London 1971, S. 148 f.

sich gegeben hat. Man mag sich auch dem Urteil *Schumpeters*, der dem Marxismus durchaus freundlich gesonnen war, voll anschließen, daß die Beiträge *Lenins* zur Öko-nomie unbedeutend gewesen sind.[5] Der von *Lenin* stammende oder ihm zugeschriebene Ausspruch beschreibt jedenfalls auf zutreffende Weise, wie *Keynes* vor mehr als einem halben Jahrhundert richtig gesehen hat[6], den empfindlichsten Punkt einer freiheitlichen Ordnung. Das Währungssystem ist der wirksamste Hebel, die Freiheit zu beseitigen.

Die Erklärungen der Anhänger von Demokratie und liberalem Wirtschaftssystem zur Interdependenz von Währungssystem und freiheitlicher Ordnung sind trotz unserer Er-fahrungen in der Regel weniger eindeutig, verkennen oft die zentrale ordnungspolitische Bedeutung des Zusammenhangs oder zeichnen sich gar durch Ignoranz aus. Hinreichen-des Anschauungsmaterial für diese Feststellung bietet die in den letzten Jahren geführte wissenschaftliche und – mehr noch – öffentliche Debatte zum *Phillips*-Theorem[7], bei ei-nem von Land zu Land unterschiedlichen wirtschaftspolitischen Hintergrund. Für die deutsche Szene dürfte grob skizziert gelten: Nach dem zweiten Weltkrieg bis Mitte der sechziger Jahre war der Primat der Währungspolitik als Stabilitätsinstrument im wesent-lichen unbestritten. Dieser Primat wurde durch einen zunehmenden Einfluß *Keynesscher* Gedanken auf die Wirtschaftspolitik relativiert oder gar zugunsten der Beschäftigungs-politik aufgegeben. Ausdruck dafür ist das Gesetz zur Förderung von Stabilität und Wachstum der Wirtschaft aus dem Jahr 1967, das die Administration und die Noten-bank – im Rahmen ihrer Aufgabe – verpflichtet, währungs- und konjunkturpolitische Ziele gleichzeitig zu verfolgen. Bei tatsächlichen oder vermeintlichen Zielkonflikten ha-ben maßgebliche Politiker das, das sie unter Vollbeschäftigung verstehen, einem stabilen Preisniveau vorgezogen – im irrigen Glauben, es gäbe für sie eine solche Wahl. An dieser Stelle sollen nicht die intellektuellen Defekte, sondern nur die Bedenkenlosigkeit einer Wirtschaftspolitik aufgezeigt werden, die bei vergleichsweise geringen Schwierigkeiten die Stabilität des Währungssystems zu opfern bereit ist.

2. Die frühzeitige Erkennung der Inflationsgefahren durch von Hayek

Es gehört zu den bleibenden Verdiensten *Friedrich August von Hayeks*, daß er frühzei-tig auf die Gefährdung der freiheitlichen Ordnung durch die Währungspolitik nicht nur aufmerksam gemacht, sondern auch ihre Wurzeln gründlich analysiert hat. Im Hinblick auf gewollte oder ungewollte Mißverständnisse sollte zunächst festgehalten werden: Die Gefahren der Inflation hat *von Hayek* – wie andere Liberale – stets betont, die der Defla-tion aber keineswegs übersehen. Daß die Deflation und eine von ihr induzierte Massen-arbeitslosigkeit eine Bedrohung für die freiheitliche Ordnung bedeutet, war ihm nicht nur bewußt, er hat es auch deutlich genug geschrieben. Allerdings hielt und hält er die In-flation in einem bestimmten, noch zu erläuternden Sinn für die größere Gefahr – auch zu einer Zeit, als die Verharmlosung der Inflation zum politischen Ritual und zur wissen-

---

[5] *J. A. Schumpeter*, Geschichte der ökonomischen Analyse, Göttingen 1965, S. 1408.

[6] Hierin stimmen *Keynes* und *von Hayek* – wie mir scheint – völlig überein. Symptomatisch dafür dürfte sein, daß *von Hayek* den Untergliederungen seines Buches «Die Verfassung der Freiheit» – in 3 Teilen und 24 Kapiteln – 27 Mottos aus Publikationen anderer Autoren voranstellt, bei de-nen er nur einmal *Keynes* im hier erwähnten Zusammenhang zitiert (XXI. Kapitel «Der wäh-rungspolitische Rahmen»).

[7] Zur wissenschaftlichen Debatte vgl.: *A. M. Santomero – J. S. Seater*, The Inflation – Unemploy-ment Trade-off: A Critique of the Literature, in: Journal of Economic Literature, Vol. XVI (1978), S. 499 ff.

schaftlichen Mode wurde.[8] Scharfsichtig wandte er sich gegen diese Strömung, zunächst ohne sichtbaren Erfolg – ähnlich wie in seiner Kontroverse mit *Keynes* in den dreißiger Jahren.[9] Als seine Erkenntnisse durch die Erfahrung bestätigt wurden und eine Besinnung oder gar ein Meinungsumschwung einsetzte, war schwerer, teilweise irreparabler Schaden entstanden. Überhaupt haften dem Wirken *von Hayeks* nach meinem Dafürhalten ein wenig tragische Züge an: Mit einer hohen Sensibilität für aufkommende Gefahren hat er, oft als einsamer Rufer in der Wüste, vergeblich vor bestimmten Entwicklungen gewarnt. Erst negative Erfahrungen mit ihren unvermeidlichen Kosten und sozialen Folgen führten zur Umkehr – sofern es nicht schon zu spät war – und zur Bestätigung seiner Kassandrarufe, die zum Zeitpunkt ihrer Verlautbarung fast immer inopportun und unpopulär gewesen sind.

Das Bewußtsein dafür, daß eine Geldentwertung mit mäßigen Preisniveauerhöhungen, die «schleichende» Inflation, ein Übel ist, mag in den letzten Jahren in Politik und Wissenschaft zugenommen haben. Die rationale Begründung für diese Erkenntnis ist gleichwohl ziemlich konfus. Deshalb scheint es nicht überflüssig, an die vor Jahrzehnten entwickelte Analyse *von Hayeks* anzuknüpfen, die sich in bemerkenswerter Übereinstimmung mit der neuesten Entwicklung der Inflationstheorie befindet. Die Ausgangsfrage lautet: Warum ist eine Inflation mit geringen Preisniveausteigerungsraten nicht nur ein Übel, sondern auch in einem bestimmten Sinn gefährlicher als eine Deflation? Eine profunde Antwort auf diese Frage erfordert mehr als eine Kenntnis traditioneller quantitätstheoretischer Zusammenhänge. Ein entscheidendes Erklärungselement sind die Erwartungen von Wirtschaftssubjekten, deren analytische Berücksichtigung das wichtigste Unterscheidungsmerkmal klassischer und moderner Geldtheorie sein dürfte.

Die Bedeutung von Erwartungen für die Währungspolitik hat *von Hayek* bereits vor Jahrzehnten so unübertrefflich herausgearbeitet, daß mir in dieser Kürze nichts Besseres als seine Formulierungen bekannt sind:

«Inflation und Deflation rufen beide ihre eigenartigen Wirkungen durch unerwartete Preisniveauänderungen hervor und beide müssen Erwartungen zweimal enttäuschen. Das erste Mal, wenn die Preise sich als höher oder niedriger erweisen, als erwartet wurde, und das zweite Mal, wenn diese Preisveränderungen, wie es früher oder später kommen muß, nun schon erwartet werden und nicht mehr die Wirkung haben, die ihr unvorhergesehenes Auftreten hatte. Der Unterschied ist, daß bei Inflation die angenehme Wirkung zuerst kommt und die Reaktion später, während bei der Deflation die erste Wirkung auf das Geschäftsleben depressiv ist. Die Wirkungen beider kehren sich jedoch von selbst um. Eine Zeitlang werden die Kräfte, die jede dieser Wirkungen hervorbringen, selbstverstärkend wirken und der Zeitraum, in dem sich die Preise schneller bewegen, als erwartet wird, kann dadurch verlängert werden. Aber wenn sich die Preisbewegungen in derselben Richtung fortsetzen, müssen die Erwartungen sie einholen. Sobald das geschieht, ändert sich der Charakter der Wirkungen.»[10]

Bezieht man – wie in der Theorie heute allgemein üblich geworden – Erwartungen ein, wird verständlich, warum eine milde Inflation gefährlicher als eine Deflation ist. Eine mäßige Inflation wirkt wie ein Rauschmittel zunächst angenehm und stimulierend – ein Paradigma, das wohl von *Wilhelm Röpke* stammt –, während eine Deflation unmittelbar schmerzt; die als wohltätig empfundenen Wirkungen der Inflation halten aber, sobald sie

---

[8] F. A. *von Hayek*, Die Verfassung der Freiheit, Tübingen 1971, S. 416 ff.; das Original dieser Übersetzung ist 1960 erschienen.

[9] Vgl. dazu: *J. R. Hicks*, The Hayek Story, in: *J. R. Hicks*, Critical Essays in Monetary Theory, Oxford 1967, S. 203 ff.

[10] F. A. *von Hayek*, Die Verfassung der Freiheit, a.a.O., S. 416 f.

vorausgesehen werden, nicht an. Deshalb besteht die ohne weiteres evidente Gefahr, daß Deflationen sofort bekämpft, mäßige Inflationen dagegen eine Zeitlang toleriert werden. «Da die Inflation psychologisch und politisch um so viel schwerer zu verhindern ist als Deflation und gleichzeitig technisch um so viel leichter zu vermeiden, sollte der Nationalökonom immer die Gefahren der Inflation betonen.»[11]

Dazu besteht schon deswegen Anlaß, weil die langfristigen Wirkungen einer «schleichenden» Inflation sich letztlich nicht vom Ergebnis einer «galoppierenden» Inflation unterscheiden. Dauerhafte Preisniveauerhöhungen jeglichen Ausmaßes provozieren Beschneidungen privater Freiheiten durch staatliche Eingriffe, die auf die zwangsläufigen Umverteilungen des realen Einkommens und Vermögens als Folge nicht voll vorausseh-barer inflatorischer Prozesse zurückgehen. Das trifft – erstens – für das Verhältnis des Staates zu seinen Bürgern zu. Die reale Verschuldung des Staates wird durch eine Inflation abgebaut, die in einem progressiven Steuersystem seinen Realeinkommensanteil zugleich erhöht. Das ökonomische Interesse des Staates an einer Inflation ist offenkundig und historisch auch belegbar.[12] Zweitens können die anfänglichen Wohltaten einer unerwarteten Inflation nur perpetuiert werden, wenn sich der Preisniveauanstieg fortlaufend beschleunigt und sich die Erwartungen deshalb niemals erfüllen. Die wirtschaftspolitische Wahl ist also, entweder bei ständig steigendem Inflationstempo von der «schleichenden» über die «trabende» zur «galoppierenden» Inflation überzugehen – eine Konsequenz, die *von Hayek* klar gesehen hat[13], bevor sie als Akzelerationshypothese vor einigen Jahren neu «entdeckt» wurde[14] – oder die Inflation zu stoppen und damit eine Rezession oder gar Depression herbeizuführen. Man könnte auch sagen: Ist eine mäßige Inflation in Gang gekommen, muß eine Regierung – je länger, um so mehr – sich zwischen einem Zusammenbruch der Geldwirtschaft oder der Massenarbeitslosigkeit entscheiden. Will sie den ersten Weg vermeiden, der auch ihre Existenz gefährdet, produziert eine einmal in Gang gekommene Inflation zwangsläufig Arbeitslosigkeit, diese provoziert staatliche Interventionen – eine völlige Umkehr des Ursachen- und Wirkungszusammenhanges in der bisher vorherrschenden Sicht des Faches, ganz zu schweigen von der der Wirtschaftspolitiker. Die reale Einkommens- und Vermögensumverteilung durch Inflation ist, so sehr sie auch unmittelbar zu Einschränkungen der individuellen Freiheit führt, nicht die einzige und nicht einmal die wichtigste Inflationswirkung. Schwerer wiegen die Fehlallokationen der Produktionsfaktoren, die die freiheitliche Ordnung mehr indirekt bedrohen.

Die Preisniveaustabilisierung, das heißt angesichts der Realität in den letzten Dezennien: die Inflationsbekämpfung, wird damit zu einer ordnungspolitisch vordringlichen Aufgabe, von deren Lösung die Existenz einer freiheitlichen Ordnung abhängt. Die Gefährlichkeit der schleichenden Inflation erfordert, selbst geringe Inflationsraten auf Dauer nicht zuzulassen, letztlich also, einen anhaltenden Preisniveauanstieg überhaupt zu vermeiden. Das wirksamste Mittel der Inflationsbekämpfung in paradox klingender Formulierung ist unstreitig, eine Inflation nicht erst zuzulassen. Soweit bereits Inflation herrscht, kommt es darauf an, sie abzubauen, auch wenn ihre wohltätigen Wirkungen in der Vergangenheit einen Tribut – in Form von temporärer Arbeitslosigkeit – verlangen, dessen Aufbringung allenfalls zeitlich unterschiedlich verteilt werden kann. In dieser Ein-

---

[11] *F. A. von Hayek*, Die Verfassung der Freiheit, a.a.O., S. 419.
[12] Vgl.: *R. Gaettens*, Inflationen. Das Drama der Geldentwertungen vom Altertum bis zur Gegenwart, München 1955.
[13] *F. A. von Hayek*, Die Verfassung der Freiheit, a.a.O., S. 424.
[14] Vgl. dazu: *A. Woll*, Das Phillips-Theorem, in: *T. Pütz* (Hrsg.), Studien zum Inflationsproblem, Berlin 1975, S. 101 ff.

schätzung gab und gibt es unter den konsequenten Verfechtern des marktwirtschaftlichen Systems, soweit sie sich zu diesem Problem geäußert haben, so gut wie keinen Dissens. Einige Indizien sprechen dafür, daß über diesen Kreis hinaus die ordnungspolitische Bedeutung der Währungspolitik neuerdings stärker als bisher gesehen wird.

II. Zur Gestaltung des Währungssystems in einer freiheitlichen Ordnung

1. Gestaltung des Währungssystems als Aufgabe

Einigkeit über das Ziel enthebt nicht von einer Antwort auf die Frage, wie ein Währungssystem in einer freiheitlichen Ordnung auszusehen hat, dem in Vergangenheit und Gegenwart als wichtigste Aufgabe zufällt, eine Inflation zu verhindern oder zu unterbinden. Eine allgemeingültige Antwort dürfte nicht möglich sein, weil es entscheidend darauf ankommt, wie sich Stoff- und Marktwert der Geldzeichen zueinander verhalten. Zwei Extremfälle sind denkbar: Stoff- und Marktwert decken sich oder der Stoffwert ist so gering, daß er praktisch gleich Null gesetzt werden kann. Im ersten Fall ist Geld ein Gut wie andere Güter, im zweiten Fall ein «Gut», das sich qualitativ – um nicht zu sagen: in seinem Wesen – von anderen Gütern deutlich unterscheidet. Diese Alternative durchzieht wie ein roter Faden die Dogmen- und Wirtschaftsgeschichte zu monetären Problemen, sei es in theoretischen Analysen zur Produktionskosten- und Quantitätstheorie des Geldes, sei es in politischen Erörterungen zur Münz- oder Papierwährung. Die umfangreichen, weitgehend bekannten Diskussionen auch nur andeutungsweise nachzuzeichnen, ist hier weder möglich noch nötig. Im Zuge der wirtschaftlichen und technischen Entwicklung seit dem frühen 19. Jahrhundert sind unübersehbare und unüberschreitbare Daten gesetzt worden: der Übergang von der «vollwertigen» Münze über «gedeckte» Banknoten zu «stoffwertlosem» Geld. Im Verlaufe dieser Entwicklung hat sich auch das Währungssystem in deutlich erkennbaren Stufen geändert. Diese Stufen sollen im Hinblick auf die beschriebene Aufgabe des Währungssystems in einer freiheitlichen Ordnung skizziert werden.

2. Neuere Entwicklungsphasen des Währungssystems

Die erste Phase, der Übergang von der «vollwertigen» Münze zur «gedeckten» Banknote, beginnt in der Mitte des vergangenen Jahrhunderts in England. Damit wird nicht behauptet, daß die Inflation zuvor unbekannt gewesen sei. Tatsächlich lassen sich Inflationen bis zu den überlieferten Ursprüngen der Menschheitsgeschichte zurückverfolgen.[15] Hier geht es allein darum, die Bedeutung des verbreiteten Auftretens von bestimmten Geldformen für das Währungssystem herauszustellen. Im England der ersten Hälfte des 19. Jahrhunderts kamen mit der industriellen Entwicklung verstärkt Banken auf, die über ihre Depositen Kredite in Form von Banknoten, das heißt ein Zahlungsversprechen, vergaben. Kreditaufblähungen und Krisen häuften sich in den zwanziger und dreißiger

---

[15] Vgl.: *R. Gaettens*, Inflationen . . ., a.a.O.

Jahren allerdings ebenso wie Bankenzusammenbrüche.[16] Der Mißbrauch des Kredits im etymologischen Sinn des Wortes ließ sich nicht bestreiten. Dem setzte die *Peelsche* Bank Act von 1844 ein Ende: Die private Notenausgabe wurde beschränkt, das Monopol der Notenemission durch die Bank von England vorbereitet. Dieses Gesetz hat man im Schrifttum als Sieg der Currency- über die Banking-Schule bezeichnet. Dies trifft für einzelne Bestimmungen des Gesetzes – wie die Trennung der Bank von England in ein Issue- und ein Banking-Department, die teilweise bald ihre praktische Bedeutung verlor – gewiß zu, nicht jedoch für die hier interessierende Frage nach der Gestaltung des Währungssystems. In den entscheidenden Punkten – Einschränkung der privaten Notenausgabe, Vereinheitlichung der Noten und staatliches Emissionsmonopol – gab es keine grundlegenden Meinungsverschiedenheiten. *Tooke*, Haupt der Banking-Schule, stimmte mit seinen Kritikern überein, die immer wiederholten: «freedom of banking is freedom of swindling.»[17] Um dem Banknotenschwindel Einhalt zu gebieten, mußte die Bank von England den Wert der umlaufenden Banknoten in Gold und Silber halten («gedeckte» Banknoten), mit Ausnahme einer kleinen Quote von 14 Mill. £, für deren Deckung Staatskonsols genügten (fiduziäre Emission). Das englische Notenbanksystem hat sich weltweit durchgesetzt. Es galt – und gilt – nicht nur als Recht, sondern auch als Pflicht der Regierung, die Notenemission zu etablieren und zu überwachen, anstatt sie dem Prinzip des freien Wettbewerbs zu überlassen. Dies ist auch heute noch die herrschende Meinung liberaler Nationalökonomen. Der Grundsatz einer reichlichen und billigen Warenproduktion hat, wie *Wilhelm Röpke* hundert Jahre später schrieb, bei der Geldproduktion keinen Sinn.[18]

Die zweite Phase, der Übergang vom «gedeckten» zum «stoffwertlosen» Geld, setzte nach der letzten Jahrhundertwende ein. In der ersten Phase blieb das Metall – Gold oder Silber – die eigentliche Valuta, weil die zentrale Notenbank auf Verlangen die Deckung gegen Banknoten einlösen mußte. Das änderte sich in der zweiten Phase durch zwei Maßnahmen: Erstens wurden die Noten zum gesetzlichen Zahlungsmittel erklärt und ein Zwangskurs (z. B. Mark gleich Mark) festgesetzt, so daß weder eine Bezahlung in Metall verlangt werden konnte noch ein Disagio der Papier- gegenüber der Metallwährung möglich war; dies geschah in Deutschland – durch eine Novelle zum Reichsbankgesetz von 1875, das dem englischen Muster folgte – im Jahre 1910.[19] Zweitens hob man die Einlösungspflicht der zentralen Notenbank auf, in Deutschland mit Beginn des ersten Weltkriegs. Als «Deckung» für die Notenausgabe genügten Schuldverschreibungen des Staates. Es bedarf keiner Begründung, daß in dieser zweiten Entwicklungsphase des Währungssystems der Inflation überhaupt keine Grenzen mehr gesetzt und Inflationsraten astronomischen Ausmaßes möglich wurden, an denen gemessen staatliche Münzverschlechterungen früherer Jahrhunderte harmlose Erscheinungen gewesen waren. Das Aufkommen und der temporäre Bestand des Faschismus in Europa, damit die Beseitigung einer freiheitlichen Ordnung, dürften ohne diese währungspolitische Entwicklung nicht erklärbar sein. Daß die staatliche Geldproduktion irgendwelchen Kontrollen unterworfen werden muß, ist bald – nicht nur unter liberalen Nationalökonomen – Allgemeingut geworden.

---

[16] Zu Einzelheiten vgl.: *J. Kulischer*, Allgemeine Wirtschaftsgeschichte des Mittelalters und der Neuzeit, Bd. II, 2. A., Darmstadt 1958, S. 528 ff.

[17] *C. Rist*, Geschichte der Geld- und Kredittheorien von John Law bis heute, Bern 1947, S. 199.

[18] *W. Röpke*, Die Lehre von der Wirtschaft, 9. A., Erlenbach-Zürich und Stuttgart 1961, S. 139.

[19] Vgl.: *J. von Spindler – W. Becker – O. E. Starke*, Die Deutsche Bundesbank. Grundzüge des Notenbankwesens und Kommentar zum Gesetz über die Deutsche Bundesbank, 4. A., Stuttgart u. a. 1973, S. 9.

Die dritte Phase, die nach dem zweiten Weltkrieg beginnt – in den USA schon früher –, ist gekennzeichnet durch Versuche, die Notenemission vor Zugriffen der Regierung zu sichern und die Knappheit einer «stoffwertlosen» Geldmenge gegenüber dem Güterangebot zu gewährleisten. Diesem Ziel sollen eine autonome Notenbank und/oder Notenemissionsvorschriften dienen. Ein gutes Beispiel für diese Bestrebungen bietet das Währungssystem in der Bundesrepublik Deutschland. Die Notenbank erhielt unter dem Einfluß der Siegermächte – anders als nach dem ersten Weltkrieg – eine von der Regierung unabhängige Position, die allerdings durch einfaches Gesetz beseitigt werden könnte. Der Staat muß sich – von eng begrenzten Ausnahmen abgesehen – am Kapitalmarkt verschulden, wodurch grosso modo die Allokation der Produktionsfaktoren, aber nicht das Preisniveau beeinflußt wird. Rechtliche Autonomie bedeutet nicht zwangsläufig auch eine tatsächliche von der Regierung oder pressure groups, die z.B. durch ihnen genehme personelle Besetzungen der Notenbankleitung Abhängigkeiten schaffen können. Die Kontrolle der Notenemission ist bisher weniger stark ausgeprägt. Während in den ersten Jahren nach der Währungsreform der Gesetzgeber noch Emissionshöchstgrenzen für zweckmäßig hielt, glaubt er nunmehr, sich auf das Ermessen der Notenbankleitung beim Ziel, «die Währung zu sichern», verlassen zu können. Vielen bereits scheint oder schien eine autonome Notenbank eine hinreichende Garantie gegen Inflation.

Dieses Ermessen ist gegenwärtig jedoch der hauptsächliche Angriffspunkt liberaler Nationalökonomen, insbesondere der sogenannten Monetaristen unter der Führung *Milton Friedmans*, weil die Erfahrung zeigt – insbesondere in den USA und in der Bundesrepublik Deutschland –, daß die Autonomie keine Garantie für ein stabiles Preisniveau ist. Im Anschluß an *Henry Simons*, der schon vor Jahrzehnten einen ähnlichen Vorschlag unterbreitete[20], schlagen die «Monetaristen» vor, die Geldmenge jährlich um bestimmte Raten – meist werden 5 v.H. genannt – zu erhöhen.[21] Die Aufgabe der Notenbank wäre rein technischer Natur. Diskretionäre Entscheidungen dürfte sie – an die Regelungen zur Geldmengenexpansion gebunden – nicht fällen. Dieser Vorschlag basiert auf der Quantitätstheorie, nach der eine Geldmenge, die langfristig stärker als die Produkteinheit steigt – jeweils pro Kopf – eine notwendige und hinreichende Bedingung der Inflation ist. Sollte die konstante Rate der Geldmengenausweitung vom Wirtschaftswachstum abweichen, sei das im Hinblick auf die Vorhersehbarkeit der Währungspolitik ein unbedeutendes Übel gegenüber dem gegenwärtigen Zustand, für den in allen Ländern unvorhersehbare und starke Geldmengenschwankungen charakteristisch sind. «... Eine *stetige* und bekannte Rate der Geldmengenerhöhung (ist) wesentlicher als der exakte numerische Wert der Zuwachsrate.»[22] Auf die Darlegung weiterer Einzelheiten des Vorschlags und noch offener Fragen, die in den letzten Jahren in Wissenschaft und Praxis lebhaft erörtert worden sind, kann verzichtet werden. Eine nicht unbeträchtliche Mehrheit unter den liberalen Nationalökonomen erhofft sich von einer regelgebundenen Notenemission eine Lösung des Inflationsproblems und setzt sich deshalb für eine Verwirklichung entsprechender Vorschriften in den einzelnen Ländern ein.

[20] *H. C. Simons*, Rules versus Authority in Monetary Policy, in: The Journal of Political Economy, Vol. XLIV (1936), S. 1 ff.

[21] Vgl. u. a.: *M. Friedman*, Die optimale Geldmenge, in: *M. Friedman*, Die optimale Geldmenge und andere Essays, München 1970, S. 9 ff.

[22] *M. Friedman*, Die optimale Geldmenge, a.a.O., S. 72.

III. Zum Konkurrenzgeldsystem

1. Die währungspolitischen Positionen von Hayeks

Die währungspolitische Einstellung *von Hayeks* lag bis vor kurzem auf der eben aufgezeichneten Linie. Er konstatierte, daß die Handhabung der Währungspolitik durch die Regierungen in den letzten Jahrzehnten erheblich zur Instabilität beigetragen hat und fragte, ob die Tauschmittelproduktion nicht den spontanen Kräften des Marktes überlassen werden könnte, um eindeutig zu antworten: «Es ist wichtig, sich von Anbeginn darüber klar zu sein, daß das heute nicht nur politisch undurchführbar ist, sondern wahrscheinlich gar nicht wünschenswert wäre, auch wenn es möglich wäre.»[23] Auch seine Erwägungen zum Vorschlag von *Henry Simons* lassen ein hohes Maß an Übereinstimmung erkennen, sofern die Währungsbehörde nicht autonom ist und keine Einigkeit über die währungspolitischen Ziele besteht. Eine unabhängige, gegen politischen Druck vollkommen geschützte Notenbank, die den eindeutigen Auftrag hätte, das Preisniveau zu stabilisieren, bei einer Wirtschaftspolitik, die den Primat der Währungspolitik anerkennt – das könnte jedoch auch gegenüber einer Regelbindung die bessere Lösung sein, weil es ihm zweckmäßiger scheint, die Ziele der Währungspolitik statt ihre Mittel festzulegen.[24]

Vor wenigen Jahren hat *von Hayek* in einem aufsehenerregenden Schritt seine bisherige Einstellung aufgegeben: Den einzig möglichen Weg, die Inflation zu stoppen und die freiheitliche Ordnung zu retten, sieht er heute darin, das staatliche Notenmonopol zu beseitigen und durch private, miteinander konkurrierende Geldemittenten zu ersetzen.[25] «Die Frage, die wir in Betracht ziehen müssen, ist, ob der Wettbewerb zwischen den Emittenten von klar unterscheidbaren und aus *verschiedenen* Einheiten bestehenden Geldarten uns nicht besseres Geld liefern würde, als wir es jemals hatten, und damit bei weitem die Unbequemlichkeiten aufwiegen würde, die eine (allerdings für die meisten Menschen gar nicht eintretende) Konfrontation mit mehr als einer Geldart mit sich bringen könnte.»[26] Er ist überzeugt, daß sich ein funktionierendes Währungssystem durch die spontanen Kräfte des Marktes entwickeln würde, dem nicht die Defekte des bestehenden Systems – Dauerinflation und daraus folgende wirtschaftliche Instabilität, undisziplinierte Staatsausgaben und Währungsgebrauch nur in einem Land – anhaften. Diese Überzeugung wird im einzelnen begründet, worauf hier nicht eingegangen zu werden braucht; dabei kann *von Hayek* eine Reihe von Fragen – wie er selbst einräumt – nicht oder noch nicht beantworten. Seine Überzeugung und den «wahrscheinlichen Charakter der individuellen Entscheidungen» versucht er «aus unserer allgemeinen Kenntnis der Zwecke herzuleiten, für die die Leute Geld begehren, und der Art und Weise, wie sie in ähnlichen Situationen handeln.»[27]

Das Aufsehen, das der Vorschlag von Hayeks erregt hat, geht nicht allein – und vielleicht nicht so sehr – auf die Originalität seiner Gedanken zurück, sondern auch auf die

---

[23] F. A. *von Hayek*, Die Verfassung der Freiheit, a.a.O., S. 409.

[24] F. A. *von Hayek*, Die Verfassung der Freiheit, a.a.O., S. 419 ff.

[25] F. A. *Hayek*, Choice in Currency. A Way to Stop Inflation, The Institute of Economic Affairs, Occasional Paper 48, London 1976. Derselbe, Denationalisation of Money. An Analysis of the Theory and Practice of Concurrent Currency, The Institute of Economic Affairs, Hobart Paper Special, London 1976. Ergänzte deutsche Übersetzung: Entnationalisierung des Geldes. Eine Analyse der Theorie und Praxis konkurrierender Umlaufmittel, Tübingen 1977.

[26] F. A. *von Hayek*, Entnationalisierung des Geldes . . ., a.a.O., S. 35.

[27] F. A. *von Hayek*, Entnationalisierung des Geldes . . ., a.a.O., S. 54.

radikale Abkehr eines weltweit renommierten Nationalökonomen von seinen früheren Überzeugungen und auf die damit bezogene Gegenposition zu ebenso anerkannten Fachvertretern, insbesondere zu Milton Friedman, dem Haupt der «Monetaristen». Daß sich zwei führende Liberale in der Beurteilung der Gestaltung des Währungssystems derzeit gegenüberstehen, beruht nach meiner Auffassung auf unterschiedlichen Einschätzungen zur Relevanz der Quantitätstheorie, die von Hayek – ohne ihre fundamentalen Einsichten jemals zu bestreiten – anders als Friedman immer sehr skeptisch beurteilt hat.[28] *Der Gedanke, das staatliche Notenmonopol durch private Bankenkonkurrenz zu ersetzen, ist wohl nicht so ungewöhnlich, wie von Hayek meint.*[29] *Nicht nur im neueren Schrifttum, wie in dem von Hayek bekannten Beitrag von Benjamin Klein*[30] *– und der anschließenden Diskussion*[31] *–, sondern auch in früheren Publikationen ist er aufgetaucht und erörtert worden. Entsprechende Vorschläge intendieren nicht immer auf eine Ausweitung der Geldmenge; sie sind gelegentlich – wie bei von Hayek – auch als Rezept gegen die Inflation gedacht.*[32]

2. Probleme eines Konkurrenzgeldsystems

Unter liberalen Nationalökonomen besteht Übereinstimmung, daß ein Konkurrenzgeldsystem einem staatlichen Monopol vorzuziehen ist, wenn es zwei Anforderungen entspräche: Es müßte – erstens – politisch realisierbar sein und – zweitens – in der behaupteten Weise funktionieren. Das heißt: Die Einwände, die *von Hayek* früher gegen ein Konkurrenzgeldsystem selbst vorgetragen hat[33], sind die Maßstäbe seines heutigen Vorschlags. Eine eindeutige wissenschaftliche Aussage zugunsten einer Seite läßt sich wohl kaum treffen. Entscheidend dürfte sein, inwieweit künftige Verhaltensweisen staatlicher Instanzen und privater Entscheidungsträger richtig eingeschätzt werden.

Im Hinblick auf die politischen Möglichkeiten brauchen keine Worte darüber verloren zu werden, daß ein Monopolist nicht an einer Beseitigung seiner Position interessiert sein kann. Auf die Einsicht der Regierungen oder selbst auf die unabhängiger Notenbanken zu vertrauen wäre wirklich Utopie. Die Frage kann nur sein, ob sich das Konkurrenzgeldsystem als Alternative zum Staatsmonopol im Bewußtsein der Öffentlichkeit soweit durchsetzen läßt, daß es sich politisch verwirklichen läßt oder gar realisiert werden muß. *Von Hayek* weist auf die Spätwirkungen der Freihandelsidee von *Adam Smith* hin – ebenso wie auf die Folgen der «*Keynesianische*» Propaganda für Inflationen – um Hoffnungen für sein Konzept zu wecken.[34] Jeder, der die politischen Anforderungen des *Hayekschen* Vorschlages vorurteilsfrei prüft, wird zu eigenen Einstellungen kommen. Bemerkenswert scheint, daß *von Hayek* auch bei Liberalen, insbesondere bei den Monetaristen, wenig Gegenliebe findet. Man kann sich schwer vorstellen, daß ein Konzept, das im

[28] F. A. *von Hayek*, Preise und Produktion, Wien 1931, S. 4; im Vergleich dazu: Derselbe, Entnationalisierung des Geldes . . ., a.a.O., S. 65.

[29] F. A. *von Hayek*, Entnationalisierung des Geldes . . ., a.a.O., S. X ff. und 6.

[30] B. *Klein*, The Competitive Supply of Money, in: Journal of Money, Credit and Banking (JMC), Vol. VI (1974), S. 423 ff.

[31] G. *Tullock*, Competing Monies, in: JMC, Vol. VII (1975), S. 491 ff., B. *Klein*, Competing Monies. A Comment, in: JMC, Vol. VIII (1976), S. 513 ff.

[32] Vgl. z.B.: H. *Rittershausen*, Wirtschaft, Das Fischer Lexikon, Bd. 8, Frankfurt a. M. 1958, S. 153. Eine knappe Zusammenfassung der umfangreichen Literatur zur «Bankfreiheit» findet sich bei: J. *Welcker*, Die Organisation des Geld- und Bankwesens, Tübingen 1977, S. 115 ff.

[33] Vgl. Fn. 23.

[34] F. A. *von Hayek*, Entnationalisierung des Geldes . . ., a.a.O., S. 129 ff.

eigenen Lager auf Widerstand stößt, zum Allgemeingut einer breiten Öffentlichkeit avanciert. Wird sich gleichwohl eines Tages erweisen, daß *von Hayek* die Rolle der Kassandra nicht nur – wie bisher – gegenüber geistigen Gegnern, sondern auch gegenüber Gleichgesinnten wahrnehmen mußte?

Selbst dann, wenn der Vorschlag *von Hayeks* politisch umgesetzt würde, bleibt die Frage, ob sein Währungssystem die prognostizierten Ergebnisse zeitigt, insbesondere die Inflation als Bedrohung einer freiheitlichen Ordnung beseitigen kann. Ist ein Konkurrenzgeldsystem überhaupt wünschenswert? Zu diesem Punkt sind wir nicht bloß auf Einschätzungen künftigen Verhaltens angewiesen. Erstens scheint es zweckmäßig, die historischen Berichte aus Zeiten des «free-banking-system», insbesondere aus der ersten Hälfte des 19. Jahrhunderts in England, auszuwerten. Eine Durchsicht der umfangreichen Literatur vermittelt den Eindruck, daß es neben zeitbedingten Besonderheiten allgemeingültige, bisher nicht ausgeschöpfte Erfahrungen gibt, die auch heute noch bedeutsam sein dürften. Zu diesen Erfahrungen könnte gehören, daß eine Bankenkonkurrenz nicht ohne weiteres eine hohe Geldqualität gewährleistet – auch dann nicht, wenn man die Informationswirkungen moderner Kommunikationssysteme in Rechnung stellt. Zweitens läßt sich das währungspolitische Ziel, die Sicherung der freiheitlichen Ordnung durch die Ausschaltung der Inflation, nur erreichen, wenn die privaten Banken – jede einzeln oder zumindest in ihrer Gesamtheit – garantieren könnten, daß das von ihnen ausgegebene Geld in seiner Kaufkraft konstant bleibt. Obwohl *von Hayek* diesem Punkt einige Aufmerksamkeit gewidmet hat, bleibt als fundamentales Problem: Da nicht nur derzeit, sondern auch in inflationsfreien Zeiten Banken alles tun, die reale Kaufkraft ihrer Aktiva zu sichern, ohne dazu jemals imstande gewesen zu sein, ist schwer einzusehen, wie Banken bei Emissionskonkurrenz ihre Aktiva vor Kaufkraftverlusten schützen könnten.

Wer *von Hayek* nicht nur im Ziel, sondern auch in der Wahl der Mittel beipflichtet, wird sich für eine Beseitigung des staatlichen Notenmonopols einsetzen und eine kompetitive private Emission befürworten. Dieser Weg dürfte steinig und nicht ohne weiteres erfolgversprechend sein, nicht zuletzt, weil er mit Vorurteilen gepflastert ist. Doch auch der andere Weg, die Bindung des staatlichen Monopols an feste Regeln, ist kaum mehr als ein Vorschlag, wenngleich dieser in der modernen ökonomischen Theorie fest verankert ist und seine Durchsetzung etwas größere Erfolgsaussichten zu haben scheint. Eine dauerhafte adäquate Lösung des aufgezeigten Problems ist nicht in greifbarer Nähe: Die von der Inflation ausgehende Gefahr für die freiheitliche Ordnung besteht unvermindert fort. *Friedrich August von Hayek* hat unser Gewissen erneut dafür geschärft – wie immer man zu seinem Vorschlag stehen mag –, daß wir für diese wichtige Aufgabe nicht mehr viel Zeit haben.

Summary

The Monetary System of a Liberal Order

The monetary system and the liberal order are connected inseparably. Monetary disturbances lead to economic instabilities, which are able to ruin a liberal order. The enemies of the liberal order have understood this point far better than its protagonists. The main danger is caused by inflation, which has been going on steadily for about sixty years. The consequences of inflation provoke growing government interventions, which in turn restrict individual freedom. *Friedrich August von Hayek* realized this at an early stage and warned strenuously of this development. Though the aim to stop inflation is no object of controversy among the adherents of a free society, the ways and means of reaching this aim are. The monetarists, under the leadership of *Milton Friedman*, propose to fix the growth rate of money, because central banks are too often inclined to purport discretionary policies with regard to the creation of money. Apart from this, the proposal of the monetarists would not touch the government monopoly of money as it has developed over the last hundred years. Compared with this, *Hayek* wants to abolish the government monopoly of money and to replace it by competition in currency supplied by private issuers. *Hayek's* proposal raises two problems: Has his scheme got a political chance? And will it have the predicted outcome? In any case, Professor *Hayek's* proposal demonstrates the necessity of creating a monetary system which is able to secure the liberal order.

Walter Hamm

Freiheitsbeschränkung durch staatliche Struktur- und Forschungspolitik

> «Es gibt vielleicht keine wichtigere Anwendung unserer Hauptthesen, als daß der Fortschritt des Wissens dort am schnellsten sein wird, wo wissenschaftliche Arbeit nicht durch eine einheitliche Idee von ihrer sozialen Nützlichkeit bestimmt ist».
>
> «Nirgends ist die Freiheit wichtiger als dort, wo unsere Unwissenheit am größten ist – mit anderen Worten an den Grenzen des Wissens, wo niemand voraussagen kann, was einen Schritt vor uns liegt».
>
> *F. A. von Hayek*, Die Verfassung der Freiheit, S. 479 f.

Die staatliche Forschungsförderung in der Bundesrepublik Deutschland befindet sich auf einem Weg, der die individuelle Freiheit in ernster Weise bedroht. Staatliche Forschungspolitik müsse als «antizipative Strukturpolitik» begriffen werden, schrieb Bundesfinanzminister *Matthöfer* 1975 im Vorwort zu einer Veröffentlichung des heutigen Bundesministers für Forschung und Technologie *Hauff*, die den bezeichnenden Untertitel «Technologiepolitik als Strukturpolitik» trägt[1]. Drei Jahre später ist *Matthöfer* noch deutlicher geworden: Er traue sich zu, die «notwendigen Strukturen» zu kennen, die die Bundesrepublik brauche, um international wettbewerbsfähig zu bleiben. Zukunftsträchtige wirtschaftliche und technische Entwicklungen sollten gezielt durch erheblich steigende staatliche Forschungsmittel angestrebt werden. Bei dieser Aufgabe berieten 1.200 Sachverständige die Bundesregierung gegen ein geringes Tagegeld. «Ich will Investitionslenkung betreiben. Diesen Vorwurf nehme ich gern auf mich.» Außer durch unternehmerische Entscheidungen im Markt müßten wirtschaftliche Strukturen mehr als bisher politisch beeinflußt werden[2].

Noch umfassender und deutlicher hat sich *Hauff* zu denselben Fragen geäußert. Er spricht von einer «Scheinkontroverse über Zulässigkeit und Nützlichkeit staatlicher Planung auf dem Gebiet von Forschung und Entwicklung» und möchte die indirekte staatliche Technologieförderung durch Übergang zur Förderung ausgewählter Schwerpunkte «zum effektiven Instrument einer aktiven Wirtschaftsstrukturpolitik weiter entwickeln»[3]. Die Produktion privatwirtschaftlicher Unternehmen orientiere sich überwiegend am bekannten, derzeitigen Bedarf und suche diesen Bedarf überwiegend mit bekannten Produkten, die auf bereits industriell eingeführten Technologien basieren, zu befriedigen. Die dem marktwirtschaftlichen System inhärente Präferenz für das Bekannte führe zu Stagnationskrisen für Unternehmen, Branchen und ganze Volkswirtschaften. «In der

---

[1] *Volker Hauff* und *Fritz W. Scharpf*, Modernisierung der Volkswirtschaft, Frankfurt/Köln 1975, S. 8.

[2] Zitiert nach einem Bericht der Frankfurter Allgemeinen Zeitung, Nr. 171, vom 10.8.1978, «Matthöfer will Investitionen lenken».

[3] *Volker Hauff*, a. a. O., S. 62 f.

Kompensation dieses für die Marktwirtschaft charakteristischen Defizits an voraus-schauender Technologieentwicklung liegt die eigentliche Aufgabe einer staatlichen For-schungs- und Technologiepolitik als Instrument des aktiven Strukturwandels»[4].

In den Augen der Forschungstechnokraten ist danach der Befund eindeutig. Die Un-ternehmer denken in einer marktwirtschaftlichen Ordnung in viel zu kurzen Fristen, er-kennen aussichtsreiche Entwicklungen nicht, kleben an bekannten Technologien, inve-stieren zuviel zur Produktion bekannter Güter mit bekannten Verfahren für einen be-kannten Bedarf und bewirken damit Stagnationskrisen. Einige aufgeklärte und wissen-schaftlich gut beratene Politiker und Beamte müssen die Unternehmer an die Hand neh-men und ihnen die zukunftsträchtigen Entwicklungspfade zeigen. Diese Vorstellungen bestimmen die praktische Politik der Bundesregierung, sind also nicht etwa unverbindli-che Absichtserklärungen. 1978 wird die Bundesregierung rund 7,75 Milliarden DM für Forschung und Entwicklung bereitstellen[5]. Gegenüber dem bisherigen Finanzplan für die Jahre 1978 bis 1982 will die Bundesregierung zur Verstärkung «zukunftsweisender Ak-zente» die Ausgaben für Forschung und Entwicklung um weitere 7 Milliarden DM erhö-hen[6]. Hieraus wird deutlich, daß die Bundesregierung auf dem Gebiet der Forschungspo-litik einen Schwerpunkt ihrer künftigen Tätigkeit sieht.

Die Gedankengänge der beiden Kabinettsmitglieder stehen in wesentlichen Punkten in diametralem Gegensatz zu den Grundvorstellungen *v. Hayeks* über eine freiheitliche Ordnung. Es erscheint nützlich und wichtig, die Überlegungen über eine praktische staat-liche Struktur- und Forschungspolitik an Hand dieser Grundvorstellungen auf ihre Stichhaltigkeit zu überprüfen und auf freiheitsfeindliche Tendenzen der neuen staatli-chen Forschungspolitik abzuklopfen.

I. Die Bedeutung der Forschung in einem Hochlohnland

Hochentwickelte Industrieländer verlieren ständig Arbeitsplätze, weil problemlos her-stellbare Massenprodukte zunehmend aus Niedriglohnländern bezogen werden. Die in-ternationale Wettbewerbsfähigkeit ist in zahlreichen Industrien deshalb nur dann ge-währleistet, wenn über erfolgreiche Innovationen und strukturellen Wandel ständig von neuem ein Vorsprung gegenüber den Konkurrenten aus Niedriglohnländern hergestellt oder gesichert wird. Innovationen sind das Ergebnis von Forschung und Entwicklung. Der weltwirtschaftliche Strukturwandel kann in den Hochlohnländern nur dann be-schäftigungsneutral bewältigt werden, wenn Ausgaben für Forschung und Entwicklung und ihre Ergebnisse – Produkt- und Verfahrensinnovationen – für die Unternehmen loh-nende Investitionen sind. Seit vielen Jahren stagnieren jedoch in der Wirtschaft die Aus-gaben für Forschung und Entwicklung oder gehen sogar – geldwertbereinigt – zurück.

Die Reallöhne sind – im internationalen Vergleich – in der Bundesrepublik seit vielen Jahren so schnell gestiegen, daß sich die Arbeitsplatzverluste in Produktionsbereichen mit unterdurchschnittlichem Produktivitätszuwachs gehäuft haben und daß eine hohe Dauerarbeitslosigkeit entstanden ist. Zugleich sind die Gewinne und die Gewinnerwar-tungen so stark gesunken, daß viele Unternehmen auf riskante Vorstöße in Neuland

---

[4] *Volker Hauff*, a.a.O., S. 48 f.

[5] Vgl. Faktenbericht 1977 zum Bundesbericht Forschung, herausg. vom Bundesminister für For-schung und Technologie, Bonn 1977, S. 37.

[6] Siehe Bundesministerium der Finanzen, Finanzbericht 1979, Bonn 1978, S. 70.

mehr und mehr verzichten. Im Falle eines Fehlschlags kann die Existenz kleiner und mittlerer Unternehmen wegen des meist niedrigen Eigenkapitals und schmaler Gewinnmargen auf dem Spiel stehen.

Einerseits sind daher steigende Forschungsausgaben und Innovationen als gesamtwirtschaftlich dringend erwünscht zu bezeichnen[7]. Andererseits hat die systematisch von der Bundesregierung und von den Gewerkschaften betriebene Umverteilungspolitik zu Lasten der Unternehmensgewinne zu einer eher sinkenden Forschungsfähigkeit und -bereitschaft vieler Unternehmen geführt.

Noch ein zweiter Gesichtspunkt ist in diesem Zusammenhang anzuführen. Forschungsausgaben sind Investitionen, meist Investitionen mit langer Ausreifungszeit. In einer Phase besonders ausgeprägter Unsicherheit über die wirtschaftspolitische Zukunft, genährt von heftiger Kritik an einer freiheitlichen Ordnung im allgemeinen und an der Sozialen Marktwirtschaft im besonderen sowie von der Verketzerung privater Unternehmer und des Gewinnstrebens, sinkt die Bereitschaft zur langfristigen Festlegung von Risikokapital. Es ist verständlich, wenn die Unternehmen unter diesen Umständen lange Produktionsumwege auch in der Forschung vermeiden und sich auf schnell zu verwirklichende Verbesserungen ihrer Produkte konzentrieren. Das freimütige Bekenntnis von *Matthöfer*, staatliche Investitionslenkung über die Forschungspolitik anzustreben, verstärkt diese Unsicherheit und leistet damit einer unerwünschten Entwicklung Vorschub, die dann mit staatlichen Interventionen bekämpft wird. Die fehlende «Konstanz der Wirtschaftspolitik» (*Walter Eucken*) und das Nichtbeachten von Fernwirkungen einer einseitig orientierten Umverteilungspolitik führen die beklagten Zustände überhaupt erst herbei. Eine verfehlte Wirtschaftspolitik läßt immer neue staatliche Interventionen als notwendig erscheinen.

Einerseits kommt demnach der Forschung in dem Hochlohnland Bundesrepublik Deutschland eine besonders wichtige Rolle zu, insbesondere für die Sicherung einer ausreichenden Zahl von Arbeitsplätzen. Andererseits werden Innovatoren, wenn vielleicht auch unbewußt, unter anderem durch zahlreiche Maßnahmen der Bundesregierung entmutigt. Wegen des von vielen Investoren als zu hoch empfundenen Neuerungsrisikos sind die Innovationen unbefriedigend niedrig. Zur Bekämpfung dieses bedenklichen Zustands setzt nun die Bundesregierung nicht an den eigentlichen Ursachen – der Verunsicherung der Unternehmer und der gewinnivellierenden Verteilungspolitik – an. Solche Maßnahmen lassen sich mit Rücksicht auf die linken Flügel beider Regierungsparteien offenbar nicht durchsetzen. Auch generelle Forschungsförderungsmaßnahmen werden wegen der Gießkanneneffekte abgelehnt. Die verfügbaren Mittel würden auf diese Weise zu breit gestreut und führten nicht zu dem erstrebten Erfolg. Vielmehr wünscht die Bundesregierung eine gezielte Forschungsförderung nach Maßstäben, die sie nach ihrem Gutdünken entwickelt hat. Andere Forschungsbemühungen, die ihr unwichtig erscheinen, werden diskriminiert.

---

[7] In diesem Sinne hat sich auch der Bundesminister für Forschung und Technologie im «Fünften Forschungsbericht der Bundesregierung», Bonn 1975, S. 10, geäußert.

II. Maßnahmen der staatlichen Forschungsförderung

Nur wenige Spezialisten sind noch in der Lage, die große Zahl differenzierter und komplizierter Vorschriften über die staatliche Forschungsförderung zu durchschauen. Das weiß auch die Bundesregierung. Daß diese Vorschriften nur für einen kleinen Kreis Auserwählter verständlich und auch offensichtlich nur für sie gedacht sind, zeigt das folgende Zitat aus einer Schrift des Bundesforschungsministers: «Die staatlichen Stellen wären mit erheblichen Problemen konfrontiert, wenn sie die direkte Förderung auf eine große Zahl wenig bekannter, in ihrer Leistungsfähigkeit schwankender Unternehmen erstrecken sollten, die auch ihrerseits weniger erfahren im Umgang mit den Möglichkeiten der staatlichen Forschungsförderung sind»[8]. Wegen der großen Fülle detaillierter Regelungen können im folgenden nur die wichtigsten Grundzüge und Entwicklungstendenzen der staatlichen Forschungsförderung dargestellt werden[9].

Die Forschungspolitik der letzten zehn Jahre ist durch ein Abgehen von der indirekten Förderung und durch verstärkte Hinwendung zur direkten, projektgebundenen Förderung gekennzeichnet. Unter indirekter Förderung werden dabei allgemeine Maßnahmen, insbesondere steuerliche Hilfen und Investitionszulagen, verstanden, die allen Unternehmen gleichermaßen bei sämtlichen, von ihnen frei gewählten Forschungsvorhaben zugute kommen. Kennzeichen der direkten staatlichen Forschungsförderung ist dagegen, daß staatliche Hilfen nur für von staatlichen Organen ausgewählte Programme und Projekte bei Erfüllung bestimmter Voraussetzungen auf vorherigen Antrag zugestanden werden. Bei dieser Förderungsmethode werden lediglich die von politischen Instanzen für wichtig und dringlich gehaltenen Forschungsaktivitäten begünstigt. Diesem Urteil liegen Prognosen über die künftige wirtschaftliche Entwicklung verschiedener Branchen und über «zukunftsträchtige» Projekte zugrunde. Da mit begrenzten Mitteln die jeweils am meisten Erfolg versprechenden Vorhaben gefördert werden sollen, bedürfte es hierzu einer die gesamte Volkswirtschaft umfassenden Analyse und Vorausschau über alle Projekte. Was förderungswürdige «zukunftsorientierte Industrie- und Dienstleistungszweige»[10] sind, kann nur dann bestimmt werden, wenn eine vergleichende gesamtwirtschaftliche Übersicht über die Zukunftschancen verschiedener Wirtschaftsbereiche angestellt und Ziele für eine mittelfristige Strukturpolitik festgelegt werden.

Im einzelnen ist darauf zu verweisen, daß die Zulagen auf Forschungs- und Entwicklungsinvestitionen in Unternehmen 1973 von 10 auf 7,5 Prozent gekürzt wurden. Ende 1974 lief dann auch die 1965 eingeführte Möglichkeit der Sonderabschreibung für Forschungs- und Entwicklungsinvestitionen aus, obwohl diese Maßnahme lediglich eine Steuerverlagerung in die Zukunft bedeutete. Die Summe der für die indirekte Forschungsförderung aufgewandten Mittel hat sich infolgedessen von 428 Millionen DM im Jahre 1973 auf 85 Millionen DM 1975 vermindert. Gleichzeitig stiegen die Finanzhilfen für die direkte Förderung um fast 500 auf 1735 Millionen DM an. Die Ausfallbürgschaft des Bundes in Höhe von 50 Millionen DM gegenüber der 1975 begründeten Wagnisfinanzierungs-Gesellschaft ist die einzige – bescheidene – zusätzliche Maßnahme der indi-

---

[8] *Volker Hauff*, a. a. O., S. 55.

[9] Siehe hierzu die vom Bundesminister für Forschung und Technologie herausgegebene «Förderfibel», 3. überarbeitete Auflage, Bonn 1978. – Einen umfassenden Überblick geben *F. Bräunling* und *D.-M. Harmsen*, Die Förderungsprinzipien und Instrumente der Forschungs- und Technologiepolitik, Göttingen 1975.

[10] Im Fünften Forschungsbericht der Bundesregierung, a. a. O., S. 10, wird dieser Begriff benutzt.

rekten Forschungsförderung in den letzten Jahren, wenn man von finanziell unbedeutenden Hilfen – etwa der «Zuschüsse für Vertragsforschung» (1978 etwa 2 Millionen DM) und der finanziellen Unterstützung von Technologie- und Innovationsberatungsstellen – absieht. Neuerdings ist unter anderem geplant, in kleinen und mittleren Unternehmen die Investitionszulage für die ersten 500 000 DM der begünstigten Anschaffungs- oder Herstellungskosten im Wirtschaftsjahr auf 15 Prozent zu verdoppeln.

Allerdings ist zu beachten, daß in der Forschung und Entwicklung die Personalausgaben mit weitem Abstand an der Spitze aller Kostenarten liegen. In einigen Branchen und in den meisten kleinen und mittleren Unternehmen erreichen die der Forschung dienenden Investitionsausgaben nur eine ganz geringe Höhe. Die Begünstigung der Investitionsausgaben hat daher nur bescheidene Bedeutung. Deswegen mehren sich die Forderungen, neben Investitionszulagen auch generelle Zulagen für die Personalausgaben in den Forschungsabteilungen zu gewähren[11].

Ungleich großzügiger geht die Bundesregierung demgegenüber bei der direkten Forschungsförderung vor. Bei diesen Förderungsverfahren werden die Forschungsvorhaben von Unternehmen zum großen Teil zu 100 Prozent gefördert, in den anderen Fällen werden die Kosten zu rund 50 Prozent aus Steuermitteln ersetzt[12]. Die vergleichsweise geringe indirekte Förderung der Forschung einerseits und die massive direkte Förderung der staatlich gewünschten Forschung andererseits führen zu einer Umlenkung in der angewandten Forschung.

Die Forschungskapazitäten in den Unternehmen sind begrenzt und lassen sich allenfalls mittelfristig ausweiten. Nach Feststellungen des Stifterverbands für die Deutsche Wissenschaft gehen die eigenfinanzierten Aufwendungen für Forschung und Entwicklung in der gewerblichen Wirtschaft seit 1972 – geldwertbereinigt – zurück[13]. Die erhebliche Vergrößerung der projektgebundenen staatlichen Fördermittel führt also dazu, daß die aus privater Initiative entspringende Forschung zum Teil verdrängt wird[14]. Da anzunehmen ist, daß forschende Unternehmen zu analysieren pflegen, in welcher Einsatzrichtung verfügbare Forschungsressourcen vermutlich das beste betriebswirtschaftliche Ergebnis liefern, ist damit zu rechnen, daß die Kapazitäten als Folge massiver direkter Forschungsförderungsmaßnahmen des Staates weniger effizient eingesetzt werden. Hierauf wird noch einzugehen sein.

Die direkte staatliche Forschungsförderung beschränkte sich ursprünglich auf ganz

---

[11] Vgl. Sachverständigenrat zur Begutachtung der gesamtwirtschaftlichen Entwicklung, Jahresgutachten 1976/77, Textziffer 328; Bundesverband der Deutschen Industrie, Zukunftsorientierte Forschungspolitik, Köln 1978, S. 33, und *Ernst Biekert,* Arzneimittelforschung 1978, Pharma Dialog, Heft 54, Frankfurt 1978, S. 20.

[12] Siehe *Volker Hauff,* a. a. O., S. 54. – Eine genaue Aufschlüsselung enthält für die Jahre 1973 bis 1976 der Faktenbericht 1977, a. a. O., S. 14. Mit Ausnahme des Jahres 1976 entfielen jeweils mehr als die Hälfte der Ausgaben des Bundesministeriums für Forschung und Technologie für Forschungs- und Entwicklungsprojekte auf die hundertprozentige Erstattung der Kosten gewerblicher Unternehmen. Insgesamt entfielen 1976 von den Gesamtausgaben für geförderte Projekte in Höhe von 1,8 Milliarden DM 500 Millionen DM auf die Eigenbeteiligung der Industrieunternehmen.

[13] Siehe das Jahresgutachten 1977/78 des Sachverständigenrats zur Begutachtung der gesamtwirtschaftlichen Entwicklung, Stuttgart/Mainz 1977, S. 136 und Textziffer 280. Dort wird darauf verwiesen, daß nicht einmal die Verdoppelung der direkten und indirekten staatlichen Fördermittel zwischen 1971 und 1975 ausreichte, den Rückgang der Unternehmensausgaben auszugleichen.

[14] Diese Ansicht vertritt auch *Helge Majer,* Industrieforschung in der Bundesrepublik Deutschland, Tübingen 1978, S. 161.

wenige Förderungsbereiche, nämlich auf Forschungsprojekte zur friedlichen Nutzung der Kernenergie, auf die Luft- und Raumfahrt und auf die elektronische Datenverarbeitung. In allen diesen Fällen mußte und muß Forschung entweder in Konkurrenz zu aus militärischen Gründen hochsubventionierten ausländischen Wettbewerbern betrieben werden (z. B. Luft- und Raumfahrt), oder es handelte sich um Grundlagenforschung ungewöhnlich kostspieliger Art, die auch im Ausland staatlich gefördert wird (Kernenergietechnik), oder es ging darum, den im wesentlichen nachkriegsbedingten beträchtlichen Vorsprung ausländischer Konkurrenten einzuholen (Datenverarbeitung).

Die direkte staatliche Forschungsförderung hatte also einen die privatwirtschaftlichen Aktivitäten ergänzenden Charakter; sie beschränkte sich auf Gebiete, auf denen sich privatwirtschaftlich geführte Unternehmen keine rentable Nutzung ihrer Forschungskapazitäten ausrechnen konnten und auf denen die einzusetzenden Mittel die Kräfte einzelner Unternehmen bei weitem überstiegen.

Seit 1969 hat sich diese Anlage der staatlichen Forschungspolitik von Grund auf geändert[15]. Schritt für Schritt wurde die direkte Forschungsförderung auf zahlreiche weitere Schwerpunkte und Projekte ausgeweitet. Ausgangspunkt hierfür ist «ein Gesamtkonzept einer künftigen regionalen und sektoralen Industriestruktur»[16], in das die Maßnahmen der Forschungspolitik eingepaßt werden. Außerdem wurde geprüft, in welcher Weise politische Ziele (z. B. im Bereich der Regional-, Arbeitsmarkt-, Bildungs- und Umweltschutzpolitik) durch Vergabe von Forschungsprojekten gefördert werden können. Das Ergebnis dieser Überlegungen sind nicht weniger als 14 Forschungsförderungsprogramme für folgende Bereiche: Datenverarbeitung, Meeresforschung, Energieforschung, Sonnenenergie, Rohstofforschung, elektronische Bauelemente, Nahverkehr, Weltraumforschung, Luftfahrt, Humanisierung des Arbeitslebens, Information und Dokumentation, Gesundheitsforschung, Grundlagenforschung, Förderung kleiner und mittlerer Unternehmen. Jedes der Forschungsprogramme umfaßt rund 100 Seiten. Wer feststellen will, ob ein konkretes Projekt nach einem dieser Programme gefördert wird, muß meist mehrere hundert Seiten durcharbeiten, die oft mit schwer verständlichen Bedingungen gespickt sind und sorgfältiger Prüfung bedürfen. Da ständig neue Programme entwickelt werden und andere auslaufen, da eine große Anzahl detaillierter Förderungsbedingungen zu beachten ist (über die sich Interessenten in einer besonderen «Förderfibel» überblickartig informieren können) und da ohne Erfahrungen mit der Auslegung dieser Bestimmungen nicht auszukommen ist, finden sich Unternehmen, die sich keinen eigenen Spezialisten leisten können, mit diesen Vorschriften nicht zurecht. Mittelständische Unternehmen sind daher besonders benachteiligt. Die Forschungspolitik der Bundesregierung hat sogar einen ganz neuen Beruf entstehen lassen: den Forschungsförderungsberater.

Außerordentlich kompliziert und umfangreich sind die Verwaltungsarbeiten, die direkt geförderte Unternehmen nach Genehmigung ihrer Anträge zu erledigen haben. Die laufende Berichterstattung, die Verwendungsnachweise und die Abrechnung erfordern die Beachtung zahlreicher gesetzlicher und anderer Vorschriften, von Merkblättern und Hinweisen; Formulare sind auszufüllen, Erläuterungen zu geben und Nachweise zu erbringen[17]. Auch diese Anforderungen schrecken verständlicherweise mittelständische Unternehmer ab. Der unproduktive Aufwand, der in den Unternehmen und in der öffentlichen Verwaltung durch die einseitige Ausweitung der direkten Forschungsförderung

---

[15] *Hauff* hat die neuen Ziele der Forschungs- und Technologiepolitik (a. a. O., S. 75 ff.) eingehend geschildert.

[16] *Volker Hauff*, a. a. O., S. 75.

[17] Siehe Bundesverband der Deutschen Industrie, Zukunftsorientierte Forschungspolitik, Köln 1978, S. 26.

erzeugt wird, ist beträchtlich. Daß nach allen bisherigen Erfahrungen ein über die Setzung allgemeiner Regeln weit hinausgehender, auf Einzelfallentscheidungen bezogener maßgeblicher Einfluß staatlicher Organe auf wichtige unternehmerische Entscheidungen die bestmögliche Nutzung des dezentralen Wissens behindert, dadurch den technischen und organisatorischen Fortschritt beeinträchtigt und zu Unwirtschaftlichkeiten führt, bleibt unbeachtet[18].

III. Freiheitsfeindliche Tendenzen der staatlichen Forschungspolitik

Eine Vorbemerkung erscheint angebracht, damit Mißverständnisse vermieden werden. Daß staatliche Instanzen bei der Verfolgung politischer Ziele gezwungen sein können, innerhalb gewisser Grenzen Forschung anzuregen und finanziell zu fördern, ist unbestritten. Offen ist allein die Grenze, bis zu der die direkte Forschungsförderung mit einem freiheitlichen Gesellschaftssystem zu vereinbaren ist. Zunächst ist daher zu ermitteln, inwieweit direkte staatliche Forschungsförderung neben den aus einzelwirtschaftlicher Initiative entspringenden Forschungsaktivitäten zweckmäßig ist[19].

Erstens gibt es Bereiche, in denen die öffentliche Hand der einzige oder nahezu der einzige Nachfrager ist. Dies gilt etwa für neue Waffensysteme oder Nahverkehrstechniken. Die Forschung und Entwicklung auf derartigen Gebieten ist privatwirtschaftlich erst dann vertretbar, wenn mit nachhaltigem Interesse des einzigen Nachfragers zu rechnen ist. In vielen Fällen wird sich staatliche Forschungsförderung als notwendig erweisen, private Unternehmen zu der staatlich gewünschten Forschung zu veranlassen.

Zweitens können Forschung und Entwicklung auf einigen Gebieten unrentabel, aus politischen Gründen aber dennoch erwünscht sein. Das gilt zum Beispiel für nationale Prestigeobjekte, etwa auf dem Gebiet der Raumfahrt.

Drittens wird direkte staatliche Forschungsförderung dort zweckmäßig sein, wo es um die Finanzierung einer besonders kostspieligen Grundlagenforschung und angewandten Forschung geht (Kernkrafttechnik als Beispiel).

Viertens kann die privatwirtschaftliche Rentabilität von Forschungsvorhaben deswegen nicht oder noch nicht gegeben sein, weil Erträge erst in ferner Zukunft zu erwarten sind oder weil ungewöhnlich hohe Risiken vorliegen. Werden aus politischen Gründen gleichwohl forscherische Aktivitäten gewünscht, so wird die öffentliche Hand ebenfalls eine finanzielle Förderung vorsehen müssen.

Häufig haben staatliche Instanzen die Wahl, ob sie politisch als dringlich angesehene Forschungen und Entwicklungen indirekt über preisliche Anreize und allgemeine Forschungsförderung oder direkt durch projektgebundene finanzielle Hilfen anregen wollen. Derzeit wird zuwenig darauf geachtet, daß beispielsweise forscherische Aktivität mit dem Ziel der Energieeinsparung und der Erschließung neuer Energiegewinnungsmethoden oder die Suche nach umweltschonenden Produktionsverfahren auch durch Energiepreiserhöhungen und Umweltschutzabgaben angeregt werden könnte. Die Wahl zwischen verschiedenen technischen Methoden bliebe den im Wettbewerb untereinander stehenden Unternehmen überlassen, die sich dabei auch externer technischer Berater be-

---

[18] Siehe *F. A. von Hayek*, Die Verfassung der Freiheit, a. a. O., S. 37 ff.
[19] Siehe hierzu *Walter Hamm*, Strukturpolitik, sektorale, in: Handwörterbuch der Wirtschaftswissenschaft, Band 7, 1977, S. 483.

dienen können. Die staatliche Administration würde nicht mit einer Aufgabe belastet, die sie nicht erfüllen kann, nämlich der Auswahl der am meisten Erfolg versprechenden Forschungsvorhaben. Die Diskriminierung jener Unternehmen, die keine projektgebundene Hilfe für ihren Lösungsversuch erhalten, unterbliebe. Der Wettbewerb zwischen den forschenden Unternehmen würde nicht verzerrt.

Es genügt daher nicht, forschungsrelevante politische Ziele aufzustellen, für deren Verfolgung forschende Unternehmen sich derzeit tatsächlich oder vermeintlich keine Rentabilität ausrechnen können. Zumindest wäre zu prüfen, ob die preisliche Neubewertung knapper Ressourcen, beispielsweise durch Umweltschutzabgaben, die forscherische Privatinitiative nicht am wirksamsten mobilisierte und ob deshalb auf direkte, projektgebundene Forschungsförderung mit allen ihren Nachteilen verzichtet werden kann. Auch unter Berücksichtigung dieses Tatbestands wird es jedoch in den erwähnten vier Fällen häufig notwendig sein, den Weg der direkten staatlichen Forschungsförderung zu verfolgen.

Derzeit gehen die projektgebundenen staatlichen Hilfen ganz wesentlich über den so abgesteckten Bereich hinaus, und sie sollen, wie eingangs dargelegt, zum Zwecke staatlicher Strukturpolitik und staatlicher Investitionslenkung wesentlich ausgedehnt werden. Welche Gefahren hiervon für eine freiheitliche Ordnung ausgehen, ist im folgenden darzustellen. Die Gedanken, die *F. A. von Hayek* in seiner «Verfassung der Freiheit» entwickelt hat, bieten sich hierfür als besonders gut geeignete Orientierungsmarken an.

a) «Anmaßung von Wissen»

Die Entwicklung der deutschen Forschungspolitik erfüllt mit ganz besonderer Klarheit jenen Tatbestand, den *F. A. von Hayek* mit «Anmaßung von Wissen» gekennzeichnet hat. Bundesfinanzminister *Matthöfer* traut sich, wie eingangs zitiert, zu, die «notwendigen Strukturen» zu kennen, die die Bundesrepublik braucht, um wettbewerbsfähig zu bleiben. Daß schon die allernächste Zukunft ins Dunkel getaucht ist und sich prognostischen menschlichen Bemühungen entzieht, daß deswegen die behaupteten Kenntnisse nicht vorhanden sein können und daß insbesondere die internationale Wettbewerbsfähigkeit deutscher Unternehmen von unbekannten Änderungen Dutzender von Variablen abhängt, wird geflissentlich übersehen.

Wie sollen «zukunftsträchtige Strukturen» der gesamten deutschen Wirtschaft durch «antizipative Strukturpolitik» systematisch angestrebt werden, wenn völlige Unklarheit etwa über die Wechselkursentwicklung, über die Anlagedispositionen der erdölfördernden Länder, über die künftige Lohnpolitik, die Veränderung der internationalen Lohnrelationen, die Entdeckung neuer und Erschöpfung bekannter Rohstoffvorkommen, die Entwicklung wichtiger Preise und Preisrelationen, Veränderungen der Nachfrage etc. besteht? Auch 1.200 beratende Fachleute können dem Bundesfinanzminister bei der Lösung einer so weitgesteckten Frage nicht helfen. Unzählige Beispiele beweisen dies. *Matthöfer* geht daran vorbei, daß das zu analysierende Objekt ein höchst komplexes Phänomen ist, das sich zuverlässigen wissenschaftlichen Voraussagen entzieht.

F. A. von Hayek hat mit Nachdruck darauf verwiesen, daß bei gesellschaftlichen Phänomenen «die konkreten Umstände, von denen die individuellen Ereignisse abhängen, in der Regel so zahlreich sind, daß wir sie praktisch nie alle ermitteln können und daß folglich nicht nur das Ideal ‹Voraussage und Kontrolle› weitgehend unerreichbar ist, sondern auch die Hoffnung, wir könnten durch Beobachtung regelmäßige Beziehungen zwischen den individuellen Ereignissen entdecken, illusorisch bleibt»[20]. Eine hochentwickelte, in die weltwirtschaftliche Arbeitsteilung stark verflochtene Volkswirtschaft ist in ganz ausgeprägtem Maße ein «komplexes Phänomen». Handeln staatliche Instanzen so, als ob sie es in der Wirtschaft mit einfachen Phänomenen zu tun hätten, dann sind Störungen und Fehlentwicklungen vorprogrammiert. Die Hoffnung, staatliche Fehldispositionen würden marktwirtschaftliche Gegenkräfte zur Überwindung solcher Störungen mobilisieren, ist ein schwacher Trost. Erstens lassen sich staatlich bewirkte Fehllenkungen von Produktivkräften nicht ungeschehen machen und nur unter gesamtwirtschaftlichen Verlusten heilen. Außerdem legen ständig zunehmende und unvorhersehbare staatliche Interventionen mehr und mehr die marktwirtschaftlichen Abwehrkräfte lahm. In der Forschungspolitik müßte sich die staatliche Lenkung der Forschung nach Vorstellungen über eine «antizipative Strukturpolitik» besonders nachteilig auswirken, weil sich Fehlentwicklungen auf diesem Gebiet nur über längere Zeiträume hinweg heilen lassen. Forscher lassen sich nicht beliebig umsetzen. In der Rede aus Anlaß der Verleihung des Nobel-Gedächtnispreises ist *F. A. von Hayek* den Gründen für die Anmaßung von Wissen nachgegangen, die die deutsche Forschungspolitik in so eindeutiger Weise bestimmt[21]. Er hat vor der Illusion gewarnt, mit ökonometrischen Methoden künftige ökonomische Ereignisse berechnen zu wollen, weil es absurd wäre, anzunehmen, daß sich die große Zahl der für jegliche Voraussagen erforderlichen Variablen und deren ständige Änderungen im Zeitablauf bestimmen ließen. Nachdrücklich hat *von Hayek* auf die Grenzen sozialwissenschaftlicher Voraussagen verwiesen. In der Wirtschaftswissenschaft sei «oft das, was oberflächlich betrachtet als das wissenschaftlichste Verfahren erscheint, in Wirklichkeit das unwissenschaftlichste»[22]. Werde «der bewußten Lenkung nach wissenschaftlichen Prinzipien» mehr anvertraut, als die wissenschaftliche Methode leisten kann, so könne dies «beklagenswerte Folgen haben»[23].

Dieser Satz verdient es ganz besonders, von den deutschen Forschungspolitikern beherzigt zu werden. Auch wenn die Bundesregierung noch einige tausend weitere Sachverständige als Gutachter heranzöge, würde sich an dem Grundproblem, nämlich an der Unsicherheit von Prognosen, nichts ändern können. Niemand kann heute die konkreten Forschungsvorhaben nennen, die morgen oder übermorgen zu international wettbewerbsfähigen Strukturen in den verschiedenen Branchen führen. Der Voraussage ganz bestimmter Ereignisse stehen unüberwindbare Hindernisse entgegen. Der selbstbewußten Aussage *Matthöfers* fehlt damit die Grundlage. Staatliches «Handeln, das davon ausgeht, wir besäßen die wissenschaftliche Kenntnis zu solchen Voraussagen», wäre «ein ernstes Hindernis» für eine erfolgreiche Politik[24]. Der Einwand, auch Unternehmer seien bei langfristigen Dispositionen auf Prognosen angewiesen, sticht nicht. Es ist ein Unterschied, ob viele Unternehmer selbstverantwortlich entscheiden oder ob eine einzige staatliche Instanz verbindlich die künftige Entwicklung bestimmt. Im ersten Fall gilt das Prinzip der Fehlerkompensation, und es besteht die Gewähr für unablässige Korrekturen unternehmerischer Entscheidungen. Im zweiten Fall ist die Fehlerkompensation ausgeschlossen. Außerdem gestehen staatliche Planungsstellen ungern Irrtümer ein; einen Zwang zu raschen Korrekturen sich abzeichnender Fehler gibt es nicht. Der wichtigste Vorzug der dezentralen marktwirtschaftlichen Steuerung gegenüber zentraler behördlicher Lenkung besteht darin, daß der einzelne Marktteilnehmer nur kleine Teilausschnitte

---

[20] *F. A. von Hayek*, Die Theorie komplexer Phänomene, Tübingen 1972, S. 25.
[21] Siehe *F. A. von Hayek*, Die Anmaßung von Wissen, in: Ordo, Band 26, Stuttgart 1975, S. 12 ff.
[22] *F. A. von Hayek*, Die Anmaßung von Wissen, a. a. O., S. 17.
[23] Ebenda, S. 17.
[24] Ebenda, S. 19.

der Volkswirtschaft zu übersehen braucht und sich im übrigen an den Informationen orientieren kann, die das Preissystem liefert.

Inwiefern muß die seit einem Jahrzehnt verfolgte Grundlinie der Forschungspolitik als freiheitsfeindlich eingestuft werden? Zwar handelt es sich auf dem Gebiet der Forschungsförderung nicht um ein befehlswirtschaftliches Vorgehen staatlicher Stellen. Auch Prämien, Anreize und finanzielle Sanktionen können jedoch so dosiert werden, daß Unternehmer nicht anders können, als den Wünschen staatlicher Stellen auf dem Gebiet der Forschung zu folgen. Nur scheinbar besteht dann noch Wahlfreiheit für die Unternehmen. Da die Forschungskapazitäten begrenzt sind, im Gegenteil in den letzten Jahren sogar rückläufige Forschungsausgaben (preisbereinigt) in der Wirtschaft festzustellen sind, haben sich die staatlichen Zielvorstellungen in der Forschungspolitik voll durchgesetzt. Von staatlichen Organen nicht gewünschte oder als weniger dringlich empfundene Forschungsaufgaben sind zurückgedrängt worden. Verantwortliche Politiker lassen im übrigen keinen Zweifel daran, daß sie entschlossen sind, ihre strukturpolitischen Zukunftsvorstellungen auch gegen Widerstreben durchzusetzen[25]. Es kann daher durchaus davon gesprochen werden, daß die unternehmerische Entscheidungsfreiheit überall dort mit staatlichem (willkürlichem) Zwang (im Sinne *von Hayeks*) eingeschränkt werden soll, wo sie staatlichen Vorstellungen über anzustrebende «Strukturen» widersprechen. Die erhebliche Vergrößerung der Steuer- und Soziallasten für Unternehmen, die dadurch stark geschrumpften Gewinne, die Einschränkung der indirekten Forschungsförderung und die beträchtliche Ausweitung der projektgebundenen Förderung haben die Voraussetzungen hierfür geschaffen.

Freiheitsbeschränkend ist die neue Linie der Forschungspolitik auch noch aus einem zweiten Grund. Die staatliche Lenkung der Forschung läuft zugleich auf eine partielle Steuerung des künftigen Güterangebots hinaus. Staatliches Gutdünken, und nicht Abstimmungsprozesse auf Märkten, bestimmen unternehmerische Aktivitäten. Auch die Freiheit der Käufer wird daher durch die staatliche Forschungslenkung berührt.

b) Begrenzungen in der Verwertung individuellen Wissens

Die Kehrseite der «Anmaßung von Wissen» und ihre unmittelbare Folge sind Beschränkungen der individuellen Freiheit, selbstgewählte Ziele mit unabhängig gewählten Mitteln – im Rahmen der vom Staat gesetzten «allgemeinen Regeln» – verfolgen zu können. Diese Beschränkungen der individuellen Freiheit müssen gerade in der Forschung und Entwicklung zu erheblichen Nachteilen führen:

– Bestimmen staatliche Instanzen maßgeblich Richtung und Intensität der Forschung, so werden auf dem Gebiet der Forschung vorwiegend nur die Ideen und das Wissen einiger weniger genutzt werden. Ein wesentlicher Teil des dezentralen Wissens, das sonst die Forschungsaktivitäten gelenkt hätte, wird notwendigerweise schlechter genutzt werden, weil es selbst mit höchstentwickelten Informationsgewinnungs- und -verarbeitungssystemen nicht aufbereitet und einer zentralen Instanz nutzungsgerecht zugeleitet werden könnte. «Kein menschlicher Verstand (kann) all das Wissen umfassen, das das Handeln der Gesellschaft lenkt»[26]. Eine umfassende Verwertung des individuellen Wissens ist da-

---

[25] «Gegenüber einem Staat, der seine Koordinationsmängel überwindet, der weiß, was er wirtschaftspolitisch will und der sein Instrumentarium konsequent und wirksam einzusetzen vermag, (werden) nur wenige Unternehmen noch geneigt sein . . . , Kooperation und Verständigung zu verweigern.» Vorstand der SPD (Herausgeber), Ökonomisch-politischer Orientierungsrahmen für die Jahre 1975–1985, Bonn 1975, S. 71.

[26] *F. A. v. Hayek*, Die Verfassung der Freiheit, a. a. O., S. 4.

her nur so möglich, daß man sich eines unpersönlichen nicht von individuellen Urteilen abhängigen, die individuellen Bemühungen koordinierenden Mechanismus bedient[27]. Die weitverbreitete Unkenntnis dieser Vorgänge, «bei denen mehr Wissen verwertet wird, als irgendein Einzelner oder eine organisierte Gruppe besitzen kann, bringt die Nationalökonomen in ständigen Gegensatz zu den Bestrebungen anderer Fachleute, die die Macht zu lenken fordern, weil sie glauben, daß ihre Spezialkenntnisse nur so voll zur Geltung kommen»[28]. Die individuelle Freiheit zum Handeln wird auf diese Weise eingeschränkt.

– Fortschritt führt immer ins Unbekannte; seine Ergebnisse sind nicht voraussagbar. Deshalb kann der Fortschritt – entgegen den Vorstellungen planungsgläubiger Politiker – nicht geplant werden[29], und deshalb weist auch staatlich kommandierte und reglementierte Forschung so geringe Fortschrittsraten auf, wie sich vor allem in den Ostblockstaaten zeigt, die auf ständigen «Technologietransfer» aus den marktwirtschaftlich organisierten Ländern angewiesen sind. Entscheidend für eine hohe Effizienz der Forschung, der Suche nach neuen Problemlösungen, der «Kombination von Wissen und Fähigkeit» ist, «daß jeder einzelne die Möglichkeit hat, nach seinen besonderen Kenntnissen zu handeln»[30]. «Freiheit ist wesentlich, um Raum für das Unvorhersehbare und Unvoraussagbare zu lassen»[31]. Da für die Forschung zuständige Beamte nicht wissen können, welches Unternehmen eine bestimmte Aufgabe am besten zu lösen vermag, ist es ratsam, auch auf diesem Gebiet dem wettbewerblichen Suchprozeß das Feld zu öffnen. Die Auffassung, daß staatliche Maßnahmen eher den Innovationsprozeß verlangsamen und daß die Marktkräfte und der Wettbewerb die entscheidenden Antriebskräfte für Innovationen sind, haben auch Manager aus der Bundesrepublik Deutschland, aus Frankreich, Großbritannien und Japan vertreten, die von der US-amerikanischen National Science Foundation im Auftrag der amerikanischen Regierung auf die Wirkung forschungsanregender staatlicher Maßnahmen angesprochen worden sind[32]. Empirische Untersuchungen in den USA haben sogar gezeigt, daß die staatlichen Forschungsförderungsmaßnahmen «provide some of the most outstanding cases of failure and waste»[33]. «The heavier the hand of government the more likely an escalation of costs»[34].

– Eine weitere schwerwiegende Begrenzung bei der Verwertung individuellen Wissens ist darin zu sehen, daß die direkte staatliche Forschungsförderung fast ausschließlich wenigen Großunternehmen zugute kommt. Hierfür gibt es mehrere Gründe:

Erstens hält sich hartnäckig das empirisch eindeutig widerlegte[35] Vorurteil, wonach wichtige Erfindungen vor allem großen Unternehmen mit umfangreichen Forschungsabteilungen zu verdanken seien.

Zweitens ist es für die staatliche Verwaltung am einfachsten, wenn sie mit wenigen großen Unternehmen zusammenarbeitet. Kein Rechnungshof wird Einspruch erheben,

---

[27] Vgl. ebenda, S. 4.
[28] Ebenda, S. 4.
[29] Vgl. ebenda, S. 51 f.
[30] Ebenda, S. 37.
[31] Ebenda, S. 38.
[32] Siehe den Bericht im «Blick durch die Wirtschaft», Nr. 92, vom 6. 5. 1978 «Förderungsmaßnahmen im Spiegel der Wirtschaft». Bei *John Jewkes, David Sawers* und *Richard Stillerman*, The Sources of Invention, 2. Aufl., London 1969, S. 228, heißt es: «Competition strengthens the total flow of new ideas».
[33] Ebenda, S. 226.
[34] Ebenda, S. 213.
[35] Siehe insbesondere ebenda, S. 226 und passim, vor allem S. 205 ff.

wenn trotz umfassender finanzieller Förderung von Großunternehmen keine befriedigenden Ergebnisse erzielt werden. Träte derselbe Umstand bei kleinen, unbekannten, wenngleich unter Fachleuten renommierten Unternehmen ein, müßten die Beamten vermutlich mit dem Vorwurf rechnen, sie hätten das zu fördernde Unternehmen nicht sorgfältig genug ausgesucht.

Drittens ist in der administrativen Abwicklung der staatlichen Forschungsförderung ein ernstes Hindernis für die Beteiligung kleiner und mittelständischer Unternehmen zu sehen. Nur Großunternehmen können sich die Spezialisten leisten, die in der Lage sind, sich im Gewirr der Vorschriften zurechtzufinden[36]. Das ist nicht nur in der Bundesrepublik Deutschland so, sondern gilt auch für andere große Industrieländer[37], muß also als unvermeidbarer Nachteil projektgebundener staatlicher Forschungsförderung angesehen werden.

Viertens besteht auch bei den kleinen und mittleren Unternehmen nur eine sehr geringe Bereitschaft, sich auf die höchst komplizierten und arbeitsaufwendigen, ohne Spezialkenntnisse gar nicht zu erfüllenden Vorbedingungen für die direkte staatliche Forschungsförderung einzulassen.

Die Folge ist, daß eine einseitige projektgebundene Hilfe wichtige innovatorische Kräfte von der staatlichen Forschungsförderung weitgehend ausschließt. Die Konzentration der Forschung in wenigen Großunternehmen wird begünstigt[38]. In großen Forschungslaboratorien wird jedoch die Entfaltungsmöglichkeit, Spontaneität und Kreativität des einzelnen Forschers oft beeinträchtigt[39]. Die einseitige Förderung der Forschung in Großunternehmen behindert daher ebenfalls die Verwertung individuellen Wissens. Die in kleinen und mittleren Unternehmen verbleibende Forschungspotenz wird vernachlässigt. Die Erfolgschancen der Forschung sinken.

– Ein wichtiges – negatives – Kennzeichen staatlicher Forschungsförderung ist die geringe Anpassungsfähigkeit und Beweglichkeit bei der Verfolgung konkreter Forschungsziele. Zwar konzentriert sich die staatliche Forschungsförderung, zumindest bisher, vor allem auf langfristige Forschungsprojekte. Gleichwohl kommt es auch auf solchen Gebieten, etwa in der Kernreaktorforschung, zu unerwarteten Entwicklungen und zu Neuentdeckungen, die Abweichungen vom bisherigen Kurs nahelegen können. Ob die staatliche Forschungsverwaltung so wendig ist, daß sie neues Wissen ständig erfaßt, auswertet und in veränderte Fragestellungen umsetzt, ist zumindest zu bezweifeln. Unternehmen, die sich im Wettbewerb behaupten müssen und nach erfolgreichen Wettbewerbsvorstößen streben, sind dagegen zu einem hohen Maß an Beweglichkeit und Anpassungsbereitschaft gezwungen. Auch hier liegt eine Ursache für die begrenzte Verwertung individuellen Wissens. Sollen diese Nachteile vermieden werden, dann drängt es sich geradezu auf, die direkte staatliche Forschungsförderung auf das unvermeidbare Ausmaß zu beschränken, dem Wissen und der Phantasie der Individuen mehr Entfaltungsmöglichkeiten zu eröffnen und durch mehr Freiheit auch bessere Ergebnisse für die Volkswirtschaft zu erzielen. Bei ihren Bemühungen, die Forschung zu fördern, sollten die staatlichen Instanzen nicht unabsichtlich verhindern, was sie zu erreichen versuchen[40].

---

[36] Vgl. oben Abschnitt 2. und Fußnote 5.
[37] Siehe «Förderungsmaßnahmen im Spiegel der Wirtschaft», in: Blick durch die Wirtschaft, Nr. 92, vom 6.5.1978.
[38] Diese Ansicht vertritt auch *Volker Hauff*, a.a.O., S. 55.
[39] Auf ein Beispiel hierfür verweisen *John Jewkes* u.a., a.a.O., S. 206 f.
[40] Siehe *John Jewkes* u.a., a.a.O., S. 228.

c) Fehlende Gleichheit vor dem Gesetz

Bedenklich an der immer weiter um sich greifenden projektgebundenen staatlichen Forschungsförderung ist weiterhin, daß die Gesetze und Verordnungen zwar formal auf alle Forscher und Unternehmen gleichermaßen anzuwenden sind, dennoch aber faktisch eine Ungleichbehandlung bewirken. In anderem Zusammenhang war bereits dargelegt worden, daß Großunternehmen eindeutig bevorzugt werden, daß die Diskriminierung der kleinen und mittleren Unternehmen eine unvermeidbare Folge des gewählten Förderverfahrens ist und daß die Bundesregierung diese Benachteiligung vieler Unternehmen weiterpraktiziert, obwohl sie die unerwünschten Folgewirkungen kennt. Erst neuerdings wird versucht, auch mittelständischen Unternehmen wenigstens bescheidene Hilfen zuteil werden zu lassen. Persönliche Freiheit ist jedoch nur dann wirklich gesichert, wenn Gesetze für alle gleichermaßen gelten[41] und wenn sie nicht so konstruiert sind, daß einzelne Gruppen diskriminiert werden.

d) Weite behördliche Ermessensspielräume statt allgemeiner Regeln

Im Bereich der projektgebundenen staatlichen Forschungsförderung besteht ganz im Gegensatz zur direkten Forschungsförderung ein ungewöhnlich großer Ermessensspielraum für Behörden. Ob ein konkretes Projekt von der Sache her in eines der laufenden Forschungsprogramme einbezogen werden kann, ob zahlreiche komplizierte Anforderungen erfüllt sind und ob mit einem erfolgreichen Abschluß des Projekts im Sinne staatlich gesetzter Maßstäbe zu rechnen ist, entzieht sich weitgehend der Nachprüfung. Überdies bleibt stets die Möglichkeit, daß die Prüfinstanz auf die begrenzten öffentlichen Mittel und auf – ihrer Ansicht nach – dringlichere Projekte als Ablehnungsgrund verweist. Je weiter das behördliche Ermessen, desto breiter ist die Lücke, durch die «jedermanns Freiheit verloren gehen kann»[42].

Dieser umfassende Ermessensspielraum von Behörden wäre weniger ärgerlich, wenn die indirekte Forschungsförderung ein größeres Gewicht hätte und diese Art von Forschung nicht wesentlich geringer begünstigte, als es für die projektgebundene Forschung zutrifft. Da beides nicht der Fall ist und da infolgedessen von einer beträchtlichen Diskriminierung der indirekt geförderten Forschung und der auf sie im wesentlichen angewiesenen kleinen und mittleren Unternehmen gesprochen werden muß, werden die durch Ermessensentscheidungen Benachteiligten besonders hart getroffen.

Weite Ermessensspielräume leisten ferner einer Entwicklung Vorschub, bei der der Forschungswettbewerb zu einem Akquisitionswettbewerb bei öffentlichen Stellen entartet[43]. Gute Kontakte zu den maßgeblichen Beamten und zu den Gutachtern können entscheidend sein. Unternehmer oder Einzelforscher, die solche lobbyistischen Fähigkeiten nicht beherrschen, werden benachteiligt sein. Noch größer wird die Macht der Forschungsförderungsbehörden dann, wenn Unternehmen von öffentlichen Forschungsaufträgen abhängig werden[44].

Alle diese Gefahren bestehen nicht, wenn die Forschung nach allgemeinen Regeln staatlich gefördert wird, was bei indirekter Förderung der Fall ist. Die Unternehmen ent-

---

[41] *F. A. von Hayek* hat hierauf mit Nachdruck verwiesen (Die Verfassung der Freiheit, a. a. O., S. 272 ff.).

[42] Ebenda, S. 275.

[43] Siehe *Helge Majer*, Industrieforschung . . . , a. a. O., S. 162.

[44] Siehe ebenda, S. 162.

scheiden frei und nach eigenen Maßstäben, sind keinerlei Ermessensentscheidungen ausgesetzt und werden auch nicht von staatlichem Willen abhängig. «Was eine freie gegenüber einer unfreien Gesellschaft auszeichnet, ist, daß in ihr jedes Individuum einen anerkannten, sich deutlich von dem öffentlichen Bereich abzeichnenden privaten Bereich hat und der private Einzelne nicht Befehlen untersteht, sondern nur den Regeln zu gehorchen braucht, die für alle gleichermaßen anwendbar sind»[45].

IV. Gesamtwirtschaftliche Folgen einer freiheitsbeschränkenden staatlichen Forschungsförderung – Zusammenfassung und Schlußfolgerungen

Die Bundesregierung verfolgt mit ihrer Forschungspolitik eine Linie, bei der ein zentraler Wille mehr und mehr die Richtung der privaten Forschungsaktivitäten beeinflussen und lenken soll. Mit schnell steigenden projektgebundenen Hilfen einerseits und einem fühlbaren Abbau allgemeiner Maßnahmen der Forschungsförderung soll dieses Ziel erreicht werden.

Hinter diesen Bestrebungen steht der falsche Glaube, «daß sich der Bereich unseres Unwissens ständig vermindere und wir daher eine umfassendere und bewußtere Lenkung aller menschlichen Tätigkeiten anstreben könnten. Aus diesem Grunde werden die Menschen, die vom Fortschritt des Wissens berauscht sind, so oft zu Feinden der Freiheit»[46]. Nicht nachdrücklich genug kann demgegenüber betont werden, daß die Vorherrschaft dieser Ideen in der praktischen Forschungspolitik sachlich unbegründet ist und zu bedenklichen gesamtwirtschaftlichen Folgen führen wird.

Sachlich unbegründet sind diese Ideen, weil auch mit erheblichen wissenschaftlichen Erkenntnisfortschritten im Einzelfall das Haupthindernis für eine zentrale Lenkung der Forschung nicht ausgeräumt werden kann, nämlich die aus der Komplexität sozialer Phänomene sich ergebende Ungewißheit künftiger Ereignisse und Entwicklungen.

Bedenkliche gesamtwirtschaftliche Folgen verschiedener Art werden bei der zunehmend interventionistischen, die Forschungsaktivitäten in staatlich gewünschte Richtungen umlenkenden Politik der Bundesregierung unvermeidlich sein:

– Wird in der Forschungspolitik verstärkt staatliche Macht eingesetzt – Macht, die «den Anspruch erhebt, überlegenes Wissen zu besitzen»[47], so wird die Entwicklung des Fortschritts gehemmt. Bei massiven direkten staatlichen Forschungsanreizen und real sinkenden Forschungsausgaben in der Wirtschaft wird einzelwirtschaftlich bestimmte Forschung zugunsten kollektiv bestimmter Forschung vermindert[48]. Damit werden, wie dargelegt, weniger Wissen, weniger Ideen und weniger individuelle Fähigkeiten in der Forschung frei zum Zuge kommen.

– Als Folge der massiven direkten staatlichen Forschungsförderung muß mit Fehlallokationen der in Forschung und Entwicklung eingesetzten Produktivkräfte gerechnet werden. Innerhalb der forschenden Unternehmen werden die Aktivitäten in Bereiche

---

[45] F. A. von Hayek, Die Verfassung der Freiheit, a. a. O., S. 270.
[46] Ebenda, S. 35.
[47] Ebenda, S. 88.
[48] Siehe hierzu auch Helge Majer, Industrieforschung, a. a. O., S. 161.

umgelenkt, die vergleichsweise geringe gesamtwirtschaftliche Vorteile versprechen. Auch durch Abwerbung von Forschungspersonal von seiten der staatlich besonders stark geförderten Unternehmen aus nicht begünstigten Betrieben wird es zur Konzentrierung der Forschungsaktivitäten dort kommen, wo staatliche Instanzen auf Grund vager strukturpolitischer Prognosen verstärkte Forschung und Entwicklung für nützlich halten. Von den Märkten ausgehende Impulse werden infolgedessen zum Teil verdrängt.

– Ausgaben für die Forschung gehören zu denjenigen Investitionen, die für die nachhaltige internationale Wettbewerbsfähigkeit eines Hochlohnlandes von besonders großer Bedeutung sind. Eine Forschungspolitik, die vorhandenes individuelles Wissen und die Kreativität der Forscher und Unternehmer nicht voll zur Entfaltung kommen läßt, schwächt die heimische Wirtschaftskraft, vermindert die Zahl der Arbeitsplätze und führt damit zu nachteiligen beschäftigungspolitischen Wirkungen.

– Eine staatliche Forschungspolitik mit strukturbestimmendem, investitionslenkendem Charakter (wie von Bundesfinanzminister *Matthöfer* beabsichtigt) wird alle jene gesamtwirtschaftlich nachteiligen Folgen hervorrufen, die in der umfangreichen Debatte über kollektive Investitionslenkung herausgearbeitet worden sind[49].

– Zentrales Prognostizieren und darauf aufbauende staatliche Forschungslenkung führen dazu, daß die bei dezentralem einzelwirtschaftlichem Planen zu erwartende Fehlerkompensation ausgeschaltet und die rasche Anpassung an Datenänderungen verhindert wird. Kollektive Fehlentscheidungen wirken in einer Richtung; dagegen ist es unwahrscheinlich, daß alle selbständig planenden Unternehmen den gleichen Fehler machen. Es kommt also zur Streuung des Risikos[50]. Das gesamtwirtschaftliche Ergebnis der forscherischen·Bemühungen wird daher bei kollektiver Forschungsplanung geschmälert.

– Staatliche Forschungslenkung beschränkt den Wettbewerb. Behörden treffen Entscheidungen, die sonst in wettbewerblichen Prozessen fallen. Eine gleichmäßige Förderung aller grundsätzlich für ein konkretes Projekt geeigneten Unternehmen wird regelmäßig nicht möglich sein. «Daher kommt es zu Diskriminierungen und höchstens zufällig zur Förderung der besonders leistungsfähigen Unternehmer»[51]. Eine ineffiziente Verwendung von Forschungsressourcen ist auch insofern vorprogrammiert.

– Projektgebundene staatliche Hilfen kommen nahezu ausschließlich Großunternehmen zugute. Auch insoweit wird der Wettbewerb verfälscht – zum Nachteil einzelner Forscher und mittelständischer Unternehmer, die nach empirischen Ermittlungen einen erheblichen Anteil an wichtigen Erfindungen haben.

– Die staatlichen Forschungsförderungsinstanzen unterliegen nicht dem Zwang, mit angeregten Innovationen den künftigen Bedarf treffen zu müssen. Staatliche Bedarfsvorstellungen können sich als irrig herausstellen. Da derzeit allenfalls schlecht funktionierende Sanktionen bei Fehlentscheidungen bestehen, gibt es auch keinen Zwang zu ständigen Korrekturen von Forschungsprogrammen und -zielen in Anpassung an Veränderungen auf Märkten.

– Häufig fehlt es bei staatlicher Forschungsförderung an der Abstimmung politischer Ziele und Maßnahmen. Beispielsweise werden derzeit neue Schienenstrecken für hohe Geschwindigkeiten bei Verwendung der herkömmlichen Technik gebaut. Die Nutzungsdauer dieser erst Ende der achtziger Jahre verfügbaren Strecken soll bis tief in das nächste Jahrtausend reichen. Daneben werden Forschungsmittel für eine ganz neue

---

[49] Siehe hierzu *Walter Hamm*, Kollektive Investitionslenkung, in: Ordo, Band 27, 1976, S. 134 ff., insbesondere S. 158 ff., und die dort zitierte Literatur.
[50] Ebenda, S. 171. Siehe auch *Vera C. Lutz*, Zentrale Planung für die Marktwirtschaft, Tübingen 1973, S. 124 f.
[51] Ebenda, S. 160.

Technik bereitgestellt, die den traditionellen Schienenverkehr ersetzen soll (Magnet-schwebetechnik). Auch für neue Techniken im öffentlichen Nahverkehr sind erhebliche Forschungsmittel unzweckmäßig eingesetzt worden (computergesteuerte Kabinenbahn).

– Andere projektgebundene Förderprogramme haben sich trotz Milliardenaufwands an Steuermitteln als Fehlschläge erwiesen – offensichtlich deswegen, weil ungeeignete Verfahren hartnäckig weiterverfolgt worden sind. Hier ist insbesondere an Großrechen-anlagen, an Weltraumraketen und an die Reaktortechnik zu erinnern. Erhebliche finan-zielle Mittel und Forschungskapazitäten sind aussichtsreicheren Verwendungsmöglich-keiten entzogen worden.

– Die staatliche Forschungsförderung richtet sich nur auf wenige Schwerpunkte. Einen umfassenden Überblick über aussichtsreiche Forschungsrichtungen (die zum Teil in un-bekanntes Neuland führen und Produkte betreffen, deren Verwendungsmöglichkeit noch offen ist, wie etwa bei potientiellen Arzneimitteln) können staatliche Organe sich nicht verschaffen. Auch Bemühungen um eine ausreichende «Prognosekapazität» kön-nen aus der Natur der Sache heraus nicht weiterhelfen. Die Forschungsaktivitäten wer-den daher als Folge der strukturbestimmenden staatlichen Forschungslenkung zuneh-mend einseitig kanalisiert. Schon die Vernachlässigung eines Teils der von Behörden nicht erkannten aussichtsreichen Forschungsrichtungen kann sich für eine Volkswirt-schaft als nachteilig erweisen.

– Große technische Fortschritte sind oft Zufallsergebnisse, jedenfalls nicht das Ergeb-nis bewußter, zielgerichteter Suche nach einem neuen Produkt. Derartige Aktivitäten werden von der staatlichen projektgebundenen Hilfe nicht erfaßt; sie entziehen sich ihrer Natur nach dem planerischen Zugriff.

– Eigenverantwortliche, abseits staatlicher Forschungsprogramme liegende Aktivitä-ten werden finanziell benachteiligt. Die unternehmerische Initiative wird auf diese Weise zum Teil umgelenkt. Prämiiert werden jene Unternehmen, die dem Willen der staatlichen Behörden folgen.

– Wird die wirtschaftspolitische Verunsicherung der Unternehmer beseitigt und neues Vertrauen in einen geradlinigen, die freiheitliche Wirtschaftsordnung sichernden Kurs der Wirtschaftspolitik geschaffen, kann verstärkt mit langfristigen Forschungsinvesti-tionen der Unternehmen gerechnet werden. In freiheitlichen Wirtschaftsordnungen ist der eindeutige Beweis erbracht worden, daß sie – insgesamt gesehen – mehr Fortschritt und technisches Wissen produzieren, als es bei staatlich reglementierter Forschung der Fall ist. Andernfalls bedürften die Ostblockstaaten nicht eines ständigen umfassenden Transfers von technologischen Neuerungen aus dem Westen. Die Behauptung *Hauffs*, in marktwirtschaftlich organisierten Volkswirtschaften produzierten die Unternehmen überwiegend bekannte Erzeugnisse mit bekannten Methoden für einen bekannten Be-darf[52], erscheint daher einseitig und ist durch die Erfahrung der letzten drei Jahrzehnte zweifelsfrei widerlegt. In dieser Feststellung kann daher auch kein überzeugender Grund für eine staatlich gelenkte Forschung erblickt werden. Empirisch eindeutig durch interna-tionale Vergleiche nachweisbar ist die Tatsache, daß gerade in Ländern mit staatlich ge-lenkter Forschung das von *Hauff* fälschlich für die Marktwirtschaft angenommene «cha-rakteristische Defizit für vorausschauende Technologieentwicklung»[53] besteht.

Die gesamtwirtschaftlichen Folgen des einseitigen Vordringens projektgebundener Forschungsförderung sind nach alledem bedenklich. Überschätzung des Wissens einiger Technokraten und Unkenntnis der Vorzüge wettbewerblicher Prozesse sind die Ursachen für die Fehlsteuerung in der Forschungspolitik. Der Wettbewerb ist «ein Verfahren zur

---

[52] *Volker Hauff*, a. a. O., S. 48.
[53] Ebenda, S. 49.

Entdeckung von Tatsachen», «die ohne sein Bestehen entweder unbekannt bleiben oder doch zumindest nicht genutzt werden würden»[54]. Behörden können wettbewerbliche Prozesse nicht simulieren und nur einen Bruchteil des individuellen Wissens in ihren Entscheidungen berücksichtigen. Alles spricht daher für den Abbau direkter projektgebundener Forschungsförderung – mit Ausnahme weniger oben genannter Bereiche. Die beste Lösung bestünde unzweifelhaft in einer steuerlichen Entlastung der Unternehmen, durch die sie instand gesetzt werden, selbstverantwortlich auch zunehmend risikoreichere und geringere Trefferquoten versprechende Forschung zu betreiben. Erweist sich dieses Verfahren aus verteilungspolitischen Gründen derzeit als nicht realisierbar, sollte der Schwerpunkt eindeutig auf die indirekte staatliche Forschungsförderung gelegt werden, die den Unternehmen und Forschern die Wahl läßt, auf welchen Gebieten und für welche Zwecke sie ihre Forschungskapazität einsetzen. Derzeit wird Forschungspolitik in der Bundesrepublik Deutschland zunehmend mit untauglichen Mitteln betrieben.

Summary

Restraints to Freedom through Regional, Sectoral, and Research Policy of the State

The government of the Federal Republic of Germany is planning to direct private research and management according to state-set priorities. It has been explicitly confirmed that the intention behind this is the control of capital investment. The financial means provided to that end will be increased by DM 7 billion over the next few years. Direct subsidizing of projects considered necessary and important by the state has largely superseded the general type of government research promotion, e. g. via tax incentives.

Von Hayek's reflections reveal that such authoritarian influence on research activities stems from a «pretence of knowledge» and will allow but the consideration and application of a small fraction of the comprehensive decentralized knowledge. The procedure means a restraint to freedom, if premiums and incentives are measured to make entrepreneurs comply with the requests of the government. Government control of research amounts to a partial control of future supply and diverts entrepreneurial initiative from the consumers' priorities perceptible in the market. Therefore, preference should be given to a government research promotion that is based on general rules leaving competence and responsibility for the selection of research projects entirely to the enterprises.

---

[54] F. A. von Hayek, Der Wettbewerb als Entdeckungsverfahren, a. a. O., S. 249.

Namenregister

Sachregister

Anschriften der Autoren

Dr. Lucas Beltrán, Professor (Catedrático de Economia Politica), Av. Concha Espina, 10, E – Madrid – 16

Dr. James M. Buchanan, Professor, Virginia Polytechnic Institute and State University, Blacksburg, Virginia 24061, USA

Dr. Gerard Curzon, Professor, Institut Universitaire de Hautes Études Internationales, 132, Rue de Lausanne, CH-1211 Genève 21

Dr. Victoria Curzon Price, Professor am Institut Universitaire d'Etudes Européennes, Villa Moynier, 122, Rue de Lausanne, CH-1211 Genève 21

Dr. Gottfried Dietze, Professor, The Johns Hopkins University, Baltimore, Maryland 21218, USA

Dr. Milton Friedman, Professor, Hoover Institution on War, Revolution and Peace, Stanford, California 94305, USA

Dr. Helmut Gröner, Professor an der Universität Bayreuth, Kanalstraße 3, D-8580 Bayreuth

Dr. Walter Hamm, Professor an der Universität Marburg, Universitätsstraße 7, D-3550 Marburg

Dr. Norbert Horn, Professor an der Universität Bielefeld, Fakultät für Rechtswissenschaft, Postfach 8640, D-4800 Bielefeld

Dr. Otmar Issing, Professor an der Universität Würzburg, Sanderring 2, D-8700 Würzburg

Dr. Israel M. Kirzner, Professor, New York University, 538 Tisch Hall, Washington Square, New York, N.Y. 10003, USA

Dr. Ludwig M. Lachmann, Professor, University of Witwatersrand, 40 Kerry Road, Parkview Johannesburg 2193, Republik Südafrika

On. Dr. Giovanni Malagodi, Presidente d'onore del partito liberale italiano, Minister a. D., Viale Bruno Buozzi, I-109/A Roma, Italien

Dr. Wernhard Möschel, Professor an der Universität Tübingen, Wilhelmstraße 7, D-7400 Tübingen 1

Dr. Chiaki Nishiyama, Professor, Rikkyo University, Center of Modern Economics, 3-chome Nishi-Ikebukuro, Toshima, Tokyo, Japan

Sir Karl Popper F.R.S., F.B.A., Prof. Dr., The London School of Economics and Political Science (University of London), Houghton Street, London, WC2A 2 AE, Großbritannien

Dr. Charles K. Rowley, Professor, The University of Newcastle upon Tyne, Department of Economics, The University Newcastle upon Tyne NE1 7RU, Großbritannien

Dr. Hans Heinrich Rupp, Professor an der Universität Mainz, Am Marienpfad 29, D-6500 Mainz 1

Dr. Dieter Schmidtchen, Professor an der Universität des Saarlandes, Spichererbergstraße 21, D-6600 Saarbrücken

Dr. Alfred Schüller, Professor an der Universität Marburg, Forschungsstelle zum Vergleich wirtschaftlicher Lenkungssysteme, Barfüßer Tor 2, D-3550 Marburg

Arthur Seldon, B. Com., Examiner of Economics, University of London, The Institute of Economic Affairs, 2 Lord North Street, Westminster, London SW1P 3LB, Großbritannien

Dr. Klaus Stern, Professor an der Universität Köln, Institut für öffentliches Recht und Verwaltungslehre, Gyrhofstr. 8 c, D-5000 Köln 41

Dr. George J. Stigler, Professor, The University of Chicago, 5836 Greenwood Avenue, Chicago, Illinois 60637, USA

Dr. Gilbert Tixier, Professor, Université Paris-Val de Marne (Paris XII), 58, Avenue Didier, F-94210 La Varenne Saint Hilaire, Frankreich

Dr. Egon Tuchtfeldt, Professor an der Universität Bern, Alpenstraße 45, CH-3626 Hünibach bei Thun, Schweiz

Dr. Christian Watrin, Professor an der Universität zu Köln, Arndtstraße 9, D-5000 Köln-Rodenkirchen 50

Dr. Hans Willgerodt, Professor an der Universität zu Köln, Hubertushöhe 7, D-5060 Bergisch-Gladbach 1

Dr. Artur Woll, Professor an der Gesamthochschule Siegen, Theodor-Storm-Straße 29 A, D-6380 Bad Homburg

Dr. Michael Zöller, Universität München, Schloßgartenweg 2, D-8045 Ismaning

Anschriften der Schriftleitung

Professor Dr. Fritz W. Meyer, Am Hagmättle 3, D-7800 Freiburg-Littenweiler

Professor Dr. Hans Otto Lenel, Universität, Haus Recht und Wirtschaft, D-6500 Mainz

Professor Dr. Hans Willgerodt, Hubertushöhe 7, D-5060 Bergisch-Gladbach 1

Fachliteratur

— Eine Auswahl —

Internationale Wirtschaftsordnung

Herausgegeben von Prof. Dr. Helmut Gröner, Bayreuth, und Prof. Dr. Alfred Schüller, Marburg
Mit Beiträgen zahlreicher Fachspezialisten
1978. X, 278 S., 2 Abb., 3 Übers., 8 Tab., kart. DM 36,—

Im vorliegenden Sammelband setzt sich eine Reihe namhafter Autoren mit der derzeitigen weltwirtschaftlichen Situation und den Erfolgsaussichten der angestrebten Korrekturen im Wirtschaftsverkehr zwischen den Nationen auseinander und diskutiert eingehend als Alternative zu der feststellbaren interventionistischen Grundtendenz eine auf marktwirtschaftlichen Prinzipien aufgebaute internationale Wirtschaftsordnung. Dabei wird herausgearbeitet, daß ein marktwirtschaftliches Weltwirtschaftssystem besser geeignet ist, den Erfordernissen insbesondere der Entwicklungsländer nachhaltig gerecht zu werden, als das über eine Vielzahl von Eingriffen gelingen kann. Dazu ist es jedoch erforderlich, bestehende Wettbewerbsbeschränkungen abzubauen und in den nationalen Wirtschaftspolitiken, vor allem auf dem Geldsektor, mehr Disziplin als bisher walten zu lassen.

Weltwirtschaftsordnung und Wirtschaftswissenschaft

Vorträge der Festveranstaltung des Fachbereichs Wirtschaftswissenschaften der Philipps-Universität Marburg a. d. Lahn aus Anlaß des 450jährigen Jubiläums am 26. Mai 1977

Von Prof. Dr. Herbert Giersch, Prof. Dr. Hans-Günther Krüsselberg, Prof. Dr. Erich Priewasser, Prof. Dr. Jochen Röpke, Prof. Dr. Alfred Schüller
Zusammengestellt von Prof. Dr. Bernd Schiemenz, Marburg/Lahn
1978. VI, 89 S., kart. DM 24,—

In der vorliegenden Schrift weisen Wissenschaftler und leitende Männer der Praxis auf Wege hin, wie unter Beibehaltung bewährter weltwirtschaftlicher Ordnungsgrundsätze drängende Probleme der Außenhandels- und Währungspolitik gelöst werden können.

Erinnerungen

Von Ludwig v. Mises
Mit einem Vorwort von Margit v. Mises, New York, und einer Einleitung von F. A. v. Hayek, Freiburg/Br.
Mit einem Porträt und einer Bibliographie der Veröffentlichungen von Ludwig v. Mises
1978. XVI, 112 S., 1 Abb., kart. DM 34,—

Ludwig v. Mises (1881—1973) ist erst spät als einer der bedeutendsten Nationalökonomen seiner Zeit voll gewürdigt worden. Die vorliegenden Lebenserinnerungen schildern die erste seiner beiden Lebensepochen, die Wiener Jahre bis zu seiner Emigration in die Vereinigten Staaten.
Nobelpreisträger F. A. v. Hayek, lange Jahre Weggefährte von L. v. Mises sowohl in Österreich als auch in den Vereinigten Staaten, unternimmt in einem Einleitungskapitel eine Würdigung der wissenschaftlichen und politischen Bedeutung Mises' aus heutiger Sicht.

Gustav Fischer Verlag
Stuttgart · New York